PHILOSOPHY OF MATHEMATICS

EDITED AND WITH AN INTRODUCTION BY
PAUL BENACERRAF AND HILARY PUTNAM

Philosophy of Mathematics

SELECTED READINGS

PRENTICE-HALL, INC.   ENGLEWOOD CLIFFS   NEW JERSEY

PRENTICE–HALL PHILOSOPHY SERIES
Arthur E. Murphy, PH.D., *Editor*

PRENTICE-HALL INTERNATIONAL, INC., *London*
PRENTICE-HALL OF AUSTRALIA, PTY., LTD., *Sydney*
PRENTICE-HALL OF CANADA, LTD., *Toronto*
PRENTICE-HALL OF INDIA (PRIVATE) LTD., *New Delhi*
PRENTICE-HALL OF JAPAN, INC., *Tokyo*

Current printing (last digit):
12   11   10   9   8   7   6   5   4   3

PRINTED IN THE UNITED STATES OF AMERICA
66377—C

Contents

v

Introduction

1. GENERAL REMARKS

It would be difficult to say just what comprises the philosophy of mathematics—what questions, views, general areas should be covered in such a book as this. With that as our excuse, we have not tried to bring together a collection of selections which could be said to cover the field in a comprehensive way. We have tried rather to bring together selections which we felt were interesting in their own right, and which offered interesting comparisons when read together, all with the proviso that the issues discussed in them were in most cases central to the field. If we have succeeded, then we are certain that the reader has an adequate introduction to the philosophy of mathematics.

The divisions we have chosen are largely arbitrary, as the following remarks will indicate, and no importance should be attached to a particular article's being in this section rather than that. With this much said, we can state that the motivation behind the sections is roughly as follows: We included in Part 1 those selections which centered around three traditionally important views on the nature of mathematics: logicism, intuitionism, and formalism. This is not to say that other articles in the book do not bear on these views. For example, the article by Hempel in Part 3 is itself a very clear and lucid exposition of logicism. Like the other pieces in Part 3, however, it discusses the view on a (mathematically) less technical plane and is therefore more readily accessible to people with no formal training in logic than the papers in Part 1. The discussion of the three aforementioned views is thus the unifying thread that runs through the section called "The Foundations of Mathematics."

Questions concerning the existence of "abstract entities" in general and mathematical existence in particular (we leave open here the question of whether mathematical existence is a different sort of existence or the existence of a different sort of thing, or both, or neither) are discussed principally in Part 2. But it is clear to anyone with the slightest familiarity with these matters that intuitionism, at least, is a view concerning mathematical existence, at least insofar as it includes conditions on what is to count as *proofs* of the existence of certain mathematical structures, entities, etc. Therefore, an adequate consideration of these questions (adequate in that it takes in the leading points of view) would include items from Part 1 as well.

The first three sections further overlap in that the third, "Mathematical Truth," contains, besides the Hempel selection just mentioned, the quasi-intuitionistic piece by Poincaré. Nagel and Quine ("Truth by Convention") discuss conventionalism, a view also expressed by Carnap in connection with mathematical existence and truth in his article in Part 2. The Gasking-Castañeda controversy is seemingly on a different subject altogether—the relation of mathematics to the world—but there is nevertheless an obvious connection with conventionalistic viewpoints: If mathematics is somehow a very general way of describing the world, then the part played by conventions in determining mathematical truth is correspondingly diminished by the part played by a (possibly) recalcitrant world.

We feel that such overlap is unavoidable. The division into problems is, at best, a guide for the reader. It is evident that one's view on the nature of mathematical truth (if there is indeed such a beast) will affect one's views on mathematical existence, and will constitute a position on the "Foundations of Mathematics." In spite of this extensive overlap, however, there is also a distinction that can be made among the articles in the first three sections. They divide rather naturally into two groups: on the one hand, we have the items in Part 1 plus the two pieces by Gödel, and on the other, we have the rest.

The first of these groups contains contributions belonging to what we should like to call the "epistemology of mathematics." With the possible exception of the selections by Frege and Russell, the authors of these pieces devote a good part of their attention to the question of what an acceptable mathematics *should* be like: what methods, practices, proofs, etc., are *legitimate* and therefore justifiably used. They don't take existing mathematics and mathematical activity as sacrosanct and immune from criticism; according to them, there are justifiable and unjustifiable methods in mathematics, and acceptable results are those that are obtainable by justifiable methods. In fact, a good portion of the effort of the mathematician should be devoted to trying to recast intuitively desirable and acceptable results in forms which show them to be ultimately acceptable. If the author in question is an intuitionist, then it will be his view, e.g., that what part of real analysis cannot be obtained by intuitionistic methods ought to be discarded. But in most cases, it is vitally important to carry on the search for intuitionistic proofs of as yet unobtained classical theorems.

And what we have seen to be true of the intuitionist is also true of formalists (Hilbert, von Neumann, Curry). Members of this latter group are concerned about the legitimacy of references to infinite collections, structures, etc., in mathematics. More particularly, the concern takes the form of a fear that such reference, since it is to things so far from what we are capable of experiencing, might lead to contradictions (presumably because the candle of intuition casts but a dim light from such a distance). What then becomes important for the formalist is the search for a proof that these "infinitistic" methods form a consistent whole. The proof must, of course, be one which does not employ these questioned methods. So here again there appears a restriction on what methods should be countenanced in mathematics. And so on for the others. (Gödel also belongs to this group because, although he does not *advocate* any of the restrictive policies, he certainly discusses them. And furthermore, his work in pure logic has had a crucial effect on the tenability of some forms of these positions.) The other feature characterizing the members of this group is that they are all primarily mathematicians rather than philosophers. And we say this without in any way wishing to play down their philosophical contributions, any more than we would be inclined to deny the mathematical contributions made by members of the other group. The first group consists, therefore, of mathematicians who criticize the very foundations of their subject. These are the "epistemologists." (Poincaré really belongs in group one, if we are to judge from the bulk of his work, but the passages we have chosen assimilate him more to the second.)

In contrast with the "epistemologists of mathematics," there are those who accept mathematics as, if not sacrosanct, then at least not their province to criticize. For them the task is a much different one: they do not want to *promulgate* certain mathematical methods as *acceptable*; they want to *describe* the *accepted* ones. Mathematics is something given and to be accounted for, explained and accurately described. For them, epistemology is not a tool to help sort the good mathematics from the bad—it is a scheme within which mathematics as such must fit ("Mathematical propositions are analytic", "Mathematical statements are true by convention", etc.). One way of describing the difference between these two groups is to say that, for one group, the epistemological principles have a higher priority or centrality than most particular bits of mathematics, and hence can be used as a critical tool, whereas, for the other group, just the reverse is the case: existing mathematics is used as a touchstone for the formation of an epistemology, one of whose conditions of adequacy will be its ability to put all of mathematics in the proper perspective. To put it somewhat crudely, if some piece of mathematics doesn't fit the scheme, then a writer in the first group will tend to throw out the mathematics, whereas one in the second will tend to throw out the scheme.

Of course, matters are not quite that neat. For both groups there is a constant interplay between epistemological principle and mathematical activity. Members of the first group will sometimes start with some paradigm cases of acceptable mathematical practice (e.g., intuitionists and formalists both start with parts of number theory) and then try to arrive at principles which will account for the validity of this starting point. These principles are then used either to criticize what fails to conform to them, or as a guide for the erection of standards that further proofs must meet, especially proofs of those "theorems" already "proved" but not "acceptably" so. Similarly, it would be an exaggeration to saddle the second group with absolutely every- thing a mathematician might produce. Their account of mathematics might very well force them to renounce and denounce some piece of mathematics as unacceptable. But by and large this is very unlikely. Ayer, Hempel, Nagel, Gasking, Castañeda, and Alston are all prepared to take mathematics pretty much as is. Russell and the Carnap of "Logicism" present a problem, depending on how seriously one takes their discussions of the vicious circle principle and impredicative definitions. There is no question that the Carnap of "Empiricism, Semantics, and Ontology" has abandoned any *critical* function for epistemology. Quine and Goodman are also borderline cases, almost professionally so. Insofar as he has abandoned his ontic qualms, however, Quine presents no problem. Goodman, on the other hand, occupies a rather complicated position, indicating that no non-Goodmanominalistic mathematics is acceptable, indeed *intelligible*, to him, but that people who are able to do this with a clear (ontic) conscience may do so. But leaving the borderline cases straddling the border line, Heyting, Brouwer, Hilbert, von Neumann, Curry, and Poincaré (in other passages than those we are present- ing, alas) are quite clearly on the other side. Kreisel belongs, if anywhere, to this latter group, for he has strong constructivistic leanings. The "if anywhere" is inserted because Kreisel's function has been more or less to reconstruct and make mathematical sense of the philosophical pronounce- ments of the members of this latter group. And it is quite conceivable that he should wish to see just how much of extant mathematics one can obtain on this or that restriction without much caring whether or not one adopts the restriction. This would make his, as it were, a metatask.

But so much for this distinction. It is rather vague, but we hope, never- theless, somewhat suggestive, and it should be of some help in understanding how the writings of the authors included in this collection are related. What becomes of interest, once one has seen the distinction, is the way in which one can view the discussions included in this book as continuous with one another. At first sight, it might appear that the two groups did not even discuss the same problems. But it should be seen that Hilbert is just as much concerned with the determinants of "mathematical truth" as are, say, Ayer and Nagel. The position he adopts is a rather different one from those they favor, but all three should be read as writing on the same questions, or very nearly so. And similarly with Gödel and Hempel. When Gödel discusses the continuum hypothesis, he is merely discussing a particular mathematical proposition and the ways in which it might be shown to be true or false. Hempel's remarks on the nature of mathematical truth should, if cogent, be relevant to this discussion. And so on with the rest of the selections.

Consequently, it is our view that the questions we have chosen for study are intimately related. Furthermore, the authors whose discussions of these questions we have selected are, on the whole, concerned with very much the same questions, superficial differences to the contrary. These differences bespeak differences in point of view and differences in methods of attack, rather than simply different concerns. It is our view that the discussion of all these problems benefits greatly from the interplay of these differences—but only when it becomes clear what unites them as discussions of the same problems. It is our hope that reading these selections together will make this clear.

So much by way of introduction. The remainder of this Introduction will consist of remarks on a number of problems, some of which are discussed rather fully, others of which are merely touched upon by our authors. We hope that these remarks will make it easier to understand the selections and the issues involved.

2. THE ACTUAL INFINITE AND FORMALISM

Although this collection does not contain a section titled "The Infinite in Mathematics," anyone who reads the selections from the writings of Brouwer, Heyting, and Hilbert that we have included under the general title "The Foundations of Mathematics" will quickly realize that the role played by infinite structures, collections, quantities, etc., in classical mathematics has a great deal to do with the controversy between the different "schools" in the philosophy of mathematics. By the same token, the measure of success attained by Cauchy and Weierstrass in eliminating "infinite quantities" from the calculus had a great deal to do with the ideal, shared by thinkers with views as mutually antagonistic as those of Hilbert and Brouwer, of eliminating the infinite from mathematics altogether.

But why should it be deemed desirable to avoid reference to the infinite in mathematics? Sometimes it is said—even by Hilbert—that references to the infinite are "meaningless." But why should one suppose that this is so? Classical philosophers—in particular, Hume—had argued against the notion (in connection with infinite divisibility) on the basis of an identification of what is intelligible with what can be *visualized*; but the "image-in-the-head" theory of meaning no longer seems tenable, and attacks on the notion of the infinite must depend on something more reasonable than this if they are to be taken seriously.

In point of fact, it is very hard to find reasoned and even moderately detailed argument on this point. Opponents of the "actual infinite" tend to assume that the burden of proof lies on the other side. "Show us that the notion makes sense," they seem to say, where the criterion of making sense seems to be expressibility in *their* terms. We cannot discuss this issue here: suffice it to say that the reader who sympathizes with the demand of the classical empiricists that all concepts be legitimized by being "derived from experience" will probably find himself inclined to sympathize with those who doubt that any notion of an infinite structure is a clear one, whereas the reader who is either of a more realistic or of a more pragmatist turn of mind may have difficulty in seeing "what the fuss is all about."

Suppose, however, that we assume that statements about infinite structures "make sense." Are there in fact any such structures to talk about? Hilbert argues convincingly that physics provides no clear evidence for the existence of such structures: in fact, the progress of physics has, as he points out, introduced finiteness and discontinuity in area after area in which the infinite and the continuous once reigned supreme. Today even the possibility of a beginning (and an end) to "physical time" is under discussion among physicists. Thus we must agree with Hilbert that if mathematics is to be independent of dubious empirical assumptions, it must not base assertions concerning the existence of infinite structures on physical considerations.

To this Russell replied, in a slightly different context, that mathematics is concerned not with (physical) existence, but only with the *possibility* of existence. Thus, in the second edition of *Principia Mathematica* (henceforth: *PM*), Russell and Whitehead chose not to assume the so-called Axiom of Infinity, which asserts that there are infinitely many objects in the universe of discourse, but rather explicitly included it among the hypotheses of each "theorem" in whose proof it was used. If T was the "theorem" in question, then Whitehead and Russell asserted only '*if* Inf. Ax., *then* T'.

But is it clear that an infinite totality could *possibly* exist? If the Axiom of Infinity leads to a contradiction, then the theorems which list it as hypothesis are certainly not very interesting. Since these form a large part of mathematics (at least as reconstructed by Russell and Whitehead), should there not be some proof of the *consistency* of the Axiom of Infinity, whether it is to be used as a postulate of the system or only as a hypothesis of a large number of important theorems?

Here we get a parting of the ways in the philosophy of mathematics. Russell and his followers apparently regard the *possible*, if not actual, existence of infinitely many objects as self-evident, whereas for Hilbert and the formalists the consistency of this assumption must be *proved*. Moreover it must be proved by "finitist" means—that is to say, the assumption itself must obviously not figure, even in a disguised way, among the assumptions of the consistency proof. The reader will observe that this kind of question is a bit like a political question—it is not a "purely theoretical" question, in the sense of making no difference to practice, but rather it affects one's standards in mathematics, and one's program as a mathematician. Hilbert did not think that the likelihood was very great that the system of *PM* was, in fact, inconsistent: he simply felt that to take its consistency, or even the consistency of elementary number theory, without proof, was to lower the standards of mathematical exactness and to risk unpleasant surprises in the future.

3. THE "POTENTIAL INFINITE" AND INTUITIONISM

For the intuitionists, the position with respect to the infinite was different. Given a set of statements describing an infinite structure, there are two sorts of doubts that may arise. Firstly, one may doubt the *consistency* of the statements: this was Hilbert's worry. Secondly, one may doubt that the statements "pick out" a *unique* and well-defined mathematical structure. Intuitionists sometimes write as if even the notion of an "arbitrary finite magnitude" is not completely fixed in advance.[1] We know, indeed, that 1, 2, 3, are integers. We know that certain operations applied to integers lead to integers—e.g., addition, multiplication, exponentiation. But it does not follow that we have a perfectly definite notion of "any integer"—because this involves the idea of iterating an operation (say, "adding 1") an *arbitrary finite number of times*, and we need not admit that we have a clear notion of what this means. The intuitionist does not, of course, propose to do without the concept "integer"—that would be to abandon mathematics altogether. Rather he (e.g., Heyting, elaborating and formalizing Brouwer's ideas) proposes to develop a propositional calculus for dealing with concepts that do not necessarily correspond to a well-defined totality (and "statements" that do not necessarily have a truth-value). This attitude is often described as "countenancing the potential infinite but not the actual infinite." What it comes to is this:

1. A statement about an infinite structure—say, an infinite sequence of zeros and ones—may be regarded as *true* if proved and *false* if refuted, but in all other cases it is regarded as *neither true nor false*.

2. Since the structure is not thought of as well-defined, a statement about it can be proved only *if it is actually proved for a much larger class of structures*. In fact, to prove a statement about an infinite structure, we must prove the statement on the basis of verifiable statements which are either about some *finite part* of the structure (e.g., the first ten places of the sequence), or about the *rule* (if there is one) for successively producing the finite initial segments of the structure.

An example may help to make this position more clear. Consider the assertion that the sum of the first n odd numbers $(1 + 3 + \cdots + (2n - 1))$ is always a perfect square (in fact n^2). The sum of the first *one* odd numbers,

---

[1] In what follows, we present an account of intuitionism directed at the non-intuitionist. It is possibly an account acceptable to no intuitionist, but we feel that such "falsification" is justified if it helps bridge the gulf that presently exists between the intuitionist and the "classical mathematician."

i.e., 1, is a perfect square, since $1 = 1^2$. And if the sum of the first n odd numbers is n^2 then the sum of the first $n + 1$ must be $(n + 1)^2$, or $n^2 + 2n + 1$ (since the $n + 1$st odd number is $(2n - 1) + 2$, and this is equal to $2n + 1$). Thus we have proved the theorem for 1, and if we have proved the theorem for n, we can prove it for $n + 1$. Accordingly, the intuitionist—like the classical mathematician—concludes that the theorem holds for every number. The philosophical difference is that the intuitionist does not assume that the numbers are a well-defined totality. But in this case it doesn't matter. (Although there are many cases in which intuitionists are led by their position to reject classically valid proofs; e.g., proofs which assume that every statement about an infinite totality is either true or false —which amounts to assuming that the totality is well-defined—are rejected by intuitionists.) For, even if we extend the notion of an integer to cover a new "object," if all theorems proved in the preceding fashion hold for all the things previously counted as integers (notice that there need be only finitely many of these at any given time), and if the "new" integer is always "one plus" something previously counted as an integer, then the theorems in question will hold also for the "new" integer.

By way of contrast, consider the assertion that the number of "twin primes"[2] is infinite. For the classical mathematician this has a unique truth-value (even if he doesn't presently know it). But for the intuitionist it doesn't: for he has no proof of the statement, nor does he have a proof of its negation, and statements about an ill-defined totality don't have a truth-value unless they can be proved (or disproved) from a *partial* determination of the totality.

A classical mathematician can get an approximate idea of what the intuitionist has in mind in the following way: (1) *Drop* the assumption that there is a well-defined "standard model" for number theory. (2) Don't assume that we can characterize by any finite number of axioms all of the things that we would intuitively recognize as correct methods of proof. (I.e., take "number theory" itself as a concept in the process of being created.) Then there will be three classes of statements in number theory: statements which are "true," i.e., true in all models of number theory; statements which are "false," i.e., false in all models; and statements which are "neither true nor false," i.e., which are true in some models and false in others. Also, the "true" statements will all be provable—but not necessarily in any one formal system.

This explanation is, however, not intuitionistic, since an intuitionist would not accept the idea that the undecidable statements are "true in some models and false in others." Moreover, the intuitionist surely objects with reason here: for, if "number theory" is not a closed concept, then the notion

---

[2] A *prime number* is one which cannot be divided without remainder except by itself and 1. *Twin primes* are primes whose difference is 2: e.g., (5, 7), (11, 13), (17, 19), etc. Whether the number of such pairs is finite or infinite is an unsolved (and apparently hopelessly difficult) problem in number theory.

of a "model" of number theory is surely not a mathematically meaningful one even from the standpoint of classical mathematics. Yet one can still make sense of proving that a statement is "true in *all* models," namely, if one can prove that a statement is true in all models for some finite fragment of number theory, then, however the concept of "number theory" may be *enlarged* in the future, the statement in question must be, indeed, "true in all models of number theory" (since models of the whole must be models of each part). However, the idea of an infinite "model"—a *well-defined* infinite collection satisfying the axioms of a formal system—is not one acceptable to an intuitionist.

For the intuitionist, also, the problem of consistency does not arise because any statement about a "potential infinite" can be interpreted as a statement about a *finite* (but extendable) structure.[3] Thus the intuitionist and the formalist are in agreement as to the part of mathematics which is "safe"; i.e., whose consistency may be taken as evident on the basis of an interpretation; namely, the part which may be interpreted as referring only to finite structures.[4]

4. LOGICISM

Logicism (Frege-Russell-Whitehead) arose out of a concern with a different problem: the nature of mathematical truth. Logicists hoped to show, as against Kant, that mathematics did not have any "subject matter," but dealt with pure relations among concepts,[5] and that these relations were "analytic," i.e., of the same character as the principle of non-contradiction, or the rule of *modus ponens*. In contrast, Hilbert maintained that mathematics *did* have an extralogical subject matter, namely *expressions*[6] (e.g., series of strokes $|, \; ||, \; |||, \; \cdots$) and that its simplest truths (e.g., "$||$ added to $|||$ is $|||||$") were *anschaulich* (a German word which can mean both

---

[3] Strictly speaking, this is true only of free-variable statements. And even there, although the assumptions used in any one free-variable proof always have a finite model, the proof that *this* is so may require non-finitist methods. This is one problem with "finitist mathematics": the consistency of "finitist" systems is not, in general, demonstrable by strictly finitist means.

[4] We are indebted to Georg Kreisel for the remark that the intuitionist notion of the "potential infinite" has *two* classical analogues: the "ill-defined infinite set" and the "finite (but unbounded) segment."

[5] Although he is frequently charged with "platonism," Frege did not think of "concepts" as entities at all (much less, entities of a superphysical kind), and he regarded the problem of the "existence of mathematical entities" as a ridiculous one. He would have, rather, agreed with Kreisel's remark that "the problem is the objectivity of mathematics, not the existence of mathematical objects."

[6] In place of "expressions" one might, of course, use other things: e.g., tables and chairs, or musical tunes. The important thing for Hilbert was not that finitist mathematics should be literally about series of *marks* (e.g., '|', '||', '|||', etc.) but that the subject matter, whatever it might be, should be wholly finite, discriminable, and *anschaulich* in all of its relevant parts and relations.

"visual"—in colloquial German—and "self-evident" or "intuitive" in philosophical German).

Logicism had one great and undeniable achievement—it succeeded in reducing all of classical mathematics (by any reasonable standard excluding completeness) to a single formal system. This achievement was much admired by the formalists, even if they did not agree that "mathematics has been reduced to logic." Formalists held that, as a result of the work of Whitehead and Russell, one had at last a clear formalization of what it was that had to be proved consistent.

Logicists, of course, thought they had done more than just axiomatize extant mathematics. They believed that they had derived all of mathematics from pure logic, without using any extralogical assumptions, and thus shown it all to be analytic. Today most philosophers and mathematicians regard part of this dispute as purely verbal: logicists did not reduce all of mathematics to *elementary* logic, but they did reduce mathematics to elementary logic *plus* the theory of properties (or sets), properties of properties, properties of properties of properties, etc. Thus if property theory (or set theory) may be counted as part of logic, mathematics is reducible to logic. But to what extent this refutes Kant's claim and establishes mathematics as analytic is something still open to question, for several objections may be raised. (It is not our purpose here to argue these points in detail, but we feel that it is particularly important to raise objections to logicism because it is a view which has received very little criticism in the literature: of all the authors we reprint, only Wittgenstein and the intuitionists are really seriously critical of it. But the intuitionists attack it from a very different point of view, as we point out later.)

What Kant had denied was that the propositions of mathematics (arithmetic would be the relevant branch here, since he might have conceded the analyticity of algebra) were analytic. But 'analytic' for him meant either 'following from the law of non-contradiction' or being (a "logical truth") of the form 'All A are B', where "the idea of being a B is contained in the idea of being an A." A relevant example of such an analytic truth might be 'All spinsters are females'. Now, it is hardly the case that the logicist reduction of mathematics clearly shows the propositions of mathematics to be of either of these kinds. "Following from the law of non-contradiction" is itself at best a very unclear notion. The most likely (and most charitable) construal for it is something like 'whose negations are self-contradictory'. Thus construed, the question becomes that of deciding whether showing that on one set of plausible definitions arithmetic can be derived from set theory establishes that the negations of (presumably the true) arithmetic propositions are self-contradictory. It establishes, to be sure, that *if* these definitions are correct analyses of the meanings of the arithmetic terms, and *if* the set theoretic axioms are themselves analytic in the relevant sense, and *if* being derivable in first-order logic from analytic propositions via definitions representing correct analyses constitutes "following from the law of non-contradiction," *then* indeed the logicists have shown that the propositions of arithmetic follow from the law of non-contradiction. But these are very big *if*'s. Probably the biggest of them is the one concerning the analyticity of the set-theoretic axioms. In what sense would *they* be "analytic"? Many, even of those who don't doubt their consistency, would balk at their analyticity. But even should this *if* be granted, the other two loom large. The reader should refer to Quine's "Two Dogmas of Empiricism" for some objections to the first.

And of course, it is just not the case that mathematical propositions have been shown to be analytic in the second of the two Kantian senses cited (i.e., reducible to "logical truths" which have the form 'All *A* are *B*'). It might be objected that to defend Kant on this basis is to trivialize him in the process, because he surely would have widened his notion of what constitutes logic if presented with, say, quantification theory. Therefore, the claim that ought to be examined is whether mathematics is reducible to quantification theory. To this, two replies might be offered. The first is, of course, that mathematics is not so reducible. Some set theory or its equivalent is needed as well. Hence this widening would not suffice. The second might be that Kant would not have agreed to a widening of the notion of logic beyond the *monadic* predicate calculus, so that the question does not even arise. And in either case, the problem of what constitutes a correct analysis of the meaning of a mathematical term is still with us and likely to remain for a while to come.

Yet, it should not be forgotten that if today it seems somewhat arbitrary just where one draws the line between logic and mathematics, this is itself a victory for Frege, Russell, and Whitehead: before their work, the gulf between the two subjects seemed absolute.

One difficulty with calling set theory "logic" concerns the axioms of set (or property) existence; e.g., $(\exists P)(x)(\sim P(x))$ (read: 'there is a P such that for all x, x does not have P' or more simply 'there is an empty property (or set)'). In his last years, Frege came to the conclusion that such assertions of existence were not part of *logic* at all, and repudiated "logicism," which he had founded. Another difficulty is the need for an Axiom of Infinity in deriving mathematics: in order to meet this difficulty, Frege, having given up logicism, proposed to derive mathematics from *geometry* (where the Axiom of Infinity is true, since presumably there are infinitely many points) instead of from "logic."

Russell, as has already been mentioned, proposed in the second edition of *PM* not to take the Axiom of Infinity as a postulate of the system, but to list it as a hypothesis whenever it was needed to prove a theorem. But then it becomes puzzling how mathematics is *useful* (if a great many of its theorems have the form 'if Inf. Ax., then p', and "Inf. Ax."—the Axiom of Infinity—is, in fact, empirically false).

In connection with the first difficulty, it has been argued that '$(\exists P)(x)(\sim P(x))$' is a necessary truth, since there is indeed a proposition '$P(x)$' which is false for every x, namely '$x \neq x$' (or any other self-contradictory proposition). More generally, Russell has sometimes suggested that '$(\exists P)$' need not be interpreted as meaning that something "exists," as an extralogical entity, but may only be a way of indicating that there is a meaningful proposition '$P(x)$' with the specified characteristics. (Hilbert would reply: you still need the notion of the *existence* of *formulas*, i.e., *expressions*.) Sometimes Russell writes in this way: as if a property (or, as he says, "propositional function") were only a linguistic expression containing free variables (e.g., 'x', 'y',...)—or, perhaps, the meaning of such an expression. However, this interpretation of *PM* is, in fact, excluded if "impredicative definitions" are permitted. (For explanation, see the article by Carnap in Part 1.) For, if 'P' ranges only over "properties namable by formulas of *PM*" then this restriction—to objects namable in *PM*—will appear in the definition of every set. In particular, 'real number' will only be able to mean 'real number namable in *PM*'. However, under the intended interpretation of the version of *PM* which permits impredicative definitions, there is an expression which stands for the set of *all* real numbers, not just *namable* real numbers.

Strangely, Russell has never appreciated this difficulty, and calls *PM* a "no-class theory" to the present day, although his "propositional functions" are nothing but arbitrary sets (or "classes") under another name, if impredicative definitions are permitted.

Another achievement of Frege and Russell was the analysis of the concept "number." Since this analysis is presented in detail in several of our selections, we shall not review it here. However, it raises several points of disagreement between logicists and intuitionists.

According to the intuitionists, one cannot understand 'two', 'three', etc., unless one has the general notion of a *number*. On the other hand, the logicists maintain that 'two', for example, is (contextually) definable thus:

$$2(P) \equiv (\exists x)(\exists y)[P(x) \cdot P(y) \cdot x \neq y \cdot (z)(P(z) \supset \cdot z = x \vee z = y)]$$

(read: 'there are two P's if and only if there are x, y such that x is P and y is P and x is not the same thing as y and for all z, if z is P then z is the same as x or z is the same as y'.)

Here the intuitionists may, perhaps, be right. The logicist account, however, could easily be modified so as to take care of this criticism: namely, define "number" just as the logicists do[7] (roughly, a "number" is anything that can be obtained from zero—or the class of all empty classes—by

---

[7] We mean to suggest here that an intuitionist could accept the logicist definition of number in terms of the "ancestral" (a number is something that is either 0 or bears the ancestral of the successor relation to 0); not that the famous Frege–Russell definition of the ancestral would in turn be acceptable to an intuitionist.

repeatedly applying a certain "successor" operation), and then define 'zero' *not* as 'the class of all empty classes', but rather as 'the smallest *number*' (defining 'smallest' in some suitable way, or as 'the *number* which is not a successor'), 'one' as 'the *number* which is the successor of zero', 'two' as 'the *number* which is the successor of one', etc. Then the notion 'number' will be part of the definition of *each* number.[8] Of course, the definition of 'two' will be *equivalent* to the one Russell employed, but not word-by-word (or rather symbol-by-symbol) synonymous with it. So one who used the new definition could perfectly well agree with the intuitionists that the Russell definition does not express the customary meaning exactly.

Another disagreement is over the identification of numbers with sets of sets (e.g., "zero" with "the set of all empty sets"). This much discussed disagreement is pretty unimportant. In the first place, Frege[9] did not hold that "zero," "one," "two," etc., *had* to be identified with any particular entities: the important thing was the analysis of 'there are two *P*'s', 'there are three *P*'s', etc. The intuitionists accept this analysis as mathematically correct. Perhaps the intuitionist would prefer to render 'there are two *P*'s' by 'the species of *P*'s can be put in one-to-one correspondence with the numbers one, two'—however, Frege would certainly have accepted this definition.

A more important disagreement concerns the logicist claim that "mathematics can be reduced to logic." Intuitionists reject this claim on the following grounds:

1. Understanding any system of deduction involves already having the notion of *iterating an operation an arbitrary finite number of times*; and this the intuitionists regard as a fundamentally *mathematical* and not logical notion. (Recall that they also regard it as a "creative" or extendable notion —not one whose every application is completely clear and specifiable in advance.)

2. *The principle of mathematical induction* (which we used in our proof that n^2 is the sum of the first *n* odd numbers) is a fundamentally *mathematical* one (closely connected with the idea of the *iteration* of an operation), and not reducible to logic. Frege did, indeed, reduce mathematical induction to what *he* called logic—via the "definition of the ancestral" (see the Frege, Russell, and Hempel selections). This reduction, however, depends on the use of impredicative definitions, which are rejected by intuitionists, and also on the axioms of set existence, which would not be called "logic" by intuitionists even if they did accept them.

---

[8] This procedure may sound circular, but clearly it is not, provided that the expression 'zero' does not appear in the definition of 'number'; i.e., that a number be defined, e.g., as either the set of all empty sets or something bearing the ancestral of the successor relation to the set of all empty sets. *Zero* could then be identified with the "smallest" number, etc.

[9] We are indebted to Michael Dummett for this and other points in connection with Frege.

5. TAUTOLOGIES AND SETS

In his *Tractatus Logico-Philosophicus*, Wittgenstein maintained, following Russell and Frege, that mathematics was reducible to logic. Logic, in turn, was reducible to propositional calculus, according to Wittgenstein. This is correct, for the system *PM*, whenever the number of individuals is a fixed finite number, but it is correct in the infinite case only if infinitely "big" expressions[10] are permitted. The idea is, briefly, to treat universal statements as infinite conjunctions: 'Everything is *F*' is treated as 'x_1 is *F* & x_2 is *F* & $\cdots$ & $\cdots$' (where x_1, x_2, $\cdots$ are all the individuals in the universe of discourse, in some order). Now, the truths of the propositional calculus are all "tautologies"—they come out true, combinatorially, under all possible assignments of 'true' and 'false' to the "elementary propositions." Thus was born the very popular philosophical slogan that "mathematics consists wholly of tautologies."

Of course, closer examination revealed serious difficulties with the *Tractatus* view. A quantifier over properties (i.e., such an expression as 'for all properties *P*') is expanded as a conjunction with one clause for each property of individuals. But this presupposes not only that the individuals form a well-defined totality, but that the properties (or *sets* of individuals) form a well-defined totality, and similarly for sets of sets, sets of sets of sets, etc. This is already debatable for 'property' in the sense of the term in which each property corresponds to a possible "rule for selecting"; for 'property' (or rather 'set') in the sense of *arbitrary collection* (*any* collection, whether given by a rule or by "chance"), the situation is even worse. Consider, for example, the famous "continuum problem" of Cantor. This asks whether there exists some set (in the sense of *arbitrary* set) of real numbers (*arbitrary* sequences of integers) which can be put into one-to-one correspondence with neither the set of all integers nor the set of *all* real numbers. The answer 'no' has been proved by Gödel to be *consistent* with the axioms of set theory. But the answer 'yes' has just been proved by Paul J. Cohen *also* to be consistent with those axioms. In what sense then would it be true that "there really is" (or "really isn't") any such set? One might answer: 'In the sense that if you listed all the sets of real numbers, you would (or wouldn't) find one such that if you listed all the one-to-one correspondences (arbitrary sets of pairs consisting of a real number and an integer, or of two real numbers, satisfying the "one-to-one" condition) you would not find a correspondence mapping the set in question onto the integers, and you would similarly fail to find a correspondence mapping the set in question onto the real numbers.' This answer, however, is completely unhelpful for many

---

[10] One cannot even say "infinitely long," because some of the expressions that would arise at higher types if all quantifiers were "expanded" as truth-functions would be *nondenumerably* infinite, and could not be thought of as existing ("written out") in primitive notation.

reasons: e.g., the notion of "listing" all the sets of real numbers is absurd if taken literally; so is the notion of completely examining even one non-denumerably infinite and "random" collection of real numbers in detail; and then how much more absurd is the notion of examining *all* "one-to-one correspondences!"

Today, very few philosophers or mathematicians of any school would maintain that the notion of, say, an arbitrary set of sets of real numbers is a completely clear one, or that all the mathematical statements one can write down in terms of this notion have a truth-value which is well-defined in the sense of being fixed by a rule—even a non-constructive rule—which does not assume that the notion of an "arbitrary set" has already been made clear. The contention that, even in the absence of such rules, questions like the continuum problem have a definite meaning and, having a definite meaning, have a definite answer, quite independently of the state of our knowledge, forms the core of "platonism" in the philosophy of mathematics. (For a remarkably lucid and forceful statement of this position, cf. Gödel's article on the continuum problem, especially the supplementary section.)

Nevertheless, there is a respect in which this is the natural position to take. We normally do not require an effective method of verification as the *sine qua non* of meaningfulness. This was a requirement made in quite another context (empirical science) by the Vienna Circle, and long since abandoned by most of its proponents. Why should it be different with mathematics? If we think we understand what is meant by a set, a one-to-one correspondence, etc., why shouldn't we say that the continuum problem has a definite answer, no matter how far we may be from finding out what it is? What do the two have to do with one another? A split on this question normally reveals a split on the most fundamental issues in the philosophy of mathematics, on the very nature of mathematical activity.

In general, the platonists will be those who consider mathematics as the *discovery* of truths about structures which exist independently of the activity or thought of mathematicians. For others not so platonistically minded, mathematics is an activity in which the mathematician plays a more creative role. To put it crudely, propositions are true at best insofar as they follow from assumptions and definitions we have made. If we can show that a proposition is *undecidable* from the assumptions we currently accept, the question of its "truth" or "falsity" vanishes in a puff of metaphysical smoke. Our assumptions, definitions, methods of proof, constitute the rules determining the truth or falsity of the propositions formulated in their terms. If a proposition is undecidable from our current assumptions, then its "truth" is not determined by the available rules. Since nothing else is relevant, the question of truth does not arise. The platonist does not agree because, for him, the truth of mathematical propositions is not determined by the rules we adopt, but rather by the correspondence or non-correspondence between the propositions and the mathematical structures to which the terms in those propositions refer. In his view, mathematical terms and propositions have meaning above and beyond that conferred on them by the assumptions and methods of proof accepted at any one time.

To get an idea of the objections that might be raised to the platonistic way of looking at the continuum problem let us look briefly at the notion of an "arbitrary set," which is needed for the formulation of the problem. The reader may perhaps wonder: what is wrong with our preceding explanation: "arbitrary set" means "any set, whether given by a rule or by chance." The difficulty is that the notion of *chance* makes no sense in pure mathematics, except as a figure of speech. Suppose, however, we took this explanation literally: we might, for example, define an "arbitrary sequence of integers" as a sequence that *could* be generated by a "random device." One difficulty is then the word 'could.' 'Could' can only mean mathematical possibility here, since we do not want to let physical laws have any effect on mathematical truth. But "mathematical possibility" is itself a disputed notion, where infinite structures are concerned. And a further difficulty is that, according to classical mathematics, there are other infinite sets, for instance the set of all sets *of sets* of real numbers, which are so "big" that they cannot be put into one-to-one correspondence with the set of all integers or even with the set of all real numbers: such sets could not be identical with the "output" of any possible physical process, even if we were to take the notion of a "possible (actually infinite) physical process" as itself a clear one.

Again, some people say: "Why worry about possible physical models at all? You know what a *collection* is (as in 'collection of oranges') and you know what an integer is; therefore you know what is meant by 'collection of integers', and by 'collection of collections of integers', etc." This "simple-minded" point of view hardly seems satisfying, however. In the first place, our ordinary notion of a "collection" is loaded with physical connotations. If we say that these are to be disregarded, and that the members of a "collection" need not be proximate in space and time, need not be "similar" in any particular respect, etc., then we are left with the notion of something like a random listing of objects. And if we say that the members of a "collection" (a) need not be objects, numbers, etc., but may themselves be "collections", (b) need not even be capable of being listed (or for that matter, named in language), even by a random device working through an infinity of time, what notion are we supposed to form at all?

Secondly, the presence of statements (like the continuum hypothesis) corresponding to which there is no verification or refutation procedure (except looking for a proof — which is most certainly not going to do any good, if 'proof' means 'proof in present-day set theory') is, perhaps, a reason for at least suspecting an unclarity in our notion of a "set."

Here it is instructive to compare set theory with number theory. In number theory, too, there are statements which are neither provable nor refutable from the axioms of present-day mathematics. Intuitionists might agree that this shows (not by itself, of course, but together with other considerations) that we do not have a clear notion of "truth" in number theory, and that our notion of a "totality of all integers" is not precise. Most mathematicians would reject this conclusion. Yet most mathematicians feels that the notion of an "arbitrary set" is somewhat unclear. What is the reason for this difference in attitude?

Perhaps the reason is that a verification/refutation procedure is inconceivable for number theory only if we require that the procedure be effective.[11] If we take the stand that "non-constructive" procedures—i.e., procedures that require us to perform infinitely many operations in a finite time—are conceivable,[12] though not *physically* possible (owing mainly to the existence of a limit to the velocity with which physical operations can be performed), then we can say that there does "in principle" exist a verification/refutation procedure for number theory. E.g., to "verify" that an equation $P(x, y, z) = 0$ has a solution using the "procedure," we *check each ordered triple x, y, z of integers.* (Of course, this requires working forever, or else completing an infinite series of operations in a finite time.) Similarly, to check a statement of the form $(x)(\exists y)P(x, y) = 0$ (read: 'for every x there is a y such that $P(x, y) = 0$') by the "procedure," we have to substitute 0 for x, and then check through $y = 0, 1, 2, \cdots$ until we find a y_0 such that $P(0, y_0) = 0$; then we substitute 1 for x, and look for a y_1 such that $P(1, y_1) = 0$; and so on (again this requires an infinite series of operations). What this shows is: the notion of "truth" in number theory is not a dubious one if the notion of a completed actually infinite series (of, say, definitely specifiable physical operations) is itself not dubious. Since many mathematicians do not share intuitionist doubts about the clarity of the actual infinite, it is understandable that such mathematicians are willing to take the notion of number-theoretic truth as precise. E.g., Carnap argued for the legitimacy of such "non-constructive rules" in explaining the notion of number-theoretic truth in his famous book, *The Logical Syntax of Language.*

By way of contrast, we recall that *no* physical structure (not even an infinite one) can serve as a "standard model" for set theory. In addition, even if we allow "working forever," "completing infinite series in a finite time," etc., no precisely definable sequence of operations exists by means of which we could "in principle" tell (in the sense explained in connection with number theory) whether an arbitrary statement of set theory was true or false by the procedure of exhaustively checking all cases. In short, if you

---

[11] An effective procedure is (roughly) one that a computing machine could be "programed" to employ. Gödel proved the impossibility of an effective decision procedure for number theory.

[12] E.g., if one has an infinite series of operations to perform, say $S_1, S_2, S_3, \ldots$ and one is able to perform S_1 in 1 minute, S_2 in $\frac{1}{2}$ minute, S_3 in $\frac{1}{4}$ minute, etc.; then in 2 minutes one will have completed the whole infinite series.

understand such notions as *counting, adding, multiplying, seeing if two numbers are equal*, we can explain to you the notion of a "true statement of number theory" (though not if you consistently "boggle" at all quantifications over an infinite domain); but to have explained to you the notion of a "true statement of set theory" or of an "arbitrary set," it would appear that you must already have some such notion in your conceptual vocabulary.

6. MATHEMATICAL TRUTH

One is struck by the extent to which those professional philosophers (as opposed to mathematicians) who have written about the subjects of "mathematical truth" and "the existence of mathematical objects" have ignored or failed to mention almost *all* of the foregoing considerations. For instance, there has been a great deal of talk about the "existence" of "such entities as numbers": a very strange way of putting things, since number theory as such certainly does not assume that the number words "one," "two," etc., refer to anything. On the other hand, the questions of the intelligibility, preciseness, and "safety" of references to actually infinite structures and sequences of operations have been largely ignored, or given only the benefit of passing mention. Partly this has been so because much of the literature had assumed its present form before the proof by Gödel of the impossibility of effective (and hence wholly finite) "decision procedures" (verification/refutation procedures) for number theory and set theory. For example, the last part of Carnap's article "The Logicist Foundations of Mathematics" would be a perfectly acceptable answer to the difficulties about impredicative definitions (at least of sets of integers) if set theory were *decidable* (admitted of an effective decision procedure); it was the discovery of Gödel's theorem that pushed Carnap from the semi-finitist standpoint taken in that article to the use of "non-constructive" rules in his later writings, and still later into an almost platonistic attitude toward the notion of a set.

In connection with the notion of mathematical truth: the early Wittgenstein notion of a "tautology" is seen to be unhelpful once we realize that, if all of mathematics is to consist of "tautologies," then some of these must be not just infinite, but "bigger" than physical space itself, when written out in the "primitive notation!" The philosophers who have, nevertheless, gone on saying that all the truths of pure mathematics are "tautologies" have, in all probability, simply been unaware of this difficulty. Wittgenstein himself, however, did become aware of it (partly under the influence of Brouwer, according to one story), and he adopted a radically different position in his later writings.

Besides the early Wittgenstein position ("mathematics consists of tautologies"), another position on the nature of mathematical truth very popular with philosophers has been *conventionalism* (the statements of pure mathematics are "true by convention" or "true by the rules of the language").

This position is, for example, ably expounded by Nagel in "Logic without Ontology" and attacked by Quine in "Truth by Convention," and, more radically, in "Two Dogmas of Empiricism." In "Semantics, Empiricism, and Ontology," Carnap extends conventionalism to questions of mathematical existence: "sets," he appears to say, *exist by convention*. Indeed, so much of the literature of analytic philosophy has been devoted to discussions *pro* and *con* conventionalism that very little would be left of any important bearing on the philosophy of mathematics if it should turn out that conventionalism is fundamentally and completely wrong. Even Quine and the later Wittgenstein—both former conventionalists turned anti-conventionalists—try to save certain elements of the conventionalist position when they give a positive account of the nature of mathematical truth. (Roughly, the move is to replace the notion of a "convention" or "rule" by the notion of a "bare behavioristic fact" of "agreement in our judgments.")

The following difficulty with conventionalistic accounts is worth mentioning (it is not discussed by any of our authors): the statement that a mathematical system is *consistent* is itself a statement of pure mathematics, and so, if true, must be *true by convention*, if conventionalism is right and all true mathematical statements are true by convention. But isn't there something absurd about the idea of laying down a possibly inconsistent set of conventions, and then adding a further convention: "the above conventions are to be consistent"? Here we feel inclined to say: the freedom from contradiction of a set of rules (the fact that certain "programs" for computing do not lead to the "output" '1 = 0') is an objective combinatorial fact, independent of human stipulation.

7. THE EXISTENCE OF MATHEMATICAL ENTITIES

The so-called ontological problem in philosophy presents itself in many guises, or rather, has many aspects. It has received (from W. V. Quine—"On What There Is") the forthright formulation "What is there?" and the equally forthright answer (from the same author) "Everything." As anyone familiar with Quine's philosophical position well knows, the apparent simplicity of both the question and the answer is only apparent. This is the beginning of a sinewy course which starts from the view that it is not evident from a given statement what that statement *says* (implies that) there is; i.e., what there must be for the statement in question to be true. To illustrate, consider the following two statements:

(1)   She did it for Peter's sake.

(2)   She did it for Peter's brother.

Both appear to be of the same grammatical form, but, at least according to the proponents of this view, (2) presupposes (implies) the existence of some male (other than Peter), whereas (1) does not presuppose (imply) the existence of some "sake." So, apparent grammatical form is not a reliable guide to logical form. Our utterances do not wear their ontological commitments upon their linguistic sleeves. We need a key to the Pandora's box of ontological commitments that is language. We need a criterion.

Armed with such a criterion, we could dispose of the problem by answering it piecemeal. If we have some way of telling what a statement *says* there is, then our original problem reduces to that of the truth of statements. This is one which we may or may not be able to solve, but one which had been with us all along. If the statement is a mathematical one, then presumably we establish its truth or falsity in the way appropriate to statements of its kind. And if it is true, then there is what it says there is.

That such a criterion is needed should seem evident from examining statements (1) and (2). It is normal to react with suspicion to the suggestion that above and beyond the people, atomic warheads, and pleasantly striped felines whose existence we must more or less reluctantly avow, there are also "sakes." We naturally take the construction 'for Peter's sake' to differ in this respect from 'for Peter's uncle'. But in the absence of a theory to back us up, that we should so react proves nothing but our inclination to deny to "Peter's sake" the same status—existence—which we so cheerfully extend to Peter's uncle. The criterion Quine proffers is rooted in the ancient philosophical tradition of reductionism, and in its intent appears to do justice to our intuitions. The leading idea is this: what supports our intuitions about the case of Peter's sake is that we seem to be able to say the same thing without even appearing to make reference to "sakes." It might be necessary to employ circumlocutions, but as it is normally meant (1) might be paraphrased as

(3)   She did it for Peter.

This won't quite do because 'for' sometimes suggests 'at the request of', but it suffices to indicate the direction in which the paraphrase might be extended.

So, to remove an apparent commitment by paraphrase, is to show that it was *only* apparent. To complete the picture, there is a particular kind of paraphrase which is remarkably well suited to reveal ontological commitments. This is paraphrase into the notation of quantification theory: if a statement S which appears to say that there are F's fatally resists paraphrase into statements in quantificational notation which do not imply '$(\exists x)Fx$' then S is ontologically committed to F's. Such is Quine's criterion (somewhat paraphrased).

It was said previously that the road was a tortuous one. But so far everything seems straightforward enough. The twist comes when we notice that, on Quine's view, statements generally don't confront the tests of their truth or falsity singly; they do so in bunches, to which we may loosely refer as "theories" (cf. "Two Dogmas of Empiricism"). And it is the "truth" of the entire theory that we judge, and we judge it on severely pragmatic considerations, such as the degree to which it serves our interests or needs. In the particular case of *mathematical* theories, it seems to be an established fact that something like what passes for "classical mathematics" is needed in our (non-mathematical) scientific theorizing. But on Quine's criterion, these mathematical theories seem to require abstract entities as values of their bound variables of quantification. Unless we can produce "mathematical" theories which can do the same job, but which make no such demands upon our ontological consciences, we are forced to recognize reference to such entities as necessary and the entities themselves as part of the ultimate furniture of the universe.

Should ingenuity prevail and provide us with a paraphrase of that part of classical mathematics we need for scientific theorizing which does not require us to recognize entities any more abstract than tables, chairs, or kitchen cabinets, then we could use such a paraphrase to reduce the ultimate furniture of the universe to something more closely approximating the ultimate furniture of our houses. Quine sees no such paraphrase in the offing. But we may be thankful for one thing at least; that is the work of Frege, Russell, *et al.*, which has rid us once and for all of the need to make a place in our conceptual attic for entities such as integrals, irrational numbers, and even integers. The reduction of mathematics to the theory of classes allows us to confine all such items to the corner reserved for classes. Less pragmatically inclined logicists might take the reduction to have shown that numbers, etc., "were really classes all along." Quine, of course, makes no such claim. He asserts that numbers are dispensable in favor of classes. The "economy" thereby achieved is that of having a homogeneous world of abstract entities instead of a conceptually heterogeneous one cluttered with real, rational, whole, complex, positive, negative, irrational, imaginary, and what-have-you numbers in addition to the customary assortment of classes.

But not everyone feels as Quine does. There are those who take their ontological stand on principle. The nominalist is one such. Nominalism, as its name suggests, has traditionally been a thesis about names. It could with justice be stated as the view that there is no need to confuse an abstract name with the name of an abstract thing. "Redness," "heterogeneity," "the square root of -1" are abstract names, but we need not on that account suppose that there exist abstract things which they name, even if we think the names are meaningful. For a name to have meaning there need not exist something of which it is the name. Nominalism denies the legitimacy of a particular kind of inference—without any commitment whatsoever about the truth or falsity of the conclusion of such an inference. Through the ages, this view has become transmuted into the stronger one denying that there are any abstract things.

The nominalist of the latter half of the twentieth century makes no such sweeping denials, however. He directs his wrath against relations that may be employed to "generate" new (heretofore undiscovered?) elements out of those we already may have admitted. Good man that he is, he allows us to start with anything we like as the fundamental building blocks of the universe, but once we have made our choice, we are limited in the methods we may employ to generate (discover) new members. What there is, is limited to what there was in the first place and to what can be obtained from this by applying certain methods acceptable to him. These may be roughly characterized as follows: he recognizes no distinction among generated entities which does not make itself felt as a difference of "content," where a difference in "content" is one which comes down to a difference in ultimate constituency in terms of the previously chosen individuals. For example, if we start with a table, a chair, and the number three as our "individuals" then (letting '+' designate our generating relation, or in this case, operation) we are allowed to "expand" our spartan universe to include

(a)   table + chair

(b)   table + three

(c)   chair + three

(d)   (table + chair) + three

leaving us with the meager total of seven items in all. We may describe our universe by saying that, given any pair of items in it, one member of the pair differs from the other by "containing" at least one of the *original* individuals which the other does not. This is why the placement of parentheses in (d) is really superfluous. The nominalist's rule dictates the associativity of the operation of compounding new elements. Given any choice of individuals, the nominalist will be willing to recognize all additions made to the original set which satisfy this principle, but no others. In particular, what is most obviously ruled out is the employment of class membership as the generating relation, for, e.g., the table and the class whose only member is the table are distinct on set-theoretic grounds, but identical on nominalistic ones. They both "reduce" to the table.

One sees but dimly what relation this view bears to that of traditional nominalists, but if a bit of interpretation be allowed, we will make a stab at it. Goodman denies that there is anything in his nominalism which militates against abstract entities as such; they may enter the universe at ground level, as individuals. What follows is not an imputation to him of any view incompatible with those he expresses. It is only a myth, a story of what might have been (but of course was not). It is an attempt to explain the conceptual relation of latter-day nominalism to its intellectual precursor.

Imagine an empiricist, born with a blank mind, who looks about him and sees trees, grass, green patches, and people. He also hears these people discoursing on trees, grass, green patches, and people. He understands them.

Being an empiricist and knowing that he was born with a blank mind, he supposes that what language he understands and speaks, he must have learned. Insofar as it contains "names," he must have learned them either directly in connection with those things which they name (ostensively), or else indirectly, in connection with descriptions of the things which they name. The chain must end somewhere in experience. Names of individual things are the easiest things for which to account on such a view. "General names" present more of a problem, but nevertheless one which can be solved by treating them as names that apply to individual things not singly but severally. But anything which appears to be a name, but which cannot be accounted for in this way, is devoid of meaning, especially if it appears to make reference to entities with which we could not conceivably have come into contact. Classes are such entities. We can make distinctions among "entities" in terms of the notation of classes that have no counterpart in the reality with which we have had intercourse. So viewed, the distinction between Bobo the elephant, the set whose only member is Bobo, and the set whose only member is *that* set is unintelligible. There is nothing to understand. It is no distinction. And similarly for the distinction between the number five and actual collections of five *bona fide* objects. The only thing that can make a difference is a difference in individuals—and individuals are the things that we can see, touch, etc.

Applying Goodman's nominalism to such an empiricism yields a form of traditional nominalism. Goodman's view is, if you like, traditional nominalism stripped of its attendant empiricism. It is the resulting nakedness that has made it such a favored object of misunderstanding. For one might complain (with some justice) that without the company of the empiricism, or some such explanatory view, nominalism is a lonely principle indeed—devoid of a *raison d'être*.

Attention to the language Goodman employs suggests another approach to the problem, one which might cast some light on Goodman's nominalism and some other views as well. It will be recalled that he states his view in terms of a "relation that generates" new elements from the "atoms" or "individuals" of the system. If it is thought that these atoms constitute all there is before we start "generating" more, and that the generating relation of a system is just that—a mass production system for compounding new elements from our raw materials—then it is not without some justice that a sober man would object to a method of bookkeeping which allowed indefinitely many new objects to have been "made" from the same materials. Bobo, our elephant of a minute ago, is a case in point. The factory that set up shop with him as its entire stock of raw material and started flooding the market with Bobo, his unit class, the unit class of that, etc., would be compounding a felony. And if ontology is that kind of enterprise, then indeed the 'ε' of class membership should be ruled out as a manufacturing principle. But is it really? Is setting up a system (mathematical, scientific, philosophical, etc.)

sufficiently like setting up a factory with a fixed stock of raw materials to warrant being subject to the nominalist's scruple?

Many would deny that it is. It might be argued that setting up such a system is more like putting forth a theory to describe, on the basis of indirect evidence, what is to be found in some remote region of space. If such is the case, then the appropriate standard to apply to a theory is one having to do with its relation to what it purports to describe, systematize, explain, etc. Considerations of whether the "generating" relation of the system satisfied nominalistic principles would be strictly irrelevant. We are not generating new entities, we are merely attempting to describe those that there are. And what reason is there to deny that 'ε' could be employed accurately so to describe? When the task is a descriptive one, and presumably judgable by other standards, there is less temptation to complain of ontic *escroquerie*. The plausibility of nominalism comes almost entirely from its misleading term "generating relation." At least the platonist might argue thus. The description that he might give of his task would very likely parallel the foregoing. Gödel says something very much like this in both of the selections that we reprint.

But the battlefield has not yet been accurately described. There are other combatants besides Quine, the nominalist, and the platonist. We will not attempt to be exhaustive, but Carnap's position, a form of conventionalism, must be mentioned. We will not discuss it in as much detail, because we feel that it is open to fewer misunderstandings than the others might be. Carnap's view of ontology is easily stated. There are two kinds of questions that might be asked, and these two kinds are best exemplified by the two groups:

(a)   Are there numbers? Do numbers exist? Do physical objects exist?

(b)   Are there numbers x, y, z, w, such that $x > 2 \cdot (y^x + z^x = w^x)$?
       Are there any gila monsters weighing more than 20 pounds?

The first group contains what Carnap wishes to call "framework" of "external" questions, and the second, "internal" questions. Carnap argues that, although the two groups might *seem* to contain the same kinds of question, asking whether there exist things satisfying a certain description, the similarities are superficial only. Whereas questions in the second group call for normal answers, those in the first call *not* for answers but for practical decisions concerning the adoption of linguistic forms. They are really disguised ways of asking:

(a)   Should we adopt a language which involves speaking of numbers? of physical objects?

These are not "factual" questions, admitting of answers that might be true or false. They are policy questions which must be answered on the basis of the suitability of such adoption to our aims, goals, etc. Once one has decided to adopt a particular set of linguistic forms, those of number theory, for example (possibly because we want to do science and it does not appear to be feasible without them), then the internal questions are answerable in the manner appropriate to the framework in question. In the case of numbers, by providing proofs, in the case of physical objects or gila monsters, by suitable empirical techniques. At any rate, the familiar questions of ontology, concerning the existence of abstract entities, or concrete ones, vanish as real questions. Their place is taken by questions calling for decisions rather than for straightforward answers.

We wish at this point to raise only one possible difficulty concerning this position. What distinguishes an internal from an external question? For example, does "Are there tables?" call for a decision concerning the use of table talk? Or is it a *bona fide* question? How are we to tell? The answer does not emerge very clearly from Carnap's discussion.

8. WITTGENSTEIN

The selections from the writings of Wittgenstein have been put by themselves in a separate section, in this collection of readings. This should not be taken as an indication that Wittgenstein is more important in the philosophy of mathematics, or even, necessarily, as important as such seminal thinkers as Brouwer, Hilbert, or Frege. Rather it is in view of the great influence that Wittgenstein had on Russell and on the positivists, the great influence that he is currently having on "analytic philosophers," and the great difficulty of interpreting his often cryptic remarks on the subjects with which we are concerned, that it has seemed worthwhile to include substantial excerpts from his writings, and desirable to group those excerpts by themselves, rather than to struggle to make them fit one of our topic headings. Our purpose in including the reviews of his book is to facilitate discussion of Wittgenstein's later ideas in the philosophy of mathematics by providing possible starting points; we certainly do not wish to give the impression that we regard these criticisms as definitive.

The reader who encounters Wittgenstein's writing for the first time in this volume is warned that it is unwise to try to "attach a label" to Wittgenstein's position, either in the *Tractatus* or in the later writings. The desire to "fit" Wittgenstein into one or another school (usually positivism) has led to radical misinterpretation of his position, or rather positions. In the *Tractatus*, for example, Wittgenstein held that such logically valid statements as

(1) It is raining or it is not raining.

(this is, of course, a substitution-instance of '$p \lor \sim p$') are "empty" and "say nothing about the world." This has led interpreters to ascribe to Wittgenstein the position that "the truths of formal logic are empty"—even though these interpreters often have had in mind a different and wider notion of "truth of formal logic," including such propositions as

(2)   Every proposition is either true or false.

    or

(3)   Every proposition p has a unique negation $\sim p$ which is such that
    (I) p and $\sim p$ together fill up "logical space" (i.e., 'p or $\sim p$' holds in every "possible world").
    (II) p and $\sim p$ correspond to disjoint regions of "logical space" (i.e., 'p' and '$\sim p$' do not *both* hold in *any* "possible world").

In Wittgenstein's view (in the *Tractatus*), (2) and (3) are not "empty" propositions; in fact (2) and (3) are not *propositions* at all: rather they are attempts to express what "shows itself" but "cannot be said." (1) would, indeed, have traditionally been said to depend for its truth on such facts as (2) and (3): Wittgenstein preferred to say that (1) was a "tautology" (or "empty"); but he added "it must show something, that certain combinations of signs are tautologies." *What* it "must show" is, of course (2) or (3) (in the present case), but Wittgenstein could not say this because of his doctrine of the inexpressibility of such facts.

As far as we can see, this position—apart from the peculiar notion that these are things that "speak out on their own account," but that we cannot "express by means of the signs"[13]—is not *so* far removed from the quite common position (among German philosophers, at least) that such facts as (2), (3) are ultimate and neither need nor possess any further explanation. That *these* sorts of principles are "empty" is something that Wittgenstein never meant to suggest!

Wittgenstein's later position (or again, position*s*) is equally dangerous to "clarify," although it is safe to say that certain doctrines are regarded by Wittgenstein as worth extensive discussion (different forms of platonism, for example, and also different versions of conventionalism). Wittgenstein's later position is in some ways very like Quine's: Quine and Wittgenstein both have a desire to destroy "platonistic" accounts once and for all, and at the same time, a distaste (albeit an ambivalent one) for conventionalistic accounts. For example, the arguments used by Quine in "Truth by Convention" also occur scattered through Wittgenstein's writings. Wittgenstein, however, devotes more attention to the differences between different branches of mathematics (e.g., set theory, number theory, logic) than does Quine; and he would not reject the notion of an "analytic" truth, as Quine does, although he would certainly not wish to say that "mathematics consists of analytic truths," either.

What is unique to Wittgenstein is a tendency to write, at least part of the

[13] Compare Miss G. E. M. Anscombe's discussion in *An Introduction to Wittgenstein's Tractatus*, p. 77.

time, in a way that *suggests* that "what we say" somehow *determines* the truths of mathematics. Interpreters who want to make Wittgenstein a conventionalist find such passages grist for their mill; but it would probably be more reasonable (though, perhaps, not very charitable) to see this as an unfortunate way of writing produced by Wittgenstein's extreme antipathy to universals, necessary connections, etc. In discussing *general names*, for example (a topic wholly outside the philosophy of mathematics), Wittgenstein *also* writes in a way that exaggerates the importance of "how we talk": on the basis of the worst passages, one could accuse him of holding that there are objective regularities in human linguistic behavior, but no objective regularities in non-linguistic events! (E.g., Wittgenstein sometimes writes as if the things we call "green" had *nothing* in common *except* that speakers *call* them green!) In the latter case (general names), it is clear that Wittgenstein did not really want to adopt such a self-defeating position; he meant only to deny the explanatory value of, e.g., postulating a universal "greeness" to account for the fact that *this* wall and *that* wall are both *green*. In the mathematical case, it is likely that Wittgenstein never did arrive at a position on the nature of mathematical necessity (for example) with which he was satisfied. His "remarks" are private notes, published after his death and without his consent; for this reason they deserve a different kind of reading than a "finished product" that a living philosopher is prepared to defend.

Part One

SYMPOSIUM ON THE FOUNDATIONS OF MATHEMATICS

I. THE LOGICIST FOUNDATIONS OF MATHEMATICS

Rudolf Carnap

II. THE INTUITIONIST FOUNDATIONS OF MATHEMATICS

Arend Heyting

III. THE FORMALIST FOUNDATIONS OF MATHEMATICS

Johann von Neumann

The first three essays in this part form part of a symposium on the foundations of mathematics which appeared in Erkenntnis (1931), *pp.* 91–121. *They were translated by Erna Putnam and Gerald J. Massey and appear here with the kind permission of Rudolf Carnap, Arend Heyting, and Klara von-Neumann Eckart. The last of these appears in A. H. Taub, ed.*, John von Neumann Collected Works, *Vol.* 2 (*New York: Pergamon Press*, 1961).

Rudolf Carnap

The problem of the logical and epistemological foundations of mathematics has not yet been completely solved. This problem vitally concerns both mathematicians and philosophers, for any uncertainty in the foundations of the "most certain of all the sciences" is extremely disconcerting. Of the various attempts already made to solve the problem none can be said to have resolved every difficulty. These efforts, the leading ideas of which will be presented in these three papers, have taken essentially three directions: *Logicism*, the chief proponent of which is Russell; *Intuitionism*, advocated by Brouwer; and Hilbert's *Formalism*.

Since I wish to draw you a rough sketch of the salient features of the logicist construction of mathematics, I think I should not only point out those areas in which the logicist program has been completely or at least partly successful but also call attention to the difficulties peculiar to this approach. One of the most important questions for the foundations of mathematics is that of the relation between mathematics and logic. *Logicism* is the thesis that mathematics is reducible to logic, hence nothing but a part of logic. Frege was the first to espouse this view (1884). In their great work, *Principia Mathematica*, the English mathematicians A. N. Whitehead and B. Russell produced a systematization of logic from which they constructed mathematics.

We will split the logicist thesis into two parts for separate discussion:

1. The *concepts* of mathematics can be derived from logical concepts through explicit definitions.
2. The *theorems* of mathematics can be derived from logical axioms through purely logical deduction.

I. THE DERIVATION OF MATHEMATICAL CONCEPTS

To make precise the thesis that the concepts of mathematics are derivable from logical concepts, we must specify the logical concepts to be employed in the derivation. They are the following: In propositional calculus, which deals with the relations between unanalyzed sentences, the most important concepts are: the negation of a sentence p, 'not-p' (symbolized '$\sim p$'); the disjunction of two sentences, 'p or q' ('$p \vee q$'); the conjunction, 'p and q' ('$p \cdot q$'); and the implication, 'if p, then q' ('$p \supset q$'). The concepts of functional calculus are given in the form of functions, e.g., '$f(a)$' (read 'f of a') signifies that the property f belongs to the object a. The most important concepts of functional calculus are universality and existence: '$(x)f(x)$' (read 'for every x, f of x') means that the property f belongs to every object; '$(\exists x)f(x)$' (read 'there is an x such that f of x') means that f belongs to at least one object. Finally there is the concept of identity: '$a = b$' means that 'a' and 'b' are names of the same object.

Not all these concepts need be taken as undefined or primitive, for some of them are reducible to others. For example, '$p \vee q$' can be defined as '$\sim(\sim p \cdot \sim q)$' and '$(\exists x)f(x)$' as '$\sim(x)\sim f(x)$'. It is the logicist thesis, then, that the logical concepts just given suffice to define all mathematical concepts, that over and above them no specifically mathematical concepts are required for the construction of mathematics.

Already before Frege, mathematicians in their investigations of the interdependence of mathematical concepts had shown, though often without being able to provide precise definitions, that all the concepts of arithmetic are reducible to the natural numbers (i.e., the numbers 1, 2, 3, ... which are used in ordinary counting). Accordingly, the *main problem* which remained for logicism was to derive the natural numbers from logical concepts. Although Frege had already found a solution to this problem, Russell and Whitehead reached the same results independently of him and were subsequently the first to recognize the agreement of their work with Frege's. The crux of this solution is the correct recognition of the logical status of the natural numbers; they are logical attributes which belong, not to things, but to concepts. That a certain number, say 3, is the number of a concept means that three objects fall under it. We can express the very same thing with the help of the logical concepts previously given. For example, let '$2_m(f)$' mean that at least two objects fall under the concept f. Then we can define this concept as follows (where '$=_{Df}$' is the symbol for definition, read as "means by definition"):

$$2_m(f) =_{Df} (\exists x)(\exists y)[\sim(x = y) \cdot f(x) \cdot f(y)]$$

or in words: there is an x and there is a y such that x is not identical with y and f belongs to x and f belongs to y. In like manner, we define 3_m, 4_m, and so on. Then we define the number two itself thus:

$$2(f) =_{\text{Df}} 2_m(f) \cdot \sim 3_m(f)$$

or in words: at least two, but not at least three, objects fall under f. We can also define arithmetical operations quite easily. For example, we can define addition with the help of the disjunction of two mutually exclusive concepts. Furthermore, we can define the concept of natural number itself.

The derivation of the other kinds of numbers—i.e., the positive and negative numbers, the fractions, the real and the complex numbers—is accomplished, not in the usual way by adding to the domain of the natural numbers, but by the construction of a completely new domain. The natural numbers do not constitute a subset of the fractions but are merely correlated in obvious fashion with certain fractions. Thus the natural number 3 and the fraction $\frac{3}{1}$ are not identical but merely correlated with one another. Similarly we must distinguish the fraction $\frac{1}{2}$ from the real number correlated with it. In this paper, we will treat only the definition of the real numbers. Unlike the derivations of the other kinds of numbers which encounter no great difficulties, the derivation of the real numbers presents problems which, it must be admitted, neither logicism, intuitionism, nor formalism has altogether overcome.

Let us assume that we have already constructed the series of fractions (ordered according to magnitude). Our task, then, is to supply definitions of the real numbers based on this series. Some of the real numbers, the rationals, correspond in obvious fashion to fractions; the rest, the irrationals, correspond as Dedekind showed (1872) to "gaps" in the series of fractions. Suppose, for example, that we divide the (positive) fractions into two classes, the class of all whose square is less than 2, and the class comprising all the rest of the fractions. This division forms a "cut" in the series of fractions which corresponds to the irrational real number $\sqrt{2}$. This cut is called a "gap" since there is no fraction correlated with it. As there is no fraction whose square is two, the first or "lower" class contains no greatest member, and the second or "upper" class contains no least member. Hence, to every real number there corresponds a cut in the series of fractions, each irrational real number being correlated with a gap.

Russell developed further Dedekind's line of thought. Since a cut is uniquely determined by its "lower" class, Russell defined a real number as the lower class of the corresponding cut in the series of fractions. For example, $\sqrt{2}$ is defined as the class (or property) of those fractions whose square is less than two, and the rational real number $\frac{1}{3}$ is defined as the class of all fractions smaller than the fraction $\frac{1}{3}$. On the basis of these definitions, the entire arithmetic of the real numbers can be developed. This development, however, runs up against certain difficulties connected with so-called "impredicative definition," which we will discuss shortly.

The essential point of this method of introducing the real numbers is that they are *not postulated but constructed*. The logicist does not establish the existence of structures which have the properties of the real numbers by laying down axioms or postulates; rather, through explicit definitions, he produces logical constructions that have, by virtue of these definitions, the usual properties of the real numbers. As there are no "creative definitions," definition is not creation but only name-giving to something whose existence has already been established.

In similarly constructivistic fashion, the logicist introduces the rest of the concepts of mathematics, those of analysis (e.g., convergence, limit, continuity, differential, quotient, integral, etc.) and also those of set theory (notably the concepts of the transfinite cardinal and ordinal numbers). This "constructivistic" method forms part of the very texture of logicism.

II. THE DERIVATION OF THE THEOREMS OF MATHEMATICS

The second thesis of logicism is that the *theorems of mathematics* are derivable from logical axioms through logical deduction. The requisite system of logical axioms, obtained by simplifying Russell's system, contains four axioms of propositional calculus and two of functional calculus. The rules of inference are a rule of substitution and a rule of implication (the *modus ponens* of ancient logic). Hilbert and Ackermann have used these same axioms and rules of inference in their system.

Mathematical predicates are introduced by explicit definitions. Since an explicit definition is nothing but a convention to employ a new, usually much shorter, way of writing something, the *definiens* or the new way of writing it can always be eliminated. Therefore, as every sentence of mathematics can be translated into a sentence which contains only the primitive logical predicates already mentioned, this second thesis can be restated thus: Every provable mathematical sentence is translatable into a sentence which contains only primitive logical symbols and which is provable in logic.

But the derivation of the theorems of mathematics poses certain difficulties for logicism. In the first place it turns out that some theorems of arithmetic and set theory, if interpreted in the usual way, require for their proof besides the logical axioms still other special axioms known as the *axiom of infinity* and the *axiom of choice* (or multiplicative axiom). The axiom of infinity states that for every natural number there is a greater one. The axiom of choice states that for every set of disjoint non-empty sets, there is (at least) one selection-set, i.e., a set that has exactly one member in common with each of the member sets. But we are not concerned here with the content of these axioms but with their logical character. Both are existential sentences. Hence, Russell was right in hesitating to present them as logical axioms, for logic deals only with possible entities and cannot make assertions about whether something does or does not exist. Russell found a way out of this difficulty. He reasoned that since mathematics was also a purely formal science, it too could make only conditional. not categorical, statements about existence: if certain structures exist, then there also exist certain other structures whose existence follows logically from the existence of the former. For this reason he transformed a mathematical sentence, say S, the proof of which required the axiom of infinity, I, or the axiom of choice, C, into a conditional sentence; hence S is taken to assert not S, but $I \supset S$ or $C \supset S$, respectively. This conditional sentence is then derivable from the axioms of logic.

A greater difficulty, perhaps the greatest difficulty, in the construction of mathematics has to do with another axiom posited by Russell, the so-called *axiom of reducibility*, which has justly become the main bone of contention for the critics of the system of *Principia Mathematica*. We agree with the opponents of logicism that it is inadmissible to take it as an axiom. As we will discuss more fully later, the gap created by the removal of this axiom has certainly not yet been filled in an entirely satisfactory way. This difficulty is bound up with Russell's *theory of types* which we shall now briefly discuss.

We must distinguish between a "simple theory of types" and a "ramified theory of types." The latter was developed by Russell but later recognized by Ramsey to be an unnecessary complication of the former. If, for the sake of simplicity, we restrict our attention to one-place functions (properties) and abstract from many-place functions (relations), then type theory consists in the following classification of expressions into different "types": To type 0 belong the names of the objects ("individuals") of the domain of discourse (e.g., $a, b, \ldots$). To type 1 belong the properties of these objects (e.g. $f(a)$, $g(a), \ldots$). To type 2 belong the properties of these properties (e.g., $F(f), G(f), \ldots$); for example, the concept $2(f)$ defined above belongs to this type. To type 3 belong the properties of properties of properties, and so on. The basic rule of type theory is that every predicate belongs to a determinate type and can be meaningfully applied only to expressions of the next lower type. Accordingly, sentences of the form $f(a)$, $F(f)$, $2(f)$ are always meaningful, i.e., either true or false; on the other hand combinations like $f(g)$ and $f(F)$ are neither true nor false but meaningless. In particular, expressions like $f(f)$ or $\sim f(f)$ are meaningless, i.e., we cannot meaningfully say of a property either that it belongs to itself or that it does not. As we shall see, this last result is important for the elimination of the antinomies.

This completes our outline of the simple theory of types, which most proponents of modern logic consider legitimate and necessary. In his system, Russell introduced the ramified theory of types, which has not found much acceptance. In this theory the properties of each type are further subdivided into "orders." This division is based, not on the kind of objects to which the property belongs, but on the form of the definition which introduces it. Later we shall consider the reasons why Russell believed this further ramification necessary. Because of the introduction of the ramified theory of types, certain difficulties arose in the construction of mathematics, especially in the theory of real numbers. Many fundamental theorems not only could not be proved but could not even be expressed. To overcome this difficulty, Russell had to use brute force; i.e., he introduced the axiom of reducibility by means of which the different orders of a type could be reduced in certain respects to the lowest order of the type. The sole justification for this axiom was the fact that there seemed to be no other way out of this particular difficulty engendered by the ramified theory of types. Later Russell himself, influenced by Wittgenstein's sharp criticism, abandoned the axiom of reducibility in the second edition of *Principia Mathematica* (1925). But, as he still believed that one could not get along without the ramified theory of types, he despaired of the situation. Thus we see how important it would be, not only for logicism but for any attempt to solve the problems of the foundations of mathematics, to show that the simple theory of types is sufficient for the construction of mathematics out of logic. A young English mathematician and pupil of Russell, Ramsey (who unfortunately died this year, i.e., 1930), in 1926 made some efforts in this direction which we will discuss later.

III. THE PROBLEM OF IMPREDICATIVE DEFINITION

To ascertain whether the simple theory of types is sufficient or must be further ramified, we must first of all examine the reasons which induced Russell to adopt this ramification in spite of its most undesirable consequences. There were two closely connected reasons: the necessity of eliminating the logical antinomies and the so-called "vicious circle" principle. We call "logical antinomies" the contradictions which first appeared in set theory (as so-called "paradoxes") but which Russell showed to be common to all logic. It can be shown that these contradictions arise in logic if the theory of types is not presupposed. The simplest antinomy is that of the concept "impredicable." By definition a property is "impredicable" if it does not belong to itself. Now is the property "impredicable" itself impredicable? If we assume that it is, then since it belongs to itself it would be, according to the definition of "impredicable," not impredicable. If we assume that it is not impredicable, then it does not belong to itself and hence, according to the definition of "impredicable," is impredicable. According to the law of excluded middle, it is either impredicable or not, but both alternatives lead to a contradiction. Another example is Grelling's antinomy of the concept "heterological." Except that it concerns predicates rather than properties, this antinomy is completely analogous to the one just described. By definition, a predicate is "heterological" if the property designated by the predicate does not belong to the predicate itself. (For example, the word 'monosyllabic' is heterological, for the word itself is not monosyllabic.) Obviously both the assumption that the word 'heterological' is itself heterological as well as the opposite assumption lead to a contradiction. Russell and other logicians have constructed numerous antinomies of this kind.

Ramsey has shown that there are two completely different kinds of anti-nomies. Those belonging to the first kind can be expressed in logical symbols and are called "logical antinomies" (in the narrower sense). The "impredic-able" antinomy is of this kind. Ramsey has shown that this kind of antinomy is eliminated by the simple theory of types. The concept "impredicable," for example, cannot even be defined if the simple theory of types is presupposed, for an expression of the form, a property does not belong to itself ($\sim f(f)$), is not well-formed, and meaningless according to that theory.

Antinomies of the second kind are known as "semantical" or "epistem-ological" antinomies. They include our previous example, "heterological," as well as the antinomy, well-known to mathematicians, of the smallest natural number which cannot be defined in German with fewer than 100 letters. Ramsey has shown that antinomies of this second kind cannot be constructed in the symbolic language of logic and therefore need not be taken into account in the construction of mathematics from logic. The fact that they appear in word languages led Russell to impose certain restrictions on logic in order to eliminate them, viz., the ramified theory of types. But perhaps their appearance is due to some defect of our ordinary word language.

Since antinomies of the first kind are already eliminated by the simple theory of types and those of the second kind do not appear in logic, Ramsey declared that the ramified theory of types and hence also the axiom of reducibility were superfluous.

Now what about Russell's second reason for ramifying the theory of types, viz., the vicious circle principle? This principle, that "no whole may contain parts which are definable only in terms of that whole", may also be called an "injunction against impredicative definition." A definition is said to be "impredicative" if it defines a concept in terms of a totality to which the concept belongs. (The concept "impredicative" has nothing to do with the aforementioned pseudo concept "impredicable.") Russell's main reason for laying down this injunction was his belief that antinomies arise when it is violated. From a somewhat different standpoint Poincaré before, and Weyl after, Russell also rejected impredicative definition. They pointed out that an impredicatively defined concept was meaningless because of the circularity in its definition. An example will perhaps make the matter clearer:

We can define the concept "inductive number" (which corresponds to the concept of natural number including zero) as follows: A number is said to be "inductive" if it possesses all the hereditary properties of zero. A property is said to be "hereditary" if it always belongs to the number $n + 1$ whenever it belongs to the number n. In symbols,

$$\text{Ind}(x) =_{\text{Df}} (f)[(\text{Her}(f) \cdot f(0)) \supset f(x)]$$

To show that this definition is circular and useless, one usually argues as follows: In the *definiens* the expression '(f)' occurs, i.e., "for all properties (of numbers)". But since the property "inductive" belongs to the class of all properties, the very property to be defined already occurs in a hidden way in the *definiens* and thus is to be defined in terms of itself, an obviously inadmissible procedure. It is sometimes claimed that the meaninglessness of an impredicatively defined concept is seen most clearly if one tries to establish whether the concept holds in an individual case. For example, to ascertain whether the number three is inductive, we must, according to the definition, investigate whether every property which is hereditary and belongs to zero also belongs to three. But if we must do this for every property, we must also do it for the property "inductive" which is also a property of numbers. Therefore, in order to determine whether the number three is inductive, we must determine among other things whether the property "inductive" is hereditary, whether it belongs to zero, and finally—this is the crucial point —whether it belongs to three. But this means that it would be impossible to determine whether three is an inductive number.

Before we consider how Ramsey tried to refute this line of thought, we must get clear about how these considerations led Russell to the ramified theory of types. Russell reasoned in this way: Since it is inadmissible to define a property in terms of an expression which refers to "all properties," we must subdivide the properties (of type 1): To the "first order" belong those properties in whose definition the expression 'all properties' does not occur; to the "second order" those in whose definition the expression 'all properties of the first order' occurs; to the "third order" those in whose definition the expression 'all properties of the second order' occurs, and so on. Since the expression 'all properties' without reference to a determinate order is held to be inadmissible, there never occurs in the definition of a property a totality to which it itself belongs. The property "inductive," for example, is defined in this no longer impredicative way: A number is said to be "inductive" if it possesses all the hereditary properties of the first order which belong to zero.

But the ramified theory of types gives rise to formidable difficulties in the treatment of the real numbers. As we have already seen, a real number is defined as a class, or what comes to the same thing, as a property of fractions. For example, we saw that $\sqrt{2}$ is defined as the class or property of those fractions whose square is less than two. But since the expression 'for all properties' without reference to a determinate order is inadmissible under the ramified theory of types, the expression 'for all real numbers' cannot refer to all real numbers without qualification but only to the real numbers of a determinate order. To the first order belong those real numbers in whose definition an expression of the form 'for all real numbers' does not occur; to the second order belong those in whose definition such an expression occurs, but this expression must be restricted to "all real numbers of the first order," and so on. Thus there can be neither an admissible definition nor an admissible sentence which refers to all real numbers without qualification.

But as a consequence of this ramification, many of the most important definitions and theorems of real number theory are lost. Once Russell had recognized that his earlier attempt to overcome it, viz., the introduction of the axiom of reducibility, was itself inadmissible, he saw no way out of this difficulty. The *most difficult problem* confronting contemporary studies in the foundations of mathematics is this: How can we develop logic if, on the one hand, we are to avoid the danger of the meaninglessness of impredicative definitions and, on the other hand, are to reconstruct satisfactorily the theory of real numbers?

IV. ATTEMPT AT A SOLUTION

Ramsey (1926) outlined a construction of mathematics in which he courageously tried to resolve this difficulty by declaring the forbidden impredicative definitions to be perfectly admissible. They contain, he contended, a circle but the circle is harmless, not vicious. Consider, he said, the description 'the tallest man in this room'. Here we describe something in terms of a totality to which it itself belongs. Still no one thinks this description inadmissible since the person described already exists and is only singled out, not created, by the description. Ramsey believed that the same considerations applied to properties. The totality of properties already exists in itself. That we men are finite beings who cannot name individually each of infinitely many properties but can describe some of them only with reference to the totality of all properties is an empirical fact that has nothing to do with logic. For these reasons Ramsey allows impredicative definition. Consequently, he can both get along with the simple theory of types and still retain all the requisite mathematical definitions, particularly those needed for the theory of the real numbers.

Although this happy result is certainly tempting, I think we should not let ourselves be seduced by it into accepting Ramsey's basic premise; viz., that the totality of properties already exists before their characterization by definition. Such a conception, I believe, is not far removed from a belief in a platonic realm of ideas which exist in themselves, independently of *if* and *how* finite human beings are able to think them. I think we ought to hold fast to Frege's dictum that, in mathematics, only that may be taken to exist whose existence has been proved (and he meant proved in finitely many steps). I agree with the intuitionists that the finiteness of every logical-mathematical operation, proof, and definition is not required because of some accidental empirical fact about man but is required by the very nature of the subject. Because of this attitude, intuitionist mathematics has been called "anthropological mathematics." It seems to me that, by analogy, we should call Ramsey's mathematics "theological mathematics," for when he speaks of the totality of properties he elevates himself above the actually knowable and definable and in certain respects reasons from the standpoint of an infinite mind which is not bound by the wretched necessity of building every structure step by step.

We may now rephrase our crucial question thus: Can we have Ramsey's result without retaining his absolutist conceptions? His result was this: Limitation to the simple theory of types and retention of the possibility of definitions for mathematical concepts, particularly in real number theory. We can reach this result if, like Ramsey, we allow impredicative definition, but can we do this without falling into his conceptual absolutism? I will try to give an affirmative answer to this question.

Let us go back to the example of the property "inductive" for which we gave an impredicative definition:

$$\text{Ind}(x) =_{\text{Df}} (f)[(\text{Her}(f) \cdot f(0)) \supset f(x)]$$

Let us examine once again whether the use of this definition, i.e., establishing whether the concept holds in an individual case or not, really leads to circularity and is therefore impossible. According to this definition, that the number two is inductive means:

$$(f) [(\text{Her}(f) \cdot f(0)) \supset f(2)]$$

in words: Every property f which is hereditary and belongs to zero belongs also to two. How can we verify a universal statement of this kind? If we had to examine every single property, an unbreakable circle would indeed result, for then we would run headlong against the property "inductive." Establishing whether something had it would then be impossible in principle, and the concept would therefore be meaningless. But the verification of a universal logical or mathematical sentence does not consist in running through a series of individual cases, for impredicative definitions usually refer to infinite totalities. The belief that we must run through all the individual cases rests on a confusion of "numerical" generality, which refers to objects already given, with "specific" generality.[1] We do not establish specific generality by running through individual cases but by logically deriving certain properties from certain others. In our example, that the number two is inductive means that the property "belonging to two" follows logically from the property "being hereditary and belonging to zero." In symbols, '$f(2)$' can be derived for an arbitrary f from '$\text{Her}(f) \cdot f(0)$' by logical operations. This is indeed the case. First, the derivation of '$f(0)$' from '$\text{Her}(f) \cdot f(0)$' is trivial and proves the inductiveness of the number zero. The remaining steps are based on the definition of the concept "hereditary":

$$\text{Her}(f) =_{\text{Df}} (n)[f(n) \supset f(n+1)]$$

Using this definition, we can easily show that '$f(0 + 1)$' and hence '$f(1)$' are derivable from '$\text{Her}(f) \cdot f(0)$' and thereby prove that the number one is

[1] Cf. F. Kaufmann, *Das Unendliche in der Mathematik und seine Ausschaltung* (Vienna, 1930).

inductive. Using this result and our definition, we can derive '$f(1 + 1)$' and hence '$f(2)$' from 'Her(f) · $f(0)$', thereby showing that the number two is inductive. We see then that the definition of inductiveness, although impredicative, does not hinder its utility. That proofs that the defined property obtains (or does not obtain) in individual cases can be given shows that the definition is meaningful. If we reject the belief that it is necessary to run through individual cases and rather make it clear to ourselves that the complete verification of a statement about an arbitrary property means nothing more than its logical (more exactly, tautological) validity for an arbitrary property, we will come to the conclusion that impredicative definitions are logically admissible. If a property is defined impredicatively, then establishing whether or not it obtains in an individual case may, under certain circumstances, be difficult, or it may even be impossible if there is no solution to the decision problem for that logical system. But in no way does impredicativeness make such decisions impossible in principle for all cases. If the theory just sketched proves feasible, logicism will have been helped over its greatest difficulty, which consists in steering a safe course between the Scylla of the axiom of reducibility and the Charybdis of the allocation of the real numbers to different orders.

Logicism as here described has several features in common both with intuitionism and with formalism. It shares with intuitionism a constructivistic tendency with respect to definition, a tendency which Frege also emphatically endorsed. A concept may not be introduced axiomatically but must be constructed from undefined, primitive concepts step by step through explicit definitions. The admission of impredicative definitions seems at first glance to run counter to this tendency, but this is only true for constructions of the form proposed by Ramsey. Like the intuitionists, we recognize as properties only those expressions (more precisely, expressions of the form of a sentence containing one free variable) which are constructed in finitely many steps from undefined primitive properties of the appropriate domain according to determinate rules of construction. The difference between us lies in the fact that we recognize as valid not only the rules of construction which the intuitionists use (the rules of the so-called "strict functional calculus"), but in addition, permit the use of the expression 'for all properties' (the operations of the so-called "extended functional calculus").

Further, logicism has a methodological affinity with formalism. Logicism proposes to construct the logical-mathematical system in such a way that, although the axioms and rules of inference are chosen with an interpretation of the primitive symbols in mind, nevertheless, *inside the system* the chains of deductions and of definitions are carried through formally as in a pure calculus, i.e., without reference to the meaning of the primitive symbols.

Arend Heyting

The intuitionist mathematician proposes to do mathematics as a natural function of his intellect, as a free, vital activity of thought. For him, mathematics is a production of the human mind. He uses language, both natural and formalized, only for communicating thoughts, i.e., to get others or himself to follow his own mathematical ideas. Such a linguistic accompaniment is not a representation of mathematics; still less is it mathematics itself.

It would be most in keeping with the active attitude of the intuitionist to deal at once with the construction of mathematics. The most important building block of this construction is the concept of unity which is the architectonic principle on which the series of integers depends. The integers must be treated as units which differ from one another only by their place in this series. Since in his *Logischen Grundlagen der exakten Wissenschaften* Natorp has already carried out such an analysis, which in the main conforms tolerably well to the intuitionist way of thinking, I will forego any further analysis of these concepts. But I must still make one remark which is essential for a correct understanding of our intuitionist position: we do not attribute an existence independent of our thought, i.e., a transcendental existence, to the integers or to any other mathematical objects. Even though it might be true that every thought refers to an object conceived to exist independently of it, we can nevertheless let this remain an open question. In any event, such an object need not be completely independent of human thought. Even if they should be independent of individual acts of thought, mathematical objects are by their very nature dependent on human thought. Their existence is guaranteed only insofar as they can be determined by thought. They have properties only insofar as these can be discerned in them by thought. But this possibility of knowledge is revealed to us only by the act of knowing itself. Faith in transcendental existence, unsupported by concepts, must be rejected as a means of mathematical proof. As I will shortly illustrate more fully by an example, this is the reason for doubting the law of excluded middle.

Oskar Becker has dealt thoroughly with the problems of mathematical existence in his book on that subject. He has also uncovered many connections between these questions and the most profound philosophical problems.

We return now to the construction of mathematics. Although the introduction of the fractions as pairs of integers does not lead to any basic difficulties, the definition of the irrational numbers is another story. A real number is defined according to Dedekind by assigning to every rational number either the predicate 'Left' or the predicate 'Right' in such a way that the natural order of the rational numbers is preserved. But if we were to transfer this definition into intuitionist mathematics in exactly this form, we would have no guarantee that Euler's constant C is a real number. We do not need the definition of C. It suffices to know that this definition amounts to an algorithm which permits us to enclose C within an arbitrarily small rational interval. (A rational interval is an interval whose end points are rational numbers. But, as absolutely no ordering relations have been defined between C and the rational numbers, the word 'enclose' is obviously vague for practical purposes. The practical question is that of computing a series of rational intervals each of which is contained in the preceding one in such a way that the computation can always be continued far enough so that the last interval is smaller than an arbitrarily given limit.) But this algorithm still provides us with no way of deciding for an arbitrary rational number A whether it lies left or right of C or is perhaps equal to C. But such a method is just what Dedekind's definition, interpreted intuitionistically, would require.

The usual objection against this argument is that it does not matter whether or not this question can be decided, for, if it is not the case that $A = C$, then either $A < C$ or $A > C$, and this last alternative is decided after a finite, though perhaps unknown, number of steps N in the computation of C. I need only reformulate this objection to refute it. It can mean only this: either there exists a natural number N such that after N steps in the computation of C it turns out that $A < C$ or $A > C$; or there is no such N and hence, of course, $A = C$. But, as we have seen, the existence of N signifies nothing but the possibility of actually producing a number with the requisite property, and the non-existence of N signifies the possibility of deriving a contradiction from this property. Since we do not know whether or not one of these possibilities exists, we may not assert that N either exists or does not exist. In this sense, we can say that the law of excluded middle may not be used here.

In its original form, then, Dedekind's definition cannot be used in intuitionist mathematics. Brouwer, however, has improved it in the following way: Think of the rational numbers enumerated in some way. For the sake

of simplicity, we restrict ourselves to the numbers in the closed unit interval
and take always as our basis the following enumeration:

$$\text{(A)} \quad 0, 1, \frac{1}{2}, \frac{1}{3}, \frac{2}{3}, \frac{1}{4}, \frac{3}{4}, \frac{1}{5}, \frac{2}{5}, \frac{3}{5}, \frac{4}{5}, \cdots$$

A real number is determined by a cut in the series (A); i.e., by a rule which
assigns to each rational number in the series either the predicate 'Left' or the
predicate 'Right' in such a way that the natural order of the rational numbers
is preserved. At each step, however, we permit one individual number to be
left out of this mapping. For example, let the rule be so formed that the series
of predicates begins this way:

$$0, 1, \frac{1}{2}, \frac{1}{3}, \frac{2}{3}, \frac{1}{4}, \frac{3}{4}, \frac{1}{5}, \frac{2}{5}, \frac{3}{5}, \frac{4}{5}, \cdots$$

$$\text{L, R, L, L, ?, L,}$$

Here $\frac{2}{3}$ is temporarily left out of the mapping. We need not know whether
or not the predicate for $\frac{2}{3}$ is ever determined. But it is also a possibility that
$\frac{3}{4}$ should become a new excluded number and hence that $\frac{2}{3}$ would receive
the predicate 'Left'.

It is easy to give a cut for Euler's constant. Let d_n be the smallest difference
between two successive numbers in the first n numbers of (A). Now if we
compute C far enough to get a rational interval i which is smaller than d_n,
then at most one of these n numbers can fall within i. If there is such a
number, it becomes the excluded number for the cut. Thus, we can see how
closely Brouwer's definition is related to the actual computation of a real
number.

We can now take an important step forward. We can drop the requirement that the series of predicates be determined to infinity by a rule. It
suffices if the series is determined step by step in some way, e.g., by free
choices. I call such sequences "infinitely proceeding." Thus the definition of
real numbers is extended to allow infinitely proceeding sequences in addition
to rule-determined sequences. Before discussing this new definition in detail,
we will give a simple example.We begin with this"Left-Right"choice-sequence:

$$0, 1, \frac{1}{2}, \frac{1}{3}, \frac{2}{3}, \frac{1}{4}, \frac{3}{4}, \frac{1}{5}, \frac{2}{5}, \frac{3}{5}, \frac{4}{5},$$

$$\text{L, R, L, L, R, L, R, L, L,}$$

Here the question about which predicate $\frac{2}{3}$ receives cannot be answered yet,
for it must still be decided which predicate to give it. The question about the
predicate which $\frac{4}{5}$ receives, on the other hand, can be answered now by
'Right', since that choice would hold for every possible continuation of the
sequence. In general, only those questions about an infinitely proceeding

sequence which refer to every possible continuation of the sequence are susceptible of a determinate answer. Other questions, like the foregoing about the predicate for $\frac{2}{3}$, must therefore be regarded as meaningless. Thus choice-sequences supplant, not so much the individual rule-determined sequences, but rather the totality of all possible rules. A "Left-Right" choice-sequence, the freedom of choice for which is limited only by the conditions which result from the natural order of the rational numbers, determines not just one real number but the spread of all real numbers or the continuum. Whereas we ordinarily think of each real number as individually defined and only afterwards think of them all together, we here define the continuum as a totality. If we restrict this freedom of choice by rules given in advance, we obtain spreads of real numbers. For example, if we prescribe that the sequence begin in the way we have just written it, we define the spread of real numbers between $\frac{1}{2}$ and $\frac{2}{3}$. An infinitely proceeding sequence gradually becomes a rule-determined sequence when more and more restrictions are placed on the freedom of choice.

We have used the word 'spread' exactly in Brouwer's sense. His definition of a spread is a generalization of this notion. In addition to choice-sequences, Brouwer treats sequences which are formed from choice-sequences by mapping-rules. A spread involves two rules. The first rule states which choices of natural numbers are allowed after a determinate finite series of permitted choices has been made. The rule must be so drawn that at least one new permissible choice is known after each finite series of permitted choices has been made. The natural order of the rational numbers is an example of such a rule for our "Left-Right" sequence previously given. The second rule involved in a spread assigns a mathematical object to each permissible choice. The mathematical object may, of course, depend also on choices previously made. Thus it is permissible to terminate the mapping at some particular number and to assign nothing to subsequent choices. A sequence which results from a permissible choice-sequence by a mapping-rule is called an "element" of the spread.

To bring our previous example of the spread of real numbers between $\frac{1}{2}$ and $\frac{2}{3}$ under this general definition, we will replace the predicates 'Left', 'Right', and 'temporarily undetermined', by 1, 2, and 3; and we will derive the rule for permissible choices from the natural order of the rational numbers and from the requirement that the sequence begin in a particular way; and we will take identity for the mapping-rule.

A spread is not the sum of its elements (this statement is meaningless unless spreads are regarded as existing in themselves). Rather, a spread is identified with its defining rules. Two elements of a spread are said to be equal if equal objects exist at the nth place in both for every n. Equality of elements of a spread, therefore, does not mean that they are the same element. To be the same, they would have to be assigned to the same spread by the same choice-sequence. It would be impractical to call two mathematical objects equal only if they are the same object. Rather, every kind of object must receive its own definition of equality.

Brouwer calls "species" those spreads which are defined, in classical terminology, by a characteristic property of their members. A species, like a spread, is not regarded as the sum of its members but is rather identified with its defining property. Impredicative definitions are made impossible by the fact, which intuitionists consider self-evident, that only previously defined objects may occur as members of a species. There results, consequently, a step-by-step introduction of species. The first level is made up of those spread-species whose defining property is identity with an element of a particular spread. Hence, to every spread M there corresponds the spread-species of those spread-elements which are identical with some element of M.[1] A species of the first order can contain spread-elements and spread-species. In addition, a species of the second order contains species of the first order as members, and so on.

The introduction of infinitely proceeding sequences is not a necessary consequence of the intuitionist approach. Intuitionist mathematics could be constructed without choice-sequences. But the following set-theoretic theorem about the continuum shows how much mathematics would thereby be impoverished. This theorem will also serve as an example of an intuitionist reasoning process.

Let there be a rule assigning to each real number a natural number as its correlate. Assume that the real numbers a and b have different correlates, e.g., 1 and 2. Then, by a simple construction, we can determine a third number c which has the following property: in every neighborhood of c, no matter how small, there is a mapped number other than c; i.e., every finite initial segment of the cut which defines c can be continued so as to get a mapped number other than c. We define the number d by a choice-sequence thus: we begin as with c but we reserve the freedom to continue at an arbitrary choice in a way different from that for c. Obviously the correlate of d is not determined after any previously known finite number of choices. Accordingly, no definite correlate is assigned to d. But this conclusion contradicts our premise that every real number has a correlate. Our assumption that the two numbers a and b have different correlates is thus shown to be contradictory. And, since two natural numbers which cannot be distinguished are the same number, we have the following theorem: if every real number is assigned a correlate, then all the real numbers have the same correlate.

As a special result, we have: if a continuum is divided into two subspecies in such a way that every member belongs to one and only one of these subspecies, then one of the subspecies is empty and the other is identical with the continuum.

The unit continuum, for example, cannot be subdivided into the species of numbers between 0 and $\frac{1}{2}$ and the species of numbers between $\frac{1}{2}$ and 1,

[1] This definition of spread-species is taken from a communication of Professor Brouwer.

for the preceding construction produces a number for which one need never decide whether it is larger or smaller than $\frac{1}{2}$. The theorems about the continuity of a function determined in an interval are also connected with the foregoing theorem. But Brouwer's theorem about the uniform continuity of all full functions goes far beyond these results.

But what becomes of the theorem we have just proved if no infinitely proceeding sequences are allowed in mathematics? In that event, the species of numbers defined by rule-determined sequences would have to take the place of the continuum. This definition is admissible if we take it to mean that a number belongs to this species only if there is a rule which permits us actually to determine all the predicates of the sequence successively.

In this event, the foregoing proof continues to hold only if we succeed in defining the number d by a rule-determined sequence rather than by a choice-sequence. We can probably do it if we make use of certain unsolved problems; e.g., whether or not the sequence 0123456789 occurs in the decimal expansion of π. We can let the question—whether or not to deviate from the predicate series for c, at the nth predicate in the predicate sequence for d—depend on the occurrence of the preceding sequence at the nth digit after the decimal point in π. This proof obviously is weakened as soon as the question about the sequence is answered. But, in the event that it is answered, we can replace this question by a similar unanswered question, if there are any left. We can prove our theorem for rule-determined sequences only on the condition that there always remain unsolved problems. More precisely, the theorem is true if there are two numbers, determined by rule-determined sequences, such that the question about whether they are the same or different poses a demonstrably unsolvable problem. It is false if the existence of two such numbers is contradictory. But the problem raised by these conditions is insuperable. Even here choice-sequences prove to be superior to rule-determined sequences in that the former make mathematics independent of the question of the existence of unsolvable problems.

We conclude our treatment of the construction of mathematics in order to say something about the intuitionist propositional calculus. We here distinguish between propositions and assertions. An assertion is the affirmation of a proposition. A mathematical proposition expresses a certain expectation. For example, the proposition, 'Euler's constant C is rational', expresses the expectation that we could find two integers a and b such that $C = a/b$. Perhaps the word 'intention', coined by the phenomenologists, expresses even better what is meant here. We also use the word 'proposition' for the intention which is linguistically expressed by the proposition. The intention, as already emphasized above, refers not only to a state of affairs thought to exist independently of us but also to an experience thought to be possible, as the preceding example clearly brings out.

The affirmation of a proposition means the fulfillment of an intention. The assertion 'C is rational', for example, would mean that one has in fact found the desired integers. We distinguish an assertion from its corresponding proposition by the assertion sign '⊢' that Frege introduced and which Russell and Whitehead also used for this purpose. The affirmation of a proposition is not itself a proposition; it is the determination of an empirical fact, viz., the fulfillment of the intention expressed by the proposition.

A logical function is a process for forming another proposition from a given proposition. Negation is such a function. Becker, following Husserl, has described its meaning very clearly. For him negation is something thoroughly positive, viz., the intention of a contradiction contained in the original intention. The proposition 'C is not rational', therefore, signifies the expectation that one can derive a contradiction from the assumption that C is rational. It is important to note that the negation of a proposition always refers to a proof procedure which leads to the contradiction, even if the original proposition mentions no proof procedure. We use ¬ as the symbol for negation.

For the law of excluded middle we need the logical function "either-or". '$p \vee q$' signifies that intention which is fulfilled if and only if at least one of the intentions p and q is fulfilled. The formula for the law of excluded middle would be '⊢$p \vee \neg p$'. One can assert this law for a particular proposition p only if p either has been proved or reduced to a contradiction. Thus, a proof that the law of excluded middle is a general law must consist in giving a method by which, when given an arbitrary proposition, one could always prove either the proposition itself or its negation. Thus the formula '$p \vee \neg p$' signifies the expectation of a mathematical construction (method of proof) which satisfies the aforementioned requirement. Or, in other words, this formula is a mathematical proposition; the question of its validity is a mathematical problem which, when the law is stated generally, is unsolvable by mathematical means. In this sense, logic is dependent on mathematics.

We conclude with some remarks on the question of the solvability of mathematical problems. A problem is posed by an intention whose fulfillment is sought. It is solved either if the intention is fulfilled by a construction or if it is proved that the intention leads to a contradiction. The question of solvability can, therefore, be reduced to that of provability.

A proof of a proposition is a mathematical construction which can itself be treated mathematically. The intention of such a proof thus yields a new proposition. If we symbolize the proposition 'the proposition p is provable' by '$+p$', then '$+$' is a logical function, viz., "provability". The assertions '⊢p' and '⊢$+p$' have exactly the same meaning. For, if p is proved, the provability of p is also proved, and if $+p$ is proved, then the intention of a proof of p has been fulfilled, i.e., p has been proved. Nevertheless, the propositions p and $+p$ are not identical, as can best be made clear by an example. In the computation of Euler's constant C, it can happen that a particular rational value, say A, is contained for an unusually long time within the interval within which we keep more narrowly enclosing C so that we finally suspect that $C = A$; i.e., we expect that, if we continued the computation of C, we would keep on finding A within this interval. But such a suspicion is by no means a proof that it will always happen. The proposition $+(C = A)$, therefore, contains more than the proposition $(C = A)$.

If we apply negation to both of these propositions, then we get not only two different propositions, '$\neg p$' and '$\neg +p$', but also the assertions, '$\vdash \neg p$' and '$\vdash \neg +p$', are different. '$\vdash \neg +p$' means that the assumption of such a construction as $+p$ requires is contradictory. The simple expectation p, however, need not lead to a contradiction. Here is how this works in our example just cited. Assume that we have proved the contradictoriness of the assumption that there is a construction which proves that A lies within every interval that contains C ($\vdash \neg +p$). But still the assumption that in the actual computation of C we will always in fact find A within our interval need not lead to a contradiction. It is even conceivable that we might prove that the latter assumption could never be proved to be contradictory, and hence that we could assert at the same time both '$\vdash \neg +p$' and '$\vdash \neg \neg p$'. In such an event, the problem whether $C = A$ would be essentially unsolvable.

The distinction between p and $+p$ vanishes as soon as a construction is intended in p itself, for the possibility of a construction can be proved only by its actual execution. If we limit ourselves to those propositions which require a construction, the logical function of provability generally does not arise. We can impose this restriction by treating only propositions of the form 'p is provable' or, to put it another way, by regarding every intention as having the intention of a construction for its fulfillment added to it. It is in this sense that intuitionist logic, insofar as it has been developed up to now without using the function $+$, must be understood. The introduction of provability would lead to serious complications. Yet its minimal practical value would hardly make it worthwhile to deal with those complications in detail.[2] But here this notion has given us an insight into how to conceive of essentially unsolvable problems.

We will have accomplished our purpose if we have shown you that intuitionism contains no arbitrary assumptions. Still less does it contain artificial prohibitions, such as those used to avoid the logical paradoxes. Rather, once its basic attitude has been adopted, intuitionism is the only possible way to construct mathematics.

---

[2] The question dealt with in this paragraph was fully clarified only in a discussion with H. Freudenthal after the conference. The results of this discussion are reproduced in the text.

III. THE FORMALIST FOUNDATIONS OF MATHEMATICS

Johann von Neumann

I

Critical studies of the foundations of mathematics during the past few decades, in particular Brouwer's system of "intuitionism," have reopened the question of the origins of the generally supposed absolute validity of classical mathematics. Noteworthy is the fact that this question, in and of itself philosophico-epistemological, is turning into a logico-mathematical one. As a result of three important advances in the field of mathematical logic (namely: Brouwer's sharp formulation of the defects of classical mathematics; Russell's thorough and exact description of its methods (both the good and the bad); and Hilbert's contributions to the mathematical-combinatorial investigation of these methods and their relations), more and more it is unambiguous mathematical questions, not matters of taste, that are being investigated in the foundations of mathematics. As the other papers have dealt extensively both with the domain (delimited by Brouwer) of unconditionally valid (i.e., needing no justification) "intuitionist" or "finitistic" definitions and methods of proof and with Russell's formal characterization (which has been further developed by his school) of the nature of classical mathematics, we need not dwell on these topics any longer. An understanding of them is, of course, a necessary prerequisite for an understanding of the utility, tendency, and *modus procedendi* of Hilbert's theory of proof. We turn instead directly to the theory of proof.

The leading idea of Hilbert's theory of proof is that, even if the statements of classical mathematics should turn out to be false as to content, nevertheless, classical mathematics involves an internally closed procedure which operates according to fixed rules known to all mathematicians and which consists basically in constructing successively certain combinations of primitive symbols which are considered "correct" or "proved." This construction-procedure, moreover, is "finitary" and directly constructive. To see clearly the essential difference between the occasionally non-constructive handling of the "content" of mathematics (real numbers and the like) and the always constructive linking of the steps in a proof, consider this example: Assume that there exists a classical proof of the existence of a real number x with a certain very complicated and deep-seated property $E(x)$. Then it may well happen that, from this proof, we can in no way derive a procedure for constructing an x such that $E(x)$. (We shall give an example of such a proof in a moment.) On the other hand, if the proof somehow violated the conventions of mathematical inference, i.e., if it contained an error, we could, of course, find this error by a finitary process of checking. In other words, although the content of a classical mathematical sentence cannot always (i.e., generally) be finitely verified, the formal way in which we arrive at the sentence can be. Consequently, if we wish to prove the validity of classical mathematics, which is possible in principle only by reducing it to the *a priori* valid finitistic system (i.e., Brouwer's system), then we should investigate, not statements, but methods of proof. We must regard classical mathematics as a combinatorial game played with the primitive symbols, and we must determine in a finitary combinatorial way to which combinations of primitive symbols the construction methods or "proofs" lead.

As we promised, we now produce an example of a non-constructive existence proof. Let $f(x)$ be a function which is linear from 0 to $\frac{1}{3}$, from $\frac{1}{3}$ to $\frac{2}{3}$, from $\frac{2}{3}$ to 1, and so on. Let

$$f(0) = -1; \quad f\left(\frac{1}{3}\right) = -\sum_{n=1}^{n=\infty} \frac{\varepsilon_{2n}}{2^n}; \quad f\left(\frac{2}{3}\right) = \sum_{n=1}^{n=\infty} \frac{\varepsilon_{2n-1}}{2^n}; \quad \text{and} \quad f(1) = 1$$

ε_n is defined as follows: if $2k$ is the sum of two prime numbers, then $\varepsilon_k = 0$; otherwise $\varepsilon_k = 1$. Obviously $f(x)$ is continuous and calculable with arbitrary accuracy at any point x. Since $f(0) < 0$ and $f(1) > 0$, there exists an x, where $0 \leq x \leq 1$, such that $f(x) = 0$. (In fact we readily see that $\frac{1}{3} \leq x \leq \frac{2}{3}$.) However the task of finding a root with an accuracy greater than $\pm\frac{1}{6}$ encounters formidable difficulties. Given the present state of mathematics, these difficulties are insuperable, for if we could find such a root, then we could predict with certitude the existence of a root $< \frac{2}{3}$ or $> \frac{1}{3}$, according as its approximate value were $\leq \frac{1}{2}$ or $\geq \frac{1}{2}$, respectively. The former case (where the approximate value of the root is $\leq \frac{1}{2}$) excludes both that $f(\frac{1}{3}) < 0$ and that $f(\frac{2}{3}) = 0$; the latter case (where the approximate value of the root $\geq \frac{1}{2}$) excludes both that $f(\frac{1}{3}) = 0$ and that $f(\frac{2}{3}) > 0$. In other words, in the former case the value of ε_n must be 0 for all even n but not for all odd n; in the latter case the value of ε_n must be 0 for all odd n but not for all even n. Hence we would have proved that Goldbach's famous conjecture (that $2n$ is always the sum of two prime numbers), instead of holding universally, must already fail to hold for odd n in the former case and for even n in the latter. But no mathematician today can supply a proof for either case, since no one can find the solution of $f(x) = 0$ more accurately than with an error of $\frac{1}{6}$. (With an error of $\frac{1}{6}$, $\frac{1}{2}$ would be an approximate value of the root, for the root lies between $\frac{1}{3}$ and $\frac{2}{3}$, i.e., between $\frac{1}{2} - \frac{1}{6}$ and $\frac{1}{2} + \frac{1}{6}$.)

II

Accordingly, the tasks which Hilbert's theory of proof must accomplish are these:

1. To enumerate all the symbols used in mathematics and logic. These symbols, called "primitive symbols," include the symbols '$\sim$' and '$\rightarrow$' (which stand for "negation" and "implication" respectively).

2. To characterize unambiguously all the combinations of these symbols which represent statements classified as "meaningful" in classical mathematics. These combinations are called "formulas." (Note that we said only "meaningful," not necessarily "true." '1 + 1 = 2' is meaningful but so is '1 + 1 = 1', independently of the fact that one is true and the other false. On the other hand, combinations like '1 + → = 1' and '+ +1 = →' are meaningless.)

3. To supply a construction procedure which enables us to construct successively all the formulas which correspond to the "provable" statements of classical mathematics. This procedure, accordingly, is called "proving."

4. To show (in a finitary combinatorial way) that those formulas which correspond to statements of classical mathematics which can be checked by finitary arithmetical methods can be proved (i.e., constructed) by the process described in (3) if and only if the check of the corresponding statement shows it to be true.

To accomplish tasks 1–4 would be to establish the validity of classical mathematics as a short-cut method for validating arithmetical statements whose elementary validation would be much too tedious. But since this is in fact the way we use mathematics, we would at the same time sufficiently establish the empirical validity of classical mathematics.

We should remark that Russell and his school have almost completely accomplished tasks 1–3. In fact, the formalization of logic and mathematics suggested by tasks 1–3 can be carried out in many different ways. The real problem, then, is (4).

In connection with (4) we should note the following: If the "effective check" of a numerical formula establishes its truth, then that procedure can be transformed into a formal proof of the formula if tasks 1–3 really reproduce classical mathematics completely. The criterion given in (4) is, then, surely necessary, and we have only to prove that it is also sufficient. If the "effective check" of a numerical formula shows it to be false, then from that formula we can derive a relation $p = q$ where p and q are two different, effectively given numbers. Hence (according to task 3) this would give us a formal proof of $p = q$ from which we could obviously get a proof of $1 = 2$. Therefore, the sole thing we must show to establish (4) is the formal un-provability of $1 = 2$; i.e., we need investigate only this one particular false numerical relation. The unprovability of the formula $1 = 2$ by the methods described in (3) is called "consistency." The real problem, then, is that of finding a finitary combinatorial proof of consistency.

III

To be able to indicate the direction which a proof of consistency takes, we must consider formal proof procedure—as in (3)—a little more closely. It is defined as follows:

3_1. Certain formulas, characterized in an unambiguous and finitary way, are called "axioms." Every axiom is considered proved.

3_2. If a and b are two meaningful formulas, and if a and $a \rightarrow b$ have both been proved, then b also has been proved.

Note that, although (3_1) and (3_2) do indeed enable us to write down successively all provable formulas, still this process can never be finished. Further, (3_1) and (3_2) contain no procedure for deciding whether a given formula e is provable. As we cannot tell in advance which formulas must be proved successively in order ultimately to prove e, some of them might turn out to be far more complicated and structurally quite different from e itself. (Anyone who is acquainted, for example, with analytic number theory knows just how likely this possibility is, especially in the most interesting parts of mathematics.) But the problem of deciding the provability of an arbitrarily given formula by means of a (naturally finitary) general procedure, i.e., the so-called decision problem for mathematics, is much more difficult and complex than the problem discussed here.

As it would take us too far afield to give the axioms which are used in classical mathematics, the following remarks must suffice to characterize them. Although infinitely many formulas are regarded as axioms (for example, by our definition each of the formulas $1 = 1, 2 = 2, 3 = 3, \ldots$ is an axiom), they are nevertheless constructed from finitely many schemata by substitution in this manner: 'If a, b, and c are formulas, then $(a \rightarrow b) \rightarrow ((b \rightarrow c) \rightarrow (a \rightarrow c))$ is an axiom', and the like.

Now if we could succeed in producing a class R of formulas such that

(α) Every axiom belongs to R,

(β) If a and $a \rightarrow b$ belong to R, then b also belongs to R,

(γ) '$1 = 2$' does not belong to R,

then we would have proved consistency, for according to (α) and (β) every proved formula obviously must belong to R, and, according to (γ), $1 = 2$ must therefore be unprovable. The actual production of such a class at this time is unthinkable, however, for it poses difficulties comparable to those raised by the decision problem. But the following remark leads from this problem to a much simpler one: If our system were inconsistent, then there would exist a proof of $1 = 2$ in which only a finite number of axioms are used. Let the set of these axioms be called M. Then the axiom system M is already inconsistent. Hence the axiom system of classical mathematics is certainly consistent if every finite subsystem thereof is consistent. And this is surely the case if, for every finite set of axioms M, we can give a class of formulas R_M which has the following properties:

(α) Every axiom of M belongs to R_M.

(β) If a and $a \rightarrow b$ belong to R_M, then b also belongs to R_M.

(γ) $1 = 2$ does not belong to R_M.

This problem is not connected with the (much too difficult) decision problem, for R_M depends only on M and plainly says nothing about provability (with the help of all the axioms). It goes without saying that we must have an effective, finitary procedure for constructing R_M (for every effectively given finite set of axioms M) and that the proofs of (α), (β), and (γ) must also be finitary.

Although the consistency of classical mathematics has not yet been proved, such a proof has been found for a somewhat narrower mathematical system. This system is closely related to a system which Weyl proposed before the conception of the intuitionist system. It is substantially more extensive than the intuitionist system but narrower than classical mathematics.[1]

Thus Hilbert's system has passed the first test of strength: the validity of a non-finitary, not purely constructive mathematical system has been established through finitary constructive means. Whether someone will succeed in extending this validation to the more difficult and more important system of classical mathematics, only the future will tell.

---

[1] The reader can find bibliographical material, for example, in Weyl's article, "Philosophie der Mathematik," in *Handbuch der Philosophie*, Oldenbourg, Munich.

DISPUTATION

Arend Heyting

Persons of the dialogue: Class, Form, Int, Letter, Prag, Sign

Class: How do you do, Mr. Int? Did you not flee the town on this fine summer day?

Int: I had some ideas and worked them out at the library.

Class: Industrious bee! How are you getting along?

Int: Quite well. Shall we have a drink?

Class: Thank you. I bet you worked on that hobby of yours, rejection of the excluded middle, and the rest. I never understood why logic should be reliable everywhere else, but not in mathematics.

Int: We have spoken about that subject before. The idea that for the description of some kinds of objects another logic may be more adequate than the customary one has sometimes been discussed. But it was Brouwer who first discovered an object which actually requires a different form of logic, namely the mental mathematical construction [L. E. J. Brouwer 1908]. The reason is that in mathematics from the very beginning we deal with the infinite, whereas ordinary logic is made for reasoning about finite collections.

Class: I know, but in my eyes logic is universal and applies to the infinite as well as to the finite.

Int: You ought to consider what Brouwer's program was [L. E. J. Brouwer 1907]. It consisted in the investigation of mental mathematical construction as such, without reference to questions regarding the nature of the constructed

Excerpted by kind permission of the author and publisher from Arend Heyting, Intuitionism, An Introduction (*Amsterdam: North Holland Publishing Co.*, 1956).

objects, such as whether these objects exist independently of our knowledge of them. That this point of view leads immediately to the rejection of the principle of excluded middle, I can best demonstrate by an example.

Let us compare two definitions of natural numbers, say k and l.

   I. k is the greatest prime such that $k - 1$ is also a prime, or $k = 1$ if such a number does not exist.

   II. l is the greatest prime such that $l - 2$ is also a prime, or $l = 1$ if such a number does not exist.

Classical mathematics neglects altogether the obvious difference in character between these definitions. k can actually be calculated ($k = 3$), whereas we possess no method for calculating l, as it is not known whether the sequence of pairs of twin primes p, $p + 2$ is finite or not. Therefore intuitionists reject II as a definition of an integer; they consider an integer to be well-defined only if a method for calculating it is given. Now this line of thought leads to the rejection of the principle of excluded middle, for if the sequence of twin primes were either finite or not finite, II would define an integer.

Class: One may object that the extent of our knowledge about the existence or non-existence of a last pair of twin primes is purely contingent and entirely irrelevant in questions of mathematical truth. Either an infinity of such pairs exist, in which case $l = 1$; or their number is finite, in which case l equals the greatest prime such that $l - 2$ is also a prime. In every conceivable case l is defined; what does it matter whether or not we can actually calculate the number?

Int: Your argument is metaphysical in nature. If "to exist" does not mean "to be constructed", it must have some metaphysical meaning. It cannot be the task of mathematics to investigate this meaning or to decide whether it is tenable or not. We have no objection against a mathematician privately admitting any metaphysical theory he likes, but Brouwer's program entails that we study mathematics as something simpler, more immediate than metaphysics. In the study of mental mathematical constructions "to exist" must be synonymous with "to be constructed".

Class: That is to say, as long as we do not know if there exists a last pair of twin primes, II is not a definition of an integer, but as soon as this problem is solved, it suddenly becomes such a definition. Suppose on January 1, 1970 it is proved that an infinity of twin primes exists; from that moment $l = 1$. Was $l = 1$ before that date or not? [Menger 1930].

Int: A mathematical assertion affirms the fact that a certain mathematical construction has been effected. It is clear that before the construction was made, it had not been made. Applying this remark to your example, we see that before Jan. 1, 1970 it had not been proved that $l = 1$. But this is not what you mean. It seems to me that in order to clarify the sense of your question you must again refer to metaphysical concepts: to some world of mathematical things existing independently of our knowledge, where "$l = 1$" is true in some absolute sense. But I repeat that mathematics ought not to depend upon such notions as these. In fact all mathematicians and even intuitionists are convinced that in some sense mathematics bear upon eternal truths, but when trying to define precisely this sense, one gets entangled in a maze of metaphysical difficulties. The only way to avoid them is to banish them from mathematics. This is what I meant by saying that we study mathematical constructions as such and that for this study classical logic is inadequate.

Class: Here come our friends Form and Letter. Boys, we are having a most interesting discussion on intuitionism.

Letter: Could you speak about anything else with good old Int? He is completely submerged in it.

Int: Once you have been struck with the beauty of a subject, devote your life to it!

Form: Quite so! Only I wonder how there can be beauty in so indefinite a thing as intuitionism. None of your terms are well-defined, nor do you give exact rules of derivation. Thus one for ever remains in doubt as to which reasonings are correct and which are not [R. Carnap 1934, p. 41; 1937, p. 46; W. Dubislav 1932, pp. 57, 75]. In daily speech no word has a perfectly fixed meaning; there is always some amount of free play, the greater, the more abstract the notion is. This makes people miss each other's point, also in non-formalized mathematical reasonings. The only way to achieve absolute rigour is to abstract all meaning from the mathematical statements and to consider them for their own sake, as sequences of signs, neglecting the sense they may convey. Then it is possible to formulate definite rules for deducing new statements from those already known and to avoid the uncertainty resulting from the ambiguity of language.

Int: I see the difference between formalists and intuitionists mainly as one of taste. You also use meaningful reasoning in what Hilbert called metamathematics, but your purpose is to separate these reasonings from purely formal mathematics and to confine yourself to the most simple reasonings possible. We, on the contrary, are interested not in the formal side of mathematics, but exactly in that type of reasoning which appears in metamathematics; we try to develop it to its farthest consequences. This preference arises from the conviction that we find here one of the most fundamental faculties of the human mind.

Form: If you will not quarrel with formalism, neither will I with intuitionism. Formalists are among the most pacific of mankind. Any theory may be formalized and then becomes subject to our methods. Also intuitionistic mathematics may and will be thus treated [R. Carnap 1934, p. 44; 1937, p. 51].

Class: That is to say, intuitionistic mathematics ought to be studied as a part of mathematics. In mathematics we investigate the consequences of given assumptions; the intuitionistic assumptions may be interesting, but they have no right to a monopoly.

Int: Nor do we claim that; we are content if you admit the good right of our conception. But I must protest against the assertion that intuitionism starts from definite, more or less arbitrary assumptions. Its subject, constructive mathematical thought, determines uniquely its premises and places it beside, not interior to, classical mathematics, which studies another subject, whatever subject that may be. For this reason an agreement between formalism and intuitionism by means of the formalization of intuitionistic mathematics is also impossible. It is true that even in intuitionistic mathematics the finished part of a theory may be formalized. It will be useful to reflect for a moment upon the meaning of such a formalization. We may consider the formal system as the linguistic expression, in a particularly suitable language, of mathematical thought.

If we adopt this point of view, we clash against the obstacle of the fundamental ambiguousness of language. As the meaning of a word can never be fixed precisely enough to exclude every possibility of misunderstanding, we can never be mathematically sure that the formal system expresses correctly our mathematical thoughts.

However, let us take another point of view. We may consider the formal system itself as an extremely simple mathematical structure; its entities (the signs of the system) are associated with other, often very complicated, mathematical structures. In this way formalizations may be carried out inside mathematics, and it becomes a powerful mathematical tool. Of course, one is never sure that the formal system represents fully any domain of mathematical thought; at any moment the discovering of new methods of reasoning may force us to extend the formal system.

Form: For several years we have been familiar with this situation. Gödel's incompleteness theorem showed us that any consistent formal system of number-theory may be extended consistently in different ways.

Int: The difference is that intuitionism proceeds independently of the formalization, which can but follow after the mathematical construction.

Class: What puzzles me most is that you both seem to start from nothing at all. You seem to be building castles in the air. How can you know if your reasoning is sound if you do not have at your disposal the infallible criterion given by logic? Yesterday I talked with Sign, who is still more of a relativist than either of you. He is so slippery that no argument gets hold of him, and he never comes to any somewhat solid conclusion. I fear this fate for anybody who discards the support of logic, that is, of common sense.

Sign: Speak of the devil and his imp appears. Were you speaking ill of me?

Class: I alluded to yesterday's discussion. To-day I am attacking these other two damned relativists.

Sign: I should like to join you in that job, but first let us hear the reply of your opponents. Please meet my friend Prag; he will be interested in the discussion.

Form: How do you do? Are you also a philosopher of science?

Prag: I hate metaphysics.

Int: Welcome, brother!

Form: Why, I would rather not defend my own position at the moment, as our discussion has dealt mainly with intuitionism and we might easily confuse it. But I fear that you are wrong as to intuitionistic logic. It has indeed been formalized and valuable work in this field has been done by a score of authors. This seems to prove that intuitionists esteem logic more highly than you think, though it is another logic than you are accustomed to.

Int: I regret to disappoint you. Logic is not the ground upon which I stand. How could it be? It would in turn need a foundation, which would involve principles much more intricate and less direct than those of mathematics itself. A mathematical construction ought to be so immediate to the mind and its result so clear that it needs no foundation whatsoever. One may very well know whether a reasoning is sound without using any logic; a clear scientific conscience suffices. Yet it is true that intuitionistic logic has been developed. To indicate what its significance is, let me give you an illustration. Let A designate the property of an integer of being divisible by 8, B the same by 4, C the same by 2. For $8a$ we may write $4 \times 2a$; by this mathematical construction P we see that the property A entails B ($A \rightarrow B$). A similar construction Q shows $B \rightarrow C$. By effecting first P, then Q (juxtaposition of P and Q) we obtain $8a = 2 \times (2 \times 2a)$ showing $A \rightarrow C$. This process remains valid if for A, B, C we substitute arbitrary properties: If the construction P shows that $A \rightarrow B$ and Q shows that $B \rightarrow C$, then the juxtaposition of P and Q shows that $A \rightarrow C$. We have obtained a logical theorem. The process by which it is deduced shows us that it does not differ essentially from mathematical theorems; it is only more general, e.g., in the same sense that "addition of integers is commutative" is a more general statement than "$2 + 3 = 3 + 2$". This is the case for every logical theorem: it is but a mathematical theorem of extreme generality; that is to say, logic is a part of mathematics, and can by no means serve as a foundation for it. At least, this is the conception of logic to which I am naturally led; it may be possible and desirable to develop other forms of logic for other purposes.

It is the mathematical logic which I just described that has been formalized. The resulting formal system proves to have peculiar properties, very interesting when compared to those of other systems of formal logic. This fact has led to the investigations to which Mr. Form alluded, but, however interesting, they are tied but very loosely to intuitionistic mathematics.

Letter: In my opinion all these difficulties are imaginary or artificial. Mathematics is quite a simple thing. I define some signs and I give some rules for combining them; that is all.

Form: You want some modes of reasoning to prove the consistency of your formal system.

Letter: Why should I want to prove it? You must not forget that our formal systems are constructed with the aim towards applications and that in general they prove useful; this fact would be difficult to explain if every formula were deducible in them. Thereby we get a practical conviction of consistency which suffices for our work. What I contest in intuitionism is the opinion that mathematics has anything to do with the infinite. I can write down a sign, say α, and call it the cardinal number of the integers. After that I can fix rules for its manipulation in agreement with those which Mr. Class uses for this notion; but in doing this I operate entirely in the finite. As soon as the notion of infinity plays a part, obscurity and confusion penetrate into the reasoning. Thus all the intuitionistic assertions about the infinite seem to me highly ambiguous, and it is even questionable whether such a sign as $10^{10^{10}}$ has any other meaning than as a figure on paper with which we operate according to certain rules [J. Dieudonné 1949].

Int: Of course your extreme finitism grants the maximum of security against misunderstanding, but in our eyes it implies a denial of understanding which it is difficult to accept. Children in the elementary school understand what the natural numbers are and they accept the fact that the sequence of natural numbers can be indefinitely continued.

Letter: It is suggested to them that they understand.

Int: That is no objection, for every communication by means of language may be interpreted as suggestion. Also Euclid in the 20th proposition of Book IX, where he proved that the set of prime numbers is infinite, knew what he spoke about. This elementary notion of natural numbers, familiar to every thinking creature, is fundamental in intuitionistic mathematics. We do not claim for it any form of certainty or definiteness in an absolute sense, which would be unrealizable, but we contend that it is sufficiently clear to build mathematics upon.

Letter: My objection is that you do not suppose too little, as Mr. Class thinks, but far too much. You start from certain principles which you take as intuitively clear without any explanation and you reject other modes of reasoning without giving any grounds for that discrimination. For instance, to most people the principle of the excluded middle seems at least as evident as that of complete induction. Why do you reject the former and accept the latter? Such an unmotivated choice of first principles gives to your system a strongly dogmatic character.

Int: Indeed intuitionistic assertions must seem dogmatic to those who read them as assertions about facts, but they are not meant in this sense. Intuitionistic mathematics consists, as I have explained already to Mr. Class, in mental constructions; a mathematical theorem expresses a purely empirical fact, namely the success of a certain construction. "2 + 2 = 3 + 1" must be read as an abbreviation for the statement: "I have effected the mental constructions indicated by "2 + 2" and by "3 + 1" and I have found that they lead to the same result." Now tell me where the dogmatic element can come in; not in the mental construction itself, as is clear by its very nature as an activity, but no more in the statements made about the constructions, for they express purely empirical results.

Letter: Yet you contend that these mental constructions lead to some sort of truth; they are not a game of solitaire, but in some sense must be of value for mankind, or you would be wrong in annoying others with them. It is in this pretence that I see the dogmatic element. The mathematical intuition inspires you with objective and eternal truths; in this sense your point of view is not only dogmatic, but even theological [H. B. Curry 1951, p. 6].

Int: In the first instance, my mathematical thoughts belong to my individual intellectual life and are confined to my personal mind, as is the case for other thoughts as well. We are generally convinced that other people have thoughts analogous to our own and that they can understand us when we express our thoughts in words, but we also know that we are never quite sure of being faultlessly understood. In this respect, mathematics does not essentially differ from other subjects; if for this reason you consider mathematics to be dogmatic, you ought to call any human reasoning dogmatic. The characteristic of mathematical thought is, that it does not convey truth about the external world, but is only concerned with mental constructions. Now we must distinguish between the simple practice of mathematics and its valuation. In order to construct mathematical theories no philosophical preliminaries are needed, but the value we attribute to this activity will depend upon our philosophical ideas.

Sign: In the way you treat language you put the clock back. Primitive language has this floating, unsteady character you describe, and the language of daily life is still in the main of the same sort, but as soon as scientific thought begins, the formalization of language sets in. In the last decades significists have studied this process. It has not yet come to an end, for more strictly formalized languages are still being formed.

Int: If really the formalization of language is the trend of science, then intuitionistic mathematics does not belong to science in this sense of the word. It is rather a phenomenon of life, a natural activity of man, which itself is open to study by scientific methods; it has actually been studied by such methods, namely that of formalizing intuitionistic reasoning and the signific method, but it is obvious that this study does not belong to intuitionistic mathematics, nor do its results. That such a scientific examination of intuitionistic mathematics will never produce a complete and definite description of it, no more than a complete theory of other phenomena is attainable, is clearly to be seen. Helpful and interesting as these meta-intuitionistic considerations may be, they cannot be incorporated into intuitionistic mathematics itself. Of course, these remarks do not apply to formalization inside mathematics, as I described it a few moments ago.

Prag: Allow me to underline what Mr. Sign said just now. Science proceeds by formalization of language; it uses this method because it is efficient. In particular the modern completely formalized languages have appeared to be most useful. The ideal of the modern scientist is to prepare an arsenal of formal systems ready for use from which he can choose, for any theory, that system which correctly represents the experimental results. Formal systems ought to be judged by this criterion of usefulness and not by a vague and arbitrary interpretation, which is preferred for dogmatic or metaphysical reasons.

Int: It seems quite reasonable to judge a mathematical system by its usefulness. I admit that from this point of view intuitionism has as yet little chance of being accepted, for it would be premature to stress the few weak indications that it might be of some use in physics [J. L. Destouches 1951]; in my eyes its chances of being useful for philosophy, history and the social sciences are better. In fact, mathematics, from the intuitionistic point of view, is a study of certain functions of the human mind, and as such it is akin to these sciences. But is usefulness really the only measure of value? It is easy to mention a score of valuable activities which in no way support science, such as the arts, sports, and light entertainment. We claim for intuitionism a value of this sort, which it is difficult to define beforehand, but which is clearly felt in dealing with the matter. You know how philosophers struggle with the problem of defining the concept of value in art; yet every educated person feels this value. The case is analogous for the value of intuitionistic mathematics.

Form: For most mathematicians this value is affected fatally by the fact that you destroy the most precious mathematical results; a valuable method for the foundation of mathematics ought to save as much as possible of its results [D. Hilbert 1922]. This might even succeed by constructive methods; for definitions of constructiveness other than that advocated by the intuitionists are conceivable. For that matter, even the small number of actual intuitionists do not completely agree about the delimination of the constructive. The most striking example is the rejection by Griss of the notion of negation, which other intuitionists accept as perfectly clear [H. Freudenthal 1936; G. F. C. Griss 1946, p. 24; 1946A]. It seems probable, on the other hand, that a somewhat more liberal conception of the constructive might lead to the saving of the vital parts of classical mathematics.

Int: As intuitionists speak a non-formalized language, slight divergences of opinion between them can be expected. Though they have arisen sooner and in more acute forms than we could foresee, they are in no way alarming, for they all concern minor points and do not affect the fundamental ideas, about which there is complete agreement. Thus it is most unlikely that a wider conception of constructiveness could obtain the support of intuitionists. As to the mutilation of mathematics of which you accuse me, it must be taken as an inevitable consequence of our standpoint. It can also be seen as the excision of noxious ornaments, beautiful in form, but hollow in substance, and it is at least partly compensated for by the charm of subtle distinctions and witty methods by which intuitionists have enriched mathematical thought.

Form: Our discussion has assumed the form of a discussion of values. I gather from your words that you are ready to acknowledge the value of other conceptions of mathematics, but that you claim for your conception a value of its own. Is that right?

Int: Indeed, the only positive contention in the foundation of mathematics which I oppose is that classical mathematics has a clear sense; I must confess that I do not understand that. But even those who maintain that they do understand it might still be able to grasp our point of view and to value our work.

Letter: It is shown by the paradoxes that classical mathematics is not perfectly clear.

Form: Yes, but intuitionistic criticism goes much farther than is necessary to avoid the paradoxes; Mr. Int has not even mentioned them as an argument for his conception, and no doubt in his eyes consistency is but a welcome by-product of intuitionism.

Sign: You describe your activity as mental construction, Mr. Int, but mental processes are only observable through the acts to which they lead, in your case through the words you speak and the formulas you write. Does not this mean that the only way to study intuitionism is to study the formal system which it constructs?

Int: When looking at the tree over there, I am convinced I see a tree, and it costs considerable training to replace this conviction by the knowledge that in reality lightwaves reach my eyes, leading me to the construction of an image of the tree. In the same way, in speaking to you I am convinced that I press my opinions upon you, but you instruct me that in reality I produce vibrations in the air, which cause you to perform some action, e.g. to produce other vibrations. In both cases the first view is the natural one, the second is a theoretical construction. It is too often forgotten that the truth of such constructions depends upon the present state of science and that the words "in reality" ought to be translated into "according to the contemporary view of scientists". Therefore I prefer to adhere to the idea that, when describing intuitionistic mathematics, I convey thoughts to my hearers; these words ought to be taken not in the sense of some philosophical system, but in the sense of every-day life.

Sign: Then intuitionism, as a form of interaction between men, is a social phenomenon and its study belongs to the history of civilization.

Int: Its study, not its practice. Here I agree with Mr. Prag: *primum vivere, deinde philosophari,* and if we like we can leave the latter to others. Let those who come after me wonder why I built up these mental constructions and how they can be interpreted in some philosophy; I am content to build them in the conviction that in some way they will contribute to the clarification of human thought.

Prag: It is a common fault of philosophers to speak about things they know but imperfectly and we are near to being caught in that trap. Is Mr. Int willing to give us some samples of intuitionistic reasoning, in order that we may better be able to judge the quality of the stuff?

Int: Certainly, and even I am convinced that a few lessons will give you a better insight into it than lengthy discussions. May I beg those gentlemen who are interested in my explanations, to follow me to my classroom?

REFERENCES

BROUWER, L. E. J.

    1907 *Over de grondslagen der wiskunde,* Thesis, Amsterdam 1907.

    1908 "De onbetrouwbaarheid der logische principes", *Tijdschrift voor wijsbegeerte 2.*

CARNAP, R.

    1934 *Logische Syntax der Sprache,* Wien 1934.

    1937 *The Logical Syntax of Language,* London 1937.

CURRY, H. B.

    1951 *Outlines of Formalist Philosophy of Mathematics,* Amsterdam 1951.

DESTOUCHES, J. L.
1951 "Sur la mécanique classique et l'intuitionnisme," *Proc. Akad. Amsterdam* Ser. A 54, pp. 74–79 = *Indagationes math.* 13, pp. 74–79.

DIEUDONNÉ, J.
1949 "L'axiomatique dans les mathématiques modernes", *Congrès intern. de philosophie des sciences*, Paris 1949. (*Actualités scientifiques et industrielles 1137*, Paris 1951.)

DUBISLAV, W.
1932 *Die Philosophie der Mathematik in der Gegenwart*, Berlin 1932.

FREUDENTHAL, H.
1936 "Zur intuitionistischen Deutung logischer Formeln", *Compositio math.* 4, pp. 112–116.

GRISS, G. F. C.
1946 *Idealistische Filosofie*. Een humanistische levens- en wereld-beschouwing. Arnhem 1946.
1946 "Negationless intuitionistic mathematics I", *Proc. Akad. Amsterdam* 49, pp. 1127–1133 = *Indagationes math.* 8, pp. 675–681.

HILBERT, D.
1922 "Neubegründung der Mathematik", *Abhandl. mat. Seminar Hamburg Univers. 1*, pp. 157–177.

MENGER, K.
1930 "Der Intuitionismus", *Blätter deutsch. Philosophie 4*, pp. 311–325.

L. E. J. Brouwer

The subject for which I am asking your attention deals with the founda-tions of mathematics. To understand the development of the opposing theories existing in this field one must first gain a clear understanding of the concept "science"; for it is as a part of science that mathematics originally took its place in human thought.

By science we mean the systematic cataloguing by means of laws of nature of causal sequences of phenomena, i.e., sequences of phenomena which for individual or social purposes it is convenient to consider as re-peating themselves identically,—and more particularly of such causal sequences as are of importance in social relations.

That science lends such great power to man in his action upon nature is due to the fact that the steadily improving cataloguing of ever more causal sequences of phenomena gives greater and greater possibility of bringing about desired phenomena, difficult or impossible to evoke directly, by evoking other phenomena connected with the first by causal sequences. And that man always and everywhere creates order in nature is due to the fact that he not only isolates the causal sequences of phenomena (i.e., he strives to keep them free from disturbing secondary phenomena) but also supple-ments them with phenomena caused by his own activity, thus making them of wider applicability. Among the latter phenomena the results of counting and measuring take so important a place, that a large number of the natural laws introduced by science treat only of the mutual relations between the results of counting and measuring. It is well to notice in this connection that a natural law in the statement of which measurable magnitudes occur can

Inaugural address at the University of Amsterdam, read October 14, 1912. *Translated by Professor Arnold Dresden. Reprinted by the kind permission of the author and the editor from the* Bulletin of the American Mathematical Society, 20 (*November*, 1913), 81–96.

only be understood to hold in nature with a certain degree of approximation; indeed natural laws as a rule are not proof against sufficient refinement of the measuring tools.

The exceptions to this rule have from ancient times been practical arithmetic and geometry on the one hand, and the dynamics of rigid bodies and celestial mechanics on the other hand. Both these groups have so far resisted all improvements in the tools of observation. But while this has usually been looked upon as something accidental and temporal for the latter group, and while one has always been prepared to see these sciences descend to the rank of approximate theories, until comparatively recent times there has been absolute confidence that no experiment could ever disturb the exactness of the laws of arithmetic and geometry; this confidence is expressed in the statement that mathematics is "the" exact science.

On what grounds the conviction of the unassailable exactness of mathematical laws is based has for centuries been an object of philosophical research, and two points of view may here be distinguished, *intuitionism* (largely French) and *formalism* (largely German). In many respects these two viewpoints have become more and more definitely opposed to each other; but during recent years they have reached agreement as to this, that the exact validity of mathematical laws as laws of nature is out of the question. The question where mathematical exactness does exist, is answered differently by the two sides; the intuitionist says: in the human intellect, the formalist says: on paper.

In Kant we find an old form of intuitionism, now almost completely abandoned, in which time and space are taken to be forms of conception inherent in human reason. For Kant the axioms of arithmetic and geometry were synthetic a priori judgments, i.e., judgments independent of experience and not capable of analytical demonstration; and this explained their apodictic exactness in the world of experience as well as in abstracto. For Kant, therefore, the possibility of disproving arithmetical and geometrical laws experimentally was not only excluded by a firm belief, but it was entirely unthinkable.

Diametrically opposed to this is the view of formalism, which maintains that human reason does not have at its disposal exact images either of straight lines or of numbers larger than ten, for example, and that therefore these mathematical entities do not have existence in our conception of nature any more than in nature itself. It is true that from certain relations among mathematical entities, which we assume as axioms, we deduce other relations according to fixed laws, in the conviction that in this way we derive truths from truths by logical reasoning, but this non-mathematical conviction of truth or legitimacy has no exactness whatever and is nothing but a vague sensation of delight arising from the knowledge of the efficacy of the projection into nature of these relations and laws of reasoning. For the formalist therefore mathematical exactness consists merely in the method of developing the series of relations, and is independent of the significance one might want to give to the relations or the entities which they relate. And for the consistent formalist these meaningless series of relations to which mathematics are reduced have mathematical existence only when they have been represented in spoken or written language together with the mathematical-logical laws upon which their development depends, thus forming what is called symbolic logic.

Because the usual spoken or written languages do not in the least satisfy the requirements of consistency demanded of this symbolic logic, formalists try to avoid the use of ordinary language in mathematics. How far this may be carried is shown by the modern Italian school of formalists, whose leader, Peano, published one of his most important discoveries concerning the existence of integrals of real differential equations in the *Mathematische Annalen* in the language of symbolic logic; the result was that it could only be read by a few of the initiated and that it did not become generally available until one of these had translated the article into German.

The viewpoint of the formalist must lead to the conviction that if other symbolic formulas should be substituted for the ones that now represent the fundamental mathematical relations and the mathematical-logical laws, the absence of the sensation of delight, called "consciousness of legitimacy," which might be the result of such substitution would not in the least invalidate its mathematical exactness. To the philosopher or to the anthropologist, but not to the mathematician, belongs the task of investigating why certain systems of symbolic logic rather than others may be effectively projected upon nature. Not to the mathematician, but to the psychologist, belongs the task of explaining why we believe in certain systems of symbolic logic and not in others, in particular why we are averse to the so-called contradictory systems in which the negative as well as the positive of certain propositions are valid.[1]

As long as the intuitionists adhered to the theory of Kant it seemed that the development of mathematics in the nineteenth century put them in an ever weaker position with regard to the formalists. For in the first place this development showed repeatedly how complete theories could be carried over from one domain of mathematics to another: projective geometry, for example, remained unchanged under the interchange of the rôles of point and straight line, an important part of the arithmetic of real numbers remained valid for various complex number fields and nearly all the theorems of elementary geometry remained true for non-archimedian geometry, in which there exists for every straight line segment another such segment,

---

[1] See Mannoury, *Methodologisches und Philosophisches zur Elementarmathematik*, pp. 149–154.

infinitesimal with respect to the first. These discoveries seemed to indicate indeed that of a mathematical theory only the logical form was of importance and that one need no more be concerned with the material than it is necessary to think of the significance of the digit groups with which one operates, for the correct solution of a problem in arithmetic.

But the most serious blow for the Kantian theory was the discovery of non-euclidean geometry, a consistent theory developed from a set of axioms differing from that of elementary geometry only in this respect that the parallel axiom was replaced by its negative. For this showed that the phenomena usually described in the language of elementary geometry may be described with equal exactness, though frequently less compactly in the language of non-euclidean geometry; hence, it is not only impossible to hold that the space of our experience has the properties of elementary geometry but it has no significance to ask for *the* geometry which would be true for the space of our experience. It is true that elementary geometry is better suited than any other to the description of the laws of kinematics of rigid bodies and hence of a large number of natural phenomena, but with some patience it would be possible to make objects for which the kinematics would be more easily interpretable in terms of non-euclidean than in terms of euclidean geometry.[2]

However weak the position of intuitionism seemed to be after this period of mathematical development, it has recovered by abandoning Kant's apriority of space but adhering the more resolutely to the apriority of time. This neo-intuitionism considers the falling apart of moments of life into qualitatively different parts, to be reunited only while remaining separated by time, as the fundamental phenomenon of the human intellect, passing by abstracting from its emotional content into the fundamental phenomenon of mathematical thinking, the intuition of the bare two-oneness. This intuition of two-oneness, the basal intuition of mathematics, creates not only the numbers one and two, but also all finite ordinal numbers, inasmuch as one of the elements of the two-oneness may be thought of as a new two-oneness, which process may be repeated indefinitely; this gives rise still further to the smallest infinite ordinal number ω. Finally this basal intuition of mathematics, in which the connected and the separate, the continuous and the discrete are united, gives rise immediately to the intuition of the linear continuum, i.e., of the "between," which is not exhaustible by the interposition of new units and which therefore can never be thought of as a mere collection of units.

In this way the apriority of time does not only qualify the properties of arithmetic as synthetic a priori judgments, but it does the same for those of geometry, and not only for elementary two- and three-dimensional geometry, but for non-euclidean and n-dimensional geometries as well. For

[2] See Poincaré, *La Science et l'Hypothèse*, p. 104.

since Descartes we have learned to reduce all these geometries to arithmetic by means of the calculus of coordinates.

From the present point of view of intuitionism therefore all mathematical sets of units which are entitled to that name can be developed out of the basal intuition, and this can only be done by combining a finite number of times the two operations: "to create a finite ordinal number" and "to create the infinite ordinal number ω"; here it is to be understood that for the latter purpose any previously constructed set or any previously performed constructive operation may be taken as a unit. Consequently the intuitionist recognizes only the existence of denumerable sets, i.e., sets whose elements may be brought into one-to-one correspondence either with the elements of a finite ordinal number or with those of the infinite ordinal number ω. And in the construction of these sets neither the ordinary language nor any symbolic language can have any other rôle than that of serving as a non-mathematical auxiliary, to assist the mathematical memory or to enable different individuals to build up the same set.

For this reason the intuitionist can never feel assured of the exactness of a mathematical theory by such guarantees as the proof of its being non-contradictory, the possibility of defining its concepts by a finite number of words,[3] or the practical certainty that it will never lead to a misunderstanding in human relations.[4]

As has been stated above, the formalist wishes to leave to the psychologist the task of selecting the "truly-mathematical" language from among the many symbolic languages that may be consistently developed. Inasmuch as psychology has not yet begun in this task, formalism is compelled to mark off, at least temporarily, the domain that it wishes to consider as "true mathematics" and to lay down for that purpose a definite system of axioms and laws of reasoning, if it does not wish to see its work doomed to sterility. The various ways in which this attempt has actually been made all follow the same leading idea, viz., the presupposition of the existence of a world of mathematical objects, a world independent of the thinking individual, obeying the laws of classical logic and whose objects may possess with respect to each other the "relation of a set to its elements." With reference to this relation various axioms are postulated, suggested by the practice with natural finite sets; the principal of these are: "*a set is determined by its elements*"; *for any two mathematical objects it is decided whether or not one of them is contained in the other one as an element*"; "*to every set belongs another set containing as its elements nothing but the subsets of the given set*"; the axiom of selection: "*a set which is split into subsets contains at least one subset which contains one and not more than one element of each of the first subsets*"; the

---

[3] See, however, Poincaré in *Scientia*, No. XXIV, p. 6.
[4] See, however, Borel in *Revue du Mois*, No. 80, p. 221.

axiom of inclusion: "*if for any mathematical object it is decided whether a certain property is valid for it or not, then there exists a set containing nothing but those objects for which the property does hold*"; the axiom of composition: "*the elements of all sets that belong to a set of sets form a new set.*"

On the basis of such a set of axioms the formalist develops now in the first place the theory of "finite sets." A set is called finite if its elements can not be brought into one-to-one correspondence with the elements of one of its subsets; by means of relatively complicated reasoning the principle of complete induction is proved to be a fundamental property of these sets;[5] this principle states that a property will be true for all finite sets if, first, it is true for all sets containing a single element, and, second, its validity for an arbitrary finite set follows from its validity for this same set reduced by a single one of its elements. That the formalist must give an explicit proof of this principle, which is self-evident for the finite numbers of the intuitionist on account of their construction, shows at the same time that the former will never be able to justify his choice of axioms by replacing the unsatisfactory appeal to inexact practice or to intuition equally inexact for him by a proof of the non-contradictoriness of his theory. For in order to prove that a contradiction can never arise among the infinitude of conclusions that can be drawn from the axioms he is using, he would first have to show that if no contradiction had as yet arisen with the nth conclusion then none could arise with the $(n + 1)$th conclusion, and secondly, he would have to apply the principle of complete induction intuitively. But it is this last step which the formalist may not take, even though he should have proved the principle of complete induction; for this would require mathematical certainty that the set of properties obtained after the nth conclusion had been reached, would satisfy for an arbitrary n his definition for finite sets,[6] and in order to secure this certainty he would have to have recourse not only to the unpermissible application of a symbolic criterion to a concrete example but also to another intuitive application of the principle of complete induction; this would lead him to a vicious circle reasoning.

In the domain of finite sets in which the formalistic axioms have an interpretation perfectly clear to the intuitionists, unreservedly agreed to by them, the two tendencies differ solely in their method, not in their results; this becomes quite different however in the domain of infinite or transfinite sets, where, mainly by the application of the axiom of inclusion, quoted above, the formalist introduces various concepts, entirely meaningless to the intuitionist, such as for instance "*the set whose elements are the points of space,*" "*the set whose elements are the continuous functions of a variable,*"

---

[5] Compare, e.g., Zermelo, "Sur les ensembles finis et le principe de l'induction complète," *Acta Mathematica*, 32, pp. 185–193.

[6] Compare Poincaré, *Revue de Métaphysique et de Morale*, 1905, p. 834.

"the set whose elements are the discontinuous functions of a variable," and so forth. In the course of these formalistic developments it turns out that the consistent application of the axiom of inclusion leads inevitably to contradictions. A clear illustration of this fact is furnished by the so-called paradox of Burali-Forti.[7] To exhibit it we have to lay down a few definitions.

A set is called ordered if there exists between any two of its elements a relation of "higher than" or "lower than," with this understanding that if the element a is higher than the element b, then the element b is lower than the element a, and if the element b is higher than a and c is higher than b, then c is higher than a.

A well-ordered set (in the formalistic sense) is an ordered set, such that every subset contains an element lower than all others.

Two well-ordered sets that may be brought into one-to-one correspondence under invariance of the relations of "higher than" and "lower than" are said to have the same ordinal number.

If two ordinal numbers A and B are not equal, then one of them is greater than the other one, let us say A is greater than B; this means that B may be brought into one-to-one correspondence with an initial segment of A under invariance of the relations of "higher than" and "lower than." We have introduced above, from the intuitionist viewpoint, the smallest infinite ordinal number ω, i.e., the ordinal number of the set of all finite ordinal numbers arranged in order of magnitude.[8] Well-ordered sets having the ordinal number ω are called elementary series.

It is proved without difficulty by the formalist that an arbitrary subset of a well-ordered set is also a well-ordered set, whose ordinal number is less than or equal to that of the original set; also, that if to a well-ordered set that does not contain all mathematical objects a new element be added that is defined to be higher than all elements of the original set, a new well-ordered set arises whose ordinal number is greater than that of the first set.

We construct now on the basis of the axiom of inclusion the *set s which contains as elements all the ordinal numbers arranged in order of magnitude;* then we can prove without difficulty, on the one hand that s is a well-ordered set whose ordinal number can not be exceeded by any other ordinal number in magnitude, and on the other hand that it is possible, since not all mathematical objects are ordinal numbers, to create an ordinal number greater than that of s by adding a new element to s,—a contradiction.[9]

[7] Compare *Rendiconti del Circolo Matematico di Palermo*, 1897.

[8] The more general ordinal numbers of the intuitionist are the numbers constructed by means of Cantor's two principles of generation (compare *Math. Annalen*, vol. 49, p. 226).

[9] It is without justice that the paradox of Burali-Forti is sometimes classed with that of Richard, which in a somewhat simplified form reads as follows: "Does there exist a *least integer, that can not be defined by a sentence of at most twenty words*? On the one hand *yes*, for the number of sentences of at most twenty words is of course finite; on the other hand *no*, for if it should exist, it would be defined by the sentence of fifteen words formed by the words italicized above."

Although the formalists must admit contradictory results as mathematical if they want to be consistent, there is something disagreeable for them in a paradox like that of Burali-Forti because at the same time the progress of their arguments is guided by the principium contradictionis, i.e., by the rejection of the simultaneous validity of two contradictory properties. For this reason the axiom of inclusion has been modified to read as follows: "*If for all elements of a set it is decided whether a certain property is valid for them or not, then the set contains a subset containing nothing but those elements for which the property does hold.*"[10]

In this form the axiom permits only the introduction of such sets as are subsets of sets previously introduced; if one wishes to operate with other sets, their existence must be explicitly postulated. Since however in order to accomplish anything at all the existence of a certain collection of sets will have to be postulated at the outset, the only valid argument that can be brought against the introduction of a new set is that it leads to contradictions; indeed the only modifications that the discovery of paradoxes has brought about in the practice of formalism has been the abolition of those sets that had given rise to these paradoxes. One continues to operate without hesitation with other sets introduced on the basis of the old axiom of inclusion; the result of this is that extended fields of research, which are without significance for the intuitionist are still of considerable interest to the formalist. An example of this is found in the theory of potencies, of which I shall sketch the principal features here, because it illustrates so clearly the impassable chasm which separates the two sides.

Two sets are said to possess the same potency, or power, if their elements can be brought into one-to-one correspondence. The power of set A is said to be greater than that of B, and the power of B less than that of A, if it is possible to establish a one-to-one correspondence between B and a part of A, but impossible to establish such a correspondence between A and a part of B. The power of a set which has the same power as one of its subsets, is called infinite, other powers are called finite. Sets that have the same power as the ordinal number ω are called denumerably infinite and the power of such sets is called aleph-null: it proves to be the smallest infinite power. According to the statements previously made, this power aleph-null is the only infinite power of which the intuitionists recognize the existence.

Let us now consider the concept: "denumerably infinite ordinal number." From the fact that this concept has a clear and well-defined meaning for both formalist and intuitionist, the former infers the right to create the "set of all denumerably infinite ordinal numbers," the power of which he calls

---

The origin of this paradox does not lie in the axiom of inclusion but in the variable meaning of the word "*defined*" in the italicized sentence, which makes it possible to define by means of this sentence an infinite number of integers in succession.

[10] Compare Zermelo, *Math. Annalen*, vol. 65, p. 263.

aleph-one, a right not recognized by the intuitionist. Because it is possible to argue to the satisfaction of both formalist and intuitionist, first, that denumerably infinite sets of denumerably infinite ordinal numbers can be built up in various ways, and second, that for every such set it is possible to assign a denumerably infinite ordinal number, *not* belonging to this set, the formalist concludes: "aleph-one is greater than aleph-null," a proposition, that has no meaning for the intuitionist. Because it is possible to argue to the satisfaction of both formalist and intuitionist that it is impossible to construct[11] a set of denumerably infinite ordinal numbers, which could be proved to have a power less than that of aleph-one, but greater than that of aleph-null, the formalist concludes: "aleph-one is the second smallest infinite ordinal number," a proposition that has no meaning for the intuitionist.

Let us consider the concept: "real number between 0 and 1." For the formalist this concept is equivalent to "elementary series of digits after the decimal point,"[12] for the intuitionist it means "law for the construction of an elementary series of digits after the decimal point, built up by means of a finite number of operations." And when the formalist creates the "set of all real numbers between 0 and 1," these words are without meaning for the intuitionist, even whether one thinks of the real numbers of the formalist, determined by elementary series of freely selected digits, or of the real numbers of the intuitionist, determined by finite laws of construction. Because it is possible to prove to the satisfaction of both formalist and intuitionist, first, that denumerably infinite sets of real numbers between 0 and 1 can be constructed in various ways, and second that for every such set it is possible to assign a real number between 0 and 1, not belonging to the set, the formalist concludes: "the power of the continuum, i. e., the power of the set of real numbers between 0 and 1, is greater than aleph-null," a proposition which is without meaning for the intuitionist; the formalist further raises the question, whether there exist sets of real numbers between 0 and 1, whose power is less than that of the continuum, but greater than aleph-null, in other words, "whether the power of the continuum is the second smallest infinite power," and this question, which is still waiting for an answer, he considers to be one of the most difficult and most fundamental of mathematical problems.

For the intuitionist, however, the question as stated is without meaning; and as soon as it has been so interpreted as to get a meaning, it can easily be answered.

[11] If "construct" were here replaced by "define" (in the formalistic sense), the proof would *not* be satisfactory to the intuitionist. For, in Cantor's argument in *Math. Annalen*, vol. 49, it is not allowed to replace the words "können wir bestimmen" (p. 214, line 17 from top) by the words "muss es geben."

[12] Here as everywhere else in this paper, the assumption is tacitly made that there are an infinite number of digits different from 9.

If we restate the question in this form: "Is it impossible to construct[13] infinite sets of real numbers between 0 and 1, whose power is less than that of the continuum, but greater than aleph-null?" then the answer must be in the affirmative; for the intuitionist can only construct denumerable sets of mathematical objects and if, on the basis of the intuition of the linear continuum, he admits elementary series of free selections as elements of construction, then each non-denumerable set constructed by means of it contains a subset of the power of the continuum.

If we restate the question in the form: "Is it possible to establish a one-to-one correspondence between the elements of a set of denumerably infinite ordinal numbers on the one hand, and a set of real numbers between 0 and 1 on the other hand, both sets being indefinitely extended by the construction of new elements, of such a character that the correspondence shall not be disturbed by any continuation of the construction of both sets?" then the answer must also be in the affirmative, for the extension of both sets can be divided into phases in such a way as to add a denumerably infinite number of elements during each phase.[14]

If however we put the question in the following form: "Is it possible to construct a law which will assign a denumerably infinite ordinal number to every elementary series of digits and which will give certainty a priori that two different elementary series will never have the same denumerably infinite ordinal number corresponding to them?" then the answer must be in the negative; for this law of correspondence must prescribe in some way a construction of certain denumerably infinite ordinal numbers at each of the successive places of the elementary series; hence there is for each place c_ν a well-defined largest denumerably infinite number α_ν, the construction of which is suggested by that particular place; there is then also a well-defined denumerably infinite ordinal number α_ω, greater than all α_ν's and that can not therefore be exceeded by any of the ordinal numbers involved by the law of correspondence; hence the power of that set of ordinal numbers can not exceed aleph-null.

As a means for obtaining ever greater powers, the formalists define with every power μ a "set of all the different ways in which a number of selections

---

[13] If "construct" were here replaced by "define" (in the formalistic sense), and if we suppose that the problem concerning the pairs of digits in the decimal fraction development of π, discussed on p. 95, *can not be solved*, then the question of the text must be answered negatively. For, let us denote by Z the set of those infinite binary fractions, whose nth digit is 1, if the nth pair of digits in the decimal fraction development of π consists of unequal digits; let us further denote by X the set of all finite binary fractions. Then the power of $Z + X$ is greater than aleph-null, but less than that of the continuum.

[14] Calling *denumerably unfinished* all sets of which the elements can be individually realized, and in which for every denumerably infinite subset there exists an element not belonging to this subset, we can say in general, in accordance with the definitions of the text: "*All denumerably unfinished sets have the same power.*"

of power μ may be made," and they prove that the power of this set is greater than μ. In particular, when it has been proved to the satisfaction of both formalist and intuitionist that it is possible in various ways to construct laws according to which functions of a real variable different from each other are made to correspond to all elementary series of digits, but that it is impossible to construct a law according to which an elementary series of digits is made to correspond to every function of a real variable and in which there is certainty a priori that two different functions will never have the same elementary series corresponding to them, the formalist concludes: "the power c' of the set of all functions of a real variable is greater than the power c of the continuum," a proposition without meaning to the intuitionist; and in the same way in which he was led from c to c', he comes from c' to a still greater power c''.

A second method used by the formalists for obtaining ever greater powers is to define for every power μ, which can serve as a power of ordinal numbers, "the set of all ordinal numbers of power μ," and then to prove that the power of this set is greater than μ. In particular they denote by aleph-two the power of the set of all ordinal numbers of power aleph-one and they prove that aleph-two is greater than aleph-one and that it follows in magnitude immediately after aleph-one. If it should be possible to interpret this result in a way in which it would have meaning for the intuitionist, such interpretation would not be as simple in this case as it was in the preceding cases.

What has been treated so far must be considered to be the negative part of the theory of potencies; for the formalist there also exists a positive part however, founded on the theorem of Bernstein: "If the set A has the same power as a subset of B and B has the same power as a subset of A, then A and B have the same power" or, in an equivalent form: "If the set $A = A_1 + B_1 + C_1$, has the same power as the set A_1, then it also has the same power as the set $A_1 + B_1$.

This theorem is self-evident for denumerable sets. If it is to have any meaning at all for sets of higher power for the intuitionist, it will have to be interpretable as follows: "If it is possible, *first* to construct a law determining a one-to-one correspondence between the mathematical entities of type A and those of type A_1, and *second* to construct a law determining a one-to-one correspondence between the mathematical entities of type A and those of types A_1, B_1, and C_1, then it is possible to determine from these two laws by means of a finite number of operations a third law, determining a one-to-one correspondence between the mathematical entities of type A and those of types A_1 and B_1."

In order to investigate the validity of this interpretation, we quote the proof:

"From the division of A into $A_1 + B_1 + C_1$, we secure by means of the correspondence γ_1 between A and A_1 a division of A_1 into $A_2 + B_2 + C_2$, as well as a one-to-one correspondence γ_2 between A_1 and A_2. From the division of A_1 into $A_2 + B_2 + C_2$, we secure by means of the correspondence between A_1 and A_2 a division of A_2 into $A_3 + B_3 + C_3$, as well as a one-to-one correspondence γ_3 between A_2 and A_3. Indefinite repetition of this procedure will divide the set A into an elementary series of subsets $C_1, C_2, C_3, \ldots$, an elementary series of subsets $B_1, B_2, B_3, \ldots$, and a remainder set D. The correspondence γ_C between A and $A_1 + B_1$ which is desired is secured by assigning to every element of C_r the corresponding element of C_{r+1} and by assigning every other element of A to itself."

In order to test this proof on a definite example, let us take for A the set of all real numbers between 0 and 1, represented by infinite decimal fractions, for A_1 the set of those decimal fractions in which the $(2n - 1)$th digit is equal to the $2n$th digit; further a decimal fraction that does not belong to A_1 will be counted to belong to B_1 or to C_1 according as the above-mentioned equality of digits occurs an infinite or a finite number of times. By replacing successively each digit of an arbitrary element of A by a pair of digits equal to it, we secure at once a law determining a one-to-one correspondence γ_1 between A and A_1. For of the element of A_1 that corresponds to an arbitrary well-defined element of A, such as, e.g., $\pi - 3$, we can determine successively as many digits as we please; it must therefore be considered as being well-defined.

In order to determine the element corresponding to $\pi - 3$ according to the correspondence γ_C, it is now necessary to decide first whether it happens an infinite or a finite number of times in the decimal fraction development of $\pi - 3$ that a digit in an odd-numbered place is equal to the digit in the following even-numbered place; for this purpose we should either have to invent a process for constructing an elementary series of such pairs of equal digits, or to deduce a contradiction from the assumption of the existence of such an elementary series. There is, however, no ground for believing that either of these problems can be solved.[15]

Hence it has become evident that also the theorem of Bernstein, and with it the positive part of the theory of potencies, does not allow an intuitionistic interpretation.

So far my exposition of the fundamental issue, which divides the mathematical world. There are eminent scholars on both sides and the chance of reaching an agreement within a finite period is practically excluded. To speak with Poincaré: "Les hommes ne s'entendent pas, parce qu'ils ne parlent pas la même langue et qu'il y a des langues qui ne s'apprennent pas."

---

[15] Such belief could be based only on an appeal to the principium tertii exclusi, i.e., to the axiom of the existence of the "set of all mathematical properties," an axiom of far wider range even than the axioms of inclusion, quoted above. Compare in this connection Brouwer, "De onbetrouwbaarheid der logische principes," *Tijdschrift voor Wijsbegeerte*, 2e jaargang, pp. 152–158.

CONSCIOUSNESS, PHILOSOPHY, AND MATHEMATICS

L. E. J. Brouwer

The . . . point of view that there are no non-experienced truths and that logic is not an absolutely reliable instrument to discover truths, has found acceptance with regard to mathematics much later than with regard to practical life and to science. Mathematics rigorously treated from this point of view, and deducing theorems exclusively by means of introspective construction, is called intuitionistic mathematics. In many respects it deviates from classical mathematics. In the first place because classical mathematics uses logic to generate theorems, believes in the existence of unknown truths, and in particular applies the *principle of the excluded third* expressing that every mathematical assertion (i.e. every assignment of a mathematical property to a mathematical entity) either is a truth or cannot be a truth. In the second place because classical mathematics confines itself to *predeterminate* infinite sequences for which from the beginning the nth element is fixed for each n. Owing to this confinement classical mathematics, to define real numbers, has only predeterminate convergent infinite sequences of rational numbers at its disposal. Out of real numbers defined in this way, only subspecies of "ever unfinished denumerable" species of real numbers can be composed by means of introspective construction. Such ever unfinished denumerable species all being of measure zero, classical mathematics, to create the continuum out of points, needs some logical process starting from one or more axioms. Consequently we may say that classical analysis, however appropriate it be for technique and science, has less mathematical truth than intuitionistic analysis performing the said composition of the continuum by considering the species of freely proceeding convergent infinite sequences of rational numbers, without having recourse to language or logic.

Excerpted by kind permission of the publisher from 10th International Congress of Philosophy, *Amsterdam*, 1940, Proceedings I, *Fascicule II (Amsterdam: North-Holland Publishing Company*, 1940), *pp.* 1243–1249.

As a matter of course also the languages of the two mathematical schools diverge. And even in those mathematical theories which are covered by a neutral language, i.e. by a language understandable on both sides, either school operates with mathematical entities not recognized by the other one: there are intuitionist structures which cannot be fitted into any classical logical frame, and there are classical arguments not applying to any introspective image. Likewise, in the theories mentioned, mathematical entities recognized by both parties on each side are found satisfying theorems which for the other school are either false, or senseless, or even in a way contradictory. In particular, theorems holding in intuitionism, but not in classical mathematics, often originate from the circumstance that for mathematical entities belonging to a certain species, the possession of a certain property imposes a special character on their way of development from the basic intuition, and that from this special character of their way of development from the basic intuition, properties ensue which for classical mathematics are false. A striking example is the intuitionist theorem that a full function of the unity continuum, i.e. a function assigning a real number to every non-negative real number not exceeding unity, is necessarily uniformly continuous.

To elucidate the consequences of the rejection of the principle of the excluded third as an instrument to discover truths, we shall put the wording of this principle into the following slightly modified, intuitionistically more adequate form, called the *simple principle of the excluded third:*

Every assignment τ of a property to a mathematical entity can be j u d g e d, i.e. either proved or reduced to absurdity.

Then for a single such assertion τ the enunciation of this principle is non-contradictory in intuitionistic as well as in classical mathematics. For, if it were contradictory, then the absurdity of τ would be true and absurd at the same time, which is impossible. Moreover, as can easily be proved, for a *finite* number of such assertions τ the simultaneous enunciation of the principle is non-contradictory likewise. However, for the simultaneous enunciation of the principle for all elements of an *arbitrary* species of such assertions τ this non-contradictority cannot be maintained.

E.g. from the supposition, for a definite real number c_1, that the assertion: c_1 *is rational*, has been proved to be either true or contradictory, no contradiction can be deduced. Furthermore, $c_1, c_2, \ldots c_m$ being real numbers, neither the simultaneous supposition, for each of the values $1, 2, \ldots m$ of ν, that the assertion: c_ν *is rational*, has been proved to be either true or contradictory, can lead to a contradiction. However, the simultaneous supposition for *all* real numbers c that the assertion: c *is rational*, has been proved to be either true or contradictory, does lead to a contradiction.

Consequently if we formulate the *complete principle of the excluded third* as follows:

If a, b, and c are species of mathematical entities, if further both a and b form part of c, and if b consists of those elements of c which cannot belong to a, then c is identical with the union of a and b,

the latter principle is contradictory.

A corollary of the *simple* principle of the excluded third says that *if for an assignment τ of a property to a mathematical entity the non-contradictority, i.e. the absurdity of the absurdity, has been established, the truth of τ can be demonstrated likewise.*

The analogous corollary of the *complete* principle of the excluded third is the *principle of reciprocity of complementarity*, running as follows:

If a, b, and c are species of mathematical entities, if further a and b form part of c, and if b consists of the elements of c which cannot belong to a, then a consists of the elements of c which cannot belong to b.

Another corollary of the *simple* principle of the excluded third is the *simple principle of testability* saying that *every assignment τ of a property to a mathematical entity can be t e s t e d, i.e. proved to be either non-contradictory or absurd.*

The analogous corollary of the *complete* principle of the excluded third is the following *complete principle of testability:*

If a, b, d, and c are species of mathematical entities, if each of the species a, b, and d forms part of c, if b consists of the elements of c which cannot belong to a, and d of the elements of c which cannot belong to b, then c is identical with the union of b and d.

For intuitionism the principle of the excluded third and its corollaries are assertions σ about assertions τ, and these assertions σ only then are "realized", i.e. only then convey truths, if these truths have been experienced.

Each assertion τ of the possibility of a construction of bounded finite character in a finite mathematical system furnishes a case of realization of the principle of the excluded third. For every such construction can be attempted only in a finite number of particular ways, and each attempt proves successful or abortive in a finite number of steps.

If the assertion of an absurdity is called a *negative assertion*, then each negative assertion furnishes a case of realization of the principle of reciprocity of complementarity. For, let α be a negative assertion, indicating the absurdity of the assertion β. As, on the one hand, the implication of the truth of an assertion a by the truth of an assertion b implies the implication of the absurdity of b by the absurdity of a, whilst, on the other hand, the truth of β implies the absurdity of the absurdity of β, we conclude that the absurdity of the absurdity of the absurdity of β, i.e. the non-contradictory of α, implies the absurdity of β, i.e. implies α.

In consequence of this realization of the principle of reciprocity of complementarity the principles of testability and of the excluded third are equivalent in the domain of negative assertions. For, if for α the principle of testability holds, this means that either the absurdity of the absurdity of β or the non-contradictory of the absurdity of β, i.e., by the preceding paragraph, that either the absurdity of the absurdity of β or the absurdity of β, i.e. either the absurdity of α or α can be proved, so that α satisfies the principle of the excluded third.

To give some examples refuting the principle of the excluded third and its corollaries, we introduce the notion of a *drift*. By a drift we understand the union γ of a convergent fundamental sequence of real numbers $c_1(\gamma)$, $c_2(\gamma)$, . . ., called the *counting-numbers* of the drift, and the limiting-number $c(\gamma)$ of this sequence, called the *kernel* of the drift, all counting-numbers lying apart[1] from each other and from the kernel. If $c_\nu(\gamma) <_\circ c(\gamma)$ for each ν, the drift will be called *left-winged*. If $c_\nu(\gamma) \circ> c(\gamma)$ for each ν, the drift will be called *right-winged*. If the fundamental sequence $c_1(\gamma)$, $c_2(\gamma)$, . . . is the union of a fundamental sequence of *left counting-numbers* $l_1(\gamma)$, $l_2(\gamma)$, . . . such that $l_\nu(\gamma) <_\circ c(\gamma)$ for each ν, and a fundamental sequence of *right counting-numbers* $d_1(\gamma)$, $d_2(\gamma)$, . . . such that $d_\nu(\gamma) \circ> c(\gamma)$ for each ν, the drift will be called *two-winged*.

Let α be a mathematical assertion so far neither tested nor recognized as testable. Then in connection with this assertion α and with a drift γ the creating subject can generate an infinitely proceeding sequence $R(\gamma, \alpha)$ of real numbers $c_1(\gamma, \alpha)$, $c_2(\gamma, \alpha)$, . . . according to the following direction: As long as during the choice of the $c_n(\gamma, \alpha)$ the creating subject has experienced neither the truth, nor the absurdity of α, each $c_n(\gamma, \alpha)$ is chosen equal to $c(\gamma)$. But as soon as between the choice of $c_{r-1}(\gamma, \alpha)$ and that of $c_r(\gamma, \alpha)$ the creating subject has experienced either the truth or the absurdity of α, $c_r(\gamma, \alpha)$, and likewise $c_{r+\nu}(\gamma, \alpha)$ for each natural number ν, is chosen equal to $c_r(\gamma)$. This sequence $R(\gamma, \alpha)$ converges to a real number $D(\gamma, \alpha)$ which will be called a *direct checking-number of γ through α*.

Again, in connection with α and with a two-winged drift γ the creating subject can generate an infinitely proceeding sequence $S(\gamma, \alpha)$ of real numbers $\omega_1(\gamma, \alpha)$, $\omega_2(\gamma, \alpha)$, . . . according to the following direction: As long as during the choice of the $\omega_n(\gamma, \alpha)$ the creating subject has experienced neither

---

[1] If for two real numbers a and b defined by convergent infinite sequences of rational numbers $a_1, a_2, . . .$ and $b_1, b_2, . . .$ respectively, two such natural numbers m and n can be calculated that $b_\nu - a_\nu > 2^{-n}$ for $v \geq m$, we write $b \circ> a$ and $a <_\circ b$, and a and b are said to lie *apart* from each other. If $a = b$ is absurd, we write $a \neq b$. If $a <_\circ b$ is absurd, we write $a \geq b$. If both $a = b$ and $a <_\circ b$ are absurd, we write $a > b$. The absurdities of $a <_\circ b$ and $a < b$ prove to be mutually equivalent, and the absurdity of $a \geq b$ proves to be equivalent to $a < b$.

the truth, nor the absurdity of α, each $\omega_n(\gamma, \alpha)$ is chosen equal to $c(\gamma)$. But as soon as between the choice of $\omega_{r-1}(\gamma, \alpha)$ and that of $\omega_r(\gamma, \alpha)$ the creating subject has experienced the truth of α, $\omega_r(\gamma, \alpha)$, and likewise $\omega_{r+\nu}(\gamma, \alpha)$ for each natural number ν, is chosen equal to $d_r(\gamma)$. And as soon as between the choice of $\omega_{s-1}(\gamma, \alpha)$ and that of $\omega_s(\gamma, \alpha)$ the creating subject has experienced the absurdity of α, $\omega_s(\gamma, \alpha)$, and likewise $\omega_{s+\nu}(\gamma, \alpha)$ for each natural number ν, is chosen equal to $l_s(\gamma)$. This sequence $S(\gamma, \alpha)$ converges to a real number $E(\gamma, \alpha)$ which will be called an *oscillatory checking-number of γ through α*.

Let γ be a right-winged drift whose counting-numbers are rational. Then the assertion of the rationality of $D(\gamma, \alpha)$ is testable, but not judgable, and its non-contradictority is not equivalent to its truth. Furthermore we have $D(\gamma, \alpha) > c(\gamma)$, but not $D(\gamma, \alpha) \circ> c(\gamma)$.

Let γ be a two-winged drift whose right counting-numbers are rational, and whose left counting-numbers are irrational. Then the assertion of the rationality of $E(\gamma, \alpha)$ is neither judgable, nor is it testable, nor is its non-contradictority equivalent to its truth. Furthermore $E(\gamma, \alpha)$ is neither $\geq c(\gamma)$, nor $\leq c(\gamma)$.

The long belief in the universal validity of the principle of the excluded third in mathematics is considered by intuitionism as a phenomenon of history of civilization of the same kind as the old-time belief in the rationality of π or in the rotation of the firmament on an axis passing through the earth. And intuitionism tries to explain the long persistence of this dogma by two facts: firstly the obvious non-contradictority of the principle for an arbitrary single assertion; secondly the practical validity of the whole of classical logic for an extensive group of *simple everyday phenomena*. The latter fact apparently made such a strong impression that the play of thought that classical logic originally was, became a deep-rooted habit of thought which was considered not only as useful but even as aprioristic.

Obviously the field of validity of the principle of the excluded third is identical with the intersection of the fields of validity of the principle of testability and the principle of reciprocity of complementarity. Furthermore the former field of validity is a *proper* subfield of each of the latter ones, as is shown by the following examples:

Let A be the species of the direct checking-numbers of drifts with rational counting-numbers, B the species of the irrational real numbers, C the union of A and B. Then all assertions of rationality of an element of C satisfy the principle of testability, whilst there are assertions of rationality of an element of C not satisfying the principle of the excluded third. Again, all assertions of equality of two real numbers satisfy the principle of reciprocity of complementarity, whereas there are assertions of equality of two real numbers not satisfying the principle of the excluded third.

In the domain of mathematical assertions the property of absurdity, just as the property of truth, is a *universally additive property*, that is to say, if it holds for each element α of a species of assertions, it also holds for the assertion which is the union of the assertions α. *This property of universal additivity does not obtain for the property of non-contradictority.* However, non-contradictority does possess the weaker property of *finite additivity*, that is to say, if the assertions ρ and σ are non-contradictory, the assertion τ which is the union of ρ and σ, is also non-contradictory. For, let us start for a moment from the supposition ω that τ is contradictory. Then the truth of ρ would entail the contradictority of σ, which would clash with the data, so that the truth of ρ is absurd, i.e. ρ is absurd. This consequence of the supposition ω clashing with the data, the supposition ω is contradictory, i.e. τ is non-contradictory.

Application of this theorem to the special non-contradictory assertions that are the enunciations of the principle of the excluded third for a single assertion, establishes the above-mentioned non-contradictority of the simultaneous enunciation of this principle for a finite number of assertions.

Within some species of mathematical entities the absurdities of two non-equivalent[2] assertions may be equivalent. E.g. each of the following three pairs of non-equivalent assertions relative to a real number a:

> I 1. $a = a$;   I 2. either $a \leq 0$ or $a \geq 0$
>
> II 1. $a \geq 0$;   II 2. either $a = 0$ or $a \circ\!\!> 0$
>
> III 1. $a > 0$;   III 2. $a \circ\!\!> 0$

furnishes a pair of equivalent absurdities.

It occurs that within some species of mathematical entities some absurdities of constructive properties can be given a constructive form. E.g. for a natural number a the absurdity of the existence of two natural numbers different from a and from 1 and having a as their product, is equivalent to the existence, whenever a is divided by a natural number different from a and from 1, of a remainder. Likewise, for two real numbers a and b the relation $a \geq b$ introduced above as an absurdity of a constructive property can be formulated constructively as follows: Let $a_1, a_2, \ldots$ and $b_1, b_2, \ldots$ be convergent infinite sequences of rational numbers defining a and b respectively. Then, for any natural number n, a natural number m can be calculated such that $a_\nu - b_\nu \circ\!\!> -2^{-n}$ for $\nu \geq m$.

On the other hand there seems to be little hope for reducing irrationality of a real number a, or one of the relations $a \neq b$ and $a > b$ for real numbers

---

[2] By non-equivalence we understand absurdity of equivalence, just as by noncontradictority we understand absurdity of contradictority.

a and b, to a constructive property, if we remark that a direct checking-number of a drift whose kernel is rational and whose counting-numbers are irrational, is irrational without lying apart from the species of rational numbers; further that a direct checking-number of an arbitrary drift differs from the kernel of the drift without lying apart from it, and that a direct checking-number of a right-winged drift lies to the right of the kernel of the drift without lying apart from it.

It occurs that within some species of mathematical entities some non-contradictorities of constructive properties ζ can be given either a constructive form (possibly, but not necessarily, in consequence of reciprocity of complementarity holding for ζ) or the form of an absurdity of a constructive property. E.g. for real numbers a and b the non-contradictority of $a = b$ is equivalent to $a = b$, and the non-contradictority of: *either $a = b$ or $a \circ\!\!> b$*, is equivalent to $a \geq b$; further the non-contradictority of $a \circ\!\!> b$ is equivalent to the absurdity of $a \leq b$ as well as to the absurdity of: *either $a = b$ or $a <\!\circ b$*.

On the other hand, if we think of the property of non-contradictority of rationality existing for all direct checking-numbers of drifts whose counting-numbers are rational, there seems to be little hope for reducing non-contradictority of rationality of a real number to a constructive property or to an absurdity of a constructive property.

If we understand by the *simple absurdity* of the property η the absurdity of η, and by the $(n + 1)$-*fold absurdity* of η the absurdity of the n-fold absurdity of η, then a theorem established above expresses that *threefold absurdity is equivalent to simple absurdity*. And a corollary of this theorem is that *n-fold absurdity is equivalent to simple or to double absurdity according as n is odd or even.*

I should like to terminate here. I hope I have made clear that intuitionism on the one hand subtilizes logic, on the other hand denounces logic as a source of truth. Further that intuitionistic mathematics is inner architecture, and that research in foundations of mathematics is inner inquiry with revealing and liberating consequences, also in non-mathematical domains of thought.

Gottlob Frege

EACH INDIVIDUAL NUMBER IS AN INDEPENDENT OBJECT

55. Having recognized that a statement of number is an assertion about a concept, we can attempt to supplement the leibnizian definitions of the individual numbers by means of the definitions of 0 and of 1.

Right away we might say: the number 0 applies to a concept, if no object falls under that concept. Here, however, "no" appears to have been substituted for 0, with which it is synonymous. Therefore the following wording is preferable: the number 0 applies to a concept if, no matter what *a* might be, the statement always holds that *a* does not fall under this concept.

Similarly we could say: the number 1 applies to a concept *F* if it is not the case that no matter what *a* is, *a* does not fall under *F*, and if from the statements

'*a* falls under *F*' and '*b* falls under *F*'

it always follows that *a* and *b* are the same.

We must still define in general the transition from one number to the next. We will try the following formulation: the number $(n + 1)$ applies to the concept *F* if there is an object *a* which falls under *F* and such that the number *n* applies to the concept "falling under *F* but not [identical with] *a*."

56. These definitions appear so natural, following our previous results, that an explanation is called for to show why they cannot satisfy us.

The last definition will most quickly arouse hesitation, for, strictly speaking, the sense of the expression 'the number *n* applies to the concept

Translated by Michael S. Mahoney from Gottlob Frege, Grundlagen der Arithmetik (*Breslau*: 1884), *pp.* 67–104, 115–19.

G' is just as unknown to us as that of the expression 'the number $(n + 1)$ applies to the concept F'. To be sure, we can say by means of this and the next-to-last definition what

'the number $1 + 1$ applies to the concept F'

means, and then, using this, indicate the sense of the expression

'the number $1 + 1 + 1$ applies to the concept F', etc.

But, to give a crude example, we can never decide by means of our definitions, whether the number *Julius Caesar* applies to a concept, whether this well-known conqueror of Gaul is a number or not. Furthermore, we cannot prove with the help of our attempted definitions that a must equal b if a applies to the concept F and b applies to the same concept. The expression, '*the* number which applies to the concept F' would, therefore, not be justifiable, and it would consequently be completely impossible to prove a numerical equality because we could never isolate a definite number. It is only apparent that we have defined 0 and 1; as a matter of fact, we have only determined the sense of the expressions

'the number 0 applies to'

and

'the number 1 applies to';

but it is not permissible to isolate in these 0 and 1 as independent, recognizable objects.

57. Here is the place to examine somewhat more closely our statement that a statement of number involves an assertion about a concept. In the sentence 'the number 0 applies to the concept F', 0 is only a part of the predicate, if we consider the concept F as the actual subject. Therefore I have avoided calling numbers like 0, 1, 2 properties of concepts. The individual number appears as a separate independent object for the very reason that it forms only a part of the assertion. I have already called attention above to the fact that we say 'the [number] 1' and, by means of the definite article, set up 1 as an object.

This independence appears everywhere in arithmetic, e.g., in the equation '$1 + 1 = 2$'. Since the important thing here is to grasp the concept of number in such a way that it is useful for science, it needn't disturb us that in everyday usage the number appears attributively. This may always be avoided. E.g., the sentence 'Jupiter has four moons' may be rearranged to form 'The number of Jupiter's moons is four'. Here the 'is' is not to be considered merely a copula, as in the sentence 'the sky is blue'. This is shown by the fact that one can say 'the number of Jupiter's moons is four' or 'is the number four'. Here 'is' has the sense of 'is equal to', 'is the same as'.

We have, therefore, an equation which asserts that the expression 'the number of Jupiter's moons' denotes the same object as the word 'four'. And the form of the equation is the reigning one in arithmetic. The fact that nothing about Jupiter or about a moon is contained in the word 'four' is no objection to this interpretation. Neither is there anything in the name 'Columbus' to suggest discovery or America, and nonetheless the same man is called both Columbus and the discoverer of America.

58. One could object that we cannot at all represent[1] to ourselves the object which we call four or the number of Jupiter's moons as something separate and independent. However, it is not the separateness which we have given the number that is at fault. To be sure, one would like to believe that in picturing the four spots of a die something appears which corresponds to the word 'four'—but that is an illusion. Think of a green meadow and see whether the picture changes when the indefinite article is replaced by the number 'one'. Nothing is added, but there is certainly something in the picture corresponding to the word 'green'.

If one pictures for himself the printed word 'gold', one will not at first associate any number with it. Were one now to ask himself how many letters the word has, the result would be the number 4; the picture, however, will be in no way more definite, but can remain wholly unchanged. The added concept "letter of the word 'gold' " is the very thing in which we discover the number. In the case of the four spots of a die the situation is somewhat less obvious because the concept is forced upon us so directly by the similarity of the spots that we hardly notice its intrusion. The number can be *pictured* [translator's italics] neither as a separate object nor as a property of an outward thing, because it is neither something sensible nor the property of an outward thing. The situation is probably most clear in the case of the number 0. One will try in vain to picture 0 visible stars. To be sure, one can think of the sky completely covered up by clouds; but there is nothing in this picture which might correspond to the word 'star' or to the 0. One is only imagining a situation in which one may conclude: now no star may be seen.

59. Perhaps each word awakens some sort of picture for us, even a word like 'only'. The picture, however, need not correspond to the content of the word; it can be an entirely different one for different men. One will then probably imagine a situation which evokes a sentence in which the word occurs; or the spoken word might call forth the written word in one's memory.

This does not occur only in the case of particles. There can be no doubt that we lack any idea [picture] of our distance from the sun. For, even if we know the rule about the number of times we must multiply a unit of measure, nevertheless any attempt by this rule to sketch a picture which even slightly approaches the one desired is doomed to fail. This is, however, no reason to

In the sense of 'picture'.

doubt the correctness of the computation by which the distance has been found, and it in no way hinders us in basing further conclusions on this being the distance.

60. Even such a concrete thing as the earth we cannot picture in the way that we have learned it actually to be, but rather we are satisfied with a sphere of medium size, which serves us as a symbol for the earth, knowing nevertheless that the two are very different from one another. Now although our picture often does not at all meet the requirements, still we make judgments with great certainty about an object like the earth, even where its size is concerned.

Thought often leads us far beyond the imaginable without thereby depriving us of the basis for our conclusions. Even if, as it appears, thought without mental pictures is impossible for us men, still their connection with the object of thought can be wholly superficial, arbitrary, and conventional.

The unimaginability of the content of a word is no reason, then, to deny it any meaning or to exclude it from usage. That we are nevertheless inclined to do so is probably owing to the fact that we consider words individually and ask about their meaning [in isolation], for which we then adopt a mental picture. Thus a word for which we are lacking a corresponding inner picture will seem to have no content. However, we must always consider a complete sentence. Only in [the context of] the latter do the words really have a meaning. The inner pictures which somehow sway before us (in reading the sentence) need not correspond to the logical components of the judgment. It is enough if the sentence as a whole has a sense; by means of this its parts also receive their content.

This observation seems to me to be useful in throwing light on several difficult concepts, such as that of the infinitesimal,[2] and its scope is probably not limited to mathematics.

The separateness [independence] which I require for the number is not intended to mean that a number-word used outside of the context of a sentence shall denote anything, but rather I want only to exclude its use as a predicate or attribute, for such a use somewhat alters its meaning.

61. But, one might object, even if the earth is really unimaginable, still it is an external thing having a definite place. Where, however, is the number 4? It is neither outside of us nor inside of us. Taken in spatial terms, this is correct. A determination of the place of the number 4 makes no sense. But, from this it follows only that the number 4 is not a spatial object, not that it is no object at all. Not every object is somewhere. Even our mental

---

[2] What is in question here is defining the sense of an equation like

$$df(x) = g(x)dx$$

rather than finding an interval bounded by two distinct points and of length dx.

pictures[3] are in this sense not in us (subcutaneously). In us there are ganglia cells, blood particles, etc., but no mental pictures. Spatial predicates are not applicable to them: the one is neither right nor left of the other. Mental pictures have no distances between them which may be stated in millimeters. When nevertheless we refer to them as in us, we mean that they are subjective.

Even if the subjective has no spatial location, however, how is it possible for the number 4, which is objective, to be nowhere? Now I maintain that there is no contradiction here. The number 4 is, as a matter of fact, exactly the same for everyone who works with it; but this has nothing to do with spatiality. Not every objective object has a place.

IN ORDER TO OBTAIN CONCEPT OF NUMBER, ONE MUST DETERMINE THE SENSE OF A NUMERICAL EQUATION

62. How shall we have a number, then, if we can have no idea or picture of it? Only in the context of a sentence do words have meaning. We must, therefore, define the sense of a sentence in which a number-word occurs. This seems at first to leave a lot of latitude, but we have already determined that number-words are to be understood as standing for independent objects. This already specifies a class of sentences which must have a sense, the class of those sentences which express the recognition [of a number as the same number]. If for us the symbol a is to denote an object, then we must have a criterion which determines in every case whether b is the same as a, even if it is not always within our power to apply this criterion. In our present case, we must explain the sense of the statement:

'the number which applies to the concept F is the same number as that which applies to the concept G',

i.e., we must reproduce the content of this statement in another way without using the expression

'the number which applies to the concept F'.

In doing this, we give a general criterion for the equality of numbers. Once we have obtained such a means of grasping a definite number and recognizing it as such, we can assign it a number-word as its proper name.

63. *Hume*[4] has already mentioned such a means: "If two numbers are so combined that the one always has a unit which corresponds to each unit of the other, then we claim they are equal." In more recent times, the opinion seems to have found much sympathy among mathematicians, that the equality of numbers must be defined in terms of a one-to-one correspondence.

---

[3] This word understood purely psychologically, not psychophysically.

[4] Baumann, *Die Lehren von Zeit, Raum und Mathematik*, Vol. II, p. 565.

Immediately, however, there arise certain logical hesitations and difficulties, which we must not pass by without examination.

The relationship of equality does not hold only among numbers. It seems to follow from this that the relationship should be defined especially for numbers. One would think it possible to derive a criterion of when numbers are identical with one another from a previously determined concept of identity together with the concept of number, without its being necessary, for this purpose, to define a special concept of numerical identity.

Contrary to this, it should be noted that, for us, the concept of number has not yet been defined, but rather is to be determined by means of our definition of numerical identity. We intend to reconstruct the content of judgments interpretable as expressing identities each side of which is a number. We do not, therefore, want to define equality especially for this instance, but we wish rather, by means of the already familiar concept of equality, to determine that which is to be considered equal. This seems indeed to be a very unusual type of definition, which has probably not yet received sufficient attention from the logicians. Nevertheless, that it is not entirely unheard of may be shown by a few examples:

64. The judgment: 'the [straight] line a is parallel to the [straight] line b', or, symbolically:

$$a \mid\mid b,$$

can be interpreted as an equation. If we do this, we obtain the concept of direction and say: 'the direction of line a is the same as the direction of line b'. Hence, we replace the symbol '$\mid\mid$' by the more general '$=$', by distributing the particular content of the former to a and b. We split up the content in some way other than the original way and thus obtain a new concept. Often the situation is interpreted conversely, and several teachers define: parallel lines are those having the same direction. The theorem "if two straight lines are parallel to a third, then they are parallel to one another" can then be very easily proved on the basis of the similarly worded equality theorem. Unfortunately, this method reverses the natural order of things. For everything geometric must indeed be intuitive, at least originally. Now I ask whether anyone has ever had an intuition of the direction of a straight line? Of the straight line, yes, but can one also distinguish intuitively this line from its direction? Rather difficult! This concept is found only by means of a mental activity connected with intuition. On the other hand, one has a picture of parallel lines. That proof comes about only through a trick in which what is to be proved is covertly presupposed in the use of the word 'direction'; for, were the statement: 'if two straight lines are parallel to a third, then they are parallel to one another' false, then one could not change '$a \mid\mid b$' into an equation.

Thus one can obtain from the parallelism of planes a concept which corresponds to that of direction among straight lines. I have seen the name 'orientation' used for this concept. From geometric similarity there arises the concept of shape, so that, e.g., instead of 'the two triangles are similar', one says: 'the two triangles have the same shape' or 'the shape of the one triangle is equal to the shape of the other'. Similarly one can also obtain from the collinear relationship of geometric figures a concept for which a name is probably still lacking.

65. Now, in order to move, e.g., from parallelism[5] to the concept of direction, let us try the following definition: the sentence

'line *a* is parallel to line *b*'

is to be synonymous with

'the direction of line *a* is the same as the direction of line *b*'.

This definition departs from common practice insofar as it apparently defines the already familiar relation of equality, while it should in actuality introduce the expression 'the direction of line *a*', which occurs only incidentally. From this there arises a second hesitation; viz., whether, through such a stipulation, we could not become involved in contradictions with the familiar laws of equality. What are these? They will be developed as analytic truths from the concept itself. Now, Leibniz defines:[6]

"Eadem sunt, quorum unum potest substitui alteri salva veritate."
["Things are equal which may be substituted for one another without change of truth [value]."]

I will adopt this definition. Whether, like Leibniz, one says 'the same' or 'equal', is of little import. 'The same' does seem to express complete agreement, 'equal' only agreement in this respect or that. One can, however, assume a manner of speaking in which this difference is eliminated, e.g., by saying instead of 'the lines are equal in length' that 'the length of the lines is equal' or 'the same'; instead of saying 'the surfaces are equal in color' one might say 'the color of the surfaces is equal [identical]'.

And this is the way we used the word in the foregoing examples. In fact, all the laws of equality are contained in the principle of universal substitutivity.

In order to justify our proposed definition of the direction of a straight line, we would have to show, then, that

'the direction of *a*'

---

[5] In order to be able to express myself more comfortably and to be more easily understood, I speak here of parallelism. The essential parts of these discussions are very easily carried over to the case of numerical equality.

[6] *Non inelegans specimen demonstrandi in abstractis.* Erdmann edition, p. 94.

can be everywhere replaced by

'the direction of *b*',

if line *a* is parallel to line *b*. This is simplified by the fact that, at first, we know no assertion about the direction of a straight line other than its agreement with the direction of another straight line. We would therefore need to demonstrate only the substitutivity in such an equation or in contexts which would contain such equations as component parts.[7] All other statements about directions would have to be defined first, and for these definitions we can adopt the rule that the substitutivity of the direction of a straight line for that of one parallel to it must be preserved.

66. Still a third hesitation arises, however, concerning our proposed definition. In the sentence

'the direction of *a* is equal to the direction of *b*',

the direction of *a* appears as an object,[8] and we have in our definition a means of recognizing this object, should it appear in some other guise, such as the direction of *b*. However, this method is not sufficient for all cases. One cannot use it to decide whether England is the same as the direction of the earth's axis. Please excuse this apparently nonsensical example! Naturally, no one is going to confuse England with the direction of the earth's axis; but this is not owing to our definition. The latter says nothing about whether the statement

'the direction of *a* is equal to *q*'.

is to be affirmed or denied, if *q* itself is not given in the form 'the direction of *b*'. We lack the concept of direction; for, if we had this, then we could stipulate that, if *q* is not a direction, then our statement is to be denied; if *q* is a direction, then the earlier definition decides. It is now but a step away to define:

q is a direction if there is a straight line *b* whose direction is *q*.

However, it is clear that we have now come around in a circle. In order to

[7] For example, in a hypothetical judgment an equality of directions could occur either as antecedent or as consequent.

[8] The definite article points to this. A concept is for me a possible predicate in a singular thought content, an object a possible subject of the latter. [Although the terminology of "thought contents" has been adopted, Frege must not be taken to mean anything psychological by 'thought'. For Frege a "thought content" is what is asserted in a statement, asked in a question, etc. ...] If, in the sentence 'the direction of the axis of the telescope is equal to the direction of the earth's axis', we consider the direction of the telescope's axis to be the subject, then the predicate is 'equal to the direction of the earth's axis'. This is a concept. But the direction of the earth's axis is only a part of the predicate; the direction is an object, since it can also be made the subject.

apply this definition, we would first have to know in each case whether the statement

'q is equal to the direction of b'

was to be affirmed or denied.

67. If we were to say: q is a direction if it is introduced by means of the foregoing definitions, then we would be treating the manner by which the object q is introduced as a property of it, which it is not. The definition of an object, as such, really says nothing about that object; rather it stipulates the meaning of a symbol. Once that has happened, the definition becomes a judgment which treats of the object: it now no longer introduces the object but stands on equal footing with other statements about it. To choose this way out is to presuppose that an object could be given in one way only; otherwise it would not follow from the fact that q is not introduced by means of our definition that it could not be so introduced. The import of any equation would then be that what is given us in the same way should be recognized as the same. But this principle is so obvious and so unfruitful that there is little to be gained by stating it. As a matter of fact, no conclusion could be drawn from it which would not be the same as some premise. The many-sided and broad applicability of equations is based rather on the fact that something is recognizable again even though it is given in a different way.

68. Since this method fails to yield a sharply delimited concept of direction and, for the same reason, would yield no such concept of number, let us try a different tack. If line a is parallel to line b, then the extension of the concept "line parallel to line a" is the same as the extension of the concept "line parallel to line b"; and conversely: if the extensions of the aforementioned concepts are equal, then a is parallel to b. Let us try, then, to define:

the direction of line a is the extension of the concept "parallel to line a"

the shape of triangle d is the extension of the concept "similar to triangle d."

If we want to apply this to our case, then we must substitute concepts for the lines or the triangles and, for parallelism or similarity, the possibility of correlating in one-to-one fashion the objects falling under the one concept with those falling under the other. As an abbreviation, I will call the concept F equinumerous[9] with the concept G, if this possibility exists; I must,

---

[9] [Frege coined 'gleichzählig' for this. In his translation, J. L. Austin uses 'equal' and adds the following footnote: "*Gleichzählig*—an invented word, literally 'identinumerate' or 'tautarithmic'; but these are too clumsy for constant use. Other translators have used 'equinumerous'; 'equinumerates' would be better. Later writers have used 'similar' in this connection (but as a predicate of 'class' not of 'concept')."—Tr.]

however, request that this word be considered an arbitrarily chosen notational device whose meaning is not to be taken from its linguistic composition, but rather from the foregoing definition.

I define accordingly:

the number which applies to the concept F is the extension[10] of the concept "equinumerous with the concept F."

69. That this definition is correct will, at first perhaps, not be so clear. Don't we mean something other than [different from] a number by the extension of a concept? What we do mean becomes clear from the basic statements that can be made about extensions of concepts. They are the following:

1.   that they are equal,
2.   that the one encompasses more than the other.

Now the statement

'the extension of the concept "equinumerous with the concept F" is the same as the extension of the concept "equinumerous with the concept G"'

is true if and only if the statement

'the same number applies to the concept F as to the concept G'

is also true. Hence, there is complete agreement here.

To be sure, one does not say that one number encompasses more than another in the same sense that the extension of one concept encompasses more than does another; however, so is it impossible that

the extension of the concept "equinumerous with the concept F"

should encompass more than

the extension of the concept "equinumerous with the concept G"

Rather, if all concepts which are equinumerous with G are also equinumerous with F, then conversely, all concepts which are equinumerous with F are also equinumerous with G. This term 'more encompassing' should not, of course, be confused with the term 'greater', which occurs among numbers.

[10] I think we could say for 'extension of the concept' simply 'concept'. However, there might be two objections:

1. This stands in contradiction to my earlier assertion that the individual number is an object, the latter being indicated by the use of the article in expressions like "the 2," by the impossibility of speaking about ones, twos, etc. in the plural, and by the fact that the number makes up only a part of the predicate of a statement of number.

2. Concepts can have the same extension without coinciding.

Now I am of the opinion that both these objections can be met, but doing this would lead us too far astray. I presuppose that one knows what the extension of a concept is.

Certainly, it is also imaginable that the extension of the concept "equinumerous with the concept *F*" might encompass more or less than the extension of another concept; the latter, then, could not be a number according to our definition. Furthermore, it is not usual to call a number more or less encompassing than the extension of a concept. Nonetheless, there is nothing in the way of so speaking should the occasion arise.

COMPLETION AND CONFIRMATION OF OUR DEFINITION

70. Definitions are confirmed by their fruitfulness. Those definitions which could just as easily be left out without invalidating proofs should be discarded as wholly worthless.

Let us see, then, whether some of the familiar properties of numbers can be derived from our definition of the number which applies to the concept *F*. We will be satisfied here by the most simple properties.

In order to do this, it is necessary to specify somewhat more exactly the meaning of equinumerosity. We defined it in terms of one-to-one correlation; just how I want to understand this expression must now be explained, since one might easily suspect a connection with intuition.

Let us consider the following example: If a waiter wants to be sure that he is placing just as many knives as plates on the table, he need count neither of them if he places a knife immediately to the right of each plate so that each knife on the table is located to the immediate right of a plate. The plates and knives are thus correlated in one-to-one fashion with one another, in this case through the same positional relationship. If, in the sentence

'α lies immediately to the right of *A*'

we imagine all sorts of objects substituted for α and *A*, then the part of the content which remains unchanged through all this forms the essence of the relation. Let us generalize this:

When, from a thought content which concerns an object *a* and an object *b*, we remove *a* and *b*, we retain the concept of a relation, which, accordingly, requires supplementation in two places. If, in the statement

'the earth has more mass than the moon',

we remove "the earth," then we obtain the concept "having more mass than the moon." If, on the other hand, we remove the object, "the moon," we gain the concept "having less mass than the earth." Removing both at once leaves a relational concept, which has in itself no more meaning than a simple concept, and which must be supplemented to become a thought content. But this supplementation can come about in various ways: instead of the earth and moon, I can take, e.g., the sun and earth, thus also affecting a removal of the earth and moon [and disclosing the relational nature of the concept].

The individual pairs of associated objects are related—one might say as subjects—to the relational concept in a manner similar to that of the individual object and the concept under which it falls. The subject here is a composite. At times, when the relation is a reversible one [symmetric in two argument places], this is also expressed linguistically, as in the sentence 'Peleus and Thetis were the parents of Achilles'.[11]

On the other hand, it would not be possible to reformulate the statement 'the earth is greater than the moon' so as to make 'the earth and the moon' appear as a compound subject, because the 'and' always indicates a certain equality of rank. This, however, does not affect the matter at hand.

The concept of relation, like the simple concept, belongs, then, to pure logic. The particular content of the relation does not concern us here, but only its logical form. And [the truth of] whatever can be asserted about this form is analytic and is known *a priori*. This holds for the relational concepts as well as for the others.

Just as

'*a* falls under the concept *F*'

is the general form of a thought content concerning the object *a*, so can

'*a* stands in the relation ϕ to *b*'

be taken as the general form of a thought content concerning objects *a* and *b*.

71. Now if each object which falls under the concept *F* stands in the relation ϕ to an object falling under the concept *G*, and if, for each object which falls under *G*, there is an object falling under *F* which stands in the relation ϕ to it, then the objects falling under *F* and *G* are correlated with one another by means of the relation ϕ.

We may still ask what the expression

'each object which falls under *F* stands in the relation ϕ to an object falling under *G*'

means, if no object at all falls under *F*. By this I mean that the two statements

'*a* falls under *F*'

and

'*a* does not stand in the relation ϕ to any object falling under *G*'

cannot stand together, no matter what *a* denotes, so that either the first or the second or both are false. From this it follows that if there is no object falling under *F*, then "each object which falls under *F* stands in the relation ϕ to an object falling under *G*," because then the first statement

'*a* falls under *F*'

[11] Do not confuse this with the case where the 'and' only seemingly connects the subjects, but in reality, however, connects two sentences.

is always to be denied, no matter what *a* might be.

Thus

'for each object which falls under *G*, there is an object falling under *F* which stands in the relation ϕ to it'.

means that the two statements

'*a* falls under *G*'

and

'no object falling under *F* stands in the relation ϕ to *a*'

cannot stand together, whatever *a* may be.

72. We have now seen when the objects falling under the concepts *F* and *G* are correlated with one another by means of the relation ϕ. This correlation is here supposed to be one-to-one. By that I mean that the following two statements must hold:

1. If *d* stands in the relation ϕ to *a*, and if *d* stands in the relation ϕ to *e*, then, no matter what *d*, *a*, and *e* may be, *a* is always the same as *e*.
2. If *d* stands in the relation ϕ to *a*, and if *b* stands in the relation ϕ to *a*, then, whatever *d*, *b*, and *a* may be, *d* is always the same as *b*.

By these statements we have reduced one-to-one correlations to purely logical terms and can now offer the following definition:

the expression

'the concept *F* is equinumerous with the concept *G*'

is to be synonymous with the expression

'there is a relation ϕ which correlates in one-to-one fashion the objects falling under *F* with the objects falling under *G*'.

I [now] repeat [our original definition]:

the number which applies to the concept *F* is the extension of the concept "equinumerous with the concept *F*,"

and add to it:

the expression:

'*n* is a number'

is to be synonymous with the expression

'there is a concept to which the number *n* applies'.

Thus the concept of number is defined, apparently by means of itself, nevertheless without fallacy, because 'the number which applies to the concept *F*' has already been defined.

73. We want to show next, then, that the number which applies to the concept *F* is equal to the number which applies to the concept *G*, if the concept *F* is equinumerous with the concept *G*. This sounds like a tautology, but it is not, since the meaning of the word 'equinumerous' does not follow from its (linguistic) composition, but rather from the foregoing definition.

According to our definition, we must show that the extension of the concept "equinumerous with the concept *F*" is the same as that of the concept "equinumerous with the concept of *G*," if the concept *F* is equinumerous with the concept *G*. In other words, it must be shown that, under this hypothesis, the following statements always hold:

'if the concept *H* is equinumerous with the concept *F*, then it is also equinumerous with the concept *G*';

and

'if the concept *H* is equinumerous with the concept *G*, then it is also equinumerous with the concept *F*'.

The upshot of the first statement is that there is a relation which correlates in one-to-one fashion the objects falling under the concept *H* with those falling under the concept *G*, if there is a relation ϕ which correlates one-to-one the objects falling under the concept *F* with those falling under the concept *G*, and if there is a relation ψ which correlates one-to-one the objects falling under the concept *H* with those falling under the concept *F*. The following arrangement of the letters will make this easier to see

$$H\psi F\phi G.$$

Such a relation can in fact be given: it is [that] part of the thought content:

"there is an object to which *c* stands in the relation ψ and which stands in the relation ϕ to *b*"

[which remains] if we remove from it *c* and *b* (considering them as the things related). It can be shown that this relation is one-to-one and that it correlates the objects falling under the concept *H* with those falling under the concept *G*.

In a similar manner, the other theorem can also be proved.[12] Hopefully, these outlines will suffice to demonstrate that we need not borrow here any evidence from intuition, and that something may be done with our definitions.

74. We can now go on to the definitions of the individual numbers.

---

[12] Similarly for its converse: If the number which applies to the concept *F* is the same as that which applies to the concept *G*, then the concept *F* is equinumerous with the concept *G*.

Because nothing falls under the concept "unequal to itself," I define:

0 is the number which applies to the concept "unequal to itself."

Perhaps someone will take exception to my speaking about a concept here. He will perhaps object that a contradiction is contained therein and will recall the old stand-bys, wooden iron and the square circle. To my mind, these are not at all as bad as they are made out to be. Of course, they are not exactly useful, but they can't do any harm, either, as long as one doesn't require that something fall under them; and *that* one does not yet do through the mere usage of the concepts. That a concept contains a contradiction is not always obvious without some examination; but to do that, one must have [the concept] and treat it logically just like any other. All that can be demanded of a concept from the point of view of logic and for rigor in proof procedure is its precise delineation; that, for each object, it be determined whether or not it falls under the concept. This requirement is fully satisfied, then, by concepts containing a contradiction, such as "unequal to itself," for it is known of every object that it does not fall under such a concept.[13]

I use the word 'concept' in such a way that

'*a* falls under the concept *F*'

is the general form of a thought content, which concerns an object *a* and which remains decidable, whatever one may put for *a*. And in this sense,

'*a* falls under the concept "unequal to itself" '

is synonymous with

'*a* is unequal to itself'

or

'*a* is unequal to *a*'.

In defining 0, I could have taken any other concept under which nothing falls. It was up to me, however, to choose one of which this could be purely logically proved, and for this purpose "unequal to itself" presented itself most comfortably, whereby I let the previously presented definition of Leibniz hold, which is also purely logical.

75. We must now be able to prove, by means of what has already been said, that every concept under which nothing falls is equinumerous with any other concept under which nothing falls, and only with such a concept;

---

[13] Completely different from this is the definition of an object in terms of a concept under which it falls. The expression 'the greatest proper fraction' has, for example, no content, because the definite article carries with it the requirement that it refer to a definite object. On the other hand, the concept, "fraction which is less than 1 and has the property that no fraction which is less than 1 exceeds it in magnitude," is wholly unobjectionable. In fact, in order to prove that there is no such fraction, one even needs this concept, even though it contains a contradiction.

from which it follows that 0 is the number which applies to such a concept and that no object falls under a concept if the number which applies to that concept is 0.

If we assume that no object falls either under the concept F or under the concept G, then, in order to prove that they are equinumerous, we need a relation ϕ about which the following statements hold:

'each object which falls under F stands in the relation ϕ to an object which falls under G; for each object which falls under G there is one falling under F which stands in the relation ϕ to it'.

According to what was said earlier about the meaning of these expressions, every relation fulfills these conditions under our hypotheses; hence also equality, which is, moreover, one-to-one. For, both the foregoing statements required of it hold.

If, on the other hand, an object falls under G, e.g., a, whereas none falls under F, then the two statements

'a falls under G'

and

'no object falling under F stands in the relation ϕ to a'

hold for every relation ϕ; for, the first holds true according to the first assumption, and the second, according to the second. That is, if there is no object falling under F, then there is also none which would stand in any sort of relation to a. There is, therefore, no relation which would, according to our definition, correlate the objects falling under F with those falling under G; accordingly, the concepts F and G are not equinumerous.

76. I want now to define the relation in which any two adjoining members of the series of natural numbers stand to one another. The statement

'there is a concept F and an object x falling under it such that the number which applies to the concept F is n, and that the number which applies to the concept "falling under F but not identical with x" is m',

is to be synonymous with

'n immediately follows m in the series of natural numbers'.

I am avoiding the expression 'n is *the* number immediately following m', because two theorems would first have to be proved in order to justify the use of the definite article.[14] For the same reason, I am not yet saying here '$n = m + 1$'; for, by means of the equals sign, $(m + 1)$ is also designated as an object.

[14] See footnote 13.

77. Now, in order to arrive at the number 1, we must first show, that there is something which immediately follows 0 in the series of natural numbers.

Let us consider the concept—or, if you prefer—the predicate 'equal to 0'. 0 falls under this. On the other hand, no object falls under the concept "equal to 0 but not equal to 0," so that 0 is the number which applies to this concept. We have therefore, a concept "equal to 0" and an object 0 falling under it, for which it holds that:

the number which applies to the concept "equal to 0," is equal to the number which applies to the concept "equal to 0";

the number which applies to the concept "equal to 0 but not equal to 0" is 0.

Therefore, according to our definition, the number which applies to the concept "equal to 0" follows immediately after 0 in the series of natural numbers.

If we define, then,

1 is the number which applies to the concept "equal to 0,"

then we can express the last statement so:

1 immediately follows 0 in the series of natural numbers.

Perhaps it is not superfluous to note that the definition of 1 does not presuppose any observed fact[15] for its objective legitimacy, for one can easily be confused by the fact that certain subjective conditions must be fulfilled in order to enable us to give the definition, and that sense impressions cause us to do so.[16] This can, nevertheless, be the case without the derived theorems ceasing to be *a priori*. To such conditions belongs the requirement, for example, that blood flow through the brain in sufficient quantity and of the right concentration—at least as far as we know; however, the truth of our last proposition is independent of that; it continues to hold even if this flow no longer takes place. And even if all reasonable creatures should at some time simultaneously slip into hibernation, the truth of the statement would not, as it were, be suspended for the duration of this sleep, but would remain undisturbed. The truth of a statement is not its being thought.

78. I list here several theorems to be proved by means of our definitions. The reader will easily see how this may be done.

I.   If *a* immediately follows 0 in the series of natural numbers, then $a = 1$.

II.   If 1 is the number which applies to a concept, then there is an object which falls under that concept.

---

[15] A proposition that is not general.

[16] Cf. B. Erdmann, *Die Axiome der Geometrie* (1877), p. 164.

III.   If 1 is the number which applies to a concept F; if the object x falls
under the concept F, and if y falls under the concept F, then $x = y$;
i.e., x is the same as y.

IV.   If an object falls under a concept F and if, from the fact that x falls
under the concept F and that y falls under the concept F, it may always
be inferred that $x = y$, then 1 is the number which applies to the concept F.

V.   The relation that m bears to n, if and only if

"n immediately follows m in the series of natural numbers",

is a one-one relation.

Thus far it has not yet been said that for every number there is another
which immediately follows it or is immediately followed by it in the series of
natural numbers.

VI.   Every number except 0 immediately follows another number in the
series of natural numbers.

79. Now in order to be able to prove that every number (n) in the series
of natural numbers is immediately followed by a number, one must come up
with a concept to which this latter number applies. We choose for this:

"belonging to the series of natural numbers ending with n,"

but we must first define it.

To begin with I shall repeat, in somewhat different words, the definition
I gave in my *Begriffsschrift* of following in a series:

The statement

'if every object to which x stands in the relation ϕ falls under the concept
F, and if, from the fact that d falls under the concept F, it always follows,
no matter what d may be, that every object to which d stands in the
relation ϕ falls under the concept F, then y falls under the concept F,
no matter what concept F might be',

is to be synonymous with

'y follows x in the ϕ-series'

and with

'x precedes y in the ϕ-series'.

80. Several remarks concerning this definition will not be superfluous
here. Since the relation ϕ is left indeterminate, the series is not necessarily to
be thought of in the form of a spatial or temporal arrangement, although
these cases are not excluded.

Some other definition might be considered more natural, e.g., if, in proceeding from x, we always turn our attention from one object to another, to which it stands in the relation ϕ, and if, in this way, we can finally reach y, then we say that y follows x in the ϕ-series.

This is a way of looking at the matter, not a definition. Whether we reach y in the wanderings of our attention can depend on many subjective incidental circumstances; e.g., on the time we have available or on our knowledge of the things. Whether y follows x in the ϕ-series has, in general, nothing at all to do with our attention and the conditions of its progress, but rather it is a matter of objective fact: just as a green leaf reflects certain light rays whether or not they should meet my eye and summon up a sensation; just as a grain of salt is soluble in water whether or not I put it in water and observe the process; and just as it remains soluble even if it is not possible for me to experiment on it.

By means of my definition, the matter is elevated from the realm of the subjectively possible to that of the objectively definite. Indeed, the fact that from certain statements another statement follows is something objective, something independent of whatever laws may govern the wanderings of our attention; and it makes no difference whether we really make the inference or not. Here we have a criterion which decides the question, wherever it can be asked, even though we might be hindered by external difficulties from judging in individual cases whether it is applicable. That makes no difference to the issue itself.

We need not always run through all the intermediate members, from the initial member up to an object, in order to be sure that the latter follows the former. If, e.g., it is given that, in the ϕ-series, b follows a and c follows b, then we can conclude on the basis of our definition that c follows a, without even knowing the intermediate members.

Only by means of this definition of following in a series does it become possible to reduce the rule of inference from n to $(n + 1)$, which apparently is peculiar to mathematics, to general logical laws.

81. Now if we have as our relation ϕ the one in which m is related to n by the statement

'n immediately follows m in the series of natural numbers',

then we say instead of 'ϕ-series', 'series of natural numbers'.

I define further:

the statement

'y follows x in the ϕ-series or y is the same as x',

is to be synonymous with

'y belongs to the ϕ-series starting with x'

and with

'x belongs to the ϕ-series ending with y'.

According to this, a belongs to the series of natural numbers ending with n if n either follows a in the series of natural numbers or is equal to a.[17]

82. We must now show that, under a condition still to be stated, the number which applies to the concept

"belonging to the series of natural numbers ending with n"

immediately follows n in the series of natural numbers. Having this result, we will have proved that there is a number which immediately follows n in the series of natural numbers; i.e., that there is no last member of this series. Obviously, this statement cannot be established empirically or by means of induction.

It would take us too far afield to give the proof itself. We can only give a brief sketch of it here. We must prove:

1. If a immediately follows d in the series of natural numbers, and if the number which applies to the concept

    "belonging to the series of natural numbers ending with d"

    immediately follows d in the series of natural numbers, then the number which applies to the concept

    "belonging to the series of natural numbers ending with a"

    immediately follows a in the series of natural numbers.

2. We must prove that what has been asserted about d and a in the foregoing statements holds for 0, and then show that it also holds for n, if n belongs to the series of natural numbers beginning with 0. This will result from an application of my definition of

    'y follows x in the series of natural numbers',

    taking as the concept F the relation asserted above to hold between d ~~and a;~~ and substituting 0 and n for d and a.

83. In order to prove Theorem 1 of the last paragraph, we must show that a is the number which applies to the concept "belonging to the series of natural numbers ending with a, but not equal to a." And to this end, we must prove that this concept has the same extension as the concept "belonging to the series of natural numbers ending with d." For this, we need the theorem

[17] If n is not a number, then only n itself belongs to the series of natural numbers ending with n. One should not object to this expression.

that no object which belongs to the series of natural numbers beginning with 0 can follow itself in the series of natural numbers. The latter must likewise be proved by means of our definition of following in a series, as it is outlined above.[18]

For this reason, we must add the condition that n belong to the series of natural numbers beginning with 0 to the statement that the number which applies to the concept

"belonging to the series of natural numbers ending with n,"

immediately follows n in the series of natural numbers. There is a shorter way of putting this, which I shall now define:

the statement

'n belongs to the series of natural numbers beginning with 0'

is to be synonymous with

'n is a finite number'.

We can now express the last theorem thus: no finite number follows itself in the series of natural numbers.

INFINITE NUMBERS

84. In contrast to the finite numbers there are the infinite ones. The number which applies to the concept "finite number" is an infinite one. Let us denote it, say, by $\aleph_0$.[19] Were it a finite number, it could not follow itself in the series of natural numbers. One can show, however, that $\aleph_0$ does just this.

There is nothing somehow mysterious or marvellous about the infinite number $\aleph_0$ when so defined. 'The number which applies to the concept F is $\aleph_0$' says nothing more nor less than: there is a relation which establishes a one-to-one correlation between the objects falling under the concept F and the finite numbers. This has, according to our definitions, a completely clear and unambiguous sense, and that suffices to justify the use of the symbol $\aleph_0$ and to guarantee it a meaning. That we can form no mental picture of an infinite number is wholly irrelevant and would hold true of finite numbers as well. In this way, our number $\aleph_0$ is something just as determinate

---

[18] E. Schröder (*op. cit.*, p. 63) seems to look upon this theorem as the consequence of an ambiguous terminology. The difficulty which infects his whole presentation of the matter emerges here too; i.e., it is never quite clear whether the number is a symbol and, if so, what its meaning is, or whether it *is* this very meaning. From the fact that one sets up different symbols, so that the same one never recurs, it does not follow that these symbols mean different things.

[19] [Frege used '∞_1', but we adopt the aleph notation as being more in keeping with current practice.—Tr.]

as any finite number: it can be recognized without a doubt as the same and differentiated from any other.

85. Recently, in a noteworthy paper,[19] G. Cantor introduced infinite numbers. I agree with him completely in his evaluation of the view which would have only the finite numbers qualify as real. Neither these nor the fractions are sensibly perceptible and spatial, nor are the negative, irrational, and complex numbers. And if one calls real [only] that which affects the senses, or at least can have sense impressions as an immediate or distant consequence, then certainly none of these numbers is real. But we don't need such sense impressions as evidence for our theorems. A name or a symbol, which is introduced in a logically unobjectionable way, may be used by us without hesitation in our investigations, and thus our number $\aleph_0$ is just as firmly grounded as 2 or 3.

Although I believe I agree with Cantor in this matter, I do, however, deviate from him in terminology. He calls my numbers 'powers', whereas his concept[20] of number is based on ordering. To be sure, finite numbers end up being independent of order; however, this does not hold for infinite numbers. Now the linguistic usage of the word 'number' and of the question 'how many?' contains no indication of a definite order. Cantor's number answers rather the question: 'the last member is the how-manyth member of the sequence?' Therefore my terminology seems to me to agree better with linguistic usage. If one extends the meaning of a word, then one must take care that as many general statements as possible retain their validity, and particularly statements as basic as, for instance, [the one asserting] for numbers their independence of the sequence. We have needed no extension at all, because our concept of number immediately embraces infinite numbers as well.

86. In order to obtain his infinite numbers, Cantor introduces the relational concept of following in a sequence, which differs from my "following in a series." According to him, for instance, a sequence would result if one were so to order the finite positive whole numbers that the odd numbers followed one another in their own natural order, and similarly the even numbers in theirs, and it were further stipulated that all the even numbers should come after all the odd numbers. In this sequence, e.g., 0 would follow 13. There would, however, be no number immediately preceding 0. Now this case cannot occur within my definition of following in a series. It may be strictly proved, without using intuition, that, if y follows x in the ϕ-series, there is an object which immediately precedes y in this series. It seems to me, then, that exact definitions of following in a sequence and of number [in Cantor's sense] are still lacking. Thus Cantor bases himself on a somewhat mysterious "inner

[19] *Grundlagen einer allgemeinen Mannichfaltigkeitslehre* (Leipzig, 1883).

[20] This expression may appear to contradict [my earlier remarks emphasizing] the objectivity of concepts; however, only the *terminology* is subjective here.

intuition" where a proof from definitions should be striven for and would probably be found. For I think I can foresee how those concepts could be defined. In any case, I in no way wish these comments to be taken as an attack on the justifiability or fruitfulness of these concepts. On the contrary, I welcome these investigations as an extension of the science, especially because they strike a purely arithmetic path to higher infinite numbers (powers).

CONCLUSION

87. I hope in this monograph to have made it probable that arithmetic laws are analytic judgments, and therefore *a priori*. According to this, arithmetic would be only a further developed logic, every arithmetic theorem a logical law, albeit a derived one. The applications of arithmetic to the explanation of natural phenomena would be logical processing of observed facts;[21] computation would be inference. Numerical laws will not need, as Baumann[22] contends, a practical confirmation in order to be applicable in the external world; for, in the external world, the totality of space and its contents, there are no concepts, no properties of concepts, no numbers. Therefore, the numerical laws are really not applicable to the external world: they are not laws of nature. They are, however, applicable to judgments, which are true of things in the external world: they are laws of the laws of nature. They assert connections not between natural phenomena, but rather between judgments; and it is to the latter that the laws of nature belong.

88. Kant[23] evidently underestimated the value of analytic judgments—probably as the result of having too narrow a definition of the concept—although he apparently also had in mind the broader concept used here.[24] Taking his definition as a basis, the division of judgments into the analytic and the synthetic is not exhaustive. He is thinking of universal affirmative judgments. In such cases, one can speak of a concept of the subject and inquire whether the concept of the predicate—as would result from *his* definition—is contained in it. How can we do this, however, when the subject is a single object? Or when the judgment is existential? In such cases there can be, in Kant's sense, no talk of a concept of the subject. Kant seems to have thought of the concept as determined by subordinate characteristics; that, however, is one of the least fruitful notions of concept. If one surveys the foregoing definitions, one will hardly find one of this kind. The same is true of the really fruitful definitions in mathematics, e.g., of the continuity of a function. There

---

[21] Observation itself already includes a logical activity.

[22] *Die Lehren von Zeit, Raum und Mathematik*, Vol. II, p. 670.

[23] *Op. cit.*, III, p. 39ff.

[24] On p. 43 of the preceding reference [Kant] says that a synthetic statement can be understood according to the Theorem of Contradiction only if another synthetic statement is presupposed.

we don't have a series of subordinate characteristics but rather a more intimate, I should say more organic, connection between the [elements of the] definitions. The difference can be illustrated by means of a geometrical analogy. If the concepts (or their extensions) are represented by regions of a plane, then the concept defined by means of subordinate characteristics corresponds to the region which is the overlap of all the individual regions corresponding to these characteristics; it is enclosed by parts of their boundaries. Pictorially speaking, in such a definition, we delimit a region by using in a new way lines already given. In doing this, however, nothing essentially new comes out. The more fruitful definitions draw border lines which had not previously been given. What can be inferred from them cannot be seen in advance; one does not simply withdraw again from the box what one has put into it. These inferences expand our knowledge and one should, therefore, following Kant, consider them synthetic. Nevertheless, they can be proved purely logically and hence are analytic. They are in fact contained in the definitions, but like the plant in the seed, not like the rafter in the house. One often needs several definitions to prove a theorem, which consequently is contained in no single definition, but nevertheless follows in a purely logical way from all of them together.

89. I must also contradict the generality of Kant's assertion[25] that without sensible perception no object would be given us. Zero and 1 are objects that cannot be given us sensibly. And those who hold the smaller numbers to be intuitive will surely have to concede that none of the numbers greater than $1000^{1000^{1000}}$ can be given them intuitively, and that we nevertheless know a good deal about them. Perhaps Kant was using the word 'object' in a somewhat different sense; but then zero, 1, and our $\aleph_0$ disappear completely from his considerations; for, they are not concepts either, and Kant demands even of concepts that their objects be appended to them in intuition.

In order not to open myself to the criticism of carrying on a picayune search for faults in the work of a genius whom we look up to only with thankful awe, I believe I should also emphasize our areas of agreement, which are far more extensive than those of our disagreement. To touch on only the immediate points, I see a great service in Kant's having distinguished between synthetic and analytic judgments. In terming geometric truths synthetic and *a priori*, he uncovered their true essence. And this is still worth repeating today, because it is still often not recognized. If Kant erred with respect to arithmetic, this does not detract essentially, I think, from his merit. It was important for him that there should be synthetic judgments *a priori*; whether they occur only in geometry or also in arithmetic is of little importance.

90. I do not claim to have made the analytic nature of arithmetic theorems more than probable, because one can always still doubt whether their proof can

[25] *Op. cit.*, III, p. 82.

be carried out completely from purely logical laws, whether evidence of another sort has not crept in unnoticed somewhere. This doubt is also not entirely relieved by the outlines which I have given of the proofs of a few theorems; it can only be alleviated by an airtight chain of reasoning, such that no step is made which is not in conformity with one of a few rules of inference recognized as purely logical. Thus until now, hardly a single [real] proof has ever been offered, because the mathematician is satisfied if every transition to a new judgment appears to him to be correct, without asking whether this appearance is logical or intuitive. A step in such a proof is often quite complex and involves several simple inferences, in addition to which intuitive considerations can creep in. One proceeds in jumps, and from this there arises the impression of an over-rich variety of rules of inference used in mathematics. For, the greater the jumps, the more complex are the combinations of simple inferences and intuitive axioms which they can represent. Nevertheless, such a transition often occurs to us directly, without our being conscious of the intermediate steps, and since it does not present itself as one of the recognized logical rules of inference, we are immediately ready to consider this manifest transition as an intuitive one and the inferred truth as a synthetic one, even when the range of its validity extends far beyond intuition.

Proceeding in this way, it is not possible clearly to separate the synthetic, based on intuition, from the analytic. Nor will it be possible to compile with completeness and certainty the axioms of intuition needed to make every mathematical proof capable of proceeding from these axioms alone, according to logical laws.

91. The requirement of avoiding all jumps in a proof must, therefore, be imposed. That it is so difficult to satisfy is owing to the tediousness of a step-by-step procedure. Every proof, which is even slightly involved, threatens to become enormously long. In addition to this, the superfluity of logical forms expressed in language makes it difficult to extract a group of rules of inference sufficient for all cases and yet easy to survey.

In order to minimize the effects of these drawbacks, I have devised my concept writing. It strives for greater brevity and comprehensibility of expression and is manipulated in a few standard ways, as in a computation, so that no transition is permitted which does not conform to rules set up once for all.[26] No assumption can then slip in unnoticed. I have thus proved a theorem,[27] borrowing no axioms from intuition, which one would consider at first glance to be synthetic and which I shall state here as follows:

If the relation of each member of a series to its successor is one-to-one,

---

[26] It is, however, supposed to be able to express not only the logical form of a statement, as does the Boolean notation, but also its content.

[27] *Begriffsschrift*, Halle a/S., 1879, p. 86, Formula 133.

and if *m* and *y* follow *x* in this series, then *y* precedes *m* in this series, or coincides with it, or follows *m*.

From this proof, one can see that theorems which expand our knowledge can contain analytic judgments.[28]

[RECAPITULATION]

106. Let us cast a quick glance backward on the course of our investigation. After determining that a number was not a collection of things nor a property of such a collection, nor, furthermore, the subjective product of mental processes, we decided that a statement of number asserts something objective about a concept. We defined first the individual numbers 0, 1, etc., and then following in the number series. Our first attempt failed, because in it we stated the meaning of only whole assertions about concepts, and not of 0 and 1 separately, although these entered into those assertions. As a result of this, we could not prove the equality of numbers. It was shown that the numbers with which arithmetic concerns itself must be understood not as dependent attributes, but rather substantivally.[29] Thus numbers appeared to us as recognizable objects, although not physical ones nor even merely spatial ones, nor ones which we could picture in imagination. We then established the basic theorem: that the meaning of a word is not to be defined separately, but rather in the context of a statement; only by following this theorem can we, I think, avoid the physical interpretation of number, without slipping into psychological interpretation. There is only one type of statement which must have a sense for every object; that is the recognition sentences, called equations in the case of numbers. We saw that statements of number are also to be interpreted as equations. It became a question, then, of determining the sense of a numerical equation and of expressing this sense without making use of the number-words or the word 'number'. The possibility of establishing a one-to-one correspondence between the objects falling under a concept *F* and those falling under a concept *G* was found to be the content of a recognition judgment about numbers. Our definition, therefore, had to posit that possibility as synonymous with a numerical equation. We recalled similar instances: the definition of direction from parallelism, of shape from similarity, etc.

---

[28] This proof will be found to be still much too lengthy, a disadvantage which may seem to more than balance out the almost unconditional guarantee against a mistake or a loophole. My purpose at that time was to reduce everything to the smallest possible number of the simplest possible logical laws. As a result of this, I applied only one rule of inference. I pointed out even then, in the foreword (p. vii) that, for futher application, it would be recommended to admit more rules of inference. This can be done without impairing the validity of the chain of reasoning, and an important abbreviation could thereby be achieved.

[29] The difference corresponds to that between 'blue' and 'the color of the sky'.

107. The question then arose: when are we justified in interpreting a content to be that of a recognition judgment? For this, the condition must be fulfilled that in every judgment the left side of the tentatively assumed equation can be replaced by the right, without altering the truth of the judgment. Now, at first and without resorting to further definitions, no further assertion about the left or right side of such an equation is known to us beyond the assertion of their equality. Substitutivity had therefore to be proved only for equations.

A doubt still remained, however. A recognition statement must always have a sense. If we interpret the possibility of correlating in one-to-one fashion the objects falling under the concept F with those falling under the concept G as an equation, by saying for it: 'the number which applies to the concept F is equal to the number which applies to the concept G' and thereby introducing the expression 'the number which applies is the concept F', then we have a sense for the equation only if both sides have the form just mentioned. We would not be able to judge according to such a definition whether an equation only one side of which had this form was true or false. That caused us to make the following definition:

The number which applies to the concept F is the extension of the concept "concept equinumerous with the concept F,"

by which we called a concept F equinumerous with a concept G, if there exists the possibility of correlating them one-to-one.

In doing this, we presuppose that the sense of the expression 'extension of a concept' is familiar. This method of overcoming the difficulty will probably not be everywhere applauded, and some will prefer to set aside this doubt in another way. I, too, place no decisive weight on the introduction of the extension of a concept.

108. We still had to define one-to-one correspondences; we reduced them to purely logical terms. After we had outlined the proof of the theorem that the number which applies to the concept F is equal to that which applies to the concept G, if the concept F is equinumerous with the concept G, we defined 0, the expression 'n immediately follows m in the series of natural numbers', and the number 1, and we showed that 1 immediately follows 0 in the series of natural numbers. We presented a few theorems which could be easily proved at this point and then went somewhat more deeply into the following, which demonstrates the infinity of the number series:

Every number in the series of natural numbers is followed by a number.

We were thereby led to the concept "belonging to the series of natural numbers ending with n," of which we wanted to show that the number applying to it immediately follows n in the series of natural numbers. We defined it at first by means of an object y following an object x in a general ϕ-series. The sense of this expression was also reduced to purely logical terms. And thereby we succeeded in proving that the rule of inference from n to $(n + 1)$, which is usually considered a peculiarly mathematical one, is based on the general logical rules of inference.

For the proof of the infinity of the number series, we needed the theorem that no finite number follows itself in the series of natural numbers. We thus arrived at the concepts of finite and infinite numbers. We showed that the latter is basically no less justified logically than is the former. For the purposes of comparison, we drew upon Cantor's infinite numbers and his "following in a sequence," where we pointed out the difference in terminology.

109. We thus rendered the analytic and *a priori* character of arithmetic truths highly probable, arriving at an improvement on Kant's point of view. We saw further what was still lacking in order to elevate that probability to certainty and we indicated the path that must lead to this.

SELECTIONS FROM *INTRODUCTION TO MATHEMATICAL PHILOSOPHY*

Bertrand Russell

I. THE SERIES OF NATURAL NUMBERS

Mathematics is a study which, when we start from its most familiar portions, may be pursued in either of two opposite directions. The more familiar direction is constructive, towards gradually increasing complexity: from integers to fractions, real numbers, complex numbers; from addition and multiplication to differentiation and integration, and on to higher mathematics. The other direction, which is less familiar, proceeds, by analysing, to greater and greater abstractness and logical simplicity; instead of asking what can be defined and deduced from what is assumed to begin with, we ask instead what more general ideas and principles can be found, in terms of which what was our starting-point can be defined or deduced. It is the fact of pursuing this opposite direction that characterises mathematical philosophy as opposed to ordinary mathematics. But it should be understood that the distinction is one, not in the subject matter, but in the state of mind of the investigator. Early Greek geometers, passing from the empirical rules of Egyptian land-surveying to the general propositions by which those rules were found to be justifiable, and thence to Euclid's axioms and postulates, were engaged in mathematical philosophy, according to the above definition; but when once the axioms and postulates had been reached, their deductive employment, as we find it in Euclid, belonged to mathematics in the ordinary sense. The distinction between mathematics and mathematical philosophy is one which depends upon the interest inspiring the research, and upon the stage which the research has reached; not upon the propositions with which the research is concerned.

Reprinted by kind permission of the publishers from Bertrand Russell, Introduction to Mathematical Philosophy (*New York: The Macmillan Company; London: George Allen & Unwin Ltd.*, 1919), *pp.* 1–19, 194–206.

We may state the same distinction in another way. The most obvious and easy things in mathematics are not those that come logically at the beginning; they are things that, from the point of view of logical deduction, come somewhere in the middle. Just as the easiest bodies to see are those that are neither very near nor very far, neither very small nor very great, so the easiest conceptions to grasp are those that are neither very complex nor very simple (using "simple" in a *logical* sense). And as we need two sorts of instruments, the telescope and the microscope, for the enlargement of our visual powers, so we need two sorts of instruments for the enlargement of our logical powers, one to take us forward to the higher mathematics, the other to take us backward to the logical foundations of the things that we are inclined to take for granted in mathematics. We shall find that by analysing our ordinary mathematical notions we acquire fresh insight, new powers, and the means of reaching whole new mathematical subjects by adopting fresh lines of advance after our backward journey. It is the purpose of this book to explain mathematical philosophy simply and untechnically, without enlarging upon those portions which are so doubtful or difficult that an elementary treatment is scarcely possible. A full treatment will be found in *Principia Mathematica*;[1] the treatment in the present volume is intended merely as an introduction.

To the average educated person of the present day, the obvious starting-point of mathematics would be the series of whole numbers,

$$1, 2, 3, 4, \ldots \text{ etc.}$$

Probably only a person with some mathematical knowledge would think of beginning with 0 instead of with 1, but we will presume this degree of knowledge; we will take as our starting-point the series:

$$0, 1, 2, 3, \ldots n, n + 1, \ldots$$

and it is this series that we shall mean when we speak of the "series of natural numbers."

It is only at a high stage of civilisation that we could take this series as our starting-point. It must have required many ages to discover that a brace of pheasants and a couple of days were both instances of the number 2: the degree of abstraction involved is far from easy. And the discovery that 1 is a number must have been difficult. As for 0, it is a very recent addition; the Greeks and Romans had no such digit. If we had been embarking upon mathematical philosophy in earlier days, we should have had to start with something less abstract than the series of natural numbers, which we should reach as a stage on our backward journey. When the logical foundations of mathematics have grown more familiar, we shall be able to start further back,

---

[1] Cambridge University Press, vol. i, 1910; vol. ii, 1911; vol. iii, 1913. By Whitehead and Russell.

at what is now a late stage in our analysis. But for the moment the natural numbers seem to represent what is easiest and most familiar in mathematics.

But though familiar, they are not understood. Very few people are prepared with a definition of what is meant by "number," or "0," or "1." It is not very difficult to see that, starting from 0, any other of the natural numbers can be reached by repeated additions of 1, but we shall have to define what we mean by "adding 1," and what we mean by "repeated." These questions are by no means easy. It was believed until recently that some, at least, of these first notions of arithmetic must be accepted as too simple and primitive to be defined. Since all terms that are defined are defined by means of other terms, it is clear that human knowledge must always be content to accept some terms as intelligible without definition, in order to have a starting-point for its definitions. It is not clear that there must be terms which are *incapable* of definition: it is possible that, however far back we go in defining, we always *might* go further still. On the other hand, it is also possible that, when analysis has been pushed far enough, we can reach terms that really are simple, and therefore logically incapable of the sort of definition that consists in analysing. This is a question which it is not necessary for us to decide; for our purposes it is sufficient to observe that, since human powers are finite, the definitions known to us must always begin somewhere, with terms undefined for the moment, though perhaps not permanently.

All traditional pure mathematics, including analytical geometry, may be regarded as consisting wholly of propositions about the natural numbers. That is to say, the terms which occur can be defined by means of the natural numbers, and the propositions can be deduced from the properties of the natural numbers—with the addition, in each case, of the ideas and propositions of pure logic.

That all traditional pure mathematics can be derived from the natural numbers is a fairly recent discovery, though it had long been suspected. Pythagoras, who believed that not only mathematics, but everything else could be deduced from numbers, was the discoverer of the most serious obstacle in the way of what is called the "arithmetising" of mathematics. It was Pythagoras who discovered the existence of incommensurables, and, in particular, the incommensurability of the side of a square and the diagonal. It the length of the side is 1 inch, the number of inches in the diagonal is the square root of 2, which appeared not to be a number at all. The problem thus raised was solved only in our own day, and was only solved *completely* by the help of the reduction of arithmetic to logic, which will be explained in following chapters. For the present, we shall take for granted the arithmetisation of mathematics, though this was a feat of the very greatest importance.

Having reduced all traditional pure mathematics to the theory of the natural numbers, the next step in logical analysis was to reduce this theory itself to the smallest set of premisses and undefined terms from which it could be derived. This work was accomplished by Peano. He showed that the entire theory of the natural numbers could be derived from three primitive ideas and five primitive propositions in addition to those of pure logic. These three ideas and five propositions thus became, as it were, hostages for the whole of traditional pure mathematics. If they could be defined and proved in terms of others, so could all pure mathematics. Their logical "weight," if one may use such an expression, is equal to that of the whole series of sciences that have been deduced from the theory of the natural numbers; the truth of this whole series is assured if the truth of the five primitive propositions is guaranteed, provided, of course, that there is nothing erroneous in the purely logical apparatus which is also involved. The work of analysing mathematics is extraordinarily facilitated by this work of Peano's.

The three primitive ideas in Peano's arithmetic are:

0, number, successor.

By "successor" he means the next number in the natural order. That is to say, the successor of 0 is 1, the successor of 1 is 2, and so on. By "number" he means, in this connection, the class of the natural numbers.[2] He is not assuming that we know all the members of this class, but only that we know what we mean when we say that this or that is a number, just as we know what we mean when we say "Jones is a man," though we do not know all men individually.

(1)   0 is a number.
(2)   The successor of any number is a number.
(3)   No two numbers have the same successor.
(4)   0 is not the successor of any number.
(5)   Any property which belongs to 0, and also to the successor of every number which has the property, belongs to all numbers.

The last of these is the principle of mathematical induction. We shall have much to say concerning mathematical induction in the sequel; for the present, we are concerned with it only as it occurs in Peano's analysis of arithmetic.

Let us consider briefly the kind of way in which the theory of the natural numbers results from these three ideas and five propositions. To begin with, we define 1 as "the successor of 0," 2 as "the successor of 1," and so on. We can obviously go on as long as we like with these definitions, since, in virtue of (2), every number that we reach will have a successor, and, in virtue of (3), this cannot be any of the numbers already defined, because, if it were, two different numbers would have the same successor; and in virtue of (4) none of the numbers we reach in the series of successors can be 0. Thus the series of successors gives us an endless series of continually new numbers. In virtue of (5) all numbers come in this series, which begins with 0 and travels

[2] We shall use "number" in this sense in the present chapter. Afterwards the word will be used in a more general sense.

on through successive successors: for (*a*) 0 belongs to this series, and (*b*) if a number *n* belongs to it, so does its successor, whence, by mathematical induction, every number belongs to the series.

Suppose we wish to define the sum of two numbers. Taking any number *m*, we define $m + 0$ as *m*, and $m + (n + 1)$ as the successor of $m + n$. In virtue of (5) this gives a definition of the sum of *m* and *n*, whatever number *n* may be. Similarly we can define the product of any two numbers. The reader can easily convince himself that any ordinary elementary proposition of arithmetic can be proved by means of our five premisses, and if he has any difficulty he can find the proof in Peano.

It is time now to turn to the considerations which make it necessary to advance beyond the standpoint of Peano, who represents the last perfection of the "arithmetisation" of mathematics, to that of Frege, who first succeeded in "logicising" mathematics, *i.e.* in reducing to logic the arithmetical notions which his predecessors had shown to be sufficient for mathematics. We shall not, in this chapter, actually give Frege's definition of number and of particular numbers, but we shall give some of the reasons why Peano's treatment is less final than it appears to be.

In the first place, Peano's three primitive ideas—namely, "0," "number," and "successor"—are capable of an infinite number of different interpretations, all of which will satisfy the five primitive propositions. We will give some examples.

(1) Let "0" be taken to mean 100, and let "number" be taken to mean the numbers from 100 onward in the series of natural numbers. Then all our primitive propositions are satisfied, even the fourth, for, though 100 is the successor of 99, 99 is not a "number" in the sense which we are now giving to the word "number." It is obvious that any number may be substituted for 100 in this example.

(2) Let "0" have its usual meaning, but let "number" mean what we usually call "even numbers," and let the "successor" of a number be what results from adding two to it. Then "1" will stand for the number two, "2" will stand for the number four, and so on; the series of "numbers" now will be

0, two, four, six, eight ...

All Peano's five premisses are satisfied still.

(3) Let "0" mean the number one, let "number" mean the set

$$1, \frac{1}{2}, \frac{1}{4}, \frac{1}{8}, \frac{1}{16}, \ldots$$

and let "successor" mean "half." Then all Peano's five axioms will be true of this set.

It is clear that such examples might be multiplied indefinitely. In fact, given any series

$$x_0, x_1, x_2, x_3, \ldots x_n, \ldots$$

which is endless, contains no repetitions, has a beginning, and has no terms that cannot be reached from the beginning in a finite number of steps, we have a set of terms verifying Peano's axioms. This is easily seen, though the formal proof is somewhat long. Let "0" mean x_0, let "number" mean the whole set of terms, and let the "successor" of x_n mean x_{n+1}. Then

(1) "0 is a number," i.e. x_0 is a member of the set.

(2) "The successor of any number is a number," i.e. taking any term x_n in the set, x_{n+1} is also in the set.

(3) "No two numbers have the same successor," i.e. if x_m and x_n are two different members of the set, x_{m+1} and x_{n+1} are different; this results from the fact that (by hypothesis) there are no repetitions in the set.

(4) "0 is not the successor of any number," i.e. no term in the set comes before x_0.

(5) This becomes: Any property which belongs to x_0, and belongs to x_{n+1} provided it belongs to x_n, belongs to all the x's.

This follows from the corresponding property for numbers.

A series of the form

$$x_0, x_1, x_2, \ldots x_n, \ldots$$

in which there is a first term, a successor to each term (so that there is no last term), no repetitions, and every term can be reached from the start in a finite number of steps, is called a *progression*. Progressions are of great importance in the principles of mathematics. As we have just seen, every progression verifies Peano's five axioms. It can be proved, conversely, that every series which verifies Peano's five axioms is a progression. Hence these five axioms may be used to define the class of progressions: "progressions" are "those series which verify these five axioms." Any progression may be taken as the basis of pure mathematics: we may give the name "0" to its first term, the name "number" to the whole set of its terms, and the name "successor" to the next in the progression. The progression need not be composed of numbers: it may be composed of points in space, or moments of time, or any other terms of which there is an infinite supply. Each different progression will give rise to a different interpretation of all the propositions of traditional pure mathematics; all these possible interpretations will be equally true.

In Peano's system there is nothing to enable us to distinguish between these different interpretations of his primitive ideas. It is assumed that we know what is meant by "0," and that we shall not suppose that this symbol means 100 or Cleopatra's Needle or any of the other things that it might mean.

This point, that "0" and "number" and "successor" cannot be defined by means of Peano's five axioms, but must be independently understood, is important. We want our numbers not merely to verify mathematical formulæ, but to apply in the right way to common objects. We want to have ten fingers and two eyes and one nose. A system in which "1" meant 100, and "2" meant 101, and so on, might be all right for pure mathematics, but would not suit daily life. We want "0" and "number" and "successor" to have meanings which will give us the right allowance of fingers and eyes and noses. We have already some knowledge (though not sufficiently articulate or analytic) of what we mean by "1" and "2" and so on, and our use of numbers in arithmetic must conform to this knowledge. We cannot secure that this shall be the case by Peano's method; all that we can do, if we adopt his method, is to say "we know what we mean by '0' and 'number' and 'successor,' though we cannot explain what we mean in terms of other simpler concepts." It is quite legitimate to say this when we must, and at *some* point we all must; but it is the object of mathematical philosophy to put off saying it as long as possible. By the logical theory of arithmetic we are able to put it off for a very long time.

It might be suggested that, instead of setting up "0" and "number" and "successor" as terms of which we know the meaning although we cannot definite them, we might let them stand for *any* three terms that verify Peano's five axioms. They will then no longer be terms which have a meaning that is definite though undefined: they will be "variables," terms concerning which we make certain hypotheses, namely, those stated in the five axioms, but which are otherwise undetermined. If we adopt this plan, our theorems will not be proved concerning an ascertained set of terms called "the natural numbers," but concerning all sets of terms having certain properties. Such a procedure is not fallacious; indeed for certain purposes it represents a valuable generalisation. But from two points of view it fails to give an adequate basis for arithmetic. In the first place, it does not enable us to know whether there are any sets of terms verifying Peano's axioms; it does not even give the faintest suggestion of any way of discovering whether there are such sets. In the second place, as already observed, we want our numbers to be such as can be used for counting common objects, and this requires that our numbers should have a *definite* meaning, not merely that they should have certain formal properties. This definite meaning is defined by the logical theory of arithmetic.

II. DEFINITION OF NUMBER

The question "What is a number?" is one which has been often asked but has only been correctly answered in our own time. The answer was given by Frege in 1884, in his *Grundlagen der Arithmetik*.[3] Although this book is quite short, not difficult, and of the very highest importance, it attracted almost no attention, and the definition of number which it contains remained practically unknown until it was rediscovered by the present author in 1901.

In seeking a definition of number, the first thing to be clear about is what we may call the grammar of our inquiry. Many philosophers, when

---

[3] The same answer is given more fully and with more development in his *Grundgesetze der Arithmetik*, vol. i, 1893.

attempting to define number, are really setting to work to define plurality, which is quite a different thing. *Number* is what is characteristic of numbers, as *man* is what is characteristic of men. A plurality is not an instance of number, but of some particular number. A trio of men, for example, is an instance of the number 3, and the number 3 is an instance of number; but the trio is not an instance of number. This point may seem elementary and scarcely worth mentioning; yet it has proved too subtle for the philosophers, with few exceptions.

A particular number is not identical with any collection of terms having that number: the number 3 is not identical with the trio consisting of Brown, Jones, and Robinson. The number 3 is something which all trios have in common, and which distinguishes them from other collections. A number is something that characterises certain collections, namely, those that have that number.

Instead of speaking of a "collection," we shall as a rule speak of a "class," or sometimes a "set." Other words used in mathematics for the same thing are "aggregate" and "manifold." We shall have much to say later on about classes. For the present, we will say as little as possible. But there are some remarks that must be made immediately.

A class or collection may be defined in two ways that at first sight seem quite distinct. We may enumerate its members, as when we say, "The collection I mean is Brown, Jones, and Robinson." Or we may mention a defining property, as when we speak of "mankind" or "the inhabitants of London." The definition which enumerates is called a definition by "extension," and the one which mentions a defining property is called a definition by "intension." Of these two kinds of definition, the one by intension is logically more fundamental. This is shown by two considerations: (1) that the extensional definition can always be reduced to an intensional one; (2) that the intensional one often cannot even theoretically be reduced to the extensional one. Each of these points needs a word of explanation.

(1) Brown, Jones, and Robinson all of them possess a certain property which is possessed by nothing else in the whole universe, namely, the property of being either Brown or Jones or Robinson. This property can be used to give a definition by intension of the class consisting of Brown and Jones and Robinson. Consider such a formula as "x is Brown or x is Jones or x is Robinson." This formula will be true for just three x's, namely, Brown and Jones and Robinson. In this respect it resembles a cubic equation with its three roots. It may be taken as assigning a property common to the members of the class consisting of these three men, and peculiar to them. A similar treatment can obviously be applied to any other class given in extension.

(2) It is obvious that in practice we can often know a great deal about a class without being able to enumerate its members. No one man could actually enumerate all men, or even all the inhabitants of London, yet a great deal is known about each of these classes. This is enough to show that definition by

extension is not *necessary* to knowledge about a class. But when we come to consider infinite classes, we find that enumeration is not even theoretically possible for beings who only live for a finite time. We cannot enumerate all the natural numbers: they are 0, 1, 2, 3, *and so on.* At some point we must content ourselves with "and so on." We cannot enumerate all fractions or all irrational numbers, or all of any other infinite collection. Thus our knowledge in regard to all such collections can only be derived from a definition by intension.

These remarks are relevant, when we are seeking the definition of number, in three different ways. In the first place, numbers themselves form an infinite collection, and cannot therefore be defined by enumeration. In the second place, the collections having a given number of terms themselves presumably form an infinite collection: it is to be presumed, for example, that there are an infinite collection of trios in the world, for if this were not the case the total number of things in the world would be finite, which, though possible, seems unlikely. In the third place, we wish to define "number" in such a way that infinite numbers may be possible; thus we must be able to speak of the number of terms in an infinite collection, and such a collection must be defined by intension. i.e. by a property common to all its members and peculiar to them.

For many purposes, a class and a defining characteristic of it are practically interchangeable. The vital difference between the two consists in the fact that there is only one class having a given set of members, whereas there are always many different characteristics by which a given class may be defined. Men may be defined as featherless bipeds, or as rational animals, or (more correctly) by the traits by which Swift delineates the Yahoos. It is this fact that a defining characteristic is never unique which makes classes useful; otherwise we could be content with the properties common and peculiar to their members.[4] Any one of these properties can be used in place of the class whenever uniqueness is not important.

Returning now to the definition of number, it is clear that number is a way of bringing together certain collections, namely, those that have a given number of terms. We can suppose all couples in one bundle, all trios in another, and so on. In this way we obtain various bundles of collections, each bundle consisting of all the collections that have a certain number of terms. Each bundle is a class whose members are collections, i.e. classes; thus each is a class of classes. The bundle consisting of all couples, for example, is a class of classes: each couple is a class with two members, and the whole bundle of couples is a class with an infinite number of members, each of which is a class of two members.

How shall we decide whether two collections are to belong to the same

---

[4] As will be explained later, classes may be regarded as logical fictions, manufactured out of defining characteristics. But for the present it will simplify our exposition to treat classes as if they were real. [Russell's exposition of his "no-class" theory is omitted in this anthology.—Eds.]

bundle? The answer that suggests itself is: "Find out how many members each has, and put them in the same bundle if they have the same number of members." But this presupposes that we have defined numbers, and that we know how to discover how many terms a collection has. We are so used to the operation of counting that such a presupposition might easily pass unnoticed. In fact, however, counting, though familiar, is logically a very complex operation; moreover it is only available, as a means of discovering how many terms a collection has, when the collection is finite. Our definition of number must not assume in advance that all numbers are finite; and we cannot in any case, without a vicious circle, use counting to define numbers, because numbers are used in counting. We need, therefore, some other method of deciding when two collections have the same number of terms.

In actual fact, it is simpler logically to find out whether two collections have the same number of terms than it is to define what that number is. An illustration will make this clear. If there were no polygamy or polyandry anywhere in the world, it is clear that the number of husbands living at any moment would be exactly the same as the number of wives. We do not need a census to assure us of this, nor do we need to know what is the actual number of husbands and of wives. We know the number must be the same in both collections, because each husband has one wife and each wife has one husband. The relation of husband and wife is what is called "one-one."

A relation is said to be "one-one" when, if x has the relation in question to y, no other term x' has the same relation to y, and x does not have the same relation to any term y' other than y. When only the first of these two conditions is fulfilled, the relation is called "one-many"; when only the second is fulfilled, it is called "many-one." It should be observed that the number 1 is not used in these definitions.

In Christian countries, the relation of husband to wife is one-one; in Mahometan countries it is one-many; in Tibet it is many-one. The relation of father to son is one-many; that of son to father is many-one, but that of eldest son to father is one-one. If n is any number, the relation of n to $n + 1$ is one-one; so is the relation of n to $2n$ or to $3n$. When we are considering only positive numbers, the relation of n to n^2 is one-one; but when negative numbers are admitted, it becomes two-one, since n and $-n$ have the same square. These instances should suffice to make clear the notions of one-one, one-many, and many-one relations, which play a great part in the principles of mathematics, not only in relation to the definition of numbers, but in many other connections.

Two classes are said to be "similar" when there is a one-one relation which correlates the terms of the one class each with one term of the other class, in the same manner in which the relation of marriage correlates husbands with wives. A few preliminary definitions will help us to state this definition more precisely. The class of those terms that have a given relation to something or other is called the *domain* of that relation: thus fathers are the domain of the relation of father to child, husbands are the domain of the relation of husband to wife, wives are the domain of the relation of wife to husband, and husbands and wives together are the domain of the relation of marriage. The relation of wife to husband is called the *converse* of the relation of husband to wife. Similarly *less* is the converse of *greater*, *later* is the converse of *earlier*, and so on. Generally, the converse of a given relation is that relation which holds between *y* and *x* whenever the given relation holds between *x* and *y*. The *converse domain* of a relation is the domain of its converse: thus the class of wives is the converse domain of the relation of husband to wife. We may now state our definition of similarity as follows:—

One class is said to be "similar" to another when there is a one-one relation of which the one class is the domain, while the other is the converse domain.

It is easy to prove (1) that every class is similar to itself, (2) that if a class α is similar to a class β, then β is similar to α, (3) that if α is similar to β and β to γ, then α is similar to γ. A relation is said to be *reflexive* when it possesses the first of these properties, *symmetrical* when it possesses the second, and *transitive* when it possesses the third. It is obvious that a relation which is symmetrical and transitive must be reflexive throughout its domain. Relations which possess these properties are an important kind, and it is worth while to note that similarity is one of this kind of relations.

It is obvious to common sense that two finite classes have the same number of terms if they are similar, but not otherwise. The act of counting consists in establishing a one-one correlation between the set of objects counted and the natural numbers (excluding 0) that are used up in the process. Accordingly common sense concludes that there are as many objects in the set to be counted as there are numbers up to the last number used in the counting. And we also know that, so long as we confine ourselves to finite numbers, there are just *n* numbers from 1 up to *n*. Hence it follows that the last number used in counting a collection is the number of terms in the collection, provided the collection is finite. But this result, besides being only applicable to finite collections, depends upon and assumes the fact that two classes which are similar have the same number of terms; for what we do when we count (say) 10 objects is to show that the set of these objects is similar to the set of numbers 1 to 10. The notion of similarity is logically presupposed in the operation of counting, and is logically simpler though less familiar. In counting, it is necessary to take the objects counted in a certain order, as first, second, third, etc., but order is not of the essence of number: it is an irrelevant addition, an unnecessary complication from the logical point of view. The notion of similarity does not demand an order: for example, we saw that the number of husbands is the same as the number of wives, without having to establish an order of precedence among them. The notion of similarity also does not require that the classes which are similar should be finite. Take, for example, the natural numbers (excluding 0) on the one hand, and the fractions which have 1 for their numerator on the other hand: it is obvious that we can correlate 2 with $\frac{1}{2}$, 3 with $\frac{1}{3}$, and so on, thus proving that the two classes are similar.

We may thus use the notion of "similarity" to decide when two collections are to belong to the same bundle, in the sense in which we were asking this question earlier in this chapter. We want to make one bundle containing the class that has no members: this will be for the number 0. Then we want a bundle of all the classes that have one member: this will be for the number 1. Then, for the number 2, we want a bundle consisting of all couples; then one of all trios; and so on. Given any collection, we can define the bundle it is to belong to as being the class of all those collections that are "similar" to it. It is very easy to see that if (for example) a collection has three members, the class of all those collections that are similar to it will be the class of trios. And whatever number of terms a collection may have, those collections that are "similar" to it will have the same number of terms. We may take this as a *definition* of "having the same number of terms." It is obvious that it gives results conformable to usage so long as we confine ourselves to finite collections.

So far we have not suggested anything in the slightest degree paradoxical. But when we come to the actual definition of numbers we cannot avoid what must at first sight seem a paradox, though this impression will soon wear off. We naturally think that the class of couples (for example) is something different from the number 2. But there is no doubt about the class of couples: it is indubitable and not difficult to define, whereas the number 2, in any other sense, is a metaphysical entity about which we can never feel sure that it exists or that we have tracked it down. It is therefore more prudent to content ourselves with the class of couples, which we are sure of, than to hunt for a problematical number 2 which must always remain elusive. Accordingly we set up the following definition:—

The number of a class is the class of all those classes that are similar to it.

Thus the number of a couple will be the class of all couples. In fact, the class of all couples will *be* the number 2, according to our definition. At the expense of a little oddity, this definition secures definiteness and indubitableness; and it is not difficult to prove that numbers so defined have all the properties that we expect numbers to have.

We may now go on to define numbers in general as any one of the bundles into which similarity collects classes. A number will be a set of classes such as that any two are similar to each other, and none outside the set are similar to any inside the set. In other words, a number (in general) is any collection which is the number of one of its members; or, more simply still:

A number is anything which is the number of some class.

Such a definition has a verbal appearance of being circular, but in fact it is not. We define "the number of a given class" without using the notion of number in general; therefore we may define number in general in terms of "the number of a given class" without committing any logical error.

Definitions of this sort are in fact very common. The class of fathers, for example, would have to be defined by first defining what it is to be the father of somebody; then the class of fathers will be all those who are somebody's father. Similarly if we want to define square numbers (say), we must first define what we mean by saying that one number is the square of another, and then define square numbers as those that are the squares of other numbers. This kind of procedure is very common, and it is important to realize that it is legitimate and even often necessary.

We have now given a definition of numbers which will serve for finite collections. It remains to be seen how it will serve for infinite collections. But first we must decide what we mean by "finite" and "infinite," which cannot be done within the limits [here].

III. MATHEMATICS AND LOGIC

Mathematics and logic, historically speaking, have been entirely distinct studies. Mathematics has been connected with science, logic with Greek. But both have developed in modern times: logic has become more mathematical and mathematics has become more logical. The consequence is that is has now become wholly impossible to draw a line between the two; in fact, the two are one. They differ as boy and man: logic is the youth of mathematics and mathematics is the manhood of logic. This view is resented by logicians who, having spent their time in the study of classical texts, are incapable of following a piece of symbolic reasoning, and by mathematicians who have learnt a technique without troubling to inquire into its meaning or justification. Both types are now fortunately growing rarer. So much of modern mathematical work is obviously on the border-line of logic, so much of modern logic is symbolic and formal, that the very close relationship of logic and mathematics has become obvious to every instructed student. The proof of their identity is, of course, a matter of detail: starting with premises which would be universally admitted to belong to logic, and arriving by deduction at results which as obviously belong to mathematics, we find that there is no point at which a sharp line can be drawn, with logic to the left and mathematics to the right. If there are still those who do not admit the identity of logic and mathematics, we may challenge them to indicate at what point, in the successive definitions and deductions of *Principia Mathematica*, they consider that logic ends and mathematics begins. It will then be obvious that any answer must be quite arbitrary.

In the earlier chapters of this book, starting from the natural numbers, we have first defined "cardinal number" and shown how to generalise the conception of number, and have then analysed the conceptions involved in the definition, until we found ourselves dealing with the fundamentals of logic. In a synthetic, deductive treatment these fundamentals come first, and the natural numbers are only reached after a long journey. Such treatment, though formally more correct than that which we have adopted, is more difficult for the reader, because the ultimate logical concepts and propositions with which it starts are remote and unfamiliar as compared with the natural numbers. Also they represent the present frontier of knowledge, beyond which is the still unknown; and the dominion of knowledge over them is not as yet very secure.

It used to be said that mathematics is the science of "quantity." "Quantity" is a vague word, but for the sake of argument we may replace it by the word "number." The statement that mathematics is the science of number would be untrue in two different ways. On the one hand, there are recognised branches of mathematics which have nothing to do with number—all geometry that does not use co-ordinates or measurement, for example: projective and descriptive geometry, down to the point at which co-ordinates are introduced, does not have to do with number, or even with quantity in the sense of *greater* and *less*. On the other hand, through the definition of cardinals, through the theory of induction and ancestral relations, through the general theory of series, and through the definitions of the arithmetical operations, it has become possible to generalise much that used to be proved only in connection with numbers. The result is that what was formerly the single study of Arithmetic has now become divided into numbers of separate studies, no one of which is specially concerned with numbers. The most elementary properties of numbers are concerned with one-one relations, and similarity between classes. Addition is concerned with the construction of mutually exclusive classes respectively similar to a set of classes which are not known to be mutually exclusive. Multiplication is merged in the theory of "selections," *i.e.* of a certain kind of one-many relations. Finitude is merged in the general study of ancestral relations, which yields the whole theory of mathematical induction. The ordinal properties of the various kinds of number-series, and the elements of the theory of continuity of functions and the limits of functions, can be generalised so as no longer to involve any essential reference to numbers. It is a principle, in all formal reasoning, to generalize to the utmost, since we thereby secure that a given process of deduction shall have more widely applicable results; we are, therefore, in thus generalizing the reasoning of arithmetic, merely following a precept which is universally admitted in mathematics. And in thus generalising we have, in effect, created a set of new deductive systems, in which traditional arithmetic is at once dissolved and enlarged; but whether any one of these new deductive systems—for example, the theory of selections—is to be said to belong to logic or to arithmetic is entirely arbitrary, and incapable of being decided rationally.

We are thus brought face to face with the question: What is this subject, which may be called indifferently either mathematics or logic? Is there any way in which we can define it?

Certain characteristics of the subject are clear. To begin with, we do not, in this subject, deal with particular things or particular properties: we deal formally with what can be said about *any* thing or *any* property. We are prepared to say that one and one are two, but not that Socrates and Plato are two, because, in our capacity of logicians or pure mathematicians, we have never heard of Socrates and Plato. A world in which there were no such individuals would still be a world in which one and one are two. It is not open to us, as pure mathematicians or logicians, to mention anything at all, because, if we do so, we introduce something irrelevant and not formal. We may make this clear by applying it to the case of the syllogism. Traditional logic says: "All men are mortal, Socrates is a man, therefore Socrates is mortal." Now it is clear that what we *mean* to assert, to begin with, is only that the premisses imply the conclusion, not that premisses and conclusion are actually true; even the most traditional logic points out that the actual truth of the premisses is irrelevant to logic. Thus the first change to be made in the above traditional syllogism is to state it in the form: "If all men are mortal and Socrates is a man, then Socrates is mortal." We may now observe that it is intended to convey that this argument is valid in virtue of its *form*, not in virtue of the particular terms occurring in it. If we had omitted "Socrates is a man" from our premisses, we should have had a non-formal argument, only admissible because Socrates is in fact a man; in that case we could not have generalized the argument. But when, as above, the argument is *formal*, nothing depends upon the terms that occur in it. Thus we may substitute α for *men*, β for *mortals*, and x for Socrates, where α and β are any classes whatever, and x is any individual. We then arrive at the statement: "No matter what possible values x and α and β may have, if all α's are β's and x is an α, then x is a β"; in other words, "the propositional function 'if all α's are β and x is an α, then x is a β' is always true." Here at last we have a proposition of logic—the one which is only *suggested* by the traditional statement about Socrates and men and mortals.

It is clear that, if *formal* reasoning is what we are aiming at, we shall always arrive ultimately at statements like the above, in which no actual things or properties are mentioned; this will happen through the mere desire not to waste our time proving in a particular case what can be proved generally. It would be ridiculous to go through a long argument about Socrates, and then go through precisely the same argument again about Plato. If our argument is one (say) which holds of all men, we shall prove it concerning "x," with the hypothesis "if x is a man." With this hypothesis, the argument will retain its hypothetical validity even when x is not a man. But now we shall find that our argument would still be valid if, instead of supporting x to be a man, we were to suppose him to be a monkey or a goose or a Prime Minister. We shall therefore not waste our time taking as our premiss "x is a man" but shall take "x is an α," where α is any class of individuals, or "ϕx" where ϕ is any propositional function of some assigned type. Thus the absence of all mention of particular things or properties in logic or pure mathematics is a necessary result of the fact that this study is, as we say, "purely formal."

At this point we find ourselves faced with a problem which is easier to state than to solve. The problem is: "What are the constituents of a logical proposition?" I do not know the answer, but I propose to explain how the problem arises.

Take (say) the proposition "Socrates was before Aristotle." Here it seems obvious that we have a relation between two terms, and that the constituents of the proposition (as well as of the corresponding fact) are simply the two terms and the relation, i.e. Socrates, Aristotle, and *before*. (I ignore the fact that Socrates and Aristotle are not simple; also the fact that what appear to be their names are really truncated descriptions. Neither of these facts is relevant to the present issue.) We may represent the general form of such propositions by "$x R y$," which may be read "x has the relation R to y." This general form may occur in logical propositions, but no particular instance of it can occur. Are we to infer that the general form itself is a constituent of such logical propositions?

Given a proposition, such as "Socrates is before Aristotle," we have certain constituents and also a certain form. But the form is not itself a new constituent; if it were, we should need a new form to embrace both it and the other constituents. We can, in fact, turn *all* the constituents of a proposition into variables, while keeping the form unchanged. This is what we do when we use such a schema as "$x R y$," which stands for any one of a certain class of propositions, namely, those asserting relations between two terms. We can proceed to general assertions, such as "$x R y$ is sometimes true"—i.e. there are cases where dual relations hold. This assertion will belong to logic (or mathematics) in the sense in which we are using the word. But in this assertion we do not mention any particular things or particular relations; no particular things or relations can ever enter into a proposition of pure logic. We are left with pure *forms* as the only possible constituents of logical propositions.

I do not wish to assert positively that pure forms—e.g. the form "$x R y$" —do actually enter into propositions of the kind we are considering. The question of the analysis of such propositions is a difficult one, with conflicting considerations on the one side and on the other. We cannot embark upon this question now, but we may accept, as a first approximation, the view that *forms* are what enter into logical propositions as their constituents. And we may explain (though not formally define) what we mean by the "form" of a proposition as follows:—

The "form" of a proposition is that, in it, that remains unchanged when every constituent of the proposition is replaced by another.

Thus "Socrates is earlier than Aristotle" has the same form as "Napoleon is greater than Wellington," though every constituent of the two propositions is different.

We may thus lay down, as a necessary (though not sufficient) characteristic of logical or mathematical propositions, that they are to be such as can be obtained from a proposition containing no variables (i.e. no such words as *all*, *some*, *a*, *the*, etc.) by turning every constituent into a variable and asserting that the result is always true or sometimes true, or that it is always true in respect of some of the variables that the result is sometimes true in respect of the others, or any variant of these forms. And another way of stating the same thing is to say that logic (or mathematics) is concerned only with *forms*, and is concerned with them only in the way of stating that they are always or sometimes true—with all the permutations of "always" and "sometimes" that may occur.

There are in every language some words whose sole function is to indicate form. These words, broadly speaking, are commonest in languages having fewest inflections. Take "Socrates is human." Here "is" is not a constituent of the proposition, but merely indicates the subject-predicate form. Similarly in "Socrates is earlier than Aristotle," "is" and "than" merely indicate form; the proposition is the same as "Socrates precedes Aristotle," in which these words have disappeared and the form is otherwise indicated. Form, as a rule, *can* be indicated otherwise than by specific words: the order of the words can do most of what is wanted. But this principle must not be pressed. For example, it is difficult to see how we could conveniently express molecular forms of propositions (i.e. what we call "truth-functions") without any word at all. We saw . . . that one word or symbol is enough for this purpose, namely, a word or symbol expressing *incompatibility*. But without even one we should find ourselves in difficulties. This, however, is not the point that is important for our present purpose. What is important for us is to observe that form may be the one concern of a general proposition, even when no word or symbol in that proposition designates the form. If we wish to speak about the form itself, we must have a word for it; but if, as in mathematics, we wish to speak about all propositions that have the form, a word for the form will usually be found not indispensable; probably in theory it is *never* indispensable.

Assuming—as I think we may—that the forms of propositions *can* be represented by the forms of the propositions in which they are expressed without any special word for forms, we should arrive at a language in which everything formal belonged to syntax and not to vocabulary. In such a language we could express *all* the propositions of mathematics even if we did not know one single word of the language. The language of mathematical logic, if it were perfected, would be such a language. We should have symbols for variables, such as "x" and "R" and "y," arranged in various ways; and the way of arrangement would indicate that something was being said to be true of all values or some values of the variables. We should not need to know any words, because they would only be needed for giving values to the variables, which is the business of the applied mathematician, not of the pure mathematician or logician. It is one of the marks of a proposition of logic that, given a suitable language, such a proposition can be asserted in such a language by a person who knows the syntax without knowing a single word of the vocabulary.

But, after all, there are words that express form, such as "is" and "than." And in every symbolism hitherto invented for mathematical logic there are symbols having constant formal meanings. We may take as an example the symbol for incompatibility which is employed in building up truth-functions. Such words or symbols may occur in logic. The question is: How are we to define them?

Such words or symbols express what are called "logical constants." Logical constants may be defined exactly as we defined forms; in fact, they are in essence the same thing. A fundamental logical constant will be that which is in common among a number of propositions, any one of which can result from any other by substitution of terms one for another. For example, "Napoleon is greater than Wellington" results from "Socrates is earlier than Aristotle" by the substitution of "Napoleon" for "Socrates," "Wellington" for "Aristotle," and "greater" for "earlier." Some propositions can be obtained in this way from the prototype "Socrates is earlier than Aristotle" and some cannot; those that can are those that are of the form "$x \, R \, y$," i.e. express dual relations. We cannot obtain from the above prototype by term-for-term substitution such propositions as "Socrates is human" or "the Athenians gave the hemlock to Socrates," because the first is of the subject-predicate form and the second expresses a three-term relation. If we are to have any words in our pure logical language, they must be such as express "logical constants," and "logical constants" will always either be, or be derived from, what is in common among a group of propositions derivable from each other, in the above manner, by term-for-term substitution. And this which is in common is what we call "form."

In this sense all the "constants" that occur in pure mathematics are logical constants. The number 1, for example, is derivative from propositions of the form: "There is a term c such that ϕx is true when, and only when, x is c." This is a function of ϕ, and various different propositions result from giving different values to ϕ. We may (with a little omission of intermediate steps not relevant to our present purpose) take the above function of ϕ as what is meant by "the class determined by ϕ is a unit class" or "the class determined by ϕ is a member of 1" (1 being a class of classes). In this way, propositions in in which 1 occurs acquire a meaning which is derived from a certain constant logical form. And the same will be found to be the case with all mathematical constants: all are logical constants, or symbolic abbreviations whose full use in a proper context is defined by means of logical constants.

But although all logical (or mathematical) propositions can be expressed wholly in terms of logical constants together with variables, it is not the case that, conversely, all propositions that can be expressed in this way are logical. We have found so far a necessary but not a sufficient criterion of mathematical propositions. We have sufficiently defined the character of the primitive *ideas* in terms of which all the ideas of mathematics can be *defined*, but not of the primitive *propositions* from which all the propositions of mathematics can be *deduced*. This is a more difficult matter, as to which it is not yet known what the full answer is.

We may take the axiom of infinity as an example of a proposition which, though it can be enunciated in logical terms, cannot be asserted by logic to be true. All the propositions of logic have a characteristic which used to be expressed by saying that they were analytic, or that their contradictories were self-contradictory. This mode of statement, however, is not satisfactory. The law of contradiction is merely one among logical propositions; it has no special pre-eminence; and the proof that the contradictory of some proposition is self-contradictory is likely to require other principles of deduction besides the law of contradiction. Nevertheless, the characteristic of logical propositions that we are in search of is the one which was felt, and intended to be defined, by those who said that it consisted in deducibility from the law of contradiction. This characteristic, which, for the moment, we may call *tautology*, obviously does not belong to the assertion that the number of individuals in the universe is n, whatever number n may be. But for the diversity of types, it would be possible to prove logically that there are classes of n terms, where n is any finite integer; or even that there are classes of $\aleph_0$ terms. But, owing to types, such proofs ... are fallacious. We are left to empirical observation to determine whether there are as many as n individuals in the world. Among "possible" worlds, in the Leibnizian sense, there will be worlds having one, two, three, ... individuals. There does not even seem any logical necessity why there should be even one individual[5]—why, in fact, there should be any world at all. The ontological proof of the existence of God, if it were valid, would establish the logical necessity of at least one individual. But it is generally recognized as invalid, and in fact rests upon a mistaken view of existence—i.e. it fails to realize that existence can only be asserted of something described, not of something named, so that it is meaningless to argue from "this is the so-and-so" and "the so-and-so exists" to "this exists." If we reject the ontological argument, we seem driven to conclude that the existence of a world is an accident—i.e. it is not logically necessary. If that be so, no principle of logic can assert "existence" except under a hypothesis, i.e. none can be of the form "the propositional function so-and-so is sometimes true." Propositions of this form, when they occur in logic, will have to occur as hypotheses or consequences of hypotheses, not as complete asserted propositions. The complete asserted propositions of logic will all be such as affirm that some propositional function is *always* true. For example, it is always true that if p implies q and q implies r then p implies r, or that, if all α's are β's and x is an α then x is a β. Such propositions may occur in logic, and their truth is independent of the existence of the universe.

---

[5] The primitive propositions in *Principia Mathematica* are such as to allow the inference that at least one individual exists. But I now view this as a defect in logical purity.

We may lay it down that, if there were no universe, *all* general propositions would be true; for the contradictory of a general proposition ... is a proposition asserting existence, and would therefore always be false if no universe existed.

Logical propositions are such as can be known *a priori*, without study of the actual world. We only know from a study of empirical facts that Socrates is a man, but we know the correctness of the syllogism in its abstract form (i.e. when it is stated in terms of variables) without needing any appeal to experience. This is a characteristic, not of logical propositions in themselves, but of the way in which we know them. It has, however, a bearing upon the question what their nature may be, since there are some kinds of propositions which it would be very difficult to suppose we could know without experience.

It is clear that the definition of "logic" or "mathematics" must be sought by trying to give a new definition of the old notion of "analytic" propositions. Although we can no longer be satisfied to define logical propositions as those that follow from the law of contradiction, we can and must still admit that they are a wholly different class of propositions from those that we come to know empirically. They all have the characteristic which, a moment ago, we agreed to call "tautology." This, combined with the fact that they can be expressed wholly in terms of variables and logical constants (a logical constant being something which remains constant in a proposition even when *all* its constituents are changed)—will give the definition of logic or pure mathematics. For the moment, I do not know how to define "tautology."[6] It would be easy to offer a definition which might seem satisfactory for a while; but I know of none that I feel to be satisfactory, in spite of feeling thoroughly familiar with the characteristic of which a definition is wanted. At this point, therefore, for the moment, we reach the frontier of knowledge on our backward journey into the logical foundations of mathematics.

We have now come to an end of our somewhat summary introduction to mathematical philosophy. It is impossible to convey adequately the ideas that are concerned in this subject so long as we abstain from the use of logical symbols. Since ordinary language has no words that naturally express exactly what we wish to express, it is necessary, so long as we adhere to ordinary language, to strain words into unusual meanings; and the reader is sure, after a time if not at first, to lapse into attaching the usual meanings to words, thus arriving at wrong notions as to what is intended to be said. Moreover, ordinary grammar and syntax is extraordinarily misleading. This is the case, e.g. as regards numbers; "ten men" is grammatically the same form as "white men," so that 10 might be thought to be an adjective qualifying "men." It is the case, again, wherever propositional functions are involved, and in particular as regards existence and descriptions. Because language is mis-

---

[6] The importance of "tautology" for a definition of mathematics was pointed out to me by my former pupil Ludwig Wittgenstein, who was working on the problem. I do not know whether he has solved it, or even whether he is alive or dead.

leading, as well as because it is diffuse and inexact when applied to logic (for which it was never intended), logical symbolism is absolutely necessary to any exact or thorough treatment of our subject. Those readers, therefore, who wish to acquire a mastery of the principles of mathematics, will, it is to be hoped, not shrink from the labour of mastering the symbols—a labour which is, in fact, much less than might be thought. As the above hasty survey must have made evident, there are innumerable unsolved problems in the subject, and much work needs to be done. If any student is led into a serious study of mathematical logic by this little book, it will have served the chief purpose for which it has been written.

David Hilbert

As a result of his penetrating critique, Weierstrass has provided a solid foundation for mathematical analysis. By elucidating many notions, in particular those of minimum, function, and differential quotient, he removed the defects which were still found in the infinitesimal calculus, rid it of all confused notions about the infinitesimal, and thereby completely resolved the difficulties which stem from that concept. If in analysis today there is complete agreement and certitude in employing the deductive methods which are based on the concepts of irrational number and limit, and if in even the most complex questions of the theory of differential and integral equations, notwithstanding the use of the most ingenious and varied combinations of the different kinds of limits, there nevertheless is unanimity with respect to the results obtained, then this happy state of affairs is due primarily to Weierstrass's scientific work.

And yet in spite of the foundation Weierstrass has provided for the infinitesimal calculus, disputes about the foundations of analysis still go on.

These disputes have not terminated because the meaning of the *infinite*, as that concept is used in mathematics, has never been completely clarified. Weierstrass's analysis did indeed eliminate the infinitely large and the infinitely small by reducing statements about them to [statements about] relations between finite magnitudes. Nevertheless the infinite still appears in the infinite numerical series which defines the real numbers and in the concept of the real number system which is thought of as a completed totality existing all at once.

In his foundation for analysis, Weierstrass accepted unreservedly and used

---

Delivered June 4, 1925, before a congress of the Westphalian Mathematical Society in Munster, in honor of Karl Weierstrass. Translated by Erna Putnam and Gerald J. Massey from Mathematische Annalen *(Berlin) no. 95 (1925), pp. 161–90. Permission for the translation and inclusion of the article in this volume was kindly granted by the publishers, Springer Verlag.*

repeatedly those forms of logical deduction in which the concept of the infinite comes into play, as when one treats of *all* real numbers with a certain property or when one argues that *there exist* real numbers with a certain property.

Hence the infinite can reappear in another guise in Weierstrass's theory and thus escape the precision imposed by his critique. It is, therefore, *the problem of the infinite* in the sense just indicated which we need to resolve once and for all. Just as in the limit processes of the infinitesimal calculus, the infinite in the sense of the infinitely large and the infinitely small proved to be merely a figure of speech, so too we must realize that the infinite in the sense of an infinite totality, where we still find it used in deductive methods, is an illusion. Just as operations with the infinitely small were replaced by operations with the finite which yielded exactly the same results and led to exactly the same elegant formal relationships, so in general must deductive methods based on the infinite be replaced by finite procedures which yield exactly the same results; i.e., which make possible the same chains of proofs and the same methods of getting formulas and theorems.

The goal of my theory is to establish once and for all the certitude of mathematical methods. This is a task which was not accomplished even during the critical period of the infinitesimal calculus. This theory should thus complete what Weierstrass hoped to achieve by his foundation for analysis and toward the accomplishment of which he has taken a necessary and important step.

But a still more general perspective is relevant for clarifying the concept of the infinite. A careful reader will find that the literature of mathematics is glutted with inanities and absurdities which have had their source in the infinite. For example, we find writers insisting, as though it were a restrictive condition, that in rigorous mathematics only a *finite* number of deductions are admissible in a proof—as if someone had succeeded in making an infinite number of them.

Also old objections which we supposed long abandoned still reappear in different forms. For example, the following recently appeared: Although it may be possible to introduce a concept without risk, i.e., without getting contradictions, and even though one can prove that its introduction causes no contradictions to arise, still the introduction of the concept is not thereby justified. Is not this exactly the same objection which was once brought against complex-imaginary numbers when it was said: "True, their use doesn't lead to contradictions. Nevertheless their introduction is unwarranted, for imaginary magnitudes do not exist."? If, apart from proving consistency, the question of the justification of a measure is to have any meaning, it can consist only in ascertaining whether the measure is accompanied by commensurate success. Such success is in fact essential, for in mathematics as elsewhere success is the supreme court to whose decisions everyone submits.

As some people see ghosts, another writer seems to see contradictions even where no statements whatsoever have been made, viz., in the concrete world of sensation, the "consistent functioning" of which he takes as special assumption. I myself have always supposed that only statements, and hypotheses insofar as they lead through deductions to statements, could contradict one another. The view that facts and events could themselves be in contradiction seems to me to be a prime example of careless thinking.

The foregoing remarks are intended only to establish the fact that the definitive clarification of *the nature of the infinite*, instead of pertaining just to the sphere of specialized scientific interests, is needed for *the dignity of the human intellect* itself.

From time immemorial, the infinite has stirred men's *emotions* more than any other question. Hardly any other *idea* has stimulated the mind so fruitfully. Yet, no other *concept* needs *clarification* more than it does.

Before turning to the task of clarifying the nature of the infinite, we should first note briefly what meaning is actually given to the infinite. First let us see what we can learn from physics. One's first naïve impression of natural events and of matter is one of permanency, of continuity. When we consider a piece of metal or a volume of liquid, we get the impression that they are unlimitedly divisible, that their smallest parts exhibit the same properties that the whole does. But wherever the methods of investigating the physics of matter have been sufficiently refined, scientists have met divisibility boundaries which do not result from the shortcomings of their efforts but from the very nature of things. Consequently we could even interpret the tendency of modern science as emancipation from the infinitely small. Instead of the old principie *natura non facit saltus*, we might even assert the opposite, viz., "nature makes jumps."

It is common knowledge that all matter is composed of tiny building blocks called "atoms," the combinations and connections of which produce all the variety of macroscopic objects. Still physics did not stop at the atomism of matter. At the end of the last century there appeared the atomism of electricity which seems much more bizarre at first sight. Electricity, which until then had been thought of as a fluid and was considered the model of a continuously active agent, was then shown to be built up of positive and negative *electrons*.

In addition to matter and electricity, there is one other entity in physics for which the law of conservation holds, viz., energy. But it has been established that even energy does not unconditionally admit of infinite divisibility. Planck has discovered *quanta of energy*.

Hence, a homogeneous continuum which admits of the sort of divisibility needed to realize the infinitely small is nowhere to be found in reality. The infinite divisibility of a continuum is an operation which exists only in thought. It is merely an idea which is in fact impugned by the results of our observations of nature and of our physical and chemical experiments.

The second place where we encounter the question of whether the infinite is found in nature is in the consideration of the universe as a whole. Here we must consider the expanse of the universe to determine whether it embraces anything infinitely large. But here again modern science, in particular astronomy, has reopened the question and is endeavoring to solve it, not by the defective means of metaphysical speculation, but by reasons which are based on experiment and on the application of the laws of nature. Here, too, serious objections against infinity have been found. *Euclidean* geometry necessarily leads to the postulate that space is infinite. Although euclidean geometry is indeed a consistent conceptual system, it does not thereby follow that euclidean geometry actually holds in reality. Whether or not real space is euclidean can be determined only through observation and experiment. The attempt to prove the infinity of space by pure speculation contains gross errors. From the fact that outside a certain portion of space there is always more space, it follows only that space is unbounded, not that it is infinite. Unboundedness and finiteness are compatible. In so-called *elliptical* geometry, mathematical investigation furnishes the natural model of a finite universe. Today the abandonment of euclidean geometry is no longer merely a mathematical or philosophical speculation but is suggested by considerations which originally had nothing to do with the question of the finiteness of the universe. Einstein has shown that euclidean geometry must be abandoned. On the basis of his gravitational theory, he deals with cosmological questions and shows that a finite universe is possible. Moreover, all the results of astronomy are perfectly compatible with the postulate that the universe is elliptical.

We have established that the universe is finite in two respects, i.e., as regards the infinitely small and the infinitely large. But it may still be the case that the infinite occupies a justified place *in our thinking*, that it plays the role of an indispensable concept. Let us see what the situation is in mathematics. Let us first interrogate that purest and simplest offspring of the human mind, viz., number theory. Consider one formula out of the rich variety of elementary formulas of number theory, e.g., the formula

$$1^2 + 2^2 + 3^2 \cdots + n^2 = \tfrac{1}{6}n(n + 1)(2n + 1)$$

Since we may substitute any integer whatsoever for n, for example $n = 2$ or $n = 5$, this formula implicitly contains *infinitely many* propositions. This characteristic is essential to a formula. It enables the formula to represent the solution of an arithmetical problem and necessitates a special idea for its proof. On the other hand, the individual numerical equations

$$1^2 + 2^2 = \tfrac{1}{6} \cdot 2 \cdot 3 \cdot 5$$

$$1^2 + 2^2 + 3^2 + 4^2 + 5^2 = \tfrac{1}{6} \cdot 5 \cdot 6 \cdot 11$$

can be verified simply by calculation and hence individually are of no especial interest.

We encounter a completely different and quite unique conception of the notion of infinity in the important and fruitful method of *ideal elements*. The method of ideal elements is used even in elementary plane geometry. The points and straight lines of the plane originally are real, actually existent objects. One of the axioms that hold for them is the axiom of connection: one and only one straight line passes through two points. It follows from this axiom that two straight lines intersect at most at one point. There is no theorem that two straight lines always intersect at some point, however, for the two straight lines might well be parallel. Still we know that by introducing ideal elements, viz., infinitely long lines and points at infinity, we can make the theorem that two straight lines always intersect at one and only one point come out universally true. These ideal "infinite" elements have the advantage of making the system of connection laws as simple and perspicuous as possible. Moreover, because of the symmetry between a point and a straight line, there results the very fruitful principle of duality for geometry.

Another example of the use of ideal elements are the familiar *complex-imaginary* magnitudes of algebra which serve to simplify theorems about the existence and number of the roots of an equation.

Just as infinitely many straight lines, viz., those parallel to each other, are used to define an ideal point in geometry, so certain systems of infinitely many numbers are used to define an *ideal number*. This application of the principle of ideal elements is the most ingenious of all. If we apply this principle systematically throughout an algebra, we obtain exactly the same simple and familiar laws of division which hold for the familiar whole numbers 1, 2, 3, 4, ... We are already in the domain of higher arithmetic.

We now come to the most aesthetic and delicately erected structure of mathematics, viz., analysis. You already know that infinity plays the leading role in analysis. In a certain sense, mathematical analysis is a symphony of the infinite.

The tremendous progress made in the infinitesimal calculus results mainly from operating with mathematical systems of infinitely many elements. But, as it seemed very plausible to identify the infinite with the "very large", there soon arose inconsistencies which were known in part to the ancient sophists, viz., the so-called paradoxes of the infinitesimal calculus. But the recognition that many theorems which hold for the finite (for example, the part is smaller than the whole, the existence of a minimum and a maximum, the interchangeability of the order of the terms of a sum or a product) cannot be immediately and unrestrictedly extended to the infinite, marked fundamental progress. I said at the beginning of this paper that these questions have been completely clarified, notably through Weierstrass's acuity. Today, analysis is not only infallible within its domain but has become a practical instrument for using the infinite.

But analysis alone does not provide us with the deepest insight into the nature of the infinite. This insight is procured for us by a discipline which comes closer to a general philosophical way of thinking and which was designed to cast new light on the whole complex of questions about the infinite. This discipline, created by George Cantor, is set theory. In this paper, we are interested only in that unique and original part of set theory which forms the central core of Cantor's doctrine, viz., the theory of *transfinite* numbers. This theory is, I think, the finest product of mathematical genius and one of the supreme achievements of purely intellectual human activity. What, then, is this theory?

Someone who wished to characterize briefly the new conception of the infinite which Cantor introduced might say that in analysis we deal with the infinitely large and the infinitely small only as limiting concepts, as something becoming, happening, i.e., with the *potential infinite*. But this is not the true infinite. We meet the true infinite when we regard the totality of numbers 1, 2, 3, 4, ... itself as a completed unity, or when we regard the points of an interval as a totality of things which exists all at once. This kind of infinity is known as *actual infinity*.

Frege and Dedekind, the two mathematicians most celebrated for their work in the foundations of mathematics, independently of each other used the actual infinite to provide a foundation for arithmetic which was independent of both intuition and experience. This foundation was based solely on pure logic and made use only of deductions that were purely logical. Dedekind even went so far as not to take the notion of finite number from intuition but to derive it logically by employing the concept of an infinite set. But it was Cantor who systematically developed the concept of the actual infinite. Consider the two examples of the infinite already mentioned

1. 1, 2, 3, 4, ...

2. The points of the interval 0 to 1 or, what comes to the same thing, the totality of real numbers between 0 and 1.

It is quite natural to treat these examples from the point of view of their size. But such a treatment reveals amazing results with which every mathematician today is familiar. For when we consider the set of all rational numbers, i.e., the fractions $\frac{1}{2}, \frac{1}{3}, \frac{2}{3}, \frac{1}{4}, \ldots, \frac{3}{7}, \ldots$, we notice that—from the sole standpoint of its size—this set is no larger than the set of integers. Hence we say that the rational numbers can be counted in the usual way; i.e., that they are enumerable. The same holds for the set of all roots of numbers, indeed even for the set of all algebraic numbers. The second example is analogous to the first. Surprisingly enough, the set of all the points of a square or cube is no larger than the set of points of the interval 0 to 1. Similarly for the set of all continuous functions. On learning these facts for the first time, you might think that from the point of view of size there is only one unique infinite. No, indeed! The sets in examples (1) and (2) are not, as we say, "equivalent". Rather, the set (2) cannot be enumerated, for it is larger than the set (1).

We meet what is new and characteristic in Cantor's theory at this point. The points of an interval cannot be counted in the usual way, i.e., by counting 1, 2, 3, ... But, since we admit the actual infinite, we are not obliged to stop here. When we have counted 1, 2, 3, . . . , we can regard the objects thus enumerated as an infinite set existing all at once in a particular order. If, following Cantor, we call the type of this order ω, then counting continues naturally with $\omega + 1$, $\omega + 2$, . . . up to $\omega + \omega$ or $\omega \cdot 2$, and then again

$$(\omega \cdot 2) + 1, (\omega \cdot 2) + 2, (\omega \cdot 2) + 3, \ldots (\omega \cdot 2) + \omega \text{ or } \omega \cdot 3,$$

and further

$$\omega \cdot 2, \omega \cdot 3, \omega \cdot 4, \ldots, \omega \cdot \omega \text{ (or } \omega^2), \omega^2 + 1, \ldots,$$

so that we finally get this table:

$$1, 2, 3, \ldots$$
$$\omega, \omega + 1, \omega + 2, \ldots$$
$$\omega \cdot 2, (\omega \cdot 2) + 1, (\omega \cdot 2) + 2, \ldots$$
$$\omega \cdot 3, (\omega \cdot 3) + 1, (\omega \cdot 3) + 2, \ldots$$
$$\cdot$$
$$\cdot$$
$$\cdot$$
$$\omega^2, \omega^2 + 1, \ldots$$
$$\omega^2 + \omega, \omega^2 + \omega \cdot 2, \omega^2 + \omega \cdot 3, \ldots$$
$$\omega^2 \cdot 2, (\omega^2 \cdot 2) + 1, \ldots$$
$$(\omega^2 \cdot 2) + \omega, (\omega^2 \cdot 2) + (\omega \cdot 2), \ldots$$
$$\omega^3, \ldots$$
$$\omega^4, \ldots$$
$$\cdot$$
$$\cdot$$
$$\cdot$$
$$\omega^\omega, \omega^{\omega^\omega}, \omega^{\omega^{\omega^\omega}}, \ldots$$

These are Cantor's first transfinite numbers or, as he called them, the numbers of the second number class. We arrive at them simply by extending counting beyond the ordinarily enumerably infinite, i.e., by a natural and uniquely determined consistent continuation of ordinary finite counting. As until now we counted only the first, second, third, . . . member of a set, we now count also the ωth, $(\omega + 1)$st, . . . , ω^ωth member.

Given these developments one naturally wonders whether or not, by using these transfinite numbers, one can really count those sets which cannot be counted in the ordinary way.

On the basis of these concepts, Cantor developed the theory of transfinite numbers quite successfully and invented a full calculus for them. Thus, thanks to the Herculean collaboration of Frege, Dedekind, and Cantor, the infinite was made king and enjoyed a reign of great triumph. In daring flight, the infinite had reached a dizzy pinnacle of success.

But reaction was not lacking. It took in fact a very dramatic form. It set in perfectly analogously to the way reaction had set in against the development of the infinitesimal calculus. In the joy of discovering new and important results, mathematicians paid too little attention to the validity of their deductive methods. For, simply as a result of employing definitions and deductive methods which had become customary, contradictions began gradually to appear. These contradictions, the so-called paradoxes of set theory, though at first scattered, became progressively more acute and more serious. In particular, a contradiction discovered by Zermelo and Russell had a downright catastrophic effect when it became known throughout the world of mathematics. Confronted by these paradoxes, Dedekind and Frege completely abandoned their point of view and retreated. Dedekind hesitated a long time before permitting a new edition of his epoch-making treatise *Was sind und was sollen die Zahlen* to be published. In an epilogue, Frege too had to acknowledge that the direction of his book *Grundgesetze der Mathematik* was wrong. Cantor's doctrine, too, was attacked on all sides. So violent was this reaction that even the most ordinary and fruitful concepts and the simplest and most important deductive methods of mathematics were threatened and their employment was on the verge of being declared illicit. The old order had its defenders, of course. Their defensive tactics, however, were too fainthearted and they never formed a united front at the vital spots. Too many different remedies for the paradoxes were offered, and the methods proposed to clarify them were too variegated.

Admittedly, the present state of affairs where we run up against the paradoxes is intolerable. Just think, the definitions and deductive methods which everyone learns, teaches, and uses in mathematics, the paragon of truth and certitude, lead to absurdities! If mathematical thinking is defective, where are we to find truth and certitude?

There is, however, a completely satisfactory way of avoiding the paradoxes without betraying our science. The desires and attitudes which will help us find this way and show us what direction to take are these:

1. Wherever there is any hope of salvage, we will carefully investigate fruitful definitions and deductive methods. We will nurse them, strengthen them, and make them useful. No one shall drive us out of the paradise which Cantor has created for us.

2. We must establish throughout mathematics the same certitude for our deductions as exists in ordinary elementary number theory, which no one doubts and where contradictions and paradoxes arise only through our own carelessness.

Obviously these goals can be attained only after we have fully elucidated *the nature of the infinite*.

We have already seen that the infinite is nowhere to be found in reality, no matter what experiences, observations, and knowledge are appealed to. Can thought about things be so much different from things? Can thinking processes be so unlike the actual processes of things? In short, can thought be so far removed from reality? Rather is it not clear that, when we think that we have encountered the infinite in some real sense, we have merely been seduced into thinking so by the fact that we often encounter extremely large and extremely small dimensions in reality?

Does material logical deduction somehow deceive us or leave us in the lurch when we apply it to real things or events?[1] No! Material logical deduction is indispensable. It deceives us only when we form arbitrary abstract definitions, especially those which involve infinitely many objects. In such cases we have illegitimately used material logical deduction; i.e., we have not paid sufficient attention to the preconditions necessary for its valid use. In recognizing that there are such preconditions that must be taken into account, we find ourselves in agreement with the philosophers, notably with Kant. Kant taught—and it is an integral part of his doctrine—that mathematics treats a subject matter which is given independently of logic. Mathematics, therefore, can never be grounded solely on logic. Consequently, Frege's and Dedekind's attempts to so ground it were doomed to failure.

As a further precondition for using logical deduction and carrying out logical operations, something must be given in conception, viz., certain extralogical concrete objects which are intuited as directly experienced prior to all thinking. For logical deduction to be certain, we must be able to see every aspect of these objects, and their properties, differences, sequences, and contiguities must be given, together with the objects themselves, as something which cannot be reduced to something else and which requires no reduction. This is the basic philosophy which I find necessary not just for mathematics, but for all scientific thinking, understanding, and communicating. The subject matter of mathematics is, in accordance with this theory, the concrete symbols themselves whose structure is immediately clear and recognizable.

Consider the nature and methods of ordinary finitary number theory. It can certainly be constructed from numerical structures through intuitive material considerations. But mathematics surely does not consist solely of numerical equations and surely cannot be reduced to them alone. Still one could argue that mathematics is an apparatus which, when applied to integers, always yields correct numerical equations. But in that event we still need to investigate the structure of this apparatus thoroughly enough to make sure that it in fact always yields correct equations. To carry out such an investigation, we have available only the same concrete material finitary

---

[1] [Throughout this paper the German word 'inhaltlich' has been translated by the words 'material' or 'materially' which are reserved for that purpose and which are used to refer to matter in the sense of the traditional distinction between matter or content and logical form.—Tr.]

methods as were used to derive numerical equations in the construction of number theory. This scientific requirement can in fact be met, i.e., it is possible to obtain in a purely intuitive and finitary way—the way we attain the truths of number theory—the insights which guarantee the validity of the mathematical apparatus.

Let us consider number theory more closely. In number theory we have the numerical symbols

$$1, 11, 111, 11111$$

where each numerical symbol is intuitively recognizable by the fact it contains only 1's. These numerical symbols which are themselves our subject matter have no significance in themselves. But we require in addition to these symbols, even in elementary number theory, other symbols which have meaning and which serve to facilitate communication, for example the symbol 2 is used as an abbreviation for the numerical symbol 11, and the numerical symbol 3 as an abbreviation for the numerical symbol 111. Moreover, we use symbols like $+$, $=$, and $>$ to communicate statements. $2 + 3 = 3 + 2$ is intended to communicate the fact that $2 + 3$ and $3 + 2$, when abbreviations are taken into account, are the self-same numerical symbol, viz., the numerical symbol 11111. Similarly $3 > 2$ serves to communicate the fact that the symbol 3, i.e., 111, is longer than the symbol 2, i.e., 11; or, in other words, that the latter symbol is a proper part of the former.

We also use the letters a, b, c for communication. Thus $b > a$ communicates the fact that the numerical symbol b is longer than the numerical symbol a. From this point of view, $a + b = b + a$ communicates only the fact that the numerical symbol $a + b$ is the same as $b + a$. The content of this communication can also be proved through material deduction. Indeed, this kind of intuitive material treatment can take us quite far.

But let me give you an example where this intuitive method is outstripped. The largest known prime number is (39 digits)

$$p = 170\ 141\ 183\ 460\ 469\ 231\ 731\ 687\ 303\ 715\ 884\ 105\ 727$$

By a well-known method due to Euclid we can give a proof, one which remains entirely within our finitary framework, of the statement that between $p + 1$ and $p! + 1$ there exists at least one new prime number. The statement itself conforms perfectly to our finitary approach, for the expression 'there exists' serves only to abbreviate the expression: it is certain that $p + 1$ or $p + 2$ or $p + 3 \ldots$ or $p! + 1$ is a prime number. Furthermore, since it obviously comes down to the same thing to say: there exists a prime number which

1. $> p$, and at the same time is

2. $\leq p! + 1$,

we are led to formulate a theorem which expresses only a part of what the euclidean theorem expresses; viz., the theorem that there exists a prime number $>p$. Although this theorem is a much weaker statement in terms of content—it asserts only part of what the euclidean theorem asserts—and although the passage from the euclidean theorem to this one seems quite harmless, that passage nonetheless involves a leap into the transfinite when the partial statement is taken out of context and regarded as an independent statement.

How can this be? Because we have an existential statement, 'there exists'! True, we had a similar expression in the euclidean theorem, but there the 'there exists' was, as I already mentioned, an abbreviation for: either $p + 1$ or $p + 2$ or $p + 3 \ldots$ or $p! + 1$ is a prime number—just as when, instead of saying 'either this piece of chalk or this piece or this piece … or this piece is red' we say briefly 'there exists a red piece of chalk among these pieces'. A statement such as 'there exists' an object with a certain property in a finite totality conforms perfectly to our finitary approach. But a statement like 'either $p + 1$ or $p + 2$ or $p + 3 \ldots$ or (ad infinitum) … has a certain property' is itself an infinite logical product. Such an extension into the infinite is, unless further explanation and precautions are forthcoming, no more permissible than the extension from finite to infinite products in calculus. Such extensions, accordingly, usually lapse into meaninglessness.

From our finitary point of view, an existential statement of the form 'there exists a number with a certain property', has in general only the significance of a partial statement; i.e., it is regarded as part of a more determinate statement. The more precise formulation may, however, be unnecessary for many purposes.

In analyzing an existential statement whose content cannot be expressed by a finite disjunction, we encounter the infinite. Similarly, by negating a general statement, i.e., one which refers to arbitrary numerical symbols, we obtain a transfinite statement. For example, the statement that if a is a numerical symbol, then $a + 1 = 1 + a$ is universally true, is from our finitary perspective *incapable of negation*. We will see this better if we consider that this statement cannot be interpreted as a conjunction of infinitely many numerical equations by means of 'and' but only as a hypothetical judgment which asserts something for the case when a numerical symbol is given.

From our finitary viewpoint, therefore, we cannot argue that an equation like the one just given, where an arbitrary numerical symbol occurs, either holds for every symbol or is disproved by a counter example. Such an argument, being an application of the law of excluded middle, rests on the presupposition that the statement of the universal validity of such an equation is capable of negation.

At any rate, we note the following: if we remain within the domain of finitary statements, as indeed we must, we have as a rule very complicated logical laws. Their complexity becomes unmanageable when the expressions 'all' and 'there exists' are combined and when they occur in expressions nested within other expressions. In short, the logical laws which Aristotle taught and which men have used ever since they began to think, do not hold. We could, of course, develop logical laws which do hold for the domain of finitary statements. But it would do us no good to develop such a logic, for we do not want to give up the use of the simple laws of Aristotelian logic. Furthermore, no one, though he speak with the tongues of angels, could keep people from negating general statements, or from forming partial judgments, or from using *tertium non datur*. What, then, are we to do?

Let us remember that *we are mathematicians* and that as mathematicians we have often been in precarious situations from which we have been rescued by the ingenious method of ideal elements. I showed you some illustrious examples of the use of this method at the beginning of this paper. Just as $i = \sqrt{-1}$ was introduced to preserve in simplest form the laws of algebra (for example, the laws about the existence and number of the roots of an equation); just as ideal factors were introduced to preserve the simple laws of divisibility for algebraic whole numbers (for example, a common ideal divisor for the numbers 2 and $1 + \sqrt{-5}$ was introduced, though no such divisor really exists); similarly, to preserve the simple formal rules of ordinary Aristotelian logic, we must *supplement the finitary statements with ideal statements*. It is quite ironic that the deductive methods which Kronecker so vehemently attacked are the exact counterpart of what Kronecker himself admired so enthusiastically in Kummer's work on number theory which Kronecker extolled as the highest achievement of mathematics.

How do we obtain *ideal statements*? It is a remarkable as well as a favorable and promising fact that to obtain ideal statements, we need only continue in a natural and obvious fashion the development which the theory of the foundations of mathematics has already undergone. Indeed, we should realize that even elementary mathematics goes beyond the standpoint of intuitive number theory. Intuitive, material number theory, as we have been construing it, does not include the method of algebraic computation with letters. Formulas were always used exclusively for communication in intuitive number theory. The letters stood for numerical symbols and an equation communicated the fact that the two symbols coincided. In algebra, on the other hand, we regard expressions containing letters as independent structures which formalize the material theorems of number theory. In place of statements about numerical symbols, we have formulas which are themselves the concrete objects of intuitive study. In place of number-theoretic material proof, we have the derivation of a formula from another formula according to determinate rules.

Hence, as we see even in algebra, a proliferation of finitary objects takes place. Up to now the only objects were numerical symbols like 1, 11, ..., 11111. These alone were the objects of material treatment. But mathematical practice goes further, even in algebra. Indeed, even when from our finitary viewpoint a formula is valid with respect to what it signifies as, for example, the theorem that always

$$a + b = b + a,$$

where a and b stand for particular numerical symbols, nevertheless we prefer not to use this form of communication but to replace it instead by the formula

$$a + b = b + a.$$

This latter formula is in no wise an immediate communication of something signified but is rather a certain formal structure whose relation to the old finitary statements,

$$2 + 3 = 3 + 2,$$

$$5 + 7 = 7 + 5,$$

consists in the fact that, when a and b are replaced in the formula by the numerical symbols 2, 3, 5, 7, the individual finitary statements are thereby obtained, i.e., by a proof procedure, albeit a very simple one. We therefore conclude that a, b, $=$, $+$, as well as the whole formula $a + b = b + a$ mean nothing in themselves, no more than the numerical symbols meant anything. Still we can derive from that formula other formulas to which we do ascribe meaning, viz., by interpreting them as communications of finitary statements. Generalizing this conclusion, we conceive mathematics to be a stock of two kinds of formulas: first, those to which the meaningful communications of finitary statements correspond; and, secondly, other formulas which signify nothing and which are the *ideal structures of our theory*.

Now what was our goal? In mathematics, on the one hand, we found finitary statements which contained only numerical symbols, for example,

$$3 > 2, 2 + 3 = 3 + 2, 2 = 3, 1 \neq 1,$$

which from our finitary standpoint are immediately intuitable and understandable without recourse to anything else. These statements can be negated, truly or falsely. One can apply Aristotelian logic unrestrictedly to them without taking special precautions. The principle of non-contradiction holds for them; i.e., the negation of one of these statements and the statement itself cannot both be true. *Tertium non datur* holds for them; i.e., either a statement or its negation is true. To say that a statement is false is equivalent to saying that its negation is true. On the other hand, in addition to these elementary statements which present no problems, we also found more problematic finitary statements; e.g., we found finitary statements that could not be split up into partial statements. Finally, we introduced ideal statements in order that the ordinary laws of logic would hold universally. But since these ideal statements, viz., the formulas, do not mean anything insofar as they do not express finitary statements, logical operations cannot be materially applied to them as they can be to finitary statements. It is, there-fore, necessary to formalize the logical operations and the mathematical proofs themselves. This formalization necessitates translating logical relations into formulas. Hence, in addition to mathematical symbols, we must also introduce logical symbols such as

$$\&\ ,\ \vee\ ,\ \rightarrow\ ,\ \sim\ ^2$$
$$\text{(and)}\ \text{(or)}\ \text{(implies)}\ \text{(not)}$$

and in addition to the mathematical variables a, b, c, ... we must also employ logical variables, viz., the propositional variables A, B, C, ...

How can this be done? Fortunately that same preestablished harmony which we have so often observed operative in the history of the development of science, that same preestablished harmony which aided Einstein by giving him the general invariant calculus already fully developed for his gravita-tional theory, comes also to our aid: we find the logical calculus already worked out in advance. To be sure, the logical calculus was originally devel-oped from an altogether different point of view. The symbols of the logical calculus originally were introduced only in order to communicate. Still it is consistent with our finitary viewpoint to deny any meaning to logical symbols, just as we denied meaning to mathematical symbols, and to declare that the formulas of the logical calculus are ideal statements which mean nothing in themselves. We possess in the logical calculus a symbolic language which can transform mathematical statements into formulas and express logical deduction by means of formal procedures. In exact analogy to the transition from material number theory to formal algebra, we now treat the signs and operation symbols of the logical calculus in abstraction from their meaning. Thus we finally obtain, instead of material mathematical knowledge which is communicated in ordinary language, just a set of formulas containing mathematical and logical symbols which are generated successively, accord-ing to determinate rules. Certain of the formulas correspond to mathematical axioms. The rules whereby the formulas are derived from one another correspond to material deduction. Material deduction is thus replaced by a formal procedure governed by rules. The rigorous transition from a naïve to a formal treatment is effected, therefore, both for the axioms (which, though originally viewed naïvely as basic truths, have been long treated in modern axiomatics as mere relations between concepts) and for the logical calculus (which originally was supposed to be merely a different language).

We will now explain briefly how *mathematical proofs* are formalized. I have already said that certain formulas which serve as building blocks for the formal structure of mathematics are called "axioms". A mathematical

---

² [Although Hilbert's original paper used '−' as the sign for negation, we have sub-stituted '∼' for greater conformity with the notation used in other papers in this collec-tion.—Eds.]

proof is a figure which as such must be accessible to our intuition. It consists of deductions made according to the deduction schema

$$\frac{\begin{array}{c}\mathfrak{S} \\ \mathfrak{S} \to \mathfrak{T}\end{array}}{\mathfrak{T}}$$

where each premise, i.e., the formulas $\mathfrak{S}$ and $\mathfrak{S} \to \mathfrak{T}$, either is an axiom, or results from an axiom by substitution, or is the last formula of a previous deduction, or results from such a formula by substitution. A formula is said to be provable if it is the last formula of a proof.

Our program itself guides *the choice of axioms for our theory of proof*. Notwithstanding a certain amount of arbitrariness in the choice of axioms, as in geometry certain groups of axioms are qualitatively distinguishable. Here are some examples taken from each of these groups:

I. Axioms for implication
   (i) $A \to (B \to A)$
     (addition of a hypothesis)
   (ii) $(B \to C) \to \{(A \to B) \to (A \to C)\}$
     (elimination of a statement)

II. Axioms for negation
   (i) $\{A \to (B \,\&\, {\sim}B)\} \to {\sim}A$
     (law of contradiction)
   (ii) ${\sim}{\sim}A \to A$
     (law of double negation)

The axioms in groups I and II are simply the axioms of the propositional calculus.

III. Transfinite axioms
   (i) $(a)A(a) \to A(b)$
     (inference from the universal to the particular; Aristotelian axiom);
   (ii) ${\sim}(a)A(a) \to (\exists a){\sim}A(a)$
     (if a predicate does not apply universally, then there is a counter-example);
   (iii) ${\sim}(\exists a)A(a) \to (a){\sim}A(a)$
     (if there are no instances of a proposition, then the proposition is false for all a).

At this point we discover the very remarkable fact that these transfinite axioms can be derived from a single axiom which contains the gist of the so-called axiom of choice, the most disputed axiom in the literature of mathematics:

$$(\text{i}')\ \ A(a) \to A(\varepsilon A)$$

where ε is the transfinite, logical choice-function.

Then the following specifically mathematical axioms are added to those just given:

IV. Axioms for identity
   (i) $a = a$
   (ii) $a = b \rightarrow \{A(a) \rightarrow A(b)\}$,

and finally

V. Axioms for number
   (i) $a + 1 \neq 0$
   (ii) The axiom of complete induction.

Thus we are now in a position to carry out our theory of proof and to construct the system of provable formulas, i.e., mathematics. But in our general joy over this achievement and in our particular joy over finding that indispensable tool, the logical calculus, already developed without any effort on our part, we must not forget the essential condition of our work. There is just one condition, albeit an absolutely necessary one, connected with the method of ideal elements. That condition is a *proof of consistency*, for the extension of a domain by the addition of ideal elements is legitimate only if the extension does not cause contradictions to appear in the old, narrower domain, or, in other words, only if the relations that obtain among the old structures when the ideal structures are deleted are always valid in the old domain.

The problem of consistency is easily handled in the present circumstances. It reduces obviously to proving that from our axioms and according to the rules we laid down we cannot get '$1 \neq 1$' as the last formula of a proof, or, in other words, that '$1 \neq 1$' is not a provable formula. This task belongs just as much to the domain of intuitive treatment as does, for example, the task of finding a proof of the irrationality of $\sqrt{2}$ in materially constructed number theory—i.e., a proof that it is impossible to find two numerical symbols $\mathfrak{a}$ and $\mathfrak{b}$ which stand in the relation $\mathfrak{a}^2 = 2\mathfrak{b}^2$, or in other words, that one cannot produce two numerical symbols with a certain property. Similarly, it is incumbent on us to show that one cannot produce a certain kind of proof. A formalized proof, like a numerical symbol, is a concrete and visible object. We can describe it completely. Further, the requisite property of the last formula; viz., that it read '$1 \neq 1$', is a concretely ascertainable property of the proof. And since we can, as a matter of fact, prove that it is impossible to get a proof which has that formula as its last formula, we thereby justify our introduction of ideal statements.

It is also a pleasant surprise to discover that, at the very same time, we have resolved a problem which has plagued mathematicians for a long time, viz., the problem of proving *the consistency of the axioms of arithmetic*. For, wherever the axiomatic method is used, the problem of proving consistency arises. Surely in choosing, understanding, and using rules and axioms we do not want to rely solely on blind faith. In geometry and physical theory, proof of consistency is effected by reducing their consistency to that of the axioms of arithmetic. But obviously we cannot use this method to prove the consistency of arithmetic itself. Since our theory of proof, based on the method of ideal elements, enables us to take this last important step, it forms the necessary keystone of the doctrinal arch of axiomatics. What we have twice experienced, once with the paradoxes of the infinitesimal calculus and once with the paradoxes of set theory, will not be experienced a third time, nor ever again.

The theory of proof which we have here sketched not only is capable of providing a solid basis for the foundations of mathematics but also, I believe, supplies a general method for treating fundamental mathematical questions which mathematicians heretofore have been unable to handle.

In a sense, mathematics has become a court of arbitration, a supreme tribunal to decide fundamental questions—on a concrete basis on which everyone can agree and where every statement can be controlled.

The assertions of the new so-called "intuitionism"—modest though they may be—must in my opinion first receive their certificate of validity from this tribunal.

An example of the kind of fundamental questions which can be so handled is the thesis that every mathematical problem is solvable. We are all convinced that it really is so. In fact one of the principal attractions of tackling a mathematical problem is that we always hear this cry within us: There is the problem, find the answer; you can find it just by thinking, for there is no *ignorabimus* in mathematics. Now my theory of proof cannot supply a general method for solving every mathematical problem—there just is no such method. Still the proof (that the assumption that every mathematical problem is solvable is a consistent assumption) falls completely within the scope of our theory.

I will now play my last trump. The acid test of a new theory is its ability to solve problems which, though known for a long time, the theory was not expressly designed to solve. The maxim "By their fruits ye shall know them" applies also to theories. When Cantor discovered his first transfinite numbers, the so-called numbers of the second number class, the question immediately arose, as I already mentioned, whether this transfinite method of counting enables one to count sets known from elsewhere which are not countable in the ordinary sense. The points of an interval figured prominently as such a set. This question—whether the points of an interval, i.e., the real numbers, can be counted by means of the numbers of the table given previously—is the famous continuum problem which Cantor posed but failed to solve. Though some mathematicians have thought that they could dispose of this problem by denying its existence, the following remarks show how wrong they were: The continuum problem is set off from other problems by its uniqueness and inner beauty. Further, it offers the advantage over other problems of combining these two qualities: on the one hand, new methods are required for its solution since the old methods fail to solve it; on the other hand, its solution itself is of the greatest importance because of the results to be obtained.

The theory which I have developed provides a solution of the continuum problem. The proof that every mathematical problem is solvable constitutes the first and most important step toward its solution. . . .[3]

In summary, let us return to our main theme and draw some conclusions from all our thinking about the infinite. Our principal result is that the infinite is nowhere to be found in reality. It neither exists in nature nor provides a legitimate basis for rational thought—a remarkable harmony between being and thought. In contrast to the earlier efforts of Frege and Dedekind, we are convinced that certain intuitive concepts and insights are necessary conditions of scientific knowledge, that logic alone is not sufficient. Operating with the infinite can be made certain only by the finitary.

The role that remains for the infinite to play is solely that of an idea— if one means by an idea, in Kant's terminology, a concept of reason which transcends all experience and which completes the concrete as a totality— that of an idea which we may unhesitatingly trust within the framework erected by our theory.

Lastly, I wish to thank P. Bernays for his intelligent collaboration and valuable help, both technical and editorial, especially with the proof of the continuum theorem.

[3] [At this point, Hilbert sketched an attempted solution of the continuum problem. The attempt was, although not devoid of interest, never carried out. We therefore omit it here.—Eds.]

REMARKS ON THE DEFINITION AND NATURE
OF MATHEMATICS

Haskell B. Curry

This paper is a discussion, written as a result of a request of Professor Gonseth, of certain points concerning the philosophy of mathematics. It is a revision of my previous discourse, on this subject, which I now regard as inadequate. The argument is based directly on my contact with mathematics without benefit of any technical acquaintance with philosophy. I have not attempted to confine myself with what is novel; but the paper is intended to be self-contained.

The principal thesis is that mathematics may be conceived as an objective science which is independent of any except the most rudimentary philosophical assumptions. It is a body of propositions dealing with a certain subject matter; and these propositions are true insofar as they correspond with the facts. The position taken is a species of formalism, which may be called empirical formalism.

THE PROBLEM OF MATHEMATICAL TRUTH

There are three principal types of opinion as to the subject matter of mathematics, viz. realism, idealism, and formalism. We shall consider here the realist and intuitionist views, leaving formalism for the next section.

According to realism, mathematical propositions express the most general properties of our physical environment. Although this is the primitive view of mathematics, yet, on account of the essential role played by infinity in mathematics, it is untenable to-day.

On the idealistic view mathematics deal with the properties of mental

Reprinted with the kind permission of the author and editor from Dialectica, 48 (1954), 228–33. *The author has indicated to us that, although this paper appeared in* 1954, *it was written in* 1939 *and represents his views as of that time.*

objects of some sort. There are various varieties of this view according to the nature of these mental objects. The extremes are Platonism, which ascribes a reality to all the infinistic constructions of classical mathematics, and intuitionism, which depends on an *a priori* intuition of temporal succession. All forms of idealism are subject to the same fundamental criticism: in the first place they are vague, and, in the second place they depend on metaphysical assumptions from which mathematics, if it is to have the prephilosophical character above mentioned, must be free.

It is important to see that this criticism, so obvious in the case of Platonism, applies also to intuitionism. As to the vagueness, Heyting, in his Ergebnisse report, explicitly denies the possibility of an exact description of this mathematical intuition. As to the metaphysical character, it is clear from the intuitionist writings that their "ur-intuition" has the following properties: (1) it is essentially a thinking activity; (2) it is *a priori*; (3) it is independent of language; and (4) it is objective in the sense that it is the same in all thinking beings. The existence of an intuition-temporal or not-satisfying these four conditions is an outright assumption.

THE FORMALIST DEFINITION OF MATHEMATICS

According to formalism the central concept in mathematics is that of a formal system. Such a system is defined by a set of conventions, which I shall call its *primitive frame*, specifying the following: first, what the objects of the theory, which I shall call *terms*, shall be; second, how certain propositions, which I shall call *elementary propositions*, may be stated concerning these terms, i.e. what *predicates* (classes, relations, etc.), we shall take as fundamental; and third, which of these elementary propositions are true. The first and third of these sets of conventions are essentially recursive definitions; we do not specify the ultimate nature of the terms, but give simply a list of primitive terms, or tokens, together with operators and rules of formation by means of which all further terms are constructed; likewise we start with a list of elementary propositions, called *axioms*, which are true by definition, and then give *rules of procedure* by means of which further elementary theorems are derived. The proof of an elementary proposition then consists simply in showing that it satisfies the recursive definition of elementary theorem.

It should be noted that in such a formal system it is immaterial what we take for the tokens (and operators),—we may take these as discrete objects, symbols, abstract concepts, variables, or what not. Any such way of understanding a formal system we may call a representation of it. The primitive frame specifies, independently of the representation, which elementary propositions are true, and therefore determines the meaning of the fundamental predicates. In this sense the primitive frame defines the system.

One representative of particular importance is when the tokens are taken as symbols. In this representation, which is insisted on by Frege and his followers (Hilbert, Carnap, the Poles) a formal system becomes essentially equivalent to the formalized syntax of an object language. This representation has certain advantages of definiteness and concreteness. But it also has certain disadvantages. For it is necessary, as Carnap has shown, to distinguish between the symbols used as names of the terms and the specimens of those terms; usually this means that the familiar symbols are used for the latter purpose and more or less outlandish ones for the former. Since we never use the symbols of the object languages in the theory but only in the introduction, this leads to unintelligibility. Why not abolish the object language altogether and understand that the tokens are objects which we can take as symbols if we want to? Again the consideration of other sorts of representations may suggest simplifications which a syntactical representation would not. Thus the syntactical viewpoint gives rise to an extreme nominalism—as shown by the inclusion of parentheses, commas, etc., among the symbols and of expressions which are not "well formed"—which is avoidable and contrary to the spirit of mathematics.

In the study of formal systems we do not confine ourselves to the derivation of elementary propositions step by step. Rather we take the system, defined by its primitive frame, as datum, and then study it by any means at our command. In so doing we may formulate further propositions, which we call metatheoretic propositions. Like the elementary propositions these state, essentially, properties of the system; but they may also involve extraneous considerations. Insomuch as they deal with what is, in view of the primitive frame, a well defined subject matter, the question of their truth involves no difficulties beyond those inherent in compound propositions in general.

The formalist definition of mathematics is then this: mathematics is the science of formal systems. The propositions of mathematics are the propositions elementary or metatheoretic, of some formal system or set of systems. For each such proposition which does not involve extraneous considerations, we have an objective criterion of truth in the sense that an alleged proof can be checked objectively; but a proposition may be indefinite in the sense that we have no resolution process (Entscheidungsverfahren). Intuition is, of course, involved in this; viz. the intuition of recursive definitions, mathematical induction and the like; but the metaphysical nature of this intuition is irrelevant. (If extraneous considerations are involved, then we have to do with applied, not pure, mathematics—the boundary line between mathematics and other sciences is not sharp, and should not be.) It should be noted that we have not confined mathematics to a single formal system; moreover, metatheoretic propositions are included in mathematics. This answers the objections which might be raised on the ground of the incompleteness theorems of Skolem, Gödel, et al.

TRUTH AND ACCEPTABILITY

We now turn to the relation of mathematics to its application. For this purpose we introduce another kind of quasi-truth concept which applies, not to single propositions, but to systems as a whole. I shall call this *acceptability*. By acceptability, then, I mean the considerations which lead us to be interested in one formal system rather than in another.

Acceptability is usually a matter of interpreting the theory in relation to some subject matter. Such an interpretation is to be distinguished from a representation: in a representation the predicates are defined by the primitive frame; in an interpretation we associate them with certain intuitive notions, so that the question arises as to the agreement between the truth of the propositions of the formal system and that of the associated intuitive ones. Acceptability is thus relative to a purpose; and a discussion of acceptability is pointless unless the purpose is stated.

As an illustration of acceptability questions let us consider the acceptability of classical mathematics for the purpose of application in physics.

Among the criteria of acceptability we may mention the following: (1) the intuitive evidence of the premises; (2) consistency (an internal criterion); (3) the usefulness of the theory as a whole.

The intuitionists have made much of the first criterion. They point out that certain propositions of classical mathematics lack intuitive evidence; and they have constructed systems which—we can admit this without swallowing the intuitionistic metaphysics—have greater intuitive evidence than the classical. But these systems are so complicated as to be useless, and are inacceptable by criterion (3). Moreover this is the decisive consideration; for physics is an empirical science. and therefore the question of intuitive evidence is secondary. The acceptability of classical mathematics is an empirical fact, and the proper retort to the intuitionist gibe, that classical mathematics has only a heuristic value, is that so far as physics is concerned, that is all the value that an intuitionist mathematics has either.

The criterion of consistency has been stressed by Hilbert. Presumably the reason for this is that he, like the intuitionists, seeks an *a priori* justification. But aside from the fact that for physics the question of an *a priori* justification is irrelevant, I maintain that a proof of consistency is neither a necessary nor a sufficient condition for acceptability. It is obviously not sufficient. As to necessity, so long as no inconsistency is known a consistency proof, although it adds to our knowledge about the system, does not alter its usefulness. Even if an inconsistency is discovered this does not mean complete abandonment of the theory, but its modification and refinement. As a matter of fact essentially this has happened in the past; we now know, for example, that the mathematics of the eighteenth century was inconsistent, but we have not abandoned the results of the eighteenth-century mathematicians. The peculiar position of Hilbert in regard to consistency is thus no part of the formalist conception of mathematics, and it is therefore unfortunate that many persons identify formalism with what should be called Hilbertism.

Let us now cut short this discussion and summarize as follows: Acceptability is relative to a purpose, and a system acceptable for one purpose may not be for another. For example, I agree with Weyl and Gentzen that there are purposes for which intuitionistic systems are acceptable, although they are not acceptable on empirical grounds, for application to physics. Again acceptability is a different question from truth; in fact a formalist definition of mathematical truth is compatible with almost any position in regard to acceptability. In this sense formalist mathematics is compatible with various philosophical views; it is an objective science which can form part of the data of philosophy.

MATHEMATICS AND LOGIC

In current popular discussions it is said that intuitionism, formalism, and logicism are the three main views in regard to the nature of mathematics; the last is supposed to be the view that mathematics is logic. But we do not have here a third view of mathematics parallel with the other two; for to say that mathematics is logic is merely to replace one undefined term by another. When we go back of the word "logic" to its definition in the logistic systems, we find that they run the gamut from extreme Platonism to pure formalism. The question of the relation of mathematics to logic is thus a different question from the definition of mathematics; on account of the lack of space we cannot go into that question here.

Georg Kreisel

1. If one may judge from his publications, Hilbert's conception of the problem of foundations underwent marked developments.

In [8], pp. 146–156[1] (1917) he still concentrated on the "sound" and rather colourless *Independence Problem* which may be formulated as follows: given a branch of knowledge which is so well-developed as to be axiomatized, the problem is to get a clear view of the logical relationships (dependence and independence or, derivability and non-derivability) of statements of the axiomatic theory. Hilbert emphasized the consistency problem which is so to speak the weakest non-derivability result, since it is the problem of showing that there exists at least one statement which is not derivable.

But in later writings (though also in 1904, [6, pp. 247–261] the *Consistency Problem* was associated with the problem of understanding the concept of infinity. He sought such an understanding in understanding the *use of transfinite machinery* from a finitist point of view. And this he saw in the elimination of transfinite ($\varepsilon-$) symbols from proofs of formulæ not containing such symbols. He was convinced from the start that such an elimination was possible, and expressed it by saying that the problems of foundations were to be *removed* or that doubts were to be eliminated instead of saying that they were to be investigated.

We note at once that there is no evidence in Hilbert's writings of the kind of formalist view suggested by Brouwer when he called Hilbert's approach "formalism." In particular, we could say that Hilbert wanted to eliminate the use of transfinite concepts from proofs of finitist assertions instead of referring to symbols and formulæ as above. The symbols were a

[1] In general, references to Hilbert's work will be given to the reprinting in [6] or [8].

Revised by the author from an earlier version which appeared in Dialectica, 12 (1958), 346–72. *Printed here by kind permission of the author and the editor of* Dialectica.

means of representation. The real opposition between Brouwer's and Hilbert's approach was not at all between formalism and intuitive mathematics, but between (i) the conception of what constitutes a foundation[2] and (ii) between two informal ways of reasoning, namely finitist and intuitionist. In fact, Bernays repeatedly emphasized the latter point, the lack of evidence in the basic intuitionistic conception of constructive proof ([8], p. 212, or [3], p. 147): in short, it is not the restrictions imposed *by* intuitionism, but those *on* intuitionism which seem to constitute the most significant differences. Hilbert's own remarks on this opposition seem quite inept.[3]

The view above on the significant differences between Brouwer's and Hilbert's approach does not deny, of course, the popular attraction of a syntactic formulation of foundational problems. Derivability in formal systems (which codify the manipulation of symbolic representations of transfinite concepts) is "down to earth", it refers to palpable acts, to what we "actually do," while the transfinite concepts themselves are "up in the air," they are abstract, and therefore supposed to be inaccessible to exact study. Even though Hilbert was not a strict positivist like Comte ([8], p. 387), his presentation was certainly congenial to a positivist era: at least, his problems were positivistically meaningful for a more liberal conception of positivism, while the transfinite concepts themselves are senseless even for the latter. It might have been expected that deficiencies in our understanding of these concepts would reappear in our inability to solve the syntactic problems, in particular to survey those parts of the corresponding formal system which are devoid of positivist interest, namely all those formulæ which contain symbols for transfinite concepts. But equally it was to be expected that specific partial (syntactic) problems could be solved despite a lack of deeper understanding of the abstract concepts. In the following sections we shall try to "reconstruct" Hilbert's programme in the light of these observations.

Hilbert was certainly not a fanatic of crude formalism: thus while his problems concerned syntactic properties of formal systems, the solutions were to be given by intuitively correct reasoning, and he explicitly considered any formalization of *this* reasoning as unnecessary. (For qualifications, cf. Section 18.)

2. The fabric of Hilbert's conception. He asserted that there was a certain type of evident reasoning which was presupposed in all scientific thinking ([8], pp. 162–163), and finitist operations were typical of this. He believed that there were no essentially different truths in mathematics ([8], p. 157).

---

[2] Brouwer ignores non-constructive mathematics altogether and therefore does not have an analogous problem of foundations to Hilbert's.

[3] E.g., [6, p. 307]: Considering that the intended meaning of the intuitionistic disjunction is different from that of classical disjunction, the rejection of *tertium non datur* is much more like depriving non-commutative algebra of the rule $ab = ba$ than a boxer of the use of his fists.

These views lead to the hope of a final solution of the problem of foundations ([7], p. 489, 494) by a reduction of all mathematical reasoning to finitist reasoning: for if the minimum that has to be presupposed suffices for this reduction then we have a complete solution. Conversely, something of this kind is required for a "complete" solution: if there is a plurality of essentially different mathematical truths there is hardly a hope of an enumeration of such truths which convinces us as being complete; furthermore there would be the problem of their inter-relations, and so there would be no unique outstanding problem of foundations.

Next, if the finitist truths are the only[4] absolute ones ([8], p. 180), it is at least natural to regard mathematical expressions containing transfinite symbols as "ideal" elements whose sole purpose is the streamlining of the symbolism ([6], p. 280, or [8], p. 187). And in this case consistency is all that matters because, in the usual systems, if consistency is established by (finitist) methods, and a formula without transfinite symbols is derived in the system considered, then this formula can be proved by the same methods ([6], p. 304, and [3], p. 154); in other words, we have the required elimination. Conversely, if consistency is all that we demand then there is no assurance that formulæ containing transfinite symbols in an essential way have the intended interpretation, and so they must be regarded as ideal. This is established by Gödel's construction of consistent, but ω-inconsistent systems,[5] because purely universal formulæ are deductively equivalent to formulæ without transfinite symbols, and purely existential formulæ which are provable in a consistent system need not be true.

We note in passing an interesting aspect of Hilbert's idea of a *paradise*: a characteristic of Cantor's set theory (Hilbert's paradise, [6], p. 274) is the abundance of transfinite machinery which Hilbert regarded in the same paper as "ideal" elements to be used as gadgets to make life smoother.

It is plain that such concepts as "finitist," "essentially the same truth," "reduction" are not at all precise. But if one really believes in the success of the finitist reduction it was not necessary to clarify them in advance. For when the work is done one can examine what methods are actually needed, in what sense we have a reduction, and at this stage one can then decide if it is satisfactory.

3. Critique of detail. There is one point in the above picture which is not convincing even if the basic assumptions are granted. Hilbert regarded

[4] Though, I think, Hilbert does not deny this elsewhere, his emphasizing that the geometric continuum ([8], p. 159) is a concept in its own right and independent of number seems to weaken the doctrine that all absolute truths are finitist.

[5] The possibility of ω-inconsistent systems was evidently clear to Hilbert, but as late as 1930 ([6], p. 320) he wanted to show that every consistent statement of arithmetic was provable, i.e., that the usual system of arithmetic was complete. Actually he requires more, namely that consistency "looks after the rest", since a system might be complete and yet some of its theorems false.

complex numbers ([6], p. 269) as a typical example of ideal elements. Yet the reduction to pairs of real numbers does not only ensure consistency, but also gives each formula containing symbols for "ideal" elements a *meaning* in terms of real numbers. It would not seem unreasonable to demand the same for formulæ with transfinite symbols, at least in any specific context. At any rate one would thereby extract more "absolute truths" from the formal machinery.

4. Critique of basic assumptions. Of course, the first basic assumption is that a reduction to finitist methods is possible at least in the sense of a finitist consistency proof. If this assumption is false, the problems at the end of para. 2 reappear and more besides.

First, instead of having a single kind of elementary reasoning whereby we understand the use of transfinite symbols, there will now be methods of reasoning involving a hierarchy of conceptions such as, e.g. more and more abstract conceptions of a "construction," and we have a hierarchy of Hilbert programmes of *discovering the appropriate complex of such methods which is needed for understanding the use of transfinite symbols in given systems* (modified Hilbert programme).

Second, it will be necessary to ascertain that the consistency of a particular system cannot be established by finitist means, or whatever other complex of methods is being considered. For such an impossibility result it will be necessary to define the notion of *finitist proof* and even to make precise how *consistency* is to be formulated. The latter point is illustrated by the need for derivability conditions on the arithmetized proof predicate in Gödel's second undecidability theorem.

Third, when we are not dealing with an elimination of the nonfinitist methods, but with a *separation* between them, it is necessary to determine the significance of the distinction between finitist and non-finitist. An analogous problem will arise for each subclass of the constructive methods used in the analysis of the transfinite machinery.

Hilbert's own writings contain little information about the solution of these new problems. For the first problem Gentzen's use of ordinals $< \varepsilon_0$ is a good illustration of the kind of subclass of constructive methods which is particularly appropriate for the analysis of a given class of transfinite methods, in this case number theory.

It is difficult to separate the second and the third problem in practice because one can only decide whether e.g. a *definition* of finitist proof is correct if its *significance* (importance) is clear. Hilbert himself is quite unconvincing about the inherent virtues of finitist reasoning. At one time ([8], p. 160, 162) the main purpose of the finitist reduction, in fact the whole need for foundations, consisted for him in clearing the fair name of mathematics which had been sullied by the paradoxes. Now on p. 158 of the same paper he said that the paradoxes simply have nothing to do with the theory of sets of numbers:

it is hard to see why this remark, if true, has not cleared the fair name at least of analysis unless one believes that stained reputations can only be cleared with a great deal of ceremony. Von Neumann's line [15] on the subject is that finitist consistency proofs would reduce strict intuitionism *ad absurdum* (but only if one means by strict intuitionism the view that classical analysis is formally inconsistent and not merely in contradiction with intuitionistic theorems): this is at least less pious than the talk about reputations, but doing down the intuitionists is hardly a grand scientific programme.—Hilbert did emphasize the increase of information contained in proofs of a formula of the form $(Ex)(y) A(x,y)$ ([8], p. 154, 155) from a pure existence proof [intuitionistically $\sim(x) \sim (y) A(x,y)$] to $(Ex)[x \leq 12 \;\&\; (y) A(x,y)]$ to $\mu_x(y) A(x,y) = 10$. But this gives no clue to the nature of the improvement involved in replacing a non-finitist proof of a universal formula $(x) A(x)$ by a finitist one, and this is the critical case (cf. [10], p. 177).

Hilbert sometimes speaks of the reliability (Sicherheit) of finitist reasoning. As Bernays has pointed out ([8], p. 210), realistically speaking, almost the opposite is true, the chance of an oversight in long finitist arguments of metamathematics being particularly great. At any rate it seems improbable that a satisfactory characterization of "finitist proof" would be based on this notion of reliability.—We shall take up the subject in the text below.

5. *Critique of basic assumptions* (continued). In the previous paragraph we considered some problems which arise when one attempts to follow Hilbert's aim of understanding the concept of infinity by eliminating the use of transfinite machinery from proofs of finitist or, more generally, constructive assertions. But this view, that understanding a concept consists simply in the technique of reasoning about it in some well-defined context, does not seem quite adequate.

Thus e.g. the first-order theory of the addition of natural numbers has a complete formalization and hence a decision method. So, from the syntactic point of view it leaves nothing to be desired. But by the completeness theorem for the predicate calculus this theory has a model containing "non-standard" integers. Thus we do not get the degree of understanding that we should have with a system which is satisfied only by a finite set.—We may regard this as a limitation on the syntactic approach for an understanding of the concept of infinity or, at least, as illustrating the use of the notion of a *model* in this connection.

Usually Gödel's incompleteness theorems are taken as showing a limitation on the syntactic approach to an understanding of the concept of infinity. We note the superficially paradoxical fact, brought out above, that the completeness of the predicate calculus, so to speak the "adequacy" of the syntactic approach for predicate logic, leads to a limitation too. This is a point of view emphasized by Skolem.

6. Conclusion. In my opinion, Hilbert's programme, including the modified version in section 4 above and the independence problem of section 1, is a rich line of research in foundations. The general problems of section 4 seem important and somewhat more specific problems will be arrived at below in a brief analysis of the work done by Hilbert's school so far. Also, the (modified) Hilbert programme gives scope to a great variety of methods of mathematical logic including those of the topological approach, intuitionism, recursion theory, as will be seen below.

My own attitude towards the original Hilbert programme is this.

As far as piecemeal understanding is concerned, its importance consists in having led to the fruitful study of the constructive aspects of axiomatic systems. But even if it is compared only with other parts of mathematical logic and not with other mathematical disciplines, its role is not unique; cf. the studies of the distinction between first-order and higher-order reasoning, or of the set theoretical aspects of informal mathematics. My own interest in the modified Hilbert programme does not go one way only, i.e. the elimination of non-constructive methods, but I find that greater facility with the non-constructive methods comes from a study of their constructive aspects.[6]

As far as an over-all philosophical understanding is concerned, the original Hilbert programme has failed, and, as is usual with great schemes, it gives no hint of what might take its place. When asked: "What is mathematics about?", Hilbert could still have said: about the arithmetico-combinatorial facts of finitist mathematics; even though the latter may raise problems of their own, such a "reduction" could have been satisfying. Hilbert's answer is simply not true even for the very weak sense of "equivalence of content" expressed in statements of formal deducibility and nondeducibility. Furthermore, we have no idea in what sort of investigation we could even hope to find a satisfactory answer to such a question. Hilbert thought it would be supplied by pure mathematics itself ([6], p. 316). But it seems clear, as Bernays has expressed it, that the totality of pure mathematics (mathematical structures) is not itself a mathematical structure; this is not only a stumbling block to a mathematical treatment of the conception of the whole of mathematics, but even to an exhaustive treatment of the concept of natural or real number because the characterization by means of a least[7] (or largest) class

---

[6] It is remarkable that mathematicians have not yet learned to exploit the non-constructive methods effectively in the following sense: in the famous non-constructive proofs of constructive results (for references, see [10]) the elimination of the non-constructive methods used is finitist, and does not require more sophisticated notions of constructivity. We know that a more essential use of non-constructive methods must be possible, and, I believe, closer study of their constructive aspects may give one a better "feeling" for them.

[7] If is of course possible (and natural) to consider the relevant extremal clauses as primitive notions in their own right and not as part of set theory, e.g., the "and only those required by the foregoing rules" in the usual definitions of natural numbers or recursive ordinals. This is used, e.g., in Hilbert's reduction ([6], p. 302) of the principle of induction to the reversibility of the formation of numerals. The latter follows from the extremal

refers explicitly to the totality from which these classes are to be taken. If one may use for orientation the formulation of *finitist proof* sketched below, one would say this: just as it is necessary to use non-finitist concepts to study the totality of finitist proofs, so it is necessary to use non-mathematical concepts, i.e. concepts lacking the precision which permit mathematical manipulation, for a significant approach to foundations. It is not at all a question of concepts which are more "reliable" than those of current mathematics, but of concepts which provide a frame of reference for discussing the status of mathematics (cf. [4], p. 245). I do not believe that at the present time we have any concepts of this kind which we can take seriously.

7. For certain parts of non-constructive mathematics the Hilbert programme has been carried out in the originally intended sense, e.g. arithmetic without induction based on the classical predicate calculus. For this purpose a detailed syntactic analysis of the latter is used. Below we shall describe three methods of syntactic analysis, their mathematical significance, including applications to the independence problem, and their bearing on the modified Hilbert programme. We conclude with two observations on finitist proofs and the completeness of predicate logic.

I. SYNTACTIC ANALYSIS

8. We begin by considering what seems to be the main novelty of Hilbert's work in mathematical logic, without which his conception of the Hilbert programme would have been wholly unconvincing, namely his proof theory. He wanted *proof* itself to be made the object of mathematical study ([8], p. 165). Though this is needed for a syntactic (combinatorial) *formulation* of independence results, by itself it is not the crucial point for proof theory. For, clearly, the traditional independence proofs by means of models, as in the case of the parallel axiom, or even the impossibility proofs for certain constructions by means of ruler and compass, are applicable to formalized systems. Thus the consistency of the rules of set theory is proved as follows: when read in the intended manner, the axioms of, e.g. Zermelo's set theory are true of the concept of set and the rules of proof are such that true statements are transformed into true ones. Hence the formal system is consistent.

No, from the point of view of technique the crucial point is that from an early stage Hilbert had in mind a *new type of analysis* in which the detailed structure of the proof is considered. In particular, in the consideration of the so-called transfinite symbols $\varepsilon_x A(x)$, one does not define "models" for

---

clause, and in a similar way other principles of proof can be obtained from such clauses (cf. Lorenzen's induction and inversion principles). But in the application of induction the troublesome totalities reappear in the choice of properties to which induction is applied: e.g., by applying induction to certain non-elementary properties such as truth-definitions, formulæ of classical arithmetic Z can be proved which cannot be proved in Z itself.

them once and for all, but different numbers are substituted for a given symbol depending on the particular proof of the system which is analyzed. Briefly: instead of constructing a model for a system as a whole he gives a method for constructing a model for each particular proof of the system.

In short, Hilbert's conception of a mathematical theory in which *proof* itself is an object of study, does not restrict the means of independence proofs, but on the contrary enlarges it.[8] A restriction comes about only when one restricts the methods to be used in this new theory to so-called finitist or arithmetico-combinatorial methods. We observe in passing the superficially paradoxical character of the fact that up to now the significant independence proofs for classical (and intuitionistic) arithmetic have been obtained by the restricted and not by the potentially more powerful methods. We shall return to this point below.

9. Decision Problem. A very satisfactory syntactic analysis is got from a practical decision method for the theory considered. In particular it solves the independence problem of para. 1 for finite sets of statements of the theory considered. It is not the most satisfactory solution because, given the decision method, one can now ask whether given statements are independent of a certain *infinite* set of statements of the theory, and this question need not be decidable; in fact, it seems inconceivable that there is an optimal solution of the problem. Similarly, the impossibility of a decision method for a given theory is not a "catastrophe";[9] it sets a limit on how[10] clear a view one may reasonably expect to get of the structure of the theory.—This stoic view of the matter is probably universal now, perhaps largely due to the thoughtful writings of Bernays.

It is clear that if a system is consistent a (finitist) proof of decidability automatically yields a (finitist) consistency proof. As early as 1927, von Neumann doubted the decidability of the predicate calculus, though Hilbert does not seem to have been quite so definite. But in any case his actual investigations aimed at much less than decidability. We shall now describe them.

10. The ε-substitution method. The main tool in his work on predicate logic was a reformulation of the predicate calculus by means of the ε-symbol.

---

[8] Within the frame work of classical constructive mathematics (i.e., non-constructive methods of proof, but only recursive functions and predicates) we can give this the following precise sense: by means of (quantifier-free) double induction syntactic independence proofs for primitive recursive arithmetic can be obtained, but not by means of constructive models, e.g., [10] or [13].

[9] The Twenties constantly saw potential catastrophes in the doings of logicians.

[10] It is usual to measure this by the degree of undecidability of the theory. There is quite a different conception of a "partially clear view", namely that obtained by methods enumerating (subsets of the) unprovable formulæ, as afforded by incomplete interpretations (cf. para. 15).

This reformulation is not specially elegant in practice, e.g. the formula $(Ey)(z) A(y, z)$ in the usual notation is written as

$$A [\varepsilon_y A \{y, \varepsilon_z \neg A(y, z)\}, \varepsilon_z \neg A \{\varepsilon_y A [y, \varepsilon_u \neg A(y, u)], z\}],$$

but it makes *evident* a fact of logical reasoning which was basic for Hilbert's programme, namely that in logical reasoning one never makes full use of the intended meaning of the transfinite symbols, in the following sense. $\varepsilon_z A(y, z)$ is intended as a choice function (some z_1 which satisfies $A(y, z)$ if such a z_1 exists, and an arbitrary value otherwise), and on this meaning the schema

$$A(y, b) \to A [y, \varepsilon_z A(y, z)] \tag{*}$$

is valid. Also, in an obvious way, the universal and existential quantifier can be defined by the use of the ε-symbol, and the schema (*) is enough to derive the usual schemata for the quantifiers. Now the gain is this: we see immediately that in any given proof, since (*) is applied only to finitely many y, one never needs the full extension of the choice function $\varepsilon_z A(y, z)$ for all y, and, moreover, in the course of the proof one does not need its "real" values, but, e.g. if (*) were the only application of the schema in the given proof, we could simply take b for $\varepsilon_z A(y, z)$ and still have a proof. Such considerations make the elimination of the ε-symbols (from a proof of a formula without ε-symbols) at least plausible. This idea was developed by Ackermann, presented in detail in [9], for predicate logic, and for number theory by Ackermann [1].—However, for practical applications it is best to apply the simple idea directly ([10], p. 171).

There is a formulation of the substitution problem which does not use the ε-symbol at all. If distinct ε-matrices are replaced by distinct function symbols f, the ε-formulæ reduce to the form $\Phi(f_1, \ldots, f_n) = 0$ where Φ is an elementary functional. The problem is to prove $(Ef_1) \ldots (Ef_n) [\Phi(f_1, \ldots, f_n) = 0]$; it is evident if this is true at all there are functions f^* which are zero except for a finite number of arguments, and can therefore be found by trial and error. The existence of functions f seems assured by the interpretation of ε-matrices as choice functions.

It seems understandable that Hilbert assumed that the *proof* of such an elementary matter as the existence of f^* must be a relatively minor task.[11]

---

[11] In [6], p. 317, Hilbert expresses this by saying that in the case of analysis "only" the proof of the purely arithmetical statement that the method terminates, is needed. (He had of course the feeling ([8], p. 187), that a purely arithmetical truth must have a purely arithmetical proof, which is refuted by Gödel's theorem if, e.g., "arithmetical" is interpreted as: expressible in classical number theory.)—Hilbert's "only" is misplaced: for after all, the statement of consistency is also purely arithmetical, so from the very start, "only" the proof of the main contention of his life was needed. However, from a mathematician's point of view, Hilbert's excitement at his reformulation of the consistency problem in terms of the convergence of the substitution method, is very natural: the latter problem, and particularly the problem of finding bounds, has the general look of a mathematical problem, while the consistency problem does not, even if it is formulated as a combinatorial problem (cf. end of para. 10).

For, if one regards metamathematical results as the absolute truths of mathematics ([8], p. 180) and the "transfinite" formulæ as ideal elements without significance outside the frame work of a formal system, it is natural to regard the metamathematical results as significant independently of their proof: though this, of course, does not mean that the proof is easy or even of an elementary character, one may be tempted to think so, e.g. because of the double meaning of "significant" (meaningful, but also: not trivial, not easy).

Open Problem. Notwithstanding the interest of alternative analyses of predicate logic and its extensions, to be described below, an examination of the substitution method applied to analysis seems very promising at the present time. Somewhere there is a combinatorial lemma lurking in the proofs which show that the substitution method terminates and which gives information about the solution of the functional equations $\Phi(f_1, \ldots, f_m) = 0$ mentioned above.[12]

11. Cut free formalizations. Other syntactic analyses of predicate logic were developed at Göttingen by Herbrand and Gentzen. They resulted in reformulations of predicate logic specially adapted for proofs of completeness.

One essential distinction between the two is that Herbrand considers only prenex formulæ and Gentzen arbitrary[13] formulæ. Herbrand and Gentzen gave explicit (primitive recursive) instructions for converting a proof with cuts into one without. But the simplest[14] exposition of, e.g. Herbrand's reformulation of the predicate calculus goes by way of the completeness theorem: if a (prenex) formula is not provable by Herbrand's rules ([9], p. 158, *b*) then it is not valid; so if a formula is provable in the ordinary way it must be provable by Herbrand's rules. But though further constructive analysis of the completeness proof is possible (cf. [10],p. 168), without it the rule for getting an Herbrand proof is only general recursive.

Given a prenex formula, say $(x) (Ey) (z) A (x, y, z)$, we ask: how could it be false? i.e. $(Ex) (y) (Ez) \neg A(x, y, z)$. There would have to be an element α such that $(y) (Ez) \neg A(\alpha, y, z)$ and without loss of generality we may as well call it 0, i.e. $(y) (Ez) \neg A(0, y, z)$. For $y = 0$ we must have $(Ez) \neg A(0, 0, z)$;

---

[12] This "lurking lemma" has since been formulated and proved by Tait [23] for the substitution method as applied to the formalism of arithmetic. It shows in particular in a natural way how the first ε-number enters into the problem: so it represents one of three independent analyses of the role of ε_0, the other two being the computational analysis of Gödel's functionals of para. 12 below, given in detail in [24], and the analysis of infinite cut free proof trees by means of ordinals (cf. footnote 16).

[13] The existence of prenex normal forms in classical logic makes this distinction more important in the analogous treatment of intuitionistic logic.

[14] I have not studied Herbrand's own publication. The exposition is suggested by Beth's semantic tableaux [2] which are a generalization of the criteria of refutability in [9].—The proof of Herbrand's theorem in [9] gives primitive recursive instructions.

we may as well take $z = 1$; for either $z \ne 0$, then calling $z = 1$ is permissible, if $z = 0$, then we must simply regard 1 as another name for the individual called 0; we must not take $z = 0$ in general. This explains the disparateness conditions of [9], p. 173. Now in order that $\neg\, A(0, 0, 1)$, there is a certain finite set of truth distributions on the prime formulæ of $\neg\, A(0, 0, 1)$ which may be recorded in the form of a finitary tree. Let R_i be the conjunction of the ith set of prime formulæ and negations of prime formulæ with arguments 0, 1 which make $\neg\, A(0, 0, 1)$ true. Now, for each i we consider all extensions $R_{i1}, \ldots, R_{im}$ of R_i by prime formulæ with arguments 0, 1, 2 which make $\neg\, A(0, 1, 2)$ true, $\neg\, A(0, 0, 1)$ being made true automatically since R_{ij} are extensions of R_i. We record this information in a tree

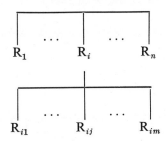

(If there is no extension of R_i, we stop the construction of R_{ij} and consider R_{i+1}, $i < n$.)

If this tree is unbounded, by the Unendlichkeitslemma, there is an infinite branch. If the prime formulæ of $(x)\,(Ey)\,(z)\,A(x, y, z)$ are given the truth values which they have on such a branch and if the variables range over the natural numbers then $\neg\, (x)\,(Ey)\,(z)\,A(x, y, z)$. (Completeness.)

If the tree is bounded, the formula $\neg\, (x)\,(Ey)\,(z)\,A(x, y, z)$ is not satisfiable at all. Now the whole tree can be converted into a *proof* of $(x)\,(Ey)\,(z)\,A(x, y, z)$. For, regard the numerals as variables. All we need are rules which allow us to infer $(x)\,(Ey)\,(z)\,A(x, y, z)$ from $A(0, 0, 1) \lor A(0, 1, 2) \lor \ldots \lor A(0, n, n + 1)$ for each n. The rules required are just Herbrand's rules. Thus we have not only a new formalization of, but also a cogent motivation for the choice of the rules.—Beth [2] has used the same idea for treating arbitrary formulæ and arriving at a variant of Gentzen's rules.

Here one conceives of a counter example to $(x)\,(Ey)\,(z)\,A(x, y, z)$ in terms of satisfying $\neg\, A\,[0, n, \varphi\,(n)]$ for some given disparate function φ and arbitrary numerals n. The impossibility of obtaining one, i.e. the breakdown of the construction above, yields a classical proof of $(x)\,(Ey)\,(z)\,A(x, y, z)$. Another conception of a counter example is to satisfy $\neg\, (x)\,(Ey)\,(z)\,A(x, y, z)$ in the prenex form $(Ex)\,(y)\,(Ez)\,\neg\, A(x, y, z)$ by a constant α and a function f, i.e. $(y)\,\neg\, A[\alpha, y, f(y)]$. The impossibility of obtaining one is expressed by $(Ey)\,A[\alpha, y, f(y)]$ and this can be expressed explicitly by means of functionals $\varphi_i(f, \alpha)$ (terms containing α and f) such that $\ldots \lor A[\alpha, \varphi_i(f, \alpha)$,

$f\{\varphi_i(f, \alpha)\}]$ ∨ ...[15]—This is only suitable for prenex formulæ (unless one uses functionals of higher type) but more suitable for arithmetic than the alternative described above.

12. Gödel's Intervention. There is a totally different analysis of classical proofs due to Gödel. First classical proofs are replaced by intuitionistic ones of (classically) equivalent theorems [5], then these proofs are analyzed by means of certain simple functionals of finite type, and these in turn are shown to be well defined by means of transfinite induction ($<\varepsilon_0$ for arithmetic with induction, $<\omega^2$ for arithmetic without). In this way the syntactic analysis is effected in several manageable steps, each of them of interest in itself.[16] For further details see Gödel's article in *Dialectica*, 12 (1958), 280–87.

II. SIGNIFICANCE OF SYNTACTIC ANALYSIS

In accordance with para. 3 and following Herbrand's lead we do not formulate the results of syntactic analysis as consistency theorems, but as interpretations in the sense of [10].

13. Mathematical Significance. To avoid repetition, we refer here to a recent discussion of this matter [10], in particular the application of an interpretation to the independence problem and other mathematical questions. To keep matters up to date we note that an interpretation in the sense of [10] of classical analysis in a quantifier-free *classical* theory of continuous functionals of finite type has been given whose constants are *recursive* continuous functionals [20].

As a result we have a new

Open Problem. To give explicit characterizations (schemata) of the particular recursive functionals actually needed for the interpretation of one of the current systems of analysis.[17]

For independence proofs it is desirable to give alternative schemata.

Digression. A totally different type of syntactic study of classical analysis is suggested by so-called predicative enterprises, e.g. [11], [16], [17]. It is evident that we do not get a model of classical analysis C simply by letting the variables of higher type[18] in a formula of C range over the sets of Wang's $\sum_\alpha$ for a fixed α[18]; for if α is not a limit number we conflict with the theorem

---

[15] This is used in [9] as an auxiliary in the proof of Herbrand's theorem. Below and in other publications we emphasize the independent significance of this step specially for the Hilbert programme for arithmetic.

[16] I regard the use of infinite induction by Schütte and Lorenzen as an intermediate step corresponding to the use of intuitionistic arithmetic in Gödel's work: it is to be supplemented by an analysis by means of ordinals.

[17] An important contribution to this problem is made in Spector's paper [22, section 10].

[18] *Type* in the sense of the simple theory of types; α is called a *level*.

of the least upper bound, and if α is a limit number we conflict with the existence of a non-denumerable set[19]. However, it seems promising to try this: given a proof in classical set theory to index the variables actually occurring in the proof by means of ordinals α so that the proof goes into a set of true statements in Spector's sense [16]. This would not give an interpretation in the sense of [10] because the statement $(Ef)\,(g)\,\mathrm{A}\,(f,g)$ is replaced by $(Ef_\alpha)\,(g_\alpha)\,\mathrm{A}\,(f,g)$, with special α, from which $(Ef)\,(g)\,\mathrm{A}\,(f,g)$ cannot in general be inferred, but nevertheless such an indexing would yield independence proofs if for certain formulæ of classical set theory there is no indexing which yields true statements (if indices α less than an appropriate bound are used).

The situation seems not unlike Euclidean geometry. For, just as in analysis, the most natural conception of a point ignores the matter of naming the point, i.e. how the real number is represented or by what constructions the point is reached from given points. But if one wants to assert the impossibility of, say, ruler and compass constructions, one introduces coordinates of a suitably restricted kind. Actually, the analogy is not complete because the field of real square root extensions of the rationals is a model of the Euclidean geometry considered, i.e. without the general continuity axiom, whereas the class of $\sum_\alpha$ sets is not a model of classical analysis if α is recursive.[19]

14. Remark on the methods used in syntactic analysis. Most of the mathematical applications of syntactic analysis, whether achieved or projected, depend little on restrictions of the metamathematical methods, except perhaps for primitive recursive bounds as in [10], p. 165. In [12] there is an attractive exposition of a non-finitist approach to the complex of Herbrand type theorems[20] for predicate calculi.—It is perhaps fair to say that the most significant results in this area were first discovered through a good understanding of finitist or intuitionistic conceptions simply because certain results are evident from a constructive meaning of the formulæ involved. But, at least once the results are known, one would expect to prove them more simply by full use of non-constructive methods.—The situation is different

[19] More precisely: (a) For countable α, Σ_α does not satisfy the axioms of classical analysis A if, as in [17], Σ_α contains an enumeration of the union of $\{\Sigma_\beta : \beta < \alpha\}$, possibly in addition to the usual ramified hierarchy (Σ_α^-). (b) For $\alpha < \omega_1$, i.e. recursive α, such an enumeration is explicitly definable in Σ_α^-. (c) Significant parts of A are realised in $\Sigma_{\alpha+\omega}^-$ (for all α) and in $\Sigma_{\omega_1}^-$, but e.g. the Cantor-Bendixson theorem is not realised in any Σ_β^-, $\beta \leq \omega_1$; for a survey cf. [21]. (d) There are denumerable α, $\alpha'(\alpha' > \alpha)$ such that, for $\beta > \alpha$, Σ_β^- satisfies A; for $\beta > \alpha'$, Σ_β^- satisfies classical set theory, and, in both cases, strong axioms of constructibility [18]. Thus the ramified theory is useful for the syntactic study of some subsystems of A by (c), for the reduction of extensions of A *to* A by (d), but not for the study *of* A itself.

[20] It should be observed that, in contrast to mere consistency problems, Herbrand-type theorems remain significant even if no restriction is imposed on the metamathematical methods in contrast to the consistency "proof" of para. 8.

at present in the study of systems of arithmetic such as Z (cf. end of para. 8).[21] There is a temptation to regard these results as artificial because the systems studied are fragments of arithmetic (by incompleteness) and may be freaks to which freakish methods are well adapted.—I do not believe that this is a fruitful account of the position; on the contrary, I believe we are here faced with a very good problem of foundations. But I do not have a satisfactory answer: we have come back to the third problem of para. 4 (cf. para. 18).

15. Modified Hilbert Programme. We take for granted Gödel's two incompleteness theorems and that finitist proof in its original sense does not go essentially beyond classical arithmetic ([8], p. 212); the latter would follow if the formulation of finitist proof sketched below is accepted. Thus it is necessary to use a hierarchy of constructive methods for the study (interpretation) of axiomatic systems. As we said above, we regard Herbrand's theorem as the paradigm for such an interpretation.[22]

The question is of course which aspects of Herbrand's theorem are essential for the present purpose, namely the understanding of transfinite symbols, and which are details, perhaps of importance elsewhere.

As in para. 11, according to Herbrand, $\mathscr{A}$, say $(x)\,(Ey)\,(z)\,A(x, y, z)$, is provable in the predicate calculus, if and only if one of a sequence of quantifier-free A_n is provable, A_n being of the form

$$A\{\alpha, \varphi_1(f), f\,[\varphi_1(f)]\} \vee \ldots \vee A\{\alpha, \varphi_{p(n)}(f), f\,[\varphi_{p(n)}(f)]\}$$

Note in passing that quite trivially the sequence could be replaced by a single formula with a constructive metamathematical quantifier $(\exists n)$, namely $(\exists n)\,A\,(n)$, where $A\,(n)$ denotes A_n. (In the case of number theory and analysis we do not even need a metamathematical quantifier, but a constructive existential quantifier $(\exists \varphi)$, φ ranging over a suitable class of recursive functionals.)

$\mathscr{A}$ and A_n are in the close relation that $\mathscr{A}$ can be proved from A_n by means of Herbrand's rules which have the property that it is *decidable*[23] for given $\mathscr{A}$ and A_n, whether $\mathscr{A}$ be so provable from A_n. What seems to me significant about this is that the logical relation between $\mathscr{A}$ and A_n considered is

---

[21] Cf. [10] and footnote 8.

[22] In the sense of [10]. The mathematical use of interpretations for independence proofs, etc., is discussed elsewhere and is here taken for granted. Tarski and Mostowski [14] have protested against my use of the word "interpretation". There are two issues: (i) It clashes with Tarski's use of the word in his book *Undecidable Theories*. (ii) Does it express at least one important meaning of the word in common use?—As to (i) there is a perfectly good word current for Tarski's meaning, namely model, and in case of doubt, one could use "formal" or "syntactic" model; also Tarski's book appeared much later than my first use of J.S.L., vol. 16 (1951), pp. 241–67. But (ii) raises a serious question if one is interested in the notion of a "reduction"; the discussion below was stimulated by Mostowski's criticism *lc*.

[23] Since in any application of Herbrand's rules the number of disjunction symbols or of free variables is reduced.

essentially more elementary than the logical relations discussed, namely those of the (undecidable) predicate calculus. In this sense A_n expresses the full content of $\mathscr{A}$.

Furthermore, as in Bernays' consistency theorem, if $\mathscr{B}$ is provable from $\mathscr{A}$ by means of transfinite symbols and $\mathscr{A}$, interpreted as one of the A_n, is finitistically true, then so is some B_m.[24]—It is natural that a good understanding of the use of transfinite symbols should include the consideration of implications $\mathscr{A} \vdash \mathscr{B}$ since their purpose is not only to produce tautologies, but also, as we said above, to step from extra-logical axioms to theorems.

This analysis led very obviously to the notion of interpretation, in particular, in finitist (constructive) systems. The conditions given are intended to express what one would reasonably expect of an understanding of transfinite symbols by, or of a reduction to, finitist (constructive) means. Whether they do so, seems a proper subject for discussion by philosophers. I myself would apply the word *reduction* only to an interpretation of a system in one of its subsystems where the primitive notions and theorems of the latter are a subset of the former.—In particular, I do not call the set theoretical definitions of natural numbers or finiteness (cf. footnote 7) a reduction because, though we now have only the one primitive notion of a set, its content is not clearly comparable with that of the others.—Further I should require the reduction to be established by (sound) methods which can be formalized in the subsystem itself.

For me the "reduction" of primitive notions is not a matter of principle. A reduction does not eliminate them since merely to see that a proposed reduction is correct one has to start with the primitive notion considered anyway. But in practice such reductions can be extraordinarily fertile if for no other reason than that they permit the formulation of new questions: of $(x)\,(Ey)\,A\,(x, y)$ we ask only if it is valid or not, of $A[\alpha, t_1\,(\alpha)] \vee \dots \vee A[\alpha, t_n(\alpha)]$ we ask what the complexity of the terms $t_i(\alpha)$ is. This is typical of the increased information contained in Herbrand's theorem. Another example is the arithmetization of the completeness theorem in [9] compared with the mere assertion of completeness. What kind of additional information is regarded as providing a satisfactory answer is a similar kind of question to the one about the significance of finitist proof; see also end of para. 18.

Open Problem. For a consistently constructive interpretation of analysis (para. 13) it is necessary to prove constructively the existence of the continuous functionals of whatever schema is produced in the solution of the open problem of para. 13. This problem is analogous to the proof of existence of Gödel's functionals in para. 12.

16. Remark. It seems desirable to discuss the bearing of an *interpretation* on Brouwer's objection that consistency leaves open the possibility that

---

[24] This is really clear for an applied predicate calculus only, cf. in note on the pure predicate calculus in the remark below.

some provable theorems are intuitively false. Remembering the difference
between the intuitionistic and truth functional meaning of the logical constants one must use an appropriate translation of classical theorems before
speaking of their being intuitively false. Gödel elucidated Brouwer's point
most elegantly: in as much as consistency does not ensure ω-consistency,
Brouwer was evidently right (even if one translates classical (Ex) A (x) into
intuitive $\sim(x) \sim$A(x)); on the other hand for classical number theory in
particular Brouwer's objection did not arise because of the translation into
Heyting's number theory. In the case of Herbrand's own interpretation the
following points should be noted. Using Hilbert's terminology it is clear that
quantifier-free formulæ, i.e. those of the elementary calculus with free variables
of [9], are regarded as the "real" elements, others as ideal and in need of an
interpretation. Now, Brouwer would certainly not accept this because on his
interpretation of propositional formulæ, the theorems of the classical propositional calculus are not valid; in particular, he interprets A v B as: A is provable
or B is provable; also he wishes to substitute for propositional letters incom-
pletely defined propositions, e.g. propositions containing a parameter ranging
over free choice sequences; under this interpretation A v $\sim$A is evidently not
valid. On the other hand, if a finitist had made Brouwer's objection, Gödel's
translation into Heyting's arithmetic would not have been sufficient, and to
answer it something like the extensions of Herbrand's theorem *lc* would have
been necessary. However, now the formulæ of the classical propositional
calculus could be regarded as "real" elements because for finitist propositions
the truth-functional interpretation of the logical connectives is applicable.

We note in passing that just as there was a Hilbert programme for understanding classical transfinite machinery from a finitist point of view so there
is an analogous programme for understanding intuitionistic machinery.
Certainly as far as independence results are concerned, the latter is more
rewarding if for no other reason than that it is less familiar.

FINITIST PROOF

17. Work is in progress[25] on a characterization of finitist proofs in the
usual sense: a formal system is described such that (i) each formal proof of
the system is recognized as a finitist proof, and (ii) each formula in the notation of the system is asserted to be provable in the system if it is provable by
finitist methods at all. The variables of the system are of two types (natural
numbers and free function variables from the natural numbers to the natural
numbers though the latter can be avoided), the constants are particular
numerals, certain constant functionals and (finitist) proof predicates, the
last two being introduced only after certain existential statements have already

---

[25] This has since been presented in the sketch [21], where the characterization of other
informal notions of proof is also considered.—My interest in a definition of "finitist proofs"
was reawakened by conversations with K. Gödel, 1955–1957.

been established. The idea corresponds closely to what Hilbert imagined the whole mathematics to be like, namely an interplay between formal proofs and metamathematics ([8], p. 174–175). Finitist proofs constitute then the least class of proofs closed under the following condition (and containing a certain obvious minimum): (i) if a proof predicate has been shown by finitist methods to satisfy the relevant existential conditions then it is finitist too, and (ii) if Prov (n, m) is a finitist proof predicate already introduced, and if, with free variable n, (Ep) Prov $[p, \ulcorner A\ (0^{(n)})\urcorner]$ is established by a finitist proof, then so is $A(n)$;—by Gödel's theorem this closure condition can be achieved only if no predicate of the system itself is both extensionally equivalent to the proof predicate of the whole system and also satisfies the conditions on a proof predicate imposed in Gödel's second undecidability theorem.

Evidently, there is no reason why the class of theorems should not be recursively enumerable: in fact, it is. A finitist could even conjecture that a particular enumeration gives precisely the class of finitistically provable theorems, e.g. in the notation of primitive recursive arithmetic, but this would be, for him, an empirical conjecture incapable of (finitist) proof.

Just as with the class of recursive functions, the only completeness properties of our class of proofs are certain closure properties, i.e. it is the least class with these closure properties.

The main open "problem" is to discover intuitively really convincing completeness properties, aided of course by more detailed information about the class itself, cf. para. 4 above.

As pointed out in para. 4, other classes of constructive proofs should be studied in addition to finitist proofs. In particular, as Bernays mentioned in [3], p. 151, the use of the first ε-number is intermediate between finitist and full intuitionist mathematics. It would be interesting to motivate the choice of some subclass of intuitionist proofs which includes the use, made e.g. in [1], of the first ε-number. (I have not done this to my own satisfaction even for the notion of finitist proof.)

18. General Remarks. Since our understanding of the notion of "constructive proof" and of its special case "finitist proof" is not too detailed, the very meaning of Hilbert's programme is not too precise. However, one can summarize what parts of Hilbert's programme are settled on the basis of our partial understanding of these notions (cf. end of section 1). If one prefers a more formal approach, one would begin with a (partial) axiomatization of the notions of "constructive proof" or "finitist proof" which contains only trivial properties of these notions, and then investigate from what additional axioms for these notions the assertions below can be formally derived.

Hilbert's programme in the wide sense wanted to establish the "adequacy" of deductive formalisms for the representation of intuitive branches of mathematics. Their inadequacy (in the case of arithmetic) is established by Gödel's first incompleteness theorem on the basis of our partial understanding of the notions involved, namely the recursive enumerability of the set of theorems of any deductive formalism in the original sense; then there is an A such that [(⌜A⌝ is a formal theorem) → A] is not formally derivable, and so the formalism cannot formally be proved to be sound if it is sound (for this A); further, it is inadequate, where by "adequacy" one means: if A then (⌜A⌝ is a theorem). It is interesting to observe that this inadequacy of the usual formalisms is connected with their surprising adequacy in another sense, namely the possibility of representing all recursive functions, at numerical arguments, by terms of the usual formal systems. As far as I know, before Gödel's work it was not even realized that all multiply recursive predicates could be defined in first order arithmetic, even when symbols for primitive recursive functions are added; although multiply recursive predicates were accepted as finitist. In fact, the schemata for recursions of higher type which Hilbert considered in [6], p. 295 and elsewhere, could, at least at first sight, be expected to "transcend" even analysis. On the other hand, as we know now, the proofs in present-day number theory can indeed be rather easily formalized in Hilbert's own formal system Z of arithmetic by means of the devices introduced by Gödel. So, while in Hilbert's days the empirical evidence (from "ordinary" number theory) for the adequacy of Z was slight, at the present time it would be overwhelming! It seems clear therefore that Hilbert's grounds for the feasibility of his programme must have rested on general philosophical considerations, perhaps the following: All that we "do" in mathematics (or: in thinking generally) is to operate with symbols, and that is all we "really" communicate to one another. (Hilbert sets great store by the "finiteness of our thoughts", both in principle ([8, p. 187]) and in proof theory, cf. para. 10 above.) As far as theorems of a transfinite character are concerned, we have proofs: their "truth" is metaphysical or poetic, and any reference to their truth must be "ultimately" reducible to assertions of formal derivability. The notion of mathematical truth can have no place in mathematics as we know it.—While it would be generally granted that this reflection itself is metaphysical or poetic it is convincing because in "ordinary" mathematics there is not the slightest hint of any practical use of the distinction between "truth" and "formal derivability" (even when rules of derivability are made explicit). The first thing to do, if one takes this distinction at all seriously, is to consider the assertion: (⌜A⌝ is a formal theorem) → A. Expressing this assertion by means of an arithmetic formula is an essential step towards the incompleteness results. Also, the truth of each such formula is evident from the interpretation of the formal rules of proof and not from the combinatorial use of these rules. In other words, each such formula is obtained from the intended meaning of the formal systems considered, i.e. accepted on the basis of this meaning, without being formally implied by the given rules (unless A itself is so implied). Each such formula would be accepted as an axiom for arithmetic. Thus we have here an illustration of how one chooses axioms for formal systems from the intended meaning of the formal systems to be considered. The part of mathematical activity concerned with a good choice of axioms had no place in Hilbert's "official" conception of mathematics. If there is any real justification for calling Hilbert's approach "formalist" it is certainly this deficiency of Hilbert's official conception of mathematics and not his use of syntactic formulations in the foundations of mathematics (cf. para. 1).

Next consider Hilbert's programme in the narrow sense, namely to prove the consistency of the usual formalizations of mathematics by finitist means. Strictly speaking, he had a number of intermediate conjectures, too, such as the decidability of arithmetic or the somewhat peculiar assertion (*): it is consistent to assume that every problem of arithmetic is solvable. But a detailed discussion seems of little more than biographical interest, since these conjectures are either settled or genuinely ill formulated: if (*) means that one may consistently add to formal arithmetic the statement:

For every closed formula A *either* A *is a formal theorem or* $\neg$A *is a formal theorem,*

then the conjecture follows trivially from Gödel's result that one may even add consistently the assertion that the formal system is inconsistent. It is unlikely that Hilbert was satisfied by this manner of establishing his conjecture. Naturally, for the narrower programme an impossibility proof requires a more detailed analysis of the notions involved than for Hilbert's general programme. In particular, Gödel's second incompleteness theorem is not conclusive until reasons are adduced which show that all finitist theorems are included among the formal theorems of the system considered. As regards a characterization of finitist proof the sketch [21] leaves open the problem of upper bounds for the set of finitist theorems, and one may have to be content to obtain bounds in stages. It is, for instance, quite likely that more convincing arguments can be given, i.e. fewer assumptions on the notion of finitist proof are needed, for showing that all finitist functions are ordinal recursive of order $< \varepsilon_0$ than, e.g. for showing that the consistency of first order arithmetic cannot be proved by finitist means. (In other words, the impossibility of a finitist proof for the ω-consistency of arithmetic may be genuinely easier to establish.) We may note in passing that current mathematics illustrates the use of different properties of intuitive intensional concepts in different theorems. Thus Gödel's first incompleteness theorem, which is concerned with Hilbert's general programme, uses substantially fewer properties of the intuitive notion of "representability" of (the syntactic) properties in a formal system than the second, which is concerned with the narrower programme. The first theorem requires that the set of theorems be representable, i.e. the formal system considered may be "identified" with its set of theorems (i.e. all we need know about it is its set of theorems), while the second requires certain (internal) properties of the proof relation to be formally derivable. This will be the case if one "identifies" the formal system with its set of production rules but not if one identifies it with the set of theorems since this set can be generated by different rules. (One could state this explicitly in the following formulation: *If a formula can be proved in* S *to express the consistency of* S, *and* S *is consistent, then this formula cannot be proved in* S; certain minimal conditions on the notion "expressing the consistency of S" are formulated in [9].)

It is to be emphasized that the remarks above do no more than assert a conviction that the notions of "constructive" and "finitist" are ripe for a systematic study. The reformulations of known theorems given above indicate that our conception of these notions is coherent because these reformulations are not forced.

We conclude with some pragmatic remarks on the choice of a significant class of constructive methods which goes beyond finitist mathematics. Here one has to recognize the following difference between the untutored notion of constructivity of the "ordinary" mathematician (interested in constructivity) and the one that seems to be forced on one if one tries to be coherent. Naïvely, "constructive" is applied to procedures or instructions for manipulating finite configurations (as in the case of finitist mathematics), but not to operations on objects of higher type or logical operations (e.g. on proofs with meaning, as in the case of intuitionistic mathematics). The naïve conception does not get into difficulties in familiar parts of mathematics, because, once constructive definitions are given, the proofs are in general quite unproblematic, cf. footnote 6 on p. 162 above. On the basis of this experience the mathematician is ill prepared to judge the constructivity of, e.g. definitions by means of recursion of the form $f(n) = g\{n, f[\tau(n)]\}$ if $\tau(n) <\cdot n$ and $f(n) = g(n, 0)$ if $\tau(n) \not<\cdot n$, where g, τ are constructive functions, $<\cdot$ a well-founded constructive ordering (but may not have been proved to be well founded by "constructive means"). This is precisely the situation in several consistency proofs for arithmetic, e.g. [1]. If one thinks in terms of (idealized) machines, the above definition is a proper instruction, provided $g, \tau, <\cdot$ are constructive, but the *proof* of well-ordering is irrelevant. It is likely that, on this naïve conception, recursion on (the usual orderings whose ordinal is) the first ε-number would be more evidently "constructive" than Gödel's simple functionals quoted in para. 12 above, which involve variables of higher type.

On the other hand, both philosophically and pragmatically, there is strong evidence that a more coherent theory of constructivity is possible if this notion is applied also to logic (inference), in particular to the interpretation of logical constants. For instance, philosophically, it is clear that there is a gap in accepting as constructive the definitions by transfinite recursion of the preceding paragraph if no condition is imposed on the proof of well-ordering: one certainly could not claim that the definition has been justified on constructive principles. Pragmatically, i.e. for the purpose of obtaining, in a systematic manner, well-rounded mathematical theories, the use of the primitive notion of a constructive proof has definitely been fruitful. One example is Gödel's use of intuitionistic logic as an intermediary in the consistency proof of arithmetic (cf. para. 12), another is the use of generalized inductive definitions based on intuitionistic logic, which explains the remarkable fact that many functions defined on inductive sets (e.g. Church-Kleene ordinal notations) are recursive: this is mysterious from the non-constructive approach to recursion theory because the inductive sets are highly non-recursive, and one sees no reason why definitions by transfinite induction on such sets should lead to recursive objects. But, also the following more isolated example is instructive.

Suppose we ask for a modification of classical arithmetic which leaves the constructive theorems (of the form $(x)(Ey)A(x, y)$ with quantifier-free A) unchanged, but makes every prenex theorem recursively satisfiable. This would express more or less what the naïve constructive mathematician described above might be after. In such a modification the class of quantifier-free theorems is the same as in classical arithmetic, while the class of theorems containing quantifiers is changed. Who would have thought of modifying only the rules for the propositional connectives, and not for quantifiers, which is precisely what is done in intuitionistic mathematics. However, if one has the concept of constructive proof and Heyting's interpretation of the logical constants, this step is inevitable. Moreover, while the general problem (of finding rules of proof valid for the constructive interpretation of the logical constants) has a high degree of determinateness,[26] the naïve constructivist's question certainly does not have a unique answer. Thus $[\sim p \to (q \vee r)]$ $\to [(\sim p \to q) \vee (\sim p \to r)]$ could be added to the propositional axiom schemata of Heyting's arithmetic, or, again, for primitive recursive $A(x)$, $\sim (x)A(x) \to (\exists x) \sim A(x)$; both these additions are nonconservative, since the former schema is not a theorem of Heyting's propositional calculus and the latter is deducible in his arithmetic only if $(\exists x) \sim A(x) \vee (x)A(x)$ is too.

More generally, even if one is primarily interested in developing systematically a smooth-running formalism, it is necessary to develop a coherent philosophical notion of constructivity. The conception itself (which applies to functions, proofs, etc.) has a degree of generality which transcends any mathematical treatment, but it is the business of pure mathematics to develop it within suitable specific contexts. In this respect it is like the notions of structure, truth, or proof. It may be remarked that I myself have come to recognize the need for, and usefulness of, a (non-finitist) notion of constructive proof only very reluctantly.

COMPLETENESS OF THE PREDICATE CALCULUS

19. I wish to emphasize two points of interest of the completeness problem; namely it illustrates (i) the mathematical treatment of a concept of great

---

[26] Even though the possibility of a (provably) complete formalization is doubtful.

generality in a specific context, as mentioned in the preceding paragraph, (ii) the limitations of a purely finitist metamathematics.

If $A(P_1, \ldots, P_n)$ is a (closed) formula of the predicate calculus whose predicate symbols are $P_1, \ldots, P_n$, then it is valid if and only if for every domain D of individuals and predicates P_i^o, $1 \leq i \leq n$, defined in D, $A(P_i^o, \ldots, P_n^o)$ is true on the usual interpretation of the logical symbols. The calculus is complete if every valid formula is provable in it. The reference to arbitrary domains here is a typical case of philosophical generality, reminiscent of the paradoxes. It would be disturbing if the paradoxes led to the formalization of logic and the justification of the formalization led back to the very notions involved in the paradoxes! Now, if one merely wishes to show that every theorem of the calculus is valid, one considers any particular set D, presumed to be well defined, and follows out the rules of the calculus with quantifiers ranging over this set; there is no generation of new sets, which is the typical step in the paradoxes. But, if one shows that every valid formula is provable, the premise itself involves quantification over all sets. As long as one has a precisely limited notation, one may expect to sharpen the result by restricting the sets for which the formula has to be valid. Gödel shows that for each $A(P_1, \ldots, P_n)$ there is a *single* set of predicates P_i^A defined over the domain D_o of natural numbers such that instead of the validity of A we merely need the truth of $A(P_1^A, \ldots, P_n^A)$ in D_o.

From a finitist point of view even this is not enough since in general the P_i^A cannot be chosen to be constructive at all. There are two finitist versions of the result, namely (a) if $A(P_1^A, \ldots, P_n^A)$ is provable in Z then $A(P_1, \ldots, P_n)$ is provable in the predicate calculus, or the stronger form (b) $A(P_1^A, \ldots, P_n^A)$ → "$A(P_1, \ldots, P_n)$ is provable in the predicate calculus", the implication being provable in Z for each A where the statement in inverted commas denotes some natural arithmetization of itself.—It should be remembered that these versions are not what Hilbert originally required ([6], p. 322) namely that if $A(P_1, \ldots, P_n)$ is not provable in the predicate calculus, $\neg A(P_1^A, \ldots, P_n^A)$ should actually be provable in Z. There is no recursively enumerable extension of the predicate calculus with this property. (Hilbert evidently assumed Z to be complete and therefore did not distinguish between these versions which are equivalent on his assumption.)

Of course, on occasions the extra information contained in the finitist versions is needed. But the finitist point of view is simply not appropriate for discussing the general problem of completeness.

REFERENCES

1. Ackermann, W., "Zur Widerspruchsfreiheit der reinen Zahlentheorie," *Math. Annalen*, 117 (1940), 162–94.
2. Beth, E. W., *Crise de la raison et la logique*. Paris, 1957.

3. Bernays, P., "Sur les questions méthodologiques actuelles de la théorie hilbertienne de la démonstration," *Les Entretiens de Zurich sur les fondements et la méthode des sciences mathématiques, 1938*, pp. 144–52, Zurich, 1941.

4. ———, "Von der Syntax der Sprache zur Philosophie der Wissenschaften," *Dialectica*, 11 (1957), 233–46.

5. Gödel, K., "Zur intuitionistischen Arithmetik und Zahlentheorie," *Ergebnisse eines mathematischen Kolloquiums*, 4 (1933), 34–38.

6. Hilbert, D., *Grundlagen der Geometrie*, 7th ed. Leipzig und Berlin, 1930.

7. ———, "Die Grundlegung der elementaren Zahlenlehre," *Math. Annalen*, 104 (1931), 485–94.

8. ———, *Gesammelte Abhandlungen*, vol. 3. Berlin, 1935.

9. ——— and Bernays, P., *Grundlagen der Mathematik*, vol. 2. Berlin, 1939.

10. Kreisel, G., "Mathematical Significance of Consistency Proofs," *J.S.L.*, 23 (1958), 155–82.

11. Lorenzen, P., *Einführung in die operative Logik und Mathematik*. Berlin-Göttingen-Heidelberg, 1955.

12. Los, J., Mostowski, A., Rasiowa, H., "A Proof of Herbrand's Theorem," *Journal de mathématiques pures et appliquées*, 35 (1956), 58–61.—Corr. 40 (1961), 129–134.

13. Mostowski, A., "On Recursive Models of Formalized Arithmetic," *Bulletin de l'Académie polonaise des sciences*, Class III, 5 (1957), 705–10.

14. ———, Review, *J.S.L.*, 22 (1957), 304–6.

15. Von Neumann, J., "Zur Hilbertschen Beweistheorie," *Math. Zeitschrift*, 26 (1927), 1–46.

16. Spector, C., "Recursive Ordinals and Predicative Set Theory," *Summaries of talks at the Summer Institute of Symbolic Logic in 1957 at Cornell University*, vol. 3, pp. 377–82.

17. Wang, Hao, "Formalization of Mathematics," *J.S.L.*, 19 (1954), 241–66.

18. Cohen, Paul J., "A Minimal Model for Set Theory," *Bull. Amer. Math. Soc.*, 69 (1963), 537–40.

19. Kreisel, G., "Interpretation of Classical Analysis by Means of Constructive Functionals of Higher Type," *Constructivity in Mathematics*. Amsterdam: North Holland Publishing Company, 1959, pp. 101–28.

20. ———, "Ordinal Logics and the Characterization of Informal Concepts of Proof," *Proceedings of the International Congress of Mathematicians, Edinburgh 1958*. Cambridge: Cambridge University Press, 1960, pp. 389–99.

21. ———, "La Prédicativité," *Bull. Soc. Math. France*, 88 (1960), 371–91.

22. Spector, C., "Provably Recursive Functionals of Analysis: a Consistency Proof of Analysis by an Extension of Principles Formulated in Current Intuitionistic Mathematics," *Proceedings of Symposia in Pure Mathematics, Amer. Math. Soc.*, 5 (1962), 1–27.

23. Tait, W. W., "Functionals Defined by Transfinite Recursion," to appear.

24. ———, "Infinitely Long Terms of Transfinite Types," *Formal Systems and Recursive Functions*, Amsterdam, North Holland Publishing Company, to appear.

ABSTRACT

Hilbert's plan for understanding the concept of infinity required the elimination of non-finitist machinery from proofs of finitist assertions. The failure of the original plan leads to a hierarchy of progressively less elementary, but still constructive methods instead of finitist ones (modified Hilbert programme). A mathematical proof of this failure requires a definition of "finitist".—The paper sketches the three principal methods for the syntactic analysis of non-constructive mathematics, the resulting consistency proofs and constructive interpretations, modelled on Herbrand's theorem, and their mathematical and logical consequences. A characterization of finitist proofs is sketched. A remark on the completeness of the predicate calculus concludes the paper. Throughout open problems and alternative approaches are emphasized.

Part Two

Part Two

W. V. Quine

A curious thing about the ontological problem is its simplicity. It can be put in three Anglo-Saxon monosyllables: 'What is there?' It can be answered, moreover, in a word—'Everything'—and everyone will accept this answer as true. However, this is merely to say that there is what there is. There remains room for disagreement over cases; and so the issue has stayed alive down the centuries.

Suppose now that two philosophers, McX and I, differ over ontology. Suppose McX maintains there is something which I maintain there is not. McX can, quite consistently with his own point of view, describe our difference of opinion by saying that I refuse to recognize certain entities. I should protest, of course, that he is wrong in his formulation of our disagreement, for I maintain that there are no entities, of the kind which he alleges, for me to recognize; but my finding him wrong in his formulation of our disagreement is unimportant, for I am committed to considering him wrong in his ontology anyway.

When *I* try to formulate our difference of opinion, on the other hand, I seem to be in a predicament. I cannot admit that there are some things which McX countenances and I do not, for in admitting that there are such things I should be contradicting my own rejection of them.

It would appear, if this reasoning were sound, that in any ontological dispute the proponent of the negative side suffers the disadvantage of not being able to admit that his opponent disagrees with him.

This is the old Platonic riddle of nonbeing. Nonbeing must in some sense be, otherwise what is it that there is not? This tangled doctrine might be

Reprinted by kind permission of the author and publisher from W. V. Quine, From a Logical Point of View (*Cambridge: Harvard University Press,* 1953), *pp.* 1–19. *Copyright* 1953 *by The President and Fellows of Harvard College.*

nicknamed *Plato's beard*; historically it has proved tough, frequently dulling the edge of Occam's razor.

It is some such line of thought that leads philosophers like McX to impute being where they might otherwise be quite content to recognize that there is nothing. Thus, take Pegasus. If Pegasus *were* not, McX argues, we should not be talking about anything when we use the word; therefore it would be nonsense to say even that Pegasus is not. Thinking to show thus that the denial of Pegasus cannot be coherently maintained, he concludes that Pegasus is.

McX cannot, indeed, quite persuade himself that any region of space-time, near or remote, contains a flying horse of flesh and blood. Pressed for further details on Pegasus, then, he says that Pegasus is an idea in men's minds. Here, however, a confusion begins to be apparent. We may for the sake of argument concede that there is an entity, and even a unique entity (though this is rather implausible), which is the mental Pegasus-idea; but this mental entity is not what people are talking about when they deny Pegasus.

McX never confuses the Parthenon with the Parthenon-idea. The Parthenon is physical; the Parthenon-idea is mental (according anyway to McX's version of ideas, and I have no better to offer). The Parthenon is visible; the Parthenon-idea is invisible. We cannot easily imagine two things more unlike, and less liable to confusion, than the Parthenon and the Parthenon-idea. But when we shift from the Parthenon to Pegasus, the confusion sets in —for no other reason than that McX would sooner be deceived by the crudest and most flagrant counterfeit than grant the nonbeing of Pegasus.

The notion that Pegasus must be, because it would otherwise be nonsense to say even that Pegasus is not, has been seen to lead McX into an elementary confusion. Subtler minds, taking the same precept as their starting point, come out with theories of Pegasus which are less patently misguided than McX's, and correspondingly more difficult to eradicate. One of these subtler minds is named, let us say, Wyman. Pegasus, Wyman maintains, has his being as an unactualized possible. When we say of Pegasus that there is no such thing, we are saying, more precisely, that Pegasus does not have the special attribute of actuality. Saying that Pegasus is not actual is on a par, logically, with saying that the Parthenon is not red; in either case we are saying something about an entity whose being is unquestioned.

Wyman, by the way, is one of those philosophers who have united in ruining the good old word 'exist'. Despite his espousal of unactualized possibles, he limits the word 'existence' to actuality—thus preserving an illusion of ontological agreement between himself and us who repudiate the rest of his bloated universe. We have all been prone to say, in our common-sense usage of 'exist', that Pegasus does not exist, meaning simply that there is no such entity at all. If Pegasus existed he would indeed be in space and time, but only because the word 'Pegasus' has spatio-temporal connotations, and not because 'exists' has spatio-temporal connotations. If spatio-temporal reference is lacking when we affirm the existence of the cube root of 27, this is simply because a cube root is not a spatio-temporal kind of thing, and not because we are being ambiguous in our use of 'exist'.[1] However, Wyman, in an ill-conceived effort to appear agreeable, genially grants us the nonexistence of Pegasus and then, contrary to what *we* meant by nonexistence of Pegasus, insists that Pegasus *is*. Existence is one thing, he says, and subsistence is another. The only way I know of coping with this obfuscation of issues is to *give* Wyman the word 'exist'. I'll try not to use it again; I still have 'is'. So much for lexicography; let's get back to Wyman's ontology.

Wyman's overpopulated universe is in many ways unlovely. It offends the aesthetic sense of us who have a taste for desert landscapes, but this is not the worst of it. Wyman's slum of possibles is a breeding ground for disorderly elements. Take, for instance, the possible fat man in that doorway; and, again, the possible bald man in that doorway. Are they the same possible man, or two possible men? How do we decide? How many possible men are there in that doorway? Are there more possible thin ones than fat ones? How many of them are alike? Or would their being alike make them one? Are no *two* possible things alike? Is this the same as saying that it is impossible for two things to be alike? Or, finally, is the concept of identity simply inapplicable to unactualized possibles? But what sense can be found in talking of entities which cannot meaningfully be said to be identical with themselves and distinct from one another? These elements are well-nigh incorrigible. By a Fregean therapy of individual concepts, some effort might be made at rehabilitation; but I feel we'd do better simply to clear Wyman's slum and be done with it.

Possibility, along with the other modalities of necessity and impossibility and contingency, raises problems upon which I do not mean to imply that we should turn our backs. But we can at least limit modalities to whole statements. We may impose the adverb 'possibly' upon a statement as a whole, and we may well worry about the semantical analysis of such usage; but little real advance in such analysis is to be hoped for in expanding our universe to include so-called *possible entities*. I suspect that the main motive for this expansion is simply the old notion that Pegasus, for example, must be because otherwise it would be nonsense to say even that he is not.

Still, all the rank luxuriance of Wyman's universe of possibles would seem to come to naught when we make a slight change in the example and speak not of Pegasus but of the round square cupola on Berkeley College. If, unless Pegasus were, it would be nonsense to say that he is not, then by the same

---

[1] The impulse to distinguish terminologically between existence as applied to objects actualized somewhere in space-time and existence (or subsistence or being) as applied to other entities arises in part, perhaps, from an idea that the observation of nature is relevant only to questions of existence of the first kind. But this idea is readily refuted by counter-instances such as 'the ratio of the number of centaurs to the number of unicorns'. If there were such a ratio, it would be an abstract entity, viz. a number. Yet it is only by studying nature that we conclude that the number of centaurs and the number of unicorns are both 0 and hence that there is no such ratio.

token, unless the round square cupola on Berkeley College were, it would be nonsense to say that it is not. But, unlike Pegasus, the round square cupola on Berkeley College cannot be admitted even as an unactualized *possible*. Can we drive Wyman now to admitting also a realm of unactualized impossibles? If so, a good many embarrassing questions could be asked about them. We might hope even to trap Wyman in contradictions, by getting him to admit that certain of these entities are at once round and square. But the wily Wyman chooses the other horn of the dilemma and concedes that it is nonsense to say that the round square cupola on Berkeley College is not. He says that the phrase 'round square cupola' is meaningless.

Wyman was not the first to embrace this alternative. The doctrine of the meaningless of contradictions runs away back. The tradition survives, moreover, in writers who seem to share none of Wyman's motivations. Still, I wonder whether the first temptation to such a doctrine may not have been substantially the motivation which we have observed in Wyman. Certainly the doctrine has no intrinsic appeal; and it has led its devotees to such quixotic extremes as that of challenging the method of proof by *reductio ad absurdum*—a challenge in which I sense a *reductio ad absurdum* of the doctrine itself.

Moreover, the doctrine of meaninglessness of contradictions has the severe methodological drawback that it makes it impossible, in principle, ever to devise an effective test of what is meaningful and what is not. It would be forever impossible for us to devise systematic ways of deciding whether a string of signs made sense—even to us individually, let alone other people —or not. For it follows from a discovery in mathematical logic due to Church that there can be no generally applicable test of contradictoriness.

I have spoken disparagingly of Plato's beard, and hinted that it is tangled. I have dwelt at length on the inconveniences of putting up with it. It is time to think about taking steps.

Russell, in his theory of so-called singular descriptions, showed clearly how we might meaningfully use seeming names without supposing that there be the entities allegedly named. The names to which Russell's theory directly applies are complex descriptive names such as 'the author of *Waverley*', 'the present King of France', 'the round square cupola on Berkeley College'. Russell analyzes such phrases systematically as fragments of the whole sentences in which they occur. The sentence 'The author of *Waverley* was a poet', for example, is explained as a whole as meaning 'Someone (better: something) wrote *Waverley* and was a poet, and nothing else wrote *Waverley*'. (The point of this added clause is to affirm the uniqueness which is implicit in the word 'the', in '*the* author of *Waverley*'.) The sentence 'The round square cupola on Berkeley College is pink' is explained as 'Something is round and square and is a cupola on Berkeley College and is pink, and nothing else is round and square and a cupola on Berkeley College'.

The virtue of this analysis is that the seeming name, a descriptive phrase, is paraphrased *in context* as a so-called incomplete symbol. No unified expression is offered as an analysis of the descriptive phrase, but the statement as a whole which was the context of that phrase still gets its full quota of meaning—whether true or false.

The unanalyzed statement 'The author of *Waverley* was a poet' contains a part, 'the author of *Waverley*', which is wrongly supposed by McX and Wyman to demand objective reference in order to be meaningful at all. But in Russell's translation, 'Something wrote *Waverley* and was a poet and nothing else wrote *Waverley*', the burden of objective reference which had been put upon the descriptive phrase is now taken over by words of the kind that logicians call bound variables, variables of quantification, namely, words like 'something', 'nothing', 'everything'. These words, far from purporting to be names specifically of the author of *Waverley*, do not purport to be names at all; they refer to entities generally, with a kind of studied ambiguity peculiar to themselves. These quantificational words or bound variables are, of course a basic part of language, and their meaningfulness, at least in context, is not to be challenged. But their meaningfulness in no way presupposes there being either the author of *Waverley* or the round square cupola on Berkeley College or any other specifically preassigned objects.

Where descriptions are concerned, there is no longer any difficulty in affirming or denying being. 'There *is* the author of *Waverley*' is explained by Russell as meaning 'Someone (or, more strictly, something) wrote *Waverley* and nothing else wrote *Waverley*'. 'The author of *Waverley* is not' is explained, correspondingly, as the alternation 'Either each thing failed to write *Waverley* or two or more things wrote *Waverley*'. This alternation is false, but meaningful; and it contains no expression purporting to name the author of *Waverley*. The statement 'The round square cupola on Berkeley College is not' is analyzed in similar fashion. So the old notion that statements of nonbeing defeat themselves goes by the board. When a statement of being or nonbeing is analyzed by Russell's theory of descriptions, it ceases to contain any expression which even purports to name the alleged entity whose being is in question, so that the meaningfulness of the statement no longer can be thought to presuppose that there be such an entity.

Now what of 'Pegasus'? This being a word rather than a descriptive phrase, Russell's argument does not immediately apply to it. However, it can easily be made to apply. We have only to rephrase 'Pegasus' as a description, in any way that seems adequately to single out our idea; say, 'the winged horse that was captured by Bellerophon'. Substituting such a phrase for 'Pegasus', we can then proceed to analyze the statement 'Pegasus is', or 'Pegasus is not', precisely on the analogy of Russell's analysis of 'The author of *Waverley* is' and 'The author of *Waverley* is not'.

In order thus to subsume a one-word name or alleged name such as 'Pegasus' under Russell's theory of description, we must, of course, be able first to translate the word into a description. But this is no real restriction. If the notion of Pegasus had been so obscure or so basic a one that no pat translation into a descriptive phrase had offered itself along familiar lines, we could still have availed ourselves of the following artificial and trivial-seeming device: we could have appealed to the *ex hypothesi* unanalyzable, irreducible attribute of *being Pegasus*, adopting, for its expression, the verb 'is-Pegasus', or 'pegasizes'. The noun 'Pegasus' itself could then be treated as derivative, and identified after all with a description: 'the thing that is-Pegasus', 'the thing that pegasizes'.[2]

If the importing of such a predicate as 'pegasizes' seems to commit us to recognizing that there is a corresponding attribute, pegasizing, in Plato's heaven or in the minds of men, well and good. Neither we nor Wyman nor McX have been contending, thus far, about the being or nonbeing of universals, but rather about that of Pegasus. If in terms of pegasizing we can interpret the noun 'Pegasus' as a description subject to Russell's theory of descriptions, then we have disposed of the old notion that Pegasus cannot be said not to be without presupposing that in some sense Pegasus is.

Our argument is now quite general. McX and Wyman supposed that we could not meaningfully affirm a statement of the form 'So-and-so is not', with a simple or descriptive singular noun in place of 'so-and-so', unless so-and-so is. This supposition is now seen to be quite generally groundless, since the singular noun in question can always be expanded into a singular description, trivially or otherwise, and then analyzed out *à la* Russell.

We commit ourselves to an ontology containing numbers when we say there are prime numbers larger than a million; we commit ourselves to an ontology containing centaurs when we say there are centaurs; and we commit ourselves to an ontology containing Pegasus when we say Pegasus is. But we do not commit ourselves to an ontology containing Pegasus or the author of *Waverley* or the round square cupola on Berkeley College when we say that Pegasus or the author of *Waverley* or the cupola in question is *not*. We need no longer labor under the delusion that the meaningfulness of a statement containing a singular term presupposes an entity named by the term. A singular term need not name to be significant.

An inkling of this might have dawned on Wyman and McX even without benefit of Russell if they had only noticed—as so few of us do—that there is a gulf between *meaning* and *naming* even in the case of a singular term which is genuinely a name of an object. The following example from Frege will serve. The phrase 'Evening Star' names a certain large physical object of spherical form, which is hurtling through space some scores of millions of miles from here. The phrase 'Morning Star' names the same thing, as was probably first established by some observant Babylonian. But the two phrases cannot be regarded as having the same meaning; otherwise that Babylonian could have dispensed with his observations and contented himself with reflecting on the

[2] For further remarks on such assimilation of all singular terms to descriptions see Quine [2], pp. 218–24.

meanings of his words. The meanings, then, being different from one another, must be other than the named object, which is one and the same in both cases.

Confusion of meaning with naming not only made McX think he could not meaningfully repudiate Pegasus; a continuing confusion of meaning with naming no doubt helped engender his absurd notion that Pegasus is an idea, a mental entity. The structure of his confusion is as follows. He confused the alleged *named object* Pegasus with the *meaning* of the word 'Pegasus', therefore concluding that Pegasus must be in order that the word have meaning. But what sorts of things are meanings? This is a moot point; however, one might quite plausibly explain meanings as ideas in the mind, supposing we can make clear sense in turn of the idea of ideas in the mind. Therefore Pegasus, initially confused with a meaning, ends up as an idea in the mind. It is the more remarkable that Wyman, subject to the same initial motivation as McX, should have avoided this particular blunder and wound up with unactualized possibles instead.

Now let us turn to the ontological problem of universals: the question whether there are such entities as attributes, relations, classes, numbers, functions. McX, characteristically enough, thinks there are. Speaking of attributes, he says: "There are red houses, red roses, red sunsets; this much is prephilosophical common sense in which we must all agree. These houses, roses, and sunsets, then, have something in common; and this which they have in common is all I mean by the attribute of redness." For McX, thus, there being attributes is even more obvious and trivial than the obvious and trivial fact of there being red houses, roses, and sunsets. This, I think, is characteristic of metaphysics, or at least of that part of metaphysics called ontology: one who regards a statement on this subject as true at all must regard it as trivially true. One's ontology is basic to the conceptual scheme by which he interprets all experiences, even the most commonplace ones. Judged within some particular conceptual scheme—and how else is judgment possible?—an ontological statement goes without saying, standing in need of no separate justification at all. Ontological statements follow immediately from all manner of casual statements of commonplace fact, just as—from the point of view, anyway, of McX's conceptual scheme—'There is an attribute' follows from 'There are red houses, red roses, red sunsets'.

Judged in another conceptual scheme, an ontological statement which is axiomatic to McX's mind may, with equal immediacy and triviality, be adjudged false. One may admit that there are red houses, roses, and sunsets, but deny, except as a popular and misleading manner of speaking, that they have anything in common. The words 'houses', 'roses', and 'sunsets' are true of sundry individual entities which are houses and roses and sunsets, and the word 'red' or 'red object' is true of each of sundry individual entities which are red houses, red roses, red sunsets; but there is not, in addition, any entity whatever, individual or otherwise, which is named by the word 'redness', nor, for that matter, by the word 'householod', 'rosehood', 'sunsethood'. That the houses and roses and sunsets are all of them red may be taken as ultimate and irreducible, and it may be held that McX is no better off, in point of real explanatory power, for all the occult entities which he posits under such names as 'redness'.

One means by which McX might naturally have tried to impose his ontology of universals on us was already removed before we turned to the problem of universals. McX cannot argue that predicates such as 'red' or 'is-red', which we all concur in using, must be regarded as names each of a single universal entity in order that they be meaningful at all. For we have seen that being a name of something is a much more special feature than being meaningful. He cannot even charge us—at least not by *that* argument—with having posited an attribute of pegasizing by our adoption of the predicate 'pegasizes'.

However, McX hits upon a different strategem. "Let us grant," he says, "this distinction between meaning and naming of which you make so much. Let us even grant that 'is red', 'pegasizes', etc., are not names of attributes. Still, you admit they have meanings. But these *meanings*, whether they are *named* or not, are still universals, and I venture to say that some of them might even be the very things that I call attributes, or something to much the same purpose in the end."

For McX, this is an unusually penetrating speech; and the only way I know to counter it is by refusing to admit meanings. However, I feel no reluctance toward refusing to admit meanings, for I do not thereby deny that words and statements are meaningful. McX and I may agree to the letter in our classification of linguistic forms into the meaningful and the meaningless, even though McX construes meaningfulness as the *having* (in some sense of 'having') of some abstract entity which he calls a meaning, whereas I do not. I remain free to maintain that the fact that a given linguistic utterance is meaningful (or *significant*, as I prefer to say so as not to invite hypostasis of meanings as entities) is an ultimate and irreducible matter of fact; or, I may undertake to analyze it in terms directly of what people do in the presence of the linguistic utterance in question and other utterances similar to it.

The useful ways in which people ordinarily talk or seem to talk about meanings boil down to two: the *having* of meanings, which is significance, and *sameness* of meaning, or synonymy. What is called *giving* the meaning of an utterance is simply the uttering of a synonym, couched, ordinarily, in clearer language than the original. If we are allergic to meanings as such, we can speak directly of utterances as significant or insignificant, and as synonymous or heteronymous one with another. The problem of explaining these adjectives 'significant' and 'synonymous' with some degree of clarity and rigor— preferably, as I see it, in terms of behavior—is as difficult as it is important.[3]

[3] See my "Two Dogmas of Empiricism" [pp. 346–65—Eds.].

But the explanatory value of special and irreducible intermediary entities called meanings is surely illusory.

Up to now I have argued that we can use singular terms significantly in sentences without presupposing that there are the entities which those terms purport to name. I have argued further that we can use general terms, for example, predicates, without conceding them to be names of abstract entities. I have argued further that we can view utterances as significant, and as synonymous or heteronymous with one another, without countenancing a realm of entities called meanings. At this point McX begins to wonder whether there is any limit at all to our ontological immunity. Does *nothing* we may say commit us to the assumption of universals or other entities which we may find unwelcome?

I have already suggested a negative answer to this question, in speaking of bound variables, or variables of quantification, in connection with Russell's theory of descriptions. We can very easily involve ourselves in ontological commitments by saying, for example, that *there is something* (bound variable) which red houses and sunsets have in common; or that *there is something* which is a prime number larger than a million. But this is, essentially, the *only* way we can involve ourselves in ontological commitments: by our use of bound variables. The use of alleged names is no criterion, for we can repudiate their namehood at the drop of a hat unless the assumption of a corresponding entity can be spotted in the things we affirm in terms of bound variables. Names are, in fact, altogether immaterial to the ontological issue, for I have shown, in connection with 'Pegasus' and 'pegasize', that names can be converted to descriptions, and Russell has shown that descriptions can be eliminated. Whatever we say with the help of names can be said in a language which shuns names altogether. To be assumed as an entity is, purely and simply, to be reckoned as the value of a variable. In terms of the categories of traditional grammar, this amounts roughly to saying that to be is to be in the range of reference of a pronoun. Pronouns are the basic media of reference; nouns, as Peirce appreciated, are propronouns. The variables of quantification, 'something', 'nothing', 'everything', range over our whole ontology, whatever it may be; and we are convicted of a particular ontological presupposition if, and only if, the alleged presuppositum has to be reckoned among the entities over which our variables range in order to render one of our affirmations true.

We may say, for example, that some dogs are white and not thereby commit ourselves to recognizing either doghood or whiteness as entities. 'Some dogs are white' says that some things that are dogs are white; and, in order that this statement be true, the things over which the bound variable 'something' ranges must include some white dogs, but need not include doghood or whiteness. On the other hand, when we say that some zoölogical species are cross-fertile we are committing ourselves to recognizing as entities the several species themselves, abstract though they are. We remain so committed at least until we devise some way of so paraphrasing the statement as to show that the seeming reference to species on the part of our bound variable was an avoidable manner of speaking.

Classical mathematics, as the example of primes larger than a million clearly illustrates, is up to its neck in commitments to an ontology of abstract entities. Thus it is that the great mediaeval controversy over universals has flared up anew in the modern philosophy of mathematics. The issue is clearer now than of old, because we now have a more explicit standard whereby to decide what ontology a given theory or form of discourse is committed to: a theory is committed to those and only those entities to which the bound variables of the theory must be capable of referring in order that the affirmations made in the theory be true.

Because this standard of ontological presupposition did not emerge clearly in the philosophical tradition, the modern philosophical mathematicians have not on the whole recognized that they were debating the same old problem of universals in a newly clarified form. But the fundamental cleavages among modern points of view on foundations of mathematics do come down pretty explicitly to disagreements as to the range of entities to which the bound variables should be permitted to refer.

The three main mediaeval points of view regarding universals are designated by historians as *realism*, *conceptualism*, and *nominalism*. Essentially these same three doctrines reappear in twentieth-century surveys of the philosophy of mathematics under the new names *logicism*, *intuitionism*, and *formalism*.

Realism, as the word is used in connection with the mediaeval controversy over universals, is the Platonic doctrine that universals or abstract entities have being independently of the mind; the mind may discover them but cannot create them. *Logicism*, represented by Frege, Russell, Whitehead, Church, and Carnap, condones the use of bound variables to refer to abstract entities known and unknown, specifiable and unspecifiable, indiscriminately.

Conceptualism holds that there are universals but they are mind-made. *Intuitionism*, espoused in modern times in one form or another by Poincaré, Brouwer, Weyl, and others, countenances the use of bound variables to refer to abstract entities only when those entities are capable of being cooked up individually from ingredients specified in advance. As Fraenkel has put it, logicism holds that classes are discovered while intuitionism holds that they are invented—a fair statement indeed of the old opposition between realism and conceptualism. This opposition is no mere quibble; it makes an essential difference in the amount of classical mathematics to which one is willing to subscribe. Logicists, or realists, are able on their assumptions to get Cantor's ascending orders of infinity; intuitionists are compelled to stop with the lowest order of infinity, and, as an indirect consequence, to abandon even some of the classical laws of real numbers. The modern controversy between logicism and intuitionism arose, in fact, from disagreements over infinity.

Formalism, associated with the name of Hilbert, echoes intuitionism in deploring the logicist's unbridled recourse to universals. But formalism also finds intuitionism unsatisfactory. This could happen for either of two opposite reasons. The formalist might, like the logicist, object to the crippling of classical mathematics; or he might, like the *nominalists* of old, object to admitting abstract entities at all, even in the restrained sense of mind-made entities. The upshot is the same: the formalist keeps classical mathematics as a play of insignificant notations. This play of notations can still be of utility—whatever utility it has already shown itself to have as a crutch for physicists and engineers. But utility need not imply significance, in any literal linguistic sense. Nor need the marked success of mathematicians in spinning out theorems, and in finding objective bases for agreement with one another's results, imply significance. For an adequate basis for agreement among mathematicians can be found simply in the rules which govern the manipulation of the notations—these syntactical rules being, unlike the notations themselves, quite significant and intelligible.[4]

I have argued that the sort of ontology we adopt can be consequential—notably in connection with mathematics, although this is only an example. Now how are we to adjudicate among rival ontologies? Certainly the answer is not provided by the semantical formula "To be is to be the value of a variable"; this formula serves rather, conversely, in testing the conformity of a given remark or doctrine to a prior ontological standard. We look to bound variables in connection with ontology not in order to know what there is, but in order to know what a given remark or doctrine, ours or someone else's, *says* there is; and this much is quite properly a problem involving language. But what there is is another question.

In debating over what there is, there are still reasons for operating on a semantical plane. One reason is to escape from the predicament noted at the beginning of this essay: the predicament of my not being able to admit that there are things which McX countenances and I do not. So long as I adhere to my ontology, as opposed to McX's, I cannot allow my bound variables to refer to entities which belong to McX's ontology and not to mine. I can, however, consistently describe our disagreement by characterizing the statements which McX affirms. Provided merely that my ontology countenances linguistic forms, or at least concrete inscriptions and utterances, I can talk about McX's sentences.

Another reason for withdrawing to a semantical plane is to find common ground on which to argue. Disagreement in ontology involves basic disagreement in conceptual schemes; yet McX and I, despite these basic disagreements, find that our conceptual schemes converge sufficiently in their intermediate and upper ramifications to enable us to communicate successfully

---

[4] See Goodman and Quine. For further discussion of the general matters touched on in the past two pages, see Bernays, Fraenkel, Black. [The article by Bernays appears in English in this book on pp. 273–85.—Eds.]

on such topics as politics, weather, and, in particular, language. Insofar as our basic controversy over ontology can be translated upward into a semantical controversy about words and what to do with them, the collapse of the controversy into question-begging may be delayed.

It is no wonder, then, that ontological controversy should end in controversy over language. But we must not jump to the conclusion that what there is depends on words. Translatability of a question into semantical terms is no indication that the question is linguistic. To see Naples is to bear a name which, when prefixed to the words 'sees Naples', yields a true sentence; still there is nothing linguistic about seeing Naples.

Our acceptance of an ontology is, I think, similar in principle to our acceptance of a scientific theory, say a system of physics: we adopt, at least insofar as we are reasonable, the simplest conceptual scheme into which the disordered fragments of raw experience can be fitted and arranged. Our ontology is determined once we have fixed upon the over-all conceptual scheme which is to accommodate science in the broadest sense; and the considerations which determine a reasonable construction of any part of that conceptual scheme, for example, the biological or the physical part, are not different in kind from the considerations which determine a reasonable construction of the whole. To whatever extent the adoption of any system of scientific theory may be said to be a matter of language, the same—but no more—may be said of the adoption of an ontology.

But simplicity, as a guiding principle in constructing conceptual schemes, is not a clear and unambiguous idea; and it is quite capable of presenting a double or multiple standard. Imagine, for example, that we have devised the most economical set of concepts adequate to the play-by-play reporting of immediate experience. The entities under this scheme—the values of bound variables—are, let us suppose, individual subjective events of sensation or reflection. We should still find, no doubt, that a physicalistic conceptual scheme, purporting to talk about external objects, offers great advantages in simplifying our over-all reports. By bringing together scattered sense events and treating them as perceptions of one object, we reduce the complexity of our stream of experience to a manageable conceptual simplicity. The rule of simplicity is indeed our guiding maxim in assigning sense data to objects: we associate an earlier and a later round sensum with the same so-called penny, or with two different so-called pennies, in obedience to the demands of maximum simplicity in our total world-picture.

Here we have two competing conceptual schemes, a phenomenalistic one and a physicalistic one. Which should prevail? Each has its advantages; each has its special simplicity in its own way. Each, I suggest, deserves to be developed. Each may be said, indeed, to be the more fundamental, though in different senses: the one is epistemologically, the other physically, fundamental.

The physical conceptual scheme simplifies our account of experience because of the way myriad scattered sense events come to be associated with single so-called objects; still there is no likelihood that each sentence about physical objects can actually be translated, however deviously and complexly, into the phenomenalistic language. Physical objects are postulated entities which round out and simplify our account of the flux of experience, just as the introduction of irrational numbers simplifies laws of arithmetic. From the point of view of the conceptual scheme of the elementary arithmetic of rational numbers alone, the broader arithmetic of rational and irrational numbers would have the status of a convenient myth, simpler than the literal truth (namely, the arithmetic of rationals) and yet containing that literal truth as a scattered part. Similarly, from a phenomenalistic point of view, the conceptual scheme of physical objects is a convenient myth, simpler than the literal truth and yet containing that literal truth as a scattered part.[5]

Now what of classes or attributes of physical objects, in turn? A platonistic ontology of this sort is, from the point of view of a strictly physicalistic conceptual scheme, as much a myth as that physicalistic conceptual scheme itself is for phenomenalism. This higher myth is a good and useful one, in turn, insofar as it simplifies our account of physics. Since mathematics is an integral part of this higher myth, the utility of this myth for physical science is evident enough. In speaking of it nevertheless as a myth, I echo that philosophy of mathematics to which I alluded earlier under the name of formalism. But an attitude of formalism may with equal justice be adopted toward the physical conceptual scheme, in turn, by the pure aesthete or phenomenalist.

The analogy between the myth of mathematics and the myth of physics is, in some additional and perhaps fortuitous ways, strikingly close. Consider, for example, the crisis which was precipitated in the foundations of mathematics, at the turn of the century, by the discovery of Russell's paradox and other antinomies of set theory. These contradictions had to be obviated by unintuitive, *ad hoc* devices; our mathematical myth-making became deliberate and evident to all. But what of physics? An antinomy arose between the undular and the corpuscular accounts of light; and if this was not as out-and-out a contradiction as Russell's paradox, I suspect that the reason is that physics is not as out-and-out as mathematics. Again, the second great modern crisis in the foundations of mathematics—precipitated in 1931 by Gödel's proof that there are bound to be undecidable statements in arithmetic—has its companion piece in physics in Heisenberg's indeterminacy principle.

In earlier pages I undertook to show that some common arguments in favor of certain ontologies are fallacious. Further, I advanced an explicit standard whereby to decide what the ontological commitments of a theory are. But the question what ontology actually to adopt still stands open, and the obvious counsel is tolerance and an experimental spirit. Let us by all means see how much of the physicalistic conceptual scheme can be reduced to a phenomenalistic one; still, physics also naturally demands pursuing,

[5] The arithmetical analogy is due to Frank, pp. 108f.

irreducible *in toto* though it be. Let us see how, or to what degree, natural science may be rendered independent of platonistic mathematics; but let us also pursue mathematics and delve into its platonistic foundations.

From among the various conceptual schemes best suited to these various pursuits, one—the phenomenalistic—claims epistemological priority. Viewed from within the phenomenalistic conceptual scheme, the ontologies of physical objects and mathematical objects are myths. The quality of myth, however, is relative; relative, in this case, to the epistemological point of view. This point of view is one among various, corresponding to one among our various interests and purposes.

BIBLIOGRAPHY

Bernays, Paul, "Sur le platonisme dans les mathématiques," *L'Enseignement mathématique*, 34 (1935–36), 52–68.

Black, Max, *The Nature of Mathematics*. London: Kegan Paul, 1933; New York: Harcourt, Brace & World, Inc., 1934.

Church, Alonzo, "A Note on the Entscheidungsproblem," *Journal of Symbolic Logic*, 1 (1936), 40f; 101f. (For a possibly more convenient presentation of the argument, see Hilbert and Bernays, vol. 2, pp. 416–21.)

Fraenkel, A. A., "Sur la notion d'existence dans les mathématiques," *L'Enseignement mathématique*, 34 (1935–36), 18–32.

Frank, Philip, *Modern Science and its Philosophy*. Cambridge, Mass.: Harvard University Press, 1949.

Gödel, Kurt, "Ueber formal unentscheidbare Sätze der Principia Mathemathica und verwandter Systeme," *Monatshefte für Mathematik und Physik*, 38 (1931), 173–98. (For an introductory account and further references see Quine [2], pp. 245ff.)

Goodman, Nelson and W. V. Quine, "Steps Toward a Constructive Nominalism," *Journal of Symbolic Logic*, 12 (1947), 105–22. (Lest the reader be led to misconstrue passages in my later writings by trying to reconcile them with the appealingly forthright opening sentence of the cited paper, let me say that I should now prefer to treat that sentence as a hypothetical statement of conditions for the construction in hand.)

Hilbert, David and Paul Bernays, *Grundlagen der Mathematik*, 2 vols. Berlin: Springer, 1934, 1939; 2nd printing, Ann Arbor, Mich.: Edwards, 1944.

Quine, W. V. [1]. *From a Logical Point of View*. Cambridge: Harvard University Press, 1953.

——— [2]. *Methods of Logic*. New York: Holt, Rinehart & Winston, Inc., 1950.

Nelson Goodman

1. INDIVIDUALS AND CLASSES

For me, as a nominalist, the world is a world of individuals. But this simple statement, I have learned from bitter experience, can be misunderstood in numberless ways. Some misunderstandings have arisen from inadequacies in my own explanations. Other misunderstandings have arisen from inadequate attention to those explanations. Conflicting arguments in bewildering variety have been brought forward to show that nominalism is bad. This paper is one more attempt to make clear what I mean by nominalism and why I think nominalism is good.

A certain amount of trouble can be blamed on emotions attaching to the word "individual". One writer[1] calls it an 'honorific' word; and I am often criticized for applying the term "individual" to something or other that is unworthy of it. Use of a different word, even a coined one, might have been advisable in order to forestall such complaints. Nevertheless, I am prepared to defend the choice of the term "individual" as entirely in accord with a common practice of adapting ordinary language to technical purposes. In some cases, what I take as an individual may indeed lack many characteristics usually associated with the term "individual", and may not count as an individual according to common usage. But the situation with respect to the term "class" is exactly parallel. According to the layman's prelogical usage,

---

[1] Victor Lowe on p. 125 of "Professor Goodman's Concept of an Individual" in the *Philosophical Review*, vol. 62 (1953), pp. 117–26.

Reprinted with the kind permission of the author and publisher from The Problem of Universals (*Notre Dame, Ind.: Notre Dame University Press*, 1956). *The Appendix to this article appeared originally in* Philosophical Studies, IX (1958), 65–66. *We reprint it with the kind permission of the author.*

children in a schoolroom make up a class, and so do people at a given social level, but Plato and this sheet of paper and the Taj Mahal do not. The term "set" in ordinary usage is perhaps even more restricted than the term "class". Yet by the logician's usage any things whatever make up a class or set. The contention that a genuine whole or individual cannot consist of widely scattered and very unlike parts misses the point as completely as would the contention that a genuine class cannot consist of widely scattered and very unlike members. In the case of "individuals" as in the case of "class", a technical usage is explicated with the help of a calculus, and the divergence from ordinary usage is expressly noted. A class for Boole need not have social cohesion; and an individual for me need not have personal integration.

Confusion of another kind has resulted from the incautious opening sentence of my joint article[2] with Quine. Although the statement "We do not believe in abstract entities" was intended more as a headline than as final doctrine, and although some reservations concerning it were almost immediately indicated[3] it has been fair game for critics ever since. Neither of us would write that sentence today, but neither of us would so change it as to affect anything beyond the first paragraph of the article in question. Quine has recently written that he would "now prefer to treat that sentence as a hypothetical statement of conditions for the construction in hand."[4] My own change would be not from the categorical to the hypothetical, but from the vaguely general to the more specific. I do not look upon abstractness as either a necessary or a sufficient test of incomprehensibility; and indeed the line between what is ordinarily called "abstract" and what is ordinarily called "concrete" seems to me vague and capricious. Nominalism for me consists specifically in the refusal to recognize classes.

What has not always been noticed is that essentially this revision is made in my book,[5] published four years later than the joint article. A key principle in this later formulation is that the nominalist rejects classes as incomprehensible, but may take anything whatever as an individual. Some misguided criticism would have been obviated had enough attention been paid to this statement; but I suspect that some of my critics feel they do me a kindness by not taking it seriously. Further explanation may help.

Nominalism as I conceive it (and I am not here speaking for Quine) does not involve excluding abstract entities, spirits, intimations of immortality, or anything of the sort; but requires only that whatever is admitted as an entity

[2] "Steps Towards a Constructive Nominalism," *Journal of Symbolic Logic*, vol. 12 (1947), pp. 105–22.

[3] See the third paragraph and the second footnote of the joint article.

[4] *From a Logical Point of View*, Harvard University Press, 1953, pp. 173–4.

[5] *The Structure of Appearance*, Harvard University Press, 1951, see especially p. 35. Incidentally (as explained in the book and later in the present article) since any nominalistic system is readily translated into a platonistic one, acceptance of most of the book by no means depends upon an acceptance of nominalism. This has been explicitly acknowledged by most of my critics.

at all be construed as an individual. A given philosopher, nominalist or not, may impose very stringent requirements upon what he will admit as an entity; but these requirements, however sound they may be and however intimately associated with traditional nominalism, are quite independent of nominalism in my sense. The nominalism I have described demands only that all entities admitted, no matter what they are, be treated as individuals. Just what this means, I shall explain in the following sections; but for the moment we may suppose that to treat entities as individuals for a system is to take them as values of the variables of lowest type in the system.

Incidentally, several of my critics have confused themselves by lumping together, without due attention to context, passages from different parts of my book. In Chapter VI, I discuss the choice of elements for a certain constructional system; but this does not turn upon the propriety of construing certain entities as individuals. Whatever we are willing to recognize as an entity at all may be construed as an individual. But in building a system, we must consider carefully what entities we are willing to recognize at all—or better, what terms we are willing to interpret as denoting and what terms we want to interpret syncategorematically. Important as the question is, nominalism does not decide it. I have never suggested that nominalism is enough to make a system acceptable. I have suggested only that platonism is enough to make it inacceptable. But more of this later.

Now, however, is nominalism consequential at all? If the nominalist is free to construe anything he pleases as an individual, can't he even construe a class as an individual?

Whatever can be construed as a class can indeed be construed as an individual, and yet a class cannot be construed as an individual. If this seems paradoxical, it can perhaps be clarified by means of an analogy. Suppose that in a certain game a player is to begin by dealing each card from his hand onto the table at either his left or his right; he may put any card on either side and may move a card from side to side if he likes. Then while it is quite true that he is free to put any card on either side, he can never get a left-hand card on the right-hand side; for a card is a left-hand card or a right-hand card according as it lies on his left or his right. Similarly, a table is an individual, or the class of its legs and top, or the class of its molecule-classes of atoms, according to the way it is construed in a system. And whether the Great Dipper is an individual or a class of stars depends upon the system we are using. We can construe anything as an individual (and aside from nominalistic scruples we can construe anything as a class); but we can no more construe a class as an individual than we can get a left-hand card on the right-hand side.

2. THE PRINCIPLE OF NOMINALISM

In brief, while the nominalist may construe anything as an individual, he refuses to construe anything as a class. But just what is the principle of this refusal? In my book I said that, roughly speaking, the nominalist sticks at a distinction of entities without a distinction of content; and some of my critics have overlooked the more explicit formulation that soon followed. The nominalist denies that two different entities can be made up of the same entities. Let us suppose, for example, that a nominalist and a platonist start with the same minimal, atomic elements[6] for their systems; merely for comparative purposes take the number of these atoms as 5. The nominalist admits also all wholes or individual sums comprised of these, and so has a universe of $2^5 - 1$, or 31, entities. He cannot concoct any more; for whatever individuals among the 31 are added together, the result is another individual among those 31. Our platonist, we may suppose, admits no sums of atoms but admits all classes of them. This, not counting the null and unit classes, gives him also 31 entities. But he further admits all classes of classes of atoms; and by this single step he welcomes into his universe $2^{31} - 1$, or over two billion, additional entities. And he has no thought of stopping there. He also admits all classes of classes of classes of atoms, and so on *ad infinitum*, climbing up through an explosively expanding universe towards a prodigiously teeming Platonic Heaven. He gets all these extra entities out of his original five by a magical process that enables him to make two or more distinct entities from exactly the same entities. And it is just here that the nominalist draws the line.

In the nominalist's world, if we start from any two distinct entities and break each of them down as far as we like (by taking parts, parts of parts, and so on), we always arrive at some entity that is contained in one but not the other of our two original entities. In the platonist's world, on the contrary, there are at least two different entities that we can so break down (by taking members, members of members, and so on) as to arrive at exactly the same entities. For instance, suppose K has two members: the class of a and b, and the class of c and d; and suppose L has two members: the class of a and c, and the class of b and d. Then although K and L are different classes, they alike break down into a, b, c, and d. Again K breaks down into the same entities as does the class having K and L as its members. These are clear cases of what the nominalist objects to as a distinction of entities without distinction of content.

This discloses the relationship between nominalism and extensionalism, which springs from a common aversion to the unwonted multiplication of entities. Extensionalism precludes the composition of more than one entity out of exactly the same entities by membership; nominalism goes further, precluding the composition of more than one entity out of the same entities by any chains of membership. For the extensionalist, two entities are identical if they break down into the same members; for the nominalist, two entities

---

[6] An atomic element—or atom—of a system is simply an element of the system that contains no lesser elements for the system. Depending on the system, an electron or a molecule or a planet might be taken as an atom.

are identical if they break down in any way into the same entities. The extensionalist's restriction upon the generation of entities is a special case of the nominalist's more thoroughgoing restriction.

Nominalism describes the world as composed of individuals. To explain nominalism we need to explain not what individuals are but rather *what constitutes describing the world as composed of them*. So to describe the world is to describe it as made up of entities no two of which break down into exactly the same entities. What this means I have just explained, but a somewhat more technical formulation may be helpful.

Suppose we have two constructional systems, having one or more (but not necessarily the same or even the same number of) atoms. Entities other than atoms are generated in system **I** as classes, and in system **II** as sum-individuals. Let us now obliterate all purely notational differences between the two systems. We may suppose from the start that each system uses but one style of variable.[7] Then let us remove all remaining tell-tale signs from system **I** other than "ε" by expansion in terms of "ε", and similarly let us remove all peculiar signs of system **II** other than "$\ll$" by expansion in terms of "$\ll$". Finally, let us put "R" in for every occurrence of "ε", "ε/ε", "$\varepsilon/\varepsilon/\varepsilon$", etc. in system **I**, and for every occurrence of "$\ll$" in system **II**. No purely notational distinction between the two systems remains; and "R" in each is irreflexive, asymmetric, and transitive. Will anything now reveal which system is which?

For each system, x is an atom if and only if nothing stands in the relation R to x[8]; and x is an atom of y (symbol: "Axy") if and only if x is an atom and is identical with or bears the relation R to y. Now in a nominalistic but not in a platonistic system, entities are the same if their atoms are the same. Thus the disguised systems will be distinguishable from each other by the fact that the nominalistic system satisfies, while the platonistic system violates, the principle:

$$(x)\,(Axy \equiv Axz) \supset y = z.\text{[9]}$$

Obviously the disguised **I** will violate this principle if the system acknowledges more than $2n - 1$ entities, where n is the number of its atoms; or again, if **I** acknowledges any unit-classes, since the unit-class and its member will have the same atoms. But even if **I** is a platonistic system so restricted as to be distinguished on neither of these two scores, it will still be detectable in its disguised version through violation of the stated principle. And if **I** admits no two such classes, then indeed it is not platonistic at all, regardless of its notation.

---

[7] The aim is to take systems as nearly alike as possible, in order to isolate the critical difference. In the following text, "ε" is to be read "is a member of", "ε/ε" is to be read "is a member of a member of, etc.; and "$\ll$" is to be read "is a proper part of".

[8] Any null class of system **I** will thus appear simply as one of the atoms of the disguised version of **I**, and thus leave no revealing trace.

[9] Both systems will satisfy the converse principle; under nominalism and platonism alike, if x and y are identical they have the same atoms.

This, I think, disposes of the charge that the distinction between nominalism and platonism is a mere matter of notation,[10] and also clarifies the nominalist's dictum: "No distinction of entities without distinction of content." For a nominalistic system, no two distinct things have the same atoms; only from different atoms can different things be generated; all non-identities between things are reducible to non-identities between their atoms.

The further question must be raised whether the distinction between nominalism and platonism can be made *purely* formal? In the case we have just considered, the problem was how to determine whether a given system is nominalistic or platonistic when we know that a given one of its relations is either ε^* or $\leqslant$. Suppose now that we are confronted with a system without knowing anything about the interpretation of its predicates; or better, suppose we are given only the arrow-diagrams of the relations of the system. Can we determine whether the system is nominalistic or platonistic? The answer is *no*. We need to know either which elements are atoms of the system or—what amounts to the same thing—which relation is the 'generating' relation[11] of the system. Take, for example, the following diagram for a system with a single relation:

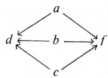

If we know that *a*, *b*, and *c* are the atoms of the system, or that the relation mapped is a generating one, then we know that the system is platonistic— since the distinct elements *d* and *f* then have exactly the same atoms. On the other hand, if we know that *a*, *b*, *c*, *d*, and *f* are all atoms of the system, then we know that the system is nominalistic. But if we do not know what the atoms are or whether the relation is a generating relation, we cannot tell whether the system is platonistic or nominalistic. Notice, though, that without such knowledge, *neither* can we tell whether a system is *extensional* or not. The system diagrammed is extensional if the relation is that of child to parent but surely not extensional if the relation is that of member to class.[12] Lest

---

[10] E.g., by Wang on p. 416 of "What is an Individual?" in *Philosophical Review*, vol. 62 (1953), pp. 413–20.

[11] Given the atoms of the system, a *generating* relation is one such that if and only if *x* is a non-atomic element of the system will there be some element *y* that stands in that relation to *x*. *The generating relation G* of a system is the relation that obtains between two elements *x* and *y* of the system if and only if *x* and *y* are connnected by a chain in which each linked pair belongs to a generating relation of the system. (Note that this does not enable us to determine whether a given relation is 'a' or 'the' generating relation of a system unless we are told what the atoms are. See further the appendix to this article.)

[12] The system diagrammed, in fact, is extensional only if it is nominalistic, although obviously this is not true of all systems. Every system, of course, is nominalistic only if it is extensional.

anyone gleefully welcome the apparent opportunity to dismiss both "nominalistic" and "extensional" as not purely formal characterizations of systems, I hasten to point out that no characterization of systems is purely formal in the sense implied. For if we are given just an arrow-diagram, without any interpretative information whatever, then we do not even know that the arrows represent relationships or that the letters represent elements. We can tell nothing at all about the system in question or even that there *is* a system in question; the diagram might be a hex sign or a complex character serving as the proper name of a single element. A classification of symbolic systems becomes significant only when at least some restrictions are imposed upon the interpretation of the symbols. The criterion for nominalism is formal to the same rather high degree as the usual criterion for extensionality.

What I have tried to do so far is to explain my version of nominalism. In outline, I have said that the nominalist insists on the world being described as composed of individuals, that to describe the world as composed of individuals is to describe it as made up of entities no two of which have the same content, and that this in turn is to describe it by means of a system for which no two distinct entities have exactly the same atoms.

Now, by way of justifying and defending the nominalism thus explained, I want to consider a number of objections to it.

3. ANSWERS TO OBJECTIONS

(i) *Objection:* The nominalism described is not really nominalism in the traditional sense.

Answer: Doubtless a good many different theses are equally legitimate descendants of earlier nominalism. I claim no more than that the principle I have set forth is one reasonable formulation of the traditional injunction against undue multiplication of entities. And I willingly submit this claim to Father Bochenski for adjudication. If he rules against me, he deprives me of nothing but a label that incites opposition.

(ii) *Objection:* The principle of nominalism set forth is false as a statement, and groundless as a stipulation; for we know from everyday experience that different things often *are* made out of the same material, or the same particles, at different times.

Answer: The catch here is the phrase "at different times". Of course, different figures are often made out of the same lump of clay at different times; and of course, the same atoms often combine into different articles at different times. Likewise, different rooms are, so to speak, often made out of the same building at different places; and the same roads sometimes make up different crossings at different places. Admittedly, it is (spatially) different parts of the building or of the roads that are comprised in the two different rooms or the two different crossings; but so likewise, it is (temporally) different

parts of the clay or the atoms that are comprised in the different figures
or the different articles. We are at liberty to disregard the temporal or any
other dimension we please; but if we were to rule out the spatial divisibility
of buildings, or of roads, then we could not very consistently speak of the
building, or a road, at different places. Similarly, if we rule out temporal
divisibility, then we cannot very consistently speak of the clay, or of the atoms,
at different times. The common experience of (different temporal parts of)
the same clay making up different figures no more discredits the principle
of nominalism than does the common experience of (different spatial parts of)
the same building making up different rooms.

A variation on this objection points to ordered pairs like *Washington,
Lincoln* and *Lincoln, Washington* as clearly illustrating the composition of
different entities out of the same individuals.[13] To be pertinent, of course,
this objection must not rest on any appeal to the logician's usual manner of
defining these ordered pairs as distinct classes of classes; for the legitimacy of
such multiple generation of classes out of the same individuals is just what is
in question. Rather the argument must be that, regardless of how ordered
pairs are defined in any formal system, we have here an everyday instance of
distinct things being composed of the same things. But surely this claim is not
true. Normally we no more conclude that we describe different composite
entities when we name two people in different order than we conclude that a
house from top to bottom and the house from bottom to top are different
entities, or that the capital of Massachusetts and the largest city in New
England are different things. We do not take the varied histories of the Battle
of Bull Run as recounting different occurrences. In daily life a multiplicity
of descriptions is no evidence for a corresponding multiplicity of things
described.

Thus I find in common experience nothing discordant with the principle
of nominalism.

(iii) *Objection:* Observance of the stated principle of nominalism is no
sufficient guarantee of soundness or sense in a philosophical system; for trash
of almost any kind can still be brought in on the ground floor as admitted
atoms of the system.

Answer: Granted. Nominalism no more guarantees philosophical
soundness than the refusal to eat poison guarantees physical well-being. Many
additional rules must be observed if we are to achieve either philosophical or
physical health. Indeed, in some cases a moderately platonistic system with a
wholesome atomic ontology may be a lesser evil than a nominalistic system
that takes monstrous vacuities as its atoms—just as a very tiny dose of poison
may be less harmful than a bullet in the head.

Nominalism is a necessary rather than a sufficient condition for an

[13] Cf. p. 110 of C. G. Hempel's article "Reflections on Nelson Goodman's *The Structure
of Appearance*", in the *Philosophical Review*, vol. 62 (1953), pp. 108–16.

acceptable philosophic system. To build well we must also exercise the most scrupulous care in choosing our raw materials. A given philosopher's choice of atoms may very likely be guided by attitudes or principles that are associated with nominalism by temperament or tradition; but such associated principles are independent of nominalism as I have defined it. Nominalism does not protect us from starting with ridiculous atoms. It does protect us from manufacturing gimcracks out of sound atoms by the popular devices of platonism. Nominalism, in other words, is a restrictive rule of processing that won't select our raw materials or help us make good things out of bad materials but will help keep us from making bad things out of good materials.

(iv) *Objection:* To keep the rule of nominalism by generating wholes, rather than classes, of individuals costs as much as it pays; for it often means forcing the imagination to accept as individuals some scattered or heterogeneous conglomerations that are never in practice recognized as single units and are surely incomprehensible if classes are.[14]

Answer: This is perhaps the most chronic complaint against nominalism: that a progressively and in the end hopelessly strained analogy is involved in extending the application of such terms as "part", "whole", and "individual" beyond the realm of well-demarcated spatio-temporally continuous lumps. Yet as I have suggested earlier, I think this objection can can be flatly and finally answered. The terminology of a system is irrelevant to the classification of the system as nominalistic or platonistic by the criterion I have explained. So long as a system admits no two distinct entities having exactly the same atoms, it is nominalistic no matter whether its generating relation is called "ε^*" or "$\ll$" or just "R", and no matter whether the values of its variables are called "classes" or "individuals" or just "entities". The words and symbols used in a system do not make it platonistic; it becomes platonistic only when it admits different entities having just the same atoms.

Thus a nominalistic system cannot put any burden on the imagination that a platonistic system does not. For the nominalist's apparatus is simply part of the platonist's apparatus. A nominalistic system can be mapped into a platonistic one. A nominalistic system is a platonistic system curtailed in a specific way.

Whatever new charges may be brought against nominalism, this best-loved of all objections now deserves to be laid to rest.

(v) *Objection:* Nominalism is trivial for a finitist and pointless for a non-finitist, since any system with a finite ontology can easily be made nominalistic while a system with an infinite ontology is repugnant to any nominalist.

Answer: Take the last point first. The nominalist is unlikely to be a non-finitist only in much the way a bricklayer is unlikely to be a

[14] This objection is urged, for example, by Lowe in the article cited in footnote 1 above; and is also put forth by Quine on p. 559 of his review of *The Structure of Appearance*, in the *Journal of Philosophy*, vol. 48 (1951), pp. 556–63.

ballet dancer. The two things are at most incongruous, not incompatible. Obviously, by the stated criterion for nominalism, some systems with infinite ontologies are nominalistic, and some systems with finite ontologies are platonistic.

But now, Hao Wang argues,[15] any finitistic platonistic system can be easily nominalized. He does not suppose that this can be done by any immediately obvious method, but refers to an ingenious device invented by Quine.[16] Now for the moment let us suppose that this device is entirely successful. Does this mean that the nominalistic program is thereby rendered pointless and trivial? On the contrary it means that an important part of the nominalistic program has been accomplished. The nominalist, after all, is looking for a nominalistic translation of everything that seems to him worth saving. The more he succeeds in finding ways of supplanting platonistic constructions by nominalistic ones, the fewer will be the cases where platonistic apparatus need be eschewed; for we can use without qualms whatever we know how to eliminate. When Wang in effect says: "So you see these occurrences of platonism are harmless after all," he completely discounts the fact that only the nominalist's efforts removed the sting. One might as well say that the program for eradicating smallpox in the United States is trivial because there is no smallpox around. In one sense, of course, any completed program is trivial—in just the sense that the goal of any program is to trivialize itself.

Unfortunately, however, the nominalistic program has not been so fully accomplished for all finite systems. Quine, after presenting his device, explicitly points out its fatal defects. The device can never be used in a system with an ontology embracing the entire universe; for more inscriptions will be needed to write out even a single universally quantified statement than there are things in the universe. Quine offers his device as an interesting but unsuccessful attempt, and drops it forthwith.

Thus Wang is wrong about the facts concerning Quine's device; and even if the facts were as Wang supposes, they would not support the conclusion he tries to draw.

(vi) *Objection:* Nominalism is impossible.

Answer: This neatly complements the charge of triviality just discussed. Call a program impossible until it is completed, and call it trivial afterwards, and you have a well-rounded defense against it. In the formal sciences we have proofs that certain problems cannot be solved—for example, the trisection of angles with straight-edge and compass alone. But nothing even resembling proof is available for the impossibility of nominalism. And parts of the program that were once confidently cited as impossible have recently been accomplished; in particular the nominalistic and even finitistic treatment of

---

[15] See the article cited in footnote 10 above.

[16] In Quine's article "On Universals" in the *Journal of Symbolic Logic*, vol. 12 (1947), pp. 78–84.

most of classical mathematics, including general definitions for "proof" and "theorem."[17]

Even if full realization of the nominalistic program ultimately does turn out to be impossible, the efforts expended on it may not be unfruitful. The impossibility of trisecting the angle with straight-edge and compass hardly detracts from the value of Euclidean geometry, or leads us to conclude that Euclid was too frugal in his choice of tools.

In the end, the nominalist may not be quite able to live within his means, but he is going to keep on trying as long as he can. Before he resorts to larceny he wants to make very sure that, and how much, he needs to steal.

(vii) *Objection:* Nominalism would hamper the development of mathematics and the other sciences by depriving them of methods they have used and are using to achieve some of their most important results.[18]

Answer: Not at all. The nominalist does not presume to restrict the scientist. The scientist may use platonistic class constructions, complex numbers, divination by inspection of entrails, or any claptrappery that he thinks may help him get the results he wants. But what he produces then becomes raw material for the philosopher, whose task is to make sense of all this: to clarify, simplify, explain, interpret in understandable terms. The practical scientist does the business but the philosopher keeps the books. Nominalism is a restraint that a philosopher imposes upon himself, just because he feels he cannot otherwise make real sense of what is put before him. He must digest what is fed him before he can assimilate it; but he does not expect it all to be pre-digested.

All the same, the advantages to the scientist of abundant and intricate apparatus are easily overestimated. Paucity of means often conduces to clarity and progress in science as well as in philosophy. Some scientists indeed—for example, certain workers in structural linguistics[19]—have even imposed the full restriction of nominalism upon themselves in order to avoid confusion and self-deception. The policy of 'no holds barred' may be exhilarating, but it can sometimes result in a terrible tangle.

(viii) *Objection:* Nominalism is bigoted. In adopting or rejecting systematic apparatus or a system-form, we ought to be governed not by a supposed insight into its intrinsic merits and defects but solely by the results we are enabled to achieve. Languages and system-forms are instruments, and instruments are to be judged by how well they work. The philosopher must not

[17] In the joint article "Steps Towards a Constructive Nominalism," cited in footnote 2 above.

[18] E.g., see p. 40 of Carnap's "Empiricism, Semantics and Ontology" in the *Revue Internationale de Philosophie*, vol. 4 (1950), pp. 20–40. (Reprinted in *Semantics and the Philosophy of Language*, ed. Linsky, University of Illinois Press, 1952, pp. 208–28.) [Pp. 233–48, this volume—Eds.]

[19] In particular, Zellig Harris and Noam Chomsky. See, for instance, the latter's "Systems of Syntactic Analysis" in the *Journal of Symbolic Logic*, vol. 18 (1953), pp. 242–56.

handicap himself by prejudiced or dogmatic repudiations of anything that will serve his purpose.

Answer: This point is strongly urged by Carnap[20] and seems also to have been responsible for Quine's somewhat tentative defection from nominalism. But surely the nominalist does not want to exclude anything that will serve the purpose of philosophy. His critics seem to conceive of that purpose as consisting of correct prediction and the control of nature. These are certainly among the major concerns of daily life, technology, and science; but they do not constitute the primary goal of philosophy—nor, I think, of science in its more philosophical aspects. Obviously a system that predicted future events correctly but reported past events erroneously would be quickly dropped by any theoretical scientist or philosopher in his right mind. But even a true and detailed account of facts past, present, and future will leave the philosopher's work undone. As I suggested a moment ago, his task is to interrelate, systematize, interpret, explain. He is driven not by practical needs but by an impractical desire to understand. He, too, will judge a system by how well it works; but a system works for him only to the extent that it clarifies. The nominalist shuns platonistic devices precisely because he feels that their use would defeat rather than serve the purpose of philosophy. A clear story cannot be told in unintelligible language.

The nominalist cannot demonstrate the need for the restrictions he imposes upon himself. He adopts the principle of nominalism in much the same spirit that he and others adopt the principle of extensionality or that logical philosophers in general adopt the law of contradiction. None of these is amenable to proof; all are stipulated as prerequisites of soundness in a philosophic system. They are usually adopted because a philosopher's conscience gives him no choice in the matter. This does not mean that he need deny that he might some time change his mind. If the neopragmatist pushes me hard enough, I will even concede that I might some day give up the law of contradiction in the interests of getting better results—although if I should give up the law I am puzzled about what the difference would then be between getting results and not getting results. But I make this concession only if the pragmatist concede in return that we might some day even give up his Law of Getting Results. Or does he want to exempt this as constituting the essence of the human mind?

Carnap protests eloquently against what he considers narrowmindedness in philosophy, concluding with the exhortation: "*Let us be cautious in making assertions and critical in examining them but tolerant in permitting linguistic forms*"; and Quine agrees that "the obvious counsel is tolerance and an experimental spirit."[21] Reluctant as I am to cast a shadow on all this sweetness and light, there are limits to my tolerance of tolerance. I admire the statesman tolerant of divergent political opinions, and the person tolerant of racial and

---

[20] In the article cited in footnote 18 above.

[21] *From a Logical Point of View* (see footnote 4 above), p. 19 [p. 195, this volume—Eds.]

educational differences; but I do not admire the accountant who is tolerant about his addition, the logician who is tolerant about his proofs, or the musician who is tolerant about his tone. In every activity, satisfactory performance requires meticulous care in some matters; and in philosophy, one of these matters is the choice of systematic apparatus or 'linguistic form'. Thus in place of Carnap's exhortation, I propose another: "*Let us, as philosophers, be utterly fastidious in choosing linguistic forms.*"

What choices fastidiousness will dictate varies with the individual philosopher. But if that were good reason for indifference, then variations in taste and belief would be good reason for indifference about quality in art and about truth in science.

4. AU REVOIR

I have explained my version of nominalism, and dealt with objections to the effect that it is not nominalism at all, that it is false or groundless, that it is too weak, that it is too strong, that it is trivial, that it is impossible, that it cripples the sciences, and that it is bigoted. Yet I by no means suppose that I have answered all the criticisms that will be or even all that have been made. Nominalism generates few entities but it arouses endless objections. The nominalist is looked upon as an intellectual vandal; and all the good neighbors rush to protect the family heirlooms against him. But the nominalist can go about his business undismayed; for his position is virtually unassailable. Every device he uses, every step he takes, is acceptable to his opponents; he makes no move that is not entirely legitimate by platonistic standards. When the nominalist and the platonist say *au revoir*, only the nominalist can be counted on to comply with the familiar parting admonition they may exchange: "Don't do anything I wouldn't do."

APPENDIX[22]

A system is nominalistic, in the precise sense I have recently defined, if no two of its entities are generated from exactly the same atoms. In order to apply this test we need to know what relation of the system is its "generating" relation, or at least what are the atoms of the system; i.e., what entities of the system do not belong to the converse domain of the generating relation.

The generating relation of a system is the proper-part relation or the ancestral of the membership or the logical sum of the two, as they occur in the system. That is, the generating relation of a system is the relation proper-part-or-ancestral-of-membership as it occurs in the system. For convenience, a subrelation of the (complete) generating relation of the system may be spoken of as a (subordinate) generating relation. Since, notation aside, the proper-part relation may itself be regarded as a subrelation of the ancestral of

[22] This appendix was first published as a note entitled "On Relations that Generate," *Philosophical Studies*, IX (1958), 65–66.

membership, there are no generating relations other than subrelations of the latter.

The point of the criterion of nominalism I have presented is its independence of notation. One may use the sign "ε" and speak of classes and yet have a nominalistic system if severe restrictions upon the admitted classes are observed. And if these restrictions are violated, one cannot escape the charge of platonism by using some other sign, say "R," in place of "ε."

Since the class of generating relations is defined by reference to a particular relation—the ancestral of membership—the criterion of nominalism falls short of being purely formal. Before we can apply the criterion we must know what the atoms of the system are or which, if any, of the relations of the system is the generating relation. But we likewise have to know this before we can determine whether a system is extensional or not. The criterion of nominalism is thus no less formal than the criterion of extensionalism. And indeed, nominalism as I define it might appropriately be termed "hyper-extensionalism."[23]

All this is a restatement of what I hoped I had made clear in my earlier article. But Professor Hempel,[24] supposing that I use the term "generating relation" in some much broader sense than I do, has complained that I do not clearly define this broader sense and has proposed the relation of parent to child as a generating relation. This relation no more meets my requirements for a generating relation than does the relation of child to parent discussed in my earlier article. Accordingly, Hempel is mistaken in saying that the system he has described, with a parent-child relation as the only one involved, will be platonistic by my criterion. Such a system has no generating relation, has all its entities as its atoms, and is therefore nominalistic.

[23] In am indebted to Professor Quine for this apt term.
[24] *Journal of Symbolic Logic*, vol. 22 (1957), pp. 206–207.

Kurt Gödel

Mathematical logic, which is nothing else but a precise and complete formulation of formal logic, has two quite different aspects. On the one hand, it is a section of Mathematics treating of classes, relations, combinations of symbols, etc., instead of numbers, functions, geometric figures, etc. On the other hand, it is a science prior to all others, which contains the ideas and principles underlying all sciences. It was in this second sense that Mathematical Logic was first conceived by Leibniz in his *Characteristica universalis*, of which it would have formed a central part. But it was almost two centuries after his death before his idea of a logical calculus really sufficient for the kind of reasoning occurring in the exact sciences was put into effect (in some form at least, if not the one Leibniz had in mind) by Frege and Peano.[1] Frege was chiefly interested in the analysis of thought and used his calculus in the first place for deriving arithmetic from pure logic. Peano, on the other hand, was more interested in its applications within mathematics and created an elegant and flexible symbolism, which permits expressing even the most complicated mathematical theorems in a perfectly precise and often very concise manner by single formulas.

It was in this line of thought of Frege and Peano that Russell's work set in. Frege, in consequence of his painstaking analysis of the proofs, had not gotten beyond the most elementary properties of the series of integers, while Peano had accomplished a big collection of mathematical theorems expressed

[1] Frege has doubtless the priority, since his first publication about the subject, which already contains all the essentials, appeared ten years before Peano's.

Reprinted with the kind permission of the author, editor, and publisher from Paul A. Schilpp, ed., The Philosophy of Bertrand Russell, *The Library of Living Philosophers, Evanston, Ill. (New York: The Tudor Publishing Company, 1944), pp. 125–53. The author wishes to note (1) that since the original publication of this paper advances have been made in some of the problems discussed and that the formulations given could be improved in several places, and (2) that the term "constructivistic" in this paper is used for a strictly anti-realistic kind of constructivism. Its meaning, therefore, is not identical with that used in current discussions on the foundations of mathematics. If applied to the actual development of logic and mathematics it is equivalent with a certain kind of "predicativity" and hence different both from "intuitionistically admissible" and from "constructive" in the sense of the Hilbert School.*

in the new symbolism, but without proofs. It was only in *Principia Mathematica* that full use was made of the new method for actually deriving large parts of mathematics from a very few logical concepts and axioms. In addition, the young science was enriched by a new instrument, the abstract theory of relations. The calculus of relations had been developed before by Peirce and Schröder, but only with certain restrictions and in too close analogy with the algebra of numbers. In *Principia* not only Cantor's set theory but also ordinary arithmetic and the theory of measurement are treated from this abstract relational standpoint.

It is to be regretted that this first comprehensive and thorough going presentation of a mathematical logic and the derivation of Mathematics from it is so greatly lacking in formal precision in the foundations (contained in *1–*21 of *Principia*), that it presents in this respect a considerable step backwards as compared with Frege. What is missing, above all, is a precise statement of the syntax of the formalism. Syntactical considerations are omitted even in cases where they are necessary for the cogency of the proofs, in particular in connection with the "incomplete symbols." These are introduced not by explicit definitions, but by rules describing how sentences containing them are to be translated into sentences not containing them. In order to be sure, however, that (or for what expressions) this translation is possible and uniquely determined and that (or to what extent) the rules of inference apply also to the new kind of expressions, it is necessary to have a survey of all possible expressions, and this can be furnished only by syntactical considerations. The matter is especially doubtful for the rule of substitution and of replacing defined symbols by their *definiens*. If this latter rule is applied to expressions containing other defined symbols it requires that the order of elimination of these be indifferent. This however is by no means always the case ($\varphi!\hat{u} = \hat{u}[\varphi!u]$, e.g., is a counter-example). In *Principia* such eliminations are always carried out by substitutions in the theorems corresponding to the definitions, so that it is chiefly the rule of substitution which would have to be proved.

I do not want, however, to go into any more details about either the formalism or the mathematical content of *Principia*,[2] but want to devote the subsequent portion of this essay to Russell's work concerning the analysis of the concepts and axioms underlying Mathematical Logic. In this field Russell has produced a great number of interesting ideas some of which are presented most clearly (or are contained only) in his earlier writings. I shall therefore frequently refer also to these earlier writings, although their content may partly disagree with Russell's present standpoint.

What strikes one as surprising in this field is Russell's pronouncedly realistic attitude, which manifests itself in many passages of his writings. "Logic is concerned with the real world just as truly as zoology, though with

---

[2] Cf. in this respect W. V. Quine's article in the Whitehead volume of this series [The Library of Living Philosophers].

its more abstract and general features," he says, e.g., in his *Introduction to Mathematical Philosophy* (edition of 1920, p. 169). It is true, however, that this attitude has been gradually decreasing in the course of time[3] and also that it always was stronger in theory than in practice. When he started on a concrete problem, the objects to be analyzed, (e.g., the classes or propositions) soon for the most part turned into "logical fictions." Though perhaps this need not necessarily mean [according to the sense in which Russell uses this term] that these things do not exist, but only that we have no direct perception of them.

The analogy between mathematics and a natural science is enlarged upon by Russell also in another respect (in one of his earlier writings). He compares the axioms of logic and mathematics with the laws of nature and logical evidence with sense perception, so that the axioms need not necessarily be evident in themselves, but rather their justification lies (exactly as in physics) in the fact that they make it possible for these "sense perceptions" to be deduced; which of course would not exclude that they also have a kind of intrinsic plausibility similar to that in physics. I think that (provided "evidence" is understood in a sufficiently strict sense) this view has been largely justified by subsequent developments, and it is to be expected that it will be still more so in the future. It has turned out that (under the assumption that modern mathematics is consistent) the solution of certain arithmetical problems requires the use of assumptions essentially transcending arithmetic, i.e., the domain of the kind of elementary indisputable evidence that may be most fittingly compared with sense perception. Furthermore it seems likely that for deciding certain questions of abstract set theory and even for certain related questions of the theory of real numbers new axioms based on some hitherto unknown idea will be necessary. Perhaps also the apparently unsurmountable difficulties which some other mathematical problems have been presenting for many years are due to the fact that the necessary axioms have not yet been found. Of course, under these circumstances mathematics may lose a good deal of its "absolute certainty;" but, under the influence of the modern criticism of the foundations, this has already happened to a large extent. There is some resemblance between this conception of Russell and Hilbert's "supplementing the data of mathematical intuition" by such axioms as, e.g., the law of excluded middle which are not given by intuition according to Hilbert's view; the borderline however between data and assumptions would seem to lie in different places according to whether we follow Hilbert or Russell.

An interesting example of Russell's analysis of the fundamental logical concepts is his treatment of the definite article "the". The problem is: what do the so-called descriptive phrases (i.e., phrases as, e.g., "the author of *Waverley*" or "the king of England") denote or signify[4] and what is the meaning of

---

[3] The above quoted passage was left out in the later editions of the *Introduction*.

[4] I use the term "signify" in the sequel because it corresponds to the German word "*bedeuten*" which Frege, who first treated the question under consideration, used in this connection.

sentences in which they occur? The apparently obvious answer that, e.g., "the author of *Waverley*" signifies Walter Scott, leads to unexpected difficulties. For, if we admit the further apparently obvious axiom, that the signification of a composite expression, containing constituents which have themselves a signification, depends only on the signification of these constituents (not on the manner in which this signification is expressed), then it follows that the sentence "Scott is the author of *Waverley*" signifies the same thing as "Scott is Scott"; and this again leads almost inevitably to the conclusion that all true sentences have the same signification (as well as all false ones).[5] Frege actually drew this conclusion; and he meant it in an almost metaphysical sense, reminding one somewhat of the Eleatic doctrine of the "One." "The True"—according to Frege's view—is analyzed by us in different ways in different propositions; "the True" being the name he uses for the common signification of all true propositions.[6]

Now according to Russell, what corresponds to sentences in the outer world is facts. However, he avoids the term "signify" or "denote" and uses "indicate" instead (in his earlier papers he uses "express" or "being a symbol for"), because he holds that the relation between a sentence and a fact is quite different from that of a name to the thing named. Furthermore, he uses "denote" (instead of "signify") for the relation between things and names, so that "denote" and "indicate" together would correspond to Frege's "*bedeuten*". So, according to Russell's terminology and view, true sentences "indicate" facts and, correspondingly, false ones indicate nothing.[7] Hence Frege's theory would in a sense apply to false sentences, since they all indicate the same thing, namely nothing. But different true sentences may indicate many different things. Therefore this view concerning sentences makes it necessary either to drop the above-mentioned principle about the signification (i.e., in Russell's terminology the corresponding one about the denotation and indication) of composite expressions or to deny that a descriptive

[5] The only further assumptions one would need in order to obtain a rigorous proof would be: (1) that' 'φ (a)" and the proposition "a is the object which has the property φ and is identical with a" mean the same thing and (2) that every proposition "speaks about something," i.e., can be brought to the form φ (a). Furthermore one would have to use the fact that for any two objects a, b, there exists a true proposition of the form φ (a, b) as, e.g., a $\neq$ b or a = a $\cdot$ b = b.

[6] Cf. "Sinn und Bedeutung," *Zeitschrift für Philosophie und philosophische Kritik*, Vol. 100 (1892), p. 35.

[7] From the indication (*Bedeutung*) of a sentence is to be distinguished what Frege called its meaning (*Sinn*) which is the conceptual correlate of the objectively existing fact (or "the True"). This one should expect to be in Russell's theory a possible fact (or rather the possibility of a fact), which would exist also in the case of a false proposition. But Russell, as he says, could never believe that such "curious shadowy" things really exist. Thirdly, there is also the psychological correlate of the fact which is called "signification" and understood to be the corresponding belief in Russell's latest book. "Sentence" in contradistinction to "proposition" is used to denote the mere combination of symbols.

phrase denotes the object described. Russell did the latter[8] by taking the view-point that a descriptive phrase denotes nothing at all but has meaning only in context; for example, the sentence "the author of *Waverley* is Scotch", is defined to mean: "There exists exactly one entity who wrote *Waverley* and whoever wrote *Waverley* is Scotch." This means that a sentence involving the phrase "the author of *Waverley*" does not (strictly speaking) assert anything about Scott (since it contains no constituent denoting Scott), but is only a roundabout way of asserting something about the concepts occurring in the descriptive phrase. Russell adduces chiefly two arguments in favor of this view, namely (1) that a descriptive phrase may be meaningfully employed even if the object described does not exist (e.g., in the sentence: "The present king of France does not exist"). (2) That one may very well understand a sentence containing a descriptive phrase without being acquainted with the object described; whereas it seems impossible to understand a sentence without being acquainted with the objects about which something is being asserted. The fact that Russell does not consider this whole question of the interpretation of descriptions as a matter of mere linguistic conventions, but rather as a question of right and wrong, is another example of his realistic attitude, unless perhaps he was aiming at a merely psychological investigation of the actual processes of thought. As to the question in the logical sense, I cannot help feeling that the problem raised by Frege's puzzling conclusion has only been evaded by Russell's theory of descriptions and that there is some-thing behind it which is not yet completely understood.

There seems to be one purely formal respect in which one may give prefer-ence to Russell's theory of descriptions. By defining the meaning of sentences involving descriptions in the above manner, he avoids in his logical system any axioms about the particle "the", i.e., the analyticity of the theorems about "the" is made explicit; they can be shown to follow from the explicit defini-tion of the meaning of sentences involving "the". Frege, on the contrary, has to assume an axiom about "the", which of course is also analytic, but only in the implicit sense that it follows from the meaning of the undefined terms. Closer examination, however, shows that this advantage of Russell's theory over Frege's subsists only as long as one interprets definitions as mere typo-graphical abbreviations, not as introducing names for objects described by the definitions, a feature which is common to Frege and Russell.

I pass now to the most important of Russell's investigations in the field of the analysis of the concepts of formal logic, namely those concerning the logical paradoxes and their solution. By analyzing the paradoxes to which Cantor's set theory had led, he freed them from all mathematical techni-calities, thus bringing to light the amazing fact that our logical intuitions (i.e., intuitions concerning such notions as: truth, concept, being, class, etc.) are

[8] He made no explicit statement about the former; but it seems it would hold for the logical system of *Principia*, though perhaps more or less vacuously.

self-contradictory. He then investigated where and how these common-sense assumptions of logic are to be corrected and came to the conclusion that the erroneous axiom consists in assuming that for every propositional function there exists the class of objects satisfying it, or that every propositional function exists "as a separate entity;"[9] by which is meant something separable from the argument (the idea being that propositional functions are abstracted from propositions which are primarily given) and also something distinct from the combination of symbols expressing the propositional function; it is then what one may call the notion or concept defined by it.[10] The existence of this concept already suffices for the paradoxes in their "intensional" form, where the concept of "not applying to itself" takes the place of Russell's paradoxical class.

Rejecting the existence of a class or concept in general, it remains to determine under what further hypotheses (concerning the propositional function) these entities do exist. Russell pointed out (*loc. cit.*) two possible directions in which one may look for such a criterion, which he called the zig-zag theory and the theory of limitation of size, respectively, and which might perhaps more significantly be called the intensional and the extensional theory. The second one would make the existence of a class or concept depend on the extension of the propositional function (requiring that it be not too big), the first one on its content or meaning (requiring a certain kind of "simplicity," the precise formulation of which would be the problem).

The most characteristic feature of the second (as opposed to the first) would consist in the non-existence of the universal class or (in the intensional interpretation) of the notion of "something" in an unrestricted sense. Axiomatic set theory as later developed by Zermelo and others can be considered as an elaboration of this idea as far as classes are concerned.[11] In particular the phrase "not too big" can be specified (as was shown by J. v. Neumann[12]) to mean: not equivalent with the universe of all things, or, to be more exact, a propositional function can be assumed to determine a class when

---

[9] In Russell's first paper about the subject: "On Some Difficulties in the Theory of Transfinite Numbers and Order Types," *Proc. London Math. Soc.*, Second Series, Vol. 4, 1906, p. 29. If one wants to bring such paradoxes as "the liar" under this viewpoint, universal (and existential) propositions must be considered to involve the class of objects to which they refer.

[10] "Propositional function" (without the clause "as a separate entity") may be understood to mean a proposition in which one or several constituents are designated as arguments. One might think that the pair consisting of the proposition and the argument could then for all purposes play the rôle of the "propositional function as a separate entity," but it is to be noted that this pair (as one entity) is again a set or a concept and therefore need not exist.

[11] The intensional paradoxes can be dealt with, e.g., by the theory of simple types or the ramified hierarchy, which do not involve any undesirable restrictions if applied to concepts only and not to sets.

[12] Cf. "Über eine Widerspruchfreiheitsfrage in der axiomatischen Mengenlehre," *Journal für reine und angewandte Mathematik*, Vol. 160, 1929, p. 227.

and only when there exists no relation (in intension, i.e., a propositional function with two variables) which associates in a one-to-one manner with each object, an object satisfying the propositional function and vice versa. This criterion, however, does not appear as the basis of the theory but as a consequence of the axioms and inversely can replace two of the axioms (the axiom of replacement and that of choice).

For the second of Russell's suggestions too, i.e., for the zig-zag theory, there has recently been set up a logical system which shares some essential features with this scheme, namely Quine's system.[13] It is, moreover, not unlikely that there are other interesting possibilities along these lines.

Russell's own subsequent work concerning the solution of the paradoxes did not go in either of the two afore-mentioned directions pointed out by himself, but was largely based on a more radical idea, the "no-class theory," according to which classes or concepts *never* exist as real objects, and sentences containing these terms are meaningful only to such an extent as they can be interpreted as a *façon de parler*, a manner of speaking about other things (cf. p. [223]). Since in *Principia* and elsewhere, however, he formulated certain principles discovered in the course of the development of this theory as general logical principles without mentioning any longer their dependence on the no-class theory, I am going to treat of these principles first.

I mean in particular the vicious circle principle, which forbids a certain kind of "circularity" which is made responsible for the paradoxes. The fallacy in these, so it is contended, consists in the circumstance that one defines (or tacitly assumes) totalities, whose existence would entail the existence of certain new elements of the same totality, namely elements definable only in terms of the whole totality. This led to the formulation of a principle which says that no totality can contain members definable only in terms of this totality, or members involving or presupposing this totality [vicious circle principle]. In order to make this principle applicable to the intensional paradoxes, still another principle had to be assumed, namely that "every propositional function presupposes the totality of its values" and therefore evidently also the totality of its possible arguments.[14] [Otherwise the concept of "not applying to itself" would presuppose no totality (since it involves no quantifications),[15] and the vicious circle principle would not prevent its application to itself.] A corresponding vicious circle principle for propositional functions which says that nothing defined in terms of a propositional function can be a possible argument of this function is then a consequence.[16] The logical system to which one is led on the basis of these principles is the

[13] Cf. "New Foundations for Mathematical Logic," *Amer. Math. Monthly*, Vol. 44, p. 70.

[14] Cf. *Principia Mathematica*, Vol. I, p. 39.

[15] Quantifiers are the two symbols (∃x) and (x) meaning respectively, "there exists an object x" and "for all objects x." The totality of objects x to which they refer is called their range.

[16] Cf. *Principia Mathematica*, Vol. I, p. 47, section IV.

theory of orders in the form adopted, e.g., in the first edition of *Principia*, according to which a propositional function which either contains quantifications referring to propositional functions of order n or can be meaningfully asserted of propositional functions of order n is at least of order n + 1, and the range of significance of a propositional function as well as the range of a quantifier must always be confined to a definite order.

In the second edition of *Principia*, however, it is stated in the Introduction (pp. XI and XII) that "in a limited sense" also functions of a higher order than the predicate itself (therefore also functions defined in terms of the predicate as, e.g., in p κ ε κ) can appear as arguments of a predicate of functions; and in appendix B such things occur constantly. This means that the vicious circle principle for propositional functions is virtually dropped. This change is connected with the new axiom that functions can occur in propositions only "through their values," i.e., extensionally, which has the consequence that any propositional function can take as an argument any function of appropriate type, whose extension is defined (no matter what order of quantifiers is used in the definition of this extension). There is no doubt that these things are quite unobjectionable even from the constructive standpoint (see p. [219]), provided that quantifiers are always restricted to definite orders. The paradoxes are avoided by the theory of simple types,[17] which in *Principia* is combined with the theory of orders (giving as a result the "ramified hierarchy") but is entirely independent of it and has nothing to do with the vicious circle principle (cf. p. [227]).

Now as to the vicious circle principle proper, as formulated on p. [217], it is first to be remarked that, corresponding to the phrases "definable only in terms of", "involving", and "presupposing", we have really three different principles, the second and third being much more plausible than the first. It is the first form which is of particular interest, because only this one makes impredicative definitions[18] impossible and thereby destroys the derivation of mathematics from logic, effected by Dedekind and Frege, and a good deal of

---

[17] By the theory of simple types I mean the doctrine which says that the objects of thought (or, in another interpretation, the symbolic expressions) are divided into types, namely: individuals, properties of individuals, relations between individuals, properties of such relations, etc. (with a similar hierarchy for extensions), and that sentences of the form: "a has the property φ," "b bears the relation R to c," etc. are meaningless, if a, b, c, R, φ are not of types fitting together. Mixed types (such as classes containing individuals and classes as elements) and therefore also transfinite types (such as the class of all classes of finite types) are excluded. That the theory of simple types suffices for avoiding also the epistemological paradoxes is shown by a closer analysis of these. (Cf. F. P. Ramsey's paper, cited in footnote 21, and A. Tarski, *Der Wahrheitsbegriff in den formalisierten Sprachen*, *Stud. phil.*, Vol. I, Lemberg, 1935, p. 399.)

[18] These are definitions of an object α by reference to a totality to which α itself (and perhaps also things definable only in terms of α) belong. As, e.g., if one defines a class α as the intersection of all classes satisfying a certain condition φ and then concludes that α is a subset also of such classes u as are defined in terms of α (provided they satisfy φ).

modern mathematics itself. It is demonstrable that the formalism of classical mathematics does not satisfy the vicious circle principle in its first form, since the axioms imply the existence of real numbers definable in this formalism only by reference to all real numbers. Since classical mathematics can be built up on the basis of *Principia* (including the axiom of reducibility), it follows that even *Principia* (in the first edition) does not satisfy the vicious circle principle in the first form, if "definable" means "definable within the system" and no methods of defining outside the system (or outside other systems of classical mathematics) are known except such as involve still more comprehensive totalities than those occurring in the systems.

I would consider this rather as a proof that the vicious circle principle is false than that classical mathematics is false, and this is indeed plausible also on its own account. For, first of all one may, on good grounds, deny that reference to a totality necessarily implies reference to all single elements of it or, in other words, that "all" means the same as an infinite logical conjunction. One may, e.g., follow Langford's and Carnap's[19] suggestion to interpret "all" as meaning analyticity or necessity or demonstrability. There are difficulties in this view; but there is no doubt that in this way the circularity of impredicative definitions disappears.

Secondly, however, even if "all" means an infinite conjunction, it seems that the vicious circle principle in its first form applies only if the entities involved are constructed by ourselves. In this case there must clearly exist a definition (namely the description of the construction) which does not refer to a totality to which the object defined belongs, because the construction of a thing can certainly not be based on a totality of things to which the thing to be constructed itself belongs. If, however, it is a question of objects that exist independently of our constructions, there is nothing in the least absurd in the existence of totalities containing members, which can be described (i.e., uniquely characterized)[20] only by reference to this totality.[21] Such a state of affairs would not even contradict the second form of the vicious circle principle, since one cannot say that an object described by reference to a totality "involves" this totality, although the description itself does; nor would it contradict the third form, if "presuppose" means "presuppose for the existence" not "for the knowability."

So it seems that the vicious circle principle in its first form applies only if one takes the constructivistic (or nominalistic) standpoint[22] toward the

[19] See Rudolf Carnap in *Erkenntnis*, Vol. 2, p. 103, and *Logical Syntax of Language*, p. 162, and C. H. Langford, *Bulletin American Mathematical Society*, Vol. 33 (1927), p. 599.

[20] An object a is said to be described by a propositional function $\varphi(x)$ if $\varphi(x)$ is true for $x = a$ and for no other object.

[21] Cf. F. P. Ramsey, "The Foundations of Mathematics," in *Proc. London Math. Soc.*, Series 2, Vol. 25 (1926), p. 338. (Reprinted in *The Foundations of Mathematics*, New York and London, 1931, p. 1.)

[22] I shall use in the sequel "constructivism" as a general term comprising both these standpoints and also such tendencies as are embodied in Russell's "no class" theory.

objects of logic and mathematics, in particular toward propositions, classes and notions, e.g., if one understands by a notion a symbol together with a rule for translating sentences containing the symbol into such sentences as do not contain it, so that a separate object denoted by the symbol appears as a mere fiction.[23]

Classes and concepts may, however, also be conceived as real objects, namely classes as "pluralities of things" or as structures consisting of a plurality of things and concepts as the properties and relations of things existing independently of our definitions and constructions.

It seems to me that the assumption of such objects is quite as legitimate as the assumption of physical bodies and there is quite as much reason to believe in their existence. They are in the same sense necessary to obtain a satisfactory system of mathematics as physical bodies are necessary for a satisfactory theory of our sense perceptions and in both cases it is impossible to interpret the propositions one wants to assert about these entities as propositions about the "data", i.e., in the latter case the actually occurring sense perceptions. Russell himself concludes in the last chapter of his book on *Meaning and Truth*, though "with hesitation," that there exist "universals," but apparently he wants to confine this statement to concepts of sense perceptions, which does not help the logician. I shall use the term "concept" in the sequel exclusively in this objective sense. One formal difference between the two conceptions of notions would be that any two different definitions of the form $\alpha(x) = \varphi(x)$ can be assumed to define two different notions α in the constructivistic sense. (In particular this would be the case for the nominalistic interpretation of the term "notion" suggested above, since two such definitions give different rules of translation for propositions containing α.) For concepts, on the contrary, this is by no means the case, since the same thing may be described in different ways. It might even be that the axiom of extensionality[24] or at least something near to it holds for concepts. The difference may be illustrated by the following definition of the number two: "Two is the notion under which fall all pairs and nothing else." There is certainly more than one notion in the constructivistic sense satisfying this condition, but there might be one common "form" or "nature" of all pairs.

Since the vicious circle principle, in its first form does apply to constructed entities, impredicative definitions and the totality of all notions or classes or propositions are inadmissible in constructivistic logic. What an impredicative definition would require is to construct a notion by a combination of a set of

---

[23] One might think that this conception of notions is impossible, because the sentences into which one translates must also contain notions so that one would get into an infinite regress. This, however, does not preclude the possibility of maintaining the above viewpoint for all the more abstract notions, such as those of the second and higher types, or in fact for all notions except the primitive terms which might be only a very few.

[24] I.e., that no two different properties belong to exactly the same things, which, in a sense, is a counterpart to Leibniz's *Principium identitatis indiscernibilium*, which says no two different things have exactly the same properties.

notions to which the notion to be formed itself belongs. Hence if one tries to effect a retranslation of a sentence containing a symbol for such an impredicatively defined notion it turns out that what one obtains will again contain a symbol for the notion in question.[25] At least this is so if "all" means an infinite conjunction; but Carnap's and Langford's idea (mentioned on p. [219]) would not help in this connection, because "demonstrability," if introduced in a manner compatible with the constructivistic standpoint towards notions, would have to be split into a hierarchy of orders, which would prevent one from obtaining the desired results.[26] As Chwistek has shown,[27] it is even possible under certain assumptions admissible within constructivistic logic to derive an actual contradiction from the unrestricted admission of impredicative definitions. To be more specific, he has shown that the system of simple types becomes contradictory if one adds the "axiom of intensionality" which says (roughly speaking) that to different definitions belong different notions. This axiom, however, as has just been pointed out, can be assumed to hold for notions in the constructivistic sense.

Speaking of concepts, the aspect of the question is changed completely. Since concepts are supposed to exist objectively, there seems to be objection neither to speaking of all of them (cf. p. [224]) nor to describing some of them by reference to all (or at least all of a given type). But, one may ask, isn't this view refutable also for concepts because it leads to the "absurdity" that there will exist properties φ such that φ (a) consists in a certain state of affairs involving all properties (including φ itself and properties defined in terms of φ), which would mean that the vicious circle principle does not hold even in its second form for concepts or propositions? There is no doubt that the totality of all properties (or of all those of a given type) does lead to situations of this kind, but I don't think they contain any absurdity.[28] It is true that such properties φ [or such propositions φ (a)] will have to contain themselves as constituents of their content [or of their meaning], and in fact in many ways, because of the properties defined in terms of φ; but this only makes it impossible to construct their meaning (i.e., explain it as an assertion about sense perceptions or any other non-conceptual entities), which is no objection for one who takes the realistic standpoint. Nor is it self-contradictory that a proper part should be identical (not merely equal) to the whole, as is seen in

---

[25] Cf. Carnap, *loc. cit.*, footnote 19 above.

[26] Nevertheless the scheme is interesting because it again shows the constructibility of notions which can be meaningfully asserted of notions of arbitrarily high order.

[27] See *Erkenntnis*, Vol. 3, p. 367.

[28] The formal system corresponding to this view would have, instead of the axiom of reducibility, the rule of substitution for functions described, e.g., in Hilbert-Bernays, *Grundlagen der Mathematik*, vol. I (1934), p. 90, applied to variables of any type, together with certain axioms of intensionality required by the concept of property which, however, would be weaker than Chwistek's. It should be noted that this view does not necessarily imply the existence of concepts which cannot be expressed in the system, if combined with a solution of the paradoxes along the lines indicated on p. [228].

the case of structures in the abstract sense. The structure of the series of integers, e.g., contains itself as a proper part and it is easily seen that there exist also structures containing infinitely many different parts, each containing the whole structure as a part. In addition there exist, even within the domain of constructivistic logic, certain approximations to this self-reflexivity of impredicative properties, namely propositions which contain as parts of their meaning not themselves but their own formal demonstrability.[29] Now formal demonstrability of a proposition (in case the axioms and rules of inference are correct) implies this proposition and in many cases is equivalent to it. Furthermore, there doubtlessly exist sentences referring to a totality of sentences to which they themselves belong as, e.g., the sentence: "Every sentence (of a given language) contains at least one relation word."

Of course this view concerning the impredicative properties makes it necessary to look for another solution of the paradoxes, according to which the fallacy (i.e., the underlying erroneous axiom) does not consist in the assumption of certain self-reflexivities of the primitive terms but in other assumptions about these. Such a solution may be found for the present in the simple theory of types and in the future perhaps in the development of the ideas sketched on pp. [216 and 229]. Of course, all this refers only to concepts. As to notions in the constructivistic sense there is no doubt that the paradoxes are due to a vicious circle. It is not surprising that the paradoxes should have different solutions for different interpretations of the terms occurring.

As to classes in the sense of pluralities or totalities it would seem that they are likewise not created but merely described by their definitions and that therefore the vicious circle principle in the first form does not apply. I even think there exist interpretations of the term "class" (namely as a certain kind of structures), where it does not apply in the second form either.[30] But for the development of all contemporary mathematics one may even assume that it does apply in the second form, which for classes as mere pluralities is, indeed, a very plausible assumption. One is then led to something like Zermelo's axiom system for set theory, i.e., the sets are split up into "levels" in such a manner that only sets of lower levels can be elements of sets of higher levels (i.e., $x \, \varepsilon \, y$ is always false if x belongs to a higher level than y). There is no reason for classes in this sense to exclude mixtures of levels in one set and transfinite levels. The place of the axiom of reducibility is now taken by the axiom of classes [Zermelo's *Aussonderungsaxiom*] which says that for each level there

[29] Cf. my paper in *Monatshefte für Mathematik und Physik*, Vol. 38 (1931), p. 173, or R. Carnap, *Logical Syntax of Language*, §35.

[30] Ideas tending in this direction are contained in the following papers by D. Mirimanoff: "Les antinomies de Russell et de Buraliforte et le problème fondamental de la théorie des ensembles," *L'Enseignment mathematique*, Vol. 19 (1917), pp. 37–52, and "Remarques sur la théorie des ensembles et les antinomies Cantoriennes," *L'Enseignment mathematique*, vol. 19 (1917), pp. 209–217, and vol. 21 (1920), pp. 29–52. Cf. in particular vol. 19, p. 212.

exists for an arbitrary propositional function $\varphi(x)$ the set of those x of this level for which $\varphi(x)$ is true, and this seems to be implied by the concept of classes as pluralities.

Russell adduces two reasons against the extensional view of classes, namely the existence of (1) the null class, which cannot very well be a collection, and (2) the unit classes, which would have to be identical with their single elements. But it seems to me that these arguments could, if anything, at most prove that the null class and the unit classes (as distinct from their only element) are fictions (introduced to simplify the calculus like the points at infinity in geometry), not that all classes are fictions.

But in Russell the paradoxes had produced a pronounced tendency to build up logic as far as possible without the assumption of the objective existence of such entities as classes and concepts. This led to the formulation of the aforementioned "no class theory," according to which classes and concepts were to be introduced as a *façon de parler*. But propositions, too, (in particular those involving quantifications)[31] were later on largely included in this scheme, which is but a logical consequence of this standpoint, since, e.g., universal propositions as objectively existing entities evidently belong to the same category of idealistic objects as classes and concepts and lead to the same kind of paradoxes, if admitted without restrictions. As regards classes this program was actually carried out, i.e., the rules for translating sentences containing class names or the term "class" into such as do not contain them were stated explicitly; and the basis of the theory, i.e., the domain of sentences into which one has to translate is clear, so that classes can be dispensed with (within the system *Principia*), but only if one assumes the existence of a concept whenever one wants to construct a class. When it comes to concepts and the interpretation of sentences containing this or some synonymous term, the state of affairs is by no means as clear. First of all, some of them (the primitive predicates and relations such as "red" or "colder") must apparently be considered as real objects;[32] the rest of them (in particular according to the second edition of *Principia*, all notions of a type higher than the first and therewith all logically interesting ones) appear as something constructed (i.e., as something not belonging to the "inventory" of the world); but neither the basic domain of propositions in terms of which finally everything is to be interpreted, nor the method of interpretation is as clear as in the case of classes (see below).

This whole scheme of the no-class theory is of great interest as one of the few examples, carried out in detail, of the tendency to eliminate assumptions about the existence of objects outside the "data" and to replace them by

---

[31] Cf. "Les paradoxes de la logique," *Rev. de Metaph. et de Morale*, Vol. 14 (1906), p. 627.

[32] In Appendix C of *Principia* a way is sketched by which these also could be constructed by means of certain similarity relations between atomic propositions, so that these latter would be the only ones remaining as real objects.

constructions on the basis of these data.[33] The result has been in this case essentially negative; i.e., the classes and concepts introduced in this way do not have all the properties required for their use in mathematics, unless one either introduces special axioms about the data (e.g., the axiom of reducibility), which in essence already mean the existence in the data of the kind of objects to be constructed, or makes the fiction that one can form propositions of infinite (and even non-denumerable) length,[34] i.e., operates with truth-functions of infinitely many arguments, regardless of whether or not one can construct them. But what else is such an infinite truth-function but a special kind of an infinite extension (or structure) and even a more complicated one than a class, endowed in addition with a hypothetical meaning, which can be understood only by an infinite mind? All this is only a verification of the view defended above that logic and mathematics (just as physics) are built up on axioms with a real content which cannot be "explained away."

What one can obtain on the basis of the constructivistic attitude is the theory of orders (cf. p. [218]); only now (and this is the strong point of the theory) the restrictions involved do not appear as *ad hoc* hypotheses for avoiding the paradoxes, but as unavoidable consequences of the thesis that classes, concepts, and quantified propositions do not exist as real objects. It is not as if the universe of things were divided into orders and then one were prohibited to speak of all orders; but, on the contrary, it is possible to speak of all existing things; only, classes and concepts are not among them; and if they are introduced as a *façon de parler*, it turns out that this very extension of the symbolism gives rise to the possibility of introducing them in a more comprehensive way, and so on indefinitely. In order to carry out this scheme one must, however, presuppose arithmetic (or something equivalent) which only proves that not even this restricted logic can be built up on nothing.

In the first edition of *Principia*, where it was a question of actually building up logic and mathematics, the constructivistic attitude was, for the most part, abandoned, since the axiom of reducibility for types higher than the first together with the axiom of infinity makes it absolutely necessary that there exist primitive predicates of arbitrarily high types. What is left of the constructive attitude is only: (1) The introduction of classes as a *façon de parler*; (2) the definition of $\sim$, $\vee$, $\cdot$, etc., as applied to propositions containing quantifiers (which incidentally proved its fecundity in a consistency proof for arithmetic); (3) the step-by-step construction of functions of orders higher than 1, which, however, is superfluous owing to the axiom of reducibility; (4) the interpretation of definitions as mere typographical abbreviations, which makes every symbol introduced by definition an incomplete symbol (not one naming an object described by the definition). But the last

---

[33] The "data" are to be understood in a relative sense here, i.e., in our case as logic without the assumption of the existence of classes and concepts.

[34] Cf. Ramsey, *loc. cit.*, footnote 21 above.

item is largely an illusion, because, owing to the axiom of reducibility, there always exist real objects in the form of primitive predicates, or combinations of such, corresponding to each defined symbol. Finally also Russell's theory of descriptions is something belonging to the constructivistic order of ideas.

In the second edition of *Principia* (or to be more exact, in the introduction to it) the constructivistic attitude is resumed again. The axiom of reducibility is dropped and it is stated explicitly that all primitive predicates belong to the lowest type and that the only purpose of variables (and evidently also of constants) of higher orders and types is to make it possible to assert more complicated truth-functions of atomic propositions,[35] which is only another way of saying that the higher types and orders are solely a *façon de parler*. This statement at the same time informs us of what kind of propositions the basis of the theory is to consist, namely of truth-functions of atomic propositions.

This, however, is without difficulty only if the number of individuals and primitive predicates is finite. For the opposite case (which is chiefly of interest for the purpose of deriving mathematics), Ramsey (*loc cit.*) took the course of considering our inability to form propositions of infinite length as a "mere accident," to be neglected by the logician. This of course solves (or rather cuts through) the difficulties; but it is to be noted that, if one disregards the difference between finite and infinite in this respect, there exists a simpler and at the same time more far-reaching interpretations of set theory (and therewith of mathematics). Namely, in case of a finite number of individuals, Russell's *aperçu* that propositions about classes can be interpreted as propositions about their elements becomes literally true, since, e.g., "$x \, \varepsilon \, m$" is equivalent to "$x = a_1, \vee \, x = a_2 \vee \ldots \vee x = a_k$" where the a_i are the elements of m; and "there exists a class such that $\ldots$" is equivalent to "there exist individuals $x_1, x_2 \ldots x_n$ such that $\ldots$,"[36] provided n is the number of individuals in the world and provided we neglect for the moment the null class which would have to be taken care of by an additional clause. Of course, by an iteration of this procedure one can obtain classes of classes, etc., so that the logical system obtained would resemble the theory of simple types except for the circumstance that mixture of types would be possible. Axiomatic set theory appears, then, as an extrapolation of this scheme for the case of infinitely many individuals or an infinite iteration of the process of forming sets.

Ramsey's viewpoint is, of course, everything but constructivistic, unless one means constructions of an infinite mind. Russell, in the second edition of *Principia*, took a less metaphysical course by confining himself to such truth-functions as can actually be constructed. In this way one is again led to the theory of orders, which, however, appears now in a new light, namely as a

---

[35] I.e., propositions of the form S(a), R(a, b), etc., where S, R are primitive predicates and a, b individuals.

[36] The x_i may, of course, as always, be partly or wholly identical with each other.

method of constructing more and more complicated truth-functions of atomic propositions. But this procedure seems to presuppose arithmetic in some form or other (see next paragraph).

As to the question of how far mathematics can be built up on this basis (without any assumptions about the data—i.e., about the primitive predicates and individuals—except, as far as necessary, the axiom of infinity), it is clear that the theory of real numbers in its present form cannot be obtained.[37] As to the theory of integers, it is contended in the second edition of *Principia* that it can be obtained. The difficulty to be overcome is that in the definition of the integers as "those cardinals which belong to every class containing 0 and containing $x + 1$ if containing x," the phrase "every class" must refer to a given order. So one obtains integers of different orders, and complete induction can be applied to integers of order n only for properties of order n; whereas it frequently happens that the notion of integer itself occurs in the property to which induction is applied. This notion, however, is of order $n + 1$ for the integers of order n. Now, in Appendix B of the second edition of *Principia*, a proof is offered that the integers of any order higher than 5 are the same as those of order 5, which of course would settle all difficulties. The proof as it stands, however, is certainly not conclusive. In the proof of the main lemma *89.16, which says that every subset α (of arbitrary high order)[38] of an inductive class β of order 3 is itself an inductive class of order 3, induction is applied to a property of β involving α [namely $\alpha - \beta \neq \Lambda$, which, however, should read $\alpha - \beta \sim\varepsilon$ Induct$_2$ because (3) is evidently false]. This property, however, is of an order > 3 if α is of an order > 3. So the question whether (or to what extent) the theory of integers can be obtained on the basis of the ramified hierarchy must be considered as unsolved at the present time. It is to be noted, however, that, even in case this question should have a positive answer, this would be of no value for the problem whether arithmetic follows from logic, if propositional functions of order n are defined (as in the second edition of *Principia*) to be certain finite (though arbitrarily complex) combinations (of quantifiers, propositional connectives, etc.), because then the notion of finiteness has to be presupposed, which fact is concealed only by taking such complicated notions as "propositional function of order n" in an unanalyzed form as primitive terms of the formalism and giving their definition only in ordinary language. The reply may perhaps be offered that in *Principia* the notion of a propositional function of order n is neither taken as primitive nor defined in terms of the notion of a finite combination, but rather quantifiers referring to propositional functions

---

[37] As to the question how far it is possible to build up the theory of real numbers, presupposing the integers, cf. Hermann Weyl, *Das Kontinuum*, reprinted, 1932.

[38] That the variable α is intended to be of undetermined order is seen from the later applications of *89.17 and from the note to *89.17. The main application is in line (2) of the proof of *89.24, where the lemma under consideration is needed for α's of arbitrarily high orders.

of order n (which is all one needs) are defined as certain infinite conjunctions and disjunctions. But then one must ask: Why doesn't one define the integers by the infinite disjunction: $x = 0 \vee x = 0 + 1 \vee x = 0 + 1 + 1 \vee \ldots$ *ad infinitum*, saving in this way all the trouble connected with the notion of inductiveness? This whole objection would not apply if one understands by a propositional function of order n one "obtainable from such truth-functions of atomic propositions as presuppose for their definition no totalities except those of the propositional functions of order $< n$ and of individuals;" this notion, however, is somewhat lacking in precision.

The theory of orders proves more fruitful if considered from a purely mathematical standpoint, independently of the philosophical question whether impredicative definitions are admissible. Viewed in this manner, i.e., as a theory built up within the framework of ordinary mathematics, where impredicative definitions are admitted, there is no objection to extending it to arbitrarily high transfinite orders. Even if one rejects impredicative definitions, there would, I think, be no objection to extend it to such transfinite ordinals as can be constructed within the framework of finite orders. The theory in itself seems to demand such an extension since it leads automatically to the consideration of functions in whose definition one refers to all functions of finite orders, and these would be functions of order ω. Admitting transfinite orders, an axiom of reducibility can be proved. This, however, offers no help to the original purpose of the theory, because the ordinal α—such that every propositional function is extensionally equivalent to a function of order α—is so great, that it presupposes impredicative totalities. Nevertheless, so much can be accomplished in this way, that all impredicativities are reduced to one special kind, namely the existence of certain large ordinal numbers (or, well-ordered sets) and the validity of recursive reasoning for them. In particular, the existence of a well-ordered set, of order type ω_1 already suffices for the theory of real numbers. In addition this transfinite theorem of reducibility permits the proof of the consistency of the Axiom of Choice, of Cantor's Continuum-Hypothesis and even of the generalized Continuum-Hypothesis (which says that there exists no cardinal number between the power of any arbitrary set and the power of the set of its subsets) with the axioms of set theory as well as of *Principia*.

I now come in somewhat more detail to the theory of simple types which appears in *Principia* as combined with the theory of orders; the former is, however, (as remarked above) quite independent of the latter, since mixed types evidently do not contradict the vicious circle principle in any way. Accordingly, Russell also based the theory of simple types on entirely different reasons. The reason adduced (in addition to its "consonance with common sense") is very similar to Frege's, who, in his system, already had assumed the theory of simpler types for functions, but failed to avoid the paradoxes, because he operated with classes (or rather functions in extension) without any restriction. This reason is that (owing to the variable it contains) a propositional function is something ambiguous (or, as Frege says, something unsaturated, wanting supplementation) and therefore can occur in a meaningful proposition only in such a way that this ambiguity is eliminated (e.g., by substituting a constant for the variable or applying quantification to it). The consequences are that a function cannot replace an individual in a proposition, because the latter has no ambiguity to be removed, and that functions with different kinds of arguments (i.e., different ambiguities) cannot replace each other; which is the essence of the theory of simple types. Taking a more nominalistic viewpoint (such as suggested in the second edition of *Principia* and in *Meaning and Truth*) one would have to replace "proposition" by "sentence" in the foregoing considerations (with corresponding additional changes). But in both cases, this argument clearly belongs to the order of ideas of the "no class" theory, since it considers the notions (or propositional functions) as something constructed out of propositions or sentences by leaving one or several constituents of them undetermined. Propositional functions in this sense are so to speak "fragments" of propositions, which have no meaning in themselves, but only insofar as one can use them for forming propositions by combining several of them, which is possible only if they "fit together," i.e., if they are of appropriate types. But, it should be noted that the theory of simple types (in contradistinction to the vicious circle principle) cannot in a strict sense follow from the constructive standpoint, because one might construct notions and classes in another way, e.g., as indicated on p. [225], where mixtures of types are possible. If on the other hand one considers concepts as real objects, the theory of simple types is not very plausible, since what one would expect to be a concept (such as, e.g., "transitivity" or the number two) would seem to be something behind all its various "realizations" on the different levels and therefore does not exist according to the theory of types. Nevertheless, there seems to be some truth behind this idea of realizations of the same concept on various levels, and one might, therefore, expect the theory of simple types to prove useful or necessary at least as a stepping-stone for a more satisfactory system, a way in which it has already been used by Quine.[39] Also Russell's "typical ambiguity" is a step in this direction. Since, however, it only adds certain simplifying symbolic conventions to the theory of types, it does not *de facto* go beyond this theory.

It should be noted that the theory of types brings in a new idea for the solution of the paradoxes, especially suited to their intensional form. It consists in blaming the paradoxes not on the axiom that every propositional function defines a concept or class, but on the assumption that every concept gives a meaningful proposition, if asserted for any arbitrary object or objects as arguments. The obvious objection that every concept can be extended to all arguments, by defining another one which gives a false proposition whenever the original one was meaningless, can easily be dealt with by pointing out that

[39] *Loc. cit.*, cf. footnote 13 above.

the concept "meaningfully applicable" need not itself be always meaningfully applicable.

The theory of simple types (in its realistic interpretation) can be considered as a carrying through of this scheme, based, however, on the following additional assumption concerning meaningfulness: "Whenever an object x can replace another object y in one meaningful proposition, it can do so in every meaningful proposition."[40] This of course has the consequence that the objects are divided into mutually exclusive ranges of significance, each range consisting of those objects which can replace each other; and that therefore each concept is significant only for arguments belonging to one of these ranges, i.e., for an infinitely small portion of all objects. What makes the above principle particularly suspect, however, is that its very assumption makes it formulation as a meaningful proposition impossible,[41] because x and y must then be confined to definite ranges of significance which are either the same or different, and in both cases the statement does not express the principle or even part of it. Another consequence is that the fact that an object x is (or is not) of a given type also cannot be expressed by a meaningful proposition.

It is not impossible that the idea of limited ranges of significance could be carried out without the above restrictive principle. It might even turn out that it is possible to assume every concept to be significant everywhere except for certain "singular points" or "limiting points," so that the paradoxes would appear as something analogous to dividing by zero. Such a system would be most satisfactory in the following respect: our logical intuitions would then remain correct up to certain minor corrections, i.e., they could then be considered to give an essentially correct, only somewhat "blurred," picture of the real state of affairs. Unfortunately the attempts made in this direction have failed so far;[42] on the other hand, the impossibility of this scheme has not been proved either, in spite of the strong inconsistency theorems of Kleene and Rosser.[43]

In conclusion I want to say a few words about the question whether (and in which sense) the axioms of *Principia* can be considered to be analytic. As to this problem it is to be remarked that analyticity may be understood in two

---

[40] Russell formulates a somewhat different principle with the same effect, in *Principia*, Vol. I, p. 95.

[41] This objection does not apply to the symbolic interpretation of the theory of types, spoken of on p. [228], because there one does not have objects but only symbols of different types.

[42] A formal system along these lines is Church's (cf. "A Set of Postulates for the Foundation of Logic," *Annals of Mathematics*, Vol. 33 (1932), p. 346, and Vol. 34 (1933), p. 839), where, however, the underlying idea is expressed by the somewhat misleading statement that the law of excluded middle is abandoned. However, this system has been proved to be inconsistent. See footnote 43.

[43] Cf. S. C. Kleene and J. B. Rosser, "The Inconsistency of Certain Formal Logics," *Annals of Math.*, Vol. 36 (1935), p. 630.

senses. First, it may have the purely formal sense that the terms occurring can be defined (either explicitly or by rules for eliminating them from sentences containing them) in such a way that the axioms and theorems become special cases of the law of identity and disprovable propositions become negations of this law. In this sense even the theory of integers is demonstrably non-analytic, provided that one requires of the rules of elimination that they allow one actually to carry out the elimination in a finite number of steps in each case.[44] Leaving out this condition by admitting, e.g., sentences of infinite (and non-denumerable) length as intermediate steps of the process of reduction, all axioms of *Principia* (including the axioms of choice, infinity and reducibility) could be proved to be analytic for certain interpretations (by considerations similar to those referred to on p. [225].[45] But this observation is of doubtful value, because the whole of mathematics as applied to sentences of infinite length has to be presupposed in order to prove this analyticity, e.g., the axiom of choice can be proved to be analytic only if it is assumed to be true.

In a second sense a proposition is called analytic if it holds, "owing to the meaning of the concepts occurring in it," where this meaning may perhaps be undefinable (i.e., irreducible to anything more fundamental).[46] It would seem that all axioms of *Principia*, in the first edition, (except the axiom of infinity) are in this sense analytic for certain interpretations of the primitive terms, namely if the term "predicative function" is replaced either by "class" (in the extensional sense) or (leaving out the axiom of choice) by "concept," since nothing can express better the meaning of the term "class" than the axiom of the classes (cf. p. [222]) and the axiom of choice, and since, on the other hand, the meaning of the term "concept" seems to imply that every propositional function defines a concept.[47] The difficulty is only that we don't perceive the concepts of "concept" and of "class" with sufficient distinctness, as is shown by the paradoxes. In view of this situation, Russell took the course

[44] Because this would imply the existence of a decision-procedure for all arithmetical propositions. Cf. A. M. Turing, *Proc. Lond. Math. Soc.*, Vol. 42 (1936), p. 230.

[45] Cf. also F. P. Ramsey, *loc. cit.* (footnote 21), where, however, the axiom of infinity cannot be obtained, because it is interpreted to refer to the individuals in the world.

[46] The two significations of the term *analytic* might perhaps be distinguished as tautological and analytic.

[47] This view does not contradict the opinion defended above that mathematics is based on axioms with a real content, because the very existence of the concept of, e.g., "class" constitutes already such an axiom; since, if one defined, e.g., "class" and "ε" to be "the concepts satisfying the axioms," one would be unable to prove their existence. "Concept" could perhaps be defined in terms of "proposition" (cf. p. [228]) (although I don't think that this would be a natural procedure); but then certain axioms about propositions, justifiable only with reference to the undefined meaning of this term, will have to be assumed. It is to be noted that this view about analyticity makes it again possible that every mathematical proposition could perhaps be reduced to a special case of a = a, namely if the reduction is effected not in virtue of the definitions of the terms occurring, but in virtue of their meaning, which can never be completely expressed in a set of formal rules.

of considering both classes and concepts (except the logically uninteresting primitive predicates) as non-existent and of replacing them by constructions of our own. It cannot be denied that this procedure has led to interesting ideas and to results valuable also for one taking the opposite viewpoint. On the whole, however, the outcome has been that only fragments of Mathematical Logic remain, unless the things condemned are reintroduced in the form of infinite propositions or by such axioms as the axiom of reducibility which (in case of infinitely many individuals) is demonstrably false unless one assumes either the existence of classes or of infinitely many "*qualitates occultae.*" This seems to be an indication that one should take a more conservative course, such as would consist in trying to make the meaning of the terms "class" and "concept" clearer, and to set up a consistent theory of classes and concepts as objectively existing entities. This is the course which the actual development of Mathematical Logic has been taking and which Russell himself has been forced to enter upon in the more constructive parts of his work. Major among the attempts in this direction (some of which have been quoted in this essay) are the simple theory of types (which is the system of the first edition of *Principia* in an appropriate interpretation) and axiomatic set theory, both of which have been successful at least to this extent, that they permit the derivation of modern mathematics and at the same time avoid all known paradoxes. Many symptoms show only too clearly, however, that the primitive concepts need further elucidation.

It seems reasonable to suspect that it is this incomplete understanding of the foundations which is responsible for the fact that Mathematical Logic has up to now remained so far behind the high expectations of Peano and others who (in accordance with Leibniz's claims) had hoped that it would facilitate theoretical mathematics to the same extent as the decimal system of numbers has facilitated numerical computations. For how can one expect to solve mathematical problems systematically by mere analysis of the concepts occurring, if our analysis so far does not even suffice to set up the axioms? But there is no need to give up hope. Leibniz did not in his writings about the *Characteristica universalis* speak of a utopian project; if we are to believe his words he had developed this calculus of reasoning to a large extent, but was waiting with its publication till the seed could fall on fertile ground.[48] He went even so far[49] as to estimate the time which would be necessary for his calculus to be developed by a few select scientists to such an extent "that humanity would have a new kind of an instrument increasing the powers of reason far more than any optical instrument has ever aided the power of

---

[48] *Die philosophischen Schriften von G. W. Leibniz*, herausgegeben von C. J. Gerhardt, Vol. 7 (1890), p. 12. Cf. also G. Vacca, "La logica di Leibniz" (section VII), *Riv. di Mat.*, Vol. 8 (1902–06), p. 72, and the preface in the first volume of the first series of *Leibniz's Sämtliche Briefe und Schriften*, herausgegeben von der Preussischen Akademie der Wissenschaften (1923–   ).

[49] Leibniz, *Philosophische Schriften* (ed. Gerhardt), Vol. 7, p. 187.

vision." The time he names is five years, and he claims that his method is not any more difficult to learn than the mathematics or philosophy of his time. Furthermore, he said repeatedly that, even in the rudimentary state to which he had developed the theory himself, it was responsible for all his mathematical discoveries; which, one should expect, even Poincaré would acknowledge as a sufficient proof of its fecundity.[50]

[50] I wish to express my thanks to Professor Alonzo Church, of Princeton University, who helped me find the correct English expressions in a number of places.

EMPIRICISM, SEMANTICS, AND ONTOLOGY[1]

Rudolf Carnap

1. THE PROBLEM OF ABSTRACT ENTITIES

Empiricists are in general rather suspicious with respect to any kind of abstract entities like properties, classes, relations, numbers, propositions, etc. They usually feel much more in sympathy with nominalists than with realists (in the medieval sense). As far as possible they try to avoid any reference to abstract entities and to restrict themselves to what is sometimes called a nominalistic language, i.e., one not containing such references. However, within certain scientific contexts it seems hardly possible to avoid them. In the case of mathematics, some empiricists try to find a way out by treating the whole of mathematics as a mere calculus, a formal system for which no interpretation is given or can be given. Accordingly, the mathematician is said to speak not about numbers, functions, and infinite classes, but merely about meaningless symbols and formulas manipulated according to given formal rules. In physics it is more difficult to shun the suspected entities, because the language of physics serves for the communication of reports and predictions and hence cannot be taken as a mere calculus. A physicist who is suspicious of abstract entities may perhaps try to declare a certain part of the language of physics as uninterpreted and uninterpretable, that part which refers to real numbers as space-time coordinates or as values

[1] I have made here some minor changes in the formulations to the effect that the term "framework" is now used only for the system of linguistic expressions, and not for the system of the entities in question.

Reprinted with the kind permission of the author and publishers from Rudolf Carnap, Meaning and Necessity, *2nd ed.* (*Chicago: The University of Chicago Press*, 1956), *pp. 205–221, and from* Revue Internationale de Philosophie, *no. 4 (1950), pp. 20–40. The slightly modified version that was printed in* Meaning and Necessity *appears here.*

of physical magnitudes, to functions, limits, etc. More probably he will just speak about all these things like anybody else but with an uneasy conscience, like a man who in his everyday life does with qualms many things which are not in accord with the high moral principles he professes on Sundays. Recently the problem of abstract entities has arisen again in connection with semantics, the theory of meaning and truth. Some semanticists say that certain expressions designate certain entities, and among these designated entities they include not only concrete material things but also abstract entities, e.g., properties as designated by predicates and propositions as designated by sentences.[2] Others object strongly to this procedure as violating the basic principles of empiricism and leading back to a metaphysical ontology of the Platonic kind.

It is the purpose of this article to clarify this controversial issue. The nature and implications of the acceptance of a language referring to abstract entities will first be discussed in general; it will be shown that using such a language does not imply embracing a Platonic ontology but is perfectly compatible with empiricism and strictly scientific thinking. Then the special question of the role of abstract entities in semantics will be discussed. It is hoped that the clarification of the issue will be useful to those who would like to accept abstract entities in their work in mathematics, physics, semantics, or any other field; it may help them to overcome nominalistic scruples.

2. LINGUISTIC FRAMEWORKS

Are there properties, classes, numbers, propositions? In order to understand more clearly the nature of these and related problems, it is above all necessary to recognize a fundamental distinction between two kinds of questions concerning the existence or reality of entities. If someone wishes to speak in his language about a new kind of entities, he has to introduce a system of new ways of speaking, subject to new rules; we shall call this procedure the construction of a linguistic *framework* for the new entities in question. And now we must distinguish two kinds of questions of existence: first, questions of the existence of certain entities of the new kind *within the framework*; we call them *internal questions*; and second, questions concerning the existence of reality *of the system of entities as a whole*, called *external questions*. Internal questions and possible answers to them are formulated with the help of the new forms of expressions. The answers may be found either by purely logical methods or by empirical methods, depending upon whether the framework is a logical or a factual one. An external question is of a problematic character which is in need of closer examination.

The world of things. Let us consider as an example the simplest kind of entities dealt with in the everyday language: the spatio-temporally ordered

---

[2] The terms "sentence" and "statement" are here used synonymously for declarative (indicative, propositional) sentences.

system of observable things and events. Once we have accepted the thing language with its framework for things, we can raise and answer internal questions; e.g., "Is there a white piece of paper on my desk?", "Did King Arthur actually live?", "Are unicorns and centaurs real or merely imaginary?", and the like. These questions are to be answered by empirical investigations. Results of observations are evaluated according to certain rules as confirming or disconfirming evidence for possible answers. (This evaluation is usually carried out, of course, as a matter of habit rather than a deliberate, rational procedure. But it is possible, in a rational reconstruction, to lay down explicit rules for the evaluation. This is one of the main tasks of a pure, as distinguished from a psychological, epistemology.) The concept of reality occurring in these internal questions is an empirical, scientific, non-metaphysical concept. To recognize something as a real thing or event means to succeed in incorporating it into the system of things at a particular space-time position so that it fits together with the other things recognized as real, according to the rules of the framework.

From these questions we must distinguish the external question of the reality of the thing world itself. In contrast to the former questions, this question is raised neither by the man in the street nor by scientists, but only by philosophers. Realists give an affirmative answer, subjective idealists a negative one, and the controversy goes on for centuries without ever being solved. And it cannot be solved because it is framed in a wrong way. To be real in the scientific sense means to be an element of the system; hence this concept cannot be meaningfully applied to the system itself. Those who raise the question of the reality of the thing world itself have perhaps in mind not a theoretical question as their formulation seems to suggest, but rather a practical question, a matter of a practical decision concerning the structure of our language. We have to make the choice whether or not to accept and use the forms of expression in the framework in question.

In the case of this particular example, there is usually no deliberate choice because we all have accepted the thing language early in our lives as a matter of course. Nevertheless, we may regard it as a matter of decision in this sense: we are free to choose to continue using the thing language or not; in the latter case we could restrict ourselves to a language of sense-data and other "phenomenal" entities, or construct an alternative to the customary thing language with another structure, or, finally, we could refrain from speaking. If someone decides to accept the thing language, there is no objection against saying that he has accepted the world of things. But this must not be interpreted as if it meant his acceptance of a *belief* in the reality of the thing world; there is no such belief or assertion or assumption, because it is not a theoretical question. To accept the thing world means nothing more than to accept a certain form of language, in other words, to accept rules for forming statements and for testing, accepting, or rejecting them. The acceptance of the thing language leads, on the basis of observations made, also to the acceptance, belief, and assertion of certain statements. But the thesis of the reality of the thing world cannot be among these statements, because it cannot be formulated in the thing language, or it seems, in any other theoretical language.

The decision of accepting the thing language, although itself not of a cognitive nature, will nevertheless usually be influenced by theoretical knowledge, just like any other deliberate decision concerning the acceptance of linguistic or other rules. The purposes for which the language is intended to be used, for instance, the purpose of communicating factual knowledge, will determine which factors are relevant for the decision. The efficiency, fruitfulness, and simplicity of the use of the thing language may be among the decisive factors. And the questions concerning these qualities are indeed of a theoretical nature. But these questions cannot be identified with the question of realism. They are not yes-no questions but questions of degree. The thing language in the customary form works indeed with a high degree of efficiency for most purposes of everyday life. This is a matter of fact, based upon the content of our experiences. However, it would be wrong to describe this situation by saying: "The fact of the efficiency of the thing language is confirming evidence for the reality of the thing world"; we should rather say instead: "This fact makes it advisable to accept the thing language".

The system of numbers. As an example of a system which is of a logical rather than a factual nature let us take the system of natural numbers. The framework for this system is constructed by introducing into the language new expressions with suitable rules: (1) numerals like "five" and sentence forms like "there are five books on the table"; (2) the general term "number" for the new entities, and sentence forms like "five is a number"; (3) expressions for properties of numbers (e.g., "odd", "prime"), relations (e.g., "greater than"), and functions (e.g., "plus"), and sentence forms like "two plus three is five"; (4) numerical variables ("m", "n", etc.) and quantifiers for universal sentences ("for every n, . . .") and existential sentences ("there is an n such that . . .") with the customary deductive rules.

Here again there are internal questions, e.g., "Is there a prime number greater than a hundred?" Here, however, the answers are found, not by empirical investigation based on observations, but by logical analysis based on the rules for the new expressions. Therefore the answers are here analytic, i.e., logically true.

What is now the nature of the philosophical question concerning the existence or reality of numbers? To begin with, there is the internal question which, together with the affirmative answer, can be formulated in the new terms, say by "There are numbers" or, more explicitly, "There is an n such that n is a number". This statement follows from the analytic statement "five is a number" and is therefore itself analytic. Moreover, it is rather trivial (in contradistinction to a statement like "There is a prime number greater than a million", which is likewise analytic but far from trivial), because it does not say more than that the new system is not empty; but this is immediately seen from the rule which states that words like "five" are substitutable for the new variables. Therefore nobody who meant the question "Are there numbers?" in the internal sense would either assert or even seriously consider a negative answer. This makes it plausible to assume that those philosophers who treat the question of the existence of numbers as a serious philosophical problem and offer lengthy arguments on either side, do not have in mind the internal question. And, indeed, if we were to ask them: "Do you mean the question as to whether the framework of numbers, *if* we were to accept it, would be found to be empty or not?", they would probably reply: "Not at all; we mean a question *prior* to the acceptance of the new framework". They might try to explain what they mean by saying that it is a question of the ontological status of numbers; the question whether or not numbers have a certain metaphysical characteristic called reality (but a kind of ideal reality, different from the material reality of the thing world) or subsistence or status of "independent entities". Unfortunately, these philosophers have so far not given a formulation of their question in terms of the common scientific language. Therefore our judgment must be that they have not succeeded in giving to the external question and to the possible answers any cognitive content. Unless and until they supply a clear cognitive interpretation, we are justified in our suspicion that their question is a pseudo-question, that is, one disguised in the form of a theoretical question while in fact it is non-theoretical; in the present case it is the practical problem whether or not to incorporate into the language the new linguistic forms which constitute the framework of numbers.

The system of propositions. New variables, "p", "q", etc., are introduced with a rule to the effect that any (declarative) sentence may be substituted for a variable of this kind; this includes, in addition to the sentences of the original thing language, also all general sentences with variables of any kind which may have been introduced into the language. Further, the general term "proposition" is introduced. "p is a proposition" may be defined by "p or not p" (or by any other sentence form yielding only analytic sentences). Therefore, every sentence of the form "... is a proposition" (where any sentence may stand in the place of the dots) is analytic. This holds, for example, for the sentence:

(*a*) "Chicago is large is a proposition".

(We disregard here the fact that the rules of English grammar require not a sentence but a that-clause as the subject of another sentence; accordingly, instead of (*a*) we should have to say "That Chicago is large is a proposition".) Predicates may be admitted whose argument expressions are sentences; these predicates may be either extensional (e.g., the customary truth-functional connectives) or not (e.g., modal predicates like "possible", "necessary", etc.). With the help of the new variables, general sentences may be formed, e.g.,

(b) "For every p, either p or not-p".

(c) "There is a p such that p is not necessary and not-p is not necessary".

(d) "There is a p such that p is a proposition".

(c) and (d) are internal assertions of existence. The statement "There are propositions" may be meant in the sense of (d); in this case it is analytic (since it follows from (a)) and even trivial. If, however, the statement is meant in an external sense, then it is non-cognitive.

It is important to notice that the system of rules for the linguistic expressions of the propositional framework (of which only a few rules have here been briefly indicated) is sufficient for the introduction of the framework. Any further explanations as to the nature of the propositions (i.e., the elements of the system indicated, the values of the variables "p", "q", etc.) are theoretically unnecessary because, if correct, they follow from the rules. For example, are propositions mental events (as in Russell's theory)? A look at the rules shows us that they are not, because otherwise existential statements would be of the form: "If the mental state of the person in question fulfils such and such conditions, then there is a p such that ...". The fact that no references to mental conditions occur in existential statements (like (c), (d), etc.) shows that propositions are not mental entities. Further, a statement of the existence of linguistic entities (e.g., expressions, classes of expressions, etc.) must contain a reference to a language. The fact that no such reference occurs in the existential statements here, shows that propositions are not linguistic entities. The fact that in these statements no reference to a subject (an observer or knower) occurs (nothing like: "There is a p which is necessary for Mr. X"), shows that the propositions (and their properties, like necessity, etc.) are not subjective. Although characterizations of these or similar kinds are, strictly speaking, unnecessary, they may nevertheless be practically useful. If they are given, they should be understood, not as ingredient parts of the system, but merely as marginal notes with the purpose of supplying to the reader helpful hints or convenient pictorial associations which may make his learning of the use of the expressions easier than the bare system of the rules would do. Such a characterization is analogous to an extra-systematic explanation which a physicist sometimes gives to the beginner. He might, for example, tell him to imagine the atoms of a gas as small balls rushing around with great speed, or the electromagnetic field and its oscillations as quasi-elastic tensions and vibrations in an ether. In fact, however, all that can accurately be said about atoms or the field is implicitly contained in the physical laws of the theories in question.[3]

[3] In my book *Meaning and Necessity* (Chicago, 1947) I have developed a semantical method which takes propositions as entities designated by sentences (more specifically, as

The system of thing properties. The thing language contains words like "red", "hard", "stone", "house", etc., which are used for describing what things are like. Now we may introduce new variables, say "f", "g", etc., for which those words are substitutable and furthermore the general term "property". New rules are laid down which admit sentences like "Red is a property", "Red is a color", "These two pieces of paper have at least one color in common" (i.e., "There is an f such that f is a color, and ..."). The last sentence is an internal assertion. It is of an empirical, factual nature. However, the external statement, the philosophical statement of the reality of properties—a special case of the thesis of the reality of universals—is devoid of cognitive content.

The systems of integers and rational numbers. Into a language containing the framework of natural numbers we may introduce first the (positive and negative) integers as relations among natural numbers and then the rational numbers as relations among integers. This involves introducing new types of variables, expressions substitutable for them, and the general terms "integer" and "rational number".

The system of real numbers. On the basis of the rational numbers, the real numbers may be introduced as classes of a special kind (segments) of rational numbers (according to the method developed by Dedekind and Frege). Here again a new type of variables is introduced, expressions substitutable for them (e.g., "$\sqrt{2}$"), and the general term "real number".

The spatio-temporal coordinate system for physics. The new entities are the space-time points. Each is an ordered quadruple of four real numbers, called its coordinates, consisting of three spatial and one temporal coordinate. The physical state of a spatio-temporal point or region is described either with the help of qualitative predicates (e.g., "hot") or by ascribing numbers as values

---

intensions of sentences). In order to facilitate the understanding of the systematic development, I added some informal, extra-systematic explanations concerning the nature of propositions. I said that the term "proposition" "is used neither for a linguistic expression nor for a subjective, mental occurrence, but rather for something objective that may or may not be exemplified in nature. ... We apply the term 'proposition' to any entities of a certain logical type, namely, those that may be expressed by (declarative) sentences in a language" (p. 27). After some more detailed discussions concerning the relation between propositions and facts, and the nature of false propositions, I added: "It has been the purpose of the preceding remarks to facilitate the understanding of our conception of propositions. If, however, a reader should find these explanations more puzzling than clarifying, or even unacceptable, he may disregard them" (p. 31) (that is, disregard these extra-systematic explanations, not the whole theory of the propositions as intensions of sentences, as one reviewer understood). In spite of this warning, it seems that some of those readers who were puzzled by the explanations, did not disregard them but thought that by raising objections against them they could refute the theory. This is analogous to the procedure of some laymen who by (correctly) criticizing the ether picture or other visualizations of physical theories, thought they had refuted those theories. Perhaps the discussions in the present paper will help in clarifying the role of the system of linguistic rules for the introduction of a framework for entities on the one hand, and that of extra-systematic explanations concerning the nature of the entities on the other.

of a physical magnitude (e.g., mass, temperature, and the like). The step from the system of things (which does not contain space-time points but only extended objects with spatial and temporal relations between them) to the physical coordinate system is again a matter of decision. Our choice of certain features, although itself not theoretical, is suggested by theoretical knowledge, either logical or factual. For example, the choice of real numbers rather than rational numbers or integers as coordinates is not much influenced by the facts of experience but mainly due to considerations of mathematical simplicity. The restriction to rational coordinates would not be in conflict with any experimental knowledge we have, because the result of any measurement is a rational number. However, it would prevent the use of ordinary geometry (which says, e.g., that the diagonal of a square with the side 1 has the irrational value $\sqrt{2}$) and thus lead to great complications. On the other hand, the decision to use three rather than two or four spatial coordinates is strongly suggested, but still not forced upon us, by the result of common observations. If certain events allegedly observed in spiritualistic séances, e.g., a ball moving out of a sealed box, were confirmed beyond any reasonable doubt, it might seem advisable to use four spatial coordinates. Internal questions are here, in general, empirical questions to be answered by empirical investigations. On the other hand, the external questions of the reality of physical space and physical time are pseudo-questions. A question like "Are there (really) space-time points?" is ambiguous. It may be meant as an internal question; then the affirmative answer is, of course, analytic and trivial. Or it may be meant in the external sense: "Shall we introduce such and such forms into our language?"; in this case it is not a theoretical but a practical question, a matter of decision rather than assertion, and hence the proposed formulation would be misleading. Or finally, it may be meant in the following sense: "Are our experiences such that the use of the linguistic forms in question will be expedient and fruitful?" This is a theoretical question of a factual, empirical nature. But it concerns a matter of degree; therefore a formulation in the form "real or not?" would be inadequate.

3. WHAT DOES ACCEPTANCE OF A KIND OF ENTITIES MEAN?

Let us now summarize the essential characteristics of situations involving the introduction of a new kind of entities, characteristics which are common to the various examples outlined above.

The acceptance of a new kind of entities is represented in the language by the introduction of a framework of new forms of expressions to be used according to a new set of rules. There may be new names for particular entities of the kind in question; but some such names may already occur in the language before the introduction of the new framework. (Thus, for example, the thing language contains certainly words of the type of "blue" and "house" before the framework of properties is introduced; and it may contain words like "ten" in sentences of the form "I have ten fingers" before the framework of numbers is introduced.) The latter fact shows that the occurrence of constants of the type in question—regarded as names of entities of the new kind after the new framework is introduced—is not a sure sign of the acceptance of the new kind of entities. Therefore the introduction of such constants is not to be regarded as an essential step in the introduction of the framework. The two essential steps are rather the following. First, the introduction of a general term, a predicate of higher level, for the new kind of entities, permitting us to say of any particular entity that it belongs to this kind (e.g., "Red is a *property*", "Five is a *number*"). Second, the introduction of variables of the new type. The new entities are values of these variables; the constants (and the closed compound expressions, if any) are substitutable for the variables.[4] With the help of the variables, general sentences concerning the new entities can be formulated.

After the new forms are introduced into the language, it is possible to formulate with their help internal questions and possible answers to them. A question of this kind may be either empirical or logical; accordingly a true answer is either factually true or analytic.

From the internal questions we must clearly distinguish external questions, i.e., philosophical questions concerning the existence or reality of the total system of the new entities. Many philosophers regard a question of this kind as an ontological question which must be raised and answered *before* the introduction of the new language forms. The latter introduction, they believe, is legitimate only if it can be justified by an ontological insight supplying an affirmative answer to the question of reality. In contrast to this view, we take the position that the introduction of the new ways of speaking does not need any theoretical justification because it does not imply any assertion of reality. We may still speak (and have done so) of "the acceptance of the new entities" since this form of speech is customary; but one must keep in mind that this phrase does not mean for us anything more than acceptance of the new framework, i.e., of the new linguistic forms. Above all, it must not be interpreted as referring to an assumption, belief, or assertion of "the reality of the entities". There is no such assertion. An alleged statement of the reality of the system of entities is a pseudo-statement without cognitive content. To be sure, we have to face at this point an important question; but it is a practical, not a theoretical question; it is the question of whether or not to accept the new linguistic forms. The acceptance cannot be judged as being either true or false because it is not an assertion. It can only be judged as being more or less expedient, fruitful, conducive to the aim for which the

---

[4] W. V. Quine was the first to recognize the importance of the introduction of variables as indicating the acceptance of entities. "The ontology to which one's use of language commits him comprises simply the objects that he treats as falling ... within the range of values of his variables" ([Notes], p. 118; compare also his [Designation] and [Universals]).

language is intended. Judgments of this kind supply the motivation for the decision of accepting or rejecting the kind of entities.[5]

Thus it is clear that the acceptance of a linguistic framework must not be regarded as implying a metaphysical doctrine concerning the reality of the entities in question. It seems to me due to a neglect of this important distinction that some contemporary nominalists label the admission of variables of abstract types as "Platonism".[6] This is, to say the least, an extremely misleading terminology. It leads to the absurd consequence, that the position of everybody who accepts the language of physics with its real number variables (as a language of communication, not merely as a calculus) would be called Platonistic, even if he is a strict empiricist who rejects Platonic metaphysics.

A brief historical remark may here be inserted. The non-cognitive character of the questions which we have called here external questions was recognized and emphasized already by the Vienna Circle under the leadership of Moritz Schlick, the group from which the movement of logical empiricism originated. Influenced by ideas of Ludwig Wittgenstein, the Circle rejected both the thesis of the reality of the external world and the thesis of its irreality as pseudo-statements;[7] the same was the case for both the thesis of the reality of universals (abstract entities, in our present terminology) and the nominalistic thesis that they are not real and that their alleged names are not names of anything but merely *flatus vocis*. (It is obvious that the apparent negation of a pseudo-statement must also be a pseudo-statement.) It is therefore not correct to classify the members of the Vienna Circle as nominalists, as is sometimes done. However, if we look at the basic anti-metaphysical and pro-scientific attitude of most nominalists (and the same holds for many materialists and realists in the modern sense), disregarding their occasional pseudo-theoretical

[5] For a closely related point of view on these questions see the detailed discussions in Herbert Feigl, "Existential Hypotheses", *Philosophy of Science*, 17 (1950), 35–62.

[6] Paul Bernays, "Sur le platonisme dans les mathématiques" (*L'Enseignement math.*, 34 (1935), 52–69). W. V. Quine, see previous footnote and a recent paper [What]. Quine does not acknowledge the distinction which I emphasize above, because according to his general conception there are no sharp boundary lines between logical and factual truth, between questions of meaning and questions of fact, between the acceptance of a language structure and the acceptance of an assertion formulated in the language. This conception, which seems to deviate considerably from customary ways of thinking, will be explained in his article [Semantics]. When Quine is the article [What] classifies my logicistic conception of mathematics (derived from Frege and Russell) as "platonic realism" (p. 33), this is meant (according to a personal communication from him) not as ascribing to me agreement with Plato's metaphysical doctrine of universals, but merely as referring to the fact that I accept a language of mathematics containing variables of higher levels. With respect to the basic attitude to take in choosing a language form (an "ontology" in Quine's terminology, which seems to me misleading), there appears now to be agreement between us: "the obvious counsel is tolerance and an experimental spirit" ([What], p. 38). [cf. pp. 183–196 of this anthology.]

[7] See Carnap, *Scheinprobleme in der Philosophie; das Fremdpsychische und der Realismus-streit*, Berlin, 1928. Moritz Schlick, *Positivismus und Realismus*, reprinted in *Gesammelte Aufsätze*, Wien, 1938.

formulations, then it is, of course, true to say that the Vienna Circle was much closer to those philosophers than to their opponents.

4. ABSTRACT ENTITIES IN SEMANTICS

The problem of the legitimacy and the status of abstract entities has recently again led to controversial discussions in connection with semantics. In a semantical meaning analysis certain expressions in a language are often said to designate (or name or denote or signify or refer to) certain extra-linguistic entities.[8] As long as physical things or events (e.g., Chicago or Caesar's death) are taken as designata (entities designated), no serious doubts arise. But strong objections have been raised, especially by some empiricists, against abstract entities as designata, e.g., against semantical statements of the following kind:

(1) "The word 'red' designates a property of things";

(2) "The word 'color' designates a property of properties of things";

(3) "The word 'five' designates a number";

(4) "The word 'odd' designates a property of numbers";

(5) "The sentence 'Chicago is large' designates a proposition".

Those who criticize these statements do not, of course, reject the use of the expressions in question, like "red" or "five"; nor would they deny that these expressions are meaningful. But to be meaningful, they would say, is not the same as having a meaning in the sense of an entity designated. They reject the belief, which they regard as implicitly presupposed by those semantical statements, that to each expression of the types in question (adjectives like "red", numerals like "five", etc.) there is a particular real entity to which the expression stands in the relation of designation. This belief is rejected as incompatible with the basic principles of empiricism or of scientific thinking. Derogatory labels like "Platonic realism", "hypostatization", or " 'Fido'-Fido principle" are attached to it. The latter is the name given by Gilbert Ryle [Meaning] to the criticized belief, which, in his view, arises by a naïve inference of analogy: just as there is an entity well known to me, viz. my dog Fido, which is designated by the name "Fido", thus there must be for every meaningful expression a particular entity to which it stands in the relation of designation or naming, i.e., the relation exemplified by "Fido"-Fido. The

---

[8] See [I]; *Meaning and Necessity* (Chicago, 1947). The distinction I have drawn in the latter book between the method of the name-relation and the method of intension and extension is not essential for our present discussion. The term "designation" is used in the present article in a neutral way; it may be understood as referring to the name-relation or to the intension-relation or to the extension-relation or to any similar relations used in other semantical methods.

belief criticized is thus a case of hypostatization, i.e., of treating as names expressions which are not names. While "Fido" is a name, expressions like "red", "five", etc., are said not to be names, not to designate anything.

Our previous discussion concerning the acceptance of frameworks enables us now to clarify the situation with respect to abstract entities as designata. Let us take as an example the statement:

(a) " 'Five' designates a number".

The formulation of this statement presupposes that our language L contains the forms of expressions which we have called the framework of numbers, in particular, numerical variables and the general term "number". If L contains these forms, the following is an analytic statement in L:

(b) "Five is a number".

Further, to make the statement (a) possible, L must contain an expression like "designates" or "is a name of" for the semantical relation of designation. If suitable rules for this term are laid down, the following is likewise analytic:

(c) " 'Five' designates five".

(Generally speaking, any expression of the form " '...' designates ..." is an analytic statement provided the term "..." is a constant in an accepted framework. If the latter condition is not fulfilled, the expression is not a statement.) Since (a) follows from (c) and (b), (a) is likewise analytic.

Thus it is clear that *if* someone accepts the framework of numbers, then he must acknowledge (c) and (b) and hence (a) as true statements. Generally speaking, if someone accepts a framework for a certain kind of entities, then he is bound to admit the entities as possible designata. Thus the question of the admissibility of entities of a certain type or of abstract entities in general as designata is reduced to the question of the acceptability of the linguistic framework for those entities. Both the nominalistic critics, who refuse the status of designators or names to expressions like "red", "five", etc., because they deny the existence of abstract entities, and the skeptics, who express doubts concerning the existence and demand evidence for it, treat the question of existence as a theoretical question. They do, of course, not mean the internal question; the affirmative answer to *this* question is analytic and trivial and too obvious for doubt or denial, as we have seen. Their doubts refer rather to the system of entities itself; hence they mean the external question. They believe that only after making sure that there really is a system of entities of the kind in question are we justified in accepting the framework by incorporating the linguistic forms into our language. However, we have seen that the external question is not a theoretical question but rather the practical question whether or not to accept those linguistic forms. This acceptance is not in need of a theoretical justification (except with respect to expediency and fruitfulness), because it does not imply a belief or assertion. Ryle says that the "Fido"-Fido principle is "a grotesque theory". Grotesque or not, Ryle is wrong in calling it a theory. It is rather the practical decision to accept certain frameworks. Maybe Ryle is historically right with respect to those whom he mentions as previous representatives of the principle, viz. John Suart Mill, Frege, and Russell. If these philosophers regarded the acceptance of a system of entities as a theory, an assertion, they were victims of the same old, metaphysical confusion. But it is certainly wrong to regard *my* semantical method as involving a belief in the reality of abstract entities, since I reject a thesis of this kind as a metaphysical pseudo-statement.

The critics of the use of abstract entities in semantics overlook the fundamental difference between the acceptance of a system of entities and an internal assertion, e.g., an assertion that there are elephants or electrons or prime numbers greater than a million. Whoever makes an internal assertion is certainly obliged to justify it by providing evidence, empirical evidence in the case of electrons, logical proof in the case of the prime numbers. The demand for a theoretical justification, correct in the case of internal assertions, is sometimes wrongly applied to the acceptance of a system of entities. Thus, for example, Ernest Nagel in [Review C.] asks for "evidence relevant for affirming with warrant that there are such entities as infinitesimals or propositions". He characterizes the evidence required in these cases—in distinction to the empirical evidence in the case of electrons—as "in the broad sense logical and dialectical". Beyond this no hint is given as to what might be regarded as relevant evidence. Some nominalists regard the acceptance of abstract entities as a kind of superstition or myth, populating the world with fictitious or at least dubious entities, analogous to the belief in centaurs or demons. This shows again the confusion mentioned, because a superstition or myth is a false (or dubious) internal statement.

Let us take as example the natural numbers as cardinal numbers, i.e., in contexts like "Here are three books". The linguistic forms of the framework of numbers, including variables and the general term "number", are generally used in our common language of communication; and it is easy to formulate explicit rules for their use. Thus the logical characteristics of this framework are sufficiently clear (while many internal questions, i.e., arithmetical questions, are, of course, still open). In spite of this, the controversy concerning the external question of the ontological reality of the system of numbers continues. Suppose that one philosopher says: "I believe that there are numbers as real entities. This gives me the right to use the linguistic forms of the numerical framework and to make semantical statements about numbers as designata of numerals". His nominalistic opponent replies: "You are wrong; there are no numbers. The numerals may still be used as meaningful expressions. But they are not names, there are no entities designated by them. Therefore the word "number" and numerical variables must not be used (unless a way were found to introduce them as merely abbreviating devices, a way of translating them into the nominalistic thing language)." I cannot think of any possible evidence that would be regarded as relevant by both philosophers, and therefore, if actually found, would decide the controversy or at least make one of the opposite theses more probable than the other. (To construe the numbers as classes or properties of the second level, according to the Frege-Russell method, does, of course, not solve the controversy, because the first philosopher would affirm and the second deny the existence of the system of classes or properties of the second level.) Therefore I feel compelled to regard the external question as a pseudo-question, until both parties to the controversy offer a common interpretation of the question as a cognitive question; this would involve an indication of possible evidence regarded as relevant by both sides.

There is a particular kind of misinterpretation of the acceptance of abstract entities in various fields of science and in semantics, that needs to be cleared up. Certain early British empiricists (e.g., Berkeley and Hume) denied the existence of abstract entities on the ground that immediate experience presents us only with particulars, not with universals, e.g., with this red patch, but not with Redness or Color-in-General; with this scalene triangle, but not with Scalene Triangularity or Triangularity-in-General. Only entities belonging to a type of which examples were to be found within immediate experience could be accepted as ultimate constituents of reality. Thus, according to this way of thinking, the existence of abstract entities could be asserted only if one could show either that some abstract entities fall within the given, or that abstract entities can be defined in terms of the types of entity which are given. Since these empiricists found no abstract entities within the realm of sense-data, they either denied their existence, or else made a futile attempt to define universals in terms of particulars. Some contemporary philosophers, especially English philosophers following Bertrand Russell, think in basically similar terms. They emphasize a distinction between the data (that which is immediately given in consciousness, e.g., sense-data, immediately past experiences, etc.) and the constructs based on the data. Existence or reality is ascribed only to the data; the constructs are not real entities; the corresponding linguistic expressions are merely ways of speech not actually designating anything (reminiscent of the nominalists' *flatus vocis*). We shall not criticize here this general conception. (As far as it is a principle of accepting certain entities and not accepting others, leaving aside any ontological, phenomenalistic and nominalistic pseudo-statements, there cannot be any theoretical objection to it.) But if this conception leads to the view that other philosophers or scientists who accept abstract entities thereby assert or imply their occurrence as immediate data, then such a view must be rejected as a misinterpretation. References to space-time points, the electromagnetic field, or electrons in physics, to real or complex numbers and their functions in mathematics, to the excitatory potential or unconscious complexes in psychology, to an inflationary trend in economics, and the like, do not imply the assertion that entities of these kinds occur as immediate data. And the same holds for references to abstract entities as designata in semantics. Some of the criticisms by English philosophers against such references give the impression that, probably due to the misinterpretation just indicated, they accuse the semanticist not so much of bad metaphysics (as some nominalists would do) but of bad psychology. The fact that they regard a semantical method involving abstract entities not merely as doubtful and perhaps wrong, but as manifestly absurd, preposterous and grotesque, and that they show a deep horror and indignation against this method, is perhaps to be explained by a misinterpretation of the kind described. In fact, of course, the semanticist does not in the least assert or imply that the abstract entities to which he refers can be experienced as immediately given either by sensation or by a kind of rational intuition. An assertion of this kind would indeed be very dubious psychology. The psychological question as to which kinds of entities do and which do not occur as immediate data is entirely irrelevant for semantics, just as it is for physics, mathematics, economics, etc., with respect to the examples mentioned above.[9]

5. CONCLUSION

For those who want to develop or use semantical methods, the decisive question is not the alleged ontological question of the existence of abstract entities but rather the question whether the use of abstract linguistic forms or, in technical terms, the use of variables beyond those for things (or phenomenal data), is expedient and fruitful for the purposes for which semantical analyses are made, viz. the analysis, interpretation, clarification, or construction of languages of communication, especially languages of science. This question is here neither decided nor even discussed. It is not a question simply of yes or no, but a matter of degree. Among those philosophers who have carried out semantical analyses and thought about suitable tools for this work, beginning with Plato and Aristotle and, in a more technical way on the basis of modern logic, with C. S. Peirce and Frege, a great majority accepted abstract entities. This does, of course, not prove the case. After all, semantics in the technical sense is still in the initial phases of its development, and we must be prepared for possible fundamental changes in methods. Let us therefore admit that the nominalistic critics may possibly be right. But if so, they will have to offer better arguments than they have so far. Appeal to ontological insight will not carry much weight. The critics will have to show that it is possible to construct a semantical method which avoids all references to abstract entities and achieves by simpler means essentially the same results as the other methods.

[9] Wilfrid Sellars ("Acquaintance and Description Again", in *Journal of Philosophy*, 46 (1949), 496–504; see pp. 502f.) analyzes clearly the roots of the mistake "of taking the designation relation of semantic theory to be a reconstruction of *being present to an experience*".

The acceptance or rejection of abstract linguistic forms, just as the acceptance or rejection of any other linguistic forms in any branch of science, will finally be decided by their efficiency as instruments, the ratio of the results achieved to the amount and complexity of the efforts required. To decree dogmatic prohibitions of certain linguistic forms instead of testing them by their success or failure in practical use, is worse than futile; it is positively harmful because it may obstruct scientific progress. The history of science shows examples of such prohibitions based on prejudices deriving from religious, mythological, metaphysical, or other irrational sources, which slowed up the developments for shorter or longer periods of time. Let us learn from the lessons of history. Let us grant to those who work in any special field of investigation the freedom to use any form of expression which seems useful to them; the work in the field will sooner or later lead to the elimination of those forms which have no useful function. *Let us be cautious in making assertions and critical in examining them, but tolerant in permitting linguistic forms.*

William P. Alston

During the past half-century many philosophers have occupied themselves with translating one linguistic expression into another, or with providing general schema for such translations. And some of them, sensitive to charges of engaging in parlor games during working hours, have tried, in various ways, to exhibit the serious value of such activities. I want to consider one very popular sort of philosophic translation—the sort which goes from sentences of the form 'There are P's' (or from other sentences which obviously imply sentences of this form, such as 'The P is R') to sentences of some other form. And I want to consider one very common explanation of the point of such translations—viz., that they enable us to avoid "ontological commitments" to P's. It will be my contention that this explanation is basically confused, and that it only succeeds in raising a dust which obstructs our view of the real point of such translations.

Let's begin by considering an example from Morton White's recent book, *Toward Reunion in Philosophy*.[1] He is speaking of the sentences 'There is a difference in age between John and Tom' and 'There is a possibility that James will come.'

"How, then, can we clarify these puzzling sentences and yet avoid the unwelcome conclusion that there are possibilities and age-differences in our universe . . .

"In the case of 'There is a difference in age between John and Tom,' we might begin by saying that we understand the relational predicate 'is as old as' and that we test statements of the form 'x is as old as y' without

---

[1] Cambridge, Mass.: Harvard University Press, 1956.

Reprinted with the kind permission of the author and the editor from Philosophical Studies 9, *no.* 1–2 (1958), 8–17.

having to see that x has some queer thing called an age, that y has one, and that these ages are identical. In that event, the belief of the ordinary man that there is a difference in age between John and Tom would be rendered in language that is not misleading by saying instead, simply, 'It is not the case that John is as old as Tom.' We might offer an analogous translation of 'There is a possibility that James will come' in which we replace it by some statement about the statement 'James will come,' for example by the statement that this statement is not certainly false. ... what we have done is to show that we *need not assert the existence* of age-differences or the existence of possibilities in communicating what we want to communicate." (pp. 68–69.)

Here are several philosophically interesting translations of this sort (which I shall call 'existential reduction'):

1. There is a possibility that James will come.
2. The statement that James will come is not certainly false.

3. There is a meaning which can be given to his remarks.
4. His remarks can be understood in a certain way.

5. There are many virtues which he lacks.
6. He might conceivably be much more virtuous than he is.

7. There are facts which render your position untenable.
8. Your position is untenable in the light of the evidence.

Now it is puzzling to me that anyone should claim that these translations "show that we need not assert the existence of" possibilities, meanings, virtues, and facts "in communicating what we want to communicate." For if the translation of (1) into (2), for example, is adequate, then they are normally used to make the same assertion. In uttering (2) we would be making the same assertion as we would make if we uttered (1), i.e., the assertion that there is a possibility that James will come. And so we would be asserting that there is a possibility (committing ourselves to the existence of a possibility) just as much by using (2) as by using (1). If, on the other hand, the translation is not adequate, it has not been shown that we can, by uttering (2), communicate what we wanted to communicate when we uttered (1). Hence the point of the translation cannot be put in terms of some assertion or commitment from which it saves us.

This dilemma has more than a passing resemblance to the "paradox of analysis," which was extensively discussed a short while ago. (If x is adequately analyzable as y, then 'x' and 'y' must be synonymous. But if so, how can we convey any information by saying 'x is y.') Some philosophers attempted (unsuccessfully in my opinion) to resolve the paradox of analysis by pointing out differences between the meanings of 'x' and 'y' which were sufficient to make the analysis informative, but not so great so to render it invalid. Similar gambits might be tried here, although the omens are no more favorable than before.

A. It may be said that (1) differs from (2) only in carrying an imputation of 'ultimate reality' to possibilities, in implying that possibilities are among the 'ultimate furniture of the universe.' Thus in replacing (1) with (2) we continue to say everything we have any need or right to say, sloughing off only the groundless, and gratuitous, attribution of ultimate reality.

Before we can accept this account we must understand what is meant by 'ultimate reality' and this is not altogether easy. What can be meant by 'taking possibilities to be ultimately real,' other than simply asserting, seriously and with full awareness of what we are doing, that, for example, there is a possibility that James will come? And this can be done by the use of (2) as well as (1).[2] But suppose that some meaning can be given to the phrase 'ultimate reality,' such that (2) does not carry with it an implication of the ultimate reality of possibilities. It is still worthy of note that no one has given adequate reason for the supposition that (1), as ordinarily used, carries any such implication either. What evidence is there that the ordinary man in uttering (1), or the scientist in uttering a sentence like 'There are fourteen electrons in this atom,' is asserting the ultimate reality of possibilities or electrons in any sense which goes beyond the serious and deliberate use of these sentences to make assertions? Of course a philosopher who utters such sentences as 'Possibilities are ultimately real,' 'Possibilities are objective entities,' etc., is asserting the *ultimate* reality of possibilities if anyone ever is. But does that justify us in saying that he is making the same assertion when he utters (1)? Well, perhaps the fact that he uses these queer sentences is an indication that his use of (1) carries a metaphysical implication. But if it does then precisely for that reason he will not admit that by using (2) he can just as well say what he wanted to say when he used (1). This is our problem all over again. Wherever (1), unlike (2), does carry a metaphysical force, the translation is not adequate. Thus the analysis would only have the virtue of showing us that we could say what we want to say without making an ontological commitment to possibilities, except where we want to make an ontological commitment to possibilities. In this case it would be less than a parlor game.

B. Alternatively, admitting that talk of 'ultimate reality' is unclear, or even unintelligible, one might locate the value of the analysis in the dissolution of this unclarity, i.e., in the fact that (2) says everything that is clearly said by (1) but without these confused suggestions of ultimate reality. But does (1) as ordinarily used carry such suggestions? Even if it does and even if this account is substantially correct, it offers no aid and comfort to the ontological interpretation. The ontological interpretation presupposes that there is an

[2] One sometimes suspects that it is some peculiar solemnity attaching to 'There is' (and especially to 'x') which leads philosophers to give sentences like (1) a metaphysical import not imputed to sentences like (2).

activity called 'admitting the (ultimate) existence of possibilities' which we might or might not perform, and the performance or nonperformance of which hinges on whether we employ (1) or (2) to say what we want to say (or on whether we use (1) with or without the realization that it can be translated by (2)). But to say that phrases like 'ultimate existence' are unintelligible is to say that we can't understand what such an activity would be, or what it would be like to perform it, and so are unable to specify what admission it is from which the translation saves us. In other words, on the present account, what the translation enables us to avoid is not certain commitments or assertions, but certain confusions. This clue will be taken up later. But first— back to the ontologist.

These moves have not proved fruitful. But there is indeed one thing, not yet explicitly mentioned, which the translation of (1) into (2) does enable us to avoid, and that is the *sentence*, (1). More generally the schema of which this translation is an instance enables us to say what we want to say without having to use any sentences of this form, i.e., any sentence beginning with 'There is (are),' followed by 'a possibility ...' 'the possibility ...' ('possibilities ...' 'some possibilities ...'), etc. And the hard-pressed ontologist may make a stand here by roundly declaring that the ability to avoid sentences of this form is what he *means* by avoiding an ontological commitment. That is, he will define 'ontological commitment to possibilities' as the inability to say what we want to say without using such sentences.

To be at all plausible this definition will have to be patched up. As it stands, we could avoid an ontological commitment to possibilities simply by introducing a new word as synonymous with 'there is,' or with 'possibility.' This makes the game too easy. The rules can be tightened by requiring that the restatement consist only of existing expressions with their established meanings. But that won't be enough. No one could consider the translation of (1) into 'The possibility exists that James will come' to constitute an evasion of an ontological commitment. The trouble is that there are a number of expressions in common use ('... exists,' 'some ...') which do essentially the same job as 'there is'; let us speak of these expressions as having an explicitly existential force.[3] The sort of translation we are trying to specify is a translation from a sentence which contains one of these expressions, along with the crucial predicate terms, into a sentence which does not. Taking account of this let us restate the definition of ontological commitment as follows:

I.   One is ontologically committed to P's if and only if he is unable to say what he wants to say without using a sentence of the form 'There is (are) a P ... (the P ..., P's ..., etc.)' or some other sentence which deviates from this form only by replacing 'there is' by some other expression with explicit existential force or by replacing 'P' by a synonym (together with

---

[3] The boundaries of this group are not precise. For example, there would be controversy over whether 'some ...' belongs here.

such grammatical changes as are required by these replacements, as in the change from 'There are some lions in this country' to 'Lions exist in this country').[4]

By a not so fortuitous circumstance this criterion is substantially equivalent to Quine's famous criterion for ontological commitment.

II. We are convicted of a particular ontological presupposition if, and only if, the alleged presuppositum has to be reckoned among the entities over which our variables range in order to render one of our affirmations true. (*From a Logical Point of View*, p. 13 [p. 191, this volume].)[5]
An entity is assumed by a theory if and only if it must be counted among the values of the variables in order that the statements affirmed in the theory be true. (*Ibid.*, p. 103.)

The equivalence can be seen as follows. The variables of a theory must range over P's in order to make the affirmations of that theory true if and only if one of those affirmations is either 'There are P's' or some statement which implies 'There are P's,' such as 'There are R's and all R's are P's.' Of course Quine's criterion applies explicitly only to "theories" which are in quantificational form. But he himself points out that the criterion is applicable to theories otherwise expressed provided they can be translated into this form. And I see no reason why any English sentence beginning with 'there is' cannot be translated into one beginning '∃x.' In fact II can be viewed as a narrower version of I, since '∃x' is one of the expressions which does essentially the same job as 'there is.' Hence although the following remarks will be explicitly directed, for the most part, to I, they will, I believe, apply equally to II.

Do we, then, adequately bring out the merits of existential reduction by saying that it enables us to avoid "ontological commitments," in the sense specified by these criteria? These criteria do point up the way in which such translations enable us to cut down the number of sentences of an explicitly existential form which we use (or to reduce the range of our variables). And in certain contexts this may be a virtue. There may be desires, widespread among logicians, which are satisfied by such reductions. And for certain purposes of theory construction or formalization it might be desirable to have as narrow a range of variable substitutions as possible. But it is at best misleading, and at worst flatly incorrect, to record this achievement by saying that we have avoided making an ontological commitment to P's, or avoided

---

[4] This criterion could be further made precise by making more explicit the scope of the 'etc.' Not any phrase containing 'possibility' can be combined with a 'there is' to produce a sentence which would normally be used to assert the existence of possibilities. Consider, for example, 'There is a man who is holding some good possibilities open for you.' More generally, what is required is that 'P' falls within the scope of the existential expression. This of course needs further clarification.

[5] Cambridge, Mass.: Harvard University Press, 1953.

asserting the existence of P's. For the achievement consists, to return to our chief example, in finding some other sentence which can be used to make the same statement which one had been making in uttering (1). And, in any ordinary sense of these terms, whether a man admits (asserts) the existence of possibilities depends on what statement he makes, not on what sentence he uses to make that statement. One admits that possibilities exist whenever he assertorially utters (1), *or any other sentence which means the same* (would ordinarily be used to make the same statement). It is a question of *what* he says, not of *how* he says it. Hence he cannot repudiate his admission by simply changing his words.[6]

A man who was afraid of policemen would be reassured if he were convinced that there are no policemen. But he would not be reassured if he were convinced that one could express all one's beliefs in a language which took not policemen, but rather policemanship, as values of variables (that one could avoid locutions like 'There is a policeman around the corner' in favor of 'Policemanship is exemplified around the corner'). Nor could we convince a scientist that the assumption of the existence of electrons can be dispensed with, simply by providing a way of translating every sentence of the form '$(\exists x)$ (x is an electron . . .)' into another sentence which has the same meaning but which does not require variables to range over electrons, though he would be convinced if we could provide a theory which did the same jobs as his electronic theory but contained no individual sentences which were synonymous with his sentences asserting the existence of electrons. That is, in any context where questions of existence arise the problem is whether or not we shall assert *that* so-and-so exists, not whether we shall choose some particular way of making this assertion. This means that assertion of existence, commitment to existence, etc., does not consist in the inflexible preference for one verbal formulation over any other, however gratifying such preferences may be to logicians, and that the use of the phrase 'ontological commitment' here is unjustifiable and misleading.

Of course Quine could say that the notational question is what he is interested in and that, ordinary usage be damned, this is what he is using 'ontological commitment' to mean. But the whole point of his using 'ontological commitment' for this purpose rather than some other phrase (and the associated use of cognate expressions like 'believe in the existence of,' 'countenance abstract entities,' etc.) is to associate, or identify, the terminological problem with existential problems as they are ordinarily conceived, and so transfer to the former the interest and importance which attaches to the latter. Otherwise why present the values of variables formula as a criterion for 'ontological commitment' instead of just as something which is interesting in its own right? The fact that Quine intends his criterion to be more than just notational in import is further brought out by (1) his insistence that

---

[6] Can there be a confusion of sentence and statement lurking in this criterion of 'ontological commitment'?

ontological questions (as he formulates them) are not different in kind from scientific questions; (2) his use of considerations other than notational convenience (queerness, unobservability) in deciding what values of variables it might be desirable to avoid.

Thus in the last analysis the ontological interpretation can offer no rationale of existential reduction other than the notational convenience attaching to the avoidance of certain verbal forms. But surely this sort of analysis has more significance than that. To get at its significance I shall relapse for a moment into ontological terminology and ask the hitherto neglected question 'Why should anyone wish to avoid an ontological commitment to, for example, possibilities?' More generally, why do the ontological analysts bend their efforts toward escaping from ontological commitments to "abstract entities" (attributes, classes, possibilities, meanings, facts, etc.) rather than to "concrete entities" (physical objects, events, persons, etc.). The reasons most commonly cited are these (Ockham's razor is not relevant here, since the question is not why we should ever try to avoid ontological commitments, but why we should aim at paring off abstract rather than concrete entities):

1. Possibilities, etc., are queer.
2. Possibilities, etc., are obscure in their nature.
3. Possibilities, etc., are unobservable (there is no empirical reason for supposing that there are any such things).

Obviously these reasons are not expressed very clearly. To say that a possibility is queer or obscure is no argument against its existence; on the contrary it is a conclusive argument for its existence. Possession of any characteristic entails, or presupposes, existence. And the unobservability of possibilities is not a matter of fact like the unobservability of mangoes on my desk or of unicorns. It is rather that we can't understand what it would be like to empirically observe a possibility.

These complaints are captious. But they do show that the objections to abstract entities would be more precisely expressed by talking not about possibilities, but about what people say about possibilities. It is because people sometimes say (and ask) such queer and obscure things about possibilities, and talk about them in empirically untestable ways, that our ontological analysts are so loath to "make an ontological commitment to possibilities," i.e., are so loath to use a sentence like (1). More specifically, the tendency to shy away from sentences like (1) is due to the fact that people who attach a great deal of importance to such sentences (and resist replacing them with sentences of other forms) are liable to:

1.   Ask such puzzling questions as 'Are possibilities eternal?' 'Can a proposition be immediately intuited?' 'What are the parts of a fact?' 'Are there negative facts as well as positive ones?'

2. Propound 'theories' which are unintelligible, or at least such that we cannot find any relevant arguments for or against them. For example, 'Possibilities contain in their essence a reference to actuality' 'Every true statement corresponds with a fact' 'Attributes have an existence independent of their exemplifications' 'Meanings are known by intuition.'

3. Take the existence (or *ultimate* existence) of such entities as problematic, subject to proof or disproof, even after ordinary sentences like (1) have been accepted, without giving an intelligible account of the difference between asserting ultimate existence in this problematic sense and simply assenting to the ordinary sentence.

But if (1) and (2) are synonymous, why should (1) and not (2) suffer this abuse, and how can the replacement of (1) with (2) alleviate the situation? It is at this point that the real virtue of this sort of translation can be seen. Consider the following parallels:

There is a possibility that James will come	There is a fruit that James will eat
There is a meaning which can be given to his words	There is a chair which can be given to his aunt
There are many virtues which he lacks	There are many articles of clothing which he lacks

In each case the strong verbal similarity provides a temptation to assimilate the two sorts of existents, i.e., to suppose that we can talk of one in the same way as the other. Since chairs have spatial locations, we are apt to ask about the (ontological) locus of meanings. (See Whitehead on God as the locus of "eternal objects.") Physical objects like chairs and fruits consist of parts which can be specified, unless they are atomic; and so we are led into asking whether facts or propositions are atomic, and if not what their parts are like.[7] Since this is a story which has been often, and ably, told in the recent literature, I shall not elaborate it further. The moral to be drawn here is that the only "ontological commitment" to possibilities which there is any reason to consider undesirable is the tendency to talk about possibilities in inappropriate ways ("category mistakes").

It is the seductive grammatical family likenesses of sentences like (1) which render them objectionable, not any assertion of the existence of possibilities they carry with them, in any intelligible sense of that term. And

---

[7] There are many reasons why the grammatical similarity, which is symmetrical, leads to confusions on the left-hand rather than the right-hand side. The most important ones are these two: (1) We have, in our language a rich repertoire of locutions for talking about chairs, fruits, etc., whereas there are comparatively few ways of talking properly about possibilities, meanings, etc. Thus the pull is into the vacuum on the left. (2) Our tendency to picture everything we talk about entails a tendency to construe the unpicturable abstracta on the model of the picturable concreta.

the point of translating (1) into (2) lies in the fact that once anyone sees that what he says when he uses (1) can be just as well said by using (2), the power of the grammatical lure will be broken. To see that one can say that there is a possibility that James will come, by using either of two sentences of quite different grammatical forms, is to see that possibilities do not *have* to be talked about in the way which would be suggested by either of these forms, and hence that one does not *have* to ask about possibilities the same sort of questions one asks about chairs. To put it in a rather dangerous way, he sees that possibilities do not exist in the same way as chairs. Of course the translation doesn't prove that the same questions cannot be asked about possibilities and about chairs. It is rather that the realization that the translation holds relieves us of the compulsion to ask these questions about possibilities in spite of the impossibility of really making sense of them.

Thus we can make explicit the virtues of existential reduction, taking account of the (unconfused) motives which have led people to perform it, without having to say what we have seen to be untenable—viz., that it enables us to avoid admitting the existence of something.

This way of looking at the matter should also free us from the supposition, which the ontological account might suggest, that when we utter (1) we are inevitably saying something false, at least if we haven't seen that it can be translated into (2), whereas we wouldn't be subject to any such danger in using (2), even if we didn't realize that it is translatable into (1). This gives rise to the idea that there is something inherently objectionable about (1), a sort of ontological taint. But when we see that the point of the translation is the neutralizing of tendencies to confusions, we see that the problem is essentially a strategic one. One is not necessarily misled by (1), with or without a translation, nor is one necessarily safe from confusion by using (2). The translation is a device for removing confusions wherever they arise. They usually arise in connection with (1), in which case we show that (2) can be used to say the same thing; but the reverse procedure might conceivably be useful. Just as no sentence is necessarily misleading, so none is guaranteed, by its form, to be used without confusion. The supposition to the contrary is one of the unfortunate effects of philosophic preoccupation with artificial languages.

WHAT IS CANTOR'S CONTINUUM PROBLEM?

Kurt Gödel

1. THE CONCEPT OF CARDINAL NUMBER

Cantor's continum problem is simply the question: How many points are there on a straight line in euclidean space? An equivalent question is: How many different sets of integers do there exist?

This question, of course, could arise only after the concept of "number" had been extended to infinite sets; hence it might be doubted if this extension can be effected in a uniquely determined manner and if, therefore, the statement of the problem in the simple terms used above is justified. Closer examination, however, shows that Cantor's definition of infinite numbers really has this character of uniqueness. For whatever "number" as applied to infinite sets may mean, we certainly want it to have the property that the number of objects belonging to some class does not change if, leaving the objects the same, one changes in any way whatsoever their properties or mutual relations (e.g., their colors or their distribution in space). From this, however, it follows at once that two sets (at least two sets of changeable objects of the space-time world) will have the same cardinal number if their elements can be brought into a one-to-one correspondence, which is Cantor's definition of equality between numbers. For if there exists such a correspondence for two sets A and B it is possible (at least theoretically) to change the properties and relations of each element of A into those of the corresponding element of B, whereby A is transformed into a set completely indistinguishable from B, hence of the same cardinal number. For example, assuming a square and a line segment both completely filled with mass points (so that at each point of them exactly one mass point is situated), it follows, owing to the

This is a revised and expanded version of a paper of the same title which appeared in The American Mathematical Monthly, 54 (1947), 515–25. It is printed here with the kind permission of the author and the editor of The American Mathematical Monthly.

demonstrable fact that there exists a one-to-one correspondence between the points of a square and of a line segment and, therefore, also between the corresponding mass points, that the mass points of the square can be so rearranged as exactly to fill out the line segment, and vice versa. Such considerations, it is true, apply directly only to physical objects, but a definition of the concept of "number" which would depend on the kind of objects that are numbered could hardly be considered to be satisfactory.

So there is hardly any choice left but to accept Cantor's definition of equality between numbers, which can easily be extended to a definition of "greater" and "less" for infinite numbers by stipulating that the cardinal number M of a set A is to be called less than the cardinal number N of a set B if M is different from N but equal to the cardinal number of some subset of B. That a cardinal number having a certain property exists is defined to mean that a set of such a cardinal number exists. On the basis of these definitions, it becomes possible to prove that there exist infinitely many different infinite cardinal numbers or "powers," and that, in particular, the number of subsets of a set is always greater than the number of its elements; furthermore, it becomes possible to extend (again without any arbitrariness) the arithmetical operations to infinite numbers (including sums and products with any infinite number of terms or factors) and to prove practically all ordinary rules of computation.

But, even after that, the problem of identifying the cardinal number of an individual set, such as the linear continuum, would not be well-defined if there did not exist some systematic representation of the infinite cardinal numbers, comparable to the decimal notation of the integers. Such a systematic representation, however, does exist, owing to the theorem that for each cardinal number and each set of cardinal numbers[1] there exists exactly one cardinal number immediately succeeding in magnitude and that the cardinal number of every set occurs in the series thus obtained.[2] This theorem makes it possible to denote the cardinal number immediately succeeding the set of finite numbers by $\aleph_0$ (which is the power of the "denumerably infinite" sets), the next one by $\aleph_1$, etc.; the one immediately succeeding all $\aleph_i$ where i is an integer, by $\aleph_\omega$, the next one by $\aleph_{\omega+1}$, etc. The theory of ordinal numbers provides the means for extending this series further and further.

---

[1] As to the question of why there does not exist a set of all cardinal numbers, see footnote 15.

[2] The axiom of choice is needed for the proof of this theorem (see A. A. Fraenkel and Y. Bar-Hillel, *Foundations of Set Theory*, Amsterdam: 1958). But it may be said that this axiom, from almost every possible point of view, is as well-founded today as the other axioms of set theory. It has been proved consistent with the other axioms of set theory which are usually assumed, provided that these other axioms are consistent (see my paper cited in footnote 16). Moreover, it is possible to define in terms of any system of objects satisfying the other axioms a system of objects satisfying those axioms *and* the axiom of choice. Finally, the axiom of choice is just as evident as the other set-theoretical axioms for the "pure" concept of set explained in footnote 14.

2. THE CONTINUUM PROBLEM, THE CONTINUUM HYPOTHESIS, AND THE PARTIAL RESULTS CONCERNING ITS TRUTH OBTAINED SO FAR

So the analysis of the phrase "how many" unambiguously leads to a definite meaning for the question stated in the second line of this paper: The problem is to find out which one of the $\aleph$'s is the number of points of a straight line or (which is the same) of any other continuum (of any number of dimensions) in a euclidean space. Cantor, after having proved that this number is greater than $\aleph_0$, conjectured that it is $\aleph_1$. An equivalent proposition is this: Any infinite subset of the continuum has the power either of the set of integers or of the whole continuum. This is Cantor's continuum hypothesis.

But, although Cantor's set theory now has had a development of more than seventy years and the problem evidently is of great importance for it, nothing has been proved so far about the question what the power of the continuum is or whether its subsets satisfy the condition just stated, except (1) that the power of the continuum is not a cardinal number of a certain special kind, namely, not a limit of denumerably many smaller cardinal numbers,[3] and (2) that the proposition just mentioned about the subsets of the continuum is true for a certain infinitesimal fraction of these subsets, the analytic[4] sets.[5] Not even an upper bound, however large, can be assigned for the power of the continuum. Nor is the quality of the cardinal number of the continuum known any better than its quantity. It is undecided whether this number is regular or singular, accessible or inaccessible, and (except for König's negative result) what its character of confinality (see footnote 4) is. The only thing that is known, in addition to the results just mentioned, is a great number of consequences of, and some propositions equivalent to, Cantor's conjecture.[6]

This pronounced failure becomes still more striking if the problem is considered in its connection with general questions of cardinal arithmetic. It is easily proved that the power of the continuum is equal to $2^{\aleph_0}$. So the continum problem turns out to be a question from the "multiplication table" of cardinal numbers, namely, the problem of evaluating a certain infinite product (in fact the simplest non-trivial one that can be formed). There is, however, not one infinite product (of factors > 1) for which so much as an upper bound for its value can be assigned. All one knows about the evaluation of infinite products are two lower bounds due to Cantor and König (the latter of which implies the aforementioned negative theorem on the power of

---

[3] See F. Hausdorff, *Mengenlehre*, 1st ed. (1914), p. 68, or H. Bachmann, *Erg. Math N. F.* I (1955), p. 167. The discoverer of this theorem, J. König, asserted more than he had actualiy proved (see *Math. Ann.*, 60 (1904), p. 177).

[4] See the list of definitions pp. 268–9.

[5] See F. Hausdorff, *Mengenlehre*, 3d ed. (1935), p. 32. Even for complements of analytic sets the question is undecided at present, and it can be proved only that they either have the power $\aleph_0$ or $\aleph_1$ or continuum or are finite (see C. Kuratowski, *Topologie*, I, Warszawa-Lwow, 1933, p. 246).

[6] See W. Sierpinski, *Hypothèse du Continu* (Warsaw: 1934; 2nd ed.; New York: 1956).

the continuum), and some theorems concerning the reduction of products with different factors to exponentiations and of exponentiations to exponentiations with smaller bases or exponents. These theorems reduce[7] the whole problem of computing infinite products to the evaluation of $\aleph_\alpha^{\mathrm{cf}(\aleph_\alpha)}$ and the performance of certain fundamental operations on ordinal numbers, such as determining the limit of a series of them. All products and powers, can easily be computed[8] if the "generalized continuum hypothesis" is assumed; i.e., if it is assumed that $2^{\aleph_\alpha} = \aleph_{\alpha+1}$ for every α, or, in other terms, that the number of subsets of a set of power $\aleph_\alpha$ is $\aleph_{\alpha+1}$. But, without making any undemonstrated assumption, it is not even known whether or not $m < n$ implies $2^m < 2^n$ (although it is trivial that it implies $2^m \leqq 2^n$), nor even whether $2^{\aleph_0} < 2^{\aleph_1}$.

3. RESTATEMENT OF THE PROBLEM ON THE BASIS OF AN ANALYSIS OF THE FOUNDATIONS OF SET THEORY AND RESULTS OBTAINED ALONG THESE LINES

This scarcity of results, even as to the most fundamental questions in this field, to some extent may be due to purely mathematical difficulties; it seems, however (see Section 4), that there are also deeper reasons involved and that a complete solution of these problems can be obtained only by a more profound analysis (than mathematics is accustomed to giving) of the meanings of the terms occurring in them (such as "set", "one-to-one correspondence", etc.) and of the axioms underlying their use. Several such analyses have already been proposed. Let us see then what they give for our problem.

First of all there is Brouwer's intuitionism, which is utterly destructive in its results. The whole theory of the $\aleph$'s greater than $\aleph_1$ is rejected as meaningless.[9] Cantor's conjecture itself receives several different meanings, all of which, though very interesting in themselves, are quite different from the original problem. They lead partly to affirmative, partly to negative answers.[10] Not everything in this field, however, has been sufficiently clarified. The "semi-intuitionistic" standpoint along the lines of H. Poincaré and H. Weyl[11] would hardly preserve substantially more of set theory.

---

[7] This reduction can be effected, owing to the results and methods of a paper by A. Tarski published in *Fund. Math.*, 7 (1925), 1.

[8] For regular numbers $\aleph_\alpha$, one obtains immediately:

$$\aleph_\alpha^{\mathrm{cf}(\aleph_\alpha)} = \aleph_\alpha \aleph_\alpha = 2^{\aleph_\alpha} = \aleph_{\alpha+1}.$$

[9] See L. E. J. Brouwer, *Atti del IV Congresso Internationale dei Matematici* (Roma, 1908), p. 569.

[10] See L. E. J. Brouwer, *Over de gondslagen der wiskunde* (Amsterdam and Leipzig, 1907), I, 9; III, 2.

[11] See H. Weyl, *Das Kontinuum*, 2nd ed. 1932. If the procedure of construction of sets described there (p. 20) is iterated, a sufficiently large (transfinite) number of times, one gets exactly the real numbers of the model for set theory mentioned in Section 4, in which the continuum hypothesis is true. But this iteration is not possible within the limits of the semi-intuitionistic standpoint.

However, this negative attitude toward Cantor's set theory, and toward classical mathematics, of which it is a natural generalization, is by no means a necessary outcome of a closer examination of their foundations, but only the result of a certain philosophical conception of the nature of mathematics, which admits mathematical objects only to the extent to which they are in-interpretable as our own constructions or, at least, can be completely given in mathematical intuition. For someone who considers mathematical objects to exist independently of our constructions and of our having an intuition of them individually, and who requires only that the general mathematical concepts must be sufficiently clear for us to be able to recognize their soundness and the truth of the axioms concerning them, there exists, I believe, a satisfactory foundation of Cantor's set theory in its whole original extent and meaning, namely axiomatics of set theory interpreted in the way sketched below.

It might seem at first that the set-theoretical paradoxes would doom to failure such an undertaking, but closer examination shows that they cause no trouble at all. They are a very serious problem, not for mathematics, however, but rather for logic and epistemology. As far as sets occur in mathematics (at least in the mathematics of today, including all of Cantor's set theory), they are sets of integers, or of rational numbers (i.e., of pairs of integers), or of real numbers (i.e., of sets of rational numbers), or of functions of real numbers (i.e., of sets of pairs of real numbers), etc. When theorems about all sets (or the existence of sets in general) are asserted, they can always be interpreted without any difficulty to mean that they hold for sets of integers as well as for sets of sets of integers, etc. (respectively, that there either exist sets of integers, or sets of sets of integers, or ... etc., which have the asserted property). This concept of set,[12] however, according to which a set is something obtainable from the integers (or some other well-defined objects) by iterated application[13] of the operation "set of",[14] not something obtained by

---

[12] It must be admitted that the spirit of the modern abstract disciplines of mathematics, in particular of the theory of categories, transcends this concept of set, as becomes apparent, e.g., by the self-applicability of categories (see the paper by S. MacLane in *Symp. on Foundations of Mathematics*, Warsaw, 1959). It does not seem, however, that anything is lost from the mathematical content of the theory if categories of different levels are distinguished. If there existed mathematically interesting proofs that would not go through under this interpretation, then the paradoxes of set theory would become a serious problem for mathematics.

[13] This phrase is meant to include transfinite iteration; i.e., the totality of sets obtained by finite iteration is considered to be itself a set and a basis for further applications of the operation "set of".

[14] The operation "set of x's" (where the variable "x" ranges over some given kind of objects) cannot be defined satisfactorily (at least not in the present state of knowledge), but can only be paraphrased by other expressions involving again the concept of set, such as: "multitude of x's", "combination of any number of x's", "part of the totality of x's", where a "multitude" ("combination", "part") is conceived of as something which exists in itself no matter whether we can define it in a finite number of words (so that random sets are not excluded).

dividing the totality of all existing things into two categories, has never led to any antinomy whatsoever; that is, the perfectly "naïve" and uncritical working with this concept of set has so far proved completely self-consistent.[15]

But, furthermore, the axioms underlying the unrestricted use of this concept of set or, at least, a subset of them which suffices for all mathematical proofs devised up to now (except for theorems about the existence of extremely large cardinal numbers, see footnote 20), have been formulated so precisely in axiomatic set theory[16] that the question of whether some given proposition follows from them can be transformed, by means of mathematical logic, into a purely combinatorial problem concerning the manipulation of symbols which even the most radical intuitionist must acknowledge as meaningful. So Cantor's continuum problem, no matter what philosophical standpoint is taken, undeniably retains at least this meaning: to find out whether an answer, and if so which answer, can be derived from the axioms of set theory as formulated in the systems cited.

Of course, if it is interpreted in this way, there are (assuming the consistency of the axioms) *a priori* three possibilities for Cantor's conjecture: It may be demonstrable, disprovable, or undecidable.[17] The third alternative (which is only a precise formulation of the foregoing conjecture, that the difficulties of the problem are probably not purely mathematical), is the most likely. To seek a proof for it is, at present, perhaps the most promising way of attacking the problem. One result along these lines has been obtained already, namely, that Cantor's conjecture is not disprovable from the axioms of set theory, provided that these axioms are consistent (see Section 4).

It is to be noted, however, that on the basis of the point of view here adopted, a proof of the undecidability of Cantor's conjecture from the accepted axioms of set theory (in contradistinction, e.g., to the proof of the transcendency of π) would by no means solve the problem. For if the meanings of the primitive terms of set theory as explained on page 262 and in footnote 14 are accepted as sound, it follows that the set-theoretical concepts and theorems describe some well-determined reality, in which Cantor's conjecture

[15] It follows at once from this explanation of the term "set" that a set of all sets or other sets of a similar extension cannot exist, since every set obtained in this way immediately gives rise to further applications of the operation "set of" and, therefore, to the existence of larger sets.

[16] See, e.g., P. Bernays, "A system of axiomatic set theory," *J. Symb. Log.*, 2 (1937), 65; 6 (1941), 1; 7 (1942), 65, 133; 8 (1943), 89. J. von Neumann, "Eine Axiomatisierung der Mengenlehre," *J. reine u. angew. Math.*, 154 (1925), 219; cf. also *Ibid.*, 160 (1929), 227; *Math. Zs.*, 27 (1928), 669. K. Gödel, *The Consistency of the Continuum Hypothesis (Ann. Math. Studies* No. 3), 1940, 2nd ed., 1951. P. Bernays and A. A. Fraenkel, *Axiomatic Set Theory* (Amsterdam, 1958). By including very strong axioms of infinity, much more elegant axiomatizations have recently become possible. (See the paper by Bernays cited in footnote 20.)

[17] In case the axioms were inconsistent the last one of the four *a priori* possible alternatives for Cantor's conjecture would occur, namely, it would then be both demonstrable and disprovable by the axioms of set theory.

must be either true or false. Hence its undecidability from the axioms being assumed today can only mean that these axioms do not contain a complete description of that reality. Such a belief is by no means chimerical, since it is possible to point out ways in which the decision of a question, which is undecidable from the usual axioms, might nevertheless be obtained.

First of all the axioms of set theory by no means form a system closed in itself, but, quite on the contrary, the very concept of set[18] on which they are based suggests their extension by new axioms which assert the existence of still further iterations of the operation "set of". These axioms can be formulated also as propositions asserting the existence of very great cardinal numbers (i.e., of sets having these cardinal numbers). The simplest of these strong "axioms of infinity" asserts the existence of inaccessible numbers (in the weaker or stronger sense) $> \aleph_0$. The latter axiom, roughly speaking, means nothing else but that the totality of sets obtainable by use of the procedures of formation of sets expressed in the other axioms forms again a set (and, therefore, a new basis for further applications of these procedures).[19] Other axioms of infinity have first been formulated by P. Mahlo.[20] These axioms show clearly, not only that the axiomatic system of set theory as used today is incomplete, but also that it can be supplemented without arbitrariness by new axioms which only unfold the content of the concept of set explained above.

It can be proved that these axioms also have consequences far outside the domain of very great transfinite numbers, which is their immediate subject matter: each of them, under the assumption of its consistency, can be shown to increase the number of decidable propositions even in the field of Diophantine equations. As for the continuum problem, there is little hope of

[18] Similarly the concept "property of set" (the second of the primitive terms of set theory) suggests continued extensions of the axioms referring to it. Furthermore, concepts of "property of property of set" etc. can be introduced. The new axioms thus obtained, however, as to their consequences for propositions referring to limited domains of sets (such as the continuum hypothesis) are contained (as far as they are known today) in the axioms about sets.

[19] See E. Zermelo, *Fund. Math.*, 16 (1930), 29.

[20] See *Ber. Verh. Sächs. Ges. Wiss.*, 63 (1911), 190–200; 65 (1913), 269–76. From Mahlo's presentation of the subject, however, it does not appear that the numbers he defines actually exist. In recent years considerable progress has been made as to the axioms of infinity. In particular, some have been formulated that are based on principles entirely different from those of Mahlo, and Dana Scott has proved that one of them implies the negation of proposition A (mentioned on p. 266). So the consistency proof for the continuum hypothesis explained on p. 266 does *not* go through if this axiom is added. However, that these axioms are implied by the general concept of set in the same sense as Mahlo's has not been made clear yet. See A. Tarski, *Proc. Intn'l Congress for Logic*, Stanford, 1960, p. 134; D. Scott, *Bull. Pol. Ac. Sci.*, Warsaw, April, 1961; W. P. Hanf and D. Scott, *AMS Notices*, 8 (1961), 445. Mahlo's axioms have been derived by Azriel Levy from a general principle about the system of all sets. See *Pac. Jour. of Math.*, 10 (1960), 233. See also P. Bernays, *Essays in the Foundations of Mathematics Dedicated to A. A. Fraenkel*, 1961, p. 1, where almost all set-theoretical axioms are derived from Levy's principle.

solving it by means of those axioms of infinity which can be set up on the basis of Mahlo's principles (the aforementioned proof for the undisprovability of the continuum hypothesis goes through for all of them without any change). But there exist others based on different principles (see footnote 20); also there may exist, besides the usual axioms, the axioms of infinity, and the axioms mentioned in footnote 18, other (hitherto unknown) axioms of set theory which a more profound understanding of the concepts underlying logic and mathematics would enable us to recognize as implied by these concepts (see, e.g., footnote 23).

Secondly, however, even disregarding the intrinsic necessity of some new axiom, and even in case it has no intrinsic necessity at all, a probable decision about its truth is possible also in another way, namely, inductively by studying its "success." Success here means fruitfulness in consequences, in particular in "verifiable" consequences, i.e., consequences demonstrable without the new axiom, whose proofs with the help of the new axiom, however, are considerably simpler and easier to discover, and make it possible to contract into one proof many different proofs. The axioms for the system of real numbers, rejected by the intuitionists, have in this sense been verified to some extent, owing to the fact that analytical number theory frequently allows one to prove number-theoretical theorems which, in a more cumbersome way, can subsequently be verified by elementary methods. A much higher degree of verification than that, however, is conceivable. There might exist axioms so abundant in their verifiable consequences, shedding so much light upon a whole field, and yielding such powerful methods for solving problems (and even solving them constructively, as far as that is possible) that, no matter whether or not they are intrinsically necessary, they would have to be accepted at least in the same sense as any well-established physical theory.

4. SOME OBSERVATIONS ABOUT THE QUESTION: IN WHAT SENSE AND IN WHICH DIRECTION MAY A SOLUTION OF THE CONTINUUM PROBLEM BE EXPECTED?

But are such considerations appropriate for the continuum problem? Are there really any clear indications for its unsolvability by the accepted axioms? I think there are at least two:

The first results from the fact that there are two quite differently defined classes of objects both of which satisfy all axioms of set theory that have been set up so far. One class consists of the sets definable in a certain manner by properties of their elements;[21] the other of the sets in the sense of arbitrary multitudes, regardless of if, or how, they can be defined. Now, before it has

---

[21] Namely, definable by certain procedures, "*in terms* of ordinal numbers" (i.e., roughly speaking, under the assumption that for each ordinal number a symbol denoting it is given). See my papers cited in footnotes 16 and 24. The paradox of Richard, of course, does not apply to this kind of definability, since the totality of ordinals is certainly not denumerable.

been settled what objects are to be numbered, and on the basis of what one-to-one correspondences, one can hardly expect to be able to determine their number, expect perhaps in the case of some fortunate coincidence. If, however, one believes that it is meaningless to speak of sets except in the sense of extensions of definable properties, then, too, he can hardly expect more than a small fraction of the problems of set theory to be solvable without making use of this, in his opinion essential, characteristic of sets, namely, that they are extensions of definable properties. This characteristic of sets, however, is neither formulated explicitly nor contained implicitly in the accepted axioms of set theory. So from either point of view, if in addition one takes into account what was said in Section 2, it may be conjectured that the continuum problem cannot be solved on the basis of the axioms set up so far, but, on the other hand, may be solvable with the help of some new axiom which would state or imply something about the definability of sets.[22]

The latter half of this conjecture has already been verified; namely, the concept of definability mentioned in footnote 21 (which itself is definable in axiomatic set theory) makes it possible to derive, in axiomatic set theory, the generalized continuum hypothesis from the axiom that every set is definable in this sense.[23] Since this axiom (let us call it "A") turns out to be demonstrably consistent with the other axioms, under the assumption of the consistency of these other axioms, this result (regardless of the philosophical position taken toward definability) shows the consistency of the continuum hypothesis with the axioms of set theory, provided that these axioms themselves are consistent.[24] The proof in its structure is similar to the consistency-proof of non-euclidean geometry by means of a model within euclidean geometry. Namely, it follows from the axioms of set theory that the sets definable in the aforementioned sense form a model of set theory in which the proposition A and, therefore, the generalized continuum hypothesis is true.

A second argument in favor of the unsolvability of the continuum problem on the basis of the usual axioms can be based on certain facts (not known at Cantor's time) which seem to indicate that Cantor's conjecture will turn out

[22] D. Hilbert's program for a solution of the continuum problem (see *Math. Ann.*, 95 (1926), 161), which, however, has never been carried through, also was based on a consideration of all possible definitions of real numbers.

[23] On the other hand, from an axiom in some sense opposite to this one, the negation of Cantor's conjecture could perhaps be derived. I am thinking of an axiom which (similar to Hilbert's completeness axiom in geometry) would state some maximum property of the system of all sets, whereas axiom A states a minimum property. Note that only a maximum property would seem to harmonize with the concept of set explained in footnote 14.

[24] See my monograph cited in footnote 16 and my paper in *Proc. Nat. Ac. Sci.*, 25 (1939), 220. I take this opportunity to correct a mistake in the notation and a misprint which occurred in this paper: in lines 25–29, p. 221; 4–6 and 10, p. 222; 11–19, p. 223, the letter α should be replaced (at all places where it occurs) by μ. Also, in Theorem 6, p. 222, the symbol "$\equiv$" should be inserted between $\phi_\alpha(x)$ and $\phi_{\bar{\alpha}}(x')$. For a carrying through of the proof in all details, the paper cited in footnote 16 is to be consulted.

to be wrong,[25] while, on the other hand, a disproof of it is demonstrably impossible on the basis of the axioms being assumed today.

One such fact is the existence of certain properties of point sets (asserting an extreme rareness of the sets concerned) for which one has succeeded in proving the existence of non-denumerable sets having these properties, but no way is apparent in which one could expect to prove the existence of examples of the power of the continuum. Properties of this type (of subsets of a straight line) are: (1) being of the first category on every perfect set,[26] (2) being carried into a zero set by every continuous one-to-one mapping of the line onto itself.[27] Another property of a similar nature is that of being coverable by infinitely many intervals of any given lengths. But in this case one has so far not even succeeded in proving the existence of non-denumerable examples. From the continuum hypothesis, however, it follows in all three cases that there exist, not only examples of the power of the continuum,[28] but even such as are carried into themselves (up to denumerably many points) by *every* translation of the straight line.[29]

Other highly implausible consequences of the continuum hypothesis are that there exist: (1) subsets of a straight line of the power of the continuum which are covered (up to denumerably many points) by *every* dense set of intervals;[30] (2) infinite dimensional subsets of Hilbert space which contain no non-denumerable finite-dimensional subset (in the sense of Menger-Urysohn);[31] (3) an infinite sequence A^i of decompositions of any set M of the power of the continuum into continuum many mutually exclusive sets A^i_x such that, in whichever way a set $A^i_{x_i}$ is chosen for each i, $\prod\limits_{i=0}^{\infty} (M - A^i_{x_i})$ is denumerable.[32] (1) and (3) are very implausible even if "power of the continuum" is replaced by "$\aleph_1$".

One may say that many results of point-set theory obtained without using the continuum hypothesis also are highly unexpected and implausible.[33] But, true as that may be, still the situation is different there, in that, in most of those instances (such as, e.g., Peano's curves), the appearance to the contrary can be explained by a lack of agreement between our intuitive geometrical concepts and the set-theoretical ones occurring in the theorems. Also, it is very

[25] Views tending in this direction have been expressed also by N. Lusin in *Fund. Math.*, 25 (1935), 129ff. See also W. Sierpinski, *Ibid.*, p. 132.

[26] See W. Sierpinski, *Fund. Math.*, 22 (1934), 270, and C. Kuratowski, *Topologie*, I, p. 269ff.

[27] See N. Lusin and W. Sierpinski, *Bull. Internat. Ac. Sci.*, Cracovie 1918, p. 35; and W. Sierpinski, *Fund. Math.*, 22 (1934), 270.

[28] For the third case see *loc. cit.* footnote 6, p. 39, Theorem 1, of the first edition.

[29] See W. Sierpinski, *Ann. Scuol. Norm. Sup.*, Pisa 4 (1935), 43.

[30] See N. Lusin, *C.R. Paris*, 158 (1914), 1259.

[31] See W. Hurewicz, *Fund. Math.*, 19 (1932), 8.

[32] See S. Braun and W. Sierpinski, *Fund. Math.*, 19 (1932), 1, proposition (Q). This proposition is equivalent with the continuum hypothesis.

[33] See, e.g., L. Blumenthal, *Am. Math. Monthly*, 47 (1940), 346.

suspicious that, as against the numerous plausible propositions which imply the negation of the continuum hypothesis, not one plausible proposition is known which would imply the continuum hypothesis. I believe that adding up all that has been said one has good reason for suspecting that the role of the continuum problem in set theory will be to lead to the discovery of new axioms which will make it possible to disprove Cantor's conjecture.

DEFINITIONS OF SOME OF THE TECHNICAL TERMS

Definitions 4–15 refer to subsets of a straight line, but can be literally transferred to subsets of euclidean spaces of any number of dimensions if "interval" is identified with "interior of a parallelepipedon."

1. I call *the character of confinality* of a cardinal number m (abbreviated by "cf(m)") the smallest number n such that m is the sum of n numbers $< m$.

2. A cardinal number m is *regular* if cf(m) $= m$, otherwise singular.

3. An infinite cardinal number m is *inaccessible* if it is regular and has no immediate predecessor (i.e., if, although it is a limit of numbers $< m$, it is not a limit of fewer than m such numbers); it is *strongly inaccessible* if each product (and, therefore, also each sum) of fewer than m numbers $< m$ is $< m$. (See W. Sierpinski and A. Tarski, *Fund. Math.*, 15 (1930), p. 292; A. Tarski, *ibid.*, 30 (1938), p. 68.)

    It follows from the generalized continuum hypothesis that these two concepts are equivalent. $\aleph_0$ is evidently inaccessible, and also strongly inaccessible. As for finite numbers, 0 and 2 and no others are strongly inaccessible. A definition of inaccessibility, applicable to finite numbers, is this: m is inaccessible if (1) any sum of fewer than m numbers $< m$ is $< m$, and (2) the number of numbers $< m$ is m. This definition, for transfinite numbers, agrees with that given above, and for finite numbers yields 0, 1, 2 as inaccessible. So inaccessibility and strong inaccessibility turn out not to be equivalent for finite numbers. This casts some doubt on their equivalence for transfinite numbers, which follows from the generalized continuum hypothesis.

4. A set of intervals is *dense* if every interval has points in common with some interval of the set. (The end-points of an interval are not considered as points of the interval.)

5. A *zero-set* is a set which can be covered by infinite sets of intervals with arbitrarily small lengths-sum.

6. A *neighborhood* of a point P is an interval containing P.

7. A subset A of B is *dense in B* if every neighborhood of any point of B contains points of A.

8. A point P is in the *exterior* of A if it has a neighborhood containing no point of A.

9. A subset A of B is *nowhere dense in B* if those points of B which are in the exterior of A are dense in B, or (which is equivalent) if for no interval I the intersection IA is dense in IB.

10. A subset A of B is *of the first category in B* if it is the sum of denumerably many sets nowhere dense in B.

11. A set A is *of the first category on B* if the intersection AB is of the first category in B.

12. A point P is called *a limit point* of a set A if any neighborhood of P contains infinitely many points of A.

13. A set A is called *closed* if it contains all its limit points.

14. A set is *perfect* if it is closed and has no isolated point (i.e., no point with a neighborhood containing no other point of the set).

15. *Borel-sets* are defined as the smallest system of sets satisfying the postulates:
    (1) The closed sets are Borel-sets.
    (2) The complement of a Borel-set is a Borel-set.
    (3) The sum of denumerably many Borel-sets is a Borel-set.

16. A set is *analytic* if it is the orthogonal projection of some Borel-set of a space of next higher dimension. (Every Borel-set therefore is, of course, analytic.)

SUPPLEMENT TO THE SECOND EDITION

Since the publication of the preceding paper, a number of new results have been obtained; I would like to mention those that are of special interest in connection with the foregoing discussions.

1. A. Hajnal has proved[34] that, if $2^{\aleph_0} \neq \aleph_2$ could be derived from the axioms of set theory, so could $2^{\aleph_0} = \aleph_1$. This surprising result could greatly facilitate the solution of the continuum problem, should Cantor's continuum hypothesis be demonstrable from the axioms of set theory, which, however, probably is not the case.

2. Some new consequences of, and propositions equivalent with, Cantor's hypothesis can be found in the new edition of W. Sierpinski's book.[35] In the first edition, it had been proved that the continuum hypothesis is equivalent with the proposition that the euclidean plane is the sum of denumerably many "generalized curves" (where a generalized curve is a point set definable

---

[34] See *Zeitschr. f. math. Log. u. Grundl. d. Math.*, II (1956), 131.
[35] See footnote 6.

by an equation $y = f(x)$ in some cartesian coordinate system). In the second edition, it is pointed out[36] that the euclidean plane can be proved to be the sum of fewer than continuum many generalized curves under the much weaker assumption that the power of the continuum is not an inaccessible number. A proof of the converse of this theorem would give some plausibility to the hypothesis $2^{\aleph_0} =$ the smallest inaccessible number $> \aleph_0$. However, great caution is called for with regard to this inference, because the paradoxical appearance in this case (like in Peano's "curves") is due (at least in part) to a transference of our geometrical intuition of curves to something which has only some of the characteristics of curves. Note that nothing of this kind is involved in the counterintuitive consequences of the continuum hypothesis mentioned on p. 267.

3. C. Kuratowski has formulated a strengthening of the continuum hypothesis,[37] whose consistency follows from the consistency-proof mentioned in Section 4. He then drew various consequences from this new hypothesis.

4. Very interesting new results about the axioms of infinity have been obtained in recent years (see footnotes 20 and 16).

In opposition to the viewpoint advocated in Section 4 it has been suggested[38] that, in case Cantor's continuum problem should turn out to be undecidable from the accepted axioms of set theory, the question of its truth would lose its meaning, exactly as the question of the truth of Euclid's fifth postulate by the proof of the consistency of non-euclidean geometry became meaningless for the mathematician. I therefore would like to point out that the situation in set theory is very different from that in geometry, both from the mathematical and from the epistemological point of view.

In the case of the axiom of the existence of inaccessible numbers, e.g., (which can be proved to be undecidable from the von Neumann–Bernays axioms of set theory provided that it is consistent with them) there is a striking asymmetry, mathematically, between the system in which it is asserted and the one in which it is negated.[39]

Namely, the latter (but not the former) has a model which can be defined and proved to be a model in the original (unextended) system. This means that the former is an extension in a much stronger sense. A closely related fact is that the assertion (but not the negation) of the axiom implies new theorems about integers (the individual instances of which can be verified by computation). So the criterion of truth explained on p. 264 is satisfied, to some extent, for the assertion, but not for the negation. Briefly speaking, only the assertion

---

[36] See p. 207 of the 2nd ed., or *Fund. Math.*, 38 (1951), 9. Related results by C. Kuratowski and R. Sikorski are given in *Fund. Math.*, 38 (1951), 15 and 18.

[37] See *Fund. Math.*, 35 (1948), 131.

[38] See Alfred Errera, *Atti Accad. Ligure*, 9 (1952), 176–83.

[39] The same asymmetry also occurs on the lowest levels of set theory, where the consistency of the axioms in question is less subject to being doubted by skeptics.

yields a "fruitful" extension, while the negation is sterile outside its own very limited domain. Cantor's continuum hypothesis, too, can be shown to be sterile for number theory and to be true in a model constructible in the original system, whereas for some other assumption about the power of the continuum this perhaps is not so. On the other hand neither one of those asymmetries applies to Euclid's fifth postulate. To be more precise, both it and its negation are extensions in the weak sense.

As far as the epistemological situation is concerned, it is to be said that by a proof of undecidability a question loses its meaning only if the system of axioms under consideration is interpreted as a hypothetico-deductive system; i.e., if the meanings of the primitive terms are left undetermined. In geometry, e.g., the question as to whether Euclid's fifth postulate is true retains its meaning if the primitive terms are taken in a definite sense, i.e., as referring to the behavior of rigid bodies, rays of light, etc. The situation in set theory is similar, the difference is only that, in geometry, the meaning usually adopted today refers to physics rather than to mathematical intuition and that, therefore, a decision falls outside the range of mathematics. On the other hand, the objects of transfinite set theory, conceived in the manner explained on p. 262 and in footnote 14, clearly do not belong to the physical world and even their indirect connection with physical experience is very loose (owing primarily to the fact that set-theoretical concepts play only a minor role in the physical theories of today).

But, despite their remoteness from sense experience, we do have something like a perception also of the objects of set theory, as is seen from the fact that the axioms force themselves upon us as being true. I don't see any reason why we should have less confidence in this kind of perception, i.e., in mathematical intuition, than in sense perception, which induces us to build up physical theories and to expect that future sense perceptions will agree with them and, moreover, to believe that a question not decidable now has meaning and may be decided in the future. The set-theoretical paradoxes are hardly any more troublesome for mathematics than deceptions of the senses are for physics. That new mathematical intuitions leading to a decision of such problems as Cantor's continuum hypothesis are perfectly possible was pointed out earlier (pp. 264–5).

It should be noted that mathematical intuition need not be conceived of as a faculty giving an *immediate* knowledge of the objects concerned. Rather it seems that, as in the case of physical experience, we *form* our ideas also of those objects on the basis of something else which *is* immediately given. Only this something else here is *not*, or not primarily, the sensations. That something besides the sensations actually is immediately given follows (independently of mathematics) from the fact that even our ideas referring to physical objects contain constituents qualitatively different from sensations or mere combinations of sensations, e.g., the idea of object itself, whereas, on the other hand, by our thinking we cannot create any qualitatively new elements, but only reproduce and combine those that are given. Evidently the "given" underlying mathematics is closely related to the abstract elements contained in our empirical ideas.[40] It by no means follows, however, that the data of this second kind, because they cannot be associated with actions of certain things upon our sense organs, are something purely subjective, as Kant asserted. Rather they, too, may represent an aspect of objective reality, but, as opposed to the sensations, their presence in us may be due to another kind of relationship between ourselves and reality.

However, the question of the objective existence of the objects of mathematical intuition (which, incidentally, is an exact replica of the question of the objective existence of the outer world) is not decisive for the problem under discussion here. The mere psychological fact of the existence of an intuition which is sufficiently clear to produce the axioms of set theory and an open series of extensions of them suffices to give meaning to the question of the truth or falsity of propositions like Cantor's continuum hypothesis. What, however, perhaps more than anything else, justifies the acceptance of this criterion of truth in set theory is the fact that continued appeals to mathematical intuition are necessary not only for obtaining unambiguous answers to the questions of transfinite set theory, but also for the solution of the problems of finitary number theory[41] (of the type of Goldbach's conjecture),[42] where the meaningfulness and unambiguity of the concepts entering into them can hardly be doubted. This follows from the fact that for every axiomatic system there are infinitely many undecidable propositions of this type.

It was pointed out earlier (p. 265) that, besides mathematical intuition, there exists another (though only probable) criterion of the truth of mathematical axioms, namely their fruitfulness in mathematics and, one may add, possibly also in physics. This criterion, however, though it may become decisive in the future, cannot yet be applied to the specifically set-theoretical axioms (such as those referring to great cardinal numbers), because very little is known about their consequences in other fields. The simplest case of an application of the criterion under discussion arises when some set-theoretical axiom has number-theoretical consequences verifiable by computation up to any given integer. On the basis of what is known today, however, it is not possible to make the truth of any set-theoretical axiom reasonably probable in this manner.

[40] Note that there is a close relationship between the concept of set explained in footnote 14 and the categories of pure understanding in Kant's sense. Namely, the function of both is "synthesis," i.e., the generating of unities out of manifolds (e.g., in Kant, of the idea of *one* object out of its various aspects).

[41] Unless one is satisfied with inductive (probable) decisions, such as verifying the theorem up to very great numbers, or more indirect inductive procedures (see pp. 265, 272).

[42] I.e., universal propositions about integers which can be decided in each individual instance.

POSTSCRIPT

Shortly after the completion of the manuscript of this paper the question of whether Cantor's Continuum Hypothesis is provable from the von Neumann-Bernays axioms of set theory (the axiom of choice included) was settled in the negative by Paul J. Cohen. A sketch of the proof will appear shortly in the *Proceedings of the National Academy of Sciences*. It turns out that for a wide range of $\aleph_\tau$, the equality $2^{\aleph_0} = \aleph_\tau$ is consistent and an extension in the weak sense (that is, it implies no new number-theoretical theorems). Whether for a suitable concept of "standard" definition there exist definable $\aleph_\tau$ not excluded by König's theorem (see p. 260 above) for which this is not so is still an open question (of course, it must be assumed that the existence of the $\aleph_\tau$ in question is either demonstrable or has been postulated).

ON PLATONISM IN MATHEMATICS[1]

Paul Bernays

With your permission, I shall now address you on the subject of the present situation in research in the foundations of mathematics.

Since there remain open questions in this field, I am not in a position to paint a definitive picture of it for you. But it must be pointed out that the situation is not so critical as one could think from listening to those who speak of a foundational crisis. From certain points of view, this expression can be justified; but it could give rise to the opinion that mathematical science is shaken at its roots.

The truth is that the mathematical sciences are growing in complete security and harmony. The ideas of Dedekind, Poincaré, and Hilbert have been systematically developed with great success, without any conflict in the results.

It is only from the philosophical point of view that objections have been raised. They bear on certain ways of reasoning peculiar to analysis and set theory. These modes of reasoning were first systematically applied in giving a rigorous form to the methods of the calculus. [According to them,] the objects of a theory are viewed as elements of a totality such that one can reason as follows: For each property expressible using the notions of the theory, it is [an] objectively determinate [fact] whether there is or there is not an element of the totality which possesses this property. Similarly, it follows from this point of view that either all the elements of a set possess a given property, or there is at least one element which does not possess it.

[1] Lecture delivered June 18, 1934, in the cycle of *Conférences internationales des Sciences mathématiques* organized by the University of Geneva, in the series on Mathematical Logic.

Translated from the French by C. D. Parsons from L'enseignement mathematique, *Vol.* 34 (1935), *pp.* 52–69. *Permission for the translation and inclusion of this paper in this book was kindly granted by the author and the editor of* L'enseignement mathématique.

An example of this way of setting up a theory can be found in Hilbert's axiomatization of geometry. If we compare Hilbert's axiom system to Euclid's, ignoring the fact that the Greek geometer fails to include certain [necessary] postulates, we notice that Euclid speaks of figures to be *constructed*,[2] whereas, for Hilbert, system of points, straight lines, and planes exist from the outset. Euclid postulates: One can join two points by a straight line; Hilbert states the axiom: Given any two points, there exists a straight line on which both are situated. "Exists" refers here to existence in the system of straight lines.

This example shows already that the tendency of which we are speaking consists in viewing the objects as cut off from all links with the reflecting subject.

Since this tendency asserted itself especially in the philosophy of Plato, allow me to call it "platonism."

The value of platonistically inspired mathematical conceptions is that they furnish models of abstract imagination. These stand out by their simplicity and logical strength. They form representations which extrapolate from certain regions of experience and intuition.

Nonetheless, we know that we can arithmetize the theoretical systems of geometry and physics. For this reason, we shall direct our attention to platonism in arithmetic. But I am referring to arithmetic in a very broad sense, which includes analysis and set theory.

The weakest of the "platonistic" assumptions introduced by arithmetic is that of the totality of integers. The *tertium non datur* for integers follows from it; viz.: if P is a predicate of integers, either P is true of each number, or there is at least one exception.

By the assumption mentioned, this disjunction is an immediate consequence of the logical principle of the excluded middle; in analysis it is almost continually applied.

For example, it is by means of it that one concludes that for two real numbers a and b, given by convergent series, either $a = b$ or $a < b$ or $b < a$; and likewise: a sequence of positive rational numbers either comes as close as you please to zero or there is a positive rational number less than all the members of the sequence.

At first sight, such disjunctions seem trivial, and we must be attentive in order to notice that an assumption slips in.

But analysis is not content with this modest variety of platonism; it reflects it to a stronger degree with respect to the following notions: set of numbers, sequence of numbers, and function. It abstracts from the possibility of giving definitions of sets, sequences, and functions. These notions are used in a "quasi-combinatorial" sense, by which I mean: in the sense of an analogy of the infinite to the finite.

Consider, for example, the different functions which assign to each member of the finite series 1, 2, ..., n a number of the same series. There are

[2] [Translator's italics.]

n^n functions of this sort, and each of them is obtained by n independent determinations. Passing to the infinite case, we imagine functions engendered by an infinity of independent determinations which assign to each integer an integer, and we reason about the totality of these functions.

In the same way, one views a set of integers as the result of infinitely many independent acts deciding for each number whether it should be included or excluded. We add to this the idea of the totality of these sets. Sequences of real numbers and sets of real numbers are envisaged in an analogous manner. From this point of view, constructive definitions of specific functions, sequences, and sets are only ways to pick out an object which exists independently of, and prior to, the construction.

The axiom of choice is an immediate application of the quasi-combinatorial concepts in question. It is generally employed in the theory of real numbers in the following special form. Let

$$M_1, M_2 \ldots$$

be a sequence of non-empty sets of real numbers, then there is a sequence

$$a_1, a_2, \ldots$$

such that for every index n, a_n is an element of M_n.

The principle becomes subject to objections if the effective construction of the sequence of numbers is demanded.

A similar case is that of Poincaré's impredicative definitions. An impredicative definition of a real number appeals to the hypothesis that all real numbers have a certain property P, or the hypothesis that there exists a real number with the property T.

This kind of definition depends on the assumption of [the existence of] the totality of sequences of integers, because a real number is represented by a decimal fraction, that is to say, by a special kind of sequence of integers.

It is used in particular to prove the fundamental theorem that a bounded set of real numbers always has a least upper bound.

In Cantor's theories, platonistic conceptions extend far beyond those of the theory of real numbers. This is done by iterating the use of the quasi-combinatorial concept of a function and adding methods of collection. This is the well-known method of set theory.

The platonistic conceptions of analysis and set theory have also been applied in modern theories of algebra and topology, where they have proved very fertile.

This brief summary will suffice to characterize platonism and its application to mathematics. This application is so widespread that it is not an exaggeration to say that platonism reigns today in mathematics.

But on the other hand, we see that this tendency has been criticized in principle since its first appearance and has given rise to many discussions. This criticism was reinforced by the paradoxes discovered in set theory, even though these antinomies refute only extreme platonism.

We have set forth only a restricted platonism which does not claim to be more than, so to speak, an ideal projection of a domain of thought. But the matter has not rested there. Several mathematicians and philosophers interpret the methods of platonism in the sense of conceptual realism, postulating the existence of a world of ideal objects containing all the objects and relations of mathematics. It is this absolute platonism which has been shown untenable by the antinomies, particularly by those surrounding the Russell Zermelo paradox.

If one hears them for the first time, these paradoxes in their purely logical form can seem to be plays on words without serious significance. Nonetheless one must consider that these abbreviated forms of the paradoxes are obtained by following out the consequences of the various requirements of absolute platonism.

The essential importance of these antinomies is to bring out the impossibility of combining the following two things: the idea of the totality of all mathematical objects and the general concepts of set and function; for the totality itself would form a domain of elements for sets, and arguments and values for functions.

We must therefore give up absolute platonism. But it must be observed that this is almost the only injunction which follows from the paradoxes. Some will think that this is regrettable, since the paradoxes are appealed to on every side. But avoiding the paradoxes does not constitute a univocal program. In particular, restricted platonism is not touched at all by the antinomies.

Still, the critique of the foundations of analysis receives new impetus from this source, and among the different possible ways of escaping from the paradoxes, eliminating platonism offered itself as the most radical.

Let us look and see how this elimination can be brought about. It is done in two steps, corresponding to the two essential assumptions introduced by platonism. The first step is to replace by constructive concepts the concepts of a set, a sequence, or a function, which I have called quasi-combinatorial. The idea of an infinity of independent determinations is rejected. One emphasizes that an infinite sequence or a decimal fraction can be given only by an arithmetical law, and one regards the continuum as a set of elements defined by such laws.

This procedure is adapted to the tendency toward a complete arithmetization of analysis. Indeed, it must be conceded that the arithmetization of analysis is not carried through to the end by the usual method. The conconceptions which are applied there are not completely reducible, as we have seen, to the notion of integer and logical concepts.

Nonetheless, if we pursue the thought that each real number is defined by an arithmetical law, the idea of the totality of real numbers is no longer indispensable, and the axiom of choice is not at all evident. Also, unless we introduce auxiliary assumptions—as Russell and Whitehead do—we must do without various usual conclusions. Weyl has made these consequences very clear in his book *Das Kontinuum*.

Let us proceed to the second step of the elimination. It consists in renouncing the idea of the totality of integers. This point of view was first defended by Kronecker and then developed systematically by Brouwer.

Although several of you heard in March [1934] an authentic exposition of this method by Professor Brouwer himself, I shall allow myself a few words of explanation.

A misunderstanding about Kronecker must first be dissipated, which could arise from his often-cited aphorism that the integers were created by God, whereas everything else in mathematics is the work of man. If that were really Kronecker's opinion, he ought to admit the concept of the totality of integers.

In fact, Kronecker's method, as well as that of Brouwer, is characterized by the fact that it avoids the supposition that there exists a series of natural numbers forming a determinate ideal object.

According to Kronecker and Brouwer, one can speak of the series of numbers only in the sense of a process that is never finished, surpassing each limit which it reaches.

This point of departure carries with it the other divergences, in particular those concerning the application and interpretation of logical forms: Neither a general judgment about integers nor a judgment of existence can be interpreted as expressing a property of the series of numbers. A general theorem about numbers is to be regarded as a sort of prediction that a property will present itself for each construction of a number; and the affirmation of the existence of a number with a certain property is interpreted as an incomplete communication of a more precise proposition indicating a [particular] number having the property in question or a method for obtaining such a number; Hilbert calls it a "partial judgment."

For the same reasons the negation of a general or existential proposition about integers does not have precise sense. One must strengthen the negation to arrive at a mathematical proposition. For example, it is to give a strengthened negation of a proposition affirming the existence of a number with a property P to say that a number with the property P cannot be given, or further, that the assumption of a number with this property leads to a contradiction. But for such strengthened negations the law of the excluded middle is no longer applicable.

The characteristic complications to be met with in Brouwer's "intuitionistic" method come from this.

For example, one may not generally make use of disjunctions like these: a series of positive terms is either convergent or divergent; two convergent sums represent either the same real number or different ones.

In the theory of integers and of algebraic numbers, we can avoid these difficulties and manage to preserve all the essential theorems and arguments.

In fact, Kronecker has already shown that the core of the theory of algebraic fields can be developed from his methodological point of view without appeal to the totality of integers.[3]

As for analysis, you know that Brouwer has developed it in accord with the requirements of intuitionism. But here one must abandon a number of the usual theorems, for example, the fundamental theorem that every continuous function has a maximum in a closed interval. Very few things in set theory remain valid in intuitionist mathematics.

We would say, roughly, that intuitionism is adapted to the theory of numbers; the semiplatonistic method, which makes use of the idea of the totality of integers but avoids quasi-combinatorial concepts, is adapted to the arithmetic theory of functions, and the usual platonism is adequate for the geometric theory of the continuum.

There is nothing astonishing about this situation, for it is a familiar procedure of the contemporary mathematician to restrict his assumptions in each domain of the science to those which are essential. By this restriction, a theory gains methodological clarity, and it is in this direction that intuitionism proves fruitful.

But as you know, intuitionism is not at all content with such a role; it opposes the usual mathematics and claims to represent the only true mathematics.

On the other hand, mathematicians generally are not at all ready to exchange the well-tested and elegant methods of analysis for more complicated methods unless there is an overriding necessity for it.

We must discuss the question more deeply. Let us try to portray more distinctly the assumptions and philosophic character of the intuitionistic method.

What Brouwer appeals to is evidence. He claims that the basic ideas of intuitionism are given to us in an evident manner by pure intuition. In relying on this, he reveals his partial agreement with Kant. But whereas for Kant there exists a pure intuition with respect to space and time, Brouwer acknowledges only the intuition of time, from which, like Kant, he derives the intuition of number.

As for this philosophic position, it seems to me that one must concede to Brouwer two essential points: first, that the concept of integer is of intuitive origin. In this respect nothing is changed by the investigations of the logicists,[4]

---

[3] To this end, Kronecker set forth in his lectures a manner of introducing the notion of algebraic number which has been almost totally forgotten, although it is the most elementary way of defining this notion. This method consists in representing algebraic numbers by the changes of sign of irreducible polynomials in one variable with rational integers as coefficients; starting from that definition, one introduces the elementary operations and relations of magnitude for algebraic numbers and proves that the ordinary laws of calculation hold; finally one shows that a polynomial with algebraic coefficients having values with different signs for two algebraic arguments a and b has a zero between a and b.

[4] [I have rendered '*logiciens*' throughout as 'logicists'.—Trans.]

to which I shall return later. Second, one ought not to make arithmetic and geometry correspond in the manner in which Kant did. The concept of number is more elementary than the concepts of geometry.

Still it seems a bit hasty to deny completely the existence of a geometrical intuition. But let us leave that question aside here; there are other, more urgent ones. Is it really certain that the evidence given by arithmetical intuition extends exactly as far as the boundaries of intuitionist arithmetic would require? And finally: Is it possible to draw an exact boundary between what is evident and what is only plausible?

I believe that one must answer these two questions negatively. To begin with, you know that men and even scholars do not agree about evidence in general. Also, the same man sometimes rejects suppositions which he previously regarded as evident.

An example of a much-discussed question of evidence, about which there has been controversy up to the present, is that of the axiom of parallels. I think that the criticism which has been directed against that axiom is partly explained by the special place which it has in Euclid's system. Various other axioms had been omitted, so that the parallels axiom stood out from the others by its complexity.

In this matter I shall be content to point out the following: One can have doubts concerning the evidence of geometry, holding that it extends only to topological facts or to the facts expressed by the projective axioms. One can, on the other hand, claim that geometric intuition is not exact. These opinions are self-consistent, and all have arguments in their favor. But to claim that metric geometry has an evidence restricted to the laws common to Euclidean and Bolyai-Lobachevskian geometry, an exact metrical evidence which yet would not guarantee the existence of a perfect square, seems to me rather artificial. And yet it was the point of view of a number of mathematicians.

Our concern here has been to underline the difficulties to be encountered in trying to describe the limits of evidence.

Nevertheless, these difficulties do not make it impossible that there should be anything evident beyond question, and certainly intuitionism offers some such. But does it confine itself completely within the region of this elementary evidence? This is not completely indubitable, for the following reason: Intuitionism makes no allowance for the possibility that, for very large numbers, the operations required by the recursive method of constructing numbers can cease to have a concrete meaning. From two integers k, l one passes immediately to k^l; this process leads in a few steps to numbers which are far larger than any occurring in experience, e.g., $67^{(257^{729})}$.

Intuitionism, like ordinary mathematics, claims that this number can be represented by an Arabic numeral. Could not one press further the criticism which intuitionism makes of existential assertions and raise the question: What does it mean to claim the existence of an Arabic numeral for the foregoing number, since in practice we are not in a position to obtain it?

Brouwer appeals to intuition, but one can doubt that the evidence for it really is intuitive. Isn't this rather an application of the general method of analogy, consisting in extending to inaccessible numbers the relations which we can concretely verify for accessible numbers? As a matter of fact, the reason for applying this analogy is strengthened by the fact that there is no precise boundary between the numbers which are accessible and those which are not. One could introduce the notion of a "practicable" procedure, and implicitly restrict the import of recursive definitions to practicable operations. To avoid contradictions, it would suffice to abstain from applying the principle of the excluded middle to the notion of practicability. But such abstention goes without saying for intuitionism.

I hope I shall not be misunderstood: I am far from recommending that arithmetic be done with this restriction. I am concerned only to show that intuitionism takes as its basis propositions which one can doubt and in principle do without, although the resulting theory would be rather meager.

It is therefore not absolutely indubitable that the domain of complete evidence extends to all of intuitionism. On the other hand, several mathematicians recognize the complete evidence of intuitionistic arithmetic and moreover maintain that the concept of the series of numbers is evident in the following sense: The affirmation of the existence of a number does not require that one must, directly or recursively, give a bound for this number. Besides, we have just seen how far beyond a really concrete presentation such a limitation would be.

In short, the point of view of intuitive evidence does not decide uniquely in favor of intuitionism.

In addition, one must observe that the evidence which intuitionism uses in its arguments is not always of an immediate character. Abstract reflections are also included. In fact, intuitionists often use statements, containing a general hypothesis, of the form 'If every number n has the property $A(n)$, then B holds'.

Such a statement is interpreted intuitionistically in the following manner: 'If it is proved that every number n possesses the property $A(n)$, then B.' Here we have a hypothesis of an abstract kind, because since the methods of demonstration are not fixed in intuitionism, the condition that something is proved is not intuitively determined.

It is true that one can also interpret the given statement by viewing it as a partial judgment, i.e., as the claim that there exists a proof of B from the given hypothesis, a proof which would be effectively given.[5] (This is approximately the sense of Kolmogorov's interpretation of intuitionism.) In any case, the argument must start from the general hypothesis, which cannot be intuitively fixed. It is therefore an abstract reflection.

In the example just considered, the abstract part is rather limited. The

[5] ["... c'est à dire comme une indication d'un raisonnement conduisant de la dite hypothèse à la conclusion B, raisonnement qu'on présente effectivement."]

abstract character becomes more pronounced if one superposes hypotheses; i.e., when one formulates propositions like the following: 'If from the hypothesis that $A(n)$ is valid for every n, one can infer B, then C holds', or 'If from the hypothesis that A leads to a contradiction, a contradiction follows, then B', or briefly 'If the absurdity of A is absurd, then B'. This abstractness of statements can be still further increased.

It is by the systematic application of these forms of abstract reasoning that Brouwer has gone beyond Kronecker's methods and succeeded in establishing a general intuitionistic logic, which has been systematized by Heyting.

If we consider this intuitionistic logic, in which the notions of consequence are applied without reservation, and we compare the method used here with the usual one, we notice that the characteristic general feature of intuitionism is not that of being founded on pure intuition, but rather [that of being founded] on the relation of the reflecting and acting subject to the whole development of science.

This is an extreme methodological position. It is contrary to the customary manner of doing mathematics, which consists in establishing theories detached as much as possible from the thinking subject.

This realization leads us to doubt that intuitionism is the sole legitimate method of mathematical reasoning. For even if we admit that the tendency away from the [thinking] subject has been pressed too far under the reign of platonism, this does not lead us to believe that the truth lies in the opposite extreme. Keeping both possibilities in mind, we shall rather aim to bring about in each branch of science, an adaptation of method to the character of the object investigated.

For example, for number theory the use of the intuitive concept of a number is the most natural. In fact, one can thus establish the theory of numbers without introducing an axiom, such as that of complete induction, or axioms of infinity like those of Dedekind and Russell.

Moreover, in order to avoid the intuitive concept of number, one is led to introduce a more general concept, like that of a proposition, a function, or an arbitrary correspondence, concepts which are in general not objectively defined. It is true that such a concept can be made more definite by the axiomatic method, as in axiomatic set theory, but then the system of axioms is quite complicated.

You know that Frege tried to deduce arithmetic from pure logic by viewing the latter as the general theory of the universe of mathematical objects. Although the foundation of this absolutely platonistic enterprise was undermined by the Russell-Zermelo paradox, the school of logicists has not given up the idea of incorporating arithmetic in a system of logic. In place of absolute platonism, they have introduced some initial assumptions. But because of these, the system loses the character of pure logic.

In the system of *Principia Mathematica*, it is not only the axioms of infinity and reducibility which go beyond pure logic, but also the initial

conception of a universal domain of individuals and of a domain of predicates. It is really an *ad hoc* assumption to suppose that we have before us the
universe of things divided into subjects and predicates, ready-made for
theoretical treatment.

But even with such auxiliary assumptions, one cannot successfully incorporate the whole of arithmetic into the system of logic. For, since this
system is developed according to fixed rules, one would have to be able to
obtain by means of a fixed series of rules all the theorems of arithmetic. But
this is not the case; as Gödel has shown, arithmetic goes beyond each given
formalism. (In fact, the same is true of axiomatic set theory.)

Besides, the desire to deduce arithmetic from logic derives from the
traditional opinion that the relation of logic to arithmetic is that of general
to particular. The truth, it seems to me, is that mathematical abstraction does
not have a lesser degree than logical abstraction, but rather another direction.

These considerations do not detract at all from the intrinsic value of that
research of logicists which aims at developing logic systematically and
formalizing mathematical proofs. We were concerned here only with defending
the thesis that for the theory of numbers, the intuitive method is more suitable.

On the other hand, for the theory of the continuum, given by analysis, the
intuitionist method seems rather artificial. The idea of the continuum is a
geometrical idea which analysis expresses in terms of arithmetic.

Is the intuitionist method of representing the continuum better adapted
to the idea of the continuum than the usual one?

Weyl would have us believe this. He reproaches ordinary analysis for
decomposing the continuum into single points. But isn't this reproach better
addressed to semiplatonism, which views the continuum as a set of arithmetical laws? The fact is that for the usual method there is a completely
satisfying analogy between the manner in which a particular point stands out
from the continuum and the manner in which a real number defined by an
arithmetical law stands out from the set of all real numbers, whose elements
are in general only implicitly involved, by virtue of the quasi-combinatorial
concept of a sequence.

This analogy seems to me to agree better with the nature of the continuum
than that which intuitionism establishes between the fuzzy character of the
continuum and the uncertainties arising from unsolved arithmetical problems.

It is true that in the usual analysis the notion of a continuous function,
and also that of a differentiable function, have a generality going far beyond
our intuitive representation of a curve. Nevertheless in this analysis, we can
establish the theorem of the maximum of a continuous function and Rolle's
theorem, thus rejoining the intuitive conception.

Intuitionist analysis, even though it begins with a much more restricted
notion of a function, does not arrive at such simple theorems; they must
instead be replaced by more complex ones. This stems from the fact that on the
intuitionistic conception, the continuum does not have the character of a

totality, which undeniably belongs to the geometric idea of the continuum. And it is this characteristic of the continuum which would resist perfect arithmetization.

These considerations lead us to notice that the duality of arithmetic and geometry is not unrelated to the opposition between intuitionism and platonism. The concept of number appears in arithmetic. It is of intuitive origin, but then the idea of the totality of numbers is superimposed. On the other hand, in geometry the platonistic idea of space is primordial, and it is against this background that the intuitionist procedures of constructing figures take place.

This suffices to show that the two tendencies, intuitionist and platonist, are both necessary; they complement each other, and it would be doing oneself violence to renounce one or the other.

But the duality of these two tendencies, like that of arithmetic and geometry, is not a perfect symmetry. As we have noted, it is not proper to make arithmetic and geometry correspond completely: the idea of number is more immediate to the mind than the idea of space. Likewise, we must recognize that the assumptions of platonism have a transcendent character which is not found in intuitionism.

It is also this transcendent character which requires us to take certain precautions in regard to each platonistic assumption. For even when such a supposition is not at all arbitrary and presents itself naturally to the mind, it can still be that the principle from which it proceeds permits only a restricted application, outside of which one would fall into contradiction.

We must be all the more careful in the face of this possibility, since the drive for simplicity leads us to make our principles as broad as possible. And the need for a restriction is often not noticed.

This was the case, as we have seen, for the principle of totality, which was pressed too far by absolute platonism. Here it was only the discovery of the Russell-Zermelo paradox which showed that a restriction was necessary.

Thus it is desirable to find a method to make sure that the platonistic assumptions on which mathematics is based do not go beyond permissible limits. The assumptions in question reduce to various forms of the principle of totality and of the principle of analogy or of the permanence of laws. And the condition restricting the application of these principles is none other than that of the consistency of the consequences which are deduced from the fundamental assumptions.

As you know, Hilbert is trying to find ways of giving us such assurances of consistency, and his proof theory has this as its goal.

This theory relies in part on the results of the logicists. They have shown that the arguments applied in arithmetic, analysis, and set theory can be formalized. That is, they can be expressed in symbols and as symbolic processes which unfold according to fixed rules. To primitive propositions correspond initial formulae, and to each logical deduction corresponds a sequence of formulae derivable from one another according to given rules. In this formalism, a platonistic assumption is represented by an initial formula or by a rule establishing a way of passing from formulae already obtained to others. In this way, the investigation of the possibilities of proof reduces to problems like those which are found in elementary number theory. In particular, the consistency of the theory will be proved if one succeeds in proving that it is impossible to deduce two mutually contradictory formulae A and Ā (with the bar representing negation). This statement which is to be proved is of the same structure as that, for example, asserting the impossibility of satisfying the equation $a^2 = 2b^2$ by two integers a and b.

Thus by symbolic reduction, the question of the consistency of a theory reduces to a problem of an elementary arithmetical character.

Starting from this fundamental idea, Hilbert has sketched a detailed program of a theory of proof, indicating the leading ideas of the arguments (for the main consistency proofs). His intention was to confine himself to intuitive and combinatorial considerations; his "finitary point of view" was restricted to these methods.

In this framework, the theory was developed up to a certain point. Several mathematicians have contributed to it: Ackermann, von Neumann, Skolem, Herbrand, Gödel, Gentzen.

Nonetheless, these investigations have remained within a relatively restricted domain. In fact, they did not even reach a proof of the consistency of the axiomatic theory of integers. It is known that the symbolic representation of this theory is obtained by adding to the ordinary logical calculus formalizations of Peano's axioms and the recursive definitions of sum $(a + b)$ and product $(a \cdot b)$.

Light was shed on this situation by a general theorem of Gödel, according to which a proof of the consistency of a formalized theory cannot be represented by means of the formalism considered. From this theorem, the following more special proposition follows: It is impossible to prove by elementary combinatorial methods the consistency of a formalized theory which can express every elementary combinatorial proof of an arithmetical proposition.

Now it seems that this proposition applies to the formalism of the axiomatic theory of numbers. At least, no attempt made up to now has given us any example of an elementary combinatorial proof which cannot be expressed in this formalism, and the methods by which one can, in the cases considered, translate a proof into the aforementioned formalism, seem to suffice in general.

Assuming that this is so,[6] we arrive at the conclusion that means more powerful than elementary combinatorial methods are necessary to prove

---

[6] In trying to demonstrate the possibility of translating each elementary combinatorial proof of an arithmetical proposition into the formalism of the axiomatic theory of numbers, we are confronted with the difficulty of delimiting precisely the domain of elementary combinatorial methods.

the consistency of the axiomatic theory of numbers. A new discovery of Gödel and Gentzen leads us to such a more powerful method. They have shown (independently of one another) that the consistency of intuitionist arithmetic implies the consistency of the axiomatic theory of numbers. This result was obtained by using Heyting's formalization of intuitionist arithmetic and logic. The argument is conducted by elementary methods, in a rather simple manner. In order to conclude from this result that the axiomatic theory of numbers is consistent, it suffices to assume the consistency of intuitionist arithmetic.

This proof of the consistency of axiomatic number theory shows us, among other things, that intuitionism, by its abstract arguments, goes essentially beyond elementary combinatorial methods.

The question which now arises is whether the strengthening of the method of proof theory obtained by admitting the abstract arguments of intuitionism would put us into a position to prove the consistency of analysis. The answer would be very important and even decisive for proof theory, and even, it seems to me, for the role which is to be attributed to intuitionistic methods.

Research in the foundations of mathematics is still developing. Several basic questions are open, and we do not know what we shall discover in this domain. But these investigations excite our curiosity by their changing perspectives, and that is a sentiment which is not aroused to the same degree by the more classical parts of science, which have attained greater perfection.

I wish to thank Professor Wavre, who was kind enough to help me improve the text of this lecture for publication. I also thank M. Rueff, who was good enough to look over the first draft to improve the French.

Part Three

Part Three

THE *A PRIORI*

Alfred Jules Ayer

The view of philosophy which we have adopted may, I think, fairly be described as a form of empiricism. For it is characteristic of an empiricist to eschew metaphysics, on the ground that every factual proposition must refer to sense-experience. And even if the conception of philosophizing as an activity of analysis is not to be discovered in the traditional theories of empiricists, we have seen that it is implicit in their practice. At the same time, it must be made clear that, in calling ourselves empiricists, we are not avowing a belief in any of the psychological doctrines which are commonly associated with empiricism. For, even if these doctrines were valid, their validity would be independent of the validity of any philosophical thesis. It could be established only by observation, and not by the purely logical considerations upon which our empiricism rests.

Having admitted that we are empiricists, we must now deal with the objection that is commonly brought against all forms of empiricism; the objection, namely, that it is impossible on empiricist principles to account for our knowledge of necessary truths. For, as Hume conclusively showed, no general proposition whose validity is subject to the test of actual experience can ever be logically certain. No matter how often it is verified in practice, there still remains the possibility that it will be confuted on some future occasion. The fact that a law has been substantiated in $n - 1$ cases affords no logical guarantee that it will be substantiated in the nth case also, no matter how large we take n to be. And this means that no general proposition referring to a matter of fact can ever be shown to be necessarily and universally true. It can at best be a probable hypothesis. And this, we shall find, applies not only to general

Excerpted and reprinted with the kind permission of the author and publishers from Alfred Jules Ayer, Language, Truth and Logic (*London: Victor Gollancz, Ltd*, 1958; *New York: Dover Publications, Inc.*), *pp. 71–87.*

propositions, but to all propositions which have a factual content. They can none of them ever become logically certain. This conclusion, which we shall elaborate later on, is one which must be accepted by every consistent empiricist. It is often thought to involve him in complete scepticism; but this is not the case. For the fact that the validity of a proposition cannot be logically guaranteed in no way entails that it is irrational for us to believe it. On the contrary, what is irrational is to look for a guarantee where none can be forthcoming; to demand certainty where probability is all that is obtainable. We have already remarked upon this, in referring to the work of Hume. And we shall make the point clearer when we come to treat of probability, in explaining the use which we make of empirical propositions. We shall discover that there is nothing perverse or paradoxical about the view that all the "truths" of science and common sense are hypotheses; and consequently that the fact that it involves this view constitutes no objection to the empiricist thesis.

Where the empiricist does encounter difficulty is in connection with the truths of formal logic and mathematics. For whereas a scientific generalization is readily admitted to be fallible, the truths of mathematics and logic appear to everyone to be necessary and certain. But if empiricism is correct no proposition which has a factual content can be necessary or certain. Accordingly the empiricists must deal with the truths of logic and mathematics in one of the two following ways: he must say either that they are not necessary truths, in which case he must account for the universal conviction that they are; or he must say that they have no factual content, and then he must explain how a proposition which is empty of all factual content can be true and useful and surprising.

If neither of these courses proves satisfactory, we shall be obliged to give way to rationalism. We shall be obliged to admit that there are some truths about the world which we can know independently of experience; that there are some properties which we can ascribe to all objects, even though we cannot conceivably observe that all objects have them. And we shall have to accept it as a mysterious inexplicable fact that our thought has this power to reveal to us authoritatively the nature of objects which we have never observed. Or else we must accept the Kantian explanation which, apart from the epistemological difficulties which we have already touched on, only pushes the mystery a stage further back.

It is clear that any such concession to rationalism would upset the main argument of this book. For the admission that there were some facts about the world which could be known independently of experience would be incompatible with our fundamental contention that a sentence says nothing unless it is empirically verifiable. And thus the whole force of our attack on metaphysics would be destroyed. It is vital, therefore, for us to be able to show that one or other of the empiricist accounts of the propositions of logic and mathematics is correct. If we are successful in this, we shall have destroyed the foundations of rationalism. For the fundamental tenet of rationalism is that thought is an independent source of knowledge, and is moreover a more trustworthy source of knowledge than experience; indeed some rationalists have gone so far as to say that thought is the only source of knowledge. And the ground for this view is simply that the only necessary truths about the world which are known to us are known through thought and not through experience. So that if we can show either that the truths in question are not necessary or that they are not "truths about the world," we shall be taking away the support on which rationalism rests. We shall be making good the empiricist contention that there are no "truths of reason" which refer to matters of fact.

The course of maintaining that the truths of logic and mathematics are not necessary or certain was adopted by Mill. He maintained that these propositions were inductive generalizations based on an extremely large number of instances. The fact that the number of supporting instances was so very large accounted, in his view, for our believing these generalizations to be necessarily and universally true. The evidence in their favor was so strong that it seemed incredible to us that a contrary instance should ever arise. Nevertheless it was in principle possible for such generalizations to be confuted. They were highly probable, but, being inductive generalizations, they were not certain. The difference between them and the hypotheses of natural science was a difference in degree and not in kind. Experience gave us very good reason to suppose that a "truth" of mathematics or logic was true universally; but we were not possessed of a guarantee. For these "truths" were only empirical hypotheses which had worked particularly well in the past; and, like all empirical hypotheses, they were theoretically fallible.

I do not think that this solution of the empiricist's difficulty with regard to the propositions of logica and mathematics is acceptable. In discussing it, it is necessary to make a distinction which is perhaps already enshrined in Kant's famous dictum that, although there can be no doubt that all our knowledge begins with experience, it does not follow that it all arises out of experience.[1] When we say that the truths of logic are known independently of experience, we are not of course saying that they are innate, in the sense that we are born knowing them. It is obvious that mathematics and logic have to be learned in the same way as chemistry and history have to be learned. Nor are we denying that the first person to discover a given logical or mathematical truth was led to it by an inductive procedure. It is very probable, for example, that the principle of the syllogism was formulated not before but after the validity of syllogistic reasoning had been observed in a number of particular cases. What we are discussing, however, when we say that logical and mathematical truths are known independently of experience, is not a historical question concerning the way in which these truths were originally discovered, not a psychological question concerning the way in which each of us comes to learn them, but an epistemological question. The contention of Mill's which

[1] *Critique of Pure Reason*, 2nd ed., Introduction, section i.

we reject is that the propositions of logic and mathematics have the same status as empirical hypotheses; that their validity is determined in the same way. We maintain that they are independent of experience in the sense that they do not owe their validity to empirical verification. We may come to discover them through an inductive process; but once we have apprehended them we see that they are necessarily true, that they hold good for every conceivable instance. And this serves to distinguish them from empirical generalizations. For we know that a proposition whose validity depends upon experience cannot be seen to be necessarily and universally true.

In rejecting Mill's theory, we are obliged to be somewhat dogmatic. We can do no more than state the issue clearly and then trust that his contention will be seen to be discrepant with the relevant logical facts. The following considerations may serve to show that of the two ways of dealing with logic and mathematics which are open to the empiricist, the one which Mill adopted is not the one which is correct.

The best way to substantiate our assertion that the truths of formal logic and pure mathematics are necessarily true is to examine cases in which they might seem to be confuted. It might easily happen, for example, that when I came to count what I had taken to be five pairs of objects, I found that they amounted only to nine. And if I wished to mislead people I might say that on this occasion twice five was not ten. But in that case I should not be using the complex sign "$2 \times 5 = 10$" in the way in which it is ordinarily used. I should be taking it not as the expression of a purely mathematical proposition, but as the expression of an empirical generalization, to the effect that whenever I counted what appeared to me to be five pairs of objects I discovered that they were ten in number. This generalization may very well be false. But if it proved false in a given case, one would not say that the mathematical proposition "$2 \times 5 = 10$" had been confuted. One would say that I was wrong in supposing that there were five pairs of objects to start with, or that one of the objects had been taken away while I was counting, or that two of them had coalesced, or that I had counted wrongly. One would adopt as an explanation whatever empirical hypothesis fitted in best with the accredited facts. The one explanation which would in no circumstances be adopted is that ten is not always the product of two and five.

To take another example: if what appears to be a Euclidean triangle is found by measurement not to have angles totalling 180 degrees, we do not say that we have met with an instance which invalidates the mathematical proposition that the sum of the three angles of a Euclidean triangle is 180 degrees. We say that we have measured wrongly, or, more probably, that the triangle we have been measuring is not Euclidean. And this is our procedure in every case in which a mathematical truth might appear to be confuted. We always preserve its validity by adopting some other explanation of the occurrence.

The same thing applies to the principles of formal logic. We may take an example relating to the so-called law of excluded middle, which states that a proposition must be either true or false, or, in other words, that it is impossible that a proposition and its contradictory should neither of them be true. One might suppose that a proposition of the form "*x* has stopped doing *y*" would in certain cases constitute an exception to this law. For instance, if my friend has never yet written to me, it seems fair to say that it is neither true nor false that he has stopped writing to me. But in fact one would refuse to accept such an instance as an invalidation of the law of excluded middle. One would point out that the proposition "My friend has stopped writing to me" is not a simple proposition, but the conjunction of the two propositions "My friend wrote to me in the past" and "My friend does not write to me now": and, furthermore, that the proposition "My friend has not stopped writing to me" is not, as it appears to be, contradictory to "My friend has stopped writing to me," but only contrary to it. For it means "My friend wrote to me in the past, and he still writes to me." When, therefore, we say that such a proposition as "My friend has stopped writing to me" is sometimes neither true nor false, we are speaking inaccurately. For we seem to be saying that neither it nor its contradictory is true. Whereas what we mean, or anyhow should mean, is that neither it nor its apparent contradictory is true. And its apparent contradictory is really only its contrary. Thus we preserve the law of excluded middle by showing that the negating of a sentence does not always yield the contradictory of the proposition originally expressed.

There is no need to give further examples. Whatever instance we care to take, we shall always find that the situations in which a logical or mathematical principle might appear to be confuted are accounted for in such a way as to leave the principle unassailed. And this indicates that Mill was wrong in supposing that a situation could arise which would overthrow a mathematical truth. The principles of logic and mathematics are true universally simply because we never allow them to be anything else. And the reason for this is that we cannot abandon them without contradicting ourselves, without sinning against the rules which govern the use of language, and so making our utterances self-stultifying. In other words, the truths of logic and mathematics are analytic propositions or tautologies. In saying this we are making what will be held to be an extremely controversial statement, and we must now proceed to make its implications clear.

The most familiar definition of an analytic proposition, or judgment, as he called it, is that given by Kant. He said[2] that an analytic judgment was one in which the predicate B belonged to the subject A as something which was covertly contained in the concept of A. He contrasted analytic with synthetic judgments, in which the predicate B lay outside the subject A, although it did stand in connection with it. Analytic judgments, he explains, "add nothing through the predicate to the concept of the subject, but merely break it up into those constituent concepts that have all along been thought in it,

[2] *Critique of Pure Reason*, 2nd ed., Introduction, sections iv and v.

although confusedly." Synthetic judgments, on the other hand, "add to the concept of the subject a predicate which has not been in any wise thought in it, and which no analysis could possibly extract from it." Kant gives "all bodies are extended" as an example of an analytic judgment, on the ground that the required predicate can be extracted from the concept of "body," "in accordance with the principle of contradiction"; as an example of a synthetic judgment, he gives "all bodies are heavy." He refers also to "7 + 5 = 12" as a synthetic judgment, on the ground that the concept of twelve is by no means already thought in merely thinking the union of seven and five. And he appears to regard this as tantamount to saying that the judgment does not rest on the principle of contradiction alone. He holds, also, that through analytic judgments our knowledge is not extended as it is through synthetic judgments. For in analytic judgments "the concept which I already have is merely set forth and made intelligible to me."

I think that this is a fair summary of Kant's account of the distinction between analytic and synthetic propositions, but I do not think that it succeeds in making the distinction clear. For even if we pass over the difficulties which arise out of the use of the vague term "concept," and the unwarranted assumption that every judgment, as well as every German or English sentence, can be said to have a subject and a predicate, there remains still this crucial defect. Kant does not give one straightforward criterion for distinguishing between analytic and synthetic propositions; he gives two distinct criteria, which are by no means equivalent. Thus his ground for holding that the proposition "7 + 5 = 12" is synthetic is, as we have seen, that the subjective intension of "7 + 5" does not comprise the subjective intension of "12"; whereas his ground for holding that "all bodies are extended" is an analytic proposition is that it rests on the principle of contradiction alone. That is, he employs a psychological criterion in the first of these examples, and a logical criterion in the second, and takes their equivalence for granted. But, in fact, a proposition which is synthetic according to the former criterion may very well be analytic according to the latter. For, as we have already pointed out, it is possible for symbols to be synonymous without having the same intensional meaning for anyone: and accordingly from the fact that one can think of the sum of seven and five without necessarily thinking of twelve, it by no means follows that the proposition "7 + 5 = 12" can be denied without self-contradiction. From the rest of his argument, it is clear that it is this logical proposition, and not any psychological proposition, that Kant is really anxious to establish. His use of the psychological criterion leads him to think that he has established it, when he has not.

I think that we can preserve the logical import of Kant's distinction between analytic and synthetic propositions, while avoiding the confusions which mar his actual account of it, if we say that a proposition is analytic when its validity depends solely on the definitions of the symbols it contains, and synthetic when its validity is determined by the facts of experience. Thus, the proposition "There are ants which have established a system of slavery" is a synthetic proposition. For we cannot tell whether it is true or false merely by considering the definitions of the symbols which constitute it. We have to resort to actual observation of the behaviour of ants. On the other hand, the proposition "Either some ants are parasitic or none are" is an analytic proposition. For one need not resort to observation to discover that there either are or are not ants which are parasitic. If one knows what is the function of the words "either," "or," and "not," then one can see that any proposition of the form "Either p is true or p is not true" is valid, independently of experience. Accordingly, all such propositions are analytic.

It is to be noticed that the proposition "Either some ants are parasitic or none are" provides no information whatsoever about the behavior of ants, or, indeed, about any matter of fact. And this applies to all analytic propositions. They none of them provide any information about any matter of fact. In other words, they are entirely devoid of factual content. And it is for this reason that no experience can confute them.

When we say that analytic propositions are devoid of factual content; and consequently that they say nothing, we are not suggesting that they are senseless in the way that metaphysical utterances are senseless. For, although they give us no information about any empirical situation, they do enlighten us by illustrating the way in which we use certain symbols. Thus if I say, "Nothing can be colored in different ways at the same time with respect to the same part of itself," I am not saying anything about the properties of any actual thing; but I am not talking nonsense. I am expressing an analytic proposition, which records our determination to call a color expanse which differs in quality from a neighboring color expanse a different part of a given thing. In other words, I am simply calling attention to the implications of a certain linguistic usage. Similarly, in saying that if all Bretons are Frenchmen, and all Frenchmen Europeans, then all Bretons are Europeans, I am not describing any matter of fact. But I am showing that in the statement that all Bretons are Frenchmen, and all Frenchmen Europeans, the further statement that all Bretons are Europeans is implicitly contained. And I am thereby indicating the convention which governs our usage of the words "if" and "all."

We see, then, that there is a sense in which analytic propositions do give us new knowledge. They call attention to linguistic usages, of which we might otherwise not be conscious, and they reveal unsuspected implications in our assertions and beliefs. But we can see also that there is a sense in which they may be said to add nothing to our knowledge. For they tell us only what we may be said to know already. Thus, if I know that the existence of May Queens is a relic of tree-worship, and I discover that May Queens still exist in England, I can employ the tautology "If p implies q, and p is true, q is true" to show that there still exists a relic of tree-worship in England. But in saying that there are still May Queens in England, and that the existence of May

Queens is a relic of tree-worship, I have already asserted the existence in England of a relic of tree-worship. The use of the tautology does, indeed, enable me to make this concealed assertion explicit. But it does not provide me with any new knowledge, in the sense in which empirical evidence that the election of May Queens had been forbidden by law would provide me with new knowledge. If one had to set forth all the information one possessed, with regard to matters of fact, one would not write down any analytic propositions. But one would make use of analytic propositions in compiling one's encyclopædia, and would thus come to include propositions which one would otherwise have overlooked. And, besides enabling one to make one's list of information complete, the formulation of analytic propositions would enable one to make sure that the synthetic propositions of which the list was composed formed a self-consistent system. By showing which ways of combining propositions resulted in contradictions, they would prevent one from including incompatible propositions and so making the list self-stultifying. But insofar as we had actually used words as "all" and "or" and "not" without falling into self-contradiction, we might be said already to know what was revealed in the formulation of analytic propositions illustrating the rules which govern our usage of these logical particles. So that here again we are justified in saying that analytic propositions do not increase our knowledge.

The analytic character of the truths of formal logic was obscured in the traditional logic through its being insufficiently formalized. For in speaking always of judgments, instead of propositions, and introducing irrelevant psychological questions, the traditional logic gave the impression of being concerned in some specially intimate way with the workings of thought. What it was actually concerned with was the formal relationship of classes, as is shown by the fact that all its principles of inference are subsumed in the Boolean class-calculus, which is subsumed in its turn in the propositional calculus of Russell and Whitehead.[3] Their system, expounded in *Principia Mathematica*, makes it clear that formal logic is not concerned with the properties of men's minds, much less with the properties of material objects, but simply with the possibility of combining propositions by means of logical particles into analytic propositions, and with studying the formal relationship of these analytic propositions, in virtue of which one is deducible from another. Their procedure is to exhibit the propositions of formal logic as a deductive system, based on five primitive propositions, subsequently reduced in number to one. Hereby the distinction between logical truths and principles of inference, which was maintained in the Aristotelian logic, very properly disappears. Every principle of inference is put forward as a logical truth and every logical truth can serve as a principle of inference. The three Aristotelian "laws of thought," the law of identity, the law of excluded middle, and the law of non-contradiction, are incorporated in the system, but they are not

[3] Vide Karl Menger, "Die Neue Logik," *Krise und Neuaufbau in den Exakten Wissenschaften*, pp. 94–6; and Lewis and Langford, *Symbolic Logic*, Chapter v.

considered more important than the other analytic propositions. They are not reckoned among the premises of the system. And the system of Russell and Whitehead itself is probably only one among many possible logics, each of which is composed of tautologies as interesting to the logician as the arbitrarily selected Aristotelian "laws of thought."[4]

A point which is not sufficiently brought out by Russell, if indeed it is recognized by him at all, is that every logical proposition is valid in its own right. Its validity does not depend on its being incorporated in a system, and deduced from certain propositions which are taken as self-evident. The construction of systems of logic is useful as a means of discovering and certifying analytic propositions, but it is not in principle essential even for this purpose. For it is possible to conceive of a symbolism in which every analytic proposition could be seen to be analytic in virtue of its form alone.

The fact that the validity of an analytic proposition in no way depends on its being deducible from other analytic propositions is our justification for disregarding the question whether the propositions of mathematics are reducible to propositions of formal logic, in the way that Russell supposed.[5] For even if it is the case that the definition of a cardinal number as a class of classes similar to a given class is circular, and it is not possible to reduce mathematical notions to purely logical notions, it will still remain true that the propositions of mathematics are analytic propositions. They will form a special class of analytic propositions, containing special terms, but they will be none the less analytic for that. For the criterion of an analytic proposition is that its validity should follow simply from the definition of the terms contained in it, and this condition is fulfilled by the propositions of pure mathematics.

The mathematical propositions which one might most pardonably suppose to be synthetic are the propositions of geometry. For it is natural for us to think, as Kant thought, that geometry is the study of the properties of physical space, and consequently that its propositions have factual content. And if we believe this, and also recognize that the truths of geometry are necessary and certain, then we may be inclined to accept Kant's hypothesis that space is the form of intuition of our outer sense, a form imposed by us on the matter of sensation, as the only possible explanation of our *a priori* knowledge of these synthetic propositions. But while the view that pure geometry is concerned with physical space was plausible enough in Kant's day, when the geometry of Euclid was the only geometry known, the subsequent invention of non-Euclidean geometries has shown it to be mistaken. We see now that the axioms of a geometry are simply definitions, and that the theorems of a geometry are simply the logical consequences of these definitions. A geometry is not in itself about physical space; in itself it cannot be said to be "about" anything. But we can use a geometry to reason about physical space. That is

[4] Vide Lewis and Langford, *Symbolic Logic*, Chapter vii, for an elaboration of this point.
[5] Vide *Introduction to Mathematical Philosophy*, Chapter ii.

to say, once we have given the axioms a physical interpretation, we can proceed to apply the theorems to the objects which satisfy the axioms.[6] Whether a geometry can be applied to the actual physical world or not, is an empirical question which falls outside the scope of the geometry itself. There is no sense, therefore, in asking which of the various geometries known to us are false, and which are true. Insofar as they are all free from contradiction, they are all true. What one can ask is which of them is the most useful on any given occasion, which of them can be applied most easily and most fruitfully to an actual empirical situation. But the proposition which states that a certain application of a geometry is possible is not itself a proposition of that geometry. All that the geometry itself tells us is that if anything can be brought under the definitions, it will also satisfy the theorems. It is therefore a purely logical system, and its propositions are purely analytic propositions.

It might be objected that the use made of diagrams in geometrical treatises shows that geometrical reasoning is not purely abstract and logical, but depends on our intuition of the properties of figures. In fact, however, the use of diagrams is not essential to completely rigorous geometry. The diagrams are introduced as an aid to our reason. They provide us with a particular application of the geometry, and so assist us to perceive the more general truth that the axioms of the geometry involve certain consequences. But the fact that most of us need the help of an example to make us aware of those consequences does not show that the relation between them and the axioms is not a purely logical relation. It shows merely that our intellects are unequal to the task of carrying out very abstract processes of reasoning without the assistance of intuition. In other words, it has no bearing on the nature of geometrical propositions, but is simply an empirical fact about ourselves. Moreover, the appeal to intuition, though generally of psychological value, is also a source of danger to the geometer. He is tempted to make assumptions which are accidentally true of the particular figure he is taking as an illustration, but do not follow from his axioms. It has, indeed, been shown that Euclid himself was guilty of this, and consequently that the presence of the figure is essential to some of his proofs.[7] This shows that his system is not, as he presents it, completely rigorous, although of course it can be made so. It does not show that the presence of the figure is essential to a truly rigorous geometrical proof. To suppose that it did would be to take as a necessary feature of all geometries what is really only an incidental defect in one particular geometrical system.

We conclude, then, that the propositions of pure geometry are analytic. And this leads us to reject Kant's hypothesis that geometry deals with the form of intuition of our outer sense. For the ground for this hypothesis was that it alone explained how the propositions of geometry could be both true *a priori* and synthetic: and we have seen that they are not synthetic. Similarly

[6] Cf. H. Poincaré, *La Science et l'Hypothèse*, Part II, Chapter iii.
[7] Cf. M. Black, *The Nature of Mathematics*, p. 154.

our view that the propositions of arithmetic are not synthetic but analytic leads us to reject the Kantian hypothesis[8] that arithmetic is concerned with our pure intuition of time, the form of our inner sense. And thus we are able to dismiss Kant's transcendental æsthetic without having to bring forward the epistemological difficulties which it is commonly said to involve. For the only argument which can be brought in favour of Kant's theory is that it alone explains certain "facts." And now we have found that the "facts" which it purports to explain are not facts at all. For while it is true that we have *a priori* knowledge of necessary propositions, it is not true, as Kant supposed, that any of these necessary propositions are synthetic. They are without exception analytic propositions, or, in other words, tautologies.

We have already explained how it is that these analytic propositions are necessary and certain. We saw that the reason why they cannot be confuted in experience is that they do not make any assertion about the empirical world. They simply record our determination to use words in a certain fashion. We cannot deny them without infringing the conventions which are pre-supposed by our very denial, and so falling into self-contradiction. And this is the sole ground of their necessity. As Wittgenstein puts it, our justification for holding that the world could not conceivably disobey the laws of logic is simply that we could not say of an unlogical world how it would look.[9] And just as the validity of an analytic proposition is independent of the nature of the external world; so is it independent of the nature of our minds. It is perfectly conceivable that we should have employed different linguistic conventions from those which we actually do employ. But whatever these conventions might be, the tautologies in which we recorded them would always be necessary. For any denial of them would be self-stultifying.

We see, then, that there is nothing mysterious about the apodeictic certainty of logic and mathematics. Our knowledge that no observation can ever confute the proposition "$7 + 5 = 12$" depends simply on the fact that the symbolic expression "$7 + 5$" is synonymous with "12," just as our knowledge that every oculist is an eye-doctor depends on the fact that the symbol "eye-doctor" is synonymous with "oculist." And the same explanation holds good for every other *a priori* truth.

What is mysterious at first sight is that these tautologies should on occasion be so surprising, that there should be in mathematics and logic the possibility of invention and discovery. As Poincaré says: "If all the assertions which mathematics puts forward can be derived from one another by formal logic, mathematics cannot amount to anything more than an immense tautology. Logical inference can teach us nothing essentially new, and if every-thing is to proceed from the principle of identity, everything must be reducible to it. But can we really allow that these theorems which fill so many books

---

[8] This hypothesis is not mentioned in the *Critique of Pure Reason*, but was maintained by Kant at an earlier date.

[9] *Tractatus Logico-Philosophicus*, 3·031.

serve no other purpose than to say in a round-about fashion 'A = A'?"[10]
Poincaré finds this incredible. His own theory is that the sense of invention
and discovery in mathematics belongs to it in virtue of mathematical induction, the principle that what is true for the number 1, and true for $n + 1$
when it is true for n,[11] is true for all numbers. And he claims that this is a
synthetic *a priori* principle. It is, in fact, *a priori*, but it is not synthetic. It is
a defining principle of the natural numbers, serving to distinguish them from
such numbers as the infinite cardinal numbers, to which it cannot be applied.[12]
Moreover, we must remember that discoveries can be made, not only in
arithmetic, but also in geometry and formal logic, where no use is made of
mathematical induction. So that even if Poincaré were right about mathematical induction, he would not have provided a satisfactory explanation of
the paradox that a mere body of tautologies can be so interesting and so
surprising.

The true explanation is very simple. The power of logic and mathematics
to surprise us depends, like their usefulness, on the limitations of our reason.
A being whose intellect was infinitely powerful would take no interest in
logic and mathematics.[13] For he would be able to see at a glance everything
that his definitions implied, and, accordingly, could never learn anything
from logical inference which he was not fully conscious of already. But our
intellects are not of this order. It is only a minute proportion of the consequences of our definitions that we are able to detect at a glance. Even so
simple a tautology as "91 × 79 = 7189" is beyond the scope of our immediate apprehension. To assure ourselves that "7189" is synonymous with
"91 × 79" we have to resort to calculation, which is simply a process of
tautological transformation—that is, a process by which we change the form
of expressions without altering their significance. The multiplication tables
are rules for carrying out this process in arithmetic, just as the laws of logic
are rules for the tautological transformation of sentences expressed in logical
symbolism or in ordinary language. As the process of calculation is carried
out more or less mechanically, it is easy for us to make a slip and so unwit-
tingly contradict ourselves. And this accounts for the existence of logical and
mathematical "falsehoods," which otherwise might appear paradoxical.
Clearly the risk of error in logical reasoning is proportionate to the length and
the complexity of the process of calculation. And in the same way, the more
complex an analytic proposition is, the more chance it has of interesting and
surprising us.

It is easy to see that the danger of error in logical reasoning can be
minimized by the introduction of symbolic devices, which enable us to

---

[10] *La Science et l'Hypothèse*, Part I, Chapter i.

[11] This was wrongly stated in previous editions as "true for n when it is true for $n + 1$."

[12] Cf. B. Russell's *Introduction to Mathematical Philosophy*, Chapter iii, p. 27.

[13] Cf. Hans Hahn, "Logik, Mathematik und Naturerkennen," *Einheitswissenschaft*,
Heft II, p. 18. "Ein allwissendes Wesen braucht keine Logik und keine Mathematik."

express highly complex tautologies in a conveniently simple form. And this gives us an opportunity for the exercise of invention in the pursuit of logical enquiries. For a well-chosen definition will call our attention to analytic truths, which would otherwise have escaped us. And the framing of definitions which are useful and fruitful may well be regarded as a creative act.

Having thus shown that there is no inexplicable paradox involved in the view that the truths of logic and mathematics are all of them analytic, we may safely adopt it as the only satisfactory explanation of their *a priori* necessity. And in adopting it we vindicate the empiricist claim that there can be no *a priori* knowledge of reality. For we show that the truths of pure reason, the proportions which we know to be valid independently of all experience, are so only in virtue of their lack of factual content. To say that a proposition is true *a priori* is to say that it is a tautology. And tautologies, though they may serve to guide us in our empirical search for knowledge, do not in themselves contain any information about any matter of fact.

Ernest Nagel

The fact that the world we inhabit exhibits periodicities and regularities has been frequently celebrated by poets, philosophers, and men of affairs. That frost will destroy a fruit crop, that a convex lens will concentrate the heat of the sun, or that populations tend to increase toward a fixed maximum, are typical of the uniformities discoverable in innumerable sectors of the physical and social environment; and however we may formulate such uniformities, no philosophy which construes them as anything else than discoveries will conform with the long experience of mankind. Every form of naturalism, to whatever extent it may emphasize the impermanence of many of these regularities or note the selective human activities involved in discovering them, will recognize them as basic features of the world; and even when it attempts to account for them, it will do so only by exhibiting a more pervasive, if more subtle, pattern in the behavior of bodies.

Nevertheless, no demonstrable ground has yet been found which can guarantee that such regularities will continue indefinitely or that the propositions asserting them are necessary. If, as many philosophers have maintained, the proper objects of scientific knowledge are principles capable of *a priori* validation, both the history of science and the analysis of its methods supply ample evidence to show that no science of nature has ever achieved what is thus proclaimed as its true objective. There are, indeed, relatively few practicing scientists today who place any credence in arguments claiming to prove that any principle about an identifiable subject matter is at once logically necessary and empirical in content.

No such general agreement can be found, even among lifelong students

Excerpted and reprinted with the kind permission of the author and the publisher from Y. H. Krikorian, ed., Naturalism and the Human Spirit (*New York: Columbia University Press,* 1944).

of the subject, concerning the status of various logical and mathematical principles constantly employed in responsible inquiries. Indeed, it is difficult to ascertain which natural structures, if any, such propositions express; and it is often no less difficult to exhibit clearly and without self-deception the grounds upon which they are acknowledged. In any event, many of the sharp divisions between professed naturalists are centered around the different interpretations which they assign to principles as familiar as the so-called "laws of thought," the basic assumptions of arithmetic or the axioms of geometry. Thus, one classical form of naturalism maintains, for example, that the principle of noncontradiction is a necessary truth which is descriptive of the limiting structure of everything both actual and possible; another form of naturalism holds this principle to be a contingent, but highly reliable, conclusion based on an empirical study of nature; and a third type of naturalism takes this principle to be void of factual content and an arbitrary specification for the construction of symbolic systems. Analogous differences among naturalists occur in their interpretation of more complicated and recondite mathematical notions.

Such disagreements among those professing naturalism is not a source of embarrassment to them, since naturalism is not a tightly integrated system of philosophy; perhaps the sole bond uniting all varieties of naturalists is that temper of mind which seeks to understand the flux of events in terms of the behaviors of identifiable bodies. Nevertheless, a naturalistic philosophy must be consistent with its own assumptions. If it professes to accept the methods employed by the various empirical sciences for obtaining knowledge about the world, it cannot with consistency claim to have *a priori* insight into the most pervasive structure of things. If it aims to give a coherent and adequate account of the various principles employed in acquiring scientific knowledge, it cannot maintain that all of them are empirical generalizations when some are not subject to experimental refutation. And if it admits that logical principles have a recognizable function in certain contexts (namely, in inquiry), it cannot consistently hold those principles to be completely arbitrary simply on the ground that they are void of factual content when considered apart from those contexts.

No one seriously doubts that logic and mathematics are used in specific contexts in identifiable ways, however difficult it may be to ascertain those ways in any detail. Does it not therefore seem reasonable to attempt to understand the significance of logico-mathematical concepts and principles in terms of the operations associated with them in those contexts and to reject interpretations of their "ultimate meaning" which appear gratuitous and irrelevant in the light of such an analysis? Such, at any rate, is the point of view of the present essay. In what follows, the difficulties and futilities of some nonoperational interpretations of logical principles will first be noted; the limitations of certain naturalistic but narrowly empirical approaches to logic will then be discussed; and finally, an operational interpretation of a small number of logical and mathematical notions will be sketched. However, and this is perhaps the common fate of essays such as the present one, no more than the outline of an argument will be found in the sequel. The present essay contributes no unfamiliar analyses. Its sole objective is to make plausible the view that the rôle of the logico-mathematical disciplines in inquiry can be clarified without requiring the invention of a hypostatic subject matter for them; and to suggest that a naturalism free from speculative vagaries and committed to a thoroughgoing operational standpoint expresses the temper of modern mathematico-experimental science.

I

1. Among the principles which Aristotle believed "hold good for everything that is" and therefore belong to the science of being qua being, he counted certain axioms of logic. These principles, according to him, were to be asserted as necessary truths and were not to be maintained as hypotheses, since "a principle which every one must have who knows anything about being is not a hypothesis." One such principle is that "the same attribute cannot at the same time belong and not belong to the same subject in the same respect."

Aristotle's formulation of the principle contains the qualification "in the same respect." This qualification is important, for it makes possible the defense of the principle against all objections. For suppose one were to deny the principle on the ground that an object, a penny for example, is both sensibly circular in shape and sensibly noncircular. The standard reply to this alleged counterexample is that the penny is circular when viewed from a direction perpendicular to its face and noncircular when viewed from a direction inclined to the face, and that since the different shapes do not occur "in the same respect" the principle has not been invalidated. But if one were now to ask for an unequivocal specification, antecedent to applying the principle, of a definite "same respect" with regard to the penny, so that the principle might then be subjected to a clear-cut test, a skillful defender of the principle as an ontological truth would refuse to supply the desired stipulation. For he would recognize that if a "respect" is first specified, it is always possible to find within that respect a way of apparently violating the principle.

For example, suppose a "same respect" is specified as viewing the penny from a direction perpendicular to its face. The penny will, nevertheless, subtend an angle of thirty degrees and also an angle of sixty degrees. To this, the obvious and proper retort is: "But not at the same distance from the face of the penny." Nevertheless, the principle is saved only by a new restriction upon what is to be understood by "the same respect"; the defender of the principle has altered his *initial* specification of what is the *same* respect. It is, of course, possible, when an attribute is suitably specified, to discover a set of conditions under which a thing does not both have and not have that attribute. The crucial point is that in specifying both the attribute and the conditions, *the principle is employed as a criterion* for deciding whether the specification of the attribute is suitable and whether those conditions are in fact sufficiently determinate. Because of the manner in which the qualification "the same respect" is used, the principle cannot be put to a genuine test, since no proposed case for testing the principle will be judged as admissible which violates the principle to be tested. In brief, conformity to the principle is the condition for a respect being "the same respect."[1]

Analogous comments are relevant for the phrases "same attribute," "belong," and "not belong," which are contained in Aristotle's formulation of the principle. For example, how is one to tell in a disputed instance of the principle whether an attribute is "the same" or not? If someone were to maintain that a penny has a diameter of $\frac{11}{16}$ of an inch and also a diameter of $\frac{12}{16}$ of an inch, he would be told that the assertion is impossible, because even though the attributes are not "the same," in predicating the former one implicitly excludes the latter; and he would, perhaps, be asked whether the measurements were carefully made, whether the same systems of units was really employed, and so forth. In short, since the assertion in effect maintains "the same attribute" to belong and also not to belong to the same subject, it is absurd. But let us press the question why, if the penny has the first of these attributes, it cannot have the other. The impossibility is not simply an empirical one, which rests on inductive arguments; for if it were, the supposition would not be absurd, contrary to the hypothesis, that an unexpected observation may one day discover the penny's diameter to have both dimensions. The impossibility arises from the fact that we use the expressions "length of $\frac{11}{16}$ inches" and "length of $\frac{12}{16}$ inches" in such a way—in part because of the manner in which they may have been defined in relation to one another—that each formulates a different outcome of measurement. We may be sure that no penny will ever turn up with a diameter having both dimensions, because what it means for the diameter to have one of the attributes of dimension is specified in terms of the absence of the other attribute. The principle of contradiction is impregnable against attack, because the "sameness" and the "difference" of attributes are specified in terms of the conformity of attributes to the principle.

Accordingly, the interpretation of the principle as an ontological truth

---

[1] The point at issue involves noting the difference between the following two statements: "However an attribute is selected, it is possible to find a respect such that a given attribute does not at the same time belong and not belong to a given subject in that respect," and "It is possible to find a respect such that, however an attribute is selected, the given attribute does not at the same time belong and not belong to a given subject in that respect." The hypothetical defender of the principle can successfully maintain the first, though not the second, because he undertakes to specify the "sameness" of respects only after he has selected an attribute—that is, after the principle is used to determine a respect, which will thus automatically satisfy the principle.

neglects its function as a norm or regulative principle for introducing distinctions and for instituting appropriate linguistic usage. To maintain that the principle is descriptive of the structure of antecedently determinate "facts" or "attributes" is to convert the outcome of employing the principle into a condition of its employment. The Aristotelian view is thus a gratuitous and irrelevant interpretation of one function of this logical law.

2. More recent advocates of an ontological interpretation of logical principles argue their claim in terms of the conception of logical relations as invariants of all possible worlds—a conception also sponsored by Leibnitz. "Pure logic and pure mathematics," according to an influential proponent of this view, "aim at being true in all possible worlds, not only in this higgledy-piggledy job-lot of a world in which chance has imprisoned us." Reason, according to this interpretation, is an investigation into the very heart and immutable essence of all things actual and possible: "Mathematics takes us into the region of absolute necessity, to which not only the actual world but every possible world must conform." As another version puts it, logic is the most general of all the sciences: "Rules of logic are the rules of operation or transformation according to which all possible objects, physical, psychological, neutral, or complexes can be combined. Thus, logic is an exploration of the field of most general abstract possibility." According to this view, then, logical principles are "principles of being," as well as "principles of inference"; they formulate the most general nature of things, they are universally applicable, and they express the limiting and necessary structure of all existence.

Two issues raised by these brief citations from contemporary literature require comment.

a. When logical principles are asserted to hold for "all possible worlds," what is to be understood by the adjective "possible"? The crux of the matter lies in ascertaining whether "possible worlds" can be specified without using the principles of logic as the *exclusive* means of specification. For if a "possible world" is one whose sole identifiable trait is its conformity to the principles of logic, the view under consideration asserts no more than this: the subject matter of logical principles is whatever conforms to them. In that case no "possible world" could fail to satisfy the principles of logic, since anything which failed to do so would not, by hypothesis, be a possible world.

The point involved is so fundamental that it is desirable to illustrate it in another way. Consider any abstract set of postulates E, for example, Hilbert's postulates for Euclidean geometry, containing the *uninterpreted* terms P, L, and N. It is clearly not significant to ask whether E is true as long as these terms have this character. But physical experiments become relevant for deciding the truth or falsity of E if, for example, L is used to denote the paths of light-rays, P the intersections of two such paths, and N the surfaces determined in another way by any two intersecting paths. Nevertheless, an experimental inquiry can be undertaken only if the paths of light-rays can be identified in some manner *other* than by the sole require-ment that light-rays are things satisfying the formal demands contained in *E*. For if a different method for identifying light-rays did not exist, it would not be possible to ascertain whether a particular physical configuration is such a path without first establishing that the configuration conforms to the implicit specifications of *E*—that is, without first ascertaining the truth of *E* for that configuration. Accordingly, since by definition nothing could be a path of a light-ray which did not satisfy *E*, the question whether *E* is true of all paths of light-rays would not be a matter to be settled by experiment.[2] It is evident, therefore, that if the question of the truth of a set of principles is to be a factual or experimental issue, their subject matter must be identi-fiable in terms of some other characteristic than that it satisfies those principles.

Let us apply these considerations to the formula: "Not both *P* and non-*P*." If it is simply a formula in some uninterpreted symbolic system, the question whether the formula is true in "all possible worlds" cannot arise. On the other hand, if its constituent symbols are interpreted in some manner, great care must be used in deriving further conclusions from the fact that on one such interpretation the formula expresses a "necessary truth." Thus, suppose that the letter "*P*" is taken to denote any "proposition" and that the other expressions in the formula are assigned their usual meanings; the formula will then express the principle of noncontradiction. But either there is some way of identifying propositions other than by the criterion that anything is a proposition which satisfies the formula, or there is not. On the first alternative, the assertion that the formula holds for all propositions will be a statement strictly analogous to general hypotheses in the empirical sciences; the evidence for the assertion, considerable though it may be, will be only partially com-plete, and in any case there will be no reason to regard the formula as expressing a necessary truth. On the second alternative, the assertion will be an implicit definition of what a proposition is; the principle of noncontra-diction will be a necessary truth, since nothing could be a proposition which does not conform to it.[3]

The view that logic is the science of all possible worlds thus suffers from a fundamental ambiguity. If the only way of identifying a "possible world"

[2] Of course, the question whether *a particular physical configuration* is the path of a light-ray (that is, whether it satisfies *E*) would remain an experimental issue.

[3] This discussion is obviously oversimplified. Thus, if the formula is a logical conse-quence of some set of axioms which are used as implicit definitions for propositions, then the principle of noncontradiction will be a necessary truth even though it now falls under the first of the above two alternatives. However, the point of the discussion is not affected by the neglect of such complications. In the present essay the word "proposition" is used loosely, and is frequently employed interchangeably with the word "statement." It is, of course, important in many contexts to distinguish between a proposition and a statement, since the former is often taken to be the "meaning" of the latter. However, the issues under discussion are fairly neutral with respect to the different views which are current concerning what propositions are, so that no serious confusions need arise from the loose use of the word.

is on the basis of its conformity to the canons of logic, logic is indeed the science of all possible worlds. But the view is then no more than a misleading formulation of the fact that logical principles are employed as stipulations or postulates, which define what we understand by the consistency of discourse.

b. The second point requiring comment bears on the view that logical principles express the limiting and necessary structures of all things. If the domain of application of logical principles is identified on the basis of the actual use to which those principles are put, this view cannot be construed literally. For it is not things and their actual relations which are said to be logically consistent or inconsistent with one another, but propositions or statements about them; and it is to the latter that principles such as the principle of noncontradiction are relevant. No one will hesitate to acknowledge that "The table on which I am now writing is brown" and "The table on which I am now writing is white" are mutually inconsistent statements. But this inconsistency cannot, according to the view under discussion, be predicated of two "facts," "states of affairs," or "objects"; for if there were such facts the view would be self-refuting. Accordingly, inconsistency is something which can be located only in discourse, among statements, not among things in general. And if so much is admitted, an obvious dialectic requires that consistency be localized in a similar domain, in discourse and among statements.

But dialectic aside and bearing in mind only the identifiable functions of logical principles, there is no obvious warrant for the claim that the latter are the rules in accordance with which all possible objects can be transformed or combined. Certainly they are not rules of operation upon things in any familiar or literal sense of "transformation of things"—unless, indeed, the things said to be transformed and combined are elements of discourse, constellations of signs of varying degrees of complexity. The "pervasive traits" and "limiting structures" of all "possible worlds" which logic is alleged to formulate thus appear to be traits of discourse when it has been ordered in a certain way. The interpretation of logical principles as ontological invariants seems therefore, on closer view, to be an extraneous ornamentation upon the functions they actually exercise. But the regulative rôle of logical principles, suggested by the foregoing discussion, will be exhibited more clearly in the sequel.

II

Empirically minded naturalists, convinced that propositions concerning matters of fact must be supported by sensory observation, but convinced also that logical principles have factual content, have not had an easy time in accounting for the apparent universality and necessity of these principles. The interpretation of logical principles widely accepted by both traditional and contemporary empiricists is that they are hypotheses about traits of minds and things, based on inductive arguments from experience.

> I readily admit [Mill declared] that these three general propositions [the Laws of Thought] are universally true of all phenomena. I also admit that if there are any inherent necessities of thought, these are such. . . . Whether the three so-called Fundamental Laws are laws of our thoughts by the native structure of the mind, or merely because we perceive them to be universally true of observed phenomena, I will not positively decide: but they are laws of our thoughts now, and invincibly so.

More recent writers concerned with defending an empirical philosophy, though they may reject Mill's psychological atomism and sensationalism, frequently do not differ from him on the view that logical principles are inductive truths. The following is a sufficiently forthright contemporary statement of this conception.

> *Logical* validity is grounded on *natural* fact. . . . When we are in doubt as to the logical validity of an argument, there is only one test. If the class of such arguments gives us materially true conclusions from materially true premises, it is valid, if not, it is invalid. . . . The crucial question which this frankly empirical approach to logic must face is whether it can explain the formal characters of logical inference. The experimental hypothesis attempts the explanation by showing that those inferential procedures which have brought knowledge in the past exhibit a certain invariant *order* whose metaphysical correlate is to be sought in the *serial* characters of existence. . . . The laws of logic . . . cannot be disproved, but they may become inapplicable and meaningless. We can say nothing about the *probability* of this being so, but we can just conceive of the possibility that the so-called *a priori* laws of logic may not enable us to organize our experience. That is why they are not formal or empty. That is why they tell us something about the *actual* world. That is why we can say that every additional application of logic to existence is an experimental verification of its invariance.

However attractive such an interpretation of logical principles may appear to a consistent empirical naturalism—to a philosophy which appreciates the limitations natural structures place upon our thought and action, but which nevertheless finds no warrant for the assertion that *a priori* knowledge of such structures is possible—there are insuperable difficulties involved in it. These difficulties arise in the main because those who profess such an interpretation misconceive the character of empirical or scientific method.

1. Little need be said in refutation of the view that logical principles formulate the "inherent necessities of thought" and are generalized descriptions of the operations of minds. Surely the actual occurrence in the same person of beliefs in logically incompatible propositions makes nonsense of the claim that the principle of noncontradiction expresses a universal fact of

psychology. Moreover, if logical principles were true descriptions of anthropological behavior, they would be contingent truths, refutable on evidence drawn from the observation of human behavior; but in that case, the necessity which is so generally attributed to logical principles, however much this may be disguised by calling their contradictories "unbelievable," would be left unexplained.

2. The view under consideration maintains that the validity of a type of inference sanctioned by logic can be established only by presenting empirical evidence to show that an inference of that form always leads from materially true premises to materially true conclusions. It must be admitted, of course, that a valid inference is often defined as one which invariably yields true conclusions from true premises. But it by no means follows that an inference ever is or can be established as valid in the manner proposed. Suppose, for example, "A" and "If A then B" are asserted as true statements (the expression "if . . . then" being used in some one of the customary ways), so that the conclusion that "B" is true may be drawn in accordance with the familiar rule of *ponendo ponens*. Let us now imagine that as a matter of fact "B" is false and that we are therefore urged by someone to abandon the rule as a universal logical principle. Would not such a suggestion be dismissed as grotesque and as resting upon some misunderstanding? Would we not retort that in the case supposed "A" or "If A then B" must have been asserted as true mistakenly or that if this is no mistake then the assertion of the falsity of "B" must be an error? Would we not, in any event, maintain that statements of the form: "If A and (if A then B) then B" are necessarily true, since not to acknowledge them as such is to run counter to the established usage of the expressions "and" and "if . . . then"?

Proponents of the view under discussion often declare that in interpreting logical principles as empirical hypotheses they are offering a justification for logic in terms of the procedures and standards of adequacy employed in the most advanced natural sciences. It is worth noting, therefore, that not a single instance can be cited from the history of science which would support the conception that the validity of logical principles is ever established by the suggested method. Is it not significant that whenever consequences derived from premises believed to be true are in disagreement with the facts of experimental observation, it is not the logical principles in accordance with which those consequences were drawn that are rejected as experimentally unwarranted? Indeed, it is not apparent how the suggested method for establishing the validity of logical principles could operate in any typical inquiry. For the truth of most premises employed in the sciences cannot be established except on the basis of an investigation of the consequences which are drawn from them—drawn in accordance with and with the help of logical principles. For example, the principles of Newtonian mechanics, which constitute part of the premises in many physical inquiries, cannot be established as adequate to their subject matter unless it is first discovered what these principles imply.

This will be even more obvious if we note that these premises employ such complex notions as differential coefficients, real numbers, and point masses; the premises cannot be construed as "descriptions" of matters of fact accessible to a direct observation, that is, as statements whose truth or falsity may be settled prior to examining their logical consequences. The proposed method for establishing the validity of arguments is thus clearly not a feasible one, since no experimental control can be instituted for determining the alleged material truth of logical principles.

It follows that no "metaphysical correlate" to logical principles need be sought in the "serial character of existence." And if logical principles do not function as contingent hypotheses about matters of fact, if they are not to be established inductively on the ground of their conformity to "certain structural and functional invariants of nature," there is no clear sense in which "every additional application of logic to existence is an experimental verification of its invariance." Logical principles are compatible with any order which the flux of events may exhibit; they could not be in disagreement with anything which inquiry may disclose, and if they should ever require revision, the grounds for such alterations must lie elsewhere than in the subject matter of the natural sciences. To be sure, should the cosmos become a chaos to the extent of making the continued existence of reflective thought impossible, the use of logical principles would thereby also become impossible. But as the above discussion indicates, the continued employment of those principles is not contingent upon the invariance of structures other than those which sustain the continuance of reflective inquiry.

3. In spite of its profession of allegiance to scientific methods as the canonical techniques of competent inquiry, the empiricistic interpretation of logic is based upon an inadequate conception of what is involved in those methods. Indeed, even when, as has already been noted, those subscribing to this interpretation explicitly reject Mill's psychological atomism, they do not always successfully free themselves from his over-simple views on the formation of scientific concepts. Two closely related points require brief discussion in this connection: the narrow criterion of meaningful discourse which is explicitly or tacitly assumed by many empirical naturalists; and the inadequate conception which they hold of the rôle of symbolic constructions in the conduct of inquiry.

a. It has often been maintained that the theoretical sciences deem to be ultimately meaningful only the statements which either formulate directly observable relations of qualities and things or can be translated without remainder into statements that do so. According to another version of this thesis, every meaningful statement must consist of terms which either denote simple, directly experienceable qualities and relations or are compounded out of terms denoting such simples. Even false hypotheses, so it has been urged on occasion, are meaningful only because they formulate the structure of some actual observable situation—a structure which happens to be wrongly attributed to a given situation. Since the familiar logical and mathematical principles seem so obviously significant, and since in their usual formulation they are ostensibly about the relations which properties of things bear to one another, the interpretation of these principles as empirical hypotheses is sometimes deduced as a corollary from this general view.

Little need be said to show the inadequacy of the suggested criterion of meaning. If it were applied consistently, most of the theories employed in the various positive sciences would have to be dismissed as in fact meaningless; and indeed, those who have accepted the criterion have been consistent enough to exclude almost all general statements as not expressing "genuine propositions." For in the first place, to the extent that theoretical propositions have the form of unrestricted universals, they do not formulate the explicit outcome of any actual series of direct observations. And in the second place, many theoretical statements contain terms (such as "point-particle," "light-wave," "electron," "gene," and the like) which denote nothing that can be directly observed and cannot be construed as being explicitly definable with the help of only such terms as do so. Moreover, there is surely no evidence for the claim that for every false hypothesis there is a situation for which it is true.[4] It is clear that underlying the suggested criterion of meaningful discourse is an ill-concealed reproductive psychology of abstraction and that in any case those who employ it cannot do justice to the actual procedures of the sciences.

A naturalism which is based on modern scientific methods cannot afford to propose illiberal restrictions upon inquiry. It must recognize that no formula can be constructed which will express once for all "*the* meaning" of any portion of scientific discourse. Instead of attempting to construct such formulae, it must turn seriously to the analysis of specific uses and functions of specific systems of expressions in specific contexts. It will have to note that statements in scientific discourse always occur as elements in a system of symbols and operations, and it will therefore attempt to understand the significance of statements in terms of the complicated uses to which they are subject. It will, accordingly, not assume dogmatically that the directly observed qualities and relations of the explicit subject matter of a science must consti-tute the sole and ultimate reference of every significant complex of its symbols. It will surely recognize that according to standard scientific procedure evidence taken from sensory observation must be relevant to propositions alleged to be about matters of fact: such propositions must entail conse-quences, obtained by logical operations in determinate ways, which can be experimentally tested when the appropriate circumstances occur. It will thus accept the pragmatic maxim that there is no difference between the objects of

---

[4] For example, within the framework of the Newtonian analysis of motion, an indefinite number of false hypotheses for gravitational attraction can be constructed, since a false theory of gravitation is obtained if the exponent "2" in Newton's formula is replaced by a different numeral. Are these different theories to be dismissed as meaningless because there do not happen to exist an infinity of situations for which these theories are true?

beliefs and conceptions where there is no possible difference in observable behavior. But it will not, therefore, insist that all significant statements must be descriptive of what can be directly observed. And it will remain sensitive to the possibility that even statements about the explicit subject matter of a science may involve a reference to the operations (overt and symbolic) performed in inquiries into that subject matter.

b. Nowhere is the systematic undervaluation of the constructive function of thought in inquiry more glaring than in the widespread neglect of the rôle played by symbolic manipulations in scientific procedure. The more comprehensive and integrated a theoretical system is, the more obvious does the need for for such manipulations appear. For especially in the theories of modern science symbols usually occur which refer to nothing that can be directly experienced; and the significance for matters of direct experience of the conceptual constructions which enter into those theories cannot be made explicit except with the help of extensive symbolic transformations. Accordingly, no statement detached from the symbolic system to which it is integral can be evaluated for its empirical validity, and no isolated concept can be judged as warranted on the basis of the essentially irrelevant criterion of pictorial suggestiveness. But since calculation or symbolic manipulation thus acquires an indispensable though intermediary rôle in inquiry, the need for reliable techniques of constructing and expanding symbolic systems becomes progressively more pressing; the institution of an entire department of investigation devoted to the formal study of symbolic systems is the practically inevitable consequence.

It is a common and tempting assumption that in performing a chain of calculations one is at the same time tracing out the existential connections between things, so that the formal pattern of symbolic transformations reproduces in some manner the structure of the subject matter under investigation. However, the specific mode in which theories are constructed and bodies of knowledge are integrated is only partially determined by experimental findings. Various norms or ideals—such as the desire for a certain degree of precision, for intellectual economy and notational convenience, or for a certain type of comprehensiveness—also control the direction of inquiry and the articulation of theories. Many symbolic constructions and operations are therefore indices of the standards regulating the course of systematic investigations, and are not merely indications of the expected conclusions of experiment or of the intrinsic relations between phases of subject matter. A myopic concern with the sensory warrants for scientific findings—such as often characterizes traditional empiricism—easily leads to neglect of this aspect of systematic scientific formulations; the traits of discourse are then identified as traits of subject matter,[5] and principles whose function it is to institute a desired

---

[5] An example of such a transference is found in the claim that, because the consistency of a set of formal postulates is established by exhibiting a group of related objects—a so-called "concrete model"—satisfying those postulates, logical traits (such as consistency)

order into inquiry are not distinguished from statements about the explicit subject matter of inquiry. When the identification is made, the construction of symbolic systems (including the use of hypotheses) is in effect viewed as an inessential scaffolding for attaining some form of intuitive knowledge. When the distinction is not made, logical principles are in effect deprived of their identifiable functions.

III

The preceding discussion has, in the main, been negative. There remains the task of making explicit the suggestions it contains concerning an alternative interpretation of some logical and mathematical notions. Nothing like a systematic account of logic and mathematics can be attempted, and only a small number of logical principles and mathematical terms will be briefly examined. But even such an examination may exhibit the fruitfulness of an operational analysis of formal concepts and may make plausible the view that the content of the formal disciplines has a regulative function in inquiry.

Although logic is one of the oldest intellectual disciplines, considerable difference of opinion exists as the scope of logical theory and as to which concepts and principles properly belong to logic. The present discussion will be confined to such admittedly formal principles as the so-called laws of thought and other "necessary truths" and to principles of inference such as the principle of *ponendo ponens*. The discussion will be facilitated if at the outset two senses are distinguished in which logical principles are commonly asserted: as principles which are explicitly about symbolism or language; and as necessary truths whose ostensible subject matter is usually some nonlinguistic realm.[6]

a. The three laws of thought are employed in the first sense in cases something like the following. Suppose that in a bit of reasoned discourse the term "animal" occurs several times. The argument will clearly be a cogent one only if in each of its occurrences the word retains a fixed "meaning" —that is, only if it is used as a name for the same kind of object. The requirement that in a given context a term must continue to be used in essentially the same manner, is expressed as the principle of identity. Analogously, the principle of noncontradiction requires that in a given context a term must not

---

must represent pervasive ontological or empirical invariants. In point of fact, however, not only can some postulate sets be established without recourse to empirical facts in the indicated manner; most postulate systems cannot be shown to be consistent by genuinely empirical methods. But what is perhaps more to the point, this argument for identifying logical with existential properties fails to observe that consistency is demanded of symbolic systems as part of an ideal for the organization of statements and is not a trait subsisting in nature independently of symbolic formulations.

[6] This distinction roughly corresponds to the difference noted in much current literature between "meta-logical" statements and statements in the "object-language" of a science.

be applied to a given thing and also denied to it; and the principle of excluded middle is formulated in a corresponding way.

When stated in this manner, these principles are obviously *prescriptive* for the use of language, and as such are not *descriptive* of actual usage. They specify minimal conditions for discourse without confusion, for they state at least some of the requirements for a precise language. Everyday language, and to some extent even the specialized languages of the sciences, are vague in some measure, so that they do not entirely conform to the requirement set by these principles.[7] Although fairly effective communication is nevertheless possible in connection with many pursuits, situations do arise in which a greater precision in the use of language is required. The laws of thought thus formulate an ideal to be achieved—an ideal which is capable of being attained at least approximately—and they indicate the direction in which the maximum of desired precision may be obtained.

Few will deny that the laws of thought as here formulated have a regulative function. Nevertheless, the admission is often qualified by the claim that if the ideal these laws formulate is a reasonable one, not an arbitrary norm, there must be an objective ground—a "structural invariant"—which lends them authority. Moreover, it is sometimes urged that this ideal must be a necessary and inescapable one, since otherwise a genuine alternative to it would be possible; however, communication would be impossible if language were so employed as to conform, for example, to the denial of the principle of identity. But this latter argument for the intrinsic necessity of these principles is surely circular. For if by "communication" is understood processes similar to those in which we are familiarly engaged when talking, writing, or carrying on research—processes which illustrate the use of symbols in at least partial conformity to the laws of thought—communication would indeed be impossible were the requirements set by these laws satisfied in no degree; but communication would not be possible simply because these laws are analytic of what is understood by the word "communication." Whatever might be the human needs which communication satisfies, the desire to communicate and the desire to enforce the ideal specified by the laws are directed toward the same end. It must, nevertheless, be acknowledged that the ideal of precision in using language is not an arbitrary one. It is not arbitrary, because communication and inquiry are directed to the achievement of certain objectives, and these objectives are best attained when language is employed in a manner approximating as closely as possible the norms expressed by the laws of thought. The assertion that this is so requires support by empirical evidence —evidence which it is possible to produce. But the available evidence is drawn from the study of the behavior of men engaged in inquiry; it does not come from a consideration of structural invariants found in other domains.

---

[7] Thus, if the term "red" is vague, there is a class of colors concerning which it is indeterminate whether the term applies to them or not, so that the principle of excluded middle fails in this case.

The three laws of thought are, however, not the only principles of logic explicitly dealing with symbolism, and some consideration must now be given to that important class of principles known as rules of inference—of which the rule of *ponendo ponens* is, perhaps, the most familiar. The first point to note in connection with such principles is that it is possible to specify accurately what rules govern the valid inferences in a language, only when the "meanings" of certain terms in that language are precise—that is, when terms like "and," "or," and "if—then" are used in determinate ways. In fact, however, the ordinary usage of such terms is vague and unclear. Everyday language, in the main, is employed according to routine habits which are fixed and stable over a narrow range but, which are indeterminate in many crucial cases; accordingly, inferences are drawn and sanctioned on the basis of crude intuitive considerations as to what is "really meant" by the terms involved.[8] The explicit formulation of canons of inference serves to clarify vague intent; and what is, perhaps, less commonly recognized, such formulations help to fix usages when they have previously been unsettled: they serve as proposals for modifying old usages and instituting new ones.

The various modern systems of formal logic must, accordingly, be viewed, not as accounts of the "true nature" of an antecedently identifiable relation of "implication," but as alternative proposals for specifying usages and for performing inferences. The adoption of a system such as is found in White-head and Russell's *Principia Mathematica* is in effect the adoption of a set of regulative principles for developing more inclusive and determinate habits for using language than are illustrated in everyday discourse. No known recent system of formal logic is or can be just a faithful transcription of those inferential canons which are embodied in common discourse, though in the construction of these systems hints may be taken from current usage; for the entire *raison d'être* for such systems is the need for precision and inclusiveness where common discourse is vague and incomplete, even if as a consequence their adoption as regulative principles involves a modification of our inferential habits.

The question naturally arises whether the conventions which explicitly formulated rules of inference institute are entirely arbitrary—whether, in other words, the adoption of one set of regulative principles for reconstructing linguistic behavior is as "justifiable" as the adoption of a different set. The issue raised does not refer to the construction of various abstract

---

[8] For example, everyone who has an elementary knowledge of English would agree that the rule of *ponendo ponens* is a correct canon of inference. On the other hand, a person unsophisticated by training in formal logic and not committed to one of the modern logical systems, may hestiate to accept the rule that a statement of the form "Either A or B" is a consequence of "A," where "A" and "B" are any statements; and he will probably seriously doubt the correctness of the rule that "If A then (if B then C)" follows from "If A and B, then C," where "A," "B," and "C" are any statements. The hesitation and the doubt must be attributed to the fact that "or," "and," and "if—then" are frequently used ambiguously and have fairly clear and determinate meanings only in relatively few contexts.

"uninterpreted" symbolic calculi, for which diverging rules of "inference" or "transformation" may be developed; for it is usually admitted that the arbitrariness of such abstract systems can be limited only by the formal requirements of symbolic construction. The issue refers to the ground upon which one system of regulative principles is to be preferred to another system, when such principles are to be employed in the conduct of scientific inquiry. But this manner of putting the question suggests its own answer. If everyday language requires completion and reorganization for the sake of attaining the ends of inquiry, the "justification" for a proposed set of regulative principles will not be arbitrary and can be given only in terms of the adequacy of the proposed changes as means or instruments for attaining the envisaged ends. Thus, if inquiry is directed toward achieving a system of physics which will be coherent, comprehensive, and economical in its use of certain types of assumption and operation, one set of canons for inference will be preferable to another if the former leads to a closer approximation to this goal than does the latter. The choice between alternative systems of regulative principles will then not be arbitrary and will have an objective basis; the choice will not, however, be grounded on the allegedly greater inherent necessity of one system of logic over another, but on the relatively greater adequacy of one of them as an instrument for achieving a certain systematization of knowledge.[9]

It is needless to dwell further on the function of rules of inference: their primary rôle is to guide the development of discourse in a certain direction, namely, in the deduction of the consequences of sets of statements; they thereby contribute to making the use of language more determinate and precise and to attaining the goals of specific inquiries. It must be admitted, however, that it is frequently difficult to exhibit adequate evidence for the superior efficacy of one type of inferential system over another, especially when the specific goals of inquiry are themselves vague and are conceived, in part at least, in aesthetic terms.[10] The point to be stressed is that however great this difficulty may be, it can be resolved only by considering the specific functions of such logical principles in determinate contexts of inquiry; it cannot be resolved by investigating the causal factors which lead men to adopt those principles or by a genetic account of inferential habits.

For example, the view has been advanced that certain simple forms of inference are generated by physiological mechanisms sharing a common character with mechanisms present in the subject matter of inquiry in which those inferences are used; and it is sometimes said that a theory of logic is "naturalistic" only if it holds that rational operations "grow out of" the

---

[9] Something more will be said on this point below. These remarks should not, however, be taken to mean that all habits of inference, and in particular language itself, have been instituted on the basis of a deliberate convention. How language first arose and how some of our common modes of inference actually came into being, are questions of fact about which there is in general little reliable information and concerning which everyone seems to be equally in the dark.

[10] For example, when a theory is required to be "simple" and "elegant."

more pervasive biological and physical ones. It may be safely assumed that there are causes and physical conditions for habits of inference, even when we happen to be ignorant of them. It is not evident, however, especially since habits of inference may change though the subject matter in connection with which they are employed does not, that the mechanism underlying a specific habit of inference is identical with the mechanism involved in that subject matter. And it is even less evident how, even if this were the case, the causal account would enable us to evaluate inferential principles, since the cogency of such an account is established only with the help of those principles. Suggestions for inferential canons may indeed be obtained from observations of natural processes; but the fact that a principle may have been suggested in this way does not explain its normative function. Again, the known facts about the earth's history make it most reasonable to assume that the higher and more complex activities of men did not always exist and that they have been developed out of more primitive ones; and it would certainly be a matter of great interest to learn just how this has come about. However, in the present state of our knowledge a genetic account of logical operations is at best a highly speculative and dubious one; and what is more to the point, even if a well-supported genetic account were available, it would contribute little or nothing to an understanding of the present functioning of logical principles or to the explanation of the grounds of their authority. In the absence of a detailed knowledge of the past, the reaffirmation of the historical and structural continuity of our rational behavior with the activities of other organisms is an act of piety; it does not increase the clarifying force of an experimentally orientated naturalism.[11]

b. Logical principles are also asserted as necessary truths which do not refer to linguistic subject matter. Thus, "Everything is identical with itself" and "If A then A" (where "A" is any statement) are formulations of the principle of identity; "Nothing has and also lacks a given property" and "It is not the case that A and not-A" (where "A" is any statement) are formulations of the principle of noncontradiction; while "If A and (if A then B), then B," and "If (if A then B) then (if not-B then not-A)" (where "A" and "B" are any statements) are examples of other principles usually regarded as necessary. These principles are ostensibly about things, their attributes and their relations, not about symbols for them; they are held to be necessary truths, because their denials are self-contradictory.

The first point to note about these logical laws is that if they are asserted as necessary truths, they are asserted to be such in some more or less precisely

---

[11] These comments should not be construed as a rejection of some form of "the principle of continuity" as a fruitful guide and norm in inquiry. Nor should they be taken as denying that the study of simpler and more basic biological behavior may provide an illuminating context and essential clews for the understanding of the "higher" functions. These remarks are included simply as a protest against frequent abuses of a useful postulate of procedure.

formulated language, whether in the crudely precise language of everyday use or in some more exact artificial symbolic system. And it is not difficult to show that although their subject matter is not the language of which they are parts, they occur in that language because of the habits of usage or the tacit or explicit rules which govern that language. For example, if the characterizations "true" and "false" are employed in the customary manner, no statement can properly (that is, without contravening that usage) be characterized as both true and false; and if the word "not" is so used in connection with acts of affirming and denying statements that a false statement is rejected as not true, the principle of noncontradiction is instituted as a necessary truth. More generally, if a precise usage is fixed for a number of expressions in a symbolic system, statements constructed out of some of these expressions will usually occur such that to deny them is to misuse those expressions. Accordingly, the laws which are regarded as necessary in a given language may be viewed as implicit definitions of the ways in which certain recurrent expressions are to be used or as consequences of other postulates for such usages. No language is so utterly flexible in its formal structure that no limits exist as to the way expressions in it can be combined and used. The necessary statements of a language help to specify what these limits are. But to the extent to which ordinary language is not precise, which statements in it are necessary cannot be determined exactly. The so-called systems of "pure logic" do not suffer from this fault; they can therefore be used as norms for instituting a more precise employment of language in situations in which such precision is essential for the task at hand. Indeed, as is well known, one result of such instituted precision is to facilitate the process of deriving consequences from premises and to supply dependable means for checking inferences.

This function of logical laws—to serve as instruments for establishing connections between statements which are usually not themselves logically necessary—is too familiar to require more than passing mention. A point worth observing, however, is that the necessary laws of logic can be reformulated so as to become principles of inference, having as their explicit subject matter the relations of expressions in a symbolic system. For it can be shown that a given language may be so reconstructed that it no longer will contain necessary truths—without thereby affecting the original possibilities for deducing statements which are not necessary—provided that corresponding to the necessary truths initially in the language appropriate rules of inference are introduced. The cost of such a reconstruction may be prohibitive in terms of the inconveniences and complexities which arise from it.[12]

[12] For example, the necessary truth "if (if A then B), then (if not-B then not-A)" could be eliminated from our language, provided that we introduce the rule that a statement of the form "if not-B then not-A" is deducible from a statement of the form "if A then B." On the other hand, it is usually assumed that when "A," "B," "C," "D" are any statements, they may be combined to form the new statements "if A then B," "if C then D," and "if (if A then B), then (if C then D)"; accordingly, since "not-A" and "not-B" are statements, "if (if A then B), then (if not-B then not-A)" must be accepted as a statement

Nevertheless, the theoretical possibility of making it helps to show that the function of necessary truths is to regulate and control the process of deduction. It follows that the previous comments on rules of inference apply with equal force to laws expressing necessary connections.

A few final remarks concerning the grounds for accepting logical laws must be made. The main stress which is to be made in this connection is that any "justification" of such laws can be given only in terms of the adequacy of the language in which they are part to the specific tasks for which that language is employed. This point can be enforced by recalling that in the empirical sciences it is not possible to perform experiments which would subject isolated statements to a crucial test, since every experiment actually tests a vaguely delimited system of theoretical and factual assumptions involved in the experiment and the statement. Analogously, it is not feasible to "justify" a law of logic by confronting it with specific observational data; the belief that it is possible to do so is part of the heritage of traditional empiricism. On the other hand, since logical laws are implicit laws for specifying the structure of a language, and since their explicit function is to link systematically statements to which data of observation are relevant, logical laws may be evaluated on the basis of their effectiveness in yielding systems of a desired kind. Thus, it has recently been suggested that in order to develop the theory of subatomic phenomena in a manner conforming both to experimental evidence and to certain ideals of economy and elegance, a "logic" different from those normally employed may have to be instituted.[13] The suggestion is still in a speculative stage, and it is interesting only as a possibility. Nevertheless, it calls attention to the fact in a striking way that under the pressure of factual observation and norms of convenience familiar language habits may come to be revised; and it indicates that the acceptance of logical principles as canonical need be neither on arbitrary grounds nor on grounds of their allegedly inherent authority, but on the ground that they effectively achieve certain postulated ends.

It must be emphasized, however, that this way of justifying logical principles has nothing in common with the view which construes them as descriptive of an intrinsic and pervasive structure of things. It has been argued that just as in geometry there are intrinsically different kinds of surface and each kind imposes "certain limits on the range of alternative coordinate systems which can be used to map it out," so "the objective structure of the system of fact imposes some limitation on the alternative

---

on the basis of the stipulation just mentioned. Hence, if the occurrence of such necessary truths is to be prevented, more complicated rules must be introduced for combining statements to form new ones.

[13] See Garrett Birkhoff and John von Neumann, "The Logic of Quantum Mechanics," *Annals of Mathematics*, XXXVII (1936), 823–43. The proposed logical system involves abandoning certain rules of inference which seem truistic both to "common sense" and to those accustomed to the system of *Principia Mathematica*.

systems of language or symbolism which are capable of representing it."
The conclusion drawn from this argument by analogy is that propositions
which would describe this structure "would almost inevitably take the
form of propositions which formulate certain very abstract and general
and widespread linguistic usages"; and since logical principles do "formulate" these usages, there can be only one genuinely valid logic, only one
absolute system of necessary truths. But even if one accepts the questionable
analogy which underlies the argument, elementary considerations of scientific
procedure must lead one to reject the conception of "*the* objective structure
of *the* system of fact" capable of being known without the mediation of any
selective symbolic system. The study of scientific inquiry requires us to admit
that structures cannot be known independently of activities of symbolization;
that structures considered for investigation are selected on the basis of special
problems; that the various structures discovered are not, according to the
best evidence, all parts of one coherent pattern; and that the precise manner
in which our theories are formulated is controlled by specifically human
postulates no less than by experimental findings. The attempt to justify
logical principles in terms of their supposed conformity to an absolute
structure of facts thus completely overlooks their actual function of formulating and regulating the pursuit of human ideals. If the preceding discussion
has any merit, however, the reasonable view is that the relative success of a
system of logic in doing these things is the sole identifiable and objective
basis for measuring its worth.

TRUTH BY CONVENTION

W. V. Quine

The less a science has advanced, the more its terminology tends to rest on an uncritical assumption of mutual understanding. With increase of rigor this basis is replaced piecemeal by the introduction of definitions. The interrelationships recruited for these definitions gain the status of analytic principles; what was once regarded as a theory about the world becomes reconstrued as a convention of language. Thus it is that some flow from the theoretical to the conventional is an adjunct of progress in the logical foundations of any science. The concept of simultaneity at a distance affords a stock example of such development: in supplanting the uncritical use of this phrase by a definition. Einstein so chose the definitive relationship as to verify conventionally the previously paradoxical principle of the absoluteness of the speed of light. But whereas the physical sciences are generally recognized as capable only of incomplete evolution in this direction, and as destined to retain always a nonconventional kernel of doctrine, developments of the past few decades have led to a widespread conviction that logic and mathematics are purely analytic or conventional. It is less the purpose of the present inquiry to question the validity of this contrast than to question its sense.

I

A definition, strictly, is a convention of notational abbreviation.[1] A *simple* definition introduces some specific expression, e.g., 'kilometer', or

[1] Cf. Russell, *Principles of Mathematics* (Cambridge, 1903), p. 429.

Reprinted with the kind permission of the author, the editor, and the publisher from Otis H. Lee, ed., Philosophical Essays for A. N. Whitehead (*New York: Longmans, Green & Co., Inc.*, 1936). *Some minor corrections have been made by the author, particularly on p. 337.*

'*e*', called the *definiendum*, as arbitrary shorthand for some complex expression, e.g., 'a thousand meters' or '$\lim_{n \to \infty} \left(1 + \dfrac{1}{n}\right)^n$', called the *definiens*. A *contextual* definition sets up indefinitely many mutually analogous pairs of definienda and definientia according to some general scheme; an example is the definition whereby expressions of the form '$\dfrac{\sin\,---}{\cos\,---}$' are abbreviated as 'tan ---'. From a formal standpoint the signs thus introduced are wholly arbitrary; all that is required of a definition is that it be theoretically immaterial, i.e., that the shorthand which it introduces admit in every case of unambiguous elimination in favor of the antecedent longhand.[2]

Funtionally a definition is not a premiss to theory, but a license for rewriting theory by putting definiens for definiendum or vice versa. By allowing such replacements a definition transmit truth: it allows true statements to be translated into new statements which are true by the same token. Given the truth of the statement 'The altitude of Kibo exceeds six thousand meters', the definition of 'kilometer' makes for the truth of the statement 'The altitude of Kibo exceeds six kilometers'; given the truth of the statement '$\dfrac{\sin \pi}{\cos \pi} = \dfrac{\sin \pi}{\cos \pi}$,' of which logic assures us in its earliest pages, the contextual definition cited above makes for the truth of the statement 'tan π $= \dfrac{\sin \pi}{\cos \pi}$.' In each case the statement inferred through the definition is true only because it is shorthand for another statement which was true independently of the definition. Considered in isolation from all doctrine, including logic, a definition is incapable of grounding the most trivial statement; even 'tan $\pi = \dfrac{\sin \pi}{\cos \pi}$,' is a definitional transformation of an antecedent self-identity, rather than a spontaneous consequence of the definition.

What is loosely called a logical consequence of definitions is therefore more exactly describable as a logical truth definitionally abbreviated: a statement which becomes a truth of logic when definienda are replaced by definientia. In this sense 'tan $\pi = \dfrac{\sin \pi}{\cos \pi}$,' is a logical consequence of the contextual definition of the tangent. 'The altitude of Kibo exceeds six kilometers' is not *ipso facto* a logical consequence of the given definition of 'kilometer'; on the other hand it would be a logical consequence of a quite suitable but

---

[2] From the present point of view a contextual definition may be recursive, but can then count among its definienda only those expressions in which the argument of recursion has a constant value, since otherwise the requirement of eliminability is violated. Such considerations are of little consequence, however, since any recursive definition can be turned into a direct one by purely logical methods. Cf. Carnap, *Logische Syntax der Sprache*, Vienna, 1934, pp. 23, 79.

unlikely definition introducing 'Kibo' as an abbreviation of the phrase 'the totality of such African terrain as exceeds six kilometers in altitude', for under this definition the statement in question is an abbreviation of a truth of logic, viz., 'The altitude of the totality of such African terrain as exceeds six kilometers in altitude exceeds six kilometers.'

Whatever may be agreed upon as the exact scope of logic, we may expect definitional abbreviations of logical truths to be reckoned as logical rather than extralogical truths. This being the case, the preceding conclusion shows logical consequences of definitions to be themselves truths of logic. To claim that mathematical truths are conventional in the sense of following logically from definitions is therefore to claim that mathematics is part of logic. The latter claim does not represent an arbitrary extension of the term 'logic' to include mathematics; agreement as to what belongs to logic and what belongs to mathematics is supposed at the outset, and it is then claimed that definitions of mathematical expressions can so be framed on the basis of logical ones that all mathematical truths become abbreviations of logical ones.

Although signs introduced by definition are formally arbitrary, more than such arbitrary notational convention is involved in questions of definability; otherwise any expression might be said to be definable on the basis of any expressions whatever. When we speak of definability, or of finding a definition for a given sign, we have in mind some traditional usage of the sign antecedent to the definition in question. To be satisfactory in this sense a definition of the sign not only must fulfill the formal requirement of unambiguous eliminability, but must also conform to the traditional usage in question. For such conformity it is necessary and sufficient that every context of the sign which was true and every context which was false under traditional usage be construed by the definition as an abbreviation of some other statement which is correspondingly true or false under the established meanings of its signs. Thus when definitions of mathematical expressions on the basis of logical ones are said to have been framed, what is meant is that definitions have been set up whereby every statement which so involves those mathematical expressions as to be recognized traditionally as true, or as false, is construed as an abbreviation of another correspondingly true or false statement which lacks those mathematical expressions and exhibits only logical expressions in their stead.[3]

An expression will be said to occur *vacuously* in a given statement if its replacement therein by any and every other grammatically admissible expression leaves the truth or falsehood of the statement unchanged. Thus for any statement containing some expressions vacuously there is a class of statements, describable as *vacuous variants* of the given statement, which are like

[3] Note that an expression is said to be defined, in terms, e.g., of logic, not only when it is a single sign whose elimination from a context in favor of logical expressions is accomplished by a single application of one definition, but also when it is a complex expression whose elimination calls for successive application of many definitions.

it in point of truth or falsehood, like it also in point of a certain skeleton of symbolic make-up, but diverse in exhibiting all grammatically possible variations upon the vacuous constituents of the given statement. An expression will be said to occur *essentially* in a statement if it occurs in all the vacuous variants of the statement, i.e., if it forms part of the aforementioned skeleton. (Note that though an expression occurs non-vacuously in a statement it may fail of essential occurrence because some of its parts occur vacuously in the statement.)

Now let S be a truth, let the expressions E_i occur vacuously in S, and let the statements S_i be the vacuous variants of S. Thus the S_i will likewise be true. On the sole basis of the expressions belonging to a certain class α, let us frame a definition for one of the expressions F occurring in S outside the E_i. S and the S_i thereby become abbreviations of certain statements S' and S_i' which exhibit only members of α instead of those occurrences of F, but which remain so related that the S_i' are all the results of replacing the E_i in S_i' by any other grammatically admissible expressions. Now since our definition of F is supposed to conform to usage, S' and the S_i' will, like S and the S_i, be uniformly true; hence the S_i' will be vacuous variants of S', and the occurrences of the E_i in S' will be vacuous. The definition thus makes S an abbreviation of a truth S' which, like S, involves the E_i vacuously, but which differs from S in exhibiting only members of α instead of the occurrences of F outside the E_i. Now it is obvious that an expression cannot occur essentially in a statement if it occurs only within expressions which occur vacuously in the statement; consequently F, occurring in S' as it does only within the E_i if at all, does not occur essentially in S'; members of α occur essentially in its stead. Thus if we take F as any non-member of α occurring essentially in S, and repeat the above reasoning for each such expression, we see that, through definitions of all such expressions in terms of members of α, S becomes an abbreviation of a truth S'' involving only members of α essentially.

Thus if in particular we take α as the class of all logical expressions, the above tells us that if logical definitions be framed for all non-logical expressions occurring essentially in the true statement S, S becomes an abbreviation of a truth S'' involving only logical expressions essentially. But if S'' involves only logical expressions essentially, and hence remains true when everything except that skeleton of logical expressions is changed in all grammatically possible ways, then S'' depends for its truth upon those logical constituents alone, and is thus a truth of logic. It is therefore established that if all non-logical expressions occurring essentially in a true statement S be given definitions on the basis solely of logic, then S becomes an abbreviation of a truth S'' of logic. In particular, then, if all mathematical expressions be defined in terms of logic, all truths involving only mathematical and logical expressions essentially become definitional abbreviations of truths of logic.

Now a mathematical truth, e.g., 'Smith's age plus Brown's equals Brown's age plus Smith's,' may contain non-logical, non-mathematical expressions. Still any such mathematical truth, or another whereof it is a definitional abbreviation, will consist of a skeleton of mathematical or logical expressions filled in with non-logical, non-mathematical expressions all of which occur vacuously. Thus every mathematical truth either is a truth in which only mathematical and logical expressions occur essentially, or is a definitional abbreviation of such a truth. Hence, granted definitions of all mathematical expressions in terms of logic, the preceding conclusion shows that all mathematical truths become definitional abbreviations of truths of logic—therefore truths of logic in turn. For the thesis that mathematics is logic it is thus sufficient that all mathematical notation be defined on the basis of logical notation.

If on the other hand some mathematical expressions resist definition on the basis of logical ones, then every mathematical truth containing such recalcitrant expressions must contain them only inessentially, or be a definitional abbreviation of a truth containing such expressions only inessentially, if all mathematics is to be logic: for though a logical truth, e.g., the above one about Africa, may involve non-logical expressions, it or some other logical truth whereof it is an abbreviation must involve only logical expressions essentially. It is of this alternative that those[4] avail themselves who regard mathematical truths, insofar as they depend upon non-logical notions, as elliptical for hypothetical statements containing as tacit hypotheses all the postulates of the branch of mathematics in question. Thus, suppose the geometrical terms 'sphere' and 'includes' to be undefined on the basis of logical expressions, and suppose all further geometrical expressions defined on the basis of logical expressions together with 'sphere' and 'includes', as with Huntington.[5] Let Huntington's postulates for (Euclidean) geometry, and all the theorems, be expanded by thoroughgoing replacement of definienda by definientia, so that they come to contain only logical expressions and 'sphere' and 'includes', and let the conjunction of the thus expanded postulates be represented as 'Hunt (sphere, includes).' Then, where 'Φ (sphere, includes)' is any of the theorems, similarly expanded into primitive terms, the point of view under consideration is that 'Φ (sphere, includes),' insofar as it is conceived as a mathematical truth, is to be construed as an ellipsis for 'If Hunt (spheres, includes) then Φ (sphere, includes).' Since 'Φ (sphere, includes)' is a logical consequence of Huntington's postulates, the above hypothetical statement is a truth of logic; it involves the expressions 'sphere' and 'includes' inessentially, in fact vacuously, since the logical deducibility of the theorems from the postulates is independent of the meanings of 'sphere' and 'includes' and survives the replacement of those expressions by any other grammatically

[4] E.g., Russell, *op. cit.*, pp. 420–30; Behmann, "Sind die mathematischen Urteile analytisch oder synthetisch?" *Erkenntnis*, 4 (1934), pp. 8–10.
[5] "A Set of Postulates for Abstract Geometry," *Mathematische Annalen*, 73 (1913), pp. 522–59.

admissible expressions whatever. Since, granted the fitness of Huntington's postulates, all and only those geometrical statements are truths of geometry which are logical consequences in this fashion of 'Hunt (sphere, includes),' all geometry becomes logic when interpreted in the above manner as a conventional ellipsis for a body of hypothetical statements.

But if, as a truth of mathematics, 'Φ (sphere, includes)' is short for 'If Hunt (sphere, includes) then Φ (sphere, includes),' still there remains, as part of this expanded statement, the original statement 'Φ (sphere, includes)'; this remains as a presumably true statement within some body of doctrine, say for the moment "non-mathematical geometry," even if the title of mathematical truth be restricted to the entire hypothetical statement in question. The body of all such hypothetical statements, describable as the "theory of deduction of non-mathematical geometry," is of course a part of logic; but the same is true of any "theory of deduction of sociology," "theory of deduction of Greek mythology," etc., which we might construct in parallel fashion with the aid of any set of postulates suited to sociology or to Greek mythology. The point of view toward geometry which is under consideration thus reduces merely to an exclusion of geometry from mathematics, a relegation of geometry to the status of sociology or Greek mythology; the labelling of the "theory of deduction of non-mathematical geometry" as "mathematical geometry" is a verbal *tour de force* which is equally applicable in the case of sociology or Greek mythology. To incorporate mathematics into logic by regarding all recalcitrant mathematical truths as elliptical hypothetical statements is thus in effect merely to restrict the term 'mathematics' to exclude those recalcitrant branches. But we are not interested in renaming. Those disciplines, geometry and the rest, which have traditionally been grouped under mathematics are the objects of the present discussion, and it is with the doctrine that mathematics in this sense is logic that we are here concerned.[6]

Discarding this alternative and returning, then, we see that if some mathematical expressions resist definition on the basis of logical ones, mathematics will reduce to logic only if, under a literal reading and without the gratuitous annexation of hypotheses, every mathematical truth contains (or is an abbreviation of one which contains) such recalcitrant expressions only inessentially if at all. But a mathematical expression sufficiently troublesome to have resisted trivial contextual definition in terms of logic can hardly be expected to occur thus idly in all its mathematical contexts. It would thus appear that for the tenability of the thesis that mathematics is logic it is not only sufficient but also necessary that all mathematical expressions be capable of definition on the basis solely of logical ones.

Though in framing logical definitions of mathematical expressions the ultimate objective be to make all mathematical truths logical truths, attention

[6] Obviously the foregoing discussion has no bearing upon postulate method as such, nor upon Huntington's work.

is not to be confined to mathematical and logical truths in testing the conformity of the definitions to usage. Mathematical expressions belong to the general language, and they are to be so defined that all statements containing them, whether mathematical truths, historical truths, or falsehoods under traditional usage, come to be construed as abbreviations of other statements which are correspondingly true or false. The definition introducing 'plus' must be such that the mathematical truth 'Smith's age plus Brown's equals Brown's age plus Smith's' becomes an abbreviation of a logical truth, as observed earlier; but it must also be such that 'Smith's age plus Brown's age equals Jones' age' becomes an abbreviation of a statement which is empirically true or false in conformity with the county records and the traditional usage of 'plus'. A definition which fails in this latter respect is no less Pickwickian than one which fails in the former; in either case nothing is achieved beyond the transient pleasure of a verbal recreation.

But for these considerations, contextual definitions of any mathematical expressions whatever could be framed immediately in purely logical terms, on the basis of any set of postulates adequate to the branch of mathematics in question. Thus, consider again Huntington's systematization of geometry. It was remarked that, granted the fitness of Huntington's postulates, a statement will be a truth of geometry if and only if it is logically deducible from 'Hunt (sphere, includes)' without regard to the meanings of 'sphere' and 'includes'. Thus 'Φ (sphere, includes)' will be a truth of geometry if and only if the following is a truth of logic: 'If α is any class and R any relation such that Hunt (α, R), then Φ (α, R).' For 'sphere' and 'includes' we might then adopt the following contextual definition: Where '$---$' is any statement containing 'α' or 'R' or both, let the statement 'If α is any class and R any relation such that Hunt (α, R), then $---$' be abbreviated as that expression which is got from '$---$' by putting 'sphere' for 'α' and 'includes' for 'R' throughout. (In the case of a compound statement involving 'sphere' and 'includes', this definition does not specify whether it is the entire statement or each of its constituent statements that is to be accounted as shorthand in the described fashion; but this ambiguity can be eliminated by stipulating that the convention apply only to whole contexts.) 'Sphere' and 'includes' thus receive contextual definition in terms exclusively of logic, for any statement containing one or both of those expressions is construed by the definition as an abbreviation of a statement containing only logical expressions (plus whatever expressions the original statement may have contained other than 'sphere' and 'includes'). The definition satisfies past usage of 'sphere' and 'includes' to the extent of verifying all truths and falsifying all falsehoods of geometry; all those statements of geometry which are true, and only those, become abbreviations of truths of logic.

The same procedure could be followed in any other branch of mathematics, with the help of a satisfactory set of postulates for the branch. Thus nothing further would appear to be wanting for the thesis that mathematics is logic. And the royal road runs beyond that thesis, for the described method of logicizing a mathematical discipline can be applied likewise to any non-mathematical theory. But the whole procedure rests on failure to conform the definitions to usage; what is logicized is not the intended subject-matter. It is readily seen, e.g., that the suggested contextual definition of 'sphere' and 'includes', though transforming purely geometrical truths and falsehoods respectively into logical truths and falsehoods, transforms certain empirical truths into falsehoods and vice versa. Consider, e.g., the true statement 'A baseball is roughly a sphere,' more rigorously 'The whole of a baseball, except for a certain very thin, irregular peripheral layer, constitutes a sphere.' According to the contextual definition, this statement is an abbreviation for the following: 'If α is any class and R any relation such that Hunt (α, R), then the whole of a baseball, except for a thin peripheral layer, constitutes an [a member of] α.' This tells us that the whole of a baseball, except for a thin peripheral layer, belongs to every class α for which a relation R can be found such that Huntington's postulates are true of α and R. Now it happens that 'Hunt (α, includes)' is true not only when α is taken as the class of all spheres, but also when α is restricted to the class of spheres a foot or more in diameter;[7] yet the whole of a baseball, except for a thin peripheral layer, can hardly be said to constitute a sphere a foot or more in diameter. The statement is therefore false, whereas the preceding statement, supposedly an abbreviation of this one, was true under ordinary usage of words. The thus logicized rendering of any other discipline can be shown in analogous fashion to yield the sort of discrepancy observed just now for geometry, provided only that the postulates of the discipline admit, like those of geometry, of alternative applications; and such multiple applicability is to be expected of any postulate set.[8]

Definition of mathematical notions on the basis of logical ones is thus a more arduous undertaking than would appear from a consideration solely of the truths and falsehoods of pure mathematics. Viewed *in vacuo*, mathematics is trivially reducible to logic through erection of postulate systems into contextual definitions; but "cette science n'a pas uniquement pour objet de contempler éternellement son propre nombril."[9] When mathematics is recognized as capable of use, and as forming an integral part of general language, the definition of mathematical notions in terms of logic becomes a task whose completion, if theoretically possible at all, calls for mathematical genius of a high order. It was primarily to this task that Whitehead and Russell addressed themselves in their *Principia Mathematica*. They adopt a meager

---

[7] Cf. Huntington, *op. cit.*, p. 540.

[8] Note that a postulate set is superfluous if it *demonstrably* admits of one and only one application: for it then embodies an adequate defining property for each of its constituent primitive terms. Cf. Tarski, "Einige methodologische Untersuchungen über die Definierbarkeit der Begriffe," *Erkenntnis*, 5 (1934), p. 85 (*Satz* 2).

[9] Poincaré, *Science et Méthode*, Paris, 1908, p. 199.

logical language as primitive, and on its basis alone they undertake to endow mathematical expressions with definitions which conform to usage in the full sense described above: definitions which not only reduce mathematical truths and falsehoods to logical ones, but reduce *all* statements, containing the mathematical expressions in question, to equivalent statements involving logical expressions instead of the mathematical ones. Within *Principia* the program has been advanced to such a point as to suggest that no fundamental difficulties stand in the way of completing the process. The foundations of arithmetic are developed in *Principia*, and therewith those branches of mathematics are accommodated which, like analysis and theory of number, spring from arithmetic. Abstract algebra proceeds readily from the relation theory of *Principia*. Only geometry remains untouched, and this field can be brought into line simply by identifying n-dimensional figures with those n-adic arithmetical relations ("equations in n variables") with which they are correlated through analytic geometry.[10] Some question Whitehead and Russell's reduction of mathematics to logic,[11] on grounds for whose exposition and criticism there is not space; the thesis that all mathematics reduces to logic is, however, substantiated by *Principia* to a degree satisfactory to most of us. There is no need here to adopt a final stand in the matter.

If for the moment we grant that all mathematics is thus definitionally constructible from logic, then mathematics becomes true by convention in a relative sense: mathematical truths become conventional transcriptions of logical truths. Perhaps this is all that many of us mean to assert when we assert that mathematics is true by convention; at least, an *analytic* statement is commonly explained merely as one which proceeds from logic and definitions, or as one which, on replacement of definienda by definientia, becomes a truth of logic.[12] But in strictness we cannot regard mathematics as true purely by convention unless all those logical principles to which mathematics is supposed to reduce are likewise true by convention. And the doctrine that mathematics is *analytic* accomplishes a less fundamental simplification for philosophy than would at first appear, if it asserts only that mathematics is a conventional transcription of logic and not that logic is convention in turn: for if in the end we are to countenance any *a priori* principles at all which are independent of convention, we should not scruple to admit a few more, nor attribute crucial importance to conventions which serve only to diminish the number of such principles by reducing some to others.

But if we are to construe logic also as true by convention, we must rest

[10] Cf. Study, *Die realistische Weltansicht und die Lehre vom Raume*, Brunswick, 1914, pp. 86–92.

[11] Cf., e.g., Dubislav, "Ueber das Verhältnis der Logik zur Mathematik," *Annalen der Philosophie*, 5 (1925), pp. 193–208; Hilbert, *Die Grundlagen der Mathematik*, Leipzig, 1928, pp. 12, 21.

[12] Cf. Frege, *Grundlagen der Arithmetik*, Breslau, 1884, p. 4; Behmann, *op. cit.*, p. 5. Carnap, *op. cit.*, uses the term in essentially the same sense but subject to more subtle and rigorous treatment.

logic ultimately upon some manner of convention other than definition: for it was noted earlier that definitions are available only for transforming truths, not for founding them. The same applies to any truths of mathematics which, contrary to the supposition of a moment ago, may resist definitional reduction to logic; if such truths are to proceed from convention, without merely being reduced to antecedent truths, they must proceed from conventions other than definitions. Such a second sort of convention, generating truths rather than merely transforming them, has long been recognized in the use of postulates.[13] Application of this method to logic will occupy the next section; customary ways of rendering postulates and rules of inference will be departed from, however, in favor of giving the whole scheme the explicit form of linguistic convention.

II

Let us suppose an approximate maximum of definition to have been accomplished for logic, so that we are left with about as meager as possible an array of primitive notational devices. There are indefinitely many ways of framing the definitions, all conforming to the same usage of the expressions in question; apart from the objective of defining much in terms of little, choice among these ways is guided by convenience or chance. Different choices involve different sets of primitives. Let us suppose our procedure to be such as to reckon among the primitive devices the *not*-idiom, the *if*-idiom ('If ... then ...'), the *every*-idiom ('No matter what x may be, ---x---'), and one or two more as required. On the basis of this much, then, all further logical notation is to be supposed defined; all statements involving any further logical notation become construed as abbreviations of statements whose logical constituents are limited to those primitives.

'Or', as a connective joining statements to form new statements, is amenable to the following contextual definition in terms of the *not*-idiom and the *if*-idiom: A pair of statements with 'or' between is an abbreviation of the statement made up successively of these ingredients: first, 'If'; second, the first statement of the pair, with 'not' inserted to govern the main verb (or, with 'it is false that' prefixed); third, 'then'; fourth, the second statement of the pair. The convention becomes clearer if we use the prefix '$\sim$' as an artificial notation for denial, thus writing '$\sim$ ice is hot' instead of 'Ice is not hot' or 'It is false that ice is hot.' Where '---' and '—' are any statements, our definition then introduces '--- or —' as an abbreviation of 'If $\sim$ --- then —.' Again 'and', as a connective joining statements, can be defined contextually by construing '--- and —' as an abbreviation for '$\sim$ if --- then

---

[13] The function of postulates as conventions seems to have been first recognized by Gergonne, "Essai sur la théorie des définitions," *Annales des mathématiques pures et appliquées* (1819). His designation of them as "implicit definitions," which has had some following in the literature, is avoided here.

$\sim$ ——.' Every such idiom is what is known as a *truth-function*, and is characterized by the fact that the truth or falsehood of the complex statement which it generates is uniquely determined by the truth or falsehood of the several statements which it combines. All truth-functions are known to be constructible in terms of the *not*- and *if*-idioms as in the above examples.[14] On the basis of the truth-functions, then, together with our further primitives—the *every*-idiom *et al.*—all further logical devices are supposed defined.

A word may, through historical or other accidents, evoke a train of ideas bearing no relevance to the truth or falsehood of its context; in point of *meaning*, however, as distinct from connotation, a word may be said to be determined to whatever extent the truth or falsehood of its contexts is determined. Such determination of truth or falsehood may be outright, and to that extent the meaning of the word is absolutely determined; or it may be relative to the truth or falsehood of statements containing other words, and to that extent the meaning of the word is determined relatively to those other words. A definition endows a word with complete determinacy of meaning relative to other words. But the alternative is open to us, on introducing a new word, of determining its meaning *absolutely* to whatever extent we like by specifying contexts which are to be true and contexts which are to be false. In fact, we need specify only the former: for falsehood may be regarded as a derivative property depending on the word '$\sim$', in such wise that falsehood of '——' means simply truth of '$\sim$——.' Since all contexts of our new word are meaningless to begin with, neither true nor false, we are free to run through the list of such contexts and pick out as true such ones as we like; those selected become true by fiat, by linguistic convention. For those who would question them we have always the same answer, 'You use the word differently.' The reader may protest that our arbitrary selection of contexts as true is subject to restrictions imposed by the requirement of *consistency*—e.g., that we must not select both '——' and '$\sim$——'; but this consideration, which will receive a clearer status a few pages hence, will be passed over for the moment.

Now suppose in particular that we abstract from existing usage of the locutions 'if-then', 'not' (or '$\sim$'), and the rest of our logical primitives, so that for the time being these become meaningless marks, and the erstwhile statements containing them lose their status as statements and become likewise meaningless, neither true nor false; and suppose we run through all those erstwhile statements, or as many of them as we like, segregating various of them arbitrarily as true. To whatever extent we carry this process, we to that extent determine meaning for the initially meaningless marks 'if',

---

[14] Sheffer, ("A Set of Five Independent Postulates for Boolean Algebras," *Trans. Amer. Math. Soc.*, 14 (1913), pp. 481–88) has shown ways of constructing these two, in turn, in terms of one; strictly, therefore, such a one should supplant the two in our ostensibly minimal set of logical primitives. Exposition will be facilitated, however, by retaining the redundancy.

'then', '$\sim$', and the rest. Such contexts as we render true are true by convention.

We saw earlier that if all expressions occurring essentially in a true statement S and not belonging to a class α are given definitions in terms solely of members of α, then S becomes a definitional abbreviation of a truth S'' involving only members of a α essentially. Now let α comprise just our logical primitives, and let S be a statement which, under ordinary usage, is true and involves only logical expressions essentially. Since all logical expressions other than the primitives are defined in terms of the primitives, it then follows that S is an abbreviation of a truth S'' involving only the primitives essentially. But if one statement S is a definitional abbreviation of another S'', the truth of S proceeds wholly from linguistic convention if the truth of S'' does so. Hence if, in the above process of arbitrarily segregating statements as true by way of endowing our logical primitives with meaning, *we assign truth to those statements which, according to ordinary usage, are true and involve only our primitives essentially*, then not only will the latter statements be true by convention, but so will all statements which are true under ordinary usage and involve only logical expressions essentially. Since, as remarked earlier, every logical truth involves (or is an abbreviation of another which involves) only logical expressions essentially, the described scheme of assigning truth makes all logic true by convention.

Not only does such assignment of truth suffice to make all those statements true by convention which are true under ordinary usage and involve only logical expressions essentially, but it serves also to make all those statements false by convention which are false under ordinary usage and involve only logical expressions essentially. This follows from our explanation of the falsehood of '---' as the truth of '$\sim$---', since '---' will be false under ordinary usage if and only if '$\sim$---' is true under ordinary usage. The described assignment of truth thus goes far towards fixing all logical expressions in point of meaning, and fixing them in conformity with usage. Still many statements containing logical expressions remain unaffected by the described assignments: all those statements which, from the standpoint of ordinary usage, involve some non-logical expressions essentially. There is hence room for supplementary conventions of one sort or another over and above the described truth-assignments, by way of completely fixing the meanings of our primitives—and fixing them, it is to be hoped, in conformity with ordinary usage. Such supplementation need not concern us now; the described truth-assignments provide partial determinations which, as far as they go, conform to usage and which go far enough to make all logic true by convention.

But we must not be deceived by schematism. It would appear that we sit down to a list of expressions and check off as arbitrarily true all those which, under ordinary usage, are true statements involving only our logical primitives essentially; but this picture wanes when we reflect that the number of such statements is infinite. If the convention whereby those statements are singled out as true is to be formulated in finite terms, we must avail ourselves of conditions finite in length which determine infinite classes of expressions.[15]

Such conditions are ready at hand. One, determining an infinite class of expressions all of which, under ordinary usage, are true statements involving only our primitive *if*-idiom essentially, is the condition of being obtainable from

(1)   'If if p then q then if if q then r then if p then r'

by putting a statement for 'p', a statement for 'q', and a statement for 'r'. In more customary language the form (1) would be expanded, for clarity, in some such fashion as this: 'If it is the case that if p then q, then, if it is the case further that if q then r, then, if p, r.' The form (1) is thus seen to be the principle of the syllogism. Obviously it is true under ordinary usage for all substitutions of statements for 'p', 'q', and 'r'; hence such results of substitution are, under ordinary usage, true statements involving only the *if*-idiom essentially. One infinite part of our program of assigning truth to all expressions which, under ordinary usage, are true statements involving only our logical primitives essentially, is thus accomplished by the following convention:

(I)   Let all results of putting a statement for 'p', a statement for 'q', and a statement for 'r' in (1) be true.

Another infinite part of the program is disposed of by adding this convention:

(II)   Let any expression be true which yields a truth when put for 'q' in the result of putting a truth for 'p' in 'If p then q.'

Given truths '---' and 'If --- then ---', (II) yields the truth of '---'. That (II) conforms to usage, i.e., that from statements which are true under ordinary usage (II) leads only to statements which are likewise true under ordinary usage, is seen from the fact that under ordinary usage a statement '---' is always true if statements '---' and 'If --- then ---' are true. Given all the truths yielded by (I), (II) yields another infinity of truths which, like the former, are under ordinary usage truths involving only the *if*-idiom essentially. How this comes about is seen roughly as follows. The truths yielded by (I), being of the form of (1), are complex statements of the form 'If --- then ---'. The statement '---' here may in particular be of the form (1) in turn, and hence likewise be true according to (I). Then, by (II), '---'

---

[15] Such a condition, if effective, constitutes a *formal system*. Usually we assign such meanings to the signs as to construe the expressions of the class as statements, specifically true statements, theorems; but this is neither intrinsic to the system nor necessary in all cases for a useful application of the system.

becomes true. In general '——' will not be of the form (1), hence would not have been obtainable by (I) alone. Still '——' will in every such case be a statement which, under ordinary usage, is true and involves only the *if*-idiom essentially; this follows from the observed conformity of (I) and (II) to usage, together with the fact that the above derivation of '——' demands nothing of '——' beyond proper structure in terms of 'if-then'. Now our stock of truths embraces not only those yielded by (I) alone, i.e., those having the form (1), but also all those thence derivable by (II) in the manner in which '——' has just now been supposed derived.[16] From this increased stock we can derive yet further ones by (II), and these likewise will, under ordinary usage, be true and involve only the *if*-idiom essentially. The generation proceeds in this fashion *ad infinitum*.

When provided only with (I) as an auxiliary source of truth, (II) thus yields only truths which under ordinary usage are truths involving only the *if*-idiom essentially. When provided with further auxiliary sources of truths, however, e.g., the convention (III) which is to follow, (II) yields truths involving further locutions essentially. Indeed, the effect of (II) is not even confined to statements which, under ordinary usage, involve only logical locutions essentially; (II) also legislates regarding other statements, to the extent of specifying that no two statements '———' and 'If ——— then ——' can both be true unless '——' is true. But this overflow need not disturb us, since it also conforms to ordinary usage. In fact, it was remarked earlier that room remained for supplementary conventions, over and above the described truth-assignments, by way of further determining the meanings of our primitives. This overflow accomplishes just that for the *if*-idiom; it provides, with regard even to a statement 'If ——— then ——' which from the standpoint of ordinary usage involves non-logical expressions essentially, that the statement is not to be true if '———' is true and '——' not.

But present concern is with statements which, under ordinary usage, involve only our logical primitives essentially; by (I) and (II) we have provided for the truth of an infinite number of such statements, but by no means all. The following convention provides for the truth of another infinite set of such statements; these, in contrast to the preceding, involve not only the *if*-idiom but also the *not*-idiom essentially (under ordinary usage).

(III) Let all results of putting a statement for 'p' and a statement for 'q', in 'If p then if $\sim p$ then q' or 'If if $\sim p$ then p then p,' be true.[17]

Statements generated thus by substitution in 'If p then if $\sim p$ then q' are statements of hypothetical form in which two mutually contradictory statements occur as premises; obviously such statements are trivially true, under

---

[16] The latter in fact comprise all and only those statements which have the form 'If if if if q then r then if p then r then s then if if p then q then s'.

[17] (1) and the two formulae in (III) are Łukasiewicz's three postulates for the propositional calculus.

ordinary usage, not matter what may figure as conclusion. Statements generated by substitution in 'If [it is the case that] if $\sim p$ then p, then p' are likewise true under ordinary usage, for one reasons as follows: Grant the hypothesis, viz., that if $\sim p$ then p; then we must admit the conclusion, viz., that p, since even denying it we admit it. Thus all the results of substitution referred to in (III) are true under ordinary usage no matter what the substituted statements may be; hence such results of substitution are, under ordinary usage, true statements, involving nothing essentially beyond the *if*-idiom and the *not*-idiom ('$\sim$').

From the infinity of truths adopted in (III), together with those already at hand from (I) and (II), infinitely more truths are generated by (II). It happens, curiously enough, that (III) adds even to our stock of statements which involve only the *if*-idiom essentially (under ordinary usage); there are truths of that description which, though lacking the *not*-idiom, are reached by (I)–(III) and not by (I) and (II). This is true, e.g., of any instance of the principle of identity, say

(2)   'If time is money then time is money'.

It will be instructive to derive (2) from (I)–(III), as an illustration of the general manner in which truths are generated by those conventions. (III), to begin with, directs that we adopt these statements as true:

(3)   'If time is money then if time is not money then time is money'.

(4)   'If if time is not money then time is money then time is money'.

(I) directs that we adopt this as true:

(5)   'If if time is money then if time is not money then time is money then if if if time is not money then time is money then time is money then if time is money then time is money'.

(II) tells us that, in view of the truth of (5) and (3), this is true:

(6)   'If if if time is not money then time is money then time is money then if time is money then time is money'.

Finally (II) tells us that, in view of the truth of (6) and (4), (2) is true.

If a statement S is generated by (I)–(III), obviously only the structure of S in terms of 'if-then' and '$\sim$' was relevant to the generation; hence all those variants S_i of S which are obtainable by any grammatically admissible substitutions upon constituents of S not containing 'if', 'then', or '$\sim$', are likewise generated by (I)–(III). Now it has been observed that (I)–(III) conform to usage, i.e., generate only statements which are true under ordinary usage; hence S and all the S_i are uniformly true under ordinary usage, the S_i are therefore vacuous variants of S, and hence only 'if', 'then', and '$\sim$' occur essentially in S. Thus (I)–(III) generate only statements which under ordinary usage are truths involving only the *if*-diom and the *not*-idiom essentially.

It can be shown also that (I)–(III) generate *all* such statements.[18] Consequently (I)–(III), aided by our definitions of logical locutions in terms of our primitives, are adequate to the generation of all statements which under ordinary usage are truths which involve any of the so-called truth-functions but nothing else essentially: for it has been remarked that all the truth-functions are definable on the basis of the *if*-idiom and the *not*-idiom. All such truths thus become true by convention. They comprise all those statements which are instances of any of the principles of the so-called propositional calculus.

To (I)–(III) we may now add a further convention or two to cover another of our logical primitives—say the *every*-idiom. A little more in this direction, by way of providing for our remaining primitives, and the program is completed; all logic, in some sense, becomes true by convention. The conventions with which I–III would thus be supplemented would be more complex than I–III. The set of conventions would be an adaptation of one of the various existing systematizations of general logistic, in the same way in which I–III are an adaptation of a systematization of the propositional calculus.

The systematization chosen must indeed leave some logical statements undecided, by Gödel's theorem, if we set generous bounds to the logical vocabulary. But no matter; logic still becomes true by convention insofar as it gets reckoned as true on any account.

Let us now consider the protest which the reader raised earlier, viz., that our freedom in assigning truth by convention is subject to restrictions imposed by the requirement of consistency.[19] Under the fiction, implicit in an earlier stage of our discussion, that we check off our truths one by one in an exhaustive list of expressions, consistency in the assignment of truth is nothing more than a special case of conformity to usage. If we make a mark in the margin opposite an expression '−−−', and another opposite '∼−−−', we sin only against the established usage of '∼' as a denial sign. Under the latter usage

---

[18] The proof rests essentially upon Łukasiewicz's proof (in his *Elementy logiki matematycznej*, Warsaw, 1929) that his three postulates for the propositional calculus, viz., (1) and the formulae in (III), are *complete*. Adaptation of his result to present purposes depends upon the fact, readily established, that any formula generable by his two rules of inference (the so-called rule of substitution and a rule answering to (II)) can be generated by applying the rules in such order that all applications of the rule of substitution precede all applications of the other rule. This fact is relevant because of the manner in which the rule of substitution has been absorbed, here, into (I) and (III). The adaptation involves also two further steps, which however present no difficulty: we must make connection between Łukasiewicz's *formulae*, containing variables 'p', 'q', etc., and the concrete *statements* which constitute the present subject-matter; also between *completeness*, in the sense (Post's) in which Łukasiewicz uses the term, and the generability of all statements which under ordinary usage are truths involving only the *if*-idiom or the *not*-idiom essentially.

[19] So, e.g., Poincaré, *op. cit.*, pp. 162–63, 195–98; Schlick, *Allgemeine Erkenntnislehre*, Berlin, 1925, pp. 36, 327.

'---' and '∼---' are not both true; in taking them both by convention as true we merely endow the sign '∼', roughly speaking, with a meaning other than denial. Indeed, we might so conduct our assignments of truth as to allow no sign of our language to behave analogously to the denial locution of ordinary usage; perhaps the resulting language would be inconvenient, but conventions are often inconvenient. It is only the objective of ending up with our mother tongue that dissuades us from marking both '---' and '∼---', and this objective would dissuade us also from marking 'It is always cold on Thursday.'

The requirement of consistency still retains the above status when we assign truth wholesale through general conventions such as (I)–(III). Each such convention assigns truth to an infinite sheaf of the entries in our fictive list, and in this function the conventions cannot conflict; by overlapping in their effects they reinforce one another, by not overlapping they remain indifferent to one another. If some of the conventions specified entries to which truth was *not* to be assigned, genuine conflict might be apprehended; such negative conventions, however, have not been suggested. (II) was, indeed, described earlier as specifying that 'If ---then ---' is not to be true if '---' is true and '---' not; but within the framework of the conventions of truth-assignment this apparent proscription is ineffectual without antecedent proscription of '---'. Thus any inconsistency among the general conventions will be of the sort previously considered, viz., the arbitrary adoption of both '---' and '∼---' as true; and the adoption of these was seen merely to impose some meaning other than denial upon the sign '∼'. As theoretical restrictions upon our freedom in the conventional assignment of truth, requirements of consistency thus disappear. Preconceived usage may lead us to stack the cards, but does not enter the rules of the game.

III

Circumscription of our logical primitives in point of meaning, through conventional assignment of truth to various of their contexts, has been seen to render all logic true by convention. Then if we grant the thesis that mathematics is logic, i.e., that all mathematical truths are definitional abbreviations of logical truths, it follows that mathematics is true by convention.

If on the other hand, contrary to the thesis that mathematics is logic, some mathematical expressions resist definition in terms of logical ones, we can extend the foregoing method into the domain of these recalcitrant expressions: we can circumscribe the latter through conventional assignment of truth to various of their contexts, and thus render mathematics conventionally true in the same fashion in which logic has been rendered so. Thus, suppose some mathematical expressions to resist logical definition, and suppose them to be reduced to as meager as possible a set of mathematical primitives. In terms of these and our logical primitives, then, all further mathematical devices are supposed defined; all statements containing the latter become abbreviations of statements containing by way of mathematical notation only the primitives. Here, as remarked earlier in the case of logic, there are alternative courses of definition and therewith alternative sets of primitives; but suppose our procedure to be such as to count 'sphere' and 'includes' among the mathematical primitives. So far we have a set of conventions, (I)–(III) and a few more, let us call them (IV)–(VII), which together circumscribe our logical primitives and yield all logic. By way of circumscribing the further primitives 'sphere' and 'includes', let us now add this convention to the set:

(VIII)   Let 'Hunt (sphere, includes)' be true.

Now we saw earlier that where 'Φ (sphere, includes)' is any truth of geometry, supposed expanded into primitive terms, the statement

(7)   'If Hunt (sphere, includes) then Φ (sphere, includes)'

is a truth of logic. Hence (7) is one of the expressions to which truth is assigned by the conventions (I)–(VII). Now (II) instructs us, in view of convention (VIII) and the truth of (7), to adopt 'Φ (sphere, includes)' as true. In this way each truth of geometry is seen to be present among the statements to which truth is assigned by the conventions (I)–(VII).

We have considered four ways of construing geometry. One way consisted of straightforward definition of geometrical expressions in terms of logical ones, within the direction of development represented by *Principia Mathematica*; this way, presumably, would depend upon identification of geometry with algebra through the correlations of analytic geometry, and definition of algebraic expressions on the basis of logical ones as in *Principia Mathematica*. By way of concession to those who have fault to find with certain technical points in *Principia*, this possibility was allowed to retain a tentative status. The other three ways all made use of Huntington's postulates, but are sharply to be distinguished from one another. The first was to include geometry in logic by construing geometrical truths as elliptical for hypothetical statements bearing 'Hunt (sphere, includes)' as hypothesis; this was seen to be a mere evasion, tantamount, under its verbal disguise, to the concession that geometry is not logic after all. The next procedure was to define 'sphere' and 'includes' contextually in terms of logical expressions by construing 'Φ (sphere, includes)' in every case as an abbreviation of 'If α is any class and R any relation such that Hunt (α, R), then Φ (α, R)'. This definition was condemned on the grounds that it fails to yield the intended usage of the defined terms. The last procedure finally, just now presented, renders geometry true by convention without making it part of logic. Here 'Hunt (sphere, includes)' is made true by fiat, by way of conventionally delimiting the meanings of "sphere" and "includes." The truths of geometry then emerge not as truths of logic, but in parallel fashion to the truths of logic.

This last method of accommodating geometry is available also for any other branch of mathematics which may resist definitional reduction to logic. In each case we merely set up a conjunction of postulates for that branch as true by fiat, as a conventional circumscription of the meanings of the constituent primitives, and all the theorems of the branch thereby become true by convention: the convention thus newly adopted together with the conventions (I)–(VII). In this way all mathematics becomes conventionally true, not by becoming a definitional transcription of logic, but by proceeding from linguistic convention in the same way as does logic.

But the method can even be carried beyond mathematics, into the so-called empirical sciences. Having framed a maximum of definitions in the latter realm, we can circumscribe as many of our "empirical" primitives as we like by adding further conventions to the set adopted for logic and mathematics; a corresponding portion of "empirical" science then becomes conventionally true in precisely the manner observed above for geometry.

The impossibility of defining any of the "empirical" expressions in terms exclusively of logical and mathematical ones may be recognized at the outset: for if any proved to be so definable, there can be no question but that it would thenceforward be recognized as belonging to pure mathematics. On the other hand vast numbers of "empirical" expressions are of course definable on the basis of logical and mathematical ones together with other "empirical" ones. Thus 'momentum' is defined as 'mass times velocity'; 'event' may be defined as 'referent of the *later*-relation', i.e., 'whatever is later than something'; 'instant' may be defined as 'maximal class of events no one of which is later than any other event of the class';[20] 'time' as 'the class of all instants'; and so on. In these examples 'momentum' is defined on the basis of mathematical expressions together with the further expressions 'mass' and 'velocity'; 'event', 'instant', and 'time' are all defined on the basis ultimately of logical expressions together with the one further expression 'later than'.

Now suppose definition to have been performed to the utmost among such non-logical, non-mathematical expressions, so that the latter are reduced to as few "empirical" primitives as possible.[21] *All* statements then become abbreviations of statements containing nothing beyond the logical and mathematical primitives and these "empirical" ones. Here, as before, there are alternatives of definition and therewith alternative sets of primitives; but suppose our primitives to be such as to include 'later than', and consider the totality of those statements which under ordinary usage are truths

---

[20] Russell, *Our Knowledge of the External World*, p. 126.

[21] In *Der logische Aufbau der Welt*, Berlin, 1928, Carnap has pursued his program with such amazing success as to provide grounds for expecting all the expressions to be definable ultimately in terms of logic and mathematics plus just one "empirical" primitive, representing a certain dyadic relation described as *recollection of resemblance*. But for the present cursory considerations no such spectacular reducibility need be presupposed.

involving only 'later than' and mathematical or logical expressions essentially. Examples of such statements are 'Nothing is later than itself'; 'If Pompey died later than Brutus and Brutus died later than Caesar then Pompey died later than Caesar.' All such statements will be either very general principles, like the first example, or else instances of such principles, like the second example. Now it is a simple matter to frame a small set of general statements from which all and only the statements under consideration can be derived by means of logic and mathematics. The conjunction of these few general statements can then be adopted as true by fiat, as 'Hunt (sphere, includes)' was adopted in (VIII); their adoption is a conventional circumscription of the meaning of the primitive 'later than'. Adoption of this convention renders all those statements conventionally true which under ordinary usage are truths essentially involving any logical or mathematical expressions, or 'later than', or any of the expressions which, like 'event', 'instant', and 'time', are defined on the basis of the foregoing, and inessentially involving anything else.

Now we can pick another of our "empirical" primitives, perhaps 'body' or 'mass' or 'energy', and repeat the process. We can continue in this fashion to any desired point, circumscribing one primitive after another by convention, and rendering conventionally true all statements which under ordinary usage are truths essentially involving only the locutions treated up to that point. If in disposing successively of our "empirical" primitives in the above fashion we take them up in an order roughly describable as leading from the general to the special, then as we progress we may expect to have to deal more and more with statements which are true under ordinary usage only with reservations, only with a probability recognized as short of certainty. But such reservations need not deter us from rendering a statement true by convention; so long as under ordinary usage the presumption is rather for than against the statement, our convention conforms to usage in verifying it. In thus elevating the statement from putative to conventional truth, we still retain the right to falsify the statement tomorrow if those events should be observed which would have occasioned its repudiation while it was still putative: for conventions are commonly revised when new observations show the revision to be convenient.

If in describing logic and mathematics as true by convention what is meant is that the primitives *can* be conventionally circumscribed in such fashion as to generate all and only the so-called truths of logic and mathematics, the characterization is empty; our last considerations show that the same might be said of any other body of doctrine as well. If on the other hand it is meant merely that the speaker adopts such conventions for those fields but not for others, the characterization is uninteresting; while if it is meant that it is a general practice to adopt such conventions explicitly for those fields but not for others, the first part of the characterization is false.

Still, there is the apparent contrast between logico-mathematical truths and others that the former are *a priori*, the latter *a posteriori*; the former

have "the character of an inward necessity," in Kant's phrase, the latter
do not. Viewed behavioristically and without reference to a metaphysical
system, this contrast retains reality as a contrast between more and less
firmly accepted statements; and it obtains antecedently to any *post facto*
fashioning of conventions. There are statements which we choose to surrender
last, if at all, in the course of revamping our sciences in the face of new discoveries; and among these there are some which we will not surrender at
all, so basic are they to our whole conceptual scheme. Among the latter are
to be counted the so-called truths of logic and mathematics, regardless of
what further we may have to say of their status in the course of a subsequent
sophicated philosophy. Now since these statements are destined to be
maintained independently of our observations of the world, we may as well
make use here of our technique of conventional truth-assignment and thereby
forestall awkward metaphysical questions as to our *a priori* insight into
necessary truths. On the other hand this purpose would not motivate extension of the truth-assignment process into the realm of erstwhile contingent
statements. On such grounds, then, logic and mathematics may be held to be
conventional while other fields are not; it may be held that it is philosophically
important to circumscribe the logical and mathematical primitives by conventions of truth-assignment which yield logical and mathematical truths, but
that it is idle elaboration to carry the process further. Such a characterization
of logic and mathematics is perhaps neither empty nor uninteresting nor false.

In the adoption of the very conventions (I)–(III) etc. whereby logic itself
is set up, however, a difficulty remains to be faced. Each of these conventions
is general, announcing the truth of every one of an infinity of statements
conforming to a certain description; derivation of the truth of any specific
statement from the general convention thus requires a logical inference,
and this involves us in an infinite regress. E.g., in deriving (6) from (3) and
(5) on the authority of (II) we *infer*, from the general announcement (II) and
the specific premiss that (3) and (5) are true statements, the conclusion that

(7)   (6) is to be true.

An examination of this inference will reveal the regress. For present purposes
it will be simpler to rewrite (II) thus:

(II′)   No matter what x may be, no matter what y may be, no matter what
z may be, if x and z are true [statements] and z is the result of putting
x for 'p' and y for 'q' in 'If p then q' then y is to be true.

We are to take (II′) as a premiss, then, and in addition the premiss that
(3) and (5) are true. We may also grant it as known that (5) is the result of
putting (3) for 'p' and (6) for 'q' in 'If p then q.' Our second premiss may thus
be rendered compositely as follows:

(8)   (3) and (5) are true and (5) is the result of putting (3) for 'p' and (6) for
'q' in 'If p then q.'

From these two premises we propose to infer (7). This inference is obviously sound logic; as logic, however, it involves use of (II′) and others of the conventions from which logic is supposed to spring. Let us try to perform the inference on the basis of those conventions. Suppose that our convention (IV), passed over earlier, is such as to enable us to infer specific instances from statements which, like (II′), involve the *every*-idiom; i.e., suppose that (IV) entitles us in general to drop the prefix 'No matter what x [or y, etc.] may be' and simultaneously to introduce a concrete designation instead of 'x' [or 'y', etc.] in the sequel. By invoking (IV) three times, then, we can infer the following from (II′):

(9) If (3) and (5) are true and (5) is the result of putting (3) for 'p' and (6) for 'q' in 'If p then q' then (6) is to be true.

It remains to infer (7) from (8) and (9). But this is an inference of the kind for which (II′) is needed; from the fact that

(10) (8) and (9) are true and (9) is the result of putting (8) for 'p' and (7) for 'q' in 'If p then q'

we are to infer (7) with help of (II′). But the task of getting (7) from (10) and (II′) is exactly analogous to our original task of getting (6) from (8) and (II′); the regress is thus under way.[22] (Incidentally the derivation of (9) from (II′) by (IV), granted just now for the sake of argument, would encounter a similar obstacle; so also the various unanalyzed steps in the derivation of (8).)

In a word, the difficulty is that if logic is to proceed *mediately* from conventions, logic is needed for inferring logic from the conventions. Alternatively, the difficulty which appears thus as a self-presupposition of doctrine can be framed as turning upon a self-presupposition of primitives. It is supposed that the *if*-idiom, the *not*-idiom, the *every*-idiom, and so on, mean nothing to us initially, and that we adopt the conventions (I)–(VII) by way of circumscribing their meaning; and the difficulty is that communication of (I)–(VII) themselves depends upon free use of those very idioms which we are attempting to circumscribe, and can succeed only if we are already conversant with the idioms. This becomes clear as soon as (I)–(VII) are rephrased in rudimentary language, after the manner of (II′).[23] It is important to note that

---

[22] Cf. Lewis Carroll, "What the Tortoise Said to Achilles," *Mind*, 4, N. S. (1895), pp. 278–80.

[23] Incidentally the conventions presuppose also some further locutions, e.g., 'true' ('a true statement'), 'the result of putting ... for ... in ...', and various nouns formed by displaying expressions in quotation marks. The linguistic presuppositions can of course be reduced to a minimum by careful rephrasing; (II′), e.g., can be improved to the following extent:

(II″) No matter what x may be, no matter what y may be, no matter what z may be, if x is true then if z is true then if z is the result of putting x for 'p' in the result of putting y for 'q' in 'If p then q' then y is true.

This involves just the *every*-idiom, the *if*-idiom, 'is', and the further locutions mentioned above.

this difficulty besets only the method of wholesale truth-assignment, not that of definition. It is true, e.g., that the contextual definition of 'or' presented at the beginning of the second section was communicated with the help of logical and other expressions which cannot be expected to have been endowed with meaning at the stage where logical expressions are first being introduced. But a definition has the peculiarity of being theoretically dispensable; it introduces a scheme of abbreviation, and we are free, if we like, to forego the brevity which it affords until enough primitives have been endowed with meaning, through the method of truth-assignment or otherwise, to accommodate full exposition of the definition. On the other hand the conventions of truth-assignment cannot be thus withheld until preparations are complete, because they are needed in the preparations.

If the truth-assignments were made one by one, rather than an infinite number at a time, the above difficulty would disappear; truths of logic such as (2) would simply be asserted severally by fiat, and the problem of inferring them from more general conventions would not arise. This course was seen to be closed to us, however, by the infinitude of the truths of logic.

It may still be held that the conventions (I)–(VIII), etc., are *observed* from the start, and that logic and mathematics thereby become conventional. It may be held that we can adopt conventions through behavior, without first announcing them in words; and that we can return and formulate our conventions verbally afterward, if we choose, when a full language is at our disposal. It may be held that the verbal formulation of conventions is no more a prerequisite of the adoption of the conventions than the writing of a grammar is a prerequisite of speech; that explicit exposition of conventions is merely one of many important uses of a completed language. So conceived, the conventions no longer involve us in vicious regress. Inference from general conventions is no longer demanded initially, but remains to the subsequent sophisticated stage where we frame general statements of the conventions and show how various specific conventional truths, used all along, fit into the general conventions as thus formulated.

It must be conceded that this account accords well with what we actually do. We discourse without first phrasing the conventions; afterwards, in writings such as this, we formulate them to fit our behavior. On the other hand it is not clear wherein an adoption of the conventions, antecedently to their formulation, consists; such behavior is difficult to distinguish from that in which conventions are disregarded. When we first agree to understand 'Cambridge' as referring to Cambridge in England failing a suffix to the contrary, and then discourse accordingly, the rôle of linguistic convention is intelligible; but when a convention is incapable of being communicated until after its adoption, its rôle is not so clear. In dropping the attributes of deliberateness and explicitness from the notion of linguistic convention we risk depriving the latter of any explanatory force and reducing it to an idle label. We may wonder what one adds to the bare statement that the truths of logic and mathematics are *a priori*, or to the still barer behavioristic statement that they are firmly accepted, when he characterizes them as true by convention in such a sense.

The more restricted thesis discussed in the first section, viz., that mathematics is a conventional transcription of logic, is far from trivial; its demonstration is a highly technical undertaking and an important one, irrespectively of what its relevance may be to fundamental principles of philosophy. It is valuable to show the reducibility of any principle to another through definition of erstwhile primitives, for every such achievement reduces the number of our presuppositions and simplifies and integrates the structure of our theories. But as to the larger thesis that mathematics and logic proceed wholly from linguistic conventions, only further clarification can assure us that this asserts anything at all.

TWO DOGMAS OF EMPIRICISM

W. V. Quine

Modern empiricism has been conditioned in large part by two dogmas. One is a belief in some fundamental cleavage between truths which are *analytic*, or grounded in meanings independently of matters of fact, and truths which are *synthetic*, or grounded in fact. The other dogma is *reductionism*: the belief that each meaningful statement is equivalent to some logical construct upon terms which refer to immediate experience. Both dogmas, I shall argue, are ill-founded. One effect of abandoning them is, as we shall see, a blurring of the supposed boundary between speculative metaphysics and natural science. Another effect is a shift toward pragmatism.

1. BACKGROUND FOR ANALYTICITY

Kant's cleavage between analytic and synthetic truths was foreshadowed in Hume's distinction between relations of ideas and matters of fact, and in Leibniz's distinction between truths of reason and truths of fact. Leibniz spoke of the truths of reason as true in all possible worlds. Picturesqueness aside, this is to say that the truths of reason are those which could not possibly be false. In the same vein we hear analytic statements defined as statements whose denials are self-contradictory. But this definition has small explanatory value; for the notion of self-contradictoriness, in the quite broad sense needed for this definition of analyticity, stands in exactly the same need of clarification as does the notion of analyticity itself. The two notions are the two sides of a single dubious coin.

Kant conceived of an analytic statement as one that attributes to its subject no more than is already conceptually contained in the subject. This formulation has two shortcomings: it limits itself to statements of subject-predicate form, and it appeals to a notion of containment which is left at a metaphorical level. But Kant's intent, evident more from the use he makes of the notion of analyticity than from his definition of it, can be restated thus: a statement is analytic when it is true by virtue of meanings and independently of fact. Pursuing this line, let us examine the concept of *meaning* which is presupposed.

Meaning, let us remember, is not to be identified with naming.[1] Frege's example of 'Evening Star' and 'Morning Star', and Russell's of 'Scott' and 'the author of *Waverley*', illustrate that terms can name the same thing but differ in meaning. The distinction between meaning and naming is no less important at the level of abstract terms. The terms '9' and 'the number of the planets' name one and the same abstract entity but presumably must be regarded as unlike in meaning; for astronomical observation was needed, and not mere reflection on meanings, to determine the sameness of the entity in question.

The above examples consist of singular terms, concrete and abstract. With general terms, or predicates, the situation is somewhat different but parallel. Whereas a singular term purports to name an entity, abstract or concrete, a general term does not; but a general term is *true of* an entity, or of each of many, or of none.[2] The class of all entities of which a general term is true is called the *extension* of the term. Now paralleling the contrast between the meaning of a singular term and the entity named, we must distinguish equally between the meaning of a general term and its extension. The general terms 'creature with a heart' and 'creature with kidneys', for example, are perhaps alike in extension but unlike in meaning.

Confusion of meaning with extension, in the case of general terms, is less common than confusion of meaning with naming in the case of singular terms. It is indeed a commonplace in philosophy to oppose intension (or meaning) to extension, or, in a variant vocabulary, connotation to denotation.

The Aristotelian notion of essence was the forerunner, no doubt, of the modern notion of intension or meaning. For Aristotle it was essential in men to be rational, accidental to be two-legged. But there is an important difference between this attitude and the doctrine of meaning. From the latter point of view it may indeed be conceded (if only for the sake of argument) that rationality is involved in the meaning of the word 'man' while two-leggedness is not; but two-leggedness may at the same time be viewed as involved in the meaning of 'biped' while rationality is not. Thus from the point of view of the doctrine of meaning it makes no sense to say of the actual individual, who is at once a man and a biped, that his rationality is essential and his two-leggedness accidental or vice versa. Things had essences,

[1] See above, pp. 188–9 [This volume].
[2] See above, pp. 189–90.

for Aristotle, but only linguistic forms have meanings. Meaning is what essence becomes when it is divorced from the object of reference and wedded to the word.

For the theory of meaning a conspicuous question is the nature of its objects: what sort of things are meanings? A felt need for meant entities may derive from an earlier failure to appreciate that meaning and reference are distinct. Once the theory of meaning is sharply separated from the theory of reference, it is a short step to recognizing as the primary business of the theory of meaning simply the synonymy of linguistic forms and the analyticity of statements; meanings themselves, as obscure intermediary entities, may well be abandoned.[3]

The problem of analyticity then confronts us anew. Statements which are analytic by general philosophical acclaim are not, indeed, far to seek. They fall into two classes. Those of the first class, which may be called *logically true*, are typified by:

(1)   No unmarried man is married.

The relevant feature of this example is that it not merely is true as it stands, but remains true under any and all reinterpretations of 'man' and 'married'. If we suppose a prior inventory of *logical* particles, comprising 'no', 'un-', 'not', 'if', 'then', 'and', etc., then in general a logical truth is a statement which is true and remains true under all reinterpretations of its components other than the logical particles.

But there is also a second class of analytic statements, typified by:

(2)   No bachelor is married.

The characteristic of such a statement is that it can be turned into a logical truth by putting synonyms for synonyms; thus (2) can be turned into (1) by putting 'unmarried man' for its synonym 'bachelor'. We still lack a proper characterization of this second class of analytic statements, and therewith of analyticity generally, inasmuch as we have had in the above description to lean on a notion of "synonymy" which is no less in need of clarification than analyticity itself.

In recent years Carnap has tended to explain analyticity by appeal to what he calls state-descriptions.[4] A state-description is any exhaustive assignment of truth values to the atomic, or noncompound, statements of the language. All other statements of the language are, Carnap assumes, built up of their component clauses by means of the familiar logical devices, in such a way that the truth-value of any complex statement is fixed for each state-description by specifiable logical laws. A statement is then explained as analytic when it comes out true under every state-description. This account is an adaptation of Leibniz's "true in all possible worlds." But note that this

    [3] See above, p. 190ff.
    [4] Carnap [2], pp. 9ff; [3], pp. 70ff.

version of analyticity serves its purpose only if the atomic statements of the language are, unlike 'John is a bachelor' and 'John is married', mutually independent. Otherwise there would be a state-description which assigned truth to 'John is a bachelor' and to 'John is married', and consequently 'No bachelors are married' would turn out synthetic rather than analytic under the proposed criterion. Thus the criterion of analyticity in terms of state-descriptions serves only for languages devoid of extralogical synonym-pairs, such as 'bachelor' and 'unmarried man'—synonym-pairs of the type which give rise to the "second class" of analytic statements. The criterion in terms of state-descriptions is a reconstruction at best of logical truth, not of analyticity.

I do not mean to suggest that Carnap is under any illusions on this point. His simplified model language with its state-descriptions is aimed primarily not at the general problem of analyticity but at another purpose, the clarification of probability and induction. Our problem, however, is analyticity; and here the major difficulty lies not in the first class of analytic statements, the logical truths, but rather in the second class, which depends on the notion of synonymy.

2. DEFINITION

There are those who find it soothing to say that the analytic statements of the second class reduce to those of the first class, the logical truths, by *definition*; 'bachelor', for example, is *defined* as 'unmarried man'. But how do we find that 'bachelor' is defined as 'unmarried man'? Who defined it thus and when? Are we to appeal to the nearest dictionary, and accept the lexicographer's formulation as law? Clearly this would be to put the cart before the horse. The lexicographer is an empirical scientist, whose business is the recording of antecedent facts; and if he glosses 'bachelor' as 'unmarried man' it is because of his belief that there is a relation of synonymy between those forms, implicit in general or preferred usage prior to his own work. The notion of synonymy presupposed here has still to be clarified, presumably in terms relating to linguistic behavior. Certainly the "definition" which is the lexicographer's report of an observed synonymy cannot be taken as the ground of the synonymy.

Definition is not, indeed, an activity exclusively of philologists. Philosophers and scientists frequently have occasion to "define" a recondite term by paraphrasing it into terms of a more familiar vocabulary. But ordinarily such a definition, like the philologist's, is pure lexicography, affirming a relation of synonymy antecedent to the exposition in hand.

Just what it means to affirm synonymy, just what the interconnections may be which are necessary and sufficient in order that two linguistic forms be properly describable as synonymous, is far from clear; but, whatever these interconnections may be, ordinarily they are grounded in usage. Definitions reporting selected instances of synonymy come then as reports upon usage.

There is also, however, a variant type of definitional activity which does not limit itself to the reporting of preëxisting synonymies. I have in mind what Carnap calls *explication*—an activity to which philosophers are given, and scientists also in their more philosophical moments. In explication the purpose is not merely to paraphrase the definiendum into an outright synonym, but actually to improve upon the definiendum by refining or supplementing its meaning. But even explication, though not merely reporting a preëxisting synonymy between definiendum and definiens, does rest nevertheless on *other* preëxisting synonymies. The matter may be viewed as follows. Any word worth explicating has some contexts which, as wholes, are clear and precise enough to be useful; and the purpose of explication is to preserve the usage of these favored contexts while sharpening the usage of other contexts. In order that a given definition be suitable for purposes of explication, therefore, what is required is not that the definiendum in its antecedent usage be synonymous with the definiens, but just that each of these favored contexts of the definiendum, taken as a whole in its antecedent usage, be synonymous with the corresponding context of the definiens.

Two alternative definientia may be equally appropriate for the purposes of a given task of explication and yet not be synonymous with each other; for they may serve interchangeably within the favored contexts but diverge elsewhere. By cleaving to one of these definientia rather than the other, a definition of explicative kind generates, by fiat, a relation of synonymy between definiendum and definiens which did not hold before. But such a definition still owes its explicative function, as seen, to preëxisting synonymies.

There does, however, remain still an extreme sort of definition which does not hark back to prior synonymies at all: namely, the explicitly conventional introduction of novel notations for purposes of sheer abbreviation. Here the definiendum becomes synonymous with the definiens simply because it has been created expressly for the purpose of being synonymous with the definiens. Here we have a really transparent case of synonymy created by definition; would that all species of synonymy were as intelligible. For the rest, definition rests on synonymy rather than explaining it.

The word 'definition' has come to have a dangerously reassuring sound, owing no doubt to its frequent occurrence in logical and mathematical writings. We shall do well to digress now into a brief appraisal of the role of definition in formal work.

In logical and mathematical systems either of two mutually antagonistic types of economy may be striven for, and each has its peculiar practical utility. On the one hand we may seek economy of practical expression—ease and brevity in the statement of multifarious relations. This sort of economy calls usually for distinctive concise notations for a wealth of concepts. Second, however, and oppositely, we may seek economy in grammar and vocabulary; we may try to find a minimum of basic concepts such that, once a distinctive notation has been appropriated to each of them, it becomes possible to express any desired further concept by mere combination and iteration of our basic notations. This second sort of economy is impractical in one way, since a poverty in basic idioms tends to a necessary lengthening of discourse. But it is practical in another way: it greatly simplifies theoretical discourse *about* the language, through minimizing the terms and the forms of construction wherein the language consists.

Both sorts of economy, though *prima facie* incompatible, are valuable in their separate ways. The custom has consequently arisen of combining both sorts of economy by forging in effect two languages, the one a part of the other. The inclusive language, though redundant in grammar and vocabulary, is economical in message lengths, while the part, called primitive notation, is economical in grammar and vocabulary. Whole and part are correlated by rules of translation whereby each idiom not in primitive notation is equated to some complex built up of primitive notation. These rules of translation are the so-called *definitions* which appear in formalized systems. They are best viewed not as adjuncts to one language but as correlations between two languages, the one a part of the other.

But these correlations are not arbitrary. They are supposed to show how the primitive notations can accomplish all purposes, save brevity and convenience, of the redundant language. Hence the definiendum and its definiens may be expected, in each case, to be related in one or another of the three ways lately noted. The definiens may be a faithful paraphrase of the definiendum into the narrower notation, preserving a direct synonymy[5] as of antecedent usage; or the definiens may, in the spirit of explication, improve upon the antecedent usage of the definiendum; or finally, the definiendum may be a newly created notation, newly endowed with meaning here and now.

In formal and informal work alike, thus, we find that definition—except in the extreme case of the explicitly conventional introduction of new notations—hinges on prior relations of synonymy. Recognizing then that the notion of definition does not hold the key to synonymy and analyticity, let us look further into synonymy and say no more of definition.

3. INTERCHANGEABILITY

A natural suggestion, deserving close examination, is that the synonymy of two linguistic forms consists simply in their interchangeability in all contexts without change of truth value—interchangeability, in Leibniz's phrase, *salva veritate*.[6] Note that synonyms so conceived need not even be free from vagueness, as long as the vaguenesses match.

---

[5] According to an important variant sense of 'definition', the relation preserved may be the weaker relation of mere agreement in reference. But definition in this sense is better ignored in the present connection, being irrelevant to the question of synonymy.

[6] Cf. Lewis [1], p. 373.

But it is not quite true that the synonyms 'bachelor' and 'unmarried man' are everywhere interchangeable *salva veritate*. Truths which become false under substitution of 'unmarried man' for 'bachelor' are easily constructed with the help of 'bachelor of arts' or 'bachelor's buttons'; also with the help of quotation, thus:

'Bachelor' has less than ten letters.

Such counterinstances can, however, perhaps be set aside by treating the phrases 'bachelor of arts' and 'bachelor's buttons' and the quotation ' 'bachelor' ' each as a single indivisible word and then stipulating that the interchangeability *salva veritate* which is to be the touchstone of synonymy is not supposed to apply to fragmentary occurrences inside of a word. This account of synonymy, supposing it acceptable on other counts, has indeed the drawback of appealing to a prior conception of "word" which can be counted on to present difficulties of formulation in its turn. Nevertheless some progress might be claimed in having reduced the problem of synonymy to a problem of wordhood. Let us pursue this line a bit, taking "word" for granted.

The question remains whether interchangeability *salva veritate* (apart from occurrences within words) is a strong enough condition for synonymy, or whether, on the contrary, some heteronymous expressions might be thus interchangeable. Now let us be clear that we are not concerned here with synonymy in the sense of complete identity in psychological associations or poetic quality; indeed no two expressions are synonymous in such a sense. We are concerned only with what may be called *cognitive* synonymy. Just what this is cannot be said without successfully finishing the present study; but we know something about it from the need which arose for it in connection with analyticity in §1. The sort of synonymy needed there was merely such that any analytic statement could be turned into a logical truth by putting synonyms for synonyms. Turning the tables and assuming analyticity, indeed, we could explain cognitive synonymy of terms as follows (keeping to the familiar example): to say that 'bachelor' and 'unmarried man' are cognitively synonymous is to say no more nor less than that the statement:

(3)   All and only bachelors are unmarried men

is analytic.[7]

What we need is an account of cognitive synonymy not presupposing analyticity—if we are to explain analyticity conversely with help of cognitive synonymy as undertaken in §1. And indeed such an independent account of

---

[7] This is cognitive synonymy in a primary, broad sense. Carnap ([2], pp. 56ff) and Lewis ([2], pp. 83ff) have suggested how, once this notion is at hand, a narrower sense of cognitive synonymy which is preferable for some purposes can in turn be derived. But this special ramification of concept-building lies aside from the present purposes and must not be confused with the broad sort of cognitive synonymy here concerned.

cognitive synonymy is at present up for consideration, namely, interchangeability *salva veritate* everywhere except within words. The question before us, to resume the thread at last, is whether such interchangeability is a sufficient condition for cognitive synonymy. We can quickly assure ourselves that it is, by examples of the following sort. The statement:

(4)   Necessarily all and only bachelors are bachelors

is evidently true, even supposing 'necessarily' so narrowly construed as to be truly applicable only to analytic statements. Then, if 'bachelor' and 'unmarried man' are interchangeable *salva veritate*, the result:

(5)   Necessarily all and only bachelors are unmarried men

of putting 'unmarried man' for an occurrence of 'bachelor' in (4) must, like (4), be true. But to say that (5) is true is to say that (3) is analytic, and hence that 'bachelor' and 'unmarried man' are cognitively synonymous.

Let us see what there is about the above argument that gives it its air of hocus-pocus. The condition of interchangeability *salva veritate* varies in its force with variations in the richness of the language at hand. The above argument supposes we are working with a language rich enough to contain the adverb 'necessarily', this adverb being so construed as to yield truth when and only when applied to an analytic statement. But can we condone a language which contains such an adverb? Does the adverb really make sense? To suppose that it does is to suppose that we have already made satisfactory sense of 'analytic'. Then what are we so hard at work on right now?

Our argument is not flatly circular, but something like it. It has the form, figuratively speaking, of a closed curve in space.

Interchangeability *salva veritate* is meaningless until relativized to a language whose extent is specified in relevant respects. Suppose now we consider a language containing just the following materials. There is an indefinitely large stock of one-place predicates (for example, 'F' where 'Fx' means that x is a man) and many-place predicates (for example, 'G' where 'Gxy' means that x loves y), mostly having to do with extralogical subject matter. The rest of the language is logical. The atomic sentences consist each of a predicate followed by one or more variables 'x', 'y', etc.; and the complex sentences are built up of the atomic ones by truth functions ('not', 'and', 'or', etc.) and quantification. In effect such a language enjoys the benefits also of descriptions and indeed singular terms generally, these being contextually definable in known ways.[8] Even abstract singular terms naming classes, classes of classes, etc., are contextually definable in case the assumed stock of predicates includes the two-place predicate of class membership. Such a language can be adequate to classical mathematics and indeed to scientific discourse generally, except insofar as the latter involves debatable

[8] See above, pp. 186–8.

devices such as contrary-to-fact conditionals or modal adverbs like 'necessarily'. Now a language of this type is extensional, in this sense: any two
predicates which agree extensionally (that is, are true of the same objects) are
interchangeable *salva veritate*.[9]

In an extensional language, therefore, interchangeability *salva veritate*
is no assurance of cognitive synonymy of the desired type. That 'bachelor'
and 'unmarried man' are interchangeable *salva veritate* in an extensional
language assures us of no more than that (3) is true. There is no assurance
here that the extensional agreement of 'bachelor' and 'unmarried man' rests
on meaning rather than merely on accidental matters of fact, as does the
extensional agreement of 'creature with a heart' and 'creature with kidneys'.

For most purposes extensional agreement is the nearest approximation
to synonymy we need care about. But the fact remains that extensional
agreement falls far short of cognitive synonymy of the type required for
explaining analyticity in the manner of §1. The type of cognitive synonymy
required there is such as to equate the synonymy of 'bachelor' and 'unmarried
man' with the analyticity of (3), not merely with the truth of (3).

So we must recognize that interchangeability *salva veritate*, if construed
in relation to an extensional language, is not a sufficient condition of cognitive
synonymy in the sense needed for deriving analyticity in the manner of §1.
If a language contains an intensional adverb 'necessarily' in the sense lately
noted, or other particles to the same effect, then interchangeability *salva
veritate* in such a language does afford a sufficient condition of cognitive
synonymy; but such a language is intelligible only insofar as the notion of
analyticity is already understood in advance.

The effort to explain cognitive synonymy first, for the sake of deriving
analyticity from it afterward as in §1, is perhaps the wrong approach. Instead
we might try explaining analyticity somehow without appeal to cognitive
synonymy. Afterward we could doubtless derive cognitive synonymy from
analyticity satisfactorily enough if desired. We have seen that cognitive
synonymy of 'bachelor' and 'unmarried man' can be explained as analyticity
of (3). The same explanation works for any pair of one-place predicates, of
course, and it can be extended in obvious fashion to many-place predicates.
Other syntactical categories can also be accommodated in fairly parallel
fashion. Singular terms may be said to be cognitively synonymous when
the statement of identity formed by putting '=' between them is analytic.
Statements may be said simply to be cognitively synonymous when their
biconditional (the result of joining them by 'if and only if') is analytic.[10] If
we care to lump all categories into a single formulation, at the expense of
assuming again the notion of "word" which was appealed to early in this
section, we can describe any two linguistic forms as cognitively synonymous

[9] This is the substance of Quine, *121.
[10] The 'if and only if' itself is intended in the truth-functional sense. See Carnap [2],
p. 14.

when the two forms are interchangeable (apart from occurrences within "words") *salva* (not longer *veritate* but) *analyticitate*. Certain technical questions arise, indeed, over cases of ambiguity or homonymy; let us not pause for them, however, for we are already digressing. Let us rather turn our backs on the problem of synonymy and address ourselves anew to that of analyticity.

4. SEMANTICAL RULES

Analyticity at first seemed most naturally definable by appeal to a realm of meanings. On refinement, the appeal to meanings gave way to an appeal to synonymy or definition. But definition turned out to be a will-o'-the-wisp, and synonymy turned out to be best understood only by dint of a prior appeal to analyticity itself. So we are back at the problem of analyticity.

I do not know whether the statement 'Everything green is extended' is analytic. Now does my indecision over this example really betray an incomplete understanding, an incomplete grasp of the "meanings", of 'green' and 'extended'? I think not. The trouble is not with 'green' or 'extended', but with 'analytic'.

It is often hinted that the difficulty in separating analytic statements from synthetic ones in ordinary language is due to the vagueness of ordinary language and that the distinction is clear when we have a precise artificial language with explicit "semantical rules." This, however, as I shall now attempt to show, is a confusion.

The notion of analyticity about which we are worrying is a purported relation between statements and languages: a statement S is said to be *analytic for* a language L, and the problem is to make sense of this relation generally, that is, for variable 'S' and 'L'. The gravity of this problem is not perceptibly less for artificial languages than for natural ones. The problem of making sense of the idiom 'S is analytic for L', with variable 'S' and 'L', retains its stubbornness even if we limit the range of the variable 'L' to artificial languages. Let me now try to make this point evident.

For artificial languages and semantical rules we look naturally to the writings of Carnap. His semantical rules take various forms, and to make my point I shall have to distinguish certain of the forms. Let us suppose, to begin with, an artificial language L_0 whose semantical rules have the form explicitly of a specification, by recursion or otherwise, of all the analytic statements of L_0. The rules tell us that such and such statements, and only those, are the analytic statements of L_0. Now here the difficulty is simply that the rules contain the word 'analytic', which we do not understand! We understand what expressions the rules attribute analyticity to, but we do not understand what the rules attribute to those expressions. In short, before we can understand a rule which begins 'A statement S is analytic for language L_0 if and only if ...', we must understand the general relative term 'analytic for'; we must understand 'S is analytic for L' where 'S' and 'L' are variables.

Alternatively we may, indeed, view the so-called rule as a conventional definition of a new simple symbol 'analytic-for-L_0', which might better be written untendentiously as 'K' so as not to seem to throw light on the interesting word 'analytic'. Obviously any number of classes K, M, N, etc. of statements of L_0 can be specified for various purposes or for no purpose; what does it mean to say that K, as against M, N, etc., is the class of the "analytic" statements of L_0?

By saying what statements are analytic for L_0 we explain 'analytic-for-L_0' but not 'analytic', not 'analytic for'. We do not begin to explain the idiom 'S is analytic for L' with variable 'S' and 'L', even if we are content to limit the range of 'L' to the realm of artificial languages.

Actually we do know enough about the intended significance of 'analytic' to know that analytic statements are supposed to be true. Let us then turn to a second form of semantical rule, which says not that such and such statements are analytic but simply that such and such statements are included among the truths. Such a rule is not subject to the criticism of containing the un-understood word 'analytic'; and we may grant for the sake of argument that there is no difficulty over the broader term 'true'. A semantical rule of this second type, a rule of truth, is not supposed to specify all the truths of the language; it merely stipulates, recursively or otherwise, a certain multitude of statements which, along with others unspecified, are to count as true. Such a rule may be conceded to be quite clear. Derivatively, afterward, analyticity can be demarcated thus: a statement is analytic if it is (not merely true but) true according to the semantical rule.

Still there is really no progress. Instead of appealing to an unexplained word 'analytic', we are now appealing to an unexplained phrase 'semantical rule'. Not every true statement which says that the statements of some class are true can count as a semantical rule—otherwise *all* truths would be "analytic" in the sense of being true according to semantical rules. Semantical rules are distinguishable, apparently, only by the fact of appearing on a page under the heading 'Semantical Rules'; and this heading is itself then meaningless.

We can say indeed that a statement is *analytic-for-L_0* if and only if it is true according to such and such specifically appended "semantical rules," but then we find ourselves back at essentially the same case which was originally discussed: 'S is analytic-for-L_0 if and only if. ...' Once we seek to explain 'S is analytic for L' generally for variable 'L' (even allowing limitation of 'L' to artificial languages), the explanation 'true according to the semantical rules of L' is unavailing; for the relative term 'semantical rule of' is as much in need of clarification, at least, as 'analytic for'.

It may be instructive to compare the notion of semantical rule with that of postulate. Relative to a given set of postulates, it is easy to say what a postulate is: it is a member of the set. Relative to a given set of semantical rules, it is equally easy to say what a semantical rule is. But given simply a notation, mathematical or otherwise, and indeed as thoroughly understood a notation as you please in point of the translations or truth conditions of its statements, who can say which of its true statements rank as postulates? Obviously the question is meaningless—as meaningless as asking which points in Ohio are starting points. Any finite (or effectively specifiable infinite) selection of statements (preferably true ones, perhaps) is as much *a* set of postulates as any other. The word 'postulate' is significant only relative to an act of inquiry; we apply the word to a set of statements just insofar as we happen, for the year or the moment, to be thinking of those statements in relation to the statements which can be reached from them by some set of transformations to which we have seen fit to direct our attention. Now the notion of semantical rule is as sensible and meaningful as that of postulate, if conceived in a similarly relative spirit—relative, this time, to one or another particular enterprise of schooling unconversant persons in sufficient conditions for truth of statements of some natural or artificial language L. But from this point of view no one signalization of a subclass of the truths of L is intrinsically more a semantical rule than another; and, if 'analytic' means 'true by semantical rules', no one truth of L is analytic to the exclusion of another.[11]

It might conceivably be protested that an artificial language L (unlike a natural one) is a language in the ordinary sense *plus* a set of explicit semantical rules—the whole constituting, let us say, an ordered pair; and that the semantical rules of L then are specifiable simply as the second component of the pair L. But, by the same token and more simply, we might construe an artificial language L outright as an ordered pair whose second component is the class of its analytic statements; and then the analytic statements of L become specifiable simply as the statements in the second component of L. Or better still, we might just stop tugging at our bootstraps altogether.

Not all the explanations of analyticity known to Carnap and his readers have been covered explicitly in the above considerations, but the extension to other forms is not hard to see. Just one additional factor should be mentioned which sometimes enters: sometimes the semantical rules are in effect rules of translation into ordinary language, in which case the analytic statements of the artificial language are in effect recognized as such from the analyticity of their specified translations in ordinary language. Here certainly there can be no thought of an illumination of the problem of analyticity from the side of the artificial language.

From the point of view of the problem of analyticity the notion of an artificial language with semantical rules is a *feu follet par excellence*. Semantical rules determining the analytic statements of an artificial language are of interest only insofar as we already understand the notion of analyticity; they are of no help in gaining this understanding.

Appeal to hypothetical languages of an artificially simple kind could

[11] The foregoing paragraph was not part of the present essay as originally published in the *Philosophical Review*, 1951. It was prompted by Martin (*see* Bibliography).

conceivably be useful in clarifying analyticity, if the mental or behavioral or cultural factors relevant to analyticity—whatever they may be—were somehow sketched into the simplified model. But a model which takes analyticity merely as an irreducible character is unlikely to throw light on the problem of explicating analyticity.

It is obvious that truth in general depends on both language and extralinguistic fact. The statement 'Brutus killed Caesar' would be false if the world had been different in certain ways, but it would also be false if the word 'killed' happened rather to have the sense of 'begat'. Thus one is tempted to suppose in general that the truth of a statement is somehow analyzable into a linguistic component and a factual component. Given this supposition, it next seems reasonable that in some statements the factual component should be null; and these are the analytic statements. But, for all its *a priori* reasonableness, a boundary between analytic and synthetic statements simply has not been drawn. That there is such a distinction to be drawn at all is an unempirical dogma of empiricists, a metaphysical article of faith.

5. THE VERIFICATION THEORY AND REDUCTIONISM

In the course of these somber reflections we have taken a dim view first of the notion of meaning, then of the notion of cognitive synonymy, and finally of the notion of analyticity. But what, it may be asked, of the verification theory of meaning? This phrase has established itself so firmly as a catchword of empiricism that we should be very unscientific indeed not to look beneath it for a possible key to the problem of meaning and the associated problems.

The verification theory of meaning, which has been conspicuous in the literature from Peirce onward, is that the meaning of a statement is the method of empirically confirming or infirming it. An analytic statement is that limiting case which is confirmed no matter what.

As urged in §1, we can as well pass over the question of meanings as entities and move straight to sameness of meaning, or synonymy. Then what the verification theory says is that statements are synonymous if and only if they are alike in point of method of empirical confirmation or infirmation.

This is an account of cognitive synonymy not of linguistic forms generally, but of statements.[12] However, from the concept of synonymy of statements we could derive the concept of synonymy for other linguistic forms, by considerations somewhat similar to those at the end of §3. Assuming the notion

---

[12] The doctrine can indeed be formulated with terms rather than statements as the units. Thus Lewis describes the meaning of a term as "*a criterion in mind*, by reference to which one is able to apply or refuse to apply the expression in question in the case of presented, or imagined, things or situations" ([2], p. 133).—For an instructive account of the vicissitudes of the verification theory of meaning, centered however on the question of meaning*fulness* rather than synonymy and analyticity, see Hempel.

of "word," indeed, we could explain any two forms as synonymous when the putting of the one form for an occurrence of the other in any statement (apart from occurrences within "words") yields a synonymous statement. Finally, given the concept of synonymy thus for linguistic forms generally, we could define analyticity in terms of synonymy and logical truth as in §1. For that matter, we could define analyticity more simply in terms of just synonymy of statements together with logical truth; it is not necessary to appeal to synonymy of linguistic forms other than statements. For a statement may be described as analytic simply when it is synonymous with a logically true statement.

So, if the verification theory can be accepted as an adequate account of statement synonymy, the notion of analyticity is saved after all. However, let us reflect. Statement synonymy is said to be likeness of method of empirical confirmation or infirmation. Just what are these methods which are to be compared for likeness? What, in other words, is the nature of the relation between a statement and the experiences which contribute to or detract from its confirmation?

The most naïve view of the relation is that it is one of direct report. This is *radical reductionism.* Every meaningful statement is held to be translatable into a statement (true or false) about immediate experience. Radical reductionism, in one form or another, well antedates the verification theory of meaning explicitly so called. Thus Locke and Hume held that every idea must either originate directly in sense experience or else be compounded of ideas thus originating; and taking a hint from Tooke (I, ch. ii) we might rephrase this doctrine in semantical jargon by saying that a term, to be significant at all, must be either a name of a sense datum or a compound of such names or an abbreviation of such a compound. So stated, the doctrine remains ambiguous as between sense data as sensory events and sense data as sensory qualities; and it remains vague as to the admissible ways of compounding. Moreover, the doctrine is unnecessarily and intolerably restrictive in the term-by-term critique which it imposes. More reasonably, and without yet exceeding the limits of what I have called radical reductionism, we may take full statements as our significant units—thus demanding that our statements as wholes be translatable into sense-datum language, but not that they be translatable term by term.

This emendation would unquestionably have been welcome to Locke and Hume and Tooke, but historically it had to await an important reorientation in semantics—the reorientation whereby the primary vehicle of meaning came to be seen no longer in the term but in the statement. This reorientation, explicit in Bentham (vol. 8, p. 247f) and Frege (§60), underlies Russell's concept of incomplete symbols defined in use;[13] also it is implicit in the verification theory of meaning, since the objects of verification are statements.

Radical reductionism, conceived now with statements as units, set itself

[13] See above, pp. 186–7.

the task of specifying a sense-datum language and showing how to translate the rest of significant discourse, statement by statement, into it. Carnap embarked on this project in the *Aufbau*.

The language which Carnap adopted as his starting point was not a sense-datum language in the narrowest conceivable sense, for it included also the notations of logic, up through higher set theory. In effect it included the whole language of pure mathematics. The ontology implicit in it (that is, the range of values of its variables) embraced not only sensory events but classes, classes of classes, and so on. Empiricists there are who would boggle at such prodigality. Carnap's starting point is very parsimonious, however, in its extralogical or sensory part. In a series of constructions in which he exploits the resources of modern logic with much ingenuity, Carnap succeeds in defining a wide array of important additional sensory concepts which, but for his constructions, one would not have dreamed were definable on so slender a basis. He was the first empiricist who, not content with asserting the reducibility of science to terms of immediate experience, took serious steps toward carrying out the reduction.

If Carnap's starting point is satisfactory, still his constructions were, as he himself stressed, only a fragment of the full program. The construction of even the simplest statements about the physical world was left in a sketchy state. Carnap's suggestions on this subject were, despite their sketchiness, very suggestive. He explained spatio-temporal point-instants as quadruples of real numbers and envisaged assignment of sense qualities to point-instants according to certain canons. Roughly summarized, the plan was that qualities should be assigned to point-instants in such a way as to achieve the laziest world compatible with our experience. The principle of least action was to be our guide in constructing a world from experience.

Carnap did not seem to recognize, however, that his treatment of physical objects fell short of reduction not merely through sketchiness, but in principle. Statements of the form 'Quality q is at point-instant $x;y;z;t$' were, according to his canons, to be apportioned truth-values in such a way as to maximize and minimize certain over-all features, and with growth of experience the truth values were to be progressively revised in the same spirit. I think this is a good schematization (deliberately oversimplified, to be sure) of what science really does; but it provides no indication, not even the sketchiest, of how a statement of the form 'Quality q is at $x;y;z;t$' could ever be translated into Carnap's initial language of sense data and logic. The connective 'is at' remains an added undefined connective; the canons counsel us in its use but not in its elimination.

Carnap seems to have appreciated this point afterward; for in his later writings he abandoned all notion of the translatability of statements about the physical world into statements about immediate experience. Reductionism in its radical form has long since ceased to figure in Carnap's philosophy.

But the dogma of reductionism has, in a subtler and more tenuous form, continued to influence the thought of empiricists. The notion lingers that to each statement, or each synthetic statement, there is associated a unique range of possible sensory events such that the occurrence of any of them would add to the likelihood of truth of the statement, and that there is associated also another unique range of possible sensory events whose occurrence would detract from that likelihood. This notion is of course implicit in the verification theory of meaning.

The dogma of reductionism survives in the supposition that each statement, taken in isolation from its fellows, can admit of confirmation or infirmation at all. My countersuggestion, issuing essentially from Carnap's doctrine of the physical world in the *Aufbau*, is that our statements about the external world face the tribunal of sense experience not individually but only as a corporate body.[14]

The dogma of reductionism, even in its attenuated form, is intimately connected with the other dogma—that there is a cleavage between the analytic and the synthetic. We have found ourselves led, indeed, from the latter problem to the former through the verification theory of meaning. More directly, the one dogma clearly supports the other in this way: as long as it is taken to be significant in general to speak of the confirmation and infirmation of a statement, it seems significant to speak also of a limiting kind of statement which is vacuously confirmed, *ipso facto*, come what may; and such a statement is analytic.

The two dogmas are, indeed, at root identical. We lately reflected that in general the truth of statements does obviously depend both upon language and upon extralinguistic fact; and we noted that this obvious circumstance carries in its train, not logically but all too naturally, a feeling that the truth of a statement is somehow analyzable into a linguistic component and a factual component. The factual component must, if we are empiricists, boil down to a range of confirmatory experiences. In the extreme case where the linguistic component is all that matters, a true statement is analytic. But I hope we are now impressed with how stubbornly the distinction between analytic and synthetic has resisted any straightforward drawing. I am impressed also, apart from prefabricated examples of black and white balls in an urn, with how baffling the problem has always been of arriving at any explicit theory of the empirical confirmation of a synthetic statement. My present suggestion is that it is nonsense, and the root of much nonsense, to speak of a linguistic component and a factual component in the truth of any individual statement. Taken collectively, science has its double dependence upon language and experience; but this duality is not significantly traceable into the statements of science taken one by one.

The idea of defining a symbol in use was, as remarked, an advance over the impossible term-by-term empiricism of Locke and Hume. The statement, rather than the term, came with Bentham to be recognized as the unit

[14] This doctrine was well argued by Duhem, pp. 303–28. Or see Lowinger, pp. 132–40.

accountable to an empiricist critique. But what I am now urging is that even in taking the statement as unit we have drawn our grid too fine. The unit of empirical significance is the whole of science.

6. EMPIRICISM WITHOUT THE DOGMAS

The totality of our so-called knowledge or beliefs, from the most casual matters of geography and history to the profoundest laws of atomic physics or even of pure mathematics and logic, is a man-made fabric which impinges on experience only along the edges. Or, to change the figure, total science is like a field of force whose boundary conditions are experience. A conflict with experience at the periphery occasions readjustments in the interior of the field. Truth-values have to be redistributed over some of our statements. Reëvaluation of some statements entails reëvaluation of others, because of their logical interconnections—the logical laws being in turn simply certain further statements of the system, certain further elements of the field. Having reëvaluated one statement we must reëvaluate some others, which may be statements logically connected with the first or may be the statements of logical connections themselves. But the total field is so underdetermined by its boundary conditions, experience, that there is much latitude of choice as to what statements to reëvaluate in the light of any single contrary experience. No particular experiences are linked with any particular statements in the interior of the field, except indirectly through considerations of equilibrium affecting the field as a whole.

If this view is right, it is misleading to speak of the empirical content of an individual statement—especially if it is a statement at all remote from the experiential periphery of the field. Furthermore it becomes folly to seek a boundary between synthetic statements, which hold contingently on experience, and analytic statements, which hold come what may. Any statement can be held true come what may, if we make drastic enough adjustments elsewhere in the system. Even a statement very close to the periphery can be held true in the face of recalcitrant experience by pleading hallucination or by amending certain statements of the kind called logical laws. Conversely, by the same token, no statement is immune to revision. Revision even of the logical law of the excluded middle has been proposed as a means of simplifying quantum mechanics; and what difference is there in principle between such a shift and the shift whereby Kepler superseded Ptolemy, or Einstein Newton, or Darwin Aristotle?

For vividness I have been speaking in terms of varying distances from a sensory periphery. Let me try now to clarify this notion without metaphor. Certain statements, though *about* physical objects and not sense experience, seem peculiarly germane to sense experience—and in a selective way: some statements to some experiences, others to others. Such statements, especially germane to particular experiences, I picture as near the periphery. But in this relation of 'germaneness" I envisage nothing more than a loose association reflecting the relative likelihood, in practice, of our choosing one statement rather than another for revision in the event of recalcitrant experience. For example, we can imagine recalcitrant experiences to which we would surely be inclined to accommodate our system by reëvaluating just the statement that there are brick houses on Elm Street, together with related statements on the same topic. We can imagine other recalcitrant experiences to which we would be inclined to accommodate our system by reëvaluating just the statement that there are no centaurs, along with kindred statements. A recalcitrant experience can, I have urged, be accommodated by any of various alternative reëvaluations in various alternative quarters of the total system; but, in the cases which we are now imagining, our natural tendency to disturb the total system as little as possible would lead us to focus our revisions upon these specific statements concerning brick houses or centaurs. These statements are felt, therefore, to have a sharper empirical reference than highly theoretical statements of physics or logic or ontology. The latter statements may be thought of as relatively centrally located within the total network, meaning merely that little preferential connection with any particular sense data obtrudes itself.

As an empiricist I continue to think of the conceptual scheme of science as a tool, ultimately, for predicting future experience in the light of past experience. Physical objects are conceptually imported into the situation as convenient intermediaries—not by definition. in terms of experience, but simply as irreducible posits[15] comparable, epistemologically, to the gods of Homer. For my part I do, qua lay physicist, believe in physical objects and not in Homer's gods; and I consider it a scientific error to believe otherwise. But in point of epistemological footing the physical objects and the gods differ only in degree and not in kind. Both sorts of entities enter our conception only as cultural posits. The myth of physical objects is epistemologically superior to most in that it has proved more efficacious than other myths as a device for working a manageable structure into the flux of experience.

Positing does not stop with macroscopic physical objects. Objects at the atomic level are posited to make the laws of macroscopic objects, and ultimately the laws of experience, simpler and more manageable; and we need not expect or demand full definition of atomic and subatomic entities in terms of macroscopic ones, any more than definition of macroscopic things in terms of sense data. Science is a continuation of common sense, and it continues the common-sense expedient of swelling ontology to simplify theory.

Physical objects, small and large, are not the only posits. Forces are another example; and indeed we are told nowadays that the boundary between energy and matter is obsolete. Moreover, the abstract entities which are the substance of mathematics—ultimately classes and classes of classes and so on up—are another posit in the same spirit. Epistemologically these are myths

[15] Cf. pp. 194–6 above.

on the same footing with physical objects and gods, neither better nor worse except for differences in the degree to which they expedite our dealings with sense experiences.

The over-all algebra of rational and irrational numbers is underdetermined by the algebra of rational numbers, but is smoother and more convenient; and it includes the algebra of rational numbers as a jagged or gerrymandered part.[16] Total science, mathematical and natural and human, is similarly but more extremely underdetermined by experience. The edge of the system must be kept squared with experience; the rest, with all its elaborate myths or fictions, has as its objective the simplicity of laws.

Ontological questions, under this view, are on a par with questions of natural science.[17] Consider the question whether to countenance classes as entities. This, as I have argued elsewhere,[18] is the question whether to quantify with respect to variables which take classes as values. Now Carnap [4] has maintained that this is a question not of matters of fact but of choosing a convenient language form, a convenient conceptual scheme or framework for science. With this I agree, but only on the proviso that the same be conceded regarding scientific hypotheses generally. Carnap (above p. 354n) has recognized that he is able to preserve a double standard for ontological questions and scientific hypotheses only by assuming an absolute distinction between the analytic and the synthetic; and I need not say again that this is a distinction which I reject.[19]

The issue over there being classes seems more a question of convenient conceptual scheme; the issue over there being centaurs, or brick houses on Elm Street, seems more a question of fact. But I have been urging that this difference is only one of degree, and that it turns upon our vaguely pragmatic inclination to adjust one strand of the fabric of science rather than another in accommodating some particular recalcitrant experience. Conservatism figures in such choices, and so does the quest for simplicity.

Carnap, Lewis, and others take a pragmatic stand on the question of choosing between language forms, scientific frameworks; but their pragmatism leaves off at the imagined boundary between the analytic and the synthetic. In repudiating such a boundary I espouse a more thorough pragmatism. Each man is given a scientific heritage plus a continuing barrage of sensory stimulation; and the considerations which guide him in warping his scientific heritage to fit his continuing sensory promptings are, where rational, pragmatic.

---

[16] Cf. p. 195 above.

[17] "L'ontologie fait corps avec la science elle-même et ne peut en être separée," Meyerson, p. 439.

[18] Above, p. 191ff.

[19] For an effective expression of further misgivings over this distinction, see White.

BIBLIOGRAPHY

Bentham, Jeremy, *Works*. Edinburgh, 1843.

Carnap, Rudolf [1]. *Der logische Aufbau der Welt*. Berlin, 1928.

—— [2]. *Meaning and Necessity*. Chicago: University of Chicago Press, 1947.

—— [3]. *Logical Foundations of Probability*. Chicago: University of Chicago Press, 1950.

—— [4]. "Empiricism, Semantics, and Ontology," *Revue internationale de philosophie*, 4 (1950), 20–40. [Reprinted in this collection, pp. 233–48.—Eds.]

Duhem, Pierre, *La Théorie physique: son objet et sa structure*. Paris, 1906.

Frege, Gottlob, *Foundations of Arithmetic*. New York: Philosophical Library, 1950. Reprint of *Grundlagen der Arithmetik* (Breslau, 1884) with English translation in parallel.

Hempel, C. G., "Problems and Changes in the Empiricist Criterion of Meaning," *Revue internationale de philosophie*, 4 (1950), 41–63.

Lewis, C. I. [1]. *A Survey of Symbolic Logic*. Berkeley, Calif.: 1918.

—— [2]. *An Analysis of Knowledge and Valuation*. LaSalle, Ill.: Open Court, 1946.

Lowinger, Armand, *The Methodology of Pierre Duhem*. New York: Columbia University Press, 1941.

Martin, R. M., "On 'Analytic'," *Philosophical Studies*, 3 (1952), 42–47.

Meyerson, Émile, *Identité et realité*, 4th ed., 1932. Paris, 1908.

Quine, W. V., *Mathematical Logic*. New York: Norton, 1940; Cambridge: Harvard University Press, 1947; rev. ed., Cambridge: Harvard University Press, 1951.

Tooke, John Horne, *The Diversions of Purley*. London, 1776; Boston, 1806.

White, Morton, "The Analytic and the Synthetic: an Untenable Dualism," in Sidney Hook, ed., *John Dewey: Philosopher of Science and Freedom*. New York: Dial Press, 1950, pp. 316–30,

ON THE NATURE OF MATHEMATICAL TRUTH

Carl G. Hempel

1. THE PROBLEM

It is a basic principle of scientific inquiry that no proposition and no theory is to be accepted without adequate grounds. In empirical science, which includes both the natural and the social sciences, the grounds for the acceptance of a theory consist in the agreement of predictions based on the theory with empirical evidence obtained either by experiment or by systematic observation. But what are the grounds which sanction the acceptance of mathematics? That is the question I propose to discuss in the present paper. For reasons which will become clear subsequently, I shall use the term "mathematics" here to refer to arithmetic, algebra, and analysis—to the exclusion, in particular, of geometry.[1]

2. ARE THE PROPOSITIONS OF MATHEMATICS SELF-EVIDENT TRUTHS?

One of the several answers which have been given to our problem asserts that the truths of mathematics, in contradistinction to the hypotheses of empirical science, require neither factual evidence nor any other justification because they are "self-evident." This view, however, which ultimately relegates decisions as to mathematical truth to a feeling of self-evidence, encounters various difficulties. First of all, many mathematical theorems are so hard to establish that even to the specialist in the particular field they appear as anything but self-evident. Secondly, it is well known that some of the most

---

[1] A discussion of the status of geometry is given in my article, "Geometry and Empirical Science," *American Mathematical Monthly*, vol. 52, pp. 7–17, 1945.

Reprinted with the kind permission of the author and the editor from The American Mathematical Monthly, *vol.* 52 (1945), *pp.* 543–56.

interesting results of mathematics—especially in such fields as abstract set theory and topology—run counter to deeply ingrained intuitions and the customary kind of feeling of self-evidence. Thirdly, the existence of mathematical conjectures such as those of Goldbach and of Fermat, which are quite elementary in content and yet undecided up to this day, certainly shows that not all mathematical truths can be self-evident. And finally, even if self-evidence were attributed only to the basic postulates of mathematics, from which all other mathematical propositions can be deduced, it would be pertinent to remark that judgments as to what may be considered as self-evident, are subjective; they may vary from person to person and certainly cannot constitute an adequate basis for decisions as to the objective validity of mathematical propositions.

3. IS MATHEMATICS THE MOST GENERAL EMPIRICAL SCIENCE?

According to another view, advocated especially by John Stuart Mill, mathematics is itself an empirical science which differs from the other branches, such as astronomy, physics, chemistry, etc., mainly in two respects: its subject matter is more general than that of any other field of scientific research, and its propositions have been tested and confirmed to a greater extent than those of even the most firmly established sections of astronomy or physics. Indeed, according to this view, the degree to which the laws of mathematics have been borne out by the past experiences of mankind is so overwhelming that—unjustifiably—we have come to think of mathematical theorems as qualitatively different from the well confirmed hypotheses or theories of other branches of science: we consider them as certain, while other theories are thought of as at best "very probable" or very highly confirmed.

But this view, too, is open to serious objections. From a hypothesis which is empirical in character—such as, for example, Newton's law of gravitation—it is possible to derive predictions to the effect that under certain specified conditions certain specified observable phenomena will occur. The actual occurrence of these phenomena constitutes confirming evidence, their non-occurrence disconfirming evidence for the hypothesis. It follows in particular that an empirical hypothesis is theoretically disconfirmable; i.e., it is possible to indicate what kind of evidence, if actually encountered, would disconfirm the hypothesis. In the light of this remark, consider now a simple "hypothesis" from arithmetic: $3 + 2 = 5$. If this is actually an empirical generalization of past experiences, then it must be possible to state what kind of evidence would oblige us to concede the hypothesis was not generally true after all. If any disconfirming evidence for the given proposition can be thought of, the following illustration might well be typical of it: We place some microbes on a slide, putting down first three of them and then another two. Afterwards we count all the microbes to test whether in this instance 3 and 2 actually added up to 5. Suppose now that we counted 6 microbes altogether. Would we consider this as an empirical disconfirmation of the given proposition, or at least as a proof that it does not apply to microbes? Clearly not; rather, we would assume we had made a mistake in counting or that one of the microbes had split in two between the first and the second count. But under no circumstances could the phenomenon just described invalidate the arithmetical proposition in question; for the latter asserts nothing whatever about the behavior of microbes; it merely states that any set consisting of $3 + 2$ objects may also be said to consist of 5 objects. And this is so because the symbols "$3 + 2$" and "5" denote the same number: they are synonymous by virtue of the fact that the symbols "2," "3," "5," and "+" are *defined* (or tacitly understood) in such a way that the above identity holds as a consequence of the meaning attached to the concepts involved in it.

4. THE ANALYTIC CHARACTER OF MATHEMATICAL PROPOSITIONS

The statement that $3 + 2 = 5$, then, is true for similar reasons as, say, the assertion that no sexagenarian is 45 years of age. Both are true simply by virtue of definitions or of similar stipulations which determine the meaning of the key terms involved. Statements of this kind share certain important characteristics: Their validation naturally requires no empirical evidence; they can be shown to be true by a mere analysis of the meaning attached to the terms which occur in them. In the language of logic, sentences of this kind are called analytic or true *a priori*, which is to indicate that their truth is logically independent of, or logically prior to, any experiential evidence.[2] And while the statements of empirical science, which are synthetic and can be validated only a posteriori, are constantly subject to revision in the light of new evidence, the truth of an analytic statement can be established definitely, once and for all. However, this characteristic "theoretical certainty" of analytic propositions has to be paid for at a high price: An analytic statement conveys no factual information. Our statement about sexagenarians, for example, asserts nothing that could possibly conflict with any factual evidence: it has no factual implications, no empirical content; and it is precisely for this reason that the statement can be validated without recourse to empirical evidence.

Let us illustrate this view of the nature of mathematical propositions by

[2] The objection is sometimes raised that without certain types of experience, such as encountering several objects of the same kind, the integers and the arithmetical operations with them would never have been invented, and that therefore the propositions of arithmetic do have an empirical basis. This type of argument, however, involves a confusion of the logical and the psychological meaning of the term "basis." It may very well be the case that certain experiences occasion psychologically the formation of arithmetical ideas and in this sense form an empirical "basis" for them; but this point is entirely irrelevant for the logical questions as to the *grounds* on which the propositions of arithmetic may be accepted as true. The point made above is that no empirical "basis" or evidence whatever is needed to establish the truth of the propositions of arithmetic.

reference to another, frequently cited, example of a mathematical—or rather logical—truth, namely the proposition that whenever $a = b$ and $b = c$ then $a = c$. On what grounds can this so-called "transitivity of identity" be asserted? Is it of an empirical nature and hence at least theoretically discon-firmable by empirical evidence? Suppose, for example, that a, b, c are certain shades of green, and that as far as we can see, $a = b$ and $b = c$, but clearly $a \neq c$. This phenomenon actually occurs under certain conditions; do we consider it as disconfirming evidence for the proposition under consideration? Undoubtedly not; we would argue that if $a \neq c$, it is impossible that $a = b$ and also $b = c$; between the terms of at least one of these latter pairs, there must obtain a difference, though perhaps only a subliminal one. And we would dismiss the possibility of empirical disconfirmation, and indeed the idea that an empirical test should be relevant here, on the grounds that identity is a transitive relation by virtue of its definition or by virtue of the basic postulates governing it.[3] Hence the principle in question is true *a priori*.

5. MATHEMATICS AS AN AXIOMATIZED DEDUCTIVE SYSTEM

I have argued so far that the validity of mathematics rests neither on its alleged self-evidential character nor on any empirical basis, but derives from the stipulations which determine the meaning of the mathematical concepts, and that the propositions of mathematics are therefore essentially "true by definition." This latter statement, however, is obviously oversimplified and needs restatement and a more careful justification.

For the rigorous development of a mathematical theory proceeds not simply from a set of definitions but rather from a set of non-definitional propositions which are not proved within the theory; these are the postulates or axioms of the theory.[4] They are formulated in terms of certain basic or primitive concepts for which no definitions are provided within the theory. It is sometimes asserted that the postulates themselves represent "implicit definitions" of the primitive terms. Such a characterization of the postulates, however, is misleading. For while the postulates do limit, in a specific sense, the meanings that can possibly be ascribed to the primitives, any self-con-sistent postulate system admits, nevertheless, many different interpretations of the primitive terms (this will soon be illustrated), whereas a set of definitions in the strict sense of the word determines the meanings of the definienda in a unique fashion.

Once the primtive terms and the postulates have been laid down, the entire theory is completely determined; it is derivable from its postulational basis in the following sense: Every term of the theory is definable in terms of the

[3] A precise account of the definition and the essential characteristics of the identity relation may be found in A. Tarski, *Introduction to Logic*, New York, 1941, Ch. III.

[4] For a lucid and concise account of the axiomatic method, see A. Tarski, loc. cit., Ch. VI.

primitives, and every proposition of the theory is logically deducible from the postulates. To be entirely precise, it is necessary also to specify the principles of logic which are to be used in the proof of the propositions, i.e. in their deduction from the postulates. These principles can be stated quite explicitly. They fall into two groups: Primitive sentences, or postulates, of logic (such as: If p and q is the case, then p is the case), and rules of deduction or inference (including, for example, the familiar modus ponens rule and the rules of substitution which make it possible to infer, from a general proposition, any one of its substitution instances). A more detailed discussion of the structure and content of logic would, however, lead too far afield in the context of this article.

6. PEANO'S AXIOM SYSTEM AS A BASIS FOR MATHEMATICS

Let us now consider a postulate system from which the entire arithmetic of the natural numbers can be derived. This system was devised by the Italian mathematician and logician G. Peano (1858–1932). The primitives of this system are the terms "0," "number," and "successor." While, of course, no definition of these terms is given within the theory, the symbol "0" is intended to designate the number 0 in its usual meaning, while the term "number" is meant to refer to the natural numbers 0, 1, 2, 3 · · · exclusively. By the successor of a natural number n, which will sometimes briefly be called n', is meant the natural number immediately following n in the natural order. Peano's system contains the following 5 postulates:

P1.   0 is a number

P2.   The successor of any number is a number

P3.   No two numbers have the same successor

P4.   0 is not the successor of any number.

P5.   If P is a property such that (a) 0 has the property P, and (b) whenever
      a number n has the property P, then the successor of n also has the
      property P, then every number has the property P.

The last postulate embodies the principle of mathematical induction and illustrates in a very obvious manner the enforcement of a mathematical "truth" by stipulation. The construction of elementary arithmetic on this basis begins with the definition of the various natural numbers. 1 is defined as the successor of 0, or briefly as $0'$; 2 as $1'$, 3 as $2'$, and so on. By virtue of P2, this process can be continued indefinitely; because of P3 (in combination with P5), it never leads back to one of the numbers previously defined, and in view of P4, it does not lead back to 0 either.

As the next step, we can set up a definition of addition which expresses in a precise form the idea that the addition of any natural number to some given number may be considered as a repeated addition of 1; the latter operation is readily expressible by means of the successor relation. This definition of addition runs as follows:

D1.   (a) $n + 0 = n$;   (b) $n + k' = (n + k)'$.

The two stipulations of this recursive definition completely determine the sum of any two integers. Consider, for example, the sum $3 + 2$. According to the definitions of the numbers 2 and 1, we have $3 + 2 = 3 + 1' = 3 + (0')'$; by D1 (b), $3 + (0')' = (3 + 0')' = ((3 + 0)')'$; but by D1 (a), and by the definitions of the numbers 4 and 5, $((3 + 0)')' = (3')' = 4' = 5$. This proof also renders more explicit and precise the comments made earlier in this paper on the truth of the proposition that $3 + 2 = 5$: Within the Peano system of arithmetic, its truth flows not merely from the definition of the concepts involved, but also from the postulates that govern these various concepts. (In our specific example, the postulates P1 and P2 are presupposed to guarantee that 1, 2, 3, 4, 5 are numbers in Peano's system; the general proof that D1 determines the sum of any two numbers also makes use of P5.) If we call the postulates and definitions of an axiomatized theory the "stipulations" concerning the concepts of that theory, then we may say now that the propositions of the arithmetic of the natural numbers are true by virtue of the stipulations which have been laid down initially for the arithmetical concepts. (Note, incidentally, that our proof of the formula "$3 + 2 = 5$" repeatedly made use of the transitivity of identity; the latter is accepted here as one of the rules of logic which may be used in the proof of any arithmetical theorem; it is, therefore, included among Peano's postulates no more than any other principle of logic.)

Now, the multiplication of natural numbers may be defined by means of the following recursive definition, which expresses in a rigorous form the idea that a product nk of two integers may be considered as the sum of k terms each of which equals n.

D2.   (a) $n \cdot 0 = 0$;   (b) $n \cdot k' = n \cdot k + n$.

It now is possible to prove the familiar general laws governing addition and multiplication, such as the commutative, associative, and distributive laws $(n + k = k + n,\ \ n \cdot k = k \cdot n;\ \ n + (k + l) = (n + k) + l,\ \ n \cdot (k \cdot l) = (n \cdot k) \cdot l; n \cdot (k + l) = (n \cdot k) + (n \cdot l))$.—In terms of addition and multiplication, the inverse operations of subtraction and division can then be defined. But it turns out that these "cannot always be performed"; i.e., in contradistinction to the sum and the product, the difference and the quotient are not defined for every couple of numbers; for example, $7 - 10$ and $7 \div 10$ are undefined. This situation suggests an enlargement of the number system by the introduction of negative and of rational numbers.

It is sometimes held that in order to effect this enlargement, we have to "assume" or else to "postulate" the existence of the desired additional kinds of numbers with properties that make them fit to fill the gaps of subtraction and division. This method of simply postulating what we want has its advantages; but, as Bertrand Russell[5] puts it, they are the same as the advantages of theft over honest toil; and it is a remarkable fact that the negative as well as the rational numbers can be obtained from Peano's primitives by the honest toil of constructing explicit definitions for them, without the introduction of any new postulates or assumptions whatsoever. Every positive and negative integer—in contradistinction to a natural number which has no sign—is definable as a certain set of ordered couples of natural numbers; thus, the integer $+ 2$ is definable as the set of all ordered couples (m, n) of natural numbers where $m = n + 2$; the integer $- 2$ is the set of all ordered couples (m, n) of natural numbers with $n = m + 2$.—Similarly, rational numbers are defined as classes of ordered couples of integers.— The various arithmetical operations can then be defined with reference to these new types of numbers, and the validity of all the arithmetical laws governing these operations can be proved by virtue of nothing more than Peano's postulates and the definitions of the various arithmetical concepts involved.

The much broader system thus obtained is still incomplete in the sense that not every number in it has a square root, and more generally, not every algebraic equation whose coefficients are all numbers of the system has a solution in the system. This suggests further expansions of the number system by the introduction of real and finally of complex numbers. Again, this enormous extension can be effected by mere definition, without the introduction of a single new postulate.[6] On the basis thus obtained, the various arithmetical and algebraic operations can be defined for the numbers of the new system, the concepts of function, of limit, of derivative and integral can be introduced, and the familiar theorems pertaining to these concepts can be proved, so that finally the huge system of mathematics as here delimited rests on the narrow basis of Peano's system: Every concept of mathematics can be defined by means of Peano's three primitives, and every proposition of mathematics can be deduced from the five postulates enriched by the definitions of the non-primitive terms.[7] These deductions can be carried out, in most cases, by means of nothing more than the principles of formal logic; the

---

[5] Bertrand Russell, *Introduction to Mathematical Philosophy*, New York and London, 1919, p. 71.

[6] For a more detailed account of the construction of the number system on Peano's basis, cf. Bertrand Russell, loc. cit., esp. Chs. I and VII.—A rigorous and concise presentation of that construction, beginning, however, with the set of all integers rather than that of the natural numbers, may be found in G. Birkhoff and S. MacLane. *A Survey of Modern Algebra*, New York, 1941, Chs. I, II, III, V.—For a general survey of the construction of the number system, cf. also J. W. Young, *Lectures on the Fundamental Concepts of Algebra and Geometry*, New York, 1911, esp. lectures X, XI, XII.

[7] As a result of very deep-reaching investigations carried out by K. Gödel it is known that arithmetic, and *a fortiori* mathematics, is an incomplete theory in the following sense: While all those propositions which belong to the classical systems of arithmetic, algebra, and analysis can indeed be derived, in the sense characterized above, from the Peano

proof of some theorems concerning real numbers, however, requires one assumption which is not usually included among the latter. This is the so-called axiom of choice. It asserts that given a class of mutually exclusive classes, none of which is empty, there exists at least one class which has exactly one element in common with each of the given classes. By virtue of this principle and the rules of formal logic, the content of all of mathematics can thus be derived from Peano's modest system—a remarkable achievement in systematizing the content of mathematics and clarifying the foundations of its validity.

7. INTERPRETATIONS OF PEANO'S PRIMITIVES

As a consequence of this result, the whole system of mathematics might be said to be true by virtue of mere definitions (namely, of the non-primitive mathematical terms) provided that the five Peano postulates are true. However, strictly speaking, we cannot, at this juncture, refer to the Peano postulates as propositions which are either true or false, for they contain three primitive terms which have not been assigned any specific meaning. All we can assert so far is that any specific interpretation of the primitives which satisfies the five postulates—i.e., turns them into true statements—will also satisfy all the theorems deduced from them. But for Peano's system, there are several—indeed, infinitely many—interpretations which will do this. For example, let us understand by 0 the origin of a half-line, by the successor of a point on that half-line the point 1 cm. behind it, counting from the origin, and by a number any point which is either the origin or can be reached from it by a finite succession of steps each of which leads from one point to its successor. It can then readily be seen that all the Peano postulates as well as the ensuing theorems turn into true propositions, although the interpretation given to the primitives is certainly not the customary one, which was mentioned earlier. More generally, it can be shown that every progression of elements of any kind provides a true interpretation, or a "model," of the Peano system. This example illustrates our earlier observation that a postulate system cannot be regarded as a set of "implicit definitions" for the primitive terms: The Peano system permits of many different interpretations,

---

postulates, there exist nevertheless other propositions which can be expressed in purely arithmetical terms, and which are true, but which cannot be derived from the Peano system. And more generally: For any postulate system of arithmetic (or of mathematics for that matter) which is not self-contradictory, there exist propositions which are true, and which can be stated in purely arithmetical terms, but which cannot be derived from that postulate system. In other words, it is impossible to construct a postulate system which is not self-contradictory, and which contains among its consequences all true propositions which can be formulated within the language of arithmetic.

This fact does not, however, affect the result outlined above, namely, that it is possible to deduce, from the Peano postulates and the additional definitions of non-primitive terms, all those propositions which constitute the classical theory of arithmetic, algebra, and analysis; and it is to these propositions that I refer above and subsequently as the propositions of mathematics.

whereas in everyday as well as in scientific language, we attach one specific meaning to the concepts of arithmetic. Thus, e.g., in scientific and in everyday discourse, the concept 2 is understood in such a way that from the statement "Mr. Brown as well as Mr. Cope, but no one else is in the office, and Mr. Brown is not the same person as Mr. Cope," the conclusion "Exactly two persons are in the office" may be validly inferred. But the stipulations laid down in Peano's system for the natural numbers, and for the number 2 in particular, do not enable us to draw this conclusion; they do not "implicitly determine" the customary meaning of the concept 2 or of the other arithmetical concepts. And the mathematician cannot acquiesce at this deficiency by arguing that he is not concerned with the customary meaning of the mathematical concepts; for in proving, say, that every positive real number has exactly two real square roots, he is himself using the concept 2 in its customary meaning, and his very theorem cannot be proved unless we presuppose more about the number 2 than is stipulated in the Peano system.

If therefore mathematics is to be a correct theory of the mathematical concepts in their intended meaning, it is not sufficient for its validation to have shown that the entire system is derivable from the Peano postulates plus suitable definitions; rather, we have to inquire further whether the Peano postulates are actually true when the primitives are understood in their customary meaning. This question, of course, can be answered only after the customary meaning of the terms "0," "natural number," and "successor" has been clearly defined. To this task we now turn.

8. DEFINITION OF THE CUSTOMARY MEANING OF THE CONCEPTS OF ARITHMETIC IN PURELY LOGICAL TERMS

At first blush, it might seem a hopeless undertaking to try to define these basic arithmetical concepts without presupposing other terms of arithmetic, which would involve us in a circular procedure. However, quite rigorous definitions of the desired kind can indeed be formulated, and it can be shown that for the concepts so defined, all Peano postulates turn into true statements. This important result is due to the research of the German logician G. Frege (1848–1925) and to the subsequent systematic and detailed work of the contemporary English logicians and philosophers B. Russell and A. N. Whitehead. Let us consider briefly the basic ideas underlying these definitions.[8]

A natural number—or, in Peano's term, a number—in its customary

---

[8] For a more detailed discussion, cf. Russell, loc. cit., Chs. II, III, IV. A complete technical development of the idea can be found in the great standard work in mathematical logic, A. N. Whitehead and B. Russell, *Principia Mathematica*, Cambridge, England, 1910–1913.—For a very precise recent development of the theory, see W. V. O. Quine, *Mathematical Logic*, New York, 1940.—A specific discussion of the Peano system and its interpretations from the viewpoint of semantics is included in R. Carnap, *Foundations of Logic and Mathematics*, International Encyclopedia of Unified Science, vol. I, no. 3, Chicago, 1939; especially sections 14, 17, 18.

meaning can be considered as a characteristic of certain *classes* of objects. Thus, e.g., the class of the apostles has the number 12, the class of the Dionne quintuplets the number 5, any couple the number 2, and so on. Let us now express precisely the meaning of the assertion that a certain class C has the number 2, or briefly, that $n(C) = 2$. Brief reflection will show that the following definiens is adequate in the sense of the customary meaning of the concept 2: There is some object x and some object y such that (1) $x \in C$ (i.e., x is an element of C) and $y \in C$, (2) $x \neq y$, and (3) if z is any object such that $z \in C$, then either $z = x$ or $z = y$. (Note that on the basis of this definition it becomes indeed possible to infer the statement "The number of persons in the office is 2" from "Mr. Brown as well as Mr. Cope, but no one else is in the office, and Mr. Brown is not identical with Mr. Cope"; C is here the class of persons in the office.) Analogously, the meaning of the statement that $n(C) = 1$ can be defined thus: There is some x such that $x \in C$, and any object y such that $y \in C$, is identical with x. Similarly, the customary meaning of the statement that $n(C) = 0$ is this: There is no object such that $x \in C$.

The general pattern of these definitions clearly lends itself to the definition of any natural number. Let us note especially that in the definitions thus obtained, the definiens never contains any arithmetical term, but merely expressions taken from the field of formal logic, including the signs of identity and difference. So far, we have defined only the meaning of such phrases as "$n(C) = 2$," but we have given no definition for the numbers 0, 1, 2, ... apart from this context. This desideratum can be met on the basis of the consideration that 2 is that property which is common to all couples, i.e., to all classes C such that $n(C) = 2$. This common property may be conceptually represented by the class of all those classes which share this property. Thus we arrive at the definition: 2 is the class of all couples, i.e., the class of all classes C for which $n(C) = 2$.—This definition is by no means circular because the concept of couple—in other words, the meaning of "$n(C) = 2$"—has been previously defined without any reference to the number 2. Analogously, 1 is the class of all unit classes, i.e., the class of all classes C for which $n(C) = 1$. Finally, 0 is the class of all null classes, i.e., the class of all classes without elements. And as there is only one such class, 0 is simply the class whose only element is the null class. Clearly, the customary meaning of any given natural number can be defined in this fashion.[9] In order to characterize the intended interpreta-

---

[9] The assertion that the definitions given above state the "customary" meaning of the arithmetical terms involved is to be understood in the logical, not the psychological sense of the term "meaning." It would obviously be absurd to claim that the above definitions express "what everybody has in mind" when talking about numbers and the various operations that can be performed with them. What is achieved by those definitions is rather a "logical reconstruction" of the concepts of arithmetic in the sense that if the definitions are accepted, then those statements in science and everyday discourse which involve arithmetical terms can be interpreted coherently and systematically in such a manner that they are capable of objective validation. The statement about the two persons in the office provides a very elementary illustration of what is meant here.

tion of Peano's primitives, we actually need, of all the definitions here referred to, only that of the number 0. It remains to define the terms "successor" and "integer."

The definition of "successor," whose precise formulation involves too many niceties to be stated here, is a careful expression of a simple idea which is illustrated by the following example: Consider the number 5, i.e., the class of all quintuplets. Let us select an arbitrary one of these quintuplets and add to it an object which is not yet one of its members. 5′, the successor of 5, may then be defined as the number applying to the set thus obtained (which, of course, is a sextuplet). Finally, it is possible to formulate a definition of the customary meaning of the concept of natural number; this definition, which again cannot be given here, expresses, in a rigorous form, the idea that the class of the natural numbers consists of the number 0, its successor, the successor of that successor, and so on.

If the definitions here characterized are carefully written out—this is one of the cases where the techniques of symbolic, or mathematical, logic prove indispensable—it is seen that the definiens of every one of them contains exclusively terms from the field of pure logic. In fact, it is possible to state the customary interpretation of Peano's primitives, and thus also the meaning of every concept definable by means of them—and that includes every concept of mathematics—in terms of the following 7 expressions, in addition to variables such as "x" and "C": *not, and, if—then; for every object x it is the case that* ...; *there is some object x such that* ...; x *is an element* of class C; *the class of all things x such that*. ... And it is even possible to reduce the number of logical concepts needed to a mere four: The first three of the concepts just mentioned are all definable in terms of "*neither—nor*," and the fifth is definable by means of the fourth and "*neither—nor*," Thus, all the concepts of mathematics prove definable in terms of four concepts of pure logic. (The definition of one of the more complex concepts of mathematics in terms of the four primitives just mentioned may well fill hundreds or even thousands of pages; but clearly this affects in no way the theoretical importance of the result just obtained; it does, however, show the great convenience and indeed practical indispensability for mathematics of having a large system of highly complex defined concepts available.)

9. THE TRUTH OF PEANO'S POSTULATES IN THEIR CUSTOMARY INTERPRETATION

The definitions characterized in the preceding section may be said to render precise and explicit the customary meaning of the concepts of arithmetic. Moreover—and this is crucial for the question of the validity of mathematics—it can be shown that the Peano postulates all turn into true propositions if the primitives are construed in accordance with the definitions just considered.

Thus, P1 (0 is a number) is true because the class of all numbers—i.e., natural numbers—was defined as consisting of 0 and all its successors. The truth of P2 (The successor of any number is a number) follows from the same definition. This is true also of P5, the principle of mathematical induction. To prove this, however, we would have to resort to the precise definition of "integer" rather than the loose description given of that definition above. P4 (0 is not the successor of any number) is seen to be true as follows: By virtue of the definition of "successor," a number which is a successor of some number can apply only to classes which contain at least one element; but the number 0, by definition, applies to a class if and only if that class is empty.— While the truth of P1, P2, P4, P5 can be inferred from the above definitions simply by means of the principles of logic, the proof of P3 (No two numbers have the same successor) presents a certain difficulty. As was mentioned in the preceding section, the definition of the successor of a number n is based on the process of adding, to a class of n elements, one element not yet contained in that class. Now if there should exist only a finite number of things altogether then this process could not be continued indefinitely, and P3, which (in conjunction with P1 and P2) implies that the integers form an infinite set, would be false. Russell's way of meeting this difficulty[10] was to introduce a special "axiom of infinity," which stipulates, in effect, the existence of infinitely many objects and thus makes P3 demonstrable. The axiom of infinity does not belong to the generally recognized laws of logic; but it is capable of expression in purely logical terms and may be treated as an additional postulate of logic.

10. MATHEMATICS AS A BRANCH OF LOGIC

As was pointed out earlier, all the theorems of arithmetic, algebra, and analysis can be deduced from the Peano postulates and the definitions of those mathematical terms which are not primitives in Peano's system. This deduction requires only the principles of logic plus, in certain cases, the axiom of choice, which asserts that for any set of mutually exclusive non-empty sets $\alpha, \beta, \ldots$, there exists at least one set which contains exactly one element from each of the sets $\alpha, \beta, \ldots$, and which contains no other elements.[11] By combining this result with what has just been said about the Peano system, the following conclusion is obtained, which is also known as *the thesis of logicism concerning the nature of mathematics*:

[10] Cf. Bertrand Russell, loc. cit., p. 24 and Ch. XIII.

[11] This only apparently self-evident postulate is used in proving certain theorems of set theory and of real and complex analysis; for a discussion of its significance and of its problematic aspects, see Russell, loc. cit., Ch. XII (where it is called the multiplicative axiom), and A. Fraenkel, *Einleitung in die Mengenlehre*, Dover Publications, New York, 1946, §16, sections 7 and 8.

Mathematics is a branch of logic. It can be derived from logic in the following sense:

a. All the concepts of mathematics, i.e. of arithmetic, algebra, and analysis, can be defined in terms of four concepts of pure logic.

b. All the theorems of mathematics can be deduced from those definitions by means of the principles of logic (including the axioms of infinity and choice).[12]

In this sense it can be said that the propositions of the system of mathematics as here delimited are true by virtue of the definitions of the mathematical concepts involved, or that they make explicit certain characteristics with which we have endowed our mathematical concepts by definition. The propositions of mathematics have, therefore, the same unquestionable certainty which is typical of such propositions as "All bachelors are unmarried," but they also share the complete lack of empirical content which is associated with that certainty: The propositions of mathematics are devoid of all factual content; they convey no information whatever on any empirical subject matter.

11. ON THE APPLICABILITY OF MATHEMATICS TO EMPIRICAL SUBJECT MATTER

This result seems to be irreconcilable with the fact that after all mathematics has proved to be eminently applicable to empirical subject matter, and that indeed the greater part of present-day scientific knowledge has been reached only through continual reliance on and application of the propositions of mathematics.—Let us try to clarify this apparent paradox by reference to some examples.

Suppose that we are examining a certain amount of some gas, whose volume v, at a certain fixed temperature, is found to be 9 cubic feet when the pressure p is 4 atmospheres. And let us assume further that the volume of the gas for the same temperature and $p = 6$ at., is predicted by means of Boyle's law. Using elementary arithmetic we reason thus: For corresponding values of v and p, $vp = c$, and $v = 9$ when $p = 4$; hence $c = 36$: Therefore, when $p = 6$, then $v = 6$. Suppose that this prediction is borne out by subsequent test. Does that show that the arithmetic used has a predictive power of its own, that its propositions have factual implications? Certainly not. All the

---

[12] The principles of logic developed in Quine's work and in similar modern systems of formal logic embody certain restrictions as compared with those logical rules which had been rather generally accepted as sound until about the turn of the 20th century. At that time, the discovery of the famous paradoxes of logic, especially of Russell's paradox (cf. Russell, loc. cit., Ch. XIII) revealed the fact that the logical principles implicit in customary mathematical reasoning involved contradictions and therefore had to be curtailed in one manner or another.

predictive power here deployed, all the empirical content exhibited stems from the initial data and from Boyle's law, which asserts that $vp = c$ for *any* two corresponding values of v and p, hence also for $v = 9$, $p = 4$, and for $p = 6$ and the corresponding value of v.[13] The function of the mathematics here applied is not predictive at all; rather, it is analytic or explicative: it renders explicit certain assumptions or assertions which are included in the content of the premises of the argument (in our case, these consist of Boyle's law plus the additional data); mathematical reasoning reveals that those premises contain—hidden in them, as it were,—an assertion about the case as yet unobserved. In accepting our premises—so arithmetic reveals—we have—knowingly or unknowingly—already accepted the implication that the p-value in question is 6. Mathematical as well as logical reasoning is a conceptual technique of making explicit what is implicitly contained in a set of premises. The conclusions to which this technique leads assert nothing that is *theoretically new* in the sense of not being contained in the content of the premises. But the results obtained may well be *psychologically new*: we may not have been aware, before using the techniques of logic and mathematics, what we committed ourselves to in accepting a certain set of assumptions or assertions.

A similar analysis is possible in all other cases of applied mathematics, including those involving, say, the calculus. Consider, for example, the hypothesis that a certain object, moving in a specified electric field, will undergo a constant acceleration of 5 feet/sec². For the purpose of testing this hypothesis, we might derive from it, by means of two successive integrations, the prediction that if the object is at rest at the beginning of the motion, then the distance covered by it at any time t is $\frac{5}{2}t^2$ feet. This conclusion may clearly be psychologically new to a person not acquainted with the subject, but it is not theoretically new; the content of the conclusion is already contained in that of the hypothesis about the constant acceleration. And indeed, here as well as in the case of the compression of a gas, a failure of the prediction to come true would be considered as indicative of the factual incorrectness of at least one of the premises involved (*f.ex.*, of Boyle's law in its application to the particular gas), but never as a sign that the logical and mathematical principles involved might be unsound.

Thus, in the establishment of empirical knowledge, mathematics (as well as logic) has, so to speak, the function of a theoretical juice extractor: the techniques of mathematical and logical theory can produce no more juice of factual information than is contained in the assumptions to which they are applied; but they may produce a great deal more juice of this kind than might have been anticipated upon a first intuitive inspection of those assumptions which form the raw material for the extractor.

---

[13] Note that we may say "hence" by virtue of the rule of substitution, which is one of the rules of logical inference.

At this point, it may be well to consider briefly the status of those mathematical disciplines which are not outgrowths of arithmetic and thus of logic; these include in particular topology, geometry, and the various branches of abstract algebra, such as the theory of groups, lattices, fields, etc. Each of these disciplines can be developed as a purely deductive system on the basis of a suitable set of postulates. If P be the conjunction of the postulates for a given theory, then the proof of a proposition T of that theory consists in deducing T from P by means of the principles of formal logic. What is established by the proof is therefore not the truth of T, but rather the fact that T is true provided that the postulates are. But since both P and T contain certain primitive terms of the theory, to which no specific meaning is assigned, it is not strictly possible to speak of the truth of either P or T; it is therefore more adequate to state the point as follows: If a proposition T is logically deduced from P, then every specific interpretation of the primitives which turns all the postulates of P into true statements, will also render T a true statement.—Up to this point, the analysis is exactly analogous to that of arithmetic as based on Peano's set of postulates. In the case of arithmetic, however, it proved possible to go a step further, namely to define the customary meanings of the primitives in terms of purely logical concepts and to show that the postulates—and therefore also the theorems—of arithmetic are unconditionally true by virtue of these definitions. An analogous procedure is not applicable to those disciplines which are not outgrowths of arithmetic: The primitives of the various branches of abstract algebra have no specific "customary meaning"; and if geometry in its customary interpretation is thought of as a theory of the structure of physical space, then its primitives have to be construed as referring to certain types of physical entities, and the question of the truth of a geometrical theory in this interpretation turns into an *empirical* problem.[14] For the purpose of applying any one of these nonarithmetical disciplines to some specific field of mathematics or empirical science, it is therefore necessary first to assign to the primitives some specific meaning and then to ascertain whether in this interpretation the postulates turn into true statements. If this is the case, then we can be sure that all the theorems are true statements too, because they are logically derived from the postulates and thus simply explicate the content of the latter in the given interpretation.—In their application to empirical subject matter, therefore, these mathematical theories no less than those which grow out of arithmetic and ultimately out of pure logic, have the function of an analytic tool, which brings to light the implications of a given set of assumptions but adds nothing to their content.

But while mathematics in no case contributes anything to the content of our knowledge of empirical matters, it is entirely indispensable as an instrument for the validation and even for the linguistic expression of such knowledge: The majority of the more far-reaching theories in empirical science—including those which lend themselves most eminently to prediction or to

[14] For a more detailed discussion of this point, cf. the article mentioned in footnote 1.

practical application—are stated with the help of mathematical concepts; the formulation of these theories makes use, in particular, of the number system, and of functional relationships among different metrical variables. Furthermore, the scientific test of these theories, the establishment of predictions by means of them, and finally their practical application, all require the deduction, from the general theory, of certain specific consequences; and such deduction would be entirely impossible without the techniques of mathematics which reveal what the given general theory implicitly asserts about a certain special case.

Thus, the analysis outlined on these pages exhibits the system of mathematics as a vast and ingenious conceptual structure without empirical content and yet an indispensable and powerful theoretical instrument for the scientific understanding and mastery of the world of our experience.

ON THE NATURE OF MATHEMATICAL REASONING

Henri Poincaré

I

The very possibility of mathematical science seems an insoluble contradiction. If this science is only deductive in appearance, from whence is derived that perfect rigour which is challenged by none? If, on the contrary, all the propositions which it enunciates may be derived in order by the rules of formal logic, how is it that mathematics is not reduced to a gigantic tautology? The syllogism can teach us nothing essentially new, and if everything must spring from the principle of identity, then everything should be capable of being reduced to that principle. Are we then to admit that the enunciations of all the theorems with which so many volumes are filled are only indirect ways of saying that A is A?

No doubt we may refer back to axioms which are at the source of all these reasonings. If it is felt that they cannot be reduced to the principle of contradiction, if we decline to see in them any more than experimental facts which have no part or lot in mathematical necessity, there is still one resource left to us: we may class them among *a priori* synthetic views. But this is no solution of the difficulty—it is merely giving it a name; and even if the nature of the synthetic views had no longer for us any mystery, the contradiction would not have disappeared; it would have only been shirked. Syllogistic reasoning remains incapable of adding anything to the data that are given it; the data are reduced to axioms, and that is all we should find in the conclusions.

No theorem can be new unless a new axiom intervenes in its demonstration; reasoning can only give us immediately evident truths borrowed from direct intuition; it would only be an intermediary parasite. Should we not

Excerpted and reprinted with the kind permission of the publisher from Henri Poincaré, Science and Hypothesis (*New York: Dover Publications, Inc.*), *pp. 1–19.*

therefore have reason for asking if the syllogistic apparatus serves only to disguise what we have borrowed?

The contradiction will strike us the more if we open any book on mathematics; on every page the author announces his intention of generalizing some proposition already known. Does the mathematical method proceed from the particular to the general, and, if so, how can it be called deductive?

Finally, if the science of number were merely analytical, or could be analytically derived from a few synthetic intuitions, it seems that a sufficiently powerful mind could with a single glance perceive all its truths; nay, one might even hope that some day a language would be invented simple enough for these truths to be made evident to any person of ordinary intelligence.

Even if these consequences are challenged, it must be granted that mathematical reasoning has of itself a kind of creative virtue, and is therefore to be distinguished from the syllogism. The difference must be profound. We shall not, for instance, find the key to the mystery in the frequent use of the rule by which the same uniform operation applied to two equal numbers will give identical results. All these modes of reasoning, whether or not reducible to the syllogism, properly so called, retain the analytical character, and *ipso facto*, lose their power.

II

The argument is an old one. Let us see how Leibnitz tried to show that two and two make four. I assume the number one to be defined, and also the operation $x + 1$—i.e., the adding of unity to a given number x. These definitions, whatever they may be, do not enter into the subsequent reasoning. I next define the numbers 2, 3, 4 by the equalities:—

$$(1) \quad 1 + 1 = 2; \qquad (2) \quad 2 + 1 = 3; \qquad (3) \quad 3 + 1 = 4,$$

and in the same way I define the operation $x + 2$ by the relation;

$$(4) \quad x + 2 = (x + 1) + 1.$$

Given this, we have:—

$$2 + 2 = (2 + 1) + 1; \text{ (def. 4).}$$
$$(2 + 1) + 1 = 3 + 1 \qquad \text{(def. 2).}$$
$$3 + 1 = 4 \qquad \text{(def. 3).}$$

whence $\qquad\qquad 2 + 2 = 4 \qquad\qquad\qquad$ Q.E.D.

It cannot be denied that this reasoning is purely analytical. But if we ask a mathematician, he will reply: "This is not a demonstration properly so called; it is a verification." We have confined ourselves to bringing together one or other of two purely conventional definitions, and we have verified their identity; nothing new has been learned. *Verification* differs from proof precisely because it is analytical, and because it leads to nothing. It leads to nothing because the conclusion is nothing but the premises translated into another language. A real proof, on the other hand, is fruitful, because the conclusion is in a sense more general than the premisses. The equality $2 + 2$ $= 4$ can be verified because it is particular. Each individual enunciation in mathematics may be always verified in the same way. But if mathematics could be reduced to a series of such verifications it would not be a science. A chess-player, for instance, does not create a science by winning a piece. There is no science but the science of the general. It may even be said that the object of the exact sciences is to dispense with these direct verifications.

III

Let us now see the geometer at work, and try to surprise some of his methods. The task is not without difficulty; it is not enough to open a book at random and to analyse any proof we may come across. First of all, geometry must be excluded, or the question becomes complicated by difficult problems relating to the rôle of the postulates, the nature and the origin of the idea of space. For analogous reasons we cannot avail ourselves of the infinitesimal calculus. We must seek mathematical thought where it has remained pure—i.e., in Arithmetic. But we still have to choose; in the higher parts of the theory of numbers the primitive mathematical ideas have already undergone so profound an elaboration that it becomes difficult to analyse them.

It is therefore at the beginning of Arithmetic that we must expect to find the explanation we seek; but it happens that it is precisely in the proofs of the most elementary theorems that the authors of classic treatises have displayed the least precision and rigour. We may not impute this to them as a crime; they have obeyed a necessity. Beginners are not prepared for real mathematical rigour; they would see in it nothing but empty, tedious subtleties. It would be waste of time to try to make them more exacting; they have to pass rapidly and without stopping over the road which was trodden slowly by the founders of the science.

Why is so long a preparation necessary to habituate oneself to this perfect rigour, which it would seem should naturally be imposed on all minds? This is a logical and psychological problem which is well worthy of study. But we shall not dwell on it; it is foreign to our subject. All I wish to insist on is, that we shall fail in our purpose unless we reconstruct the proofs of the elementary theorems, and give them, not the rough form in which they are left so as not to weary the beginner, but the form which will satisfy the skilled geometer.

DEFINITION OF ADDITION

I assume that the operation $x + 1$ has been defined; it consists in adding the number 1 to a given number x. Whatever may be said of this definition, it does not enter into the subsequent reasoning.

We now have to define the operation $x + a$, which consists in adding the number a to any given number x. Suppose that we have defined the operation $x + (a - 1)$; the operation $x + a$ will be defined by the equality: (1) $x + a = [x + (a - 1)] + 1$. We shall know what $x + a$ is when we know what $x + (a - 1)$ is, and as I have assumed that to start with we know what $x + 1$ is, we can define successively and "by recurrence" the operations $x + 2$, $x + 3$, etc. This definition deserves a moment's attention; it is of a particular nature which distinguishes it even at this stage from the purely logical definition; the equality (1), in fact, contains an infinite number of distinct definitions, each having only one meaning when we know the meaning of its predecessor.

PROPERTIES OF ADDITION

Associative.—I say that $a + (b + c) = (a + b) + c$; in fact, the theorem is true for $c = 1$. It may then be written $a + (b + 1) = (a + b) + 1$; which, remembering the difference of notation, is nothing but the equality (1) by which I have just defined addition. Assume the theorem true for $c = \gamma$, I say that it will be true for $c = \gamma + 1$. Let $(a + b) + \gamma = a + (b + \gamma)$, it follows that $[(a + b) + \gamma] + 1 = [a + (b + \gamma)] + 1$; or by def. (1)—$(a + b) + (\gamma + 1) = a + (b + \gamma + 1) = a + [b + (\gamma + 1)]$, which shows by a series of purely analytical deductions that the theorem is true for $\gamma + 1$. Being true for $c = 1$, we see that it is successively true for $c = 2$, $c = 3$, etc.

Commutative.—(1) I say that $a + 1 = 1 + a$. The theorem is evidently true for $a = 1$; we can *verify* by purely analytical reasoning that if it is true for $a = \gamma$ it will be true for $a = \gamma + 1$.[1] Now, it is true for $a = 1$, and therefore is true for $a = 2$, $a = 3$, and so on. This is what is meant by saying that the proof is demonstrated "by recurrence."

(2) I say that $a + b = b + a$. The theorem has just been shown to hold good for $b = 1$, and it may be verified analytically that if it is true for $b = \beta$, it will be true for $b = \beta + 1$. The proposition is thus established by recurrence.

DEFINITION OF MULTIPLICATION

We shall define multiplication by the equalities: (1) $a \times 1 = a$. (2) $a \times b = [a \times (b - 1)] + a$. Both of these include an infinite number of definitions; having defined $a \times 1$, it enables us to define in succession $a \times 2$, $a \times 3$, and so on.

PROPERTIES OF MULTIPLICATION

Distributive.—I say that $(a + b) \times c = (a \times c) + (b \times c)$. We can verify analytically that the theorem is true for $c = 1$; then if it is true for $c = \gamma$, it will be true for $c = \gamma + 1$. The proposition is then proved by recurrence.

[1] For $(\gamma + 1) + 1 = (1 + \gamma) + 1 = 1 + (\gamma + 1)$.—[Tr.]

Commutative.—(1) I say that $a \times 1 = 1 \times a$. The theorem is obvious for $a = 1$. We can verify analytically that if it is true for $a = a$, it will be true for $a = \alpha + 1$.

(2) I say that $a \times b = b \times a$. The theorem has just been proved for $b = 1$. We can verify analytically that if it be true for $b = \beta$ it will be true for $b = \beta + 1$.

IV

This monotonous series of reasonings may now be laid aside; but their very monotony brings vividly to light the process, which is uniform, and is met again at every step. The process is proof by recurrence. We first show that a theorem is true for $n = 1$; we then show that if it is true for $n - 1$ it is true for n, and we conclude that it is true for all integers. We have now seen how it may be used for the proof of the rules of addition and multiplication— that is to say, for the rules of the algebraical calculus. This calculus is an instrument of transformation which lends itself to many more different combinations than the simple syllogism; but it is still a purely analytical instrument, and is incapable of teaching us anything new. If mathematics had no other instrument, it would immediately be arrested in its development; but it has recourse anew to the same process—i.e., to reasoning by recurrence, and it can continue its forward march. Then if we look carefully, we find this mode of reasoning at every step, either under the simple form which we have just given to it, or under a more or less modified form. It is therefore mathematical reasoning *par excellence*, and we must examine it closer.

V

The essential characteristic of reasoning by recurrence is that it contains, condensed, so to speak, in a single formula, an infinite number of syllogisms. We shall see this more clearly if we enunciate the syllogisms one after another. They follow one another, if one may use the expression, in a cascade. The following are the hypothetical syllogisms:—The theorem is true of the number 1. Now, if it is true of 1, it is true of 2; therefore it is true of 2. Now, if it is true of 2, it is true of 3; hence it is true of 3, and so on. We see that the conclusion of each syllogism serves as the minor of its successor. Further, the majors of all our syllogisms may be reduced to a single form. If the theorem is true of $n - 1$, it is true of n.

We see, then, that in reasoning by recurrence we confine ourselves to the enunciation of the minor of the first syllogism, and the general formula which contains as particular cases all the majors. This unending series of syllogisms is thus reduced to a phrase of a few lines.

It is now easy to understand why every particular consequence of a theorem may, as I have above explained, be verified by purely analytical processes. If, instead of proving that our theorem is true for all numbers, we only wish to show that it is true for the number 6 for instance, it will be enough to establish the first five syllogisms in our cascade. We shall require 9 if we wish to prove it for the number 10; for a greater number we shall require more still; but however great the number may be we shall always reach it, and the analytical verification will always be possible. But however far we went we should never reach the general theorem applicable to all numbers, which alone is the object of science. To reach it we should require an infinite number of syllogisms, and we should have to cross an abyss which the patience of the analyst, restricted to the resources of formal logic, will never succeed in crossing.

I asked at the outset why we cannot conceive of a mind powerful enough to see at a glance the whole body of mathematical truth. The answer is now easy. A chess-player can combine for four or five moves ahead; but, however extraordinary a player he may be, he cannot prepare for more than a finite number of moves. If he applies his faculties to Arithmetic, he cannot conceive its general truths by direct intuition alone; to prove even the smallest theorem he must use reasoning by recurrence, for that is the only instrument which enables us to pass from the finite to the infinite. This instrument is always useful, for it enables us to leap over as many stages as we wish; it frees us from the necessity of long, tedious, and monotonous verifications which would rapidly become impracticable. Then when we take in hand the general theorem it becomes indispensable, for otherwise we should ever be approaching the analytical verification without ever actually reaching it. In this domain of Arithmetic we may think ourselves very far from the infinitesimal analysis, but the idea of mathematical infinity is already playing a preponderating part, and without it there would be no science at all, because there would be nothing general.

VI

The views upon which reasoning by recurrence is based may be exhibited in other forms; we may say, for instance, that in any finite collection of different integers there is always one which is smaller than any other. We may readily pass from one enunciation to another, and thus give ourselves the illusion of having proved that reasoning by recurrence is legitimate. But we shall always be brought to a full stop—we shall always come to an indemonstrable axiom, which will at bottom be but the proposition we had to prove translated into another language. We cannot therefore escape the conclusion that the rule of reasoning by recurrence is irreducible to the principle of contradiction. Nor can the rule come to us from experiment. Experiment may teach us that the rule is true for the first ten or the first hundred numbers, for instance; it will not bring us to the indefinite series of numbers, but only to a more or less long, but always limited, portion of the series.

Now, if that were all that is in question, the principle of contradiction would be sufficient, it would always enable us to develop as many syllogisms as we wished. It is only when it is a question of a single formula to embrace an infinite number of syllogisms that this principle breaks down, and there, too, experiment is powerless to aid. This rule, inaccessible to analytical proof and to experiment, is the exact type of the *a priori* synthetic intuition. On the other hand, we cannot see in it a convention as in the case of the postulates of geometry.

Why then is this view imposed upon us with such an irresistable weight of evidence? It is because it is only the affirmation of the power of the mind which knows it can conceive of the indefinite repetition of the same act, when the act is once possible. The mind has a direct intuition of this power, and experiment can only be for it an opportunity of using it, and thereby of becoming conscious of it.

But it will be said, if the legitimacy of reasoning by recurrence cannot be established by experiment alone, it is so with experiment aided by induction? We see successively that a theorem is true of the number 1, of the number 2, of the number 3, and so on—the law is manifest, we say, and it is so on the same ground that every physical law is true which is based on a very large but limited number of observations.

It cannot escape our notice that here is a striking analogy with the usual processes of induction. But an essential difference exists. Induction applied to the physical sciences is always uncertain, because it is based on the belief in a general order of the universe, an order which is external to us. Mathematical induction—i.e., proof by recurrence—is, on the contrary, necessarily imposed on us, because it is only the affirmation of a property of the mind itself.

VII

Mathematicians, as I have said before, always endeavour to generalize the propositions they have obtained. To seek no further example, we have just shown the equality, $a + 1 = 1 + a$, and we then used it to establish the equality, $a + b = b + a$, which is obviously more general. Mathematics may, therefore, like the other sciences, proceed from the particular to the general. This is a fact which might otherwise have appeared incomprehensible to us at the beginning of this study, but which has no longer anything mysterious about it, since we have ascertained the analogies between proof by recurrence and ordinary induction.

No doubt mathematical recurrent reasoning and physical inductive reasoning are based on different foundations, but they move in parallel lines and in the same direction—namely, from the particular to the general.

Let us examine the case a little more closely. To prove the equality $a + 2 = 2 + a \ldots (1)$, we need only apply the rule $a + 1 = 1 + a$, twice, and write $a + 2 = a + 1 + 1 = 1 + a + 1 = 1 + 1 + a = 2 + a \ldots (2)$.

The equality thus deduced by purely analytical means is not, however, a simple particular case. It is something quite different. We may not therefore even say in the really analytical and deductive part of mathematical reasoning that we proceed from the general to the particular in the ordinary sense of the words. The two sides of the equality (2) are merely more complicated combinations than the two sides of the equality (1), and analysis only serves to separate the elements which enter into these combinations and to study their relations.

Mathematicians therefore proceed "by construction," they "construct" more complicated combinations. When they analyze these combinations, these aggregates, so to speak, into their primitive elements, they see the relations of the elements and deduce the relations of the aggregates themselves. The process is purely analytical, but it is not a passing from the general to the particular, for the aggregates obviously cannot be regarded as more particular than their elements.

Great importance has been rightly attached to this process of "construction," and some claim to see in it the necessary and sufficient condition of the progress of the exact sciences. Necessary, no doubt, but not sufficient! For a construction to be useful and not mere waste of mental effort, for it to serve as a stepping-stone to higher things, it must first of all possess a kind of unity enabling us to see something more than the juxtaposition of its elements. Or more accurately, there must be some advantage in considering the construction rather than the elements themselves. What can this advantage be? Why reason on a polygon, for instance, which is always decomposable into triangles, and not on elementary triangles? It is because there are properties of polygons of any number of sides, and they can be immediately applied to any particular kind of polygon. In most cases it is only after long efforts that those properties can be discovered, by directly studying the relations of elementary triangles. If the quadrilateral is anything more than the juxtaposition of two triangles, it is because it is of the polygon type.

A construction only becomes interesting when it can be placed side by side with other analogous constructions for forming species of the same genus. To do this we must necessarily go back from the particular to the general, ascending one or more steps. The analytical process "by construction" does not compel us to descend, but it leaves us at the same level. We can only ascend by mathematical induction, for from it alone we can learn something new. Without the aid of this induction, which in certain respects differs from, but is as fruitful as, physical induction, construction would be powerless to create science.

Let me observe, in conclusion, that this induction is only possible if the same operation can be repeated indefinitely. That is why the theory of chess can never become a science, for the different moves of the same piece are limited and do not resemble each other.

MATHEMATICS AND THE WORLD[1]

D. A. T. Gasking

My object is to try to elucidate the nature of mathematical propositions, and to explain their relation to the everyday world of counting and measurement—of clocks, and yards of material, and income-tax forms. I should like to be able to summarize my views in a few short phrases, and then go on to defend them. Unfortunately I cannot do this, for as I shall try to demonstrate, I do not think any short statement will do to express the truth of the matter with any precision. So I shall proceed by approximations—I shall discuss several different views in the hope that in showing wnat is right and what is wrong with them, clarification will come about.

The opinions of philosophers about the nature of mathematical propositions can be divided, as can their opinions about so many things, into two main classes. There are those who try to analyze mathematical propositions away—who say that they are *really* something else (like those writers on ethics who say that goodness is really only pleasure, or those metaphysicians who say that chairs and tables are really groups of sensations, or colonies of souls). I shall call such "analyzing-away" theories "radical" theories. On the other hand there are those who insist that mathematical propositions are *sui generis*, that they cannot be analyzed into anything else, that they give information about an aspect of reality totally different from any other (compare those philosophers who maintain, e.g., that goodness is a simple unanalyzable quality, or those realists who maintain that a chair is a chair, an external material substance, known, perhaps, by means of sensations, but not to be confused with those sensations). For convenience, I shall call these

[1] A paper read at the Annual Congress of the Australasian Association of Psychology and Philosophy in Sydney University on Thursday, 15th August, 1940.

Reprinted with the kind permission of the author and editor from The Australasian Journal of of Philosophy, 18, *no.* 2 (*September*, 1940), 97–116.

types of theory which oppose any analyzing-away, "conservative". I should maintain that in general what I call "conservative" opinions in philosophy are perfectly correct, but rather unsatisfactory and unilluminating, whereas opinions of the "radical" type are untrue, but interesting and illuminating.

I shall start by considering the "radical" theories about the nature of mathematics. Those I know of fall into two main types. (1) Some people maintain that a proposition of mathematics is *really* a particularly well-founded empirical generalization of a certain type, or that it is logically on the same footing as a very well-established scientific law. Mill's theory was of this type, and many scientists I have talked to have tended to have similar opinions. Let us call these "empirical" theories about mathematics. (2) Then, on the other hand, there is a great variety of theories usually called "conventionalist", which analyze away mathematical propositions into propositions about the use of symbols. Examples: "By a mathematical proposition the speaker or writer merely expresses his intention of manipulating symbols in a certain way, and recommends or commands that others should do likewise." "A mathematical proposition is really an empirical proposition describing how educated people commonly use certain symbols." "A mathematical proposition is really a rule for the manipulation of symbols." (Ayer, for example, and C. I. Lewis have expressed opinions of this general type.)

First, for the "empirical" theories. According to these a mathematical proposition just expresses a particularly well-founded empirical generalization or law about the properties and behavior of objects, obtained by examining a large number of instances and seeing that they conform without exception to a single general pattern. The proposition "$7 + 5 = 12$", for instance, just expresses (on one version of this theory) the fact of experience that if we count up seven objects of any sort, and then five more objects, and then count up the whole lot, we always get the number twelve. Or again, it might be maintained that the geometrical proposition "equilateral triangles are equiangular" just expresses the fact that wherever, by measurement, we find the sides of a triangle to be equal, we will find, on measuring the angles with the same degree of accuracy, that the angles are equal too. It is contended that such propositions are essentially like, for example, Boyle's Law of gases, only much better founded.

But "$7 + 5 = 12$" does not mean the same as the proposition about what you get on counting groups. For it is true that $7 + 5$ does equal 12, but it is not true that on counting seven objects and then five others, and then counting the whole, you will always get twelve. People sometimes miscount, and sometimes the objects counted melt away (if they are wax) or coalesce (if they are globules of mercury). Similarly the geometrical proposition that equilateral triangles are equiangular does not mean the same as the proposition that any triangle which is equilateral by measurement will be found to be equiangular when measured. The former is true; the latter false. We sometimes make mistakes with our rulers and protractors.

To this it might be objected that this shows that the empirical proposition offered as a translation of the mathematical one is not a correct translation, but that it has not been demonstrated that it is impossible to find an empirical proposition about counting and measurement, which is a correct translation. Let us try some alternatives, then. It might be suggested that "7 + 5 = 12" means "If you count *carefully and with attention*, you will get such and such a result." But, even with the greatest care in counting, mistakes sometimes happen, at any rate with large numbers. Shall we then say: "7 + 5 = 12" means "If you count *correctly* you will get such and such results"? But, in the first place, even if you count objects correctly, you do not always get a group of seven objects and a group of five adding up to twelve. It sometimes happens that a person correctly counts seven objects, then correctly counts five, and then correctly counts the total and gets eleven. Sometimes one of the objects does disappear in the course of counting, or coalesces with another. And even if this were not so, the suggested translation would not give you a simple empirical proposition about what happened when people counted, as a translation of 7 + 5 = 12, but would give you a mere tautology. For what is the criterion of correctness in counting? Surely that when you add seven and five you should get twelve. "Correctness" has no meaning, in this context, independent of the mathematical proposition. So our suggested analysis of the meaning of "7 + 5 = 12" runs, when suitably expanded: "7 + 5 = 12" means "If you count objects *correctly* (i.e. in such a way as to get 12 on adding 7 and 5) you will, on adding 7 to 5, get 12."

No doubt there *are* important connections between mathematical propositions, and propositions about what results people will usually get on counting and measuring. But it will not do to say that a mathematical proposition means the same as, or is equivalent to, any such empirical proposition, for this reason: A mathematical proposition is "incorrigible", whereas an empirical proposition is "corrigible".

The difference between "corrigible" and "incorrigible" propositions can best be explained by examples. Most everyday assertions that we make, such as that "Mr. Smith has gone away for the day", are corrigible. By this I mean simply that, whenever we make such an assertion, however strong our grounds for making it, we should always freely withdraw it and admit it to have been false, *if* certain things were to happen. Thus my assertion, that Smith is away for the day, is corrigible, because (although I may have the excellent grounds for making it that when I met him in the street this morning he said he was on his way to the railway-station) if, for example, I were to go to his room now and find him sitting there, I should withdraw my assertion that he was away and admit it to have been false. I should take certain events as proving, if they happened, that my assertion was untrue.

A mathematical proposition such as 7 + 5 = 12, on the other hand, is incorrigible, because no future happenings whatsoever would ever prove the proposition false, or cause anyone to withdraw it. You can imagine any sort of fantastic chain of events you like, but nothing you can think of would ever, if it happened, disprove $7 + 5 = 12$. Thus, if I counted out 7 matches, and then 5 more, and then on counting the whole lot, got 11, this would not have the slightest tendency to make anyone withdraw the proposition that $7 + 5 = 12$ and say it was untrue. And even if this constantly happened, both to me and to everyone else, and not only with matches, but with books, umbrellas and every sort of object—surely even this would not make us withdraw the proposition. Surely in such a case we should not say: "the proposition $7 + 5 = 12$ has been empirically disproved; it has been found that $7 + 5$ really equals 11." There are plenty of alternative explanations to choose from. We might try a psychological hypothesis, such as this: we might say that it had been discovered by experiment that everyone had a curious psychological kink, which led him, whenever he performed counting operations of a certain sort, always to miss out one of the objects in his final count (like the subject in some experiments on hypnosis who, under suggestion, fails to see any 't's' on a printed page). Or we might prefer a physical hypothesis and say: a curious physical law of the universe has been experimentally established, namely, that whenever 5 objects are added to 7 objects, this process of addition causes one of them to disappear, or to coalesce with another object. The one thing we should *never* say, whatever happened, would be that the proposition that $7 + 5 = 12$ had been experimentally disproved. If curious things happened, we should alter our physics, but not our mathematics.

This rather sweeping assertion that mathematical propositions are completely incorrigible is, I think, an over-simplification, and needs qualifying. I shall mention the qualifications later, rather than now, for simplicity of exposition. So if you will accept it for the moment as very nearly true, I should like to draw your attention to certain of its consequences. A *corrigible* proposition gives you some information about the world—a completely *incorrigible* proposition tells you nothing. A corrigible proposition is one that you would withdraw and admit to be false if certain things happened in the world. It therefore gives you the information that *those* things (i.e. those things which would make you withdraw your proposition *if* they happened) will *not* happen. An incorrigible proposition is one which you would never admit to be false *whatever* happens: it therefore does not tell you *what* happens. The truth, for example, of the corrigible proposition that Smith is away for the day, is compatible with certain things happening (e.g. your going to his room and finding it empty) and is not compatible with certain other happenings (e.g. your going to his room and finding him there). It therefore tells you what sort of thing will happen (you will find his room empty) and what sort of thing will not happen (you will not find him in). The truth of an incorrigible proposition, on the other hand, is compatible with any and every conceivable state of affairs. (For example: whatever is your experience on counting, it is still true that $7 + 5 = 12$.) It therefore does not tell you which events will take place and which will not. That is: the proposition "7 + 5 = 12" tells you nothing about the world.

If such a proposition tells you nothing about the world, what, then, is the point of it—what does it do? I think that in a sense it is true to say that it prescribes what you are to *say*—it tells you *how to describe* certain happenings. Thus the proposition "7 + 5 = 12" does not tell you that on counting 7 + 5 you will not get 11. (This, as we have seen, is false, for you sometimes do get 11.) But it does *lay it down*, so to speak, that *if* on counting 7 + 5 you do get 11, you are to describe what has happened in some such way as this: *Either* "I have made a mistake in my counting" *or* "Someone has played a practical joke and abstracted one of the objects when I was not looking" *or* "Two of the objects have coalesced" *or* "One of the objects has disappeared", etc.

This, I think, is the truth that is in the various "conventionalist" theories of mathematics. Only, unfortunately, the formulæ expressing such theories are usually misleading and incorrect. For example, to say that: "a mathematical proposition merely expresses the speaker's or writer's determination to use symbols in a certain way", is obviously untrue. For if it were true, and if I decided to use the symbol + in such a way that 5 + 7 = 35, I would then be speaking truly if I said "5 + 7 = 35". But this proposition is not true. The truth of any mathematical proposition does not depend on my decision or determination. It is independent of my will. This formula neglects the "public" or "over-individual" character of mathematics.

Or, consider the formula: "A mathematical proposition is really an empirical statement describing the way people commonly use certain symbols." This, I think, is nearer. But it is open to the following obvious objection: If "7 + 5 = 12" were really an assertion about the common usage of symbols, then it would follow that 7 + 5 would not equal 12 if people had a different symbolic convention. But even if people did use symbols in a way quite different from the present one, the fact which we now express by "7 + 5 = 12" would still be true. No change in our language-habits would ever make this false.

This objection is, I think, sufficient to show that the suggested formula is untrue, as it stands. But we should be blind to its merits if we did not see *why* it is that no change in our language-habits would make the proposition 7 + 5 = 12 untrue. The reason is this: As we use symbols at present, this proposition is incorrigible—one which we maintain to be true whatever happens in the world, and never admit to be false under any circumstances. Imagine a world where the symbolic conventions are totally different—say on Mars. How shall we *translate* our incorrigible proposition into the Martian symbols? If our translation is to be correct—if the proposition in the Martian language is to mean the same as our "7 + 5 = 12", it *too* must be incorrigible—otherwise we should not call it a correct translation. Thus a correct Martian translation of our "7 + 5 = 12" must be a proposition which the Martians maintain to be true whatever happens. Thus 7 + 5 = 12, and any correct translation into any other symbolic convention will be incorrigible, i.e. true whatever happens. So its truth does, in a sense, depend on the empirical fact that people use symbols in certain ways. But it is an inaccurate way of stating this fact to say that it describes how people use symbols.

A better formulation is "a mathematical proposition really expresses a rule for the manipulation of symbols". But this, too, is unsatisfactory, and for the following reason: To say that it is a "rule for the manipulation of symbols" suggests that it is entirely arbitrary. A symbolic rule is something which we can decide to use or not, just as we wish. (We could easily use "hice" as the plural of "house", and get on as well as we do now.) But, it seems, we cannot just change our mathematical propositions at will, without getting into difficulties. An engineer, building a bridge, has to use the standard multiplication tables and no others, or else the bridge will collapse. Thus which mathematical system we use does not seem to be entirely arbitrary— one system works in practice, and another does not. Which system we are to use seems to depend in some way not on our decision, but on the nature of the world. To say that "7 + 5 = 12" really expresses a rule for the use of symbols, suggests that this proposition is just like " 'house' forms its plural by adding 's' ". But there *is* a difference between the two, and so the formula is misleading.

I want to conclude this paper by considering in some detail the objection that you cannot build bridges with any mathematics, and that therefore mathematics does depend on the nature of reality. Before doing so, however, I should like to mention the type of theory I called "conservative". We saw that the (radical) theory, that mathematical propositions are "really" empirical propositions about the results of counting, is untrue. But there is a close connection between the two sorts of proposition, and therefore the "empirical" theory, although untrue, has a point. It emphasises the connection between mathematical propositions and our everyday practice of counting and calculation; thus it serves as a useful corrective to that type of theory which would make mathematics too abstract and pure—a matter of pure intellect and Platonic "Forms", far from the mundane counting of change. Similarly the various "conventionalist" theories are also, strictly speaking, untrue, but they too have their point. Mathematical propositions in certain respects are *like* rules for the use of symbols, *like* empirical propositions about how symbols are used, *like* statements of intention to use symbols in certain ways. But conventionalist formulæ are untrue because mathematical propositions are not *identical* with any of these. They are what they are; they function in the way they do, and not exactly like any other sort of proposition.

And this it is which makes that sort of theories I have called "conservative" perfectly correct. Mathematical propositions are *sui generis*. But merely to say: "They are what they are" is not very helpful. Nor is it any better if this is dressed up in learned language: e.g., "Mathematical propositions state very general facts about the structure of reality; about the necessary

and synthetic relations between the universals number, shape, size, and so on."
If you are inclined to think that such answers as this, to the question "what
are mathematical propositions about?", are informative and illuminating,
ask yourself: "How does my hearer come to understand the meaning of such
phrases as 'structure of reality', 'necessary relations between universals', and
so on? How were these phrases explained to him in the first place?" Surely
he was told what was meant by "necessary relation between universals", by
being told, for example, that colour, shape, size, number, etc., are universals,
and that an example of a necessary relation between universals would be
"everything that has shape has size", "2 + 2 = 4", "two angles of an
isosceles triangle are equal", and so on. These phrases, such as "necessary
relation between universals", are *introduced* into his language *via* or *by means
of* such phrases as "2 + 2 = 4"; they are introduced *via* mathematical
propositions, among others. To use an expression of John Wisdom's,[2] they
are "made to measure". So to tell someone that mathematical propositions
are "so-and-so" does not help, if, in explaining what is meant by "so-and-so",
you have to introduce mathematical propositions, among others, as illustrative examples. Compare giving a "conservative" answer to the question
"What are mathematical propositions?" with the following example: A child
learns the meaning of the words "see", "can't see", "blindfolded" etc.,
before he learns the meaning of the word "blind". The latter word is then
introduced into his vocabulary by the explanation: "A blind man is one who
can't see in broad daylight even when not blindfolded." If the child then asks
of a blind man "why can't he see in broad daylight even when not blindfolded?", it is not much use answering "because he is blind". Like the "conservative" answer in philosophy, it may serve to stop any further questions, but
it usually leave a feeling of dissatisfaction.

Then what sort of answer *can* be given to one who is puzzled about the
nature of mathematics? Mathematical propositions are what they are, so any
radical answer equating them with something else, such as symbolic rules, or
statements of the results of counting and measurement, or of common symbolic usage, will be untrue. Such answers will be untrue, because the two sides
of the equation will have different meanings. Similarly conservative answers
will be unhelpful, because the two sides of the equation will have the same
meaning. The definiens will be useless, because it will contain terms which are
introduced into the language *via* the definiendum, and can only be explained
in terms of it. It is "made to measure". No simple formula will do. The only
way of removing the puzzle is to describe the use and function of mathematical
propositions in detail and with examples. I shall now try to do this, to some
extent, in considering the natural objection to the strictly untrue but illuminating theory: "mathematical propositions express rules for the manipulation
of symbols." The objection is that symbolic rules are essentially arbitrary,

---

[2] My debt to the lectures of Wisdom and Wittgenstein, in writing this paper, is very
great.

whereas mathematics does, to some extent at least, depend not on our choice of symbolic conventions, but on the nature of reality, because only our present system gives useful results when applied to the practical tasks of the world. Against this, I shall maintain that we could use *any* mathematical rules we liked, and still get on perfectly well in the business of life.

Example 1.—6 × 4, according to our current multiplication table, equals 24. You might argue: this cannot be merely a conventional rule for our use of symbols, for if it were we could use any other rule we liked, e.g. 6 × 4 = 12, and still get satisfactory results. But if you tried this alternative rule, you would, in fact, find your practical affairs going all wrong. A builder, for example, having measured a room to be paved with tiles, each one yard square, and having found the length of the sides to be 6 yards and 4 yards, could not use the alternative table. He could not say to himself: "The room is 6 by 4; now 6 × 4 = 12, so I shall have to get 12 tiles for this job." For, if he did, he would find he had not enough tiles to cover his floor.

But the builder could quite easily have used an arithmetic in which 6 × 4 = 12, and by measuring and counting could have paved his room perfectly well, with exactly the right number of tiles to cover the floor. How does he do it? Well, he:

(1) Measures the sides, and writes down '4' and '6'.

(2) Multiplies 4 by 6 according to a 'queer' multiplication table which gives 4 × 6 = 12.

(3) Counts out 12 tiles, lays them on the floor. And they fit perfectly.

The 'queer' multiplication table he uses gives 2 × 2 = 4, 2 × 4 = 6, 2 × 8 = 10, 4 × 4 = 9, 4 × 6 = 12 etc. The number found by multiplying a or b according to *his* table, is that which in *our* arithmetic we should get by the formula:

$$(a + 2)(b + 2)/4$$

And he could pave any other size of floor, using the queer multiplication table described, and still always get the right number of tiles to cover it.

How is this possible? He measures the sides of the room with a yardstick as follows: He lays his yardstick along the longer side, with the 'O' mark of the yardstick in the corner, and the other end of the stick, marked '36 inches', some distance along the stick. As he does this, he counts "one". He then pivots the yardstick on the 36 inches mark, and swings it round through two right angles, till it is once more lying along the side of the room—this time with the "36 inches" mark nearer to the corner from which he started, and the "O" mark further along the side. As he does this, he counts "two". But now the direction of the stick has been reversed, and it is the convention for measuring that lengths should always be measured in the same direction. So he pivots the stick about its middle and swings it round so that the '36' mark is now where the 'O' mark was, and vice-versa. As he does this, he counts "three". He then swings the stick round through two right angles, pivoting on the '36' mark, counting "four". He then reverses its direction, as before, counting "five". He swings it over again, counting "six". It now lies with its end in the corner, so he writes down the length of the side as "six yards". (If we had measured it in our way, we should have written its length down as four yards.) He then measures the shorter side in the same way, and finds the length (using his measuring technique) to be four yards. (We should have made it three.) He then multiplies 4 by 6, according to his table, making it 12, counts out 12 tiles, and lays them down. So long as he uses the technique described for measuring lengths, he will always get the right number of tiles for any room with his 'queer' multiplication table.

This example shows you that we use the method we do for multiplying lengths to get areas, because we use a certain method of measuring lengths. Our technique of calculating areas is relative to our technique of measuring lengths.

Here you might say: admitting that this is true, it is still the case that mathematics is not arbitrary, for you could not use the method of measuring we do, *and* a different multiplication table, and *still* get the right number of tiles for our room. Could we not? Let us see.

Example 2.—Suppose our 'queer' multiplication table gave 3 × 4 = 24. The builder measures the sides of a room exactly as we do, and finds that they are 3 yards and 4 yards, respectively. He then "multiplies" 3 by 4, and gets 24. He counts out 24 tiles, places them on the floor, and they fit perfectly, with none over. How does he do it?

He measures the sides as we do, and writes down '3' and '4'. He "multiplies" and gets 24. He then counts out 24 tiles as follows: He picks up a tile from his store, and counts "one". He puts the tile on to his truck and counts "two". He picks up another tile and counts "three". He puts it on his truck and counts "four". He goes on this way until he reaches a count of "twenty-four". He then takes his "twenty-four" tiles and paves the room, and they fit perfectly.

This example shows that our technique of calculating areas is relative both to a certain technique of measurement, *and* to a certain technique of counting.

At this stage you might make a further objection. You might say: Mathematics *does* tell you something about the world, and is not an arbitrary rule of symbolic usage. It tells you that *if* you both count and measure lengths in the way we do, you will not get the right number of tiles for a room unless you multiply the lengths according to our present table. It is not arbitrary, because if, for example, you measure the sides of a room as we do, and find them to be 4 and 3, and if you count tiles as we do, you would get the wrong number of tiles to pave your room if you used some other multiplication table—say one in which 3 × 4 = 24. I maintain, on the contrary, that we could quite well use such a 'queer' table, and count and measure as at present, and still get the right number of tiles. To help us to see what is involved here, let us consider a rather analogous case.

Example 3.—Imagine that the following extraordinary thing happened. You measure a room normally, and find the sides to be 6 and 4. You multiply normally and get 24. You then count out 24 tiles in the normal way. (Each tile is 1 × 1.) But when you come to try and lay the tiles in the room, you find that you can get 12 such tiles on to the floor of the room, and there are 12 tiles over. What should we say if this happened?

The first thing we should say would be: "You must have made a mistake in your measuring" or "you must have made a slip in multiplying" or "you must have counted your tiles wrongly, somehow". And we should immediately check again the measurements, calculations, and counting. But suppose that, after the most careful checking and re-checking, by large numbers of highly qualified persons, *no* mistake at all of this sort can be found anywhere. Suppose, moreover, that this happened to everyone constantly, with all sorts of rooms and tiles. What would we say then? There are still a number of ways in which we might explain this curious phenomenon. I shall mention two conceivable hypotheses:

(1) Measuring rods do not, as we supposed, stay a constant length wherever they are put. They stay the same size when put against things the same length as themselves, and also when put against things larger than themselves running from north to south. But when put against things larger than themselves running east-west, they always contract to half their previous length (and this contraction happens so smoothly that we never notice it). Thus the room is in fact 6 by 2 yards, i.e. 12 square yards, and twelve tiles are needed. When the measuring rod is put along the north south wall of six yards' length, it stays a yard long, and so we get a measurement of 6. When, however, it is put along the shorter east-west wall it contracts to half a yard in length, and can be put four times along the two-yard wall. If you now say the dimensions are 6 and 4, and multiply to get 24, you are over-estimating the real area.

(2) An alternative hypothesis: When we measure the room our yardstick always stays a constant length, and thus the area of the room is really 24 square yards. But since we can only get 12 tiles in it, each tile being 1 yard square, it follows that the tiles must *expand*, on being put into the room, to double their area. It is just a curious *physical* law that objects put into a room double their area instantaneously. We do not see this expansion because it is instantaneous. And we can never measure it, by measuring the tiles, first out of the room and then inside, because our yardstick itself expands proportionately on being taken into the room.

This example (which might easily have been put in much more detail with *ad hoc* hypotheses to cover every discrepancy) shows that, however much the practical predictions of builders' requirements are upset when we use our present multiplication table, this need never cause us to alter our present rules for multiplication. Anomalies are accounted for by saying our knowledge of the relevant *physical* laws is defective, not by saying that the multiplication table is "untrue". If, when working things out in the usual way, we found that we had constantly 12 tiles too many, we should not say that we had been wrong in thinking that $6 \times 4 = 24$. We should rather say that we had been wrong in thinking that physical objects did not expand and contract in certain ways. If things go wrong, we always change our physics rather than our mathematics.

If we see, from example 3, what we should do if things went wrong when we used our present arithmetic, we can now answer the objection it was intended to throw light on. The objection was this:

"It is wrong to say that we could use any arithmetic we liked and still get on perfectly well in our practical affairs. Mathematics is not a collection of arbitrary symbolic rules, therefore, and does tell us something about, and does depend on, the nature of reality. For if you *both* count and measure as we do, *and* use a 'queer' multiplication table, you won't get the right number of tiles to pave a room. Thus the proposition '$3 \times 4 = 12$' tells you that for a room 3 yards by 4, measured normally, you need neither more nor less than 12 tiles, counted normally. Its truth depends on this fact about the world."

But I deny this. I say we could have

(1) used our present technique of counting and measurement,

(2) multiplied according to the rule $3 \times 4 = 24$ (for example),

(3) and still have got exactly the right number of tiles to pave our room.

I therefore say that $3 \times 4 = 12$ depends on *no* fact about the world, other than some fact about the usage of symbols.

Example 4.—Imagine that we did use a 'queer' arithmetic, in which $3 \times 4 = 24$. If this was our universally accepted and standard arithmetic, we should treat the proposition $3 \times 4 = 24$ *exactly* as we now treat the proposition $3 \times 4 = 12$ of our present standard arithmetic. That is to say, if we did use this queer system, we should stick to the proposition $3 \times 4 = 24$ no matter *what* happened, and ascribe any failure of prediction of builders' requirements, and so on, *always* to a mistaken view of the physical laws that apply to the world, and *never* to the untruth of the formula $3 \times 4 = 24$. This latter proposition, if it *were* part of our mathematical system, would be *incorrigible*, exactly as $3 \times 4 = 12$ is to us now.

In example 3 we saw what would be done and said if things went wrong in using $3 \times 4 = 12$. Now *if* $3 \times 4 = 24$ were our rule, and incorrigible, and *if* in using it we found ourselves getting the wrong practical results, we should do and say exactly the same sort of thing as we did in example 3. Thus, assuming that our rule is 3 × 4 = 24, a builder measures his floor normally and writes down 3 and 4. He multiplies according to his table and gets 24. He counts out 24 tiles normally, and tries to put them in the room. He finds that he can only get 12 tiles in. What does he say? He *does not* say "I have proved by experiment that 3 × 4 does not equal 24", for his proposition 3 × 4 = 24 is *incorrigible*, and no event in the world, however extraordinary, will ever lead him to deny it, or be counted as relevant to its truth or falsity. What he does say is something like this: "The area of the room is *really* 24 square yards. Since I can only get 12 yard square tiles into it, it follows that the tiles must expand to double their area on being put into the room." (As we have seen, he might use other hypotheses, e.g. about the behavior of measuring rods. But this is probably the most convenient.)

Thus we could easily have counted and measured as at present, *and* used an arithmetic in which 3 × 4 = 24, *and* have got perfectly satisfactory results. Only, of course, to get satisfactory practical results, we should use a physics different in some respects from our present one. Thus a builder having found the area of a room to be 24 square yards would never attempt to put 24 tiles in it, for he would have learnt in his physics lessons at school that tiles put in a room double in area. He would therefore argue: "Since the tiles double in area, I must put half of 24 tiles, or 12 tiles, in the room." He would count out 12 tiles and pave the room perfectly with them.

But even here an obstinate objector might admit all this, and still maintain that mathematics was not an arbitrary convention; that it did depend on certain facts about the world. He might say: "3 × 4 = 12 is true, and it is because of this fact about the world, namely that *if* tiles and rulers do not expand and contract (except slightly with changes in temperature), and if we measure and count normally, we need exactly 12 tiles, no more and no less, to pave a room that is 3 by 4. And 3 × 4 = 24 is false, because of the 'brute fact' that *if* tiles etc. don't expand, and *if* you measure and count normally, 24 tiles are too many to pave a room that is 3 by 4."

The point that is, I think, missed by this objection could be brought out by asking: "How do we *find out* whether a tile or a yardstick has or has not expanded or contracted?" We normally have two ways of doing so. We can *watch* it growing bigger or smaller. Or we can *measure* it before and after.

Now in the case described in example 4, where our queer arithmetic gives 3 × 4 = 24, and things double in area on being put in a room, how do we find out that the things do expand? Not by watching them grow—*ex hypothesi* we do not observe this. Nor by measuring them before and after. For, since we assume that a measuring rod *also* expands on being taken into the room, the dimensions of the tile as measured by a yardstick outside the room are the same as its dimensions as measured by the same (now expanded) yardstick inside the room. In this case we find out that the tiles expand by *measuring, counting and calculating in a certain way*—by finding that the tiles each measure

1 × 1, that the room measures 3 × 4, or 24 square yards, and that we can only get 12 tiles in it. This is our sole *criterion* for saying that the tiles expand. That the tiles expand *follows from* our queer arithmetic. Similarly, as we do things at present, our criterion for saying that tiles do not expand, is that when 12 tiles measuring 1 × 1 are put into a room 3 × 4, or 12 square yards, they fit exactly. From our present arithmetic, it follows that tiles do not expand.

In example 4, where we have a 'queer' arithmetic in which 3 × 4 = 24, and a 'queer' physics, it is a "law of nature" that tiles expand on being put into a room. But it is not a "law of nature" which describes what happens in the world. Rather is it a law "by convention", analogous to that law of our present physics which says that when a body falls on the floor with a certain downward force, the floor itself exerts an equal force in the opposite direction. It is just put into the system to balance our calculations, not to describe anything that happens.

This last objection might have been put in a slightly different form. It might have been said: "3 × 4 = 12 does describe and depend on the nature of reality, because it entails a certain purely empirical proposition about what does and does not happen, namely the complex proposition: 'It is not the case *both* that tiles do not expand *and* that we need less than 12 tiles to pave a floor measuring 3 by 4'." But I should maintain that this complex proposition (of the form 'not both p and q') is not empirical; that it does not describe anything that happens in the world, because it is incorrigible. Nothing whatsoever that we could imagine happening would ever lead us, if it happened, to deny this complex proposition. Therefore it does not tell us what happens in the world. The simple propositions which are elements in this complex one—the propositions 'tiles do not expand' and 'we need less than 12 tiles to pave a 3 by 4 floor'—are both of them corrigible, and both describe the world (one of them falsely). But the complex proposition that they are not both true is incorrigible, and therefore, for the reasons given earlier, does not describe or depend on the nature of the world. There is nothing out of the ordinary about this. The propositions "my curtains are now red over their whole surface", and "my curtains are now green all over" are both of them corrigible propositions, descriptive of the world. (One is true, the other false, as a matter of fact.) But the complex proposition "my curtains are not both red and green over their whole surface" is incorrigible, because nothing would ever make me deny it, and it is therefore not descriptive of the world.

I have talked, throughout the paper, as if mathematical propositions were completely incorrigible, in the sense that *whatever* queer things happened, we should *never* alter our mathematics, and always prefer to change our physics. This was a convenient over-simplification that must now be qualified. I maintain that we *need* never alter our mathematics. But it might happen that we found our physical laws getting very complicated indeed, and might discover that, by changing our mathematical system, we could effect a very great simplification in our physics. In such a case we might decide to use a different mathematical system. (So far as I can understand, this seems to be what has actually happened in certain branches of contemporary physics.) And mathematics does depend on and reflect the nature of the world at least to this extent, that we would find certain systems enormously inconvenient and difficult to use, and certain others relatively simple and handy. Using one sort of arithmetic or geometry, for example, we might find that our physics could be reduced to a logically neat and simple system, which is intellectually satisfying, whereas using different arithmetics and geometries, we should find our physics full of very complicated *ad hoc* hypotheses. But what we find neat, simple, easy, and intellectually satisfying surely depends rather on our psychological make-up, than on the behavior of measuring rods, solids and fluids, electrical charges—the "external world".

ARITHMETIC AND REALITY[1]

Hector-Neri Castañeda

I propose to discuss whether "queer" arithmetics (to be thought of on the analogy with non-Euclidean geometries) can be effectively applied to describe the world. Since this question has been investigated at length and quite recently by Professor Douglas Gasking in his very famous and influential paper "Mathematics and the World,"[1] the first part of my discussion is devoted to an examination of Gasking's views and arguments.

1. A CONVENTIONALISTIC VIEW OF ARITHMETIC

1. *Gasking's view.* Professor Gasking has argued most persuasively for the view that mathematical propositions are like conventions or rules as to how we should describe what happens in the world. The proposition "7 + 5 = 12", e.g., "does *lay it* down, so to speak, that *if* on counting 7 + 5 you do get 11, you are to describe what has happened in some such manner as this: *Either* 'I have made a mistake in my counting' *or* 'Someone has played a practical joke and abstracted one of the objects when I was not looking' *or* 'Two of the objects have coalesced' *or* 'One of the objects has disappeared', etc." (p. 394).

Gasking's argument is non-technical and seems very clear and, therefore, very convincing. As far as I can see his view may be summarized in the following theses:

(A)   Mathematical propositions are incorrigible (p. 392, etc.);

[1] [*The Australasian Journal of Philosophy*, 1940. Reprinted in this book on pp. 390–403. Three-figured numbers in parentheses have been changed to indicate the pages of the article as reprinted in this book.]

Reprinted with the kind permission of the author and the editor from The Australasian Journal of Philosophy, 37, *no.* 2 (*August,* 1959), 92–107.

(B) They are not descriptive of the world (pp. 393ff);

(C) Their truth depends on the usage of symbols only (p. 400) but (C1) they are not simply rules for the manipulation of symbols (p. 395);

(D) their characteristic function is to formulate a way of calculating (p. 401);

(E) such a way of calculating together with a way of counting and a way of measuring constitute criteria for our descriptions of the world, i.e., arithmetical propositions are some of the rules governing our describing of reality (p. 401);

(F) there is no necessity in the boundaries separating calculations, countings, measurements, and facts; we can very well draw different contours for, say, arithmetic provided we modify accordingly our countings or measurements or our descriptions of fact (pp. 401ff).

Of course, it is unfair to represent Gasking as merely making these seven assertions. The point of his paper is to explain them as well as to argue for them. Thus, he argues to (B) from (A), and spends one third of the essay in proving (F), from which he infers (C). He speaks of queer arithmetics for what I have called different contours of arithmetic (cf. Part II below). He discusses the example of an arithmetic in which "3 × 4 = 24", and argues that we could employ it quite successfully in our ordinary problems like paving a floor.

It should be said that Gasking makes claims about mathematical propositions in general, even though his actual discussion is limited to "3 × 4 = 12", "3 × 4 = 24", "7 + 5 = 12".

2. Incorrigibility. Gasking defines: "A corrigible proposition is one that you would withdraw and admit to be false if certain things happened in the world" (393). And most people would agree with him that mathematical propositions are incorrigible in that sense. Clearly, "7 + 5 = 12" tells us nothing about events, so that "no future happening whatsoever would ever prove the proposition false, or cause anyone to withdraw it" (392).

Then Gasking goes on to say that only corrigible propositions can be informative or descriptive of the world. But he seems to assume a definition of 'informative' or 'descriptive of the world' in terms of corrigibility: "A corrigible proposition ... therefore gives you the information that *those* things (i.e., those things which would make you withdraw your proposition if they happened) *will* not happen" (393). Certainly, if that is what 'descriptive of the world' means, mathematical propositions are absolutely uninformative or nondescriptive. However, the term 'descriptive of the world' is often used in another sense, in which to say that incorrigible propositions or statements are not descriptive of the world is, among other things, to beg the question against Kant, whether there is a synthetic *a priori* or not. In fact, Gasking does continue his argument, and his defence of thesis (F) does seem like a discussion of whether arithmetical propositions can be incorrigible and synthetic, or, as he says, whether or not they "depend on the nature of reality" (397, 400 etc.).

Of course, it is not a good reply that a question is begged against Kant. Kant has been dead for close to 160 years and science, as well as philosophy, has changed tremendously since then. The point is that there are good reasons not to identify corrigibility with being descriptive of the world in the sense of "depending on the nature of reality". Just to mention two cases, we have propositions like (1) and (2) below which somewhat resist such an identification:

(1) One ought legally (i.e., according to the law) to drive on the right-hand side of the road.
(2) I have a mild eye-ache.

Proposition (1) is corrigible, but not descriptive of the world; (2) is both incorrigible and descriptive of the world.

When a person says it is illegal not to drive on the right, which is the same as (1), he could be led to withdraw his statement by finding out that the existing law requires driving on the left. Many facts enter into the truth of a proposition like (1); that there is an authority capable of legislating on such matters, that there is a procedure which has in reality been followed, etc. But (1) does not inform us of that, except in the sense that its truth *presupposes* those facts. (1) is a statement about legal obligation, whose simple denial is not the disjunction of all the statements denying those facts, but the proposition that it is not illegal not to drive on the right.

Gasking's own fellow-Wittgensteinians have been arguing that statements like (2) are not descriptive, just because they are incorrigible. They want to take them as highly developed signs of pain; but they are too well acquainted with human nature to deny that utterances like (2) can be true or false. Or when they want to deny that (2) can be descriptive or formulate knowledge and, hence, withhold the use of the adjectives 'true' and 'false' from (2), they have to fall back on "the *sincere* (or *honest*) utterance of . . .". Obviously, statements like (2) do not fail to be descriptive of the world in the sense that their truth "depends on no fact about the world, other than some fact about the usage of symbols" (400). Furthermore, it will never do to accept that other persons can describe my states of pain because they see and hear me, whereas *I* who feel the pain cannot describe them. Surely, (2) may and does in fact function as a sign of pain to my hearers; but there is no reason to suppose that because (2) functions as surrogate pain behavior *as well* it no longer serves to describe a mental state of myself.

At any rate, (2) shows that Gasking's assimilation of incorrigibility to uninformativity is far from obvious.

3. *Arithmetic and Life*. Gasking's final argument for the view that

mathematical propositions are not descriptive of the world and depend on the usage of symbols hinges entirely on his claim that "we could use *any* mathematical *rules* we liked, and still get on perfectly well in the business of life" (397, my italics in 'rules'). His argument is roughly divided into two parts to show that:

(F.1)   We could use any mathematics and compensate for deviations from the present one by means of an adequate technique of counting or measuring (397ff);

(F.2)   We could use any mathematics different from the present one and modify our physics (401–2).

3.1. *Rules*. Before examining the details of Gasking's argument it is important to note that he first speaks of "mathematical rules" and then of "mathematical propositions", as if the two expressions were synonymous. But, although we may say that rules are a species of proposition, not all propositions could be said to be rules. On the other hand, it is natural to say that a rule is not descriptive, but prescriptive; so that Gasking could at least *prima facie* be accused of begging the question.

Indeed, the typical propositions or statements of which we can say that we can use different ones and yet get on in the business of life are *rules*, particularly rules like

(1) It is unlawful to drive on the left-hand side of the road. We could certainly have a different law, making it unlawful to drive on the right, and life might be just as pleasant (or unpleasant) as it now is. However, it is not clear that arithmetical propositions like "$7 \times 5 = 35$" or "$7 + 5 = 12$" are rules. There is not a single bit of ground for saying that these are rules governing the describing of the world in the way in which (1) is a rule governing the traffic of vehicles on the road.

For one thing, rules tell us what to do or what to avoid doing, but if a storm fells 7 trees and then 5 trees it has felled 12 trees regardless of whether there are human beings or not. No action is prescribed to anybody by the proposition "7 trees and 5 different trees are 12 trees".

Secondly, rules are formulated in sentences containing a "rulish" or prescriptive term like 'ought', 'forbidden', 'required', 'illegal', 'unlawful', 'permitted', etc. It is not easy to find a place for such terms in "$7 + 5 = 12$".

There are indeed mathematical rules like "To multiply a whole number by 10^n you may (are permitted to) write n zeros to the right of that number". There are also rules for the application of mathematics like "To find out how many tiles, each 1 foot square, you need to pave a room 20×50 feet, you ought to multiply 20×50". But the important thing is that all such rules are derived from mathematical propositions asserting a given relationship between numbers. The rules are, in Kant's terminology, hypothetical imperatives; they follow from the non-rulish propositions, by means of the ordinary logic of rules or norms.[2] Similarly, once we have the proposition "7 + 5 = 12" we have the ground for the rule "If you are discussing the number which is the sum of 5 and 7, you may discuss instead the number 12", or a ground for the rule "If you put 7 apples in the basket and then 5, you may say that you put 12".

In any case, it is worth noticing that rules, i.e., real, ordinary rules like "It is not permissible to drive on the left", may be said to be:

   (i) corrigible—the legislators might not have enacted such a law;
   (ii) synthetic—in the sense that they could be disobeyed;
   (iii) not empirical—they are not discovered by observation;
   (iv) not descriptive of the world—but prescriptive;
   (v) not dependent on the usage of symbols only—enactment is necessary;
   (vi) replaceable—i.e., using different, incompatible rules we could get along in the world.

It is not difficult to see that Gasking's view of mathematical propositions as rules lets him hold that mathematical propositions are replaceable (feature vi), not empirical (feature iii), and not descriptive of the world (feature iv). One can see that the underlying movement of Gasking's argument takes him from the incorrigibility of mathematical statements to their non-empirical character, and then, since he assimilates non-empirical to non-descriptive (pp. 391f., 402), the dichotomy "either descriptive or rulish" forces him to classify them as rules.

However, once we reflect on the nature of rules it is clear that Gasking is now heading for trouble. At the bottom of the replaceability of ordinary rules lies their corrigibility. Surely, to say that the rule may be to drive on the left rather than the right is in part to say that it might have been *false* that we ought to drive on the right. Likewise, the possibility of a queer mathematics in which "7 × 5 = 75" entails that "7 × 5 = 35" *could* be false, i.e., that it is corrigible. Therefore, Gasking's argument has the perplexing characteristic that, even though he identifies corrigibility with being descriptive of the world, his strongest step involves showing that ordinary arithmetical propositions could be falsified *and so* are not descriptive of the world!

Clearly, a proposition whose truth depends on linguistic use alone, like "Bachelors are unmarried", cannot be falsified *at all*. We could drop the word 'bachelor' and use 'solor' in its stead, but the proposition 'Solors are unmarried" is exactly the same, and continues to be unfalsifiable. We may stop using words with which we could say that bachelors are unmarried, but that is not to use a queer system of family relationships.

I do not know of any way of repairing Gasking's argument. If mathe-

   [2] Cf., e.g., H. N. Castañeda, "Nota sobre la lògica de los fines y medios," *Universidad de San Carlos* (Guatemala), No. XXIX (1956); "Imperative Inference," *Philosophy and Phenomenological Research* (*forthcoming*).

matical propositions were rules he could defend their replaceability, without having to bother with whether they are corrigible or not. But I have indicated some reasons which make it difficult to disguise them as rules. I pass over the view that analytic propositions are rules and that, since mathematical propositions are analytic, they must be rules. This view begs the very question we are discussing: whether or not mathematical propositions are descriptive of the world, i.e., non-analytic.[3] However, a view can be illuminating even though it is false and the arguments for it are invalid.

3.2. *Queer Countings and Measurings.* Gasking argues that we could employ a queer arithmetic in which 6 × 4 = 12 and get on perfectly well with the business of life. He does not define a queer arithmetic, but it is clear from his discussion that he does *not* mean one or more changes of labels. In other words, to use the formula "6 × 4 = 12" is not merely to use '6' to mean the number 3, and perhaps '3' or 'w' to mean the number 6. These are trivial changes in numerical terminology. Obviously, such changes are present in our daily experience, as when we translate from English into German, or as when a person translates numbers into the binary system to make a computer work some problem. By a 'queer arithmetic' Gasking means something more exciting. Presumably, we are to think of queer arithmetics on the analogy with non-Euclidean geometries. Provisionally, just to fix the sense of the argument, we may say that a *queer arithmetic* is a system of propositions about natural numbers in which we have a different multiplication table. (This topic will be given an independent and detailed discussion in Part II of this paper.)

Gasking says that in that queer arithmetic the product $m \times n$ is the number that we obtain by the formula: $(m + 2)(n + 2)/4$. (Let us not ask now about the nature of the translation in question.) He argues that by means of a different "technique of measuring lengths" (398) a builder could pave a room 6 yards long and 4 yards wide:

> He lays his yardstick along the longer side, with the '0' mark of the yardstick in the corner, and the other end of the stick, marked '36 inches', some distance along · · · he counts 'one'. He then pivots the yardstick on the 36 inches mark, and swings it round through two right angles, till it is once more lying along the side of the room—this time with the '36 inches' mark nearer to the corner · · · he counts 'two' · · · he pivots the stick about its middle and swings it round · · · he counts 'three'. He then swings the stick round through two right angles, pivoting on the '36' mark, counting 'four'. He then reverses its direction, as before, counting 'five' · · · (397f.)

Clearly, if he were to count the tiles, after he paved the floor, the builder (hereafter to be called "Gaskon") would have to count: 'one' for the first

[3] Besides, the major premise is false. For a thorough discussion of the view that analytic propositions are rules, cf. A. Pap, *Semantics and Necessary Truth* (New Haven: Yale University Press, 1958), 170ff, 182–85.

tile, 'two-three' for the second, 'four' for the third if it is the last, or 'four-five' if it is not the last, etc. Hence, the "queer technique" of measuring requires a similarly "queer technique" of counting. (This, incidentally, shows that measuring and counting are not independent concepts or operations, as Gasking implies on p. 398.) Counting is, in fact, the simplest form of measuring, and every measuring includes it or presupposes it.

It is important to note that Gasking's talk of a "different technique" is deceptive. He is dealing with a different concept of counting and measuring. Different techniques under the same ordinary concept of counting are, e.g., (1) counting by saying 'one' 'two', 'three', etc. to different objects, (2) counting by pairs or fives, (3) weighing the totality of objects, weighing one of them, and dividing the two numbers (when the objects involved are supposed to have the same weight), etc.

In Part II, I shall show that "queer" countings either lead to contradictions or involve at most an infinity of trivial changes in numerical terminology. In the present case we may notice in passing that Gaskon is supposed to count twelve tiles as we do, in order to pave the floor. But once he has paved the room he will *have to* count in the queer way he measures to speak of 4 and 6 tiles or squares on each side, as illustrated:

	1	2–3	4–5	6	
1	1	2–3	4–5	6–7	
2–3	8–9	10–11	12–13	14–15	6 × 4 = 12
4	16–17	18–19	20–21	22	

Gaskon must count abnormally to find that the room is 6 yards long and 4 yards wide; but then he will find that he needs 22 tiles, whereas, according to his arithmetic, he needs only 12.

We should also notice that in such a queer arithmetic, in which we are supposed to have all natural numbers, we cannot employ the usual rules of addition: "2 tiles and 1 tile = 4 tiles"; on the other hand, "3 tiles and 1 tile" has no meaning. But let us postpone the development of these matters.

One can easily see that Gasking's argument looks persuasive only because he has isolated (1) the measuring of the room from the counting of the tiles or squares, and (2) multiplication from the remaining body of arithmetic. One suspects that, just as it is impossible to isolate measuring from counting, it is not possible to isolate both counting and measuring from the properties of physical objects. That is to say, all the cases that Gasking discusses are probably in the end instances of his last case: that, by changing the laws of physics, we might very well get on in the business of life with a queer arithmetic. Thus, his last argument is the fundamental one.

3.3. *Queer Physics.* Gasking's more dramatic claim is that Gaskon could count and measure the way we do, but multiply according to different tables, and yet get exactly the right number of tiles to pave his room (399). He offers both a general argument and an illustration. I quote the former in full:

> Imagine that we did use a 'queer' arithmetic, in which $3 \times 4 = 24$ $\cdots$ if we did use this queer system, we should stick to the proposition '$3 \times 4 = 24$' no matter *what* happened, and ascribe any failure of prediction of builders' requirements, and so on, *always* to a mistaken view of the physical laws that apply to the world, and *never* to the untruth of the formula '$3 \times 4 = 24$'. This latter proposition, if it *were* part of our mathematical system, would be *incorrigible*, exactly as '$3 \times 4 = 12$' is to us now. (400.)

He then goes on to illustrate. When he sees that 12 tiles are enough to pave the room, Gaskon would say, e.g., that "the tiles must expand to double their area on being put into the room" (401).

Of course, Gasking is right in everything he says here. Since mathematical propositions are incorrigible, *if* "Napoleon weighed 50 pounds at birth" were a mathematical proposition it would be incorrigible. This contrary-to-fact conditional is logically true. But from it we can infer neither (a) that "Napoleon weighed 50 pounds at birth" is a mathematical proposition, nor (b) that it is incorrigible, nor (c) that it is a legitimate candidate as a mathematical truth. Gasking's argument is simply an *ignoratio elenchi*. The issue is neither whether "$3 \times 4 = 24$" would be incorrigible, nor what we would say if certain facts did not come out right when we used that formula for prediction. The issue is whether the formula is a legitimate alternative in arithmetic—in the way in which the proposition in Riemannian geometry that there are no parallels is or is supposed to be a legitimate alternative to Euclid's postulate.

This argument also brings into focus the perplexing feature mentioned in Section 3.1. If "$3 \times 4 = 12$" is absolutely incorrigible, and this is the assumption from which Gasking is arguing, *nothing at all* could make it false, regardless of how much the description of the facts were to be changed. The only possibility would be, as was the case with the analytic proposition "bachelors are unmarried", to make a trivial terminological change—but this has been excluded by the definition of a queer arithmetic.

Even Gasking's illustration looks more plausible thanks to his method of isolating propositions and cases. For us to say meaningfully that the tiles double in size when brought into the room, they must be smaller outside the room; moreover, things inside the room must have the same constant size, everything else being equal. As Gasking correctly emphasizes:

> In this case we find that the tiles expand by *measuring, counting and calculating in a certain way*—by finding that the tiles each measure 1×1, that the room measures 3×4, or 24 square yards, and that we can only get 12 tiles in it.

This is our sole *criterion* for saying that the tiles expand. That the tiles expand *follows from* our queer arithmetic. (402, his italics.)

Let us suppose now that Gaskon draws a rectangle like the floor of the room outside the room and tries to pave it with the same tiles:

	1	2	3	4
1	1	2	3	4
2	5	6	7	8
3	9	10	11	12

$3 \times 4 = 24$; yet 12 tiles are enough

Then, inside the room, he cuts a piece of paper into three strips and each strip into four pieces. According to his "multiplication" table he should have 24. He counts the pieces of paper and finds only 12. Thus, it seems that Gaskon should say that things expand: (a) when they are brought into the room, (b) when they are taken out of the room, (c) when they are left in the room, and (d) when they are left outside the room. In other words, there is no expansion: from what size did they expand? So Gaskon can say that from his queer arithmetic it follows that the tiles *cannot* expand.

But now Gaskon has become possessed of the scientific demon. He counts 12 tiles, then he makes 4 piles of three each, so that according to his queer arithmetical proposition "$3 \times 4 = 24$" he has to say that they have doubled. He counts "one, two, three; four, five, six; seven, eight, nine; ten, eleven, and twelve", so that the additional ones vanish; but since the piles have remained intact he has both 12 and 24 tiles—yet 12 and 24 are different numbers!

Gasking may say that there is no contradiction, for there are two different operations involved, and if we distinguish them everything is all right. Well and good; but then Gaskon is bound to say that the operation '×' cannot be an abbreviation for counting, and that the only way of determining how many tiles he needs to pave the room is to measure the floor by counting the squares, as in the diagram above. He may eventually invent ordinary multiplication as a shorthand for addition. In other words, the operation Gasking represents by '×' is *either* the source of contradictions if both it and ordinary multiplication are taken to be the same operation, *or* it is an altogether different operation which can peacefully coexist with ordinary multiplication. In the latter case Gasking is not discussing a queer arithmetic, but only ordinary arithmetical operations which (i) are not shortcuts for counting, (ii) are correctly performed on numbers without contradiction, (iii) are not involved in counting and (iv) are such that the propositions formulating them are *already* incorrigible, like any other arithmetical proposition.

In other words, if Gaskon's 'queer' arithmetic involves no contradiction, it is only a terminologically different arithmetic, in which the operation $\dotplus$, defined by "$m \dotplus n = 2 (m \times n)$", has been called "multiplication" and the sign '$\times$' has been used to supplant '$\dotplus$'—in spite of the resulting ambiguity!

I conclude, therefore, that Gasking has not proved his most important claims, (B) that ordinary arithmetical propositions are not descriptive of the world, (C) that they depend on linguistic usage only and (F) that queer arithmetics could very well be applied to reality. I have pointed out a conflict between his theses (B), (C), and (F). So perhaps one of them may after all be true. Even though I have attacked Gasking's arguments for (F), it is not completely clear from my discussion that (B) and (C) are true. For one thing, all three may very well be false. In any case, I propose to examine thesis (F) on its own merits.

II ALTERNATIVE ARITHMETICS

1. *Queer Arithmetics.* Let us follow Gasking in the use of the term 'queer arithmetic'. But we must give it a precise meaning if we are to get somewhere. The following definition seems to me to be adequate for a general discussion of Gasking's problem:

Def. A *queer arithmetic* is a system of propositions about numbers which includes at least one proposition incompatible with the propositions proven in arithmetical treatises and manuals.

It should be noticed that:

(a) Peano's postulates alone do not constitute a queer arithmetic, but only an incomplete formulation of arithmetic. Those postulates (to be discussed below) formulate formal properties of the sequence of natural numbers, but do not tell us how numbers are used in counting and measuring.

(b) There are trivial changes that can be introduced in the numerals, which cannot produce a queer arithmetic. One such trivial change would be to use the sign '4' to stand for the number 3, and either the sign '3' or another sign to stand for the number 4. Clearly an infinite collection of such trivial changes does not yield a queer arithmetic. We may speak of a *trivially different arithmetic*. One such example would be to use the signs in the first row for those just underneath them:

(G1)   1, 2, 4, 6, 8, 10, 12, 14,..., $2n - 2$,...
      1, 2, 3, 4, 5, 6, 7, 8,..., n,...

(G1) is the trivially different arithmetic involved in Gaskon's queer countings and measurings discussed in Section I.3.2. above.

(c) There are (as we have seen) trivial changes in the terminology of arithmetical operations or functions. We may call "multiplication" the operation of doubling the product of two numbers, and we may speak of "semi-multiplication" for ordinary multiplication. Again, these changes may be compounded to infinity. In an excess of clarity we may call the systems obtained by such changes *trivially changed arithmetics*. One such arithmetic, we saw in I.3.3. above, misled Gasking.

2. *Ordinary Arithmetic.* The ordinary arithmetic of natural numbers can be characterized by two sets of propositions:

(A) *Peano's postulates*, which determine the natural sequence of numbers:

(P1) 1 is a number.
(P2) Every number n has an immediate successor, to be called n', which is also a number.
(P3) If two successors m' and n' are the same number, then m and n are the same number.
(P4) 1 is not the successor of any number.
(P5) Every property P is possessed by all numbers if 1 has P and if, when n has it, n' has it too.

(B) *The principles of counting*, which formulate the basic manner in which natural numbers function in experience:

(C1) To count the objects of a collection or aggregate K is to establish a one-to-one correspondence between the objects of K and a set N of numbers (or numerals), such that:
(C2) N includes 1;
(C3) there is at most one number in N whose immediate successor is not in N;
(C4) the number of objects in K is the number mentioned in (C3) if it exists; otherwise the number of objects in K is infinite;
(C5) the one-to-one correspondence may be carried out (i) by actually attaching one number (or numeral) to each object; or (ii) by forming partial non-overlapping correspondences of type (i), as when we count by twos or fives or hundreds; or (iii) by specifying a rule for actually attaching numerals to as many objects as we please.

Obviously, since, as Peano, Dedekind, etc., have shown, all formal properties of numbers follow from (P1)–(P5), a queer arithmetic worth discussing must be one which differs from ordinary arithmetic in at least one of Peano's axioms or one of the principles of counting. Otherwise, the different arithmetic is trivially different or trivially changed, or self-contradictory. Thus, there are at most ten fundamental types of queer arithmetics.

3. *Numbers and the World.* I want to argue in some detail that Gasking's claim that a queer arithmetic could be applied to describe reality is

ungrounded. Every queer arithmetic, i.e., one which does not turn out to be either an incomplete or a trivially different or changed arithmetic, is inconsistent or inadequate to help us get on in the world in all situations.

3.1. *Non-Peanian Arithmetics.* To begin with, I shall show that a queer arithmetic which contains a change in Peano's postulates requires a different concept of counting. So if, as in Gasking's final argument, we are to suppose that Gaskon has a queer arithmetic, but his counting and measuring proceed as usual, then Gaskon's computations must produce results contradictory to those which he obtains from counting.

CASE 1. If 1 is not a number we must start counting with two. Thus, when Gaskon says that he needs three tiles he actually needs two, and in general whenever he says "n objects" we can translate "n − 1 objects". Hence, (P1) cannot be the source of a queer arithmetic.

CASE 2. If we abandon (P2), at least some numbers, say 8 and 25, do not have immediate successors, or if they do their successors are not numbers. In the former situation we could not count beyond 8, for (C3) does not allow us to make a new start; aggregates with 10 and 12 objects would be uncountable. This may not be inconsistent, but will certainly make it impossible for Gaskon to pave his room—except by a lucky chance, since he could not have a way of distinguishing 12 tiles from 11 or 14. Of course, this is not the queer arithmetic Gaskon was left with, for he was supposed to know that 11 apples and 12 tiles were exactly what they are for us; he was able to count up to any number. Thus, Gaskon was supposed to be able to do the impossible.

On the other hand, if the sequence of natural numbers is only supposed to have, as it were, a hole, we find a trivially different arithmetic. If 8 has a successor, 9, which is not a number, when we count we are just to bypass 9. Arithmetic is the same as usual, except that after 8 (and before 26) all numbers are moved one place, and after 26 they are moved two places.

CASE 3. If 1 is the successor of, say, 25, (C1) and (C5) require that we stop counting at 25. Thus, abandoning (P3) takes us back to Case 2.

CASE 4. Suppose that 100 and 50 have the same successor, even though they are different. Thus, we may have the following sequence of natural numbers:

$$1, 2, \ldots, \; 50 \atop a, \ldots, 100} \!\!\!\!\!\!\Big\rangle \; 51, 52, 53 \ldots$$

According to (C2) we must count "One, two, ..."; according to (C3) we must say "fifty-one" after saying "fifty", and cannot use "a".

Thus, the segment "a, ... , 100" is altogether irrelevant, and we obtain the usual arithmetic.

On the other hand, suppose the resulting sequence were:

$$1, 2, \ldots, 50, 51, 52, \ldots, 98, 99, 100, 51, \ldots$$

If the sequence repeats in cycles after 50, according to (C1) and (C5) we cannot count beyond 100, and are back to Case 2. If the numbers following the second 51 are different, say, 101, 102, ... , we are led to contradictions because of the ambiguity of "51 apples". If one 51 is disregarded in counting we obtain the normal arithmetic.

CASE 5. Suppose that there is a property, call it R, which 1 has and if n has it n' has it too, but not all numbers have it. If only (P5) is false we get a transfinite arithmetic, but transfinite numbers are not used in counting, so our ordinary arithmetic is not queer. If no other numbers, transfinite or appendetic like "a, ... , 100" at the beginning of Case 4, are included, then the negation of (P5) produces inconsistency; for nothing could fail to have R. If besides (P5) (P4) is also false, then a situation like the one described above with the segment "a, ... , 100" preceding 51 would be possible. But this does not produce a queer arithmetic, only a "larger" arithmetic which includes ordinary arithmetic.

3.2. *Queer Countings.* Suppose now that a queer arithmetic includes both Peano's axioms and different principles of counting. Again, there are at most five basic types of queer arithmetic. I shall show that they either involve self-contradiction or prevent Gaskon from getting on in the business of life.

CASE 1. We give up the one-to-one correspondence, for example:

    (a) we count "one-two, three-four, five-six, ...",
    (b) we count "one, two-three, four-five-six".
    (c) Gasking's special technique of counting discussed in 3.2. of Part I: "One" for the first object; we say "two" for the second if it is the last, otherwise "two-three"; we say next "four" or "four-five", depending on whether the object is the last to be counted; and so on.

In some of these "countings" we just use a term like 'one-two' for '1', 'three-four' for '2', etc., so that there is no queer arithmetic, but only a trivially different one. At any rate if we are to avoid contradictions we cannot, e.g., allow that 12 apples for *us* be regarded both as 25 and as 30 apples and say that 25 and 30 are different numbers. We must have a general rule as to how the correspondence between numerals and objects is to be made. Thus, using a queer arithmetic of this sort, we should speak of $\phi(n)$ objects for every situation in which we now say that there are n objects. And the counting will have to be "$\phi(1), \phi(2), \phi(3), ... , \phi(n)$". Now, if the other numbers are disregarded we just have a trivial change in terminology; if we consider that Peano's postulates apply to the ϕ-numbers as well as to the other numbers, we do not produce a queer arithmetic, either. This only shows the well-known fact that Peano's postulates are not a complete or unique characterization of the sequence of natural numbers. Since the natural numbers are those attributed to objects in counting, the ϕ-numbers *are* the natural numbers under a new name.

Let us consider now the correlation of one numeral to several objects. In fact we often do it, as, e.g., when we count pairs or triplets or piles. But suppose we counted: "one (taking or pointing to one object), two (taking two objects), three (taking two), ...". We could not count the persons forming a monogamous marriage or the persons forming two such marriages. Clearly, the arithmetic is not queer, but we may find it difficult to determine how many tiles we have to buy for a certain room whose dimensions we cannot ascertain, unless we interpolate "fractions" and come to use the trivially different sequence "1, $1\frac{1}{2}$, 2, $2\frac{1}{2}$, ...".

CASE 2. If we never start counting with '1', we are only changing the names of the numbers.

CASE 3. If we are not to use certain numerals in counting, they have to be fixed by a rule; otherwise we may fall into contradictions, or provide no way of finding agreement, for we may count from 1 to 15 once and then count the same objects correctly, jumping, say, 8 or 10, and obtain 16 or more objects. Let the numerals to be omitted be fixed. Then we may just have a trivially different arithmetic with terminological changes after those numerals. But we may find that our arithmetic is inadequate or leads to contradiction. Suppose, e.g., that '9' is omitted. Eight apples and 1 apple will be 10 apples. If 8 and 2 are also 10, we get a contradiction; if 8 and 2 are 11 then we can use these addition tables in life, but we have only substituted '10' for '9', '11' for '10', etc.

CASE 4. We may abandon (C4) and take as the number of counted objects one whose successor is also mentioned in the counting operation. This amounts to correlating several objects to a numeral and leads us back to Case 1 above. If we take another number, then we are actually correlating several numerals to one object, which also fails to produce an applicable queer arithmetic.

CASE 5. Obviously contained in the previous cases.

3.3. *Conclusion.* Queer arithmetics in the sense defined cannot apply to the world. Thus, what I have called Gasking's thesis (F) is false, namely, that we are free to use a queer arithmetic provided we introduce certain changes in our technique of counting and measuring or in our description of the facts, i.e., our physics.

Part Four

SELECTIONS FROM *REMARKS ON THE FOUNDATIONS OF MATHEMATICS*

Ludwig Wittgenstein

I

23. "But we surely infer this proposition from that because it actually follows! We ascertain that it follows."—We ascertain that what is written here follows from what is written there. And this proposition is being used *temporally*.

24. Separate the feelings (gestures) of agreement, from what you *do* with the proof.

25. But how about when I ascertain that this pattern of lines:

(a)

is like-numbered with this pattern of angles:

(b)

Excerpted and reprinted with the kind permission of the editors, translator, and publishers from Ludwig Wittgenstein, Remarks on the Foundations of Mathematics, *translated from the German by G. E. M. Anscombe, edited by G. H. von Wright, R. Rhees, and G. E. M. Anscombe (New York: The Macmillan Company, 1956; Oxford: Basil Blackwell & Mott Ltd., 1956). The Roman numerals at the beginning of the various sections indicate the parts of the book from which the various sections were taken; the original paragraph numbers have been retained. We are greatly indebted to the editors of Wittgenstein for their many valuable suggestions concerning what we should include in these selections, many of which have been adopted. At the suggestion of Mr. Rhees, we have placed paragraph 2 of Part IV after paragraph 40 of Part V.*

(I have made the patterns memorable on purpose) by correlating them:

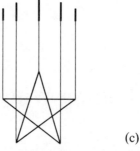

(c)

Now what do I ascertain when I look at this figure? What I see is a star with threadlike appendages.—

26. But I can make use of the figure like this: five people stand arranged in a pentagon; against the wall are wands, like the strokes in (a); I look at the figure (c) and say: "I can give each of the people a wand".

I could regard figure (c) as a schematic *picture* of my giving the five men a wand each.

27. For if I first draw some arbitrary polygon:

and then some arbitrary series of strokes

I can find out by correlating them whether I have as many angles in the top figure as strokes in the bottom one. (I do not know how it would turn out.) And so I can also say that by drawing projection-lines I have ascertained that there are as many strokes at the top of figure (c) as the star beneath has points. (Temporally!) In this way of taking it the figure is not like a mathematical proof (any more than it is a mathematical proof when I divide a bag of apples among a group of people and find that each can have just *one* apple).

I can however conceive figure (c) as a mathematical proof. Let us give names to the shapes of the patterns (a) and (b): let (a) be called a "hand", *H*, and (b) a "pentacle", *P*. I have proved that *H* has as many strokes as *P* has angles. And this proposition is once more non-temporal.

28. A proof—I might say—is a *single* pattern, at one end of which are

written certain sentences and at the other end a sentence (which we call the 'proved proposition'.)

To describe such a pattern we may say: in it the proposition ... follows from.... This is one way of describing a *design*, which might also be for example an ornament (a wallpaper design). I can say, then, "In the proof on that blackboard the proposition p follows from q and r", and that is simply a description of what can be seen there. But it is not the mathematical proposition that p follows from q and r. That has a different application. It says—as one might put it—that it makes sense to speak of a proof (pattern) in which p follows from q and r. Just as one can say that the proposition "white is lighter than black" asserts that it makes sense to speak of two objects, the lighter one white and the other black, but not of two objects, the lighter one black and the other white.

29. Let us imagine that we had given a paradigm of 'lighter' and 'darker' in the shape of a white and a black patch, and now, so to speak, we use it to deduce that red is darker than white.

30. The proposition proved by (c) now serves as a new prescription for ascertaining numerical equality: if one set of objects has been arranged in the form of a hand and another as the angles of a pentacle, we say the two sets are equal in number.

31. "But isn't that merely because we have already correlated H and P and seen that they are the same in number?"—Yes, but if they were so in one case, how do I know that they will be so again now?—"Why, because it is of the *essence* of H and P to be the same in number."—But how can you have brought *that* out by correlating them? (I thought the counting or correlation merely yielded the result that these two groups before me were —or were not—the same in number.)

—"But now, if he has an H of things and a P of things, and he actually correlates them, it surely isn't *possible* for him to get any result but that they are the same in number.—And that it is not possible can surely be seen from the proof."—But *isn't* it possible? If, e.g., he—as someone else might say—omits to draw one of the correlating lines. But I admit that in an enormous majority of cases he will always get the same result, and, if he did not get it, would think something had put him out. And if it were not like this the ground would be cut away from under the whole proof. For we decide to use the proof-picture instead of correlating the groups; we do *not* correlate them, but *instead* compare the groups with those of the proof (in which indeed two groups are correlated with one another).

32. I might also say as a result of the proof: "From now on an H and a P are called 'the same in number' ".

Or: The proof doesn't *explore* the essence of the two figures, but it does express what I am going to count as belonging to the essence of the figures from now on.——I deposit what belongs to the essence among the paradigms of language.

The mathematician creates *essence*.

33. When I say "This proposition follows from that one", that is to accept a rule. The acceptance is *based* on the proof. That is to say, I find this chain (this figure) acceptable as a *proof*.——"But could I do otherwise? Don't I *have* to find it acceptable?"—Why do you say you have to? Because at the end of the proof you say, e.g.: "Yes—I have to accept this conclusion". But that is after all only the expression of your unconditional acceptance.

I.e. (I believe): the words "I have to admit this" are used in *two kinds* of case: when we have got a proof—and also with reference to the individual steps of the proof themselves.

34. And how does it come out that the proof *compels* me? Well, in the fact that once I have got it I go ahead in such-and-such a way, and refuse any other path. All I should further say as a final argument against someone who did not want to go that way, would be: "Why, don't you see ...!"— and that is no *argument*.

35. "But, if you are right, how does it come about that all men (or at any rate all normal men) accept these patterns as proofs of these propositions?"—It is true, there is great—and interesting—agreement here.

36. Imagine you have a row of marbles, and you number them with Arabic numerals, which run from 1 to 100; then you make a big gap after every 10, and in each 10 a rather smaller gap in the middle with 5 on either side: this makes the 10 stand out clearly as 10; now you take the sets of 10 and put them one below another, and in the middle of the column you make a bigger gap, so that you have five rows above and five below; and now you number the rows from 1 to 10.—We have, so to speak, done drill with the marbles. I can say that we have unfolded properties of the hundred marbles. —But now imagine that this whole process, this experiment with the hundred marbles, were filmed. What I now see on the screen is surely not an experiment, for the picture of an experiment is not itself an experiment.—But I see the 'mathematically essential' thing about the process in the projection too! For here there appear first a hundred spots, and then they are arranged in tens, and so on and so on.

Thus I might say: the proof does not serve as an experiment; but it does serve as the picture of an experiment.

37. Put two apples on a bare table, see that no one comes near them and nothing shakes the table; now put another two apples on the table; now count the apples that are there. You have made an experiment; the result of the counting is probably 4. (We should present the result like this: when, in such-and-such circumstances, one puts first 2 apples and then

another 2 on a table, mostly none disappear and none get added.) And analogous experiments can be carried out, with the same result, with all kinds of solid bodies.—This is how our children learn sums; for one makes them put down three beans and then another three beans and then count what is there. If the result at one time were 5, at another 7 (say because, *as we should now say*, one sometimes got added, and one sometimes vanished of itself), then the first thing we said would be that beans were no good for teaching sums. But if the same thing happened with sticks, fingers, lines and most other things, that would be the end of all sums.

"But shouldn't we then still have $2 + 2 = 4$?"—This sentence would have become unusable.

38. "You only need to look at the figure

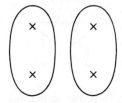

to see that $2 + 2$ are 4."—Then I only need to look at the figure

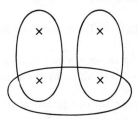

to see that $2 + 2 + 2$ are 4.

39. What do I convince anyone of, if he has followed the film projection of the experiment with the hundred marbles?

One might say, I convince him that it happened like that.—But this would not be a mathematical conviction.——But can't I say: *I impress a procedure on him*? This procedure is the regrouping of 100 things in 10 rows of 10. And this procedure can *as a matter of fact* always be carried out again. And he can rightly be convinced of that.

40. And that is how the proof (25) impresses a procedure on us by drawing projection-lines: the procedure of one-one correlation of the *H* and the *P*.—"But doesn't it also *convince* me of the fact that this[1] correlation

---

[1] Is 'this correlation' here the correlation of the patterns in the proof itself? A thing cannot be at the same time the measure and the thing measured. (Note in margin.)

is *possible*?"—If that is supposed to mean: you can always carry it out—, then that doesn't have to be true at all. But the drawing of the projection-lines convinces us that there are as many lines above as angles below; and it supplies us with a model to use in correlating such patterns.—"But surely what the model shews in this way is that it does work, not that it did work this time? In the sense in which it wouldn't have worked if the top figure had been | | | | | | instead of ₁ | | | ₁,"—How is that? doesn't it work then? Like *this* e.g.:

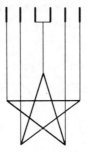

This figure too could be used to prove something. It could be used to show that groups of these forms *cannot* be given a 1-1 correlation.[2] 'A 1-1 correlation is impossible here' means, e.g., "these figures and 1-1 correlation don't fit together."

"I didn't mean it like that!"—Then show me how you mean it, and I'll do it.

But can't I say that the figure shows *how* such a correlation is possible— and mustn't it for that reason also show *that* it is possible?—

41. Now what was the point of our proposal to attach names to the five parallel strokes and the five-pointed star? What is done by their having got names? It will be a means of indicating something about the kind of use these figures have. Namely—that we recognize them as such-and-such at a glance. To do so, we don't count their strokes or angles; for us they are typical shapes, like knife and fork, like letters and numerals.

Thus, when given the order "Draw an *H*" (for example)—I can produce this shape immediately.—Now the proof teaches me a way of correlating the two shapes. (I should like to say that it is not merely these individual figures that are correlated in the proof, but the *shapes themselves*. But this surely only means that these shapes are well impressed on my mind; are impressed as paradigms.) Now isn't it possible for me to get into difficulties when I want to correlate the shapes *H* and *P*—say by there being an angle too many at the bottom or a stroke too many at the top?—"But surely not,

---

[2] On the strength of the figure I shall, e.g., try to effect one correlation, but not the other, and shall say that that one is not possible. (Note in margin.)

if you have really drawn *H* and *P* again!—And that can be proved; look at this figure."

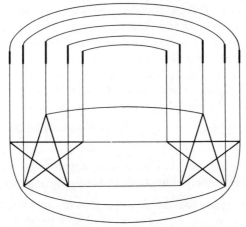

—This figure teaches me a new way of checking whether I have really drawn the same figures; but can't I still get into difficulties when I now want to use this model as a guide? But I say that I am certain I shall not normally get into any difficulties.

42. There is a puzzle which consists in making a particular figure, e.g. a rectangle, out of given pieces. The division of the figure is such that we find it difficult to discover the right arrangement of the parts. Let it for example be this:

What do you discover when you succeed in arranging it?—You discover a position—of which you did not think before.—Very well; but can't we also say: you find out that these triangles can be arranged like this?—But 'these triangles': are they the actual ones in the rectangle above, or are they triangles which have yet to be arranged like that?

43. If you say: "I should never have thought that these shapes could be arranged like that", we can't point to the solution of the puzzle and say: "Oh, you didn't think the pieces could be arranged like that?"—You would reply: "I mean, I didn't think of this way of arranging them at all".

44. Let us imagine the physical properties of the parts of the puzzle to be such that they can't come into the desired position. Not, however, that

one feels a resistance if one tries to put them in this position; but one simply tries everything else, only not *this*, and the pieces don't get into this position by accident either. This position is as it were excluded from space. As if there were e.g. a 'blind spot' in our brain here.—And *isn't* it like this when I believe I have tried all *possible* arrangements and have always passed this one by, as if bewitched?

Can't we say: the figure which shows you the solution removes a blindness, or even changes your geometry? It as it were shows you a new dimension of space. (As if a fly were shown the way out of the fly-bottle.)

45. A demon has cast a spell round this position and excluded it from our space.

46. The new position has as it were come to be out of nothingness. Where there was nothing, now there suddenly is something.

47. In what sense has the solution shewn you that such-and-such can be done? Before, you could *not* do it—and now perhaps you can.—

48. I said, "I accept such-and-such as proof of a proposition"—but is it possible for me *not* to accept the figure shewing the arrangement of the pieces as proof that these pieces can be arranged to have this periphery?

49. But now imagine that one of the pieces is lying so as to be the *mirror-image* of the corresponding part of the pattern. Now you want to arrange the figure according to the pattern; you see it must work, but you never hit on the idea of turning the piece over, and you find that you do not succeed in fitting the puzzle together.

50. A rectangle can be made of two parallelograms and two triangles. Proof:

A child would find it difficult to hit on the composition of a rectangle with these parts, and would be surprised by the fact that two sides of the parallelograms make a straight line, when the parallelograms are, after all, askew. It might strike him as if the rectangle came out of these figures by something like magic. True, he has to admit that they do form a rectangle, but it is by a trick, by a distorted arrangement, in an unnatural way.

I can imagine the child, after having put the two parallelograms together in *this* way, not believing his eyes when he sees that they fit like *that*. 'They *don't look* as if they fitted together like that.' And I could imagine its being said: It's only through some hocus-pocus that it looks to us as if *they* yielded the rectangle—in reality they have changed their nature, they aren't these parallelograms any more.

51. "You admit *this*—then you must admit *this* too."—He *must* admit it—and all the time it is possible that he does not admit it! You want to say: "if he *thinks*, he must admit it".

"I'll show you why you have to admit it."—I shall bring a case before your eyes which will determine you to judge this way if you think about it.

52. Now, how can the manipulations of the proof make him admit anything?

53. "Now you will admit that 5 consists of 3 and 2."

I will only admit it, if that is not to admit anything. Except—that I want to use *this picture*.

54. One might for example take this figure

as a proof of the fact that 100 parallelograms arranged like this must yield a straight strip. Then, when one actually does put 100 together, one gets e.g. a slightly curved strip.—But the proof has determined us to use this picture and form of expression: if they don't yield a straight strip, they were not accurately constructed.

55. Just think, how can the picture (or procedure) that you show me now oblige me always to judge in such-and-such a way?

If what we have here is an experiment, then surely *one* is too little to bind me to any judgment.

56. The one who is offering the proof says: "Look at this figure. What shall we say about it? Surely that a rectangle consists of ...?—"

Or again: "Now, surely you call this a 'parallelogram' and this a 'triangle', and *this* is what it is like for one figure to consist of others".

57. "Yes, you have convinced me that a rectangle always consists of ..."—Should I also say: "Yes, you have convinced me that *this* rectangle

(the one in the proof) consists of ..."? For wouldn't this be the more modest proposition, which you ought to grant even if perhaps you don't yet grant the general proposition? But oddly enough if *that* is what you grant, you seem to be granting, not the more modest geometrical proposition, but what is not a proposition of geometry at all. Of course not—for as regards the rectangle in the proof he didn't convince me of anything. (I shouldn't have been in any doubt about this figure, if I had seen it previously.) As far as concerns this figure I acknowledged everything of my own accord. And he merely used it to make me realize something.—But on the other hand, if he didn't convince me of anything as regards this rectangle, then how has he convinced me of a property of other rectangles?

58. "True, this shape doesn't look as if it could consist of two skew parts."

What are you surprised at? Surely not at seeing this figure. It is something *in* the figure that surprises me.—But there isn't anything going on in the figure!

What surprises me is the way straight and skew go together. It makes me as it were dizzy.

59. But I do actually say: "I have convinced myself that this figure can be constructed with these pieces", e.g. I have seen a picture of the solution of the puzzle.

Now if I say this to somebody it is surely supposed to mean: "Just try: these bits, properly arranged, really do yield the figure". I want to encourage him to do something and I forecast that he will succeed. And the forecast is founded on the ease with which we can construct the figure from the pieces as soon as we know *how*.

60. You say you are astonished at what the proof shows you. But are you astonished at its having been possible to draw these lines? No. You are only astonished when you tell yourself that two bits like this *yield* this shape. When, that is, you think yourself into the situation of seeing the result after having expected something different.

61. "*This* follows inexorably from *that*."—True, in this demonstration this issues from that.

This is a demonstration for whoever acknowledges it as a demonstration. If anyone *doesn't* acknowledge it, doesn't go by it as a demonstration, then he has parted company with us even before it comes to talk.

62.

Here we have something that looks inexorable—. And yet it can be 'inexorable' only in its consequences! For otherwise it is nothing but a picture.

What does the action at a distance—as it might be called—of this pattern consist in?

63. I have read a proof—and now I am convinced.—What if I straightway forgot this conviction?

For it is a peculiar procedure: I *go through* the proof and then accept its result.—I mean: this is simply what we *do*. This is use and custom among us, or a fact of our natural history.

APPENDIX I[3]

1. It is easy to think of a language in which there is not a form for questions, or commands, but question and command are expressed in the form of statements, e.g. in forms corresponding to our: "I should like to know if ..." and "My wish is that ...".

No one would say of a question (e.g. whether it is raining outside) that it was true or false. Of course it is English to say so of such a sentence as "I want to know whether ...". But suppose this form were always used instead of the question?—

2. The great majority of sentences that we speak, write and read, are statement sentences.

And—you say—these sentences are true or false. Or, as I might also say, the game of truth-functions is played with them. For assertion is not something that gets added to the proposition, but an essential feature of the game

[3] R. L. Goodstein writes as follows of the present section:

Part I is followed by two appendices; the first of these discusses an informal version of Gödel's non-demonstrable proposition. Apart from the very important observation (7) " 'But may there not be true propositions which are written in this (Russell's) symbolism but are not provable in Russell's system?' 'True propositions', hence propositions which are true in *another* system, i.e., can rightly be asserted in another game, ...; and a proposition which cannot be proved in Russell's system is 'true' or 'false' in a different sense from a proposition of *Principia Mathematica*," this appendix is unimportant and throws no light on Gödel's work. If the date of this appendix is 1938 as the preface tell us, then we are faced with the mystery that what Wittgenstein said on the subject in 1935 was far in advance of his standpoint three years later. For Wittgenstein with remarkable insight said in the early thirties that Gödel's results showed that the notion of a finite cardinal could not be expressed in an axiomatic system and that formal number variables must necessarily take values other than natural numbers; a view which, following Skolem's 1934 publication, of which Wittgenstein was unaware, is now generally accepted. [Review of the *Remarks*, *Mind*, vol. LXVI, pp. 549-53.]

We agree with Professor Goodstein that Appendix I is not an important part of Wittgenstein's contribution to the philosophy of mathematics. We reprint it here because we feel that the issues raised in it and further discussed in A. R. Anderson's review (cf. pp. 500ff) are interesting in their own right and therefore worthy of being discussed. We are indebted to Mr. R. Rhees for his suggestion that we include the foregoing remarks.—[Eds.]

we play with it. Comparable, say, to that characteristic of chess by which there is winning and losing in it, the winner being the one who takes the other's king. Of course, there could be a game in a certain sense very near akin to chess, consisting in making the chess moves, but without there being any winning and losing in it; or with different conditions for winning.

3. Imagine it were said: A command consists of a proposal ('assumption') and the commanding of the thing proposed.

4. Might we not do arithmetic without having the idea of uttering arithmetical *propositions*, and without ever having been struck by the similarity between a multiplication and a proposition?

Should we not shake our heads, though, when someone showed us a multiplication done wrong, as we do when someone tells us it is raining, if it is not raining?—Yes; and here is a point of connection. But we also make gestures to stop our dog, e.g. when he behaves as we do not wish.

We are used to saying "2 times 2 is 4", and the verb "is" makes this into a proposition, and apparently establishes a close kinship with everything that we call a 'proposition'. Whereas it is a matter only of a very superficial relationship.

5. Are there true propositions in Russell's system, which cannot be proved in his system?—What is called a true proposition in Russell's system, then?

6. For what does a proposition's *'being true'* mean? *'p' is true = p.* (That is the answer.)

So we want to ask something like: under what circumstances do we assert a proposition? Or: how is the assertion of the proposition used in the language-game? And the 'assertion of the proposition' is here contrasted with the utterance of the sentence e.g. as practice in elocution,—or as *part* of another proposition, and so on.

If, then, we ask in this sense: "Under what circumstances is a proposition asserted in Russell's game?" the answer is: at the end of one of his proofs, or as a 'fundamental law' (Pp.). There is no other way in this system of employing asserted propositions in Russell's symbolism.

7. "But may there not be true propositions which are written in this symbolism, but are not provable in Russell's system?"—'True propositions', hence propositions which are true in *another* system, i.e. can rightly be asserted in another game. Certainly; why should there not be such propositions; or rather: why should not propositions—of physics, e.g.—be written in Russell's symbolism? The question is quite analogous to: Can there be true propositions in the language of Euclid, which are not provable in his system, but are true?—Why, there are even propositions which are provable in Euclid's system, but are *false* in another system. May not triangles be— in another system—similar (*very* similar) which do not have equal angles?

—"But that's just a joke! For in that case they are not 'similar' to one another in the same sense!"—Of course not; and a proposition which cannot be proved in Russell's system is "true" or "false" in a different sense from a proposition of *Principia Mathematica*.

8. I imagine someone asking my advice; he says: "I have constructed a proposition (I will use '*P*' to designate it) in Russell's symbolism, and by means of certain definitions and transformations it can be so interpreted that it says: '*P* is not provable in Russell's system'. Must I not say that this proposition on the one hand is true, and on the other hand is unprovable? For suppose it were false; then it is true that it is provable. And that surely cannot be! And if it is proved, then it is proved that it is not provable. Thus it can only be true, but unprovable."

Just as we ask: " 'provable' in what system?", so we must also ask: " 'true' in what system?" 'True in Russell's system' means, as was said: proved in Russell's system; and 'false in Russell's system' means: the opposite has been proved in Russell's system.—Now what does your "suppose it is false" mean? *In the Russell sense* it means 'suppose the opposite is proved in Russell's system'; *if that is your assumption*, you will now presumably give up the interpretation that it is unprovable. And by 'this interpretation' I understand the translation into this English sentence.—If you assume that the proposition is provable in Russell's system, that means it is true *in the Russell sense*, and the interpretation "*P* is not provable" again has to be given up. If you assume that the proposition is true in the Russell sense, *the same* thing follows. Further: if the proposition is supposed to be false in some other than the Russell sense, then it does not contradict this for it to be proved in Russell's system. (What is called "losing" in chess may constitute winning in another game.)

9. For what does it mean to say that *P* and "*P* is unprovable" are the same proposition? It means that these *two* English sentences have a *single* expression in such-and-such a notation.

10. "But surely *P* cannot be provable, for, supposing it were proved, then the proposition that it is not provable would be proved." But if this were now proved, or if I believed—perhaps through an error—that I had proved it, why should I not let the proof stand and say I must withdraw my interpretation "*unprovable*"?

11. Let us suppose I prove the unprovability (in Russell's system) of *P*; then by this proof I have proved *P*. Now if this proof were one in Russell's system—I should in that case have proved at once that it belonged and did not belong to Russell's system.—That is what comes of making up such sentences.—But there is a contradiction here!—Well, then there is a contradiction here. Does it do any harm here?

12. Is there harm in the contradiction that arises when someone says: "I am lying.—So I am not lying.—So I am lying.—etc."? I mean: does it make our language less usable if in this case, according to the ordinary rules, a proposition yields its contradictory, and vice versa?—the proposition *itself* is unusable, and these inferences equally; but why should they not be made? —It is a profitless performance!—It is a language-game with some similarity to the game of thumb-catching.

13. Such a contradiction is of interest only because it has tormented people, and because this shows both how tormenting problems can grow out of language, and what kind of things can torment us.

14. A proof of unprovability is as it were a geometrical proof; a proof concerning the geometry of proofs. Quite analogous e.g. to a proof that such-and-such a construction is impossible with ruler and compass. Now such a proof contains an element of prediction, a physical element. For in consequence of such a proof we say to a man: "Don't exert yourself to find a construction (of the trisection of an angle, say)—it can be proved that it can't be done". That is to say: it is essential that the proof of unprovability should be capable of being applied in this way. It must—we might say—be a *forcible reason* for giving up the search for a proof (i.e. for a construction of such-and-such a kind).
A contradiction is unusable as such a prediction.

15. Whether something is rightly called the proposition "X is unprovable" depends on how we prove this proposition. The proof alone shows what counts as the criterion of unprovability. The proof is part of the system of operations, of the game, in which the proposition is used, and shows us its 'sense'.
Thus the question is whether the 'proof of the unprovability of P' is here a forcible reason for the assumption that a proof of P will not be found.

16. The proposition "P is unprovable" has a different sense afterwards —from before it was proved.
If it is proved, then it is the terminal pattern in the proof of unprovability. —If it is unproved, then *what* is to count as a criterion of its truth is not yet *clear*, and—we can say—its sense it still veiled.

17. Now how am I to take P as having been proved? By a proof of unprovability? Or in some other way? Suppose it is by a proof of unprovability. Now, in order to see *what* has been proved, look at the proof. Perhaps it has here been proved that such-and-such forms of proof do not lead to P.—Or suppose P has been proved in a direct way—as I should like to put it—and so in that case there follows the proposition "P is unprovable", and it must now come out how this interpretation of the symbols of P collides with the fact of the proof, and why it has to be given up here.

Suppose however that not-*P* is proved.—Proved *how*? Say by *P*'s being proved directly—for from that follows that it is provable, and hence not-*P*. What am I to say now, "*P*" or "not-*P*"? Why not both? If someone asks me "Which is the case, *P*, or not-*P*?" then I reply: *P* stands at the end of a Russellian proof, so you write *P* in the Russellian system; on the other hand, however, it is then provable and this is expressed by not-*P*, but this proposition does not stand at the end of a Russellian proof, and so does not belong to the Russellian system.——When the interpretation "*P* is unprovable" was given to' *P*, this proof of *P* was not known, and so one cannot say that *P* says: *this* proof did not exist.——Once the proof has been constructed, this has created a *new situation*: and now we have to decide whether we will call *this* a proof (a *further* proof), or whether we will still call *this* the statement of unprovability.

Suppose not-*P* is directly proved; it is therefore proved that *P* can be directly proved! So this is once more a question of interpretation—unless we now also have a direct proof of *P*. If it were like that, well, that is how it would be.

(The superstitious fear and awe of mathematicians in face of contradiction.)

18. "But suppose, now, that the proposition were *false*—and hence provable?"—Why do you call it 'false'? Because you can see a proof?—Or for other reasons? For in that case it doesn't matter. For one can quite well call the Law of Contradiction false, on the grounds that we very often make good sense by answering a question "Yes and no". And the same for the proposition '$\sim \sim p = p$' because we employ double negation as a *strengthening* of the negation and not merely as its cancellation.

19. You say: "..., so *P* is true and unprovable". That presumably means: "Therefore *P*". That is all right with me——but for what purpose do you write down this 'assertion'? (It is as if someone had extracted from certain principles about natural forms and architectural style the idea that on Mount Everest, where no one can live, there belonged a châlet in the Baroque style.) And how could you make the truth of the assertion plausible to me, since you can make no use of it except to do these bits of legerdemain?

20. Here one needs to remember that the propositions of logic are so constructed as to have *no* application as *information* in practice. So it could very well be said that they were not *propositions* at all; and one's writing them down at all stands in need of justification. Now if we append to these 'propositions' a further sentence-like structure of another kind, then we are all the more in the dark about what kind of application this system of sign-combinations is supposed to have; for the mere *ring of a sentence* is not enough to give these connections of signs any meaning.

II

1939-40

1. 'A mathematical proof must be perspicuous.' Only a structure whose reproduction is an easy task is called a "proof". It must be possible to decide with certainty whether we really have the same proof twice over, or not. The proof must be a configuration whose exact reproduction can be certain. Or again: we must be sure we can exactly reproduce what is essential to the proof. It may for example be written down in two different handwritings or colours. What goes to make the reproduction of a proof is not anything like an exact reproduction of a shade of colour or a hand-writing.

It must be easy to write down *exactly* this proof again. This is where a written proof has an advantage over a drawing. The essentials of the latter have often been misunderstood. The drawing of a Euclidian proof may be inexact, in the sense that the straight lines are not straight, the segments of circles not exactly circular, etc. etc. and at the same time the drawing is still an exact proof; and from this it can be seen that this drawing does not —e.g.—demonstrate that such a construction results in a polygon with five equal sides; that what it proves is a proposition of geometry, not one about the properties of paper, compass, ruler and pencil.

[Connects with: proof a *picture* of an experiment.]

2. I want to say: if you have a proof-pattern that cannot be taken in, and by a change in notation you turn it into one that can, then you are producing a proof, where there was none before.

Now let us imagine a proof for a Russellian proposition stating an addition like '$a + b = c$', consisting of a few thousand signs. You will say: Seeing whether this proof is correct or not is a purely external difficulty, of no mathematical interest. ("One man takes in easily what someone else takes in with difficulty or not at all" etc. etc.)

The assumption is that the definitions serve merely to abbreviate the expression for the convenience of the calculator; whereas they are part of the calculation. By their aid expressions are produced which could not have been produced without it.

3. But how about the following: "While it is true that we cannot—in the ordinary sense—multiply 234 by 537 in the Russellian calculus, still there is a Russellian calculation corresponding to this multiplication."— What kind of correspondence is this? It might be like this: we can carry out this multiplication in the Russellian calculus too, only in a different symbolism,—just as, as we should certainly say, we can carry it out in a different number system. In that case, then, we could e.g. solve the practical problems for which we use that multiplication by means of the calculation in the Russellian calculus too, only in a more roundabout way.

Now let us imagine the cardinal numbers explained as 1, 1 + 1, (1 + 1) + 1, ((1 + 1) + 1) + 1, and so on. You say that the definitions introducing the figures of the decimal system are a mere matter of convenience; the calculation 703000 × 40000101 could be done in that wearisome notation too. But is that true?—"Of course it's true! I can surely write down, construct, a calculation in that notation corresponding to the calculation in the decimal notation."—But how do I know that it corresponds to it? Well, because I have derived it from the other by a given method.—But now if I look at it again half an hour later, may it not have altered? For one cannot command a clear view of it.

Now I ask: could we also find out the truth of the proposition 7034174 + 6594321 = 13628495 by means of a proof carried out in the first notation? —Is there such a proof of this proposition?—The answer is: no.

4. But still doesn't Russell teach us *one* way of adding?

Suppose we proved by Russell's method that $(\exists\ a \ldots g)\ (\exists a \ldots l) \supset (\exists a \ldots s)$ is a tautology; could we reduce our result to $g + l$'s being s? Now this presupposes that I can take the three bits of the alphabet as representatives of the proof. But does Russell's proof show this? After all I could obviously also have carried out Russell's proof with groups of signs in the brackets whose sequence made no characteristic impression on me, so that it would not have been possible to represent the group of signs between brackets by its last term.

Even assuming that the Russellian proof were carried out with a notation such as $x_1 x_2 \ldots x_{10} x_{11} \ldots x_{100} \ldots$ as in the decimal notation, and there were 100 members in the first pair of brackets, 300 in the second and 400 in the third, does the proof itself show that $100 + 300 = 400$?—What if this proof led at one time to this result, and at another to a different one, for example $100 + 300 = 420$? What is needed in order to see that the result of the proof, if it is correctly carried out, always depends solely on the last figures of the first two pairs of brackets?

But still for small numbers Russell does teach us to add; for then we take the groups of signs in the brackets in at a glance and we can take *them* as numerals; for example 'xy', 'xyz', 'xyzuv'.

Thus Russell teaches us a new calculus for reaching 5 from 2 and 3; and that is true even if we say that a logical calculus is only—frills tacked on to the arithmetical calculus.

The *application* of the calculation must take care of itself. And that is what is correct about 'formalism'.

The reduction of arithmetic to symbolic logic is supposed to shew the point of application of arithmetic, as it were the attachment by means of which it is plugged in to its application. As if someone were shewn, first a trumpet without the mouthpiece—and then the mouthpiece, which shows how a trumpet is used, brought into contact with the human body. But the attachment which Russell gives us is on the one hand too narrow, on the other hand too wide; too general and too special. The calculation takes care of its own application.

We extend our ideas from calculations with small numbers to ones with large numbers in the same kind of way as we imagine that, if the distance from here to the sun *could* be measured with a footrule, then we should get the very result that, as it is, we get in a quite different way. That is to say, we are inclined to take the measurement of length with a footrule as a model even for the measurement of the distance between two stars.

And one says, e.g. at school: "If we imagine rulers stretching from here to the sun ..." and seems in this way to explain what we understand by the distance between the sun and the earth. And the use of such a picture is all right, so long as it is clear to us that we can measure the distance from us to the sun, and that we cannot measure it with footrules.

5. Suppose someone were to say: "The only real proof of $1000 + 1000 = 2000$ is after all the Russellian one, which shews that the expression ... is a tautology"? For can I not prove that a tautology results if I have 1000 members in each of the two first pairs of brackets and 2000 in the third? And if I can prove that, then I can look at it as a proof of the arithmetical proposition.

In philosophy it is always good to put a *question* instead of an answer to a question.

For an answer to the philosophical question may easily be unfair; disposing of it by means of another question is not.

Then should I put a *question* here, for example, instead of the answer that that arithmetical proposition cannot be proved by Russell's method?

$$\overset{1}{(\ \ )}\ \overset{2}{(\ \ )} \supset \overset{3}{(\ \ )}$$

6. The proof that $(\ )\ (\ ) \supset (\ )$ is a tautology consists in always crossing out a term of the third pair of brackets for a term of (1) or (2). And there are many methods for such collating. Or one might even say: there are many ways of establishing the success of a 1-1 correlation. One way, for example, would be to construct a star-shaped pattern for the left-hand side of the implication and another one for the right-hand side and then to compare these in their turn by making an ornament out of the two of them.

Thus the rule could be given: "If you want to know whether the numbers A and B together actually yield C, write down an expression of the form ... and correlate the variables in the brackets by writing down (or trying to) the proof that the expression is a tautology".

My objection to this is *not* that it is arbitrary to prescribe just this way of collating, but that it cannot be established in this way that $1000 + 1000 = 2000$.

7. Imagine that you had written down a 'formula' a mile long, and you showed by transformation that it was tautologous ('if *it* has not altered meanwhile', one would have to say). Now we *count* the terms in the brackets or we divide them up and make the expression into one that can be taken in, and it comes out that there are 7566 terms in the first pair of brackets, 2434 in the second, 10000 in the third. Now have I proved that $2434 + 7566 = 10000$?—That depends—one might say—on whether you are certain that the counting has really yielded the number of terms which stood between the brackets in the course of the proof.

Could one say: "Russell teaches us to write as many variables in the third pair of brackets as were in the first two together"? But really: he teaches us to write a variable in (3) for every variable in (1) and (2).

But do we learn from this what number is the sum of two given numbers? Perhaps it is said: "Of course, for in the third pair of brackets we have the paradigm, the prototype of the new number". But in what sense is $|\,|\,|\,|\,|\,|\,|\,|\,|\,|\,|\,|\,|\,|\,|\,|$ the paradigm of a number? Consider how it can be used as such.

8. Above all, the Russellian tautology corresponding to the proposition $a + b = c$ does not shew us in what notation the number c is to be written, and there is no reason why it should not be written in the form $a + b$.— For Russell does not teach us the technique of, say, adding in the decimal system.—But could we perhaps derive it from his technique?

Let us just ask the following question: Can one derive the technique of the decimal system from that of the system $1, 1 + 1, (1 + 1) + 1$, etc.?

Could this question not also be formulated as follows: if one has one technique of calculation in the one system and one in the other,—how is it shown that the two are equivalent?

9. "A proof ought to shew not merely that this is how it is, but this is how it has to be."

In what circumstances does counting show this?

One would like to say: "When the figures and the thing being counted yield a memorable configuration. When this configuration is now used in place of any fresh counting."—But here we seem to be talking only of *spatial* configurations: but if we know a series of words by heart and then co-ordinate two such series, one to one, saying for example: "First—Monday; second—Tuesday; third—Wednesday; etc."—can we not *prove* in this way that from Monday to Thursday is four days?

For the question is: What do we call a "memorable configuration"? What is the criterion for its being impressed on our minds? Or is the answer to that: "That we use it as a paradigm of identity!"?

10. We do not make *experiments* on a sentence or a proof in order to establish its properties.

How do we reproduce, how do we copy, a proof?—Not, e.g. by taking measurements of it.

Suppose a proof were so hugely long that it could not possibly be taken in? Or let us look at a different case: Let there be a long row of strokes engraved in hard rock which is our paradigm for the number that we call 1000. We call this row the proto-thousand and if we want to know whether there are a thousand men in a square, we draw lines or stretch threads. (1-1 correlation.)

Now here the sign of the number 1000 has the identity, not of a shape, but of a physical object. We could imagine a 'proto-hundred' similarly, and a proof, which we could not take in at a glance, that $10 \times 100 = 1000$.

The figure for 1000 in the system of $1 + 1 + 1 + 1 \ldots$ cannot be recognized by its *shape*.

11. |||||||||||||||||||||||||||||||||| ||||||||||||||||||
Is this pattern a proof of $27 + 16 = 43$, because one reaches '27' if one counts the strokes on the left-hand side, '16' on the right-hand side, and '43' when one counts the whole row?

Where is the queerness of calling the pattern the proof of this proposition? It lies in the kind of way this proof is to be reproduced or known again; in its not having any characteristic visual shape.

Now even if that proof has not any such visual shape, still I can copy (reproduce) it exactly—so isn't the figure a proof after all? I might e.g. have it engraved on a bit of steel and passed from hand to hand. So I should tell someone: "Here you have the proof that $27 + 16 = 43$".—Well, can't one say *after all* that he proves the proposition with the aid of the pattern? Yes; but the pattern is not the proof.

This, however, would surely be called a proof of $250 + 3220 = 3470$: one counts on from 250 and at the same time begins counting from 1 and co-ordinates the two counts:

$$251 \ldots . 1$$
$$252 \ldots . 2$$
$$253 \ldots . 3$$
$$\text{etc.}$$
$$3470 \ldots . 3220$$

That could be called a proof in 3220 steps. It is surely a proof—and can it be called perspicuous?

12. What is the invention of the decimal system really? The invention of a system of abbreviations——but what is the system of the abbreviations? Is it simply the system of the new signs or is it also a system of applying them for the purpose of abbreviation? And if it is the latter, then it *is* a new way of looking at the old system of signs.

Can we start from the system of $1 + 1 + 1 \ldots$ and learn to calculate in the decimal system through mere abbreviations of the notation?

13. Suppose that following Russell I have proved a proposition of the form $(\exists xyz \ldots)(\exists uvw \ldots) \supset (\exists abc \ldots)$—and now 'I make it perspicuous' by writing signs $x_1, x_2, x_3 \ldots$ over the variables—am I to say that following Russell I have proved an arithmetical proposition in the decimal system?

But for every proof in the decimal system there is surely a corresponding one in Russell's system!—How do we know there is? Let us leave intuition on one side.—But it can be proved.—

If a number in the decimal system is defined in terms of $1, 2, 3, \ldots 9, 0$, and the signs $0, 1 \ldots 9$ in terms of $1, 1 + 1, (1 + 1) + 1, \ldots$ can one then use the recursive explanation of the decimal system to reach a sign of the form $1 + 1 + 1 \ldots$ from any number?

Suppose someone were to say: Russellian arithmetic agrees with ordinary arithmetic up to numbers less than 10^{10}; but then it diverges from it. And now he produces a Russellian proof that $10^{10} + 1 = 10^{10}$. Now why should I not trust such a proof? How will anybody convince me that I must have miscalculated in the Russellian proof?

But then do I need a proof from another system in order to ascertain whether I have miscalculated in the first proof? Is it not enough for me to write down that proof in a way that makes it possible to take it in?

14. Is not my whole difficulty one of seeing how it is possible, without abandoning Russell's logical calculus, to reach the concept of the *set of variables* in the expression '$(\exists xyz \ldots)$', where this expression cannot be taken in?—

Well, but it can be made surveyable by writing: $(\exists x_1, x_2, x_3,$ etc.$)$. And still there is something that I do not understand: the criterion for the identity of such an expression has now surely been changed: I now see in a different way that the set of signs in two such expressions is the same.

What I am tempted to say is: Russell's proof can indeed be continued step by step, but at the end one does not rightly know what one has proved —at least not by the old criteria. By making it possible to command a clear view of the Russellian proof, I prove something about this proof.

I want to say: one need not acknowledge the Russellian technique of calculation at all—and can prove by means of a different technique of calculation that there *must* be a Russellian proof of the proposition. But in that case, of course, the proposition is no longer based upon the Russellian proof.

Or again: its being possible to imagine a Russellian proof for every proved proposition of the form $m + n = l$ does not show that the proposition is based on this proof. For it is conceivable that the Russellian proof of one proposition should not be distinguishable from the Russellian proof of another and should be called different only because they are the translations of two recognizably different proofs.

Or again: something stops being a proof when it stops being a paradigm, for example Russell's logical calculus; and on the other hand any other calculus which serves as a paradigm is acceptable.

15. It is a fact that different methods of counting practically always agree.

When I count the squares on a chess-board I practically always reach '64'.

If I know two series of words by heart, for example numerals and the alphabet, and I put them into one-one correspondence:

$$
\begin{array}{cc}
a & 1 \\
b & 2 \\
c & 3 \\
\end{array}
$$
etc.

at 'z' I practically always reach '26'.

There is such a thing as: knowing a series of words by heart. When am I said to know the poem ... by heart? The criteria are rather complicated. Agreement with a printed text is one. What would have to happen to make me doubt that I really know the *ABC* by heart? It is difficult to imagine.

But I use reciting or writing down a series of words from memory as a criterion for equality of numbers, equality of sets.

Ought I now to say: all that doesn't matter—logic still remains the fundamental calculus, only whether I have the same formula twice is of course differently established in different cases?

16. It is not logic—I should like to say—that compels me to accept a proposition of the form $(\exists \quad) (\exists \quad) \supset (\exists \quad)$, when there are a million variables in the first two pairs of brackets and two million in the third. I want to say: logic would not compel me to accept any proposition at all in this case. Something *else* compels me to accept such a proposition as in accord with logic.

Logic compels me only so far as the logical calculus compels me.

But surely it is essential to the calculus with 1000000 that this number must be capable of resolution in a sum $1 + 1 + 1 \ldots$, and in order to be certain that we have the right number of units before us, we can number the units: $\underset{1 \quad 2 \quad 3 \quad 4 \qquad\qquad 1000000}{1 + 1 + 1 + 1 + \cdots + 1}$. This notation would be like: '100,000,000,000' which also makes the numeral surveyable. And I can surely imagine someone's having a great sum of money in pennies entered in a book in which perhaps they appear as numbers of 100 places, with which I have to calculate. I should now begin to translate them into a surveyable notation, but still I should call them 'numerals', should treat them as a record of numbers. For I should even regard it as the record of a number if someone were to tell me that N has as many shillings as this vessel will hold peas. Another case again: "He has as many shillings as the Song of Songs has letters".

17. The notation '$x_1, x_2, x_3, \ldots$' gives a shape to the expression '$(\exists \ldots)$', and so to the R-proved tautology.

Let me ask the following question: Is it not conceivable that the 1-1 correlation could not be trustworthily carried out in the Russellian proof, that when, *for example*, we try to use it for adding, we regularly get a result contradicting the usual one, and that we blame this on fatigue, which makes us leave out certain steps unawares? And might we not then say:—if only we didn't get tired we should get the same result—? Because *logic* demands it? Does it demand it, then? Aren't we here rectifying logic by means of another calculus?

Suppose we took 100 steps of the logical calculus at a time and now got trustworthy results, while we don't get them if we try to take all the steps singly——one would like to say: the calculation is still based on unit steps, since 100 steps at a time is defined by means of unit steps.—But the definition says: to take 100 steps at a time is the same thing as ..., and yet we take the 100 steps at a time and *not* 100 unit steps.

Still, in the shortened calculation I am obeying a *rule*———and how was this rule justified?—What if the shortened and the unshortened proof yielded different results?

18. What I am saying surely comes to this: I can e.g. define '10' as '$1 + 1 + 1 + 1 \ldots$' and '100×2' as '$2 + 2 + 2 \ldots$' but I cannot therefore necessarily define '100×10' as '$10 + 10 + 10 \ldots$', nor yet as '$1 + 1 + 1 + 1 \ldots$'.

I can find out that 100×100 equals 10000 by means of a 'shortened' procedure. Then why should I not regard *that* as the original proof procedure?

A shortened procedure tells me what *ought* to come out with the unshortened one. (Instead of the other way round.)

19. "But the calculation is surely based on the unit steps. ..." Yes; but in a different way. For the procedure of proof is a different one.

I could say for example: $10 = 1 + 1 + 1 + 1 + 1 + 1 + 1 + 1 + 1 + 1$ *and in like manner* $100 = 10 + 10 + 10 + 10 + 10 + 10 + 10 + 10 + 10 + 10$. Have I not based the definition of 100 on the successive addition of 1? But in the same way as if I had added 100 units? Is there any need at all in my notation for a sign of the form—'1 + 1 + 1 ...' with 100 components of the sum?

The danger here seems to be one of looking at the shortened procedure as a pale shadow of the unshortened one. The rule of counting is not counting.

20. What does taking 100 steps of the calculus 'at once' consist in? Surely in one's regarding, not the unit step, but a different step, as decisive.

In ordinary addition of whole numbers in the decimal system we make steps in units, steps in tens, etc. Can one say that the procedure is founded on one of only making unit steps? One might justify it like this: the result of the addition does indeed look so—'7583'; but the explanation of this sign, its meaning, which must ultimately receive expression in its application too, is surely of this sort: 1 + 1 + 1 + 1 + 1 and so on. But is it so? Must the numerical sign be explained in this way, or this explanation receive expression implicitly in its application? I believe that if we reflect it turns out that that is not the case.

Calculating with graphs or with a slide-rule.

Of course when we check the one kind of calculation by the other, we normally get the same result. But if there are several kinds—who says, if they do not agree, which is the proper method of calculation, with its roots at the source of mathematics?

21. Where a doubt can make its appearance whether *this* is really the pattern of *this* proof, where we are prepared to doubt the identity of the proof, the derivation has lost its proving power. For the proof serves as a measure.

Could one say: it is part of proof to have an accepted criterion for the correct reproduction of a proof?

That is to say, e.g.: we must be able to be certain, it must hold as certain for us, that we have not overlooked a sign in the course of the proof. That no demon can have deceived us by making a sign disappear without our noticing, or by adding one, etc.

One might say: When it can be said: "Even if a demon had deceived us, still everything would be all right", then the prank he wanted to play on us has simply failed of its purpose.

22. Proof, one might say, does not merely show *that* it is like this, but: *how* it is like this. It shows *how* 13 + 14 yield 27.

"A proof must be capable of being taken in" means: we must be prepared to use it as our guide-line in judging.

When I say "a proof is a picture"—it can be thought of as a cinematographic picture.

We construct the proof once for all.

A proof must of course have the character of a model.

The proof (the pattern of the proof) shows us the result of a procedure (the construction); and we are convinced that a procedure regulated in *this* way always leads to this configuration.

(The proof exhibits a fact of synthesis to us.)

23. When we say that a proof is a model,—we must, of course, not be saying anything new.

Proof must be a procedure of which I say: Yes, this is how it has to be; this must come out if I proceed according to this rule.

Proof, one might say, must originally be a kind of experiment—but is then taken simply as a picture.

If I pour two lots of 200 apples together and count them, and the result is 400, that is not a proof that 200 + 200 = 400. That is to say, we should not want to take this fact as a paradigm for judging all similar situations.

To say: "these 200 apples and these 200 apples come to 400"—means: when one puts them together, none are lost or added, they behave *normally*.

24. "This is the model for the addition of 200 and 200"—not: "this is the model of the fact that 200 and 200 added together yield 400". The process of adding *did* indeed yield 400, but now we take this result as the criterion for the correct addition—or simply: for the addition—of these numbers.

The proof must be our model, our picture, of how these operations have *a result*.

The 'proved proposition' expresses what is to be read off from the proof-picture.

The proof is now our model of correctly counting 200 apples and 200 apples together: that is to say, it defines a new concept: 'the counting of 200 and 200 objects together'. Or, as we could also say: "a new criterion for nothing's having been lost or added".

The proof *defines* 'correctly counting together'.

The proof is our model for a particular *result's being yielded*, which serves as an object of comparison (yardstick) for real changes.

25. The proof convinces us of something————though what interests us is, not the mental state of conviction, but the applications attaching to this conviction.

For this reason the assertion that the proof convinces us of the truth of this proposition leaves us cold,—since this expression is capable of the most various constructions.

When I say: "the proof convinces me of something", still the proposition expressing this conviction need not be constructed in the proof. As e.g. we multiply, but do not necessarily write down the result in the form of the proposition '... × ... = ...' So we shall presumably say: the multiplication gives us this conviction without our ever uttering the *sentence* expressing it.

A psychological disadvantage of proofs that construct *propositions* is that they easily make us forget that the *sense* of the result is not to be read off from this by itself, but from the *proof*. In this respect the intrusion of the Russellian symbolism into the proofs has done a great deal of harm.

The Russellian signs veil the important forms of proof as it were to the point of unrecognizability, as when a human form is wrapped up in a lot of cloth.

26. Let us remember that in mathematics we are convinced of *grammatical* propositions; so the expression, the result, of our being convinced is that we *accept a rule*.

Nothing is more likely than that the verbal expression of the result of a mathematical proof is calculated to delude us with a myth.

27. I am trying to say something like this: even if the proved mathematical proposition seems to point to a reality outside itself, still it is only the expression of acceptance of a new measure (of reality).

Thus we take the constructability (provability) of this symbol (that is, of the mathematical proposition) as a sign that we are to transform symbols in such and such a way.

We have won through to a piece of knowledge in the proof? And the final proposition expresses this knowledge? Is this knowledge now independent of the proof (is the navel string cut)?—Well, the proposition is now used by itself and without having the proof attached to it.

Why should I not say: in the proof I have won through to a *decision*?

The proof places this decision in a system of decisions.

(I might of course also say: "the proof convinces me that this rule serves my purpose". But to say this might easily be misleading.)

28. The proposition proved by means of the proof serves as a rule—and so as a paradigm. For we *go by* the rule.

But does the proof only bring us to the point of going by this rule (accepting it), or does it also show us *how* we are to go by it?

For the mathematical proposition is to show us what it makes SENSE to say.

The proof constructs a proposition; but the point is *how* it constructs it. Sometimes, for example, it first constructs a *number* and then comes the proposition that there is such a number. When we say that the construction must *convince* us of the proposition, that means that it must lead us to apply this proposition in such-and-such a way. That it must determine us to accept this as sense, that not.

29. What is in common between the purpose of a Euclidean construction, say the bisection of a line, and the purpose of deriving a rule from rules by means of logical inferences?

The common thing seems to be that by the construction of a sign I compel the acceptance of a sign.

Could we say: "mathematics creates new *expressions*, not new propositions"?

Inasmuch, that is, as mathematical propositions are instruments taken up into the language once for all—and their proof shows the place where they stand.

But in what sense are e.g. Russell's tautologies 'instruments of language'?

Russell at any rate would not have held them to be so. His mistake, if there was one, can however only have consisted in his not paying attention to their *application*.

The proof makes one structure generate another.

It exhibits the generation of one from others.

That is all very well—but still it does quite different things in different cases! What is the *interest* of this transition?

Even if I think of a proof as something deposited in the archives of language—who says *how* this instrument is to be employed, what it is for?

30. A proof leads me to say: this *must* be like this.——Now, I understand this in the case of a Euclidean proof or the proof of '25 times 25 = 625', but is it also like this in the case of a Russellian proof, e.g. of '$\vdash p \supset q . p :$ $\supset : q$'? What does 'it *must* be like this' mean here in contrast with 'it is like this'? Should I say: "Well, I accept this expression as a paradigm for all non-informative propositions of this form"?

I go through the proof and say: "Yes, this is how it *has* to be; I must fix the use of my language in *this* way".

I want to say that the *must* corresponds to a track which I lay down in language.

31. When I said that a proof introduces a new concept, I meant something like: the proof puts a new paradigm among the paradigms of the

language; like when someone mixes a special reddish blue, somehow settles the special mixture of the colours and gives it a name.

But even if we are inclined to call a proof such a new paradigm—what is the exact similarity of the proof to such a concept-model?

One would like to say: the proof changes the grammar of our language, changes our concepts. It makes new connections, and it creates the concept of these connections. (It does not establish that they are there; they do not exist until it makes them.)

32. What concept is created by '$p \supset p$'? And yet I feel as if it would be possible to say that '$p \supset p$' serves as the sign of a concept.

'$p \supset p$' is a formula. Does a formula establish a concept? One can say: "by the formula ... such-and-such follows from this". Or again: "such-and-such follows from this in the following way: ..." But is that the sort of proposition I want? What, however, about: "Draw the consequences of this in the following way: ..."?

33. If I call a proof a model (a picture), then I must also be able to say this of a Russellian primitive proposition (as the egg-cell of a proof).

It can be asked: how did we come to utter the sentence '$p \supset p$' as a true assertion? Well, it was not used in practical linguistic intercourse,—but still there was an inclination to utter it in particular circumstances (when for example one was doing logic) *with conviction*.

But what about '$p \supset p$'? I see in it a degenerate proposition, which is on the side of truth.

I fix it as an important point to divide significant sentences at. A pivotal point of our method of description.

34. The construction of a proof begins with some signs or other, and among these some, the 'constants', must already have meaning in the language. In this way it is essential that 'v' and '$\sim$' already possess a familiar application, and the construction of a proof in *Principia Mathematica* gets its importance, its sense, from this. But the signs of the proof do *not* enable us to see this meaning.

The 'employment' of the proof has of course to do with that employment of its signs.

35. To repeat, in a certain sense even Russell's primitive propositions convince me.

Thus the conviction produced by a proof cannot simply arise from the proof-construction.

36. If I were to see the standard metre in Paris, but were not acquainted with the institution of measuring and its connection with the standard metre —could I say, that I was acquainted with the concept of the standard metre?

Is a proof not also part of an institution in this way?

A proof is an instrument—but why do I say "an instrument of language"? Is a calculation necessarily an instrument of language, then?

37. What I always do seems to be—to emphasize a distinction between the determination of a sense and the employment of a sense.

38. Accepting a proof: one may accept it as the paradigm of the pattern that arises when *these* rules are correctly applied to certain patterns. One may accept it as the correct derivation of a rule of inference. Or as a correct derivation from a correct empirical proposition; or as the correct derivation from a false empirical proposition; or simply as the correct derivation from an empirical proposition, of which we do not know whether it is true or false.

But now can I say that the conception of a proof as 'proof of constructability' of the proved proposition is in some sense a simpler, more primary, one than any other conception?

Can I therefore say: "Any proof proves *first and foremost* that this formation of signs must result when I apply these rules to these formations of signs"? Or: "The proof proves first and foremost that this formation can arise when one operates with these signs according to these transformation-rules".—

This would point to a geometrical application. For the proposition whose truth, as I say, is proved here, is a geometrical proposition—a proposition of grammar concerning the transformations of signs. It might for example be said: it is proved that it makes *sense* to say that someone has got the sign ... according to these rules from ... and ... ; but no sense etc. etc.

Or again: when mathematics is divested of all content, it would remain that certain signs can be constructed from others according to certain rules.—

The least that we have to accept would be: that these signs etc. etc.— and accepting this is a basis for accepting anything else.

I should now like to say: the sequence of signs in the proof does not necessarily carry with it any kind of acceptance. If however we do begin by accepting, this does not have to be 'geometrical' acceptance.

A proof could surely consist of only two steps: say one proposition '$(x) \cdot fx$' and one 'fa'—does the correct transition according to a rule play an important part here?

39. *What* is unshakably certain about what is proved?

To accept a proposition as unshakably certain—I want to say—means to use it as a grammatical rule: this removes uncertainty from it.

"Proof must be capable of being taken in" really means nothing but: a proof is not an experiment. We do not accept the result of a proof because it results once, or because it often results. But we see in the proof the reason for saying that this *must* be the result.

What *proves* is not that this correlation leads to this result—but that we are persuaded to take these appearances (pictures) as models for what it is like if. . . . .

The proof is our new model for what it is like if nothing gets added and nothing taken away when we count correctly etc. But these words show that I do not quite know what the proof is a model of.

I want to say: with the logic of *Principia Mathematica* it would be possible to justify an arithmetic in which $1000 + 1 = 1000$; and all that would be necessary for this purpose would be to doubt the sensible correctness of calculations. But if we do not doubt it, then it is not our conviction of the truth of logic that is responsible.

When we say in a proof: "This *must* come out"—then this is not for reasons that we do not *see*.

It is not our getting this result, but its being the end of this route, that makes us accept it.

What convinces us—*that* is the proof: a configuration that does not convince us is not the proof, even when it can be shown to exemplify the proved proposition.

That means: it must not be necessary to make a physical investigation of the proof-configuration in order to show us what has been proved.

40. If we have a picture of two men, we do not say *first* that the one appears smaller than the other, and *then* that he seems to be further away. It is, one can say, perfectly possible that the one figure's being shorter should not strike us at all, but only its being behind. (This seems to me to be connected with the question of the 'geometrical' conception of proof.)

41. "It (the proof) is the model for what is called such-and-such."

But what is the transition from '$(x) \cdot fx$' to 'fa' supposed to be a model for? At most for how inferences can be drawn from signs like '$(x) \cdot fx$'.

I thought of the model as a justification, but here it is not a justification. The pattern $(x) \cdot fx \therefore fa$ does not *justify* the conclusion. If we want to talk about a justification of the conclusion, it lies outside this schema of signs.

And yet there is something in saying that a mathematical proof creates a new concept.—Every proof is as it were an avowal of a particular employment of signs.

But what is it an avowal of? Only of *this* employment of the rules of transition from formula to formula? Or is it also an avowal in some sense, of the 'axioms'?

Could I say: I avow $p \supset p$ as a tautology?

I accept '$p \supset p$' as a maxim, e.g. of inference.

The idea that proof creates a new concept might also be roughly put as follows: a proof is not its foundations plus the rules of inference, but a *new* building—although it is an example of such and such a style. A proof is a *new* paradigm.

The concept which the proof creates may for example be a new concept of inference, a new concept of correct inferring. But as for *why* I accept this as *correct* inferring the reasons for that lie outside the proof.

The proof creates a new concept by creating or being a new sign. Or—by giving the proposition which is its result a new place. (For the proof is not a movement but a route.)

42. It must not be *imaginable* for *this* substitution in *this* expression to yield anything else. Or: I must declare it unimaginable. (The result of an experiment, however, can turn out this way or that.)

Still, the case could be imagined in which a proof altered in appearance—engraved in rock, it is stated to be the same whatever the appearance says.

Are you really saying anything but: a proof is taken as *proof*?

Proof must be a procedure plain to view. Or again: the proof is the procedure that is *plain to view*.

It is not something behind the proof, but the proof, that proves.

43. When I say: "it must first and foremost be evident that *this* substitution really yields *this* expression"—I might also say: "I must accept it as indubitable"—but then there must be good reasons for this: for example, that the same substitution practically always yields the same result etc. And isn't this exactly what surveyability consists in?

I should like to say that where surveyability is not present, i.e. where there is room for a doubt whether what we have really is the result of this substitution, the *proof* is destroyed. And not in some silly and unimportant way that has nothing to do with the *nature* of proof.

Or: logic as the foundation of all mathematics does not work, and to show this it is enough that the cogency of logical proof stands and falls with its geometrical cogency.[4]

That is to say: logical proof, e.g. of the Russellian kind, is cogent only so long as it also possesses geometrical cogency.[4] And an abbreviation of such a logical proof may have this cogency and so be a proof, when the Russellian construction, completely carried out, is not.

[4] But compare §38.—Eds.

We incline to the belief that *logical* proof has a peculiar, absolute cogency, deriving from the unconditional certainty in logic of the fundamental laws and the laws of inference. Whereas propositions proved in this way can after all not be more certain than is the correctness of the way those laws of inference are *applied*.

The logical certainty of proofs—I want to say—does not extend beyond their geometrical certainty.

44. Now if a proof is a model, then the point must be what is to count as a correct reproduction of the proof.

If, for example, the sign '| | | | | | | | | |' were to occur in a proof, it is not clear whether merely 'the same number' of strokes (or perhaps little crosses) should count as the reproduction of it, or whether some other, not too small, number does equally well. Etc.

But the question is what is to count as the criterion for the reproduction of a proof—for the identity of proofs. How are they to be compared to establish the identity? Are they the same if they look the same?

I should like, so to speak, to show that we can get away from logical proofs in mathematics.

45. "By means of suitable definitions, we can prove '25 × 25 = 625' in Russell's logic."—And can I define the ordinary technique of proof by means of Russell's? But how can one technique of proof be *defined* by means of another? How can one explain the *essence* of another? For if the one is an 'abbreviation' of the other, it must surely be a *systematic* abbreviation. Proof is surely required that I can systematically shorten the long proofs and thus once more get a system of proofs.

Long proofs at first always go along with the short ones and as it were tutor them. But in the end they can no longer follow the short ones and these show their independence.

The consideration of *long* unsurveyable logical proofs is only a means of showing how this technique—which is based on the geometry of proving—may collapse, and new techniques become necessary.

46. I should like to say: mathematics is a MOTLEY of techniques of proof. ———And upon this is based its manifold applicability and its importance.

But that comes to the same thing as saying: if you had a system like that of Russell and produced systems like the differential calculus out of it by means of suitable definitions, you would be producing a new bit of mathematics.

Now surely one could simply say: if a man had invented calculating in the decimal system—that would have been a mathematical invention!— Even if he had already got Russell's *Principia Mathematica*.—

What is it to co-ordinate one system of proofs with another? It involves a translation rule by means of which proved propositions of the one can be translated into proved propositions of the other.

Now it is possible to imagine some—or all—of the proof systems of present-day mathematics as having been co-ordinated in such a way with one system, say that of Russell. So that all proofs could be carried out in this system, even though in a roundabout way. So would there then be only the single system—no longer the many?—But then it must surely be possible to show of the *one* system that it can be resolved into the many.—*One* part of the system will possess the properties of trigonometry, another those of algebra, and so on. Thus one *can* say that different techniques are used in these parts.

I said: whoever invented calculation in the decimal notation surely made a mathematical discovery. But could he not have made this discovery all in Russellian symbols? He would, so to speak, have discovered a new *aspect*.

"But in that case the truth of true mathematical propositions can still be proved from those general foundations."—It seems to me there is a snag here. When do we say that a mathematical proposition is true?—

It seems to me as if we were introducing new concepts into the Russellian logic without knowing it.——For example, when we settle what signs of the form '$(\exists x, y, z \ldots)$' are to count as equivalent to one another, and what are not to count as equivalent.

Is it a matter of course that '$(\exists x, y, z)$' is not the same sign as '$(\exists x, y, z, n)$'?

But suppose I first introduce '$p \lor q$' and '$\sim p$' and use them to construct some tautologies—and then produce (say) the series $\sim p, \sim \sim p, \sim \sim \sim p$, etc. and introduce a notation like $\sim^1 p, \sim^2 p, \ldots \sim^{10} p. \ldots$ I should like to say: we should perhaps originally never have thought of the *possibility* of such a sequence and we have now introduced a new concept into our calculation. Here is a 'new aspect'.

It is clear that I could have introduced the concept of number in this way, even though in a very primitive and inadequate fashion—but this example gives me all I need.

In what sense can it be correct to say that one would have introduced a new concept into logic with the series $\sim p, \sim \sim p, \sim \sim \sim p$, etc.?—Well, first of all one could be said to have done it with the '*etc.*'. For this '*etc.*' stands for a law of sign formation which is new to me. A characteristic mark of this is the fact that *recursive* definition is required for the explanation of the decimal notation.

A new *technique* is introduced.

It can also be put like this: having the concept of the Russellian formation of proofs and propositions does *not* mean you have the concept of every *series* of Russellian signs.

I should like to say: Russell's foundation of mathematics postpones the introduction of new techniques—until it is finally believed that this is no longer necessary at all.

(It would perhaps be as if I were to philosophize about the concept of measurement of length for so long that it was forgotten that the actual establishment of a unit length is necessary for the measurement of length.)

47. Can what I want to say be put like *this*: "If we had learnt from the beginning to do all mathematics in Russell's system, the differential calculus, for example, would not have been invented just by our having Russell's calculus. So if someone discovered this kind of calculation *in Russell's calculus*————."

Suppose I had Russellian proofs of the propositions

$$`p \equiv \sim \sim p`$$

$$`\sim p \equiv \sim \sim \sim p`$$

$$`p \equiv \sim \sim \sim \sim p`$$

and I were now to find a shortened way of proving the proposition

$$`p \equiv \sim^{10} p`.$$

It is as if I had discovered a new kind of calculation within the old calculus. What does its having been discovered consist in?

Tell me: have I discovered a new kind of calculation if, having once learnt to multiply, I am struck by multiplications with all the factors the same, as a special branch of these calculations, and so I introduce the notation '$a^n = \ldots$'?

Obviously the mere 'shortened', or *different*, notation—'16^2' instead of '16×16'—does not amount to that. What is important is that we now merely *count* the factors.

Is '16^{15}' merely another notation for '$16 \times 16 \times 16 \times 16 \times 16 \times 16 \times 16 \times 16 \times 16 \times 16 \times 16 \times 16 \times 16 \times 16 \times 16$'?

The proof that $16^{15} = \ldots$ does not simply consist in my multiplying 16 by itself fifteen times and getting this result—the proof must show that I take the number as a factor 15 times.

When I ask "What is new about the 'new kind of calculation'—exponentiation"—that is difficult to say. The expression 'new aspect' is vague. It means that we now look at the matter differently—but the question is: what is the essential, the *important* manifestation of this 'looking at it differently'?

First of all I want to say: "It need never have *struck* anyone that in certain products all the factors are equal"—or: " 'Product of all equal factors' is a new concept"—or: "What is new consists in our classifying calculations differently". In exponentiation the essential thing is evidently that we look at the *number* of the factors. But who says we ever attended to the number of factors? It *need* not have struck us that there are products with 2, 3, 4 factors etc. although we have often worked out such products. A new aspect—but once more: what is *important* about it? For what purpose do I use what has struck me?—Well, first of all perhaps I put it down in a notation. Thus I write e.g. 'a^2' instead of '$a \times a$'. By this means I refer to the series of numbers (allude to it), which did not happen before. So I am surely setting up a new connection!—A connection—between what objects? Between the technique of counting factors and the technique of multiplying.

But in that way every proof, each individual calculation makes new connections!

But the *same* proof as shows that $a \times a \times a \times a \ldots = b$, surely also shows that $a^n = b$; it is only that we have to make the transition according to the definition of 'a^n'.—

But this transition is exactly what is new. But if it is only a transition to the old proof, how can it be important?

'It is only a different notation.' Where does it stop being—just a different notation?

Isn't it where only the one notation and not the other can be used in such-and-such a way?

It might be called "finding a new aspect", if someone writes '$a(f)$' instead of '$f(a)$'; one might say: "He *looks at* the function as an argument of its argument". Or if someone wrote '$\times (a)$' instead of '$a \times a$' one could say: "he looks at what was previously regarded as a special case of a function with two argument places as a function with *one* argument place".

If anyone does this he has certainly altered the aspect in a sense, he has for example classified *this* expression with others, compared it with others, with which it was not compared before.—But now, is that an *important* change of aspect? *No*, not so long as it does not have certain consequences.

It is true enough that I changed the aspect of the logical calculation by introducing the concept of the *number* of negations: "I never looked at it like that"—one might say. But this alteration only becomes important when it connects with the application of the sign.

Conceiving one foot as *12 inches* would indeed mean changing the aspect of 'a foot', but this change would only become important if one now also *measured* lengths in inches.

If you introduce the counting of negation signs, you bring in a new way of reproducing signs.

For arithmetic, which does talk about the equality of numbers, it is indeed a matter of complete indifference how equality of number of two classes is established—but for its inferences it is not indifferent how its signs are compared with one another, and so e.g. what is the method of establishing whether the number of figures in two numerical signs is the same.

It is not the introduction of numerical signs as abbreviations that is important, but the *method* of counting.

48. I want to give an account of the motley of mathematics.

49. "I can carry out the proof that 127 : 18 = 7.05 in Russell's system too." Why not.—But must the same result be reached in the Russellian proof as in ordinary division? The two are of course connected by means of a type of *calculation* (by rules of translation, say—); but still, is it not risky to work out the division by the new technique,—since the truth of the result is now dependent on the geometry of the rendering?

But now suppose someone says: "Nonsense—such considerations play no part in mathematics".—

—But the question is not one of uncertainty, for we *are* certain of our conclusions, but of whether we are still doing (Russellian) logic when we e.g. divide.

50. Trigonometry has its original importance in connection with measurements of lengths and angles: it is a bit of mathematics adapted to employment on measurements of lengths and angles.
Applicability to this field might also be called an 'aspect' of trigonometry.

When I divide a circle into equal sectors and determine the cosine of one of these sectors by measurement—is that a calculation or an experiment?
If a calculation—is it SURVEYABLE?

Is calculation with a slide-rule *surveyable*?

If the cosine of an angle has to be determined by measurement, is a proposition of the form 'cos α = n' a *mathematical* proposition? What is the criterion for this decision? Does the proposition say something external about our rulers etc.; or something internal about our concepts?—How is this to be decided?

Do the figures (drawings) in trigonometry belong to pure mathematics, or are they only examples of a possible *application*?

51. If there is something true about what I am trying to say, then—e.g.— calculating in the decimal notation must have its own life.—One can of course represent any decimal number in the form:

and hence carry out the four species of calculation in this notation. But the life of the decimal notation would have to be independent of calculating with unit strokes.

52. In this connection the following point constantly occurs to me: while indeed a proposition '$a : b = c$' can be *proved* in Russell's logic, still that logic does not teach us to construct a correct sentence of this form, i.e. does not teach us to *divide*. The procedure of dividing would correspond e.g. to that of a *systematic testing* of Russellian proofs with a view, say, to getting the proof of a proposition of the form '$37 \times 15 = x$'. "But the technique of such a systematic testing is in its turn founded on logic. It can surely be logically proved in turn that this technique must lead to the goal." So it is like proving in Euclid that such-and-such can be constructed in such-and-such a way.

53. If someone tries to show that mathematics is not logic, what is he trying to show? He is surely trying to say something like:—If tables, chairs, cupboards, etc. are swathed in enough paper, certainly they will look spherical in the end.

He is not trying to show that it is impossible that, for every mathematical proof, a Russellian proof can be constructed which (somehow) 'corresponds' to it, but rather that the acceptance of such a correspondence does not lean on logic.

"But surely we can always go back to the primitive logical method!" Well, assuming that we can—how is it that we don't *have* to? Or are we hasty, reckless, if we do not?

But how do we get back to the primitive expression? Do we e.g. take the route through the secondary proof and back from the end of it into the primary system, and then look to see where we have got; or do we go forward in both systems and then connect the end points? And how do we know that we reach the same result in the primary system in the two cases?

Does not proceeding in the secondary system carry the power of conviction with it?

"But at every step in the secondary system, we can imagine that it could be taken in the primary one too!"—That is just it: *we can imagine that it could be done*—without doing it.

And why do we accept the one in place of the other? On grounds of *logic*?

"But can't one prove logically that both transformations must lead to the same result?"—But what is in question here is surely the result of transformations of signs! How can logic decide this?

54. How can the proof in the stroke system prove that the proof in the decimal system is a proof?

Well—isn't it the same for the proof in the decimal system, as it is for a *construction* in Euclid of which it is proved that it really is the construction of such-and-such a figure?

Can I put it like this: "The translation of the stroke system into the decimal system presupposes a recursive definition. This definition, however, does not introduce the abbreviation of *one* expression to another. Yet of course inductive proof in the decimal system does not contain the whole set of those signs which would have to be translated by means of the recursive definition into stroke signs. Therefore this general proof cannot be translated by recursive definition into a proof in the stroke system."?

Recursive definition introduces a new sign-technique.—It must therefore make the transition to a new 'geometry'. We are taught a new method of recognizing signs. A new criterion for the identity of signs is introduced.

55. A proof shows us what OUGHT to come out.—And since every reproduction of the proof must demonstrate the same thing, while on the one hand it must reproduce the result automatically, on the other hand it must also reproduce the *compulsion* to get it.

That is: we reproduce not merely the *conditions* which once yielded this result (as in an experiment), but the result itself. And yet the proof is not a stacked game, inasmuch as it must always be capable of guiding us.

On the one hand we must be able to reproduce the proof *in toto* automatically, and on the other hand this reproduction must once more be *proof* of the result.

"Proof must be surveyable": this aims at drawing our attention to the difference between the concepts of 'repeating a proof', and 'repeating an experiment'. To repeat a proof means, not to reproduce the conditions under which a particular result was once obtained, but to repeat every step *and the result*. And although this shows that proof is something that must be capable of being reproduced *in toto* automatically, still every such reproduction must contain the force of proof, which compels acceptance of the result.

56. When do we say that one calculus 'corresponds' to another, is only an abbreviated form of the first?—"Well, when the results of the latter can be translated by means of suitable definitions into the results of the former." But has it been said how one is to calculate with these definitions? What makes us accept this translation? Is it a stacked game in the end? It is, if we are decided on only accepting the translation that leads to the accustomed result.

Why do we call a part of the Russellian calculus the part corresponding to the differential calculus?—Because the propositions of the differential calculus are proved in it.—But, ultimately, after the event.—But does that matter? Sufficient that proofs of these propositions can be found in the Russellian system! But aren't they proofs of these propositions only when their results can be translated only into *these* propositions? But is that true even in the case of multiplying in the stroke system with numbered strokes?

57. Now it must be clearly stated that calculations in the stroke notation will normally always agree with those in the decimal notation. Perhaps, in order to make sure of agreement, we shall at some point have to take to getting the stroke-calculation worked over by *several* people. And we shall do the same for calculations with still higher numbers in the decimal system.

But that of course is enough to show that it is not the proofs in the stroke notation that make the proofs in the decimal system cogent.

"Still, if we did not have the latter, we could use the former to prove the same thing."—The same thing? What is the same thing?—Well, the stroke proof will convince me of the same thing, though not in the same way.—Suppose I were to say: "The place to which a proof leads us cannot be determined independently of this proof."—Did a proof in the stroke system demonstrate to me that the proved proposition possesses the applicability given it by the proof in the decimal system—was it e.g. proved in the stroke system that the proposition is also provable in the decimal system?

58. Of course it would be nonsense to say that *one* proposition cannot have two proofs—for we do say just that. But can we not say: *this* proof shows that ... results when we do *this*; the other proof shows that this expression results when we do something else?

For is e.g. the mathematical fact that 129 is divisible by 3 independent of the fact that *this* is the result in *this* calculation? I mean: is the fact of this divisibility independent of the *calculus* in which it is a result; or is it a fact of this calculus?

Suppose it were said: "By calculating we get acquainted with the properties of numbers".

But do the properties of numbers *exist* outside the calculating?

"Two proofs prove the same when what they convince me of is the same."—And when is what they convince me of the same?—How do I know that what they convince me of is the same? Not of course by introspection.

I can be brought to accept this rule by a variety of paths.

59. "Each proof proves not merely the truth of the proposition proved, but also that it can be proved *in this way*."—But this latter can also be proved in another way.—"Yes, but the proof proves this in a particular way and in doing so proves that it can be demonstrated in this way."—But even *that* could be shown by means of a different proof.—"Yes, but then not in this way."—

But this means e.g.: this proof is a mathematical entity that cannot be replaced by any other; one can say that it can convince us of something that nothing else can, and this can be given expression by our assigning to it a proposition that we do not assign to any other proof.

60. But am I not making a crude mistake? For just this is essential to the propositions of arithmetic and to the propositions of the Russellian logic: various proofs lead to them. Even: infinitely many proofs lead to any one of them.

Is it correct to say that every proof demonstrates something to us which it alone can demonstrate? Would not—so to speak—the proved proposition then be superfluous, and the proof itself also be the thing proved?

Is it only the proved proposition that the proof convinces me of?

What is meant by: "A proof is a mathematical entity which cannot be replaced by any other"? It surely means that every single proof has a usefulness which no other one has. It might be said: "—that every proof, even of a proposition which has already been proved, is a contribution to mathematics". But why is it a contribution if its only point was to prove the proposition? Well, one can say: "the new proof shows (or *makes*) a new connection". (But in that case is there not a mathematical proposition saying that this connection exists?)

What do we *learn* when we see the new proof—apart from the proposition, which we already know anyhow? Do we learn something that cannot be expressed in a mathematical proposition?

61. How far does the application of a mathematical proposition depend on what is allowed to count as a proof of it and what is not?

I can surely say: if the proposition '137 × 373 = 46792' is true in the ordinary sense, *then there must be a multiplication-sum*, at the ends of which stand the two sides of this equation. And a multiplication-sum is a pattern satisfying certain rules.

I want to say: if I did not accept the multiplication-sum as *one* proof of the proposition, then that would mean that the application of the proposition to multiplication-sums would be gone.

62. Let us remember that it is not enough that two proofs meet in the same propositional sign. For how do we know that this sign says the same thing both times? *That* must proceed from other connections.

63. The *exact* correspondence of a correct (convincing) transition in music and in mathematics.

64. Suppose I were to set someone the problem: "Find a proof of the proposition ..."—The answer would surely be to show me certain signs. Very well: *what* condition must these signs satisfy? They must be a proof of that proposition—but is that, say, a *geometrical* condition? Or a psychological one? Sometimes it could be called a geometrical condition; where the means of proof are already prescribed and all that is being looked for is a particular arrangement.

III

15. People can be imagined to have an applied mathematics without any pure mathematics. They can e.g.—let us suppose—calculate the path described by certain moving bodies and predict their place at a given time. For this purpose they make use of a system of co-ordinates, of the equations of curves (*a form of description of actual movement*) and of the technique of calculating in the decimal system. The idea of a proposition of pure mathematics may be quite foreign to them.

Thus these people have rules in accordance with which they transform the appropriate signs (in particular, e.g. numerals) with a view to predicting the occurrence of certain events.

But when they now multiply, for example, will they not arrive at a proposition saying that the result of the multiplication is the same, however the factors are shifted round? That will not be a primary rule of notation, nor yet a proposition of their physics.

They do not *need* to obtain any such proposition—even if they allow the shift of factors.

I am imagining the matter as if this mathematics were done entirely in the form of orders. "You must do *such-and-such*"—so as to get the answer, that is, to the question 'where will this body be at such-and-such a time?' (It does not matter at all how these people have arrived at this method of prediction.)

For these people the center of gravity of mathematics is found *wholly* in *doing*.

16. But is this possible? Is it possible that they should not pronounce the commutative law (e.g.) to be a *proposition*?

But I want to say: these people are not supposed to arrive at the conception of making mathematical discoveries—but *only* of making physical discoveries.

Question: Must they make mathematical discoveries as discoveries? What do they miss if they make none? Could they (for example) use the proof of the commutative law, but without the conception of its culminating in a *proposition*, and so having a result which is in some way comparable with their physical propositions?

17. The mere picture

regarded now as four rows of five dots, now as five columns of four dots, might convince someone of the commutative law. And he might thereupon carry out multiplications, now in the one direction, now in the other.

One look at the pattern and pieces convinces him that he will be able to make them into that shape, i.e. he thereupon *undertakes* to do so.

"Yes, but only if the pieces don't change."—If they don't change, and we don't make some unintelligible mistake, or pieces disappear or get added without our noticing it.

"But it is surely essential that the pieces can as a matter of fact always be made into that shape! What would happen if they could not?"—Perhaps we should think that something had put us out. But—what then?—Perhaps we should even accept the thing as it was. And then Frege might say: "Here we have a new kind of insanity!"

18. It is clear that mathematics as a technique for transforming signs for the purpose of prediction has nothing to do with grammar.

19. The people whose mathematics was only such a technique, are now also supposed to accept proofs convincing them of the replaceability of one sign-technique by another. That is to say, they find transformations, series of pictures, on the strength of which they can venture to use one technique in place of another.

IV

5. If the intended application of mathematics is essential, how about parts of mathematics whose application—or at least *what* mathematicians take for their application—is quite fantastic? So that, as in set theory, one is doing a branch of mathematics of whose application one forms an entirely false idea. Now, isn't one doing mathematics *none the less*?

If the operations of arithmetic only served to construct a cipher, its application would of course be fundamentally different from that of our arithmetic. But would these operations then be mathematical operations at all?

Can someone who is applying a decoding rule be said to be performing mathematical operations? And yet his transformations can be so conceived. For he could surely say that he was calculating what had to come out in decoding the symbols ... with such-and-such a key. And the proposition: the signs: ..., decoded according to this rule, yield ... is a mathematical one. As is the proposition that you can get to this position from *that* one in chess.

Imagine the geometry of four-dimensional space done with a view to learning about the living conditions of spirits. Does that mean that it is not mathematics? And can I now say that it determines concepts?

Would it not sound queer to say that a child could already do thousands and thousands of multiplications—by which is supposed to be meant that it can already calculate in the unlimited number domain. And indeed this might be reckoned an extremely modest way of putting it, as it says only 'thousands and thousands' instead of 'infinitely many'.

Could people be imagined, who in their ordinary lives only calculated up to 1000 and kept calculations with higher numbers for mathematical investigations about the world of spirits?

"Whether or not this holds of the surface of a *real* sphere—it does hold for the mathematical one"—this makes it look as if the special difference between the mathematical and an empirical proposition was that, while the truth of the empirical proposition is rough and oscillating, the mathematical proposition describes *its* object precisely and absolutely. As if, in fact, the 'mathematical sphere' were a sphere. And it might e.g. be asked whether there was only *one* such sphere, or several (a Fregean question).

Does a misunderstanding about the possible application constitute an objection to the calculation as a part of mathematics?

And apart from misunderstanding,—what about mere lack of clarity?

Imagine someone who believes that mathematicians have discovered a queer thing, $\sqrt{-1}$, which when squared does yield -1, can't he nevertheless calculate quite well with complex numbers, and apply such calculations in physics? And does this make them any the less *calculations*?

In *one* respect of course his understanding has a weak foundation; but he will draw his conclusions with certainty, and his calculus will have a *solid* foundation.

Now would it not be ridiculous to say this man wasn't doing mathematics?

Someone makes an addition to mathematics, gives new definitions and discovers new theorems——and in a *certain* respect he can be said not to know what he is doing.—He has a vague imagination of having *discovered* something like a space (at which point he thinks of a room), of having opened up a kingdom, and when asked about it he would talk a great deal of nonsense.

Let us imagine the primitive case of someone carrying out enormous multiplications in order, as he says, to conquer gigantic new provinces of the domain of numbers.

Imagine calculating with $\sqrt{-1}$ invented by a madman, who, attracted merely by the paradox of the idea, does the calculation as a kind of service, or temple ritual, of the absurd. He imagines that he is writing down the impossible and operating with it.

In other words: if someone believes in mathematical *objects* and their queer properties—can't he nevertheless do mathematics? Or—isn't he also doing mathematics?

'Ideal object.' "The symbol '*a*' stands for an ideal object" is evidently supposed to assert something about the meaning, and so about the use, of '*a*'. And it means of course that this use is in a certain respect similar to that of a sign that has an object, and that it does not stand for any object. But it is interesting what the expression 'ideal object' makes of this fact.

6. In certain circumstances we might speak of an endless row of marbles. —Let us imagine such an endless straight row of marbles at equal distances from one another; we calculate the force exerted by all these marbles on a certain body according to a certain law of attraction. We regard the number yielded by this calculation as the ideal of exactness for certain measurements.

The feeling of something *queer* here comes from a misunderstanding. The kind of misunderstanding that is produced by a thumb-catching of the intellect—to which I want to call a halt.

The objection that 'the finite cannot grasp the infinite' is *really* directed against the idea of a psychological act of grasping or understanding.

Or imagine that we simply say: "This force corresponds to the attraction of an endless row of marbles which we have arranged in such-and-such a way and which attract the body according to such-and-such a law of attraction". Or again: "Calculate the force which an endless row of marbles of such-and-such a kind exerts on the body".—It certainly makes sense to give such an order. It describes a particular calculation.

What about the following question: "Calculate the weight of a pillar composed of as many slabs lying on top of one another as there are cardinal numbers; the undermost slab weighs 1 kg., and every higher one weighs half of the one just below it".

The difficulty is *not* that we can't form an image. It is easy enough to form some kind of image of an endless row, for example. The question is what use the image is to us.

Imagine infinite numbers used in a fairy tale. The dwarves have piled up as many gold pieces as there are cardinal numbers—etc. What can occur in this fairy tale must surely make sense.—

7. Imagine set theory's having been invented by a satirist as a kind of parody on mathematics.—Later a reasonable meaning was seen in it and it was incorporated into mathematics. (For if one person can see it as a paradise of mathematicians, why should not another see it as a joke?)

The question is: even as a joke isn't it evidently mathematics?—

And why is it evidently mathematics?—Because it is a game with signs according to rules?

But isn't it evident that there are concepts formed here—even if we are not clear about their application?

But how is it possible to have a concept and not be clear about its application?

8. Take the construction of the polygon of forces: isn't that a bit of applied mathematics? And where is the proposition of *pure* mathematics which is invoked in connection with this graphical calculation? Is this case not like that of the tribe which has a technique of calculating in order to make certain predictions, but no propositions of pure mathematics?

Calculation that belongs to the performance of a ceremony. For example, let the number of words in a form of blessing that is to be applied to a home be derived by a particular technique from the ages of the father and mother and the number of their children. We could imagine procedures of calculating described in such a law as the Mosaic law. And couldn't we imagine that the nation with these ceremonial prescriptions for calculating never calculated in practical life?

This would indeed be a case of *applied* calculation, but it would not serve the purpose of a prediction.

Would it be any wonder if the technique of calculating had a family of applications?

9. We only see how queer the question is whether the pattern ϕ (a particular arrangement of digits e.g. '770') will occur in the infinite expansion of π, when we try to formulate the question in a quite common or garden way: men have been trained to put down signs according to certain rules. Now they proceed according to this training and we say that it is a problem whether they will *ever* write down the pattern ϕ in following the given rule.

But what are you saying if you say that one thing is clear: either one will come on ϕ in the infinite expansion, or one will not?

It seems to me that in saying this you are yourself setting up a rule or postulate.

What if someone were to reply to a question: 'So far there is no such thing as an answer to this question'?

So, e.g., the poet might reply when asked whether the hero of his poem has a sister or not—when, that is, he has not yet decided anything about it.

The question—I want to say—changes its status, when it becomes decidable. For a connection is made then, which formerly *was not there*.

Of someone who is trained we can ask 'How *will* he interpret the rule for this case?', or again 'How *ought* he to interpret the rule for this case?' —but what if no decision about this question has been made?—Well, then the answer is, not: 'he ought to interpret it in such a way that ϕ occurs in the expansion' or: 'he ought to interpret it in such a way that it does not occur', but: 'nothing has so far been decided about this'.

However queer it sounds, the further expansion of an irrational number is a further expansion of mathematics.

We do mathematics with concepts.—And with certain concepts more than with other ones.

I want to say: it *looks* as if a ground for the decision were already there; and it has yet to be invented.

Would this come to the same thing as saying: in thinking about the technique of expansion, which we have learnt, we use the false picture of a completed expansion (of what is ordinarily called a "row") and this forces us to ask unanswerable questions?

For after all in the end every question about the expansion of $\sqrt{2}$ must be capable of formulation as a practical question concerning the technique of expansion.

And what is in question here is of course not merely the case of the expansion of a real number, or in general the production of mathematical signs, but every analogous process, whether it is a game, a dance, etc., etc.

10. When someone hammers away at us with the law of excluded middle as something which cannot be gainsaid, it is clear that there is something wrong with his question.

When someone sets up the law of excluded middle, he is as it were putting two pictures before us to choose from, and saying that one must correspond to the fact. But what if it is questionable whether the pictures can be applied here?

And if you say that the infinite expansion must contain the pattern ϕ or not contain it, you are so to speak showing us the picture of an unsurveyable series reaching into the distance.

But what if the picture began to flicker in the far distance?

11. To say of an unending series that it does *not* contain a particular pattern makes sense only under quite special conditions.

That is to say: this proposition has been given a sense for certain cases.

Roughly, for those where it is in the *rule* for this series, not to contain the pattern. ...

Further: when I calculate the expansion further, I am deriving new rules which the series obeys.

"Good,—then we can say: 'It must either reside in the rule for this series that the pattern occurs, or the opposite'." But is it like that?—"Well, doesn't the rule of expansion *determine* the series completely? And if it does so, if it allows of no ambiguity, then it must implicitly determine *all* questions about the structure of the series."—Here you are thinking of finite series.

"But surely all members of the series from the 1st up to 1,000th, up to the 10^{10}-th and so on, are determined; so surely *all* the members are determined." That is correct if it is supposed to mean that it is not the case that e.g. the so-and-so-many'th is *not* determined. But you can see that *that* gives you no information about whether a particular pattern is going to appear in the series (if it has not appeared so far). *And so we can see* that we are using a misleading *picture*.

If you want to know more about the series, you have, so to speak, to get into another dimension (as it were from the line into a surrounding plane).—But then isn't the plane *there*, just like the line, and merely something to be *explored*, if one wants to know what the facts are?

No, the mathematics of this further dimension has to be invented just as much as any mathematics.

In an arithmetic in which one does not count further than 5 the question what $4 + 3$ makes doesn't yet make sense. On the other hand the problem may very well exist of giving this question a sense. That is to say: the question makes *no more* sense than does the law of excluded middle in application to it.

12. In the law of excluded middle we think that we have already got something solid, something that at any rate cannot be called in doubt. Whereas in truth this tautology has just as shaky a sense (if I may put it like that), as the question whether p or $\sim p$ is the case.

Suppose I were to ask: what is meant by saying "the pattern ... occurs in this expansion"? The reply would be: "you surely *know* what it means. It occurs as the pattern ... in fact occurs in the expansion."—So *that* is the way it occurs?—But *what way* is that?

Imagine it were said: "Either it occurs in that way, or it does not occur in that way"!

"But don't you really understand what is meant?"—But may I not believe I understand it, and be wrong?—

For how do I know what it means to say: the pattern ... occurs in the expansion? Surely by way of examples—which show me what it is like for. ... But these examples do not show me what it is like for this pattern to occur in the expansion!

Might one not say: if I really had a right to say that these examples tell me what it is like for the pattern to occur in the expansion, then they would also have to show me what the opposite means.

13. The general proposition that that pattern does not occur in the expansion can only be a *commandment*.

Suppose we look at mathematical propositions as commandments, and even utter them as such? "Let 25^2 be 625."

Now—a commandment has an internal and an external negation.

The symbols "$(x) \cdot \phi x$" and "$(\exists x) \cdot \phi x$" are certainly useful in mathematics so long as one is acquainted with the technique of the proofs of the existence or non-existence to which the Russellian signs *here* refer. If however this is left open, then these concepts of the old logic are extremely misleading.

If someone says: "But you surely know what 'this pattern occurs in the expansion' means, namely *this*"—and points to a case of occurring,—then I can only reply that what he shows me is capable of illustrating a *variety* of facts. For that reason I can't be said to know what the proposition means just from knowing that he will certainly use it in this case.

The opposite of "there exists a law that p" is not: "there exists a law that $\sim p$". But if one expresses the first by means of P, and the second by means of $\sim P$, one will get into difficulties.

14. Suppose children are taught that the earth is an infinite flat surface; or that God created an infinite number of stars; or that a star keeps on moving uniformly in a straight line, without ever stopping.

Queer: when one takes something of this sort as a matter of course, as it were in one's stride, it loses its whole paradoxical aspect. It is as if I were to be told: Don't worry, this series, or movement, goes on without ever stopping. We are as it were excused the labour of thinking of an end.

'We won't bother about an end.'

It might also be said: 'for us the series is infinite'.

'We won't worry about an end to this series; for us it is always beyond our ken.'

15. The rational numbers cannot be *enumerated*, because they cannot be counted—but one can count with them, as with the cardinal numbers. That squint-eyed way of putting things goes with the whole system of pretence, namely that by using the new apparatus we deal with infinite sets with the same certainty as hitherto we had in dealing with finite ones.

It should not have been called 'denumerable', but on the other hand it would have made sense to say 'numerable'. And this expression also informs us of an application of the concept. For one cannot set out to enumerate the rational numbers, but one can perfectly well set out to assign numbers to them.

16. The comparison with alchemy suggests itself. We might speak of a kind of alchemy in mathematics.

Is it the earmark of this mathematical alchemy that mathematical propositions are regarded as statements about mathematical objects,—and so mathematics as the exploration of these objects?

In a certain sense it is not possible to appeal to the meaning of the signs in mathematics, just because it is only mathematics that gives them their meaning.

What is typical of the phenomenon I am talking about is that a *mysteriousness* about some mathematical concept is not *straight away* interpreted as an erroneous conception, as a mistake of ideas; but rather as something that is at any rate not to be despised, is perhaps even rather to be respected.

All that I can do, is to show an easy escape from this obscurity and this glitter of the concepts.

Strangely, it can be said that there is so to speak a solid core to all these glistening concept-formations. And I should like to say that that is what makes them into mathematical productions.

It might be said: what you see does of course look more like a gleaming Fata Morgana; but look at it from another quarter and you can see the solid body, which only looks like a gleam without a corporeal substrate when seen from that other direction.

17. 'The pattern is in the series or it is not in the series' means: either the thing looks like *this* or it does not look like this.

How does one know what is meant by the opposite of the proposition "ϕ occurs in the series", or even of the proposition "ϕ does not occur in the series"? This question sounds like nonsense, but does make sense all the same.

Namely: how do I know that I understand the proposition "ϕ occurs in this series"?

True, I can give examples illustrating the use of such statements, and also of the opposite ones. And they are examples of there being a rule prescribing the occurrence in a definite region or series of regions, or determining that such an occurrence is excluded.

If "you do it" means: you must do it, and "you do not do it" means: you must not do it—then "Either you do it, or you do not" is not the law of excluded middle.

Everyone feels uncomfortable at the thought that a proposition can state that such-and-such does not occur in an infinite series—while on the other hand there is nothing startling about a command's saying that this must not occur in this series however far it is continued.

But what is the source of this distinction between: "however far you go you will never find this"—and "however far you go you must never do this"?

On hearing the proposition one can ask: "how can we know anything like that?" but nothing analogous holds for the command.

The statement seems to overreach itself, the command not at all.

Can we imagine all mathematical propositions expressed in the imperative? For example: "Let 10 × 10 be 100".

And if you now say: "Let it be like this, or let it not be like this", you are not pronouncing the law of excluded middle—but you are pronouncing a *rule*. (As I have already said above.)

18. But is this really a way out of the difficulty? For how about all the other mathematical propositions, say '$25^2 = 625$'; isn't the law of excluded middle valid for these *inside* mathematics?

How is the law of excluded middle applied?

"Either there is a rule that prescribes it, or one that forbids it."

Assuming that there is no rule forbidding the occurrence,—why is there then supposed to be one that prescribes it?

Does it make sense to say: "While there isn't any rule forbidding the occurrence, as a matter of fact the pattern does not occur"?—And if this does not make sense, how can the opposite make sense, namely, that the pattern does occur?

Well, when I say it occurs, a picture of the series from its beginning up to the pattern floats before my mind—but if I say that the pattern does *not* occur, then no such picture is of any use to me, and my supply of pictures gives out.

What if the rule should bend in use without my noticing it? What I mean is, that I might speak of different spaces in which I use it.

The opposite of "it must not occur" is "it can occur". For a finite segment of the series, however, the opposite of "it must not occur in it" seems to be: "it must occur in it".

The queer thing about the alternative "ϕ occurs in the infinite series or it does not", is that we have to imagine the two possibilities individually, that we look for a distinct idea of each, and that *one* is not adequate for the negative and for the positive case, as it is elsewhere.

19. How do I know that the general proposition "There is ..." makes sense here? Well, if it can be used to tell something about the technique of expansion in a language game.

In *one* case what we are told is: "it must not occur"—i.e.: if it occurs you calculated wrong.

In one case what we are told is: "it can occur", i.e., no such interdict exists. In another: "it must occur in such-and-such a region (always in this place in these regions)". But the opposite of this seems to be: "it must not occur in such-and-such places"—instead of "it *need* not occur there".

But what if the rule were given that, e.g., everywhere where the formation rule for π yields 4, any arbitrary digit other than 4 can be put in its place?

Consider also the rule which forbids one digit in certain places, but otherwise leaves the choice open.

Isn't it like this? The concepts of infinite decimals in mathematical propositions are not concepts of series, but of the unlimited technique of expansion of series.

We learn an endless technique: that is to say, something is done for us first, and then we do it; we are told rules and we do exercises in following them; perhaps some expression like "and so on *ad inf.*" is also used, but what is in question here is not some gigantic extension.

These are the facts. And now what does it mean to say: "ϕ either occurs in the expansion, or does not occur"?

20. But does this mean that there is no such problem as: "Does the pattern ϕ occur in this expansion?"?—To ask this is to ask for a rule regarding the occurrence of ϕ. And the alternative of the existence or non-existence of such a rule is at any rate not a mathematical one.

Only within a mathematical structure which has yet to be erected does the question allow of a *mathematical* decision, and at the same time become a demand for such a decision.

21. Then is infinity not actual—can I not say: "these two edges of the slab meet at infinity"?

Say, not: "the circle has this property because it passes through the two points at infinity ..."; but: "the properties of the circle can be regarded in this (extraordinary) perspective".

It is essentially a perspective, and a far-fetched one. (Which does not express any reproach.) But it must always be quite clear *how far*-fetched this way of looking at it is. For otherwise its real *significance* is dark.

22. What does it mean to say: "the mathematician does not know what he is doing", or: "he knows what he is doing"?

23. Can one make infinite predictions?—Well, why should one not for example call the law of inertia one? Or the proposition that a comet describes a parabola?

In a certain sense of course the infinity of the prediction is not taken very seriously.

Now what about a *prediction* that if you expand π, however far you go, you will never come across the pattern ϕ?—Well, we could say that this is either a *non-mathematical* prediction, or alternatively a mathematical rule.

Someone who has learned to expand $\sqrt{2}$ goes to a fortune-teller, and she tells him that however far he may expand $\sqrt{2}$ he will never arrive at the pattern. . . .—Is her soothsaying a mathematical proposition? No.—Unless she says: "If you always expand correctly you will never reach it". But is that still a prediction?

Now it looks as if such a *prediction* of the correct expansion were imaginable and were distinct from a mathematical law that it *must* be thus and thus. So that in the mathematical expansion there would be a distinction between what as a matter of fact comes out like this—as it were accidentally—and what must come out.

How is it to be decided whether an infinite prediction makes sense?
At any rate not by one's saying: "I am certain I *mean* something when I say . . .".

Besides, the question is not so much whether the prediction makes some kind of sense, as: what kind of sense it makes. (That is, in what language games it occurs.)

24. "The disastrous invasion" of mathematics by logic.

In a field that has been prepared in this way *this* is a proof of existence.

The harmful thing about logical technique is that it makes us forget the special mathematical technique. Whereas logical technique is only an auxiliary technique in mathematics. For example it sets up certain connections between different techniques.

It is almost as if one tried to say that cabinet-making consisted in glueing.

25. A proof convinces you that there is a root of an equation (without giving you any idea *where*)——how do you know that you understand the proposition that there is a root? How do you know that you are really convinced of anything? You may be convinced that the application of the proved proposition will turn up. But you do not understand the proposition so long as you have not found the application.

When a proof proves in a general way that *there is* a root, then everything depends on the form in which it proves this. On what it is that here leads to this verbal expression, which is a mere shadow, and keeps mum about *essentials*. Whereas to logicians it seems to keep mum only about incidentals.

The mathematical general does not stand in the same relation to the mathematical particular as elsewhere the general to the particular.

Everything that I say really amounts to this, that one can know a proof thoroughly and follow it step by step, and yet at the same time not *understand* what it was that was proved.

And this in turn is connected with the fact that one can form a mathematical proposition in a grammatically correct way without understanding its meaning.

Now when does one understand it?—I believe: when one can apply it.

It might perhaps be said: when one has a clear picture of its application. For this, however, it is not enough to connect a clear picture with it. It would rather have been better to say: when one commands a clear view of its application. And even that is bad, for the matter is simply one of not imagining that the application is where it is not; of not being deceived by the verbal form of the proposition.

But how does it come about that one can fail to understand, or can misunderstand, a proposition or proof in this way? And what is then necessary in order to produce understanding?

There are here, I believe, cases in which someone can indeed apply the proposition (or proof), but is unable to give a clear account of the kind of application. And the case in which he is even unable to apply the proposition. (Multiplicative axiom.)

How is it as regards $0 \times 0 = 0$?

One would like to say that the understanding of a mathematical proposition is not guaranteed by its verbal form, as is the case with most nonmathematical propositions. This means—so it appears—that the words don't determine the *language-game* in which the proposition functions.

The logical notation suppresses the structure.

26. In order to see how something can be called an 'existence-proof', though it does not permit a construction of what exists, think of the different meanings of the word "where". (For example the topological and the metrical.)

For it is not merely that the existence-proof can leave the place of the 'existent' undetermined: there need not be any question of such a place.

That is to say: when the proved proposition runs: "there is a number for which ..." then it need not make sense to ask "and which number is it?", or to say "and this number is ...".

27. A proof that 777 occurs in the expansion of π, without showing where, would have to look at this expansion from a totally new point of view, so that it showed e.g. properties of regions of the expansion about which we only knew that they lay very far out. Only the picture floats before one's mind of having to assume as it were a dark zone of indeterminate length very far on in π, where we can no longer rely on our devices for calculating; and then still further out a zone where in a *different* way we can once more see something.

V

1. The rôle of propositions which deal with measures and are not 'empirical propositions'.—Someone tells me: "this stretch is two hundred and forty inches long". I say: "that's twenty foot, so it's roughly seven paces" and now I have got an idea of the length.—The transformation is founded on arithmetical propositions and on the proposition that 12 inches = 1 foot.

No one will ordinarily see this last proposition as an empirical proposition. It is said to express a convention. But measuring would entirely lose *its ordinary character* if, for example, putting 12 bits each one inch long end to end didn't ordinarily yield a length which can in its turn be preserved in a special way.

Does this mean that I have to say that the proposition '12 inches = 1 foot' asserts all those things which give measuring its present point?

No. The proposition *is grounded in* a technique. And, if you like, also in the physical and psychological facts that make the technique *possible*. But it doesn't follow that its sense is to express these conditions. The opposite of that proposition, 'twelve inches = one foot' does not say that rulers are not rigid enough or that we don't all count and calculate in the same way.

2. The proposition has the typical (but that doesn't mean *simple*) rôle of a rule.

I can use the proposition '12 inches = 1 foot' to make a prediction· namely that twelve inch-long pieces of wood laid end to end will turn out to be of the same length as one piece measured in a different way. Thus the point of that rule is, e.g., that it can be used to make certain predictions. Does it lose the character of a *rule* on that account?

Why can one make those predictions? Well,—all rulers are made alike; they don't alter much in length; nor do pieces of wood cut up into inch lengths; our memory is good enough for us not to take numbers twice in counting up to '12', and not to leave any out, and so on.

But then can the rule not be replaced by an empirical proposition saying that rulers are made in such and such ways, that people do *this* with them? One might give an ethnological account of this human institution.

Now it is evident that this account could take over the function of a rule.

If you know a mathematical proposition, that's not to say you yet know anything. If there is a confusion in our operations, if everyone calculates differently, and each one differently at different times, then there isn't any calculating yet; if we agree, then we have only set our watches, but not yet measured any time.

If you know a mathematical proposition, that's not to say you yet know *anything*.

I.e., the mathematical proposition is only supposed to supply a framework for a description.

3. How can the mere transformation of an expression be of practical consequence?

The fact that I have 25 × 25 nuts can be verified by my counting 625 nuts, but it can also be discovered in another way which is closer to the form of expression '25 × 25'. And of course it is in the linking of these two ways *of determining* a number that one point of multiplying lies.

A rule *qua* rule is detached, it stands as it were alone in its glory; although what gives it importance is the facts of daily experience.

What I have to do is [something like] to describe the office of a king; in doing which I must never fall into the error of explaining the kingly dignity by the king's usefulness, but I must leave neither his usefulness nor his dignity out of account.

I am guided in practical work by the result of transforming an expression.

But in that case how can I still say that it means the same thing whether I say "here are 625 nuts", or "here are 25 × 25 nuts"?

If you verify the proposition "here are 625 ..." then in doing that you are also verifying "here are 25 × 25 ..."; etc. But the one form is closer to one kind of verification, the other closer to another.

How can you say that "... 625 ..." and "... 25 × 25 ..." say the same thing?—Only through our arithmetic do they *become one*.

I can at one time arrive at the one, and at another time at the other kind of description, e.g. by counting. That is to say, I can arrive at either of these forms in either way; but by different routes.

It might now be asked; if the proposition "... 625 ..." was verified at one time in this way and at another time in a different way, then did it mean the same thing both times?

Or: what happens if one method of verification gives '625', but the other not '25 × 25'?—Is "... 625 ..." true and "... 25 times 25 ..." false? No.—To doubt the one means to doubt the other: that is the grammar given to these signs by our arithmetic.

If both ways of counting are supposed to justify *giving a number* then giving *one* number, even though in different forms, is all that is *provided for*. On the other hand there is no contradiction in saying: "By one method of counting I get 25 × 25 (and so 625), by the other not 625 (and so not 25 × 25)". Arithmetic has no objection to this.

For arithmetic to equate the two expressions is, one might say, a grammatical trick.

In this way arithmetic bars a particular kind of description and conducts description into other channels. (And it goes without saying that this is connected with the facts of experience.)

4. Suppose I have taught somebody to multiply; not, however, by using an explicit general rule, but only by his seeing how I work out examples for him. I can then set him a *new* question and say: "Do the same with *these* two numbers as I did with the previous ones". But I can also say: "If you do with these two what I did with the others, then you will arrive at the number ...". What kind of proposition is that?

"You will write such-and-such" is a prediction. 'If you write such-and-such, then you will have done it as I showed you' determines what he calls "following his example".

'The solution to this problem is ...'.—If I read this before I have worked out the sum,—what sort of proposition is it?

"If you do with these numbers what I did with the others, you will get ..."—that surely means: "The result of this calculation is ..."—and that is not a prediction but a mathematical proposition. But it is none the less a prediction too—A prediction of a special kind. Just as someone who at the end finds that he really does get such-and-such when he adds up the column may be really surprised; for example may exclaim: Good Lord, it does come out!

Just think of this procedure of prediction and confirmation as a special language-game—I mean: isolated from the rest of arithmetic and its application.

What is so singular about this game of prediction? What strikes me as singular would disappear if the prediction ran: "If you believe that you have gone by my example, then you will have produced *this*" or: "If everything seems correct to you, *this* will be the result". This game could be imagined in connection with the administration of a particular poison and the prediction would be that the injection affects our faculties, our memory for example, in such-and-such a way.—But if we can imagine the game with the administration of a poison, then why not with the administration of a medicine? But even then the weight of the prediction may still always rest on the fact that the *healthy* man sees *this* as the result. Or perhaps: that *this* satisfies the healthy man.

"Do as I do, and this is what you will get" doesn't of course mean: "If you do as I do then you will do as I do"—nor: "Calculate like *this*, and you will calculate like *this*".—But what does "Do as I do" mean? In the language-game—it can simply be an order: "Now do as I do!"

What is the difference between these predictions: "If you calculate correctly you will get *this* result"—and: "If you believe you are calculating correctly you will get *this* result"?

Now who says that the prediction in my language-game above does not mean the latter? It seems not to——but what *shows* this? Ask yourself *in what circumstances* the prediction would seem to predict the one thing and in what circumstances the other. For it is clear that it all depends on the rest of the circumstances.

If you predict that I shall get *this*, are you not simply predicting that I shall take this result as correct?—"But"—perhaps you say—"only because it really *is* correct!"—But what does it mean to say: "I take the calculation as correct because it is correct"?

And yet we can say: the person who is calculating in my language-game does not think of it as a peculiarity of *his* nature that he gets *this*; the fact does not appear to him as a psychological one.

I am imagining him as under the impression that he has only followed a thread that is already there, and accepting the How of the following as something that is a matter of course; and only knowing *one* explanation of his action, namely: how the thread runs.

He does indeed set himself off when he follows the rule or the examples; however, he does not regard what he does as a peculiarity of *his* course; he says, not: "so *that's* how I went", but: "so *that's* how it goes".

But now, suppose someone did say at the end of the calculation in our language-game: "so *that's* how I went"—or: "so *this* course satisfies me" —can I say he has misunderstood the whole language-game? Certainly not! So long as he does not make some further unwelcome application of it.

Isn't it the *application* of the calculation that produces this conception of its being the calculation, not ourselves, that takes this course?

Why do you want always to consider mathematics under the aspect of discovering and not of doing?

It must influence us a great deal that in calculating we use the words "correct" and "true" and "false" and the form of statements. (Shaking and nodding one's head.)

Why ought I to say that the knowledge that all human beings who have learned to calculate calculate like *this* is not *mathematical* knowledge? Because it points to a different context.

Then is calculating the results of someone else's calculating already applied mathematics?—and hence calculating my own results too?

5. There is no doubt at all that *in certain language-games* mathematical propositions play the part of rules of description, as opposed to descriptive propositions.

But that is not to say that this contrast does not shade off in all directions.

And *that* in turn is not to say that the contrast is not of the greatest importance.

What is proved by a mathematical proof is set up as an internal relation and withdrawn from doubt.

We say that a proof is a picture. But this picture stands in need of ratification, and that we give it when we work over it.—

True enough; but if it got ratification from one person, but not from another, and they could not *come to any understanding*—would what we had here be calculation?

So it is not the ratification by itself that makes it calculation but the agreement of ratifications.

For another game could quite well be imagined, in which people were prompted by expressions (similar perhaps to general rules) to let sequences of signs come to them for particular practical purposes, i.e. *ad hoc*; and that this even proved to pay. And here the 'calculations' if we choose to call them that, do not have to agree with one another. (Here we might speak of 'intuition'.)

The agreement of ratifications is the pre-condition of our language-game, it is not affirmed in it.

If a calculation is an experiment and the *conditions are fulfilled*, then we must accept whatever comes, as the result; and if a calculation is an experiment then the proposition that it yields such and such a result is after all the proposition that under such conditions this kind of sign makes its appearance. And if under these conditions one result appears at one time and another at another, we have no right to say "there's something wrong here" or "both calculations cannot be all right", but we should have to say: this calculation does not always yield the same result (*why* need not be known). But although the procedure is now just as interesting, perhaps even more interesting, what we have here *now* is no longer calculation. And this is of course a grammatical remark about the use of the word "calculation". And this grammar has of course a point.

What does it mean to reach an *understanding* about a difference in the result of calculation? It surely means to arrive at a calculation that is free of discrepancy. And if we can't reach an understanding, then the one cannot say that the other is calculating too, only with different results.

7. Now how about this—ought I to say that the same sense can only have *one* proof? Or that when a proof is found the sense alters?

Of course some people would oppose this and say: "Then the proof of a proposition cannot ever be found, for, if it has been found, it is no longer the proof of *this* proposition". But to say this is so far to say nothing at all.—

40. An addition of shapes together, so that some of the edges fuse, plays a very small part in our life.—As when

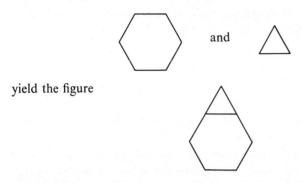

and

yield the figure

But if this were an *important* operation, our ordinary concept of arithmetical addition would perhaps be different.

It is natural for us to regard it as a geometrical fact, not as a fact of physics, that a square piece of paper can be folded into a boat or hat. But is not geometry, so understood, part of physics? No; we split geometry off from physics. The geometrical possibility from the physical one. But what if we left them together? If we simply said: "If you do this and this and this with the piece of paper then *this* will be the result"? What has to be done might be told in a rhyme. For might it not be that someone did not distinguish at all between the two possibilities? As e.g. a child who learns this technique does not. It does not know and does not consider whether these results of folding are possible only because the paper stretches, is pulled out of shape, when it is folded in such-and-such a way, or because it is *not* pulled out of shape.

And now isn't it like this in arithmetic too? Why shouldn't it be possible for people to learn to calculate without having the concepts of a mathematical and a physical fact? They merely know that this is always the result when they take care and do what they have learnt.

Let us imagine that while we were calculating the figures on paper altered erratically. A 1 would suddenly become a 6 and then a 5 and then again a 1 and so on. And I want to assume that this does not make any difference to the calculation because, as soon as I read a figure in order to calculate with it or to apply it, it once more becomes the one that we have in *our* calculating. At the same time, however, one can see quite well how the figures change during the calculations; but we are trained not to worry about this.

Of course, even if we do not make the above assumption, this calculation could lead to usable results.

Here we calculate strictly according to rules, yet this result does not *have* to come out.—I am assuming that we see no sort of regularity in the alteration of the figures.

I want to say: this calculating could really be conceived as an experiment, and we might for example say: "Let's try what will come out now if I apply this rule".

Or again: "Let us make the following experiment: we'll write the figures with ink of such-and-such a composition ... and calculate according to the rule. ..."

Now you might of course say: "In this case the manipulation of figures according to rules is not calculation."

"We are calculating only when there is a *must* behind the result."—But suppose we don't know this *must*,—is it contained in the calculation all the same? Or are we not calculating, if we do it quite naïvely?

How about the following: You aren't calculating if, when you get now this, now that result, and cannot find a mistake, you accept this and say: this simply shows that certain circumstances which are still unknown have an influence on the result.

This might be expressed like this: if calculation reveals a causal connection to you, then you are not calculating.

Our children are not only given practice in calculation but are also trained to adopt a particular attitude towards a mistake in calculating.

What I am saying comes to this, that mathematics is *normative*. But "norm" does not mean the same thing as "ideal".

IV

2. Does a calculating machine *calculate*?

Imagine that a calculating machine had come into existence by accident; now someone accidentally presses its knobs (or an animal walks over it) and it calculates the product 25 × 20.

I want to say: it is essential to mathematics that its signs are also employed in *mufti*.

It is the use outside mathematics, and so the *meaning* of the signs, that makes the sign-game into mathematics.

Just as it is not logical inference either, for me to make a change from one formation to another (say from one arrangement of chairs to another) if these arrangements have not a linguistic function apart from this transformation.

Alan Ross Anderson

The latest of Wittgenstein's books[1] consists of a collection of writings, in large part on mathematics, produced during the period 1937–1945. These fragments were written concurrently with Part I of the *Philosophical Investigations*,[2] perhaps for inclusion in the latter work, had Wittgenstein lived to complete it. It is not surprising, therefore, that there is little here that is fundamentally new. Many of the problems discussed (e.g., signs as "marks of concepts," "following a rule," the compelling character of proofs, the relation between calculation and experiment) have already been treated in the earlier volume, and though the remarks here are different in detail, they are the same in spirit. Moreover, they defy summary, the pieces chosen by the editors being in many cases cryptic, fragmentary, and unfinished.

What *is* new here is the detailed discussion of several important results in the classical foundations of mathematics (principally Cantor's theorem and Gödel's theorem, to each of which a substantial section is devoted) and of the relation of logic to mathematics. As regards logical questions, the central thesis of Wittgenstein's later philosophy ("The rules of logical inference are rules of the language-game," p. 181[3]) is well known, both from the earlier posthumous volume and from the writings of his many disciples. In the *Investigations* the thesis is applied to the "logic of our expressions" in everyday contexts; here he discusses in the same spirit the more specialized language used in talking about the foundations of mathematics.

[1] *Remarks on the Foundations of Mathematics*, ed. G. H. von Wright, R. Rhees, and G. E. M. Anscombe; German, with English translation by G. E. M. Anscombe on alternate pages (The Macmillan Company: New York, 1956).

[2] *Philosophical Investigations*, trans. G. E. M. Anscombe (New York, 1953).

[3] Page numbers, unless otherwise specified, refer to pages of the book under review.

Reprinted with the kind permission of the author and the editor from The Review of Metaphysics, 11 (*March*, 1958), 446–58.

That we are to regard the mathematical discussion as illustrative of the general thesis, is made clear at several points; for example,

> The concept of the rule for the formation of an infinite decimal is—of course —not a specifically mathematical one. It is a concept connnected with a rigidly determined *activity* in human life. The concept of this rule is not more mathematical than that of: following the rule. . . . For the expression of the rule and its sense is only a part of the language-game: following the rule. (p. 186.)

But if the special interest claimed for this volume by the editors is justified, we would expect the discussion to be substantive as well as illustrative: some light should be shed on philosophical problems in the foundations of mathematics proper. For this reason we will confine attention to Wittgenstein's views about mathematical ways of talking, leaving aside those portions of the book which repeat and elaborate the *Investigations*.[4]

It should be mentioned at the outset that Wittgenstein is concerned with a very specialized part of mathematics. (1) By "mathematics" he means calculating procedures, and (2) by "the foundations of mathematics," he means, at least when the phrase is used polemically, *Principia Mathematica* (hereafter, "*PM*"), or some closely related system, such as Frege's. The first idea is likely to elicit little sympathy from most mathematicians or logicians; nothing Wittgenstein says would lead one to guess that abstract algebra and the theory of games are part of mathematics. ("The role of the proposition: 'I must have miscalculated'. It is really the key to an understanding of the 'foundations' of mathematics" (p. 111).) And the second idea has probably not been held seriously by anyone for twenty-five years. But the target of Wittgenstein's attack need not be any particular person; he seems rather to be arguing, in many places in the book, against a putative position which has a certain plausibility, namely, that *PM* and similar formalisms provide us with ideal languages *in* which to discuss mathematics, in a way that rescues us completely from the vagueness and ambiguity of ordinary English prose.

> The curse of the invasion of mathematics by mathematical logic is that now any proposition can be represented in a mathematical symbolism, and this makes us feel obliged to understand it. Although of course this method of writing is nothing but the translation of vague ordinary prose. (p. 155.)

The idea that *PM* (or any other formalism) is an ideal language which we *use* in place of a natural language can arise easily from a number of sources.

---

[4] It should be remarked that a few pages from the *Investigations* are reprinted here, and that much of the book consists of reflections closely similar to those of the *Investigations* on "following the rule." The latter concept has been much discussed both independently and in reviews. We have therefore felt justified in neglecting these topics in favor of those more closely associated with classical work in the "foundations of mathematics."

(1) It is certainly suggested by the logicist thesis: "The fact that all Mathematics is Symbolic Logic is one of the greatest discoveries of our age; and when this fact has been established, the remainder of the principles of mathematics consists in the analysis of Symbolic Logic itself."[5] (2) Current standards of rigor in mathematics require that papers be so written that proofs could, with little difficulty, be carried out in some system of formalized set theory. And this suggests that though we do talk in the informal way, we always could say it in the ideal way, using the ideal language. (3) Perhaps more important, the notion seems to arise inevitably in the course of teaching mathematical logic. At the outset we are at pains to insist that steps not be put down simply because they seem reasonable; we require that each step be justified by citing a rule explicitly. But then in the interest of drawing attention to the interpretation of the formalism, we have students give formal proofs of expressions with intuitively plausible interpretations. Again the idea is suggested that the formal system is a language we are using.

But in thinking in this way we are likely to lose sight of the fact that throughout the whole process we have been speaking English (or English supplemented with a few technical terms). We specified the axioms and rules in English, we discussed the interpretation in English, and even what we proved was expressed in an English sentence, for example " 'p ⊃ p' is a theorem of *PM*." And having learned techniques for proving (in English) sentences of the form "*x* is a theorem of *S*," we now drop that sort of inquiry as elementary, and turn to subtler and more interesting questions about *S*, asking if it is consistent, complete, and so on. The point is that formal systems are not (or are only incidentally) systems to prove things *in*, they are systems to prove things *about*. And these proofs are carried out in whatever natural language we have in common—what Curry calls the "U-language."[6]

I do not mean that it would be impossible to use the formal systems as languages. One can readily admit (with Church,[7] for example) that it is simply an historical accident that the syntax of English is as complicated, irregular, and open-ended as it is. We *might* instead have been taught from birth to speak a language with a more regular and logically simpler structure, like some of our artificial systems. But even if it is just an historical accident, it is still true that we are constrained by the circumstance to state explicit semantical and syntactical rules in a natural language—at the outset, at least. And the interpreted formalisms are then vague to the extent that the semantical rules are vague. What we actually learn from the procedure is not so much a new formal language to talk, as a new and more careful way of using the old informal language. The ideal of rigor in artificial languages is approximated more and more closely, but never reached.

    [5] Bertrand Russell, *The Principles of Mathematics*, 2nd ed. (London, 1950), p. 5.

    [6] Haskell B. Curry, *A Theory of Formal Deducibility* (Notre Dame, 1950), pp. 11–12.

    [7] Alonzo Church, "The Need for Abstract Entities in Semantic Analysis," *Proceedings of the American Academy of Arts and Sciences*, LXXX (1951), 106–107.

The point that we never escape completely from natural languages into ideal languages, where the air is purer, is an important one, and bears repetition (though it is certainly wrong to say, as Wittgenstein does, that "the method of writing is *nothing but* the translation of vague ordinary prose"). If we forget it, we may draw unjustified parallels between the informal language we use and the formal systems about which we talk; we might for example be misled into thinking that since a contradiction spoils a formal system, the Epimenides argument must spoil English. But

> Is there harm in the contradiction that arises when someone says: "I am lying.—So I am not lying.—So I am lying.—etc."? I mean: does it make our language less usable if in this case, according to the ordinary rules, a proposition yields its contradictory, and vice versa?—the proposition *itself* is unusable, and these inferences equally; but why should they not be made?—It is a profitless performance!—It is a language-game with some similarity to the game of thumb-catching. (p. 51.)

Contradictions do make formal systems uninteresting but in natural languages we simply observe their oddness, and then ignore them hoping—indeed feeling quite confident—that their presence in English does not infect our usual mathematical procedures. Of course formal systems may suggest interesting mathematical problems, to be discussed in the idiom reserved for mathematical discourse in English. But problems about the syntax of formal systems remain mathematical problems; no 'foundation' has been given to anything:

> The *mathematical* problems of what is called foundations are no more the foundation of mathematics for us than the painted rock is the support of a painted tower. (p. 171.)

I would venture that this is the attitude of the overwhelming majority of contemporary working mathematicians, toward attempts to 'ground' mathematics in logic. The position also has certain affinities with Brouwerian intuitionism:[8] "... no science, in particular not philosophy or logic, can be a presupposition for mathematics."[9] The motivation is of course different: Brouwer considers the "basic intuition of bare two-oneness" to be fundamental to his conception of mathematics; Wittgenstein would certainly reject any such assertion. But they are agreed that "mathematical logic" is logic

---

[8] Wittgenstein also agrees with intuitionists in questioning non-constructive existence proofs. But again the motivation is different. Brouwer says that non-constructive proofs fail to establish existence; Wittgenstein says that we do not *understand* non-constructive proofs, or at least that we understand them differently, in the sense that we can't *do* the same things with constructive and non-constructive proofs (pp. 146, 155).

[9] S. C. Kleene, *Introduction to Metamathematics* (New York, 1951), p. 51.

studied mathematically,[10] and that using mathematical techniques to study the syntax of artificial languages does not somehow count as "reducing" mathematics to logic.

One might at this point object that few or no mature mathematicians or logicians are now confused on the latter point in *precisely* the way Wittgenstein envisages. No one was ever moved to give up speaking English because of the Epimenides argument—it is on the contrary just the sort of thing to stir up conversation. But I do not think this objection much to the point, even if it is true. Surely many people at one time or another (even Wittgenstein himself at one time) have had misconceptions of the kind he discusses, and it is useful to clear them up.

At least it is useful to clear them up if no further confusions are created along the way. Unfortunately, in discussing the classical work on the foundations of mathematics (I have in mind the movement beginning with Frege and Cantor, and continuing in Whitehead and Russell, Hilbert, and Gödel), confusion is created wholesale. Wittgenstein *says* he feels no antipathy toward these studies themselves, but only toward certain philosophical attitudes associated with them:

> My aim is to alter the *attitude* to contradiction and to consistency proofs. (*Not* to show that this proof shows something unimportant. How *could* that be so?) (p. 106.)

But some of the arguments designed to change our attitude toward contradictions indicate that Wittgenstein misunderstood both the content of and the motivation for a number of the results he discusses at length. These are hard words to use of a major philosopher; if true, they should be substantiated as fully as possible. What I shall do is to discuss his treatment, closely connected with his rejection of "logicism," of Gödel's theorem, as illustrative of a general misconception of the logicist and formalist programs.

The central idea of the theorem he puts as follows:

> I have constructed a proposition (I will use '*P*' to designate it) in Russell's symbolism, and by means of certain definitions and transformations it can be so interpreted that it says: '*P* is not provable in Russell's system'. Must I not say that this proposition on the one hand is true, and on the other hand is unprovable? For suppose it were false; then it is true that it is provable. And that surely cannot be! And if it is proved, then it is proved that it is not provable. Thus it can only be true, but unprovable. (p. 50.)

[10] But by way of seeing that this is no longer an important issue as between Brouwerians and, e.g., Fregeans, we observe that Church, the foremost contemporary representative of Frege's position, says that he "prefers the term 'mathematical logic,' understood as meaning logic treated by the mathematical method, especially, the formal axiomatic or logistic method" (*Introduction to Mathematical Logic* [Princeton, 1956], footnote 125).

This is not too inaccurate, as a rough paraphrase of Gödel's argument, though two pivotal points in the proof are ignored, namely, the assumption that the system is consistent (which justifies the "And surely that cannot be!"), and the fact that it is constructive. But the ensuing discussion indicates that the point has been missed:

> Just as we ask: " 'provable' in what system?", so we must also ask: " 'true' in what system?" 'True in Russell's system' means, as was said: proved in Russell's system; and 'false in Russell's system' means: the opposite has been proved in Russell's system.—Now what does your "suppose it is false" mean? *In the Russell sense* it means 'suppose the opposite is proved in Russell's system'; *if that is your assumption*, you will now presumably give up the interpretation that it is unprovable. . . . Further: if the proposition is supposed to be false in some other than the Russell sense, then it does not contradict this for it to be proved in Russell's system. (p. 51.)

There are several remarks to make.

(1) What is to be made of the claim that " 'True in Russell's system' means: proved[11] in Russell's system"? For one thing, "true," in the context of mathematical logic, is a semantical predicate, and "proved" is syntactical. Given (a) a syntactical formulation of a system, under which certain expressions are *provable*, and (b) an interpretation of the system, under which certain expressions are *true*, we may wish to know whether all the truths are provable. If so, the syntactical system is said to be *complete* relatively to the interpretation; otherwise *incomplete*. The rough content of Gödel's theorem is that if the truths are those of elementary arithmetic, and if provability is defined for a constructive and consistent formal system, then not all true statements are provable in that system—in particular, *PM* is incomplete in the sense described.

Questions about completeness arise quite naturally in the course of studying formal systems; such questions are in fact very close to the heart of mathematical logic. But Wittgenstein seems to want to legislate this class of questions out of existence, and by peculiarly un-Wittgensteinian methods at that. For surely such *use* as the phrase "true in Russell's system" has in the literature does not justify the remark under discussion. And it is in any event difficult to reconcile the comment with the claim that he is *not* saying that the proof "shews something unimportant." If the proof does not show that truth outruns provability in *PM* (provided the system is consistent), then what of importance does it show?

(2) When we "suppose it false" we do not mean to be supposing it unprovable; i.e., we are indeed supposing it false in "some other than [Wittgenstein's] Russell sense." But the claim that "if the proposition is supposed to be false in some other than the Russell sense, then it does not contradict this for it to be proved in Russell's system," again misses the point. The problem is to determine whether all those expressions which are false on

---

[11] Of course this must be construed to mean "prov*able*."

the interpretation are *provably* false in the formal system. Or in Wittgenstein's eccentric terminology, to determine whether all falsehoods in "some other than the Russell sense" are also falsehoods in the alleged "Russell sense." Gödel's answer is that they are not; and this fact can hardly be disposed of by confusing truth with provability.

(3) Nor is the fact trivial, as Wittgenstein suggests in an adjacent passage:

"But may there not be true propositions which are written in this symbolism, but are not provable in Russell's system?"—'True propositions,' hence propositions which are true in *another* system, i.e. can rightly be asserted in another game. Certainly; why should there not be such propositions; or rather: why should not propositions—of physics, e.g.—be written in Russell's symbolism? (p. 50.)

The answer to the last question is trivially that Russell's symbolism does not contain symbols for the required non-logical notions, e.g., that of mass. But even if we allow that *PM* be extended so as to express propositions of physics, the point is missed again. If Gödel's theorem showed only what Wittgenstein suggests (that there are unprovable truths expressible in *PM*), it would indeed be trivial. But the point is that *PM* was written in the hope, at the time quite reasonable, of showing that "all Mathematics is Symbolic Logic," which entails that all truths of arithmetic should be provable. We are not interested in the fact that there is *some* true proposition not provable in *PM*; we are interested rather in the fact that there is a proposition *we hoped would be provable*, which is unprovable if the system is consistent.

The reader may at this juncture feel that I am being unduly harsh in taking Wittgenstein to task for failure to discuss competently what is, after all, simply an example, and a rather abstruse and technical one to boot. But this charge would fail to take into account the rôle of examples in Wittgenstein's method. If we "look not to the meaning, but to the use," then we must get an idea of the use by detailed discussion and comparison of examples. And in this case Wittgenstein proposes to shed general light on an important locution in metamathematics:

However queer it sounds, my task as far as concerns Gödel's proof seems merely to consist in making clear what such a proposition as: "Suppose this could be proved" means in mathematics. (p. 177.)

But we are in point of clarity worse off after Wittgenstein's account than before.

Even supposing that the foregoing argument could be patched up without losing such force as it has, it is still doubtful whether one would want to draw Wittgenstein's moral:

> Let us suppose I prove the unprovability (in Russell's system) of *P*; then by this proof I have proved *P*. Now if this proof were one in Russell's system— I should in that case have proved at once that it belonged and did not belong to Russell's system.—That is what comes of making up such sentences.— But there is a contradiction here!—Well, then there is a contradiction here. Does it do any harm here? (p. 51.)

In the first place, the conclusion to draw would not be that *P* at once "belonged and did not belong" to Russell's system, but rather that Russell's system was inconsistent, a possibility for which we are always prepared in the absence of a consistency proof. But more important, it is difficult to reconcile Wittgenstein's "so what" attitude toward contradictions in mathematics with his own view of language-games.

It is in some ways instructive to compare language to a game. One is led thereby to notice that the playing-pieces (words) and the rules (grammar) are in part arbitrary. One is also led to notice that in both cases there are "moves" that are not permitted; one can violate rules of grammar as well as game rules. One notes also that in both cases there are "winning positions." In an argument, viewed as a verbal game, we have vague criteria for telling which disputant, if either, won. And as Wittgenstein remarks, what constitutes winning depends on the game. "What is called 'losing' in chess may constitute winning in another game" (p. 51). We may, as he suggests, want to produce contradictions for aesthetic reasons, say, and who is to deny us the privilege?

But now why can't we have a language-game in which one of the principal components of the winning situation would be avoidance of contradiction? I suggest that mathematics *could* be viewed as just such a game by Wittgenstein, but he distrusts the idea:

> But if you say "The point isn't understanding at all. Mathematical propositions are only positions in a game" that too is nonsense! 'Mathematics' is *not* a sharply delimited concept. (p. 155.)

But surely 'mathematics' is no *less* sharply delimited than 'speaking English'; if the latter can be regarded as a language-game, why not the former? And the fact that avoidance of contradiction *is* held essential by mathematicians is viewed as somehow perverse:

> 'Contradiction destroys the calculus'—what gives it this special position? With a little imagination, I believe, it can certainly be demolished. (p. 170.)

And again:

> Contradiction. Why just this *one* bogy? That is surely very suspicious. (p. 130.)

In trying to alter our attitudes toward contradictions, he sometimes seems to be recommending that we stop playing the consistency-game altogether:

> 'But didn't the contradiction make Frege's logic useless for giving a foundation to arithmetic?' Yes, it did. But then, who said that it had to be useful for this purpose? (p. 171.)

The straightforward answer to the last question is "Frege did," and Peano, Russell, Whitehead, and Hilbert, agreed in spirit. Wittgenstein's question indicates that he failed to grasp the motivation for the whole enterprise; i.e., he misunderstood the putative "winning position." The problem considered, in the guise of "Hilbert's program," was to find a consistent, constructive formal system in which all truths of classical mathematics could be proved. Gödel showed that the game had no winning position. Now it may be true that some writers, on the basis of a superficial familiarity with Gödel's result, tried to make something of a mystery of it. And it is no doubt in part against such writers that Wittgenstein is aiming his remarks (though one frequently wishes documentation; his opponent is always anonymous). But the way to dispel the mystery is *not* to belittle the result, or to argue that it doesn't show what it seems to show. Nor is it to suggest that the game is not worth the candle. Nor, finally, is it to use abusive *ad hominem* devices. (The phrase "the curse of mathematical logic" occurs no less than seven times; and he also remarks on "The superstitious fear and awe of mathematicians in face of contradiction" (p. 53). Adopting Wittgenstein's own analogy, one might as well say "The superstitious fear and awe of chess players in the face of checkmate.")

The way to dispel the mystery *is* to see the result as a straightforward unprovability theorem, on all fours with the theorem to the effect that one cannot trisect an arbitrary angle with straightedge and compasses. Indeed, the theorem is not even particularly surprising, once one gets over the initial shock. If we carefully limit the tools we use (to straightedge and compasses, or to constructive methods of definition), then it is not terribly surprising to find that there are things that cannot be done with these methods (trisecting an arbitrary angle, or proving an arbitrary arithmetical truth).

It is hard to avoid the conclusion that Wittgenstein failed to understand clearly the problems with which workers in the foundations have been concerned. Nor, I think, did he appreciate the real bearing of the results on the logistic thesis. For Gödel's theorem, and the line of development it culminates, have more often been cited in *favor* of Wittgenstein's position concerning the relation of logic to mathematics ("It is the use outside mathematics, and so the *meaning* of the signs, that makes the sign-game into mathematics" (p. 133). "The idea of the mechanization of mathematics. The fashion of the axiomatic system" (p. 168)). Thus Post in 1944:

[Gödel's theorems] implicitly, in all probability, justify the generalization that every symbolic logic is incomplete. . . . The conclusion is unescapable that even for such a fixed, well-defined body of mathematical propositions, *mathematical thinking is, and must remain, essentially creative.* To the writer's mind, this conclusion must inevitably result in at least a partial reversal of the entire axiomatic trend of the late nineteenth and early twentieth centuries, with a return to meaning and truth as being of the essence of mathematics.[12]

And Rogers in 1957:

[the undecidability results of Gödel and Church] ended the dream of Leibniz (and, to a certain extent, of Hilbert) of finding a mechanical method for solving all mathematical problems.[13]

In short, the principal trouble with these *Remarks* is that they are directed to the battles of twenty-five to fifty years ago—and the battle lines are no longer drawn where they once were. Ironically, the abandonment of the logicist and formalist programs, against which so much of Wittgenstein's polemic is addressed, was brought about not by dismissing the investigations as pointless or perverse, but by taking them seriously. Wittgenstein has had a profound impact on twentieth-century philosophy, though it has been exerted through his students rather than his writings. (Even the content of the *Investigations* was in large part familiar to us before its publication, though perhaps in a "more or less mangled and watered down" form, as Wittgenstein charges.) But it is very doubtful whether this application of his method to questions in the foundations of mathematics will contribute substantially to his reputation as a philosopher.

[12] E. L. Post, "Recursively Enumerable Sets of Positive Integers and Their Decision Problems," *Bulletin of the American Mathematical Society*, I (1944), p. 295.

[13] Hartley Rogers, Jr., *Theory of Recursive Functions and Effective Computability*, vol. I (mimeographed) (Massachusetts Institute of Technology, 1957), p. 14.

Michael Dummett

From time to time Wittgenstein recorded in separate notebooks thoughts that occurred to him about the philosophy of mathematics. His recently published *Bemerkungen über die Grundlagen der Mathematik*[1] consists of extracts made by the editors from five of these. Neither it nor any of these notebooks was intended by its author as a book. That it cannot be considered, and ought not to be criticized, as such is therefore unsurprising, though disappointing. Many of the thoughts are expressed in a manner which the author recognized as inaccurate or obscure; some passages contradict others; some are quite inconclusive; some raise objections to ideas which Wittgenstein held or had held which are not themselves stated clearly in the volume; other passages again, particularly those on consistency and on Gödel's theorem, are of poor quality or contain definite errors. This being so, the book has has to be treated as what it is—a selection from the jottings of a great philosopher. As Frege said of his unpublished writings, they are not all gold but there is gold in them. One of the tasks of the reader is therefore to extract the gold.

I encounter frequently in conversation the impression that this is typical of Wittgenstein's work in general; I have often heard the *Investigations* characterized as evasive and inconclusive. This seems to me a travesty of the truth; the book expresses with great clarity many forceful, profound, and quite definite ideas—though it is true that a hasty reader may sometimes be

[1] *Bemerkungen über die Grundlagen der Mathematik*. By Ludwig Wittgenstein. Edited by G. H. von Wright, R. Rhees, and G. E. M. Anscombe. With English translation (*Remarks on the Foundations of Mathematics*) by G. E. M. Anscombe, on facing pages. Oxford, Basil Blackwell, 1956. Pp. xix, 196, each version.

Reprinted with the kind permission of the author and the editor from Philosophical Review, *no. LXVIII (1959), pp. 324–48.*

bewildered by the complexity of some of the thoughts. The contrast with the present volume is marked, and is due entirely to the different origins of the two books.

In the philosophy of mathematics, Platonism stands opposed to various degrees of constructivism. According to Platonism, mathematical objects are there and stand in certain relations to one another, independently of us, and what we do is to discover these objects and their relations to one another. The constructivist usually opposes to this the picture of our making, constructing, the mathematical entities as we go along. For the Platonist, the meaning of a mathematical statement is to be explained in terms of its truth-conditions; for each statement, there is something in mathematical reality in virtue of which it is either true or false. An example of the explanation of meaning in terms of truth and falsity is the truth-table explanation of the sentential connectives. For the constructivist, the general form of an explanation of meaning must be in terms of the conditions under which we regard ourselves as justified in asserting a statement, that is, the circumstances in which we are in possession of a proof. For instance, a statement made up of two statements joined by a connective is to be explained by explaining a claim to have proved the complex statement in terms of what a claim to have proved the constituent statements consists in; thus a claim to have proved ⌜A or B⌝ will be a claim to have a method leading either to a proof of A or a proof of B. What in practice this will lead to will depend upon the degree of constructivism adopted; for example, if we confine ourselves to decidable statements, then the truth-tables will receive an acceptable interpretation and the whole classical logic will be applicable; if, on the other hand, we allow with the intuitionists a much wider range of mathematical statements to be considered as intelligible, then the law of excluded middle and many other classically valid laws will cease to hold generally. But in either case it is the notion of proof and not the notions of truth and falsity which is for the constructivist central to the account of the meaning of mathematical statements.

We may regard Platonism and the various varieties of constructivism not as rivals but merely as means of demarcating different areas of mathematics with respect not to subject matter but to methods of proof. In this case there are only the essentially mathematical problems of formulating clearly the different conceptions and investigating in detail the mathematical consequences of each. If, on the other hand, one regards the different schools as rivals, there remains the philosophical problem of deciding which of the various accounts is correct. Wittgenstein's book is intended as a contribution to the latter task only. It seems natural to suppose that the philosophical task and the mathematical go hand in hand, for the precise formulation of a conception is not irrelevant to deciding on its correctness, and unexpected consequences of adopting it may lead one to revise one's opinion as to its value. Wittgenstein will have none of this: for him philosophy and mathematics have nothing to say to one another; no mathematical discovery can have any bearing on the philosophy of mathematics.[2] It would seem that he is theoretically committed also to the converse, that no philosophical opinion could, at or at least ought to, affect the procedure of the mathematician. This comes out to some extent in his discussion of the law of excluded middle in mathematics. Against one who insisted that either the sequence "77777" occurs in the development of π or it does not, he employs arguments similar to those of the intuitionists; and yet it appears that he is not wishing to question the validity in a mathematical proof of, for example, argument by cases, but only to reprove someone who in the course of philosophical reflection wishes to insist on the law of excluded middle.[3] Yet this is not to be taken too seriously, for Wittgenstein would always be able to claim that, while he had not shown that certain mathematical procedures were *wrong*, still he had shown them not to have the interest we were inclined to attach to them. Certainly in his discussion of Cantor he displays no timidity about "interfering with the mathematicians."[4] I think that there is no ground for Wittgenstein's segregation of philosophy from mathematics but that this springs only from a general tendency of his to regard discourse as split up into a number of distinct islands with no communication between them (statements of natural science, of philosophy, of mathematics, of religion).

As Frege showed, the nominalist objection to Platonism—that talk about "abstract entities" is unintelligible—is ill-taken; if we believe in the objectivity of mathematics, then there is no objection to our thinking in terms of mathematical objects, nor to the picture of them as already there waiting to be discovered that goes with it. Nor is formalism a real alternative. The formalist insists that the content of a mathematical theorem is simply that *if* there is any domain for which the axioms hold good, then the theorem will also hold good for that domain; and he will add that so long as we do not know the axioms to be categorical, a statement of the theory need not be either true or false. But he will not reject the classical logic, since he will agree that in any particular domain for which the axioms hold, the statement will be either true or false; and furthermore, he will allow that any given statement either does or does not follow from the axioms. Since the statement that there exists a proof of a given statement from given axioms is in exactly the same position as, say, an existence-statement in number theory for which we have neither proof nor disproof, the formalist has gained no advantage; he has merely switched from one kind of mathematical object—numbers—to another—formal proofs.

Wittgenstein adopts a version (as we shall see, an extreme version) of constructivism; for him it is of the essence of a mathematical statement that it is asserted as the conclusion of a *proof*, whereas I suppose that for a Platonist a being who had *direct* apprehension of mathematical truth, not

[2] Cf. V, 13, 19; IV, 52; also *Investigations*, II, xiv; I, 124.
[3] IV, 10.
[4] I, App. II.

mediated by inferences, would not be a complete absurdity. There are many different lines of thought converging upon Wittgenstein's constructivism; I shall deal first with his conception of logical necessity.

A great many philosophers nowadays subscribe to some form of conventionalist account of logical necessity, and it is perhaps difficult to realize what a liberation was effected by this theory. The philosophical problem of necessity is twofold: what is its source, and how do we recognize it? God can ordain that something shall hold good of the actual world; but how can even God ordain that something is to hold good in all possible worlds? We know what it is to set about finding out if something *is* true; but what account can we give of the process of discovering whether it *must* be true? According to conventionalism, all necessity is imposed by us not on reality, but upon our language; a statement is necessary by virtue of our having chosen not to count anything as falsifying it. Our recognition of logical necessity thus becomes a particular case of our knowledge of our own intentions.

The conventionalism that is so widespread is, however, a modified conventionalism. On this view, although all necessity derives from linguistic conventions that we have adopted, the derivation is not always direct. Some necessary statements are straightforwardly registers of conventions we have laid down; others are more or less remote *consequences* of conventions. Thus "Nothing can at the same time be green and blue all over" is a direct register of a convention, since there is nothing in the ostensive training we give in the use of color-words which shows that we are not to call something on the borderline between green and blue "both green and blue." "Nothing can be both green and red," on the other hand, is necessary in consequence of the meanings of "green" and "red" as shown in the ostensive training. We did not need to adopt a special convention excluding the expression "both green and red" from our language, since the use by someone of this expression would already show that he had not learned what he was supposed to have learned from the ostensive training.

When applied to mathematics, this modified conventionalism results in the sort of account of mathematical truth with which we are so familiar from logical positivist writings. The axioms of a mathematical theory are necessary in virtue of their being direct registers of certain conventions we have adopted about the use of the terms of the theory; it is the job of the mathematician to discover the more or less remote consequences of our having adopted these conventions, which consequences are epitomized in the theorems. If it is inquired what is the status of the logical principles in accordance with which we pass from axioms to theorems, the reply is that to subscribe to these principles is again the expression of the adoption of linguistic conventions, in this case conventions about the use of "if," "all," and so forth. This account is entirely superficial and throws away all the advantages of conventionalism, since it leaves unexplained the status of the assertion that certain conventions have certain consequences. It appears that if we adopt the conventions registered by the axioms, together with those registered by the principles of inference, then we *must* adhere to the way of talking embodied in the theorem; and *this* necessity must be one imposed upon us, one that we meet with. It cannot itself express the adoption of a convention; the account leaves no room for any further such convention.

Wittgenstein goes in for a full-blooded conventionalism; for him the logical necessity of any statement is always the *direct* expression of a linguistic convention. That a given statement is necessary consists always in our having expressly decided to treat that very statement as unassailable; it cannot rest on our having adopted certain other conventions which are found to involve our treating it so. This account is applied alike to deep theorems and to elementary computations. To give an example of the latter, the criterion which we adopt in the first place for saying that there are n things of a certain kind is to be explained by describing the procedure of counting. But when we find that there are five boys and seven girls in a room, we say that there are twelve children altogether, without counting them all together. The fact that we are justified in doing this is not, as it were, implicit in the procedure of counting itself; rather, we have chosen to adopt a *new* criterion for saying that there are twelve children, different from the criterion of counting up all the children together. It would seem that, if we have genuinely distinct criteria for the same statement, they may clash. But the necessity of "$5 + 7 = 12$" consists just in this, that we do not count anything as a clash; if we count the children all together and get eleven, we say, "We must have miscounted."

This account is very difficult to accept, since it appears that the mathematical proof drives us along willy-nilly until we arrive at the theorem. (Of course, we learned "$5 + 7 = 12$" by rote; but we could produce an argument to prove it if the need arose.) But here Wittgenstein brings in the considerations about rules presented in the *Investigations* and elsewhere. A proof proceeds according to certain logical principles or rules of inference. We are inclined to suppose that once we have accepted the axioms from which the proof starts, we have, as it were, no further active part to play; when the proof is shown us, we are mere passive spectators. But in order to follow the proof, we have to recognize various transitions as applications of the general rules of inference. Now even if these rules had been explicitly formulated at the start, and we had given our assent to them, our doing so would not in itself constitute recognition of each transition as a correct application of the rules. Once we have the proof, we shall indeed say that anyone who does not accept it either cannot really have understood or cannot really have accepted the rules of inference; but it does not have to be the case that there was anything in what he said or did before he rejected the proof which revealed such a misunderstanding or rejection of the rule of inference. Hence at each step we are free to choose to accept or reject the proof; there is nothing in our formulation of the axioms and of the rules of inference, and nothing in our minds when we accepted these before the proof was given, which of itself shows whether we shall accept the proof or not; and hence there is nothing which *forces* us to accept the proof. If we accept the proof, we confer necessity on the theorem proved; we "put it in the archives" and will count nothing as telling against it. In doing this we are making a new decision, and not merely making explicit a decision we had already made implicitly.

A natural reaction to this is to say that it is true enough when we have not formulated our principles of inference, or have formulated them only in an imprecise form, but that it does not apply at all when we have achieved a strict formalization. Wittgenstein's hostility to mathematical logic is great; he says that it has completely distorted the thinking of philosophers.[5] Because this remark as it stands is so plainly silly, it is difficult to get a clear view of the matter. Consider a favorite example of Wittgenstein's: you train someone to obey orders of the form "Add n" with examples taken from fairly small numbers, then give him the order "Add one" and find that he adds two for numbers from 100 to 199, three for numbers from 200 to 299, and so forth. Wittgenstein says that there need have been nothing either in what you said to him during the training or in what "went on in your mind" then which of itself showed that this was not what you intended. This is certainly true, and shows something important about the concept of intention (it is a very striking case of what Wittgenstein means when he says in the *Investigations* that if God had looked into my mind, he would not have been able to see there whom I meant). But suppose the training was not given only by example, but made use also of an explicit formulation of the rule for forming from an Arabic numeral its successor. A machine can follow this rule; whence does a human being gain a freedom of choice in this matter which the machine does not possess?

It would of course be possible to argue that someone might appear to understand a rule of inference in a formal system—a substitution rule, say— and yet later reject a correct application of it; but it remains that we can see *in* the precise wording of the rule that that application was warranted. It might be replied that this is to take for granted the ordinary understanding of the words or symbols in terms of which the rule is framed; an explanation of these words or symbols would be something like Wittgenstein's idea of a rule for interpreting the rule. It is undoubtedly true and important that, while in using a word or symbol we are in some sense following a rule, this rule cannot in its turn be formulated in such a way as to leave no latitude in its interpretation, or if it can, the rules for using the words in terms of which this rule is formulated cannot in their turn be so formulated. But such considerations seem to belong to the theory of meaning in general, rather than having any particular relevance to the philosophy of mathematics. Rather, it seems that to someone who suggests that Wittgenstein's point about the scope left in deciding on the correctness of an application of a rule of inference

[5] IV, 48.

is to be countered by concentrating on rules of inference in formal systems we ought to reply by referring to what Wittgenstein calls the "motley" of mathematics.[6] He wishes, like the intuitionists, to insist that we cannot draw a line in advance round the possible forms of argument that may be used in mathematical proofs. Furthermore, it might be pointed out that a formal system does not *replace* the intuitive proofs as, frequently, a precise concept replaces a vague intuitive one; the formal system remains, as it were, answerable to the intuitive conception, and remains of interest only so long as it does not reveal undesirable features which the intuitive idea does not possess. An example would be Gödel's theorem, which shows that provability in a formal system cannot do duty as a substitute for the intuitive idea of arithmetical truth.

Suppose we are considering a statement of some mathematical theory. To avoid complications, assume that the theory is complete, that is, that it can be completely formalized, but that we are not thinking of any particular formal system. Then a Platonist will say that there exists either a proof or a disproof of the statement; the fact that the statement is true, if it is true, consists in the existence of such a proof even though we have not yet discovered it. Now if there exists a proof, let us suppose that there is somewhere an actual document, as yet unseen by human eyes, on which is written what purports to be a proof of the statement. Then Wittgenstein will reply that all the same there does not yet exist a proof, since when we discover the document it is still up to us to decide whether or not we wish to count it as a proof. It is evident that, if this is correct, then all motive for saying with the Platonist that there either *is* or *is not* a proof, that the statement must be either true or false, and so forth, has gone. What is not clear to me is that rejecting the Platonist's conception involves adopting this line about proofs; it seems to me that a man might hold that, once the proof was discovered, we had no choice but to follow it, without allowing the correctness of saying, before the proof was discovered, that either there is a proof or there is not. I will return to this later.

Wittgenstein's conception is extremely hard to swallow, even though it is not clear what one wishes to oppose to it. The proof is supposed to have the effect of persuading us, inducing us, to count such-and-such a form of words as unassailably true, or to exclude such-and-such a form of words from our language. It seems quite unclear how the proof accomplishes this remarkable feat. Another difficulty is the scarcity of examples. We naturally think that, face to face with a proof, we have no alternative but to accept the proof if we are to remain faithful to the understanding we already had of the expressions contained in it. For Wittgenstein, accepting the theorem is adopting a new rule of language, and hence our concepts cannot remain unchanged at the end of the proof. But we could have rejected the proof without doing any more violence to our concepts than is done by accepting it; in rejecting it we

6 II, 46, 48.

could have remained equally faithful to the concepts with which we started out. It seems extraordinarily difficult to take this idea seriously when we think of some particular actual proof. It may of course be said that this is because we have already accepted the proof and thereby subjected our concepts to the modification which acceptance of the proof involved; but the difficulty of believing Wittgenstein's account of the matter while reading the proof of some theorem with which one was not previously familiar is just as great. We want to say that we do not know what it would be like for someone who, by ordinary criteria, already understood the concepts employed, to reject this proof. Of course we are familiar with someone's simply not following a proof, but we are also familiar with the remedy, namely to interpolate simpler steps between each line of the proof. The examples given in Wittgenstein's book are—amazingly for him—thin and unconvincing. I think that this is a fairly sure sign that there is something wrong with Wittgenstein's account.

Consider the case of an elementary computation, for example "5 + 7 = 12." There might be people who counted as we do but did not have the concept of addition. If such a person had found out by counting that there were five boys and seven girls in a classroom, and were then asked how many children were present, he would proceed to count all the children together to discover the answer. Thus he would be quite prepared to say that on one occasion there were five boys, seven girls, and twelve children altogether, but on another occasion five boys, seven girls, and thirteen children altogether. Now if we came across such a person, we should know what kind of arguments to bring to show him that in such circumstances he must have miscounted on one occasion, and that whenever there are five boys and seven girls there are twelve children. If he accepts these arguments it will be quite true that he will have adopted a new criterion for saying that there are twelve children present, and again a new criterion for saying, "I must have miscounted." Before, he would say, "I miscounted," only when he noticed that he had, for example, counted one of the children twice over; now he will say, "I miscounted," when he has not observed anything of this kind, simply on the ground that he got the result that there were five boys, seven girls, and thirteen children. But we wish to say that even before we met this person and taught him the principles of addition, it would have been true that if he had counted five boys, seven girls, and thirteen children, he would have been wrong even according to the criteria he himself then acknowledged. That is, he must have made a mistake in counting; and if he made a mistake, then there must have been something that he did which, if he had noticed it, he himself would then have allowed as showing that he had miscounted.

If we say that if he counted five boys, seven girls, and thirteen children, then there must have been something which, if he had noticed it, he would have regarded as a criterion for having miscounted, then the effect of introducing him to the concept of addition is not to be simply described as persuading him to adopt a new criterion for having miscounted; rather, he has been induced to recognize getting additively discordant results as a *symptom* of the presence of something he already accepted as a criterion for having miscounted. That is, learning about addition leads him to say, "I miscounted," in circumstances where he would not before have said it; but if, before he had learned, he had said, "I miscounted," in those circumstances, he would have been right by the criteria he then possessed. Hence the necessity for his having miscounted when he gets additively discordant results does not, as it were, get its whole being from his now recognizing such results as a criterion for having miscounted.

If on the other hand we say that it is possible to count five boys, seven girls, and thirteen children without there being anything other than the fact of getting these results such that, if we had noticed it, we should have regarded it as a ground for saying that we had miscounted, then it appears to follow that one can make a mistake in counting (according to the criteria *we* recognize for having miscounted) without having made any particular mistake; that is, one cannot say that if one has miscounted, then either one counted this boy twice, or one counted that girl twice, or . . . . But this is absurd: one cannot make some mistake without there having been some particular mistake which one has made. It might be replied that we can choose to say that if one has miscounted, then either . . ., and that that is in fact what we do choose to say. But if a disjunction is true, then at least one of its limbs must be true; and if a statement is true, there must be something such that if we knew of it, we would regard it as a criterion for the truth of the statement. Yet the assumption from which we started is that someone counts five boys, seven girls, and thirteen children (and hence says that he must have miscounted) and that there is nevertheless nothing apart from his having got these results which (if he knew of it) he would regard as showing that he had miscounted; and hence there can be nothing which (if he knew of it) would show the truth of any one of the disjuncts of the form "He counted that boy twice," and so forth. One might put it by saying that if a disjunction is true, God must know which of the disjuncts is true; hence it cannot be right to count something as a criterion for the truth of the disjunction whose presence does not guarantee the existence of something which would show the truth of some one particular disjunct. For example, it would be wrong to regard ⌜Either if it had been the case that P, it would have been the case that Q, or if it had been the case that P, it would have been the case that not Q⌝ as a logical law, since it is perfectly possible to suppose that however much we knew about the kind of fact which we should regard as bearing on the truth of the disjunct counterfactuals, we should still know nothing which we should count as a reason for accepting either the one or the other.

It is certainly part of the meaning of the word "true" that if a statement is true, there must be something in virtue of which it is true. "There is something in virtue of which it is true" means: there is something such that if we knew of it we should regard it as a criterion (or at least as a ground) for asserting the statement. The essence of realism is this: for any statement which has a definite sense, there must be something in virtue of which either it or its negation is true. (Realism about the realm of mathematics is what we call Platonism.) Intuitionists do not at all deny the first thesis; for them one is justified in asserting a disjunction only when one has a method for arriving at something which would justify the assertion of some one particular limb of the disjunction. Rather, they deny the second thesis: there is no reason for supposing in general that, just because a statement has a quite definite use, there must be something in virtue of which either it is true or it is false. One must beware of saying that logical truths are an exception, that there is nothing in virtue of which they are true; on the contrary, for the realist we are justified in asserting ⌜P or not P⌝ because there must be something in virtue of which either P or ⌜Not P⌝ is true, and hence in any case there must be something in virtue of which ⌜P or not P⌝ is true.

Now there seems here to be one of the big differences between Wittgenstein and the intuitionists. He appears to hold that it is up to us to decide to regard any statement we happen to pick on as holding necessarily, if we choose to do so.[7] The idea behind this appears to be that, by laying down that something is to be regarded as holding necessarily, we thereby in part determine the sense of the words it contains; since we have the right to attach what sense we choose to the words we employ, we have the right to lay down as necessary any statement we choose to regard as such. Against this one would like to say that the senses of the words in the statement may have already been fully determined, so that there is no room for any further determination. Thus, if one takes a classical (realist) view, the general form of explanation of the sense of a statement consists in the stipulation of its truth-conditions (this is the view taken by Wittgenstein in the *Tractatus* and also the view of Frege). Thus the sense of the sentential operators is to be explained by means of truth-tables; it is by reference to the truth-tables that one justifies taking certain forms as logically true.

Since the intuitionist rejects the conception according to which there must be for every statement something in virtue of which either it is true or it is false (and does not regard it as possible to remedy the situation by the introduction of further truth-values), for him the fundamental form of an explanation of a statement's meaning consists in stating the criteria we recognize as justifying the assertion of the statement (in mathematics, this is in general the possession of a proof). We thus specify the sense of the sentential operators, of "or," for example, for explaining the criteria for asserting the complex statement in terms of the criteria for asserting the constituents; hence, roughly speaking, we are justified in asserting ⌜P or Q⌝ only when we are justified either in asserting P or in asserting Q. A logical law holds in

---

[7] Cf. V, 23, last par. on p. 179.

virtue of these explanations; by reference to them we see that we shall *always* be justified in asserting a statement of this form.

Wittgenstein's quite different idea, that one has the right simply to *lay down* that the assertion of a statement of a given form is to be regarded as always justified, without regard to the use that has already been given to the words contained in the statement, seems to me mistaken. If Wittgenstein were right, it appears to me that communication would be in constant danger of simply breaking down. The decision to count a particular form of statement as logically true does not affect only the sense of statements of that form; the senses of all sorts of other statements will be infected, and in a way that we shall be unable to give a direct account of, without reference to our taking the form of statement in question as logically true. Thus it will become impossible to give an account of the sense of any statement without giving an account of the sense of every statement, and since it is of the essence of language that we understand *new* statements, this means that it will be impossible to give an account of the use of our language at all. To give an example: suppose someone were to choose to regard as a logical law the counterfactual disjunction I mentioned above. We try to object to his claim that this is logically valid by observing that either he must admit that a disjunction may be true when neither limb is true, or that a counterfactual may be true when there is nothing in virtue of which it is true, that is, nothing such that if we knew of it we should regard it as a ground for asserting the counterfactual. But he may respond by denying that these consequences follow; rather, he adduces it as a consequence of the validity of the law that there must be something such that if we knew of it we should count it as a ground either for asserting ⌜If it had been the case that P, then it would have been the case that Q⌝ or for asserting ⌜If it had been the case that P, then it would have been the case that not Q.⌝ For example, he will say that there must be something in which either the bravery or the cowardice of a man consisted, even if that man had never encountered danger and hence had never had an opportunity to display either courage or cowardice. If we hold that he is entitled to regard anything as a logical law which he chooses so to regard, then we cannot deny him the right to draw this conclusion. The conclusion follows from the disjunction of counterfactuals which he elected to regard as logically true in the first place, together with statements we should all regard as logically true; and in any case, he must have the right to regard the conclusion itself as logically true if he so chooses. He will thus conclude that either a man must reveal in his behavior how he would behave in all possible circumstances, or else that there is inside him a sort of spiritual mechanism determining how he behaves in each situation.

Now we know from the rest of Wittgenstein's philosophy how repugnant such a conclusion would be to him; but what right would he have, on his own account of the matter, to object to this man's reaching this conclusion? It is all very well to say, "Say what you like once you know what the facts are"; but how are we to be sure that we can tell anyone what the facts are if it may be that the form of words we use to tell him the facts has for him a different sense as a result of his having adopted some logical law which we do not accept? It might be said that once we discover this difference in the understanding of a certain form of words, we must select another form of words which he does understand as we do and which expresses what we wanted to say; but how are we to know that there is a form of words which does the trick? If we ask him how he understands a certain statement, and he gives the same explanation of it that we should give, this is no guarantee that he in fact understands it as we do; for the mere fact that he recognizes certain forms as logically true which we do not recognize means that he may be able to construct arguments leading to the given statement as a conclusion and with premises that we accept, although we should not accept the argument; that is, he will regard himself as entitled to assert the statement in circumstances in which we should not regard ourselves as entitled to assert it. (An analogy, *not* strictly parallel, is this: we might imagine a classicist and an intuitionist giving explanations of the meaning of the existential quantifier which sounded exactly the same. Yet for all that the classicist will make existential assertions in cases in which the intuitionist will not, since he has been able to arrive at them by means of arguments which the intuitionist will not accept.) Now in the case we are imagining, it is essential to suppose that our man is not capable of giving any general kind of explanation of the words he uses such that we can, from this explanation, derive directly the meaning he attaches to any sentence composed of these words. For if he could give such an explanation, we could see from the explanation why the logical law which he accepts but we do not *is* necessary if the words in it are understood as he understands them. We should thus have a justification for taking statements of that form to be logical laws parallel to the justification of the laws of classical logic in terms of an explanation of meaning by reference to truth-conditions and the justification of intuitionist logic in terms of the explanation by reference to assertibility-conditions. But the whole point of the example was that this was a case of simply laying down a certain form of statement as logically true without the requirement of a justification of this kind.

This attitude of Wittgenstein's to logical necessity may in part explain his ambivalence about the law of excluded middle in mathematics. If a philosopher insists on the law of excluded middle, this is probably the expression of a realist (Platonist) conception of mathematics which Wittgenstein rejects: he insists that ⌜P or not P⌝ is true because he thinks that the general form of explanation of meaning is in terms of truth-conditions, and that for any mathematical statement possessing a definite sense there must be something in virtue of which either it is true or it is false. On the other hand, if a mathematician wishes to use a form of argument depending upon the law of excluded middle (for example, ⌜If P, then Q⌝; ⌜If not P, then Q⌝; therefore,

Q), Wittgenstein will not object, since the mathematician has the right to regard the form of words ⌜P or not P⌝ as holding necessarily if he chooses to do so.

To return to the example of the people who counted but did not have addition, it seems likely that someone who accepted Wittgenstein's viewpoint would wish to reject the alternative: either when one of these people counted five boys, seven girls, and thirteen children there must have been something which, if he had noticed it, would have been for him evidence of his having miscounted, or else he could have done so when there was nothing which would have shown him he had miscounted. He would reject it on the ground that it is unclear whether the alternative is being posed in *our* language or in the language of the people in question. *We* say that he must have miscounted, and hence that he must either have counted this boy twice, or . . ., and hence that there was something which if he had noticed it would have shown him that he had miscounted, and we say this just on the ground that his figures do not add up. But he would have no reason for saying it, and would assert that he had probably counted correctly. Now we must not ask whether what we say or what he says is *true*, as if we could stand outside both languages; we just *say* this, that is, we count his having got discordant results as a criterion for saying it, and he does not. Against this I wish, for the reasons I have stated, to set the conventional view that in deciding to regard a form of words as necessary, or to count such-and-such as a criterion for making a statement of a certain kind, we have a responsibility to the sense we have already given to the words of which the statement is composed.

It is easy to see from this why Wittgenstein is so obsessed in this book with an empiricist philosophy of mathematics. He does not wish to accept the empiricist account, but it has a strong allure for him; again and again he comes back to the question, "What is the difference between a calculation and an experiment?". The fact is that even if we decide to *say* that we must have made a mistake in counting when we count five boys, seven girls, and thirteen children, our mere decision to treat this result as a criterion for having made a mistake cannot of itself make it probable that in such circumstances we shall be able to find a mistake; that is, if Wittgenstein's account of the matter is correct. Nevertheless, getting such a discrepancy in counting is a very sure sign in practice that we shall be able to find a mistake, or that if we count again we shall get results that agree. It is because it is such a sure sign in practice that it is possible—or useful—for us to put "5 + 7 = 12" in the archives. Thus for Wittgenstein an empirical regularity lies behind a mathematical law.[8] The mathematical law does not *assert* that the regularity obtains, because we do not treat it as we treat an assertion of empirical fact, but as a necessary statement; all the same, what leads us to treat it in this way is the empirical regularity, since it is only because the regularity obtains that the law has a useful application.[9] What the relation is between the regularity

[8] III, 44.
[9] E.g., II, 73, 75.

and the proof which induces us to put the law in the archives Wittgenstein does not succeed in explaining.

To avoid misunderstanding, I must emphasize that I am not proposing an alternative account of the necessity of mathematical theorems, and I do not know what account should be given. I have merely attempted to give reasons for the natural resistance one feels to Wittgenstein's account, reasons for thinking that it must be wrong. But I believe that whether one accepts Wittgenstein's account or rejects it, one could not after reflecting on it remain content with the standard view which I have called modified conventionalism.

Wittgenstein's constructivism is of a much more extreme kind than that of the intuitionists. For an intuitionist, we may say that every natural number is either prime or composite because we have a method for deciding, for each natural number, whether it is prime or not. Wittgenstein would deny that we have such a method. Normally one would say that the sieve of Eratosthenes was such a method; but with a large number one would not—*could* not—use the sieve, but would resort to some more powerful criterion. It will be said that this is a mere practical, not a theoretical, matter, due to the comparative shortness of our lives. But if some fanatic devoted his life to computing, by means of the sieve, the primality of some very large number proved to be prime by more powerful means, and arrived at the conclusion that it was composite, we should not abandon our proof but say that there must be some error in his computations. This shows that we are taking the "advanced" test, and not the sieve, as the *criterion* for primality here: we use the theorem as the standard whereby we judge the computation, and not conversely. The computation is of no use to us because it is not *surveyable*. A mathematical proof, of which computations are a special case, is a proof in virtue of our using it to serve a certain purpose; namely, we put the conclusion or result in the archives, that is, treat it as unassailable and use it as a standard whereby to judge other results. Now something cannot serve this purpose, and hence is not a mathematical proof, unless we are able to exclude the possibility of a mistake's having occurred in it. We must be able to "take in" a proof, and this means that we must be certain of being able to reproduce the *same* proof. We cannot in general *guarantee* that we shall be able to repeat an experiment and get the same result as before. Admittedly, if we get a different result, we shall look for a relevant difference in the conditions of the experiment; but we did not have in advance a clear conception of just what was to count as a relevant difference. (It is not quite clear whether in saying that we must be able to reproduce a proof Wittgenstein means that one must be able to copy from the written proof before one and be certain that one has copied without error, or that one must be able to read the proof and understand it so that one could write it down without referring to the original written proof, so that the possibility of a misprint becomes more or less irrelevant. It does not seem to affect the argument which interpretation is adopted.)

Thus the computation, for a very large number proved prime by other means, of its primality by means of Eratosthenes' sieve would not be a mathematical proof but an experiment to see whether one could do such enormous computations correctly; for the computation would be unsurveyable in the sense explained. Now what the word "prime" means as applied to large numbers is shown by what we accept as the *criterion* for primality, what we take as the standard whereby to assess claims that a number is prime or is composite. The sense of the word "prime" is not therefore given once for all by the sieve of Eratosthenes. Hence we should have no right to assert that every number is either prime or composite, since for any criterion we may adopt there will be a number so large that the application of the criterion to it will not be surveyable. This throws light on Wittgenstein's insistence that the sense of a mathematical statement is determined by its proof (or disproof),[10] that finding a proof alters the concept. One is inclined to think that such a statement as "There is an odd perfect number" is fixed quite definitely in advance, and that our finding a proof or a disproof cannot alter that already determinate sense. We think this on the ground that we are in possession of a method for determining, for *any* number, whether or not it is odd and whether or not it is perfect. But suppose that the statement were to be proved, say by exhibiting a particular odd perfect number. This number would have to be very large, and it is unthinkable that it should be proved to be perfect by the simple method of computing its factors by means of the sieve and adding them all up. The proof would probably proceed by giving a new method for determining perfection, and this method would then have been adopted as our *criterion* for saying of numbers within this range whether or not they are perfect. Thus the proof determines, for numbers of this size, what the *sense* of the predicate "perfect" is to be.

This constructivism, more severe than any version yet proposed, has been called "strict finitism" by Mr. G. Kreisel and "anthropologism" by Dr. Hao Wang. It was adumbrated by Professor Paul Bernays in his *Sur le platonisme dans les mathématiques*.[11] As presented by Bernays, it would consist in concentrating on practical rather than on theoretical possibility. I have tried to explain how for Wittgenstein this is not the correct way in which to draw the contrast.

It is a matter of some difficulty to consider just what our mathematics would look like if we adopted this "anthropologistic" standpoint. Would the Peano axioms survive unaltered? "Every number has a successor" would mean, in this mathematics, that if a number is accessible (that is, if we have a notation in which it can be surveyably represented) then its successor is accessible, and this at first seems reasonable. On the other hand, it seems to lead to the conclusion that *every* number is accessible, and it is clear that, whatever

---

[10] But cf., e.g., V, 7.

[11] *L'enseignement mathématique*, XXXIV (1935), 52–69. [Reprinted in this collection, pp. 273–85.—Eds.]

notation we have, there will be numbers for which there will not be a survey-able symbol in that notation. The problem seems similar to the Greek problem of the heap: if I have something that is not a heap of sand, I cannot turn it into a heap by adding one grain of sand to it. One might solve the present difficulty by arguing as follows. Let us say that we "get to" a number if we actually write down a surveyable symbol for it. Then we may say: if I get to a number, I can get to its successor. From this it follows that if I *can* get to a number, then it is possible that I can get to its successor; that is, if a number is accessible, then its successor is possibly accessible. Unless we think that "possibly possibly p" implies "possibly p" it does not follow that if a number is accessible, its successor is accessible. We should thus have to adopt a modal logic like S2 or M which does not contain the law (in Polish notation) "CMMpMp." Another consideration pointing in the same direction is the following. "Surveyable," "accessible," and so forth, are *vague* concepts. It is often profitable to substitute for a vague concept a precise one, but that would be quite out of place here; we do not want to fix on some definite number as the last accessible number, all bigger numbers being definitely inaccessible. Now the vagueness of a vague predicate is ineradicable. Thus "hill" is a vague predicate, in that there is no definite line between hills and mountains. But we could not eliminate this vagueness by introducing a new predicate, say "eminence," to apply to those things which are neither definitely hills nor definitely mountains, since there would still remain things which were neither definitely hills nor definitely eminences, and so *ad infinitum*. Hence if we are looking for a logical theory suitable for sentences containing vague predicates, it would be natural to select a modal logic like S2 or M with infinitely many modalities (interpreting the necessity-operator as meaning "definitely"). Thus a suggestion for a propositional calculus appropriate to an anthropologistic mathematics would be one bearing to the modal system M the same relation as intuitionistic propositional calculus bears to S4. (This system would probably have to have axioms of a similar form to those origi-nally given by Heyting, namely, they would frequently be implications whose antecedent was a conjunction, and would have a rule of adjunction as primi-tive; for, as has been pointed out to me by Mr. E. J. Lemmon, under Tarski's or Gödel's translation an implication whose consequent contains implication reiterated more often than does the antecedent does not usually go over into a valid formula of M, precisely because we do not have in M "CLpLLp.") Another suggestion, made by Dr. Wang, is that anthropologistic logic would coincide with intuitionist, but that the number theory would be weaker.

Wittgenstein uses these ideas to cast doubt upon the significance attached by some philosophers to the reductionist programs of Frege and Russell. We may think that the real meaning of and justification for such an equation as "5 + 7 = 12" has been attained if we interpret it as a statement in set theory or in a higher-order predicate calculus; but the fact is that not only the proof but the statement of the proposition in the primitive notation of these theories would be so enormously long as to be quite unsurveyable. It might be replied that we can shorten both the proof and the statement by using defined symbols; but then the definitions play an essential rôle, whereas for Russell definitions are *mere* abbreviations, so that the real formal statement and formal proof are those in primitive notation. For Wittgenstein notation is not a mere outward covering for a thought which is in itself indifferent to the notation adopted. The proof in primitive notation is not what "really" justifies us in asserting "5 + 7 = 12" since we never do write down this proof; if someone were to write it down and obtain the result "5 + 7 = 11," we should—appealing to schoolroom addition as a standard—say that he must have made a mistake; we do not even write down the proof with defined symbols; what, if anything, could be called the justification of "5 + 7 = 12" would be the proof that we actually do carry out that every addition sum "could" be formulated and proved within our formal logical system, and this proof uses methods far more powerful than the rules for ordinary schoolroom addition.

I now revert to the opposing *pictures* used by Platonists and constructivists —the picture of our making discoveries within an already existing mathematical reality and the picture of our constructing mathematics as we go along. Sometimes people—including intuitionists—argue as though it were a matter of first deciding which of these pictures is correct and then drawing conclusions from this decision. But it is clear that these are only pictures, that is, that the dispute as to which is correct must find its substance elsewhere—that such a dispute ought to be capable of being expressed without reference to these pictures. On the other hand, such pictures have an enormous influence over us, and the desire to be able to form an appropriate picture is almost irresistible. If one does not believe in the objectivity of mathematical truth, one cannot accept the Platonist picture. Wittgenstein's main reason for denying the objectivity of mathematical truth is his denial of the objectivity of *proof* in mathematics, his idea that a proof does not *compel* acceptance; and what fits this conception is obviously the picture of our constructing mathematics as we go along. Now suppose that someone disagrees with Wittgenstein over this and holds that a good proof is precisely one which imposes itself upon us, not only in the sense that once we have accepted the proof we use rejection of it as a criterion for not having understood the terms in which it is expressed, but in the sense that it can be put in such a form that no one could reject it without saying something which would have been recognized before the proof was given as going back on what he had previously agreed to. Is such a person bound to adopt the Platonist picture of mathematics? Clearly not; he can accept the objectivity of mathematical proof without having to believe also in the objectivity of mathematical truth. The intuitionists, for example, usually speak as though they believed in the former without believing in the latter. It is true that A. Heyting, for instance, writes, "As the meaning of a word can never be fixed precisely enough to exclude every possibility of misunderstanding, we can never be mathematically sure that [a] formal system expresses correctly our mathematical thoughts.''[12] But intuitionists incline to write as though, while we cannot delimit in advance the realm of all possible intuitionistically valid proofs, still we can be certain for particular proofs given, and particular principles of proof enunciated, that they are intuitionistically correct. That is to say, the point involved here concerns what Wittgenstein calls the motley of mathematics; the question whether a certain statement is provable cannot be given a mathematically definite formulation since we cannot foresee in advance all possible forms of argument that might be used in mathematics. Still, I suppose that someone might deny even this, in the sense that he claimed for some particular logical framework that every theorem that could be proved intuitionistically could be proved within this framework (though perhaps the proof given might not be reproducible within the framework), and yet remain essentially an intuitionist. For the strongest arguments for intuitionism seem to be quite independent of the question of the objectivity of mathematical proof—whether the proof once given compels acceptance, and whether the concept of valid proof can be made precise. The strongest arguments come from the insistence that the general form of explanation of meaning, and hence of the logical operators in particular, is a statement not of the truth-conditions but of the assertibility-conditions. We learn the meaning of the logical operators by being *trained* in their use, and this means being trained to assert complex statements in certain kinds of situation. We cannot, as it were, extract from this training more than was put into it, and unless we are concerned with a class of decidable statements the notions of truth and falsity cannot be used to give a description of the training we receive. Hence a general account of meaning which makes essential use of the notions of truth and falsity (or of any other number of truth-values) is not of the right form for an explanation of meaning.

It is clear that considerations of this kind have nothing to do with mathematics in particular, but are of quite general application. They also have a close connection with Wittgenstein's doctrine that the meaning is the use; and I believe that the *Investigations* contains implicitly a rejection of the classical (realist) Frege-*Tractatus* view that the general form of explanation of meaning is a statement of the truth-conditions.[13] This provides a motive for the rejection by Wittgenstein and the intuitionists of the Platonist picture quite independent of any considerations about the non-objective character of mathematical proof and the motley of mathematics. On the other hand, it is not clear that someone such as I have described, who accepted the considerations about meaning but rejected the considerations about proof, would be happy with the usual constructivist picture of our making up our

[12] *Intuitionism, an Introduction* (Amsterdam, 1956), p. 4.
[13] Cf. also *Remarks*, I, App. I, 6.

mathematics. After all, the considerations about meaning do not apply only to mathematics but to all discourse; and while they certainly show something mistaken in the realist conception of thought and reality, they surely do not imply outside mathematics the extreme of subjective idealism—that we *create* the world. But it seems that we ought to interpose between the Platonist and the constructivist picture an intermediate picture, say of objects springing into being in response to our probing. We do not *make* the objects but must accept them as we find them (this corresponds to the proof imposing itself on us); but they were not already there for our statements to be true or false of before we carried out the investigations which brought them into being. (This is of course intended only as a picture; but its point is to break what seems to me the false dichotomy between the Platonist and the constructivist pictures which surreptitiously dominates our thinking about the philosophy of mathematics.)

COMMENTS ON LUDWIG WITTGENSTEIN'S *REMARKS ON THE FOUNDATIONS OF MATHEMATICS*[1]

Paul Bernays

I

The book with which the following observations are concerned is the second part of the posthumous publications of selected fragments from Wittgenstein in which he sets forth his later philosophy.[2] The necessity of making a selection and the fragmentary character which is noticeable in places are not unduly disconcerting since Wittgenstein in his publications in any case refrains from a systematic treatment and expresses his thoughts paragraph-wise—springing frequently from one theme to another. On the other hand we must admit in fairness to the author that he would doubtless have made extensive changes in the arrangement and selection of the material had he been able to complete the work himself. Besides, the editors of the book have greatly facilitated a survey of the contents by providing a very detailed table of contents and an index. The preface gives information on the origin of the different parts I–V.

Compared with the standpoint of the *Tractatus*, which indeed considerably influenced the originally very extreme doctrine of the Vienna Circle, Wittgenstein's later philosophy represents a rectification and clarification in essential respects. In particular it is the very schematic conception of the

---

[1] *Remarks on the Foundation of Mathematics*, by Ludwig Wittgenstein. Edited by G. H. von Wright, R. Rhees, G. E. M. Anscombe. Translated by G. E. M. Anscombe. Basil Blackwell, Oxford, 1956. 37s. 6d.

[2] The book was originally published in German, with the English translation attached. All pages and numbers quoted refer to the German text.

Reprinted with the kind permission of the author and the editor from Ratio, *II, no. I* (1959), 1–22. *Translated from the German.*

structure of the language of science—especially the view on the composition
of statements out of atomic propositions—which is here dropped. What
remains is the negative attitude towards speculative thinking and the
permanent tendency to disillusionize.

Thus Wittgenstein says himself, evidently with his own philosophy in
mind (p. 63, No. 18): 'Finitism and behaviorism are quite similar trends.
Both say: all we have here is merely . . . Both deny the existence of something,
both with a view to escaping from a confusion. What I am doing is, not to
show that calculations are wrong, but to subject the *interest* of calculations to
a test.' And further on he explains (p. 174, No. 16): 'My task is not to attack
Russell's logic from *within*, but from without. That is to say, not to attack it
mathematically—otherwise I should be doing mathematics—but to attack its
position, its office. My task is not to talk about Gödel's proof, for example,
but to by-pass it.'

As we see, jocularity of expression is not lacking with Wittgenstein;
and in the numerous parts written in dialogue form he often enjoys acting
the rogue.

On the other hand he does not lack *esprit de finesse*, and his formulations
contain, in addition to what is explicitly stated, many implicit suggestions.

Two problematic tendencies, however, appear throughout. The one is to
dispute away the proper rôle of thinking—reflective intending—in a behavioristic manner. David Pole, it is true, in his interesting account and exposition of Wittgenstein's later philosophy,[3] denies that Wittgenstein is a
supporter of behaviorism. This contention is justified inasmuch as Wittgenstein certainly does not deny the existence of the mental experiences of
feeling, perceiving and imagining; but with regard to thinking his attitude is
distinctly behavioristic. Here he tends everywhere towards a short circuit.
Images and perceptions are supposed in every case to be followed immediately
by behavior. 'We do it like this', that is usually the last word of understanding—or else he relies upon a need as an anthropological fact. Thought,
as such, is left out. It is characteristic in this connection that a 'proof' is
conceived as a 'picture' or 'paradigm'; and although Wittgenstein is critical
of the method of formalizing proofs, he continually takes the formal method
of proof in the Russellian system as an example. Instances of proper mathematical proofs, which are not mere calculations, which neither result merely
from showing a figure nor proceed formalistically, do not occur at all in this
book on the foundations of mathematics, a major part of which treats of
the question as to what proofs really are—although the author has evidently
concerned himself with many mathematical proofs.

One passage may be mentioned as characterizing Wittgenstein's behavioristic attitude and as an illustration of what is meant here by a short
circuit. Having rejected as unsatisfactory various attempts to characterize

[3] David Pole, *The Later Philosophy of Wittgenstein*, University of London, The Athlone
Press, 1958.

inference, he continues (p. 8, No. 17): 'Thus it is necessary to see how we perform inferences in the practice of language; what kind of operation inferring is in the language-game. For example, a regulation says: "All who are taller than six foot are to join the ... section." A clerk reads out the names of the men, and their heights. Another allots them to such and such sections. "X six foot four." "So X to the ... section." That is inference.' Here it can be seen that Wittgenstein is satisfied only with a characterization of inferring in which one passes directly from a linguistic establishment of the premisses to an action, in which, therefore, the specifically reflective element is eliminated. Language, too, appears under the aspect of behavior ('language-game').

The other problematic tendency springs from the program—already present in Wittgenstein's earlier philosophy—of strict division between the linguistic and the factual, a division also present in Carnap's *Syntax of Language*. That this division should have been retained in the new form of Wittgenstein's doctrine does not go without saying, because here the approach, compared with the earlier one, is in many respects less rigid. Signs of a certain change can in fact be observed, as, for instance, on p. 119, No. 18: 'It is clear that mathematics as a technique of transforming signs for the purpose of prediction has nothing to do with grammar.' Elsewhere (p. 125, No. 42) he even speaks of the 'synthetic character of mathematical propositions'. It is said there: 'It might perhaps be said that the synthetic character of mathematical propositions appears most obviously in the unpredictable occurrence of the prime numbers. But their being synthetic (in this sense) does not make them any the less *a priori* ... The distribution of prime numbers would be an ideal example of what could be called synthetic *a priori*, for one can say that it is at any rate not discoverable by the analysis of the concept of a prime number.' As can be seen, Wittgenstein returns here from the concept 'analytic' of the Vienna Circle to a concept-formation which is more in the Kantian sense.

A certain approach to the Kantian conception is embodied also in Wittgenstein's view that it is mathematics which first forms the character, 'creates the forms of what we call facts' (see p. 173, No. 15). In this sense Wittgenstein also strongly opposes the opinion that the propositions of mathematics have the function of empirical propositions. On the other hand he emphasizes on various occasions that the applicability of mathematics, in particular of arithmetic, rests on empirical conditions; on p. 14, No. 37, for example, he says: 'This is how our children learn sums, for we make them put down three beans and then another three beans and then count what is there. If the result were at one time five, at another time seven ..., then the first thing we should do would be to declare beans to be unsuitable for teaching sums. But if the same thing happened with sticks, fingers, strokes and most other things, then that would be the end of doing sums.—"But wouldn't it then still be that $2 + 2 = 4$?"—This sentence would then have become unusable.'

Statements like the following, however, remain important for Wittgenstein's conception (p. 160, No. 2): 'He who knows a mathematical proposition is supposed still to know *nothing*.' (The words in the German text are: 'soll noch nichts wissen'.) He repeats this twice at short intervals and adds: 'That is, the mathematical proposition is only to supply the scaffolding for a description.' In the manner of Wittgenstein we could here ask: 'Why is the person in question *supposed* to still know nothing?' What need is expressed by this 'supposed to'? It appears that only a preconceived philosophical view determines this requirement, the view, namely, that there can exist but one kind of factuality: that of concrete reality. This view conforms to a kind of nominalism as it figures also elsewhere in the discussions on the philosophy of mathematics. In order to justify such a nominalism Wittgenstein would have to go back further than he does in this book. At all events he cannot here appeal to our actual mental attitude. For indeed he attacks our tendency to regard arithmetic, for example, 'as the natural history of the domain of numbers' (see p. 117, No. 13 and p. 116, No. 11). However, he is not fully at one with himself on this point. He asks himself (p. 142, No. 16) whether 'mathematical alchemy' is characterized by the mere fact that mathematical propositions are regarded as statements about mathematical objects. 'In a certain sense it is not possible, therefore, to appeal to the meaning of signs in mathematics, because it is mathematics itself which first gives them their meaning. What is typical for the phenomenon about which I am speaking is that the *mysteriousness* about any mathematical concept is not *straight away* interpreted as a misconception, as a fallacy, but as something which is at all events not to be despised, which should perhaps even be respected. All that I can do is to show an easy escape from this obscurity and this glitter of concepts. It can be said, strangely enough, that there is so to speak a solid core in all these glistening concept-formations. And I should like to say that it is this which makes them into mathematical products.'

One may doubt whether Wittgenstein has succeeded here in showing 'an easy escape from this obscurity'; one may be more inclined to suspect that here the obscurity and the 'mysteriousness' actually have their origin in the philosophical concept-formation, i.e. in the philosophical language used by Wittgenstein.

The fundamental division between the sphere of mathematics and the sphere of facts appears in several passages in the book. In this connection Wittgenstein often speaks with a certitude which strangely contrasts with his readiness to doubt so much of what is generally accepted. The passage on p. 26, No. 80 is characteristic of this; he says here: 'But of course you cannot get to know any property of the material by imagining.' Again we read on p. 29, No. 98: 'I can calculate in the imagination, but not experiment.' From the point of view of common experience all this certainly does not go without saying. An engineer or technician has doubtless just as lively an image of materials as a mathematician has of geometrical curves, and the image which any one of us may have of a thick iron rod is no doubt such as to make it clear that the rod could not be bent by a light pressure of the hands. And in the case of technical inventing, a major rôle is certainly played by experimenting in the imagination. Wittgenstein apparently uses here without being aware of it a philosophical schema which distinguishes the *a priori* from the empirical. To what extent and in what sense this distinction, which is so important particularly in the Kantian philosophy, is justified will not be discussed here; but in any case its introduction, particularly at the present time, should not be taken too lightly. With regard to the *a priori*, Wittgenstein's viewpoint differs from the Kantian viewpoint particularly by the fact that it includes the principles of general mechanics in the sphere of the empirical. Thus he argues, for example (p. 114, No. 4): 'Why are the Newtonian laws not axioms of mathematics? Because we could quite well imagine things being otherwise ... To say of a proposition: "This could be imagined otherwise" ... ascribes the rôle of an empirical proposition to it.' The concept of 'being able to imagine otherwise', also used by Kant, has the inconvenience of ambiguity. The impossibility of imagining something may be understood in various senses. This difficulty occurs particularly in geometry. This will be discussed later.

The previously mentioned tendency of Wittgenstein to recognize only one kind of fact becomes evident not only with regard to mathematics, but also with respect to any phenomenology. Thus he discusses the proposition that white is lighter than black (p. 30, No. 105) and explains it by saying that black serves us as a paradigm of what is dark, and white as a paradigm of what is light, which makes the statement one without content. In his opinion statements about differences in brightness have content only when they refer to specific visible objects and, for the sake of clarity, differences in the brightness of colours should not be spoken about at all. This attitude obviously precludes a descriptive theory of colours.

Actually one would expect Wittgenstein to hold phenomenological views. This is suggested by the fact that he often likes to draw examples from the field of art for the purpose of comparison. It is only the philosophical program which prevents the development of an explicitly phenomenological viewpoint.

This case is an example of how Wittgenstein's method aims at eliminating a very great deal. He sees himself in the part of the free-thinker combating superstition. The latter's goal, however, is freedom of the mind; whereas it is this very mind which Wittgenstein in many ways restricts, through a mental asceticism for the benefit of an irrationality whose goal is quite undetermined.

This tendency, however, is by no means so extreme here in the later philosophy of Wittgenstein's as in the earlier form. One may already gather from the few passages quoted that Wittgenstein was probably on the way to giving mental contents more of their due.

A fact that may be connected with this is that, in contrast to the assertive form of philosophical statement throughout the *Tractatus*, a mainly aporetical attitude prevails in the present book. There lies here, it is true, a danger for philosophical pedagogics, especially as Wittgenstein's philosophy exerts a strong attraction on the younger minds. The old Greek observation that philosophical contemplation frequently begins in philosophical astonishment[4] today misleads many philosophers into holding the view that the cultivation of astonishment is in itself a philosophical achievement. One may certainly have one's doubts about the soundness of a method which requires young philosophers to be trained as it were in wondering. Wondering is heuristically fruitful only where it is the expression of an instinct of research. Naturally it cannot be demanded of any philosophy that it should make comprehensible all that is astonishing. Perhaps the various philosophical viewpoints may be characterized by what they accept as ultimate in that which is astonishing. In Wittgenstein's philosophy it is, as far as epistemological questions are concerned, sociological facts. A few quotations may serve to illustrate this (p. 13, No. 35): '. . . how does it come about that all men . . . accept these figures as proofs of these propositions? Indeed, there is here a great—and interesting —agreement.' (p. 20, No. 63): '. . . it is a peculiar procedure: I *go through* the proof and then accept its result.—I mean: this is simply how we *do* it. This is the custom among us, or a fact of our natural history.' (p. 23, No. 74): 'When one talks about *essence* one is merely noting a convention. But here one would like to retort: "There is no greater difference than between a proposition about the depth of the essence and one about a mere convention." What, however, if I reply: "To the *depth* of the essence there corresponds the *deep* need for the convention." ' (p. 122, No. 30): 'Do not look on the proof as a procedure that *compels* you, but as one that *guides* you . . . But how does it come about that it so guides *each one* of us in such a way that we are influenced by it conformably? Now how does it come about that we agree in *counting*? "That is just how we are trained", one may say, "and the agreement produced in this way is carried further by the proof." '

II

So much then for the general characterization of the present observations by Wittgenstein. Their contents, however, is by no means exhausted in the general philosophical aspects that are here raised: various specific questions concerning the foundations of philosophy are discussed in detail. We shall deal in what follows with the principal viewpoints occurring here.

Let us begin with a question which concerns the problem previously touched on, that of the distinction between the *a priori* and the empirical: the question of geometrical axioms. Wittgenstein does not deal specifically with geometrical axioms as such. Instead, he raises generally the question as

---

[4] θαυμάζειν.

to how far the axioms of a mathematical system of axioms should be self-evident. He takes as his example the parallel axiom. Let us quote a few sentences from his discussion of the subject (p. 113, No. 2): 'What do we say when such an axiom is presented to us, for example, the parallel axiom? Has experience shown us that this is how it is? ... Experience plays a part, but not the one we should *immediately expect*. For we have not, of course, made experiments and found that actually only *one* straight line through the given point fails to cut the other straight line. And yet the proposition is evident.—Suppose I now say: "It is quite indifferent why it should be evident. It is sufficient that we accept it. All that is important is how we use it" ... When the wording of the parallel axiom, for example, is given ..., the way of using this proposition, and hence its sense, is still quite undetermined. And when we say that it is evident to us, then we have by doing so already chosen, without realizing it, a certain way of using the proposition. The proposition is not a mathematical axiom if we do not employ it precisely *for this purpose*. The fact, that is, that here we do not make experiments, but accept the self-evidence, is enough to decide its use. For we are not so naïve as to let the self-evidence count instead of the experiment. It is not the fact that it appears to us self-evidently true, but the fact that we let the self-evidence count, which makes it into a mathematical proposition.'

In discussing these statements it must first be borne in mind that we have to distinguish two things: whether we recognize an axiom as geometrically valid, or whether we choose it as an axiom. The latter, of course, is not determined by the wording of the proposition. But here we are concerned with a rather technical question of deductive arrangement. However, what interests Wittgenstein here is surely the recognition of the proposition as geometrically valid. It is on this light that Wittgenstein's assertion ('that the recognition is not determined by the wording') must be considered, and it is in any case not immediately evident. He puts it so simply: 'We have not, of course, made experiments.' Admittedly, there has been no experimenting in connection with the formulation of the parallel axiom here considered, and this formulation does not lend itself to this purpose anyway. However, within the scope of the other geometrical axioms the parallel axiom is equivalent to one of the following statements of metrical geometry: 'In a triangle the sum of the angles is equal to two right angles. In a quadrilateral in which three angles are right angles the fourth angle is also a right angle. Six congruent equilateral triangles with a common vertex P (lying consecutively side by side) exactly fill up the neighborhood of point P.' Such propositions—in which, it will be noted, there is no mention of the infinite extension of a straight line— can certainly be tested by experiment. As is known, Gauss did in fact check experimentally the proposition about the sum of the angles of a triangle, making use, to be sure, of the assumption of the linear diffusion of light. This is, however, not the only possibility of such an experiment. Thus Hugo Dingler in particular has emphasized that for the concepts of the straight line, the plane and the right angle there exists a natural and, so to speak, compulsory kind of experimental realization. By means of such an experimental realization of geometrical concepts statements like in particular the second one above can be experimentally tested with great accuracy. Moreover in a less accurate way they are continually being implicitly checked by us in the normal practice of drawing figures. Our instinctive estimation of lengths and of the sizes of angles can also be considered as the result of manifold experiences, and propositions which are to serve as axioms of elementary geometry must at all events agree with that instinctive estimation.

It cannot be maintained, therefore, that our experience plays no part in the acceptance of propositions as geometrically valid. But Wittgenstein does not mean that either. This becomes clear from what follows immediately after the passage quoted (p. 114, Nos. 4 and 5): 'Does experience teach us that a straight line is possible between any two points? ... One could say: *Imagination* teaches us it. And this is where the truth lies; one has only to understand it aright. *Before* the proposition the concept is still pliable. But might not experience cause us to reject the axiom? Yes. And nevertheless it does not play the part of an empirical proposition ... Why are the Newtonian laws not axioms of mathematics? Because one could quite well imagine things being otherwise ... Something is an axiom, *not* because we recognize it as extremely probable, indeed as certain, but because we assign it a certain function, and one which conflicts with that of an empirical proposition ... The axiom, I would say, is another part of speech.' Further on (p. 124, No. 35) he says: 'What about, for example, the fundamental laws of mechanics? Whoever understands them must know on what experiences they are based. It is otherwise with the propositions of pure mathematics.'

In favour of these statements it must certainly be conceded that experience alone does not determine the theoretical recognition of a proposition. A more exact theoretical statement is always something which must be conceived beyond the facts of experience.

The view, however, that there exists in this respect such a fundamental difference between mathematical propositions and the principles of mechanics is scarcely justified. In particular the last quoted assertion that, in order to understand the basic laws of mechanics, the experience on which they are based must be known, can hardly be maintained. Of course, when mechanics is taught at the university, it is desirable that the empirical foundations should be made clear; this is, however, not for the purpose of the theoretical and practical manipulation of the laws, but for the epistemological consciousness and with an eye to the possibilities of eventually necessary modifications of the theory. Yet an engineer or productive technician in order to become skilled in mechanics and capable of handling its laws does not need to bother about how we came upon these laws. To these laws also applies what Wittgenstein so frequently emphasizes in reference to mathematical laws: that the facts of

experience which are important for the empirical motivation of these propositions by no means make up the contents of that which is asserted in the laws.
It is important for the manipulation of mechanical laws to become familiar
with the concept-formations and to obtain some sort of evidence for these
laws. This way of acquiring it is not only practically, but also theoretically
significant: the theory is fully assimilated only by the process of rational
shaping to which it is subsequently subjected. With regard to mechanics
most philosophers and many of us mathematicians have little to say here, not
having acquired mechanics in the said manner.—What distinguishes the case
of geometry from that of mechanics is the (philosophically somewhat accidental) circumstance that the acquisition of the world of concepts and of the
evidence is for the most part already completed in an (at least for us)
unconscious stage of mental development.

Ernst Mach's opposition to a rational foundation of mechanics has its
justification insofar as such a foundation endeavours to pass over the rôle
of experience in arriving at the principles of mechanics. We must keep in
mind that concept-formations and the principles of mechanics comprise
as it were an extract of experience. On the other hand it would be unjustified
to reject outright on the basis of this criticism the efforts towards a construction of mechanics that is as rational as possible.

What is specific about geometry is the phenomenological character of its
laws, and hence the important rôle of intuition. Wittgenstein points only in
passing to this aspect: '*Imagination* teaches us it. And this is where the truth
lies; one has only to understand it aright' (p. 8). The term 'imagination' is
very general, and what is said at the end of the second sentence is a qualification which shows that the author feels the theme of intuition to be a very
ticklish one. In fact it is very difficult to characterize satisfactorily the
epistemological rôle of intuition. The sharp separation of intuition and concept,
as it occurs in the Kantian philosophy, does not appear on closer examination
to be justified. In considering geometrical thinking in particular it is difficult
to distinguish clearly the share of intuition from that of conceptuality, since
we find here a formation of concepts guided so to speak by intuition, which in
the sharpness of its intentions goes beyond what is in a proper sense intuitively
evident, but which separated from intuition has not its proper content. It is
strange that Wittgenstein assigns intuition no definite epistemological rôle
although his thinking is dominated by the visual. A proof is for him always
a picture. At one time he gives a mere figure as an example of a geometrical
proof. It is also striking that he never talks about the intuitive evidence of
topological facts, such as for instance the fact that the surface of a sphere
divides the (remaining) space into an inner and an outer part in such a way
that the curve joining up an inside point with an outside one always passes
over one point on the surface of the sphere.

Questions relating to the foundations of geometry and its axioms still
belong primarily to the field of inquiry of general epistemology. What is today

called in the narrower sense mathematical foundational research is mainly directed towards the foundations of arithmetic. Here one tends to eliminate as far as possible what is specific about geometry by splitting it up into an arithmetical and a physical side. We shall leave the question open whether this procedure is justified; this question is not discussed by Wittgenstein. On the other hand he deals in great detail with the basic questions of arithmetic. Let us now take a closer look at his observations concerning this field of questions.

The viewpoint from which Wittgenstein regards arithmetic is not the usual one of the mathematician. Wittgenstein has concerned himself more with the theories on the foundations of arithmetic (in particular with the Russellian one) than with arithmetic itself. Particularly with regard to the theory of numbers, his examples seldom go beyond the numerical. An uninformed reader might well conclude that the theory of numbers consists almost entirely of numerical equations, which indeed are normally regarded not as propositions to be proved, but as simple statements. The treatment is more mathematical in the sections where he discusses questions of set theory, such as denumerability and non-denumerability, as well as the Dedekind cut theory.

Wittgenstein maintains everywhere a standpoint of strict finitism. In this respect he considers the various types of problem concerning infinity, such as exist for a finitist viewpoint, in particular the problem of the *tertium non datur* and that of impredicative definitions. The very forceful and vivid account he gives is well suited to conveying a clearer idea of the finitist's conception to those still unfamiliar with it. However, it contributes hardly anything essentially new to the argumentation; and those who consciously hold the view of classical mathematics will scarcely be convinced by it.

Let us discuss a few points in more detail. Wittgenstein deals with the question whether in the infinite expansion of π a certain sequence of numbers ϕ, such as, say, '777', ever occurs. Adopting Brouwer's viewpoint he draws attention to the possibility that to this question there may not as yet be a definite answer. In this connection he says (p. 138, No. 9): 'However strange it sounds, the further expansion of an irrational number is a further development of mathematics.' This formulation is obviously ambiguous. If it merely means that the determination of a not yet calculated decimal place of an irrational number is a contribution to the development of mathematics, then every mathematician will agree with this. But since the assertion is held to be a 'strange sounding' one, certainly something else is meant, perhaps that the course of the development of mathematics at a given time is undecided and that this undecidedness can influence also the progress of the expansion of an irrational number given by definition, so that the decision as to what figure is to be put at the ten-thousandth decimal place of π would depend on the course of the history of thought. Such a view, however, is not appropriate even according to the conception of Wittgenstein himself, for he says (p. 138, No. 9): 'The question ... changes its status when it becomes decidable.'

Now the digits in the decimal fraction expansion of π can be determined up to any chosen decimal place. Hence the view about the further development of mathematics does not contribute anything to the understanding of the situation in the case of the expansion of π. In this regard we can even say the following. Suppose we could maintain with certainty that the question of the occurrence of the sequence of numbers ϕ is undecidable, then this would imply that the figure ϕ never occurs in the expansion of π; for if it did occur, and if k were the decimal place which the last digit of ϕ has on the first occurrence in the decimal fraction expansion of π, then the question whether the figure ϕ occurs before the $(k + 1)$th place would be a decidable question and could be answered positively, and thus the initial question would be answerable. (This argument by the way does not require the principle of the *tertium non datur*.)

Further on Wittgenstein repeatedly reverts to the example of the decimal fraction expansion of π; in one place in particular (p. 185, No. 34) we find an assertion which is characteristic of his view: 'Suppose that people go on and on calculating the expansion of π. An omniscient God knows, therefore, whether by the end of the world they will have reached a figure "777". But can his *omniscience* decide whether they *would* have reached this figure after the end of the world? It cannot do so ... For him, too, the mere rule of expansion cannot decide anything that it does not decide for us.'

That is certainly not convincing. If we conceive the idea of a divine omniscience at all, then we would certainly ascribe to it the attribute of being able to survey at *one* glance a totality of which every single element is in principle accessible to us. We must pay here particular heed to the double rôle of the recursive definition of the decimal fraction expansion: on the one hand as the definitory fixing of the decimal fraction, and on the other as a means for the 'effective' calculation of decimal places. If we here take 'effective' in the usual sense, then even a divine intelligence can *effectively* calculate nothing other than what we are able to effectively calculate (no more than it would be capable of carrying out the trisection of an angle with a ruler and compass, or of deriving Gödel's underivable proposition in the related formal system); however, it is not inconceivable that this divine intelligence should be able to survey in another (not humanly effective) manner all the possible calculation results of the application of a recursive definition.

In his criticism of the theory of Dedekind's cut, Wittgenstein's main argument is that the extensional approach is mixed up in this theory with the intensional approach. This criticism is applicable in the case of certain versions of the theory where the tendency is to create the impression of a stronger character of the procedure than is actually achieved. If one wants to introduce the cuts not as mere sets of numbers, but as defining arithmetical laws of such sets, then either one must utilize a quite vague concept of the 'law', thus gaining little; or, if one sets about clarifying the concept, one meets with the difficulty which Hermann Weyl termed the vicious circle in the foundation of analysis and which for some time back was sensed instinctively by various mathematicians, who thereupon advocated a restriction of the procedure of analysis. This criticism of impredicative concept-formation even today plays a considerable rôle in the discussions on the foundations of mathematics. However, difficulties are not encountered if the extensional standpoint is consistently retained, and Dedekind's conception can certainly be understood in this sense and was probably so understood by Dedekind himself. All that is required here is that we should recognize, besides the concept of number itself, also the concept of a set of natural numbers (and in consequence of this the concept of a set of fractions, too) as an intuitively significant concept not requiring reduction. This implies a certain renunciation in respect of the goal of arithmetizing analysis, and thus geometry, too. 'But'—one could here ask in the Wittgensteinian manner—'must geometry be entirely arithmetized?' Scientists are often very dogmatic in their attempts at reductions. They are frequently inclined to treat such an attempt as completely successful even when it succeeds not in the manner intended but only in some measure and with a certain degree of approximation. Where such standpoints are en- countered, considerations of the kind suggested by Wittgenstein's book can be very valuable.

Wittgenstein's detailed discussion of Dedekind's proof is not satisfactory. Some of his objections can be disposed of simply through a clearer account of Dedekind's line of thought.

In the discussion of denumerability and non-denumerability, the reader must bear in mind that Wittgenstein always understands by cardinal number a finite cardinal number, and by a series one of the order type of the natural numbers. The polemics against the theorem of the non-denumerability of the totality of real numbers is unsatisfactory insofar as the analogy between the concepts 'non-denumerable' and 'infinite' is not brought out clearly. Corres- ponding to the way in which 'infinity of a totality G' can be defined as the property whereby to a finite number of things out of G there can always be assigned a further one, the non-denumerability of a totality G is defined by the property that to every denumerable sub-totality there can be assigned an element of G not yet contained in the sub-totality. In this sense the non- denumerability of the totality of real numbers is demonstrated by the diagonal procedure, and there is nothing foisted in here, as would appear to be the case according to Wittgenstein's argument. The theorem of the non- denumerability of the totality of real numbers is attainable without compari- son of the transfinite cardinal numbers. Besides—this is often disregarded— there exist for that theorem other proofs more geometrical than the one provided by the diagonal procedure. From the point of view of geometry we have here a rather gross fact.

It is also strange to find the author raising a question like this: 'How then do we make use of the proposition: "There is no largest [scil. finite] cardinal number."? . . . First and foremost it is to be noticed that we put the question at all, which indicates that the answer is not obvious' (p. 57, No. 5). We might think that one need not spend long searching for the answer here. Our entire analysis with its applications in physics and technology rests on the infinity of the series of numbers. The theory of probability and statistics make continually implicit use of this infinity. Wittgenstein argues as though mathematics existed almost solely for the purposes of housekeeping.

The finitist and constructive attitude on the whole taken by Wittgenstein towards the problems of the foundations of mathematics conforms to the general tendency of his philosophizing. However, it can hardly be said that he finds a confirmation for his viewpoint in the situation of the foundational investigations. All that he shows is how this standpoint has to be applied when engaging in the questions in dispute. It is generally characteristic of the situation with regard to the foundational problems that the results obtained hitherto clearly favor neither the one nor the other of the main two opposing philosophical views—the finitist-constructive and the 'Platonic'-existential view. Either of the two views can advance arguments against the other. The existential conception, however, has the advantage of enabling us to appreciate the investigations directed towards the establishment of elementary constructive methods (just as in geometry the investigation of constructions with ruler and compass has significance even for a mathematician who admits other methods of construction), while for the strictly constructivist view a large part of classical mathematics simply does not exist.

To some extent independent of the partisanship in the mentioned opposition of viewpoints are those observations of Wittgenstein's which concern the rôle of formalization, the reduction of number theory to logic, and the question of consistency. His views here show more independence, and these considerations are therefore of greater interest.

With regard to the question of consistency he asserts in particular what has meanwhile also been stressed by various other investigators in the field of foundational research: that within the bounds of a formal system the contradiction should not be considered solely as a deterrent, and that a formal system as such can still be of interest even when it leads to a contradiction. It should be observed, however, that in the former systems of Frege and Russell the contradiction already arises within a few steps, almost directly from the basic structure of the system. Furthermore, much of what Wittgenstein says in this connection overshoots the mark by a long way. Particularly unsatisfactory is the frequently quoted example of the producibility of contradictions by admitting division by nought. (One need only consider the foundation of the rule of reduction in order to see that this is not applicable in the case of the factor nought.)

Wittgenstein recognizes at all events the importance of demonstrating consistency. Yet it is doubtful whether he is sufficiently well aware of the rôle played by the condition of consistency in the reasoning of proof-theory. Thus the discussion of Gödel's theorem of non-derivability in particular suffers from the defect that Gödel's quite explicit premiss of the consistency of the considered formal system is ignored. A fitting comparison, which is drawn by Wittgenstein in connection with the Gödelian proposition, is that between a proof of formal unprovability and a proof of the impossibility of a certain construction with ruler and compass. Such a proof, Wittgenstein says, contains an element of prediction. The remark which follows, however, is strange (p. 52, No. 14): 'A contradiction is unusable as such a prediction.' Such proofs of impossibility in fact always proceed by the deduction of a contradiction.

In his considerations on the theory of numbers Wittgenstein shows a noticeable reserve towards Frege's and Russell's foundation of number theory, such as was not to be found in the earlier stages of his philosophy. Thus he says on one occasion (p. 67, No. 4): '. . . the logical calculus is only —frills tacked on to the arithmetical calculus.' This thought had hardly been formulated previously as pregnantly as here. It might be appropriate to reflect on the sense in which the assertion holds good. There is no denying that the attempt at incorporating the arithmetical, and in particular, the numerical propositions into logistic has been successful. That is to say, it has proved possible to formulate these propositions in purely logical terms and to prove them within the domain of logistic on the basis of this formulation. Whether this result may be regarded as yielding a proper philosophical understanding of the arithmetical proposition is, however, open to question, When we consider the logistical proof of an equation such as $3 + 7 = 10$. we observe that within the proof we have to carry out quite the same comparative verification which occurs in the usual counting. This necessity shows itself particularly clearly in the formalized form of logic; but it is also present when we interpret the content of the formula logically. The logical definition of three-numberedness (Dreizahligkeit), for example, is structurally so constituted that it to some extent contains within itself the element of three-numberedness. The property possessed by the predicate P (or by the class that forms the extension of P) of being three-numbered is indeed defined by the condition that there exist things x, y, z having the property P and differing each from the others, and that further everything having the property P is identical with x or y or z. Now the conclusion that for a three-numbered predicate P and a seven-numbered predicate Q, in the case that the predicates do not apply in common to one thing, the alternative $P \vee Q$ is a ten-numbered predicate, requires for its foundation just the kind of comparison that is used in elementary arithmetic—only that now an additional logical apparatus (the 'frills') comes into operation. When this is clearly realized, it appears that the proposition of the logical theory of predicates is valid because $3 + 7 = 10$, and not vice versa.

Thus in spite of the possibility of incorporating arithmetic into logistic, arithmetic constitutes the more abstract ('purer') schema; and this appears paradoxical only because of a traditional, but on closer examination unjustified view according to which logical generality is in every respect the highest generality.

Yet it might be good to look at yet another aspect of the matter. According to Frege a number (Anzahl) is to be defined as the property of a predicate. This view already presents difficulties for the normal use of the number concept; for in many contexts where a number occurs, the indication of a predicate of which it is the property proves to be highly forced. In particular it should be noted that numbers occur not only in statements: they also occur in directions and in demands or requests—such as when a housewife says to an errand-boy: 'Fetch me ten apples.'

The theoretical elaboration of this conception is not without complications either. A definite number does not generally belong as such to a predicate, but only with reference to a domain of things, a universe of discourse (apart from the many cases of extra-scientific predicates to which no definite number at all can be ascribed). Thus it would be more accurate to characterize a number as a relation between a predicate and a domain of individuals. In Frege's theory, it is true, this complication does not arise since he presupposes what might be called an absolute domain of individuals. But, as we know, it is precisely this starting point which leads to the contradiction noted by Russell. Apart from this, the Fregian conception of his predicate theory, in which the value distributions (extensions) of the predicate are treated as things quite on a par with ordinary individuals, already implies a clear deviation from our customary logic in the sense of a theoretical construction of a formal derivative frame. The idea of such a frame has retained its methodological importance, and the question as to the most favorable formation of it is still one of the main problems in foundational theory. However, with respect to such a frame one can speak of a 'logic' only in an extended sense; logic in its usual sense, stating merely the general rules for deductive reasoning, must be distinguished from the latter.

Wittgenstein's criticism of the incorporation of arithmetic into logic is, it is true, not advanced in the sense that he recognizes arithmetical theorems as stating facts *sui generis*. His tendency is rather to deny altogether that such theorems express facts. He even declares it to be the 'curse of the invasion of mathematics by mathematical logic that any proposition can now be represented in mathematical notation and we thus feel obliged to understand it, although this way of writing is really only the translation of vague, ordinary prose' (p. 155, No. 46). Indeed he recognizes calculating only as an acquired skill with practical utility. In particular, he seeks to explain away in a definitory manner what is factual about arithmetic. Thus he asks, for instance (p. 33, No. 112): 'What do I call "the multiplication 13×13"? Only the correct pattern of multiplication at the end of which comes 169? Or a "wrong multiplication" too?' Likewise, the question often arises as to what it is that we 'call calculating' (p. 97, No. 73). And on p. 92, No. 58 he argues: 'Suppose one were to say that by calculating we become acquainted with the properties

of numbers. But do the properties of numbers *exist* outside of calculating?'
The tendency is apparently to take the correct additions and multiplications
as defining calculating and to characterize them as 'correct' in a trivial manner.
But one cannot succeed in this way, i.e. one cannot express in this way the
many facts of relatedness which appear in the numerical computations. Let us
take, say, the associativity of addition. It is certainly possible to fix by
definition the addition of the single figures. But then the strange fact remains
that the addition $3 + (7 + 8)$ gives the same result as $(3 + 7) + 8$, and that
the same holds whatever numbers replace 3, 7, 8. The number-theoretic expressions are, from the definitory point of view, so to speak, over-determined.
It is indeed on this kind of over-determinateness that the many checks are
based of which we may make use in calculating.

Occasionally Wittgenstein raises the question as to whether the result of a
calculation carried out in the decimal system is also valid for the comparison
of numbers carried out by means of the direct representation with sequences
of strokes. The answer to this is to be found in the usual mathematical foundation of the method of calculating with decadic figures. Yet here Wittgenstein
touches upon something fundamental: the proofs to be given for the justification of the decadic rules of calculation rest, if they are obtained in a finitist
way, upon the assumption that every number we can form decadically is
producible also in the direct stroke notation, and that the operations of con-
catenation, etc., as also of comparison, are always performable with such
stroke sequences. From this it appears that the finitistic theory of numbers,
too, is not in the full sense 'concrete', but utilizes idealizations.

The previously mentioned assertions in which Wittgenstein speaks of the
synthetic character of mathematics are in a certain apparent contrast with the
tendency to regard numerical calculating as being characterized merely by
way of definition and to deny that arithmetical propositions have the character of facts. In this connection the following passage may be noted (p. 160,
No. 3): 'How can you maintain that "... 625 ..." and "... 25 × 25 ..."
say the same thing?—It is only through our arithmetic that they *become
one*.'

What is meant here is about the same thing that Kant had in mind in the
argument against the view that $7 + 5 = 12$ is a merely analytical proposition,
and where he contends that the concept 12 'is by no means already conceived
through my merely conceiving this union of 7 and 5', and then adds: 'That
7 *are to be* added to 5, I have, it is true, conceived in the concept of a sum
$= 7 + 5$, but not that this sum is equal to the number 12' (*Critique of Pure
Reason*, B 14ff.). The Kantian argument could be expressed in a modern
form somewhat as follows. The concept '$7 + 5$' is an individual concept
(in accordance with Carnap's terminology) expressible by the description 1_x
($x = 7 + 5$), and this concept is different from the concept '12'; the only
reason for this not being so obvious is that we involuntarily carry out the
addition of the small numbers 7 and 5 directly. We have here the case, so

often discussed in the new logic following Frege, of two terms with a different 'sense' but the same 'Bedeutung' (called 'denotation' by A. Church); in order to determine the synthetic or analytic character of a judgment one must, of course, always go by the sense, not the 'Bedeutung'. The Kantian thesis that mathematics is of a synthetic character does not at all conflict with what the Russellian school maintains when it declares the propositions of arithmetic to be analytic. We have here two entirely different concepts of the analytic— a fact which in recent times has been pointed out in particular by E. W. Beth.[5]

A further intrinsic contrast is to be found in Wittgenstein's attitude towards logistic. On the one hand, he often tends to regard proofs as formalized proofs. Thus he says on p. 93, No. 64: 'Suppose I were to set someone the problem: "Find a proof of the proposition . . . "—The solution would surely be to show me certain signs.' The distinctive and indispensable rôle of everyday language compared with that of a formalized language is not given prominence in his remarks. He often speaks of the 'language game' and by no means restricts the use of this expression to the artificial formal language, for which alone it is indeed appropriate. Our natural language has in no way the character of a game; it is peculiar to us, almost in the way our limbs are. Apparently Wittgenstein is still governed by the idea of a language of science comprehending the whole of scientific thought. In contrast with this are the highly critical remarks on usual mathematical logic. Apart from the one already mentioned concerning 'the curse of the invasion of mathematics by mathematical logic', the following in particular is worthy of notice (p. 156, No. 48): ' "Mathematical logic" has completely distorted the thinking of mathematicians and philosophers by declaring a superficial interpretation of the forms of our everyday language to be an analysis of the structures of facts. In this, of course, it has only continued to build on the Aristotelian logic.'

We shall come closer to the idea which probably underlies this criticism if we bear in mind that logical calculus was intended by various of its founders as a realization of the Leibnizian conception of the *characteristica universalis*. As to Aristotle, Wittgenstein's criticism, if we look at it more closely, is not directed against him. For all that Aristotle wanted to do with his logic was to fix the usual forms of logical arguing and to test their legitimacy. The task of the *characteristica universalis*, however, was intended to be a much larger one: to establish a concept-world which would make possible an understanding of all connections existing in reality. For an undertaking aimed at this goal, however, it cannot be taken for granted that the grammatical structures of our language have to function as the basic framework of the theory; for the categories of this grammar have a character that is at least partially anthropomorphic. Yet nothing even approaching the same value has hitherto been devised in philosophy to replace our usual logic. What

---

[5] "Over Kants Onderscheiding von synthetische en analytische Oordeelen," *De Gids*, vol. 106, 1942. Also: The "Foundations of Mathematics," *Studies in Logic*, Amsterdam, 1959, pp. 41–47.

Hegel in particular put in place of the Aristotelian logic in his rejection of it is a mere comparison of universals by way of analogies and associations, without any clearly regulative procedure. This certainly cannot pass as any sort of approach to the fulfilment of the Leibnizian ideas.

From Wittgenstein, however, we can obtain no guidance on how conventional logic may be replaced by something philosophically more efficient. He probably considered an 'analysis of the structures of facts' to be a task wrongly set. Indeed he did not look for a procedure determined by some directive rules. The 'logical compulsion', the 'inexorability of logic', the 'hardness of the logical must' are always a stumbling block for him and ever again a cause of amazement. Perhaps he does not always realize that all these terms have the character of merely a popular comparison which in many respects is inappropriate. The strictness of the logical and the exact does not limit our freedom. Our very freedom enables us to achieve precision through thought in a perceptive world of indistinctness and inexactness. Wittgenstein speaks of the 'must of kinematics' being 'much harder that the causal must' (p. 37, No. 121). Is it not an aspect of freedom that we can conceive virtual motions subject merely to kinematic laws, as well as real, causally determined motions, and can compare the former with the latter?

Enlightened humanity has sought in rational definiteness its liberating refuge from the dominating influence of the merely authoritative. At the present time, however, this has for a large part been lost to consciousness, and to many people scientific validity that has to be acknowledged appears as an oppressing authority.

In Wittgenstein's case it is certainly not this aspect which evokes his critical attitude towards scientific objectivity. Nevertheless, his tendency is to understand the intersubjective unanimity in the field of mathematics as an heteronomous one. The agreement, he believes, is to be explained by the fact that we are in the first place 'trained' in common in elementary technique and that the agreement thus created is continued through the proofs (cf. quotation on p. 195). That this kind of explanation is inadequate might occur to anybody not attracted by the impression of originality of the aspect. The mere possibility of the technique of calculating with its manifold possibilities of decomposing a computation into simpler parts cannot be regarded merely as a consequence of agreement (cf. remark on pp. 17 and 18). Furthermore, when we think of the enormously rich concept-formations towered up on each other, as for instance in function theory—where one can say of the theorems obtained at any stage what Wittgenstein once said: 'We lean on them or rest on them' (p. 124, No. 35)—we see that the conception mentioned does not in any way explain why these conceptual edifices are not continually collapsing. Considering Wittgenstein's viewpoint, it is, in fact, not surprising that he does not feel the contradiction to be something odd; but what does not appear from his account is that contradictions in mathematics are to be found only in quite peripheral extrapolations and nowhere else. In this sense one can say that the fact of mathematics does not become at all understandable through Wittgenstein's philosophy. And it is not his anthropological point of view which gives rise to the difficulty.

Where, however, does the initial conviction of Wittgenstein's arise that in the region of mathematics there is no proper knowledge about objects, but that everything here can only be techniques, standards and customary attitudes? He certainly reasons: 'There is nothing here at all to which knowing could refer.' That is bound up, as already mentioned, with the circumstance that he does not recognize any kind of phenomenology. What probably induces his opposition here are such phrases as the one which refers to the 'essence' of a colour; here the word 'essence' evokes the idea of hidden properties of the color, whereas colors as such are nothing other than what is evident in their manifest properties and relations. But this does not prevent such properties and relations from being the content of objective statements; colors are not just a nothing. Even if we do not adopt the pretensions of the philosophy of Husserl with regard to 'intuition of the essence', that does not preclude the possibility of an objective phenomenology. That in the region of colors and sounds the phenomenological investigation is still in its beginnings is certainly bound up with the fact that it has no great importance for theoretical physics, since in physics we are induced, at an early stage, to eliminate colors and sounds as qualities. Mathematics, however, can be regarded as the theoretical phenomenology of structures. In fact, what contrasts phenomenologically with the qualitative is not the quantitative, as is taught by traditional philosophy, but the structural, i.e. the forms of being aside and after, and of being composite, etc., with all the concepts and laws that relate to them.

Such a conception of mathematics leaves the attitude towards the problems of the foundations of mathematics still largely undetermined. Yet, for anyone proceeding from the Wittgensteinian conception, it can open the way to a viewpoint that does greater justice to the peculiarity and the comprehensive significance of mathematics.

Bibliography

Alston, W. P. "Ontological Commitment," *Phil. Studies,* **9** (1958). Reprinted in this anthology, pp. 249–57.

Ambrose, A. "Finitism in Mathematics I–II," *Mind* **44** (1935).
——— "Wittgenstein on some Questions in the Foundations of Mathematics," *Jour. of Phil.* **52** (1955).
——— "On Entailment and Logical Necessity," *Proc. Arist. Soc.* **56** (1955–56).

Anscombe, G. E. M. *An Introduction to Wittgenstein's* Tractatus, London: Hutchinson University Library, 1959.

Ayer, A. J. *Language, Truth and Logic,* 2nd ed., London: Gollancz, 1946.
——— "On What There Is," *Arist. Soc. Supp.,* vol. 25 (1951).

Bar-Hillel, Y. and A. A. Fraenkel. *Foundations of Set Theory,* Amsterdam: North–Holland, 1958.

Becker, O. *Grundlagen der Mathematik in geschichtlicher Entwicklung,* Freiburg and Munich: Alber, 1954.

Bennett, J. "Analytic–Synthetic," *Proc. Arist. Soc.* **59** (1958–59).
——— "A Myth about Logical Necessity," *Analysis* **21** (1960–61).
——— "On being Forced to a Conclusion," *Arist. Soc. Supp.,* vol. 35 (1961).

Bernays, P. "Sur le Platonisme dans les Mathématiques," *L'Enseignment Mathématique* **34** (1935). Translated in this anthology, pp. 274–86.
——— "Comments on Ludwig Wittgenstein's *Remarks on the Foundations of Mathematics,*" *Ratio* **2** (1959–60). Reprinted in this anthology, pp. 510–28.

Bernays, P. and A. A. Fraenkel. *Axiomatic Set Theory,* Amsterdam: North–Holland, 1958.

Bernays, P. and D. Hilbert. *Die Grundlagen der Mathematik,* Berlin: Springer, vol. 1 (1934), vol. 2 (1939).

Beth, E. W. *The Foundations of Mathematics,* Amsterdam: North–Holland, 1959.

Black, M. *The Nature of Mathematics,* New York: Harcourt, 1933.
——— "The Semantic Definition of Truth," *Analysis* **8** (1947–48).

Bolzano, B. *The Paradoxes of the Infinite,* trans. by F. Prihonsky. New Haven, Conn: Yale Univ. Press, 1950.

Boole, G. *The Mathematical Analysis of Logic,* Cambridge: Macmillan, Barclay and Macmillan, 1847; Oxford: Blackwell, 1948.
——— *An Investigation of the Laws of Thought,* London: Walton and Maberly, 1854; New York: Dover, 1951.

We are grateful to George Boolos for preparing this bibliography.—Eds.

Brodbeck, M. and H. Feigl. *Readings in the Philosopy of Science*, New York: Appleton, 1953.

Brouwer, L. E. J. "Intuitionism and Formalism," *Bull. Amer. Math. Soc.* **20** (1913). Reprinted in this anthology, pp. 66–77.

—— "Zur Begründung der intuitionistischen Mathematik," *Math. Annalen* **93** (1925), **95** (1926), **96** (1927).

—— "Über Definitionsbereiche von Funktionen," *Math. Annalen* **97** (1927).

—— "Mathematik, Wissenschaft, und Sprache," *Monatshefte für Mathematik und Physik* **36** (1929).

—— "Consciousness, Philosophy and Mathematics," *Proc. Xth International Congress of Philosophy*, Amsterdam (1948). Reprinted in this anthology, pp. 78–84.

—— "Historical Background, Principles and Methods of Intuitionism," *South African Jour. of Sci.* **49** (1952).

Cantor, G. *Contributions to the Founding of the Theory of Transfinite Numbers*, trans. by P. E. B. Jourdain. New York: Dover, date of reprint not given (original English edition published 1915).

Carnap, R. "Die Mathematik als Zweig der Logik," *Blätter für deutsche Philosophie* **4** (1930).

—— "Die Logizistische Grundlegung der Mathematik," *Erkenntnis* **2** (1931). Translated in this anthology, pp. 31–41.

—— "Die Antinomien und die Unvollständigkeit der Mathematik," *Monatshefte für Mathematik und Physik* **41** (1934).

—— *The Logical Syntax of Language*, trans. by A. Smeaton. New York: Harcourt, 1937.

—— *Foundations of Logic and Mathematics*, vol. I, No. 3 of the International Encyclopedia of Unified Science, Chicago: Univ. of Chicago Press, 1939.

—— *Introduction to Semantics*, Cambridge, Mass: Harvard Univ. Press, 1942.

—— *Formalization of Logic*, Cambridge, Mass: Harvard Univ. Press, 1943.

—— "Empiricism, Semantics and Ontology," *Revue Intern. de Phil.* **4** (1950). Reprinted in this anthology, pp. 233–48.

—— "Formal and Factual Science," in *Readings in the Philosophy of Science*, ed. by H. Feigl and M. Brodbeck. New York: Appleton, 1953.

—— *Meaning and Necessity*, enlarged ed., Chicago: Univ. of Chicago Press, 1956.

—— "The Old and the New Logic," trans. by I. Levi in *Logical Positivism*, ed. by A. J. Ayer. New York: Free Press, 1959.

Castañeda, H. N. "Arithmetic and Reality," *The Australasian Journal of Philosophy* **37**, no. 2 (August, 1959), 92–107. Reprinted in this anthology, pp. 404–17.

—— "On Mathematical Proofs and Meaning," *Mind* **70** (1961).

Chihara, C. S. "Wittgenstein and Logical Compulsion," *Analysis* **21** (1960–61).

——"Mathematical Discovery and Concept Formation," *Phil. Review* **72** (1963).

Chomsky, N. and I. Scheffler. "What is said to be," *Proc. Arist. Soc.* **59** (1958–59).

Church, A. "The Richard Paradox," *Amer. Math. Monthly* **41** (1934).

—— "A Bibliography of Symbolic Logic," *Jour. Symbolic Logic* **1** (1936) and **3** (1938).

—— "A Formulation of the Logic of Sense and Denotation," in *Structure, Method and Meaning: Essays in honor of H. M. Sheffer*, ed. by P. Henle *et al.* New York: Liberal Arts, 1951.

—— *Introduction to Mathematical Logic: Vol. I*, Princeton, N.J.: Princeton Univ. Press, 1956.

—— "Propositions and Sentences," in *The Problem of Universals*, Notre Dame, Ind.: Univ. of Notre Dame Press, 1956.

—— "Ontological Commitment," *Jour. of Phil.* **55** (1958).

Chwistek, L. "Die Nominalistische Grundlegung der Mathematik," *Erkenntnis* **3** (1932–33).

Cohen, M. R. and E. Nagel. *An Introduction to Logic and Scientific Method*, New York: Harcourt, 1934.

Curry, H. B. *Outlines of a Formalist Philosophy of Mathematics*, Amsterdam: North-Holland, 1951.

—— "Calculuses and Formal Systems," *Dialectica* **12** (1958).

—— "Remarks on the Definition and Nature of Mathematics," *Dialectica* **8** (1954). Reprinted in this anthology, pp. 152–6.

Dedekind, R. *Essays on the Theory of Numbers*, Chicago: Open Court, 1903; New York: Dover, 1963, including "Continuity and Irrational Numbers" and "The Nature and Meaning of Numbers" (translator not given).

Dubislav, W. "Über das Verhältnis der Logik zur Mathematik," *Annalen der Philosophie* 5 (1925–26).

——— "Über den sogennanten Gegenstand der Mathematik," *Erkenntnis* 1 (1930).

——— *Die Philosophie der Mathematik in der Gegenwart*, Berlin: Dunker & Dunnhaupt, 1932.

Dummett, M. A. E. "Frege on Functions: A Reply," *Phil. Review* 64 (1955).

——— "Note: Frege on Functions," *Phil. Review* 65 (1956).

——— "Nominalism," *Phil. Review* 65 (1956).

——— "Constructionalism," *Phil. Review* 66 (1957).

——— "Truth," *Proc. Arist. Soc.* 59 (1958–59).

——— "Wittgenstein's Philosophy of Mathematics," *Phil. Review* 68 (1959). Reprinted in this anthology, pp. 491–509.

Feigl, H. and M. Brodbeck. *Readings in the Philosophy of Science*, New York: Appleton, 1953.

Feigl, H. and W. Sellars. *Readings in the Philosophical Analysis*, New York: Appleton, 1949.

Findlay, J. N. "Gödelian Sentences: A Non–numerical Approach," *Mind* 51 (1942).

Fraenkel, A. A. *Einleitung in die Mengenlehre*, 3rd ed. Berlin: Springer, 1928.

——— "Die heutigen Gegensätze in der Grundlegung der Mathematik," *Erkenntnis* 1 (1930).

——— "Sur la notion d'existence dans les mathématiques," *L'Enseignment Mathématique* 34 (1935–36).

——— *Abstract Set Theory*, 2nd ed. Amsterdam: North–Holland, 1961.

Fraenkel, A. A. and Y. Bar–Hillel. *Foundations of Set Theory*, Amsterdam: North–Holland, 1958.

Fraenkel, A. A. and P. Bernays. *Axiomatic Set Theory*, Amsterdam: North–Holland, 1958.

Frege, G. *Begriffsschrift*, Halle: Nebert, 1879.

——— *The Foundations of Arithmetic*, trans. by J. L. Austin. Oxford: Blackwell, 1950.

——— *Die Grundgesetze der Arithmetik*, Jena: Pohle., vol. 1, 1893, vol. 2, 1903. Hildesheim: Olms, 1962.

——— *Translations from the Philosophical Writings*, ed. by P. Geach and M. Black. Oxford: Blackwell, 1952, including "Function and Concept," "On Concept and Object," "On Sense and Reference," "What is a Function?", "Negation," etc.

——— "The Thought," trans. by A. and M. Quinton. *Mind* 65 (1956).

Gasking, D. "Mathematics and the World," *Australasian Jour. of Psych. and Phil.* 18 (1940). Reprinted in this anthology, pp. 390–403.

Geach, P. T. "On What There Is," *Arist. Soc. Supp.*, vol. 25, 1951.

——— "Frege's *Grundlagen*," *Phil. Review* 60 (1951).

——— "On Frege's Way Out," *Mind* 65 (1956).

——— "Russell on Meaning and Denoting," *Analysis* 19 (1958–59).

——— "Frege," in *Three Philosophers*, by G. E. M. Anscombe and P. T. Geach. Oxford: Blackwell, 1961.

Gentzen, G. "Neue Fassung des Widerspruchsfreiheitsbeweises für die reine Zahlentheorie," *Forschungen zur Logik und zur Grundlegung der exacten Wissenschaften* 4 (new series) (1938).

——— "Die gegenwärtige Lage in der mathematischen Grundlagenforschungen," *Forschungen zur Logik und zur Grundlegung der exakten Wissenschaften* 4 (new series) (1938).

Gödel, K. "Zur intuitionistischen Arithmetik und Zahlentheorie," *Ergebnisse eines mathematischen Kolloquiums* 4 (1933).

——— "Eine Interpretation des intuitionistischen Aussagenkalküls," *Ergebnisse eines mathematischen Kolloquiums* 4 (1933).

—— "Zum intuitionistischen Aussagenkalkül," *Ergebnisse eines mathematischen Kolloquiums* **4** (1933).

—— *The Consistency of the Continuum Hypothesis*, Princeton, N.J.: Princeton Univ. Press, 1940.

—— "Russell's Mathematical Logic," in *The Philosophy of Bertrand Russell*, ed. by P. A. Schilpp. New York: Tudor, 1944. Reprinted in this anthology, pp. 211–32.

—— "What is Cantor's Continuum Problem?", *Amer. Math. Monthly* **54** (1947). Reprinted in this anthology, pp. 258–73.

—— "Über eine bisher noch nicht benützte Erweiterung des finiten Standpunktes," *Dialectica* **12** (1958).

—— *On Formally Undecidable Propositions of* Principia Mathematica *and Related Systems*, trans. by B. Meltzer, with an introduction by R. B. Braithwaite. Edinburgh: Oliver and Boyd, 1962.

Goodman, N. *The Structure of Appearance*, Cambridge, Mass.: Harvard Univ. Press, 1951.

—— "A World of Individuals," in *The Problem of Universals*, Notre Dame, Ind.: Univ. of Notre Dame Press, 1956. Reprinted in this anthology, pp. 197–210.

Goodman, N. and W. V. Quine. "Steps toward a Constructive Nominalism," *Jour. of Symbolic Logic* **12** (1947).

Goodstein, R. L. "Critical Notice: Wittgenstein's *Remarks on the Foundations of Mathematics*," *Mind* **66** (1957).

—— "On the Nature of Mathematical Systems," *Dialectica* **12** (1958).

—— "The Foundations of Mathematics," *Arist. Soc. Supp.*, vol. 36, 1962.

Grelling, K. "The Logical Paradoxes," *Mind* **45** (1936).

Grice, H. P. and P. F. Strawson. "In Defense of a Dogma," *Phil. Review* **65** (1956).

Hahn, H. "Logic, Mathematics and Knowledge of Nature," trans. by A. Pap in *Logical Positivism*, ed. by A. J. Ayer. New York: Free Press, 1959.

Hardy, G. H. "Mathematical Proof," *Mind* **38** (1929).

Hempel, C. G. "On the Nature of Mathematical Truth," *Amer. Math. Monthly* **52** (1945). Reprinted in this anthology, pp. 366–81.

Hempel, C. G. and P. Oppenheim. *Der Typusbegriff im Lichte der neuen Logik*, Leiden: Sijthoff, 1936.

Heyting, A. "Die intuitionistische Grundlegung der Mathematik," *Erkenntnis* **2** (1931). Translated in this anthology, pp. 42–9.

—— *Mathematische Grundlagenforschung, Intuitionismus, Beweistheorie*, Berlin: Springer, 1934.

—— "Formal Logic and Mathematics," *Synthèse* **6** (1948).

—— *Intuitionism: An Introduction*, Amsterdam: North–Holland, 1956. Excerpted in this anthology, pp. 55–65.

—— "Blick von der intuitionistischen Warte," *Dialectica* **12** (1958).

—— "Axiomatic Method and Intuitionism," in *Essays on the Foundations of Mathematics, dedicated to A. A. Fränkel on his seventieth anniversary*, ed. by Y. Bar-Hillel. Jerusalem: Magnes Press, 1961.

Hilbert, D. "Über das Unendliche," *Math. Annalen* **95** (1926). Translated in this anthology, pp. 134–51.

—— *Grundlagen der Geometrie*, 7th ed. Leipzig: Teubner, 1930.

Hilbert, D. and P. Bernays. *Die Grundlagen der Mathematik*. Berlin: Springer, vol. 1 (1934), vol. 2 (1939).

Hintikka, J. K. K. "Existential Presuppositions and Existential Commitments," *Jour. of Phil.* **56** (1959).

Kaufmann, F. *Das Unendliche in der Mathematik und seine Ausschaltung*, Vienna: Deuticke, 1930.

—— "Bemerkungen zum Grundlagenstreit in Logik und Mathematik," *Erkenntnis* **2** (1931).

Kleene, S. C. "On the Intuitionistic Logic," *Proc. Xth International Congress of Philosophy*, Amsterdam: North–Holland, 1948.

––––– *Introduction to Metamathematics*, Princeton, N.J.: Van Nostrand, 1952.

Kneale, W. "The Truths of Logic," *Proc. Arist. Soc.* **46** (1945–46).

Kneale, W. and M. *The Development of Logic*, Oxford: Clarendon Press, 1962.

Körner, S. *The Philosophy of Mathematics*, London: Hutchinson University Library, 1960.

Kreisel, G. "Some Remarks on the Foundations of Mathematics. An Expository Article," *Math. Gazette* **35** (1951).

––––– "The Diagonal Method in Formalized Arithmetic," *British Jour. for the Phil. of Sci.* **3** (1952–53).

––––– "A Variant to Hilbert's Theory of the Foundations of Arithmetic," *British Jour. for the Phil. of Sci.* **4** (1953–54).

––––– "Hilbert's Programme," *Dialectica* **12** (1958). Reprinted in this anthology, pp. 157–80.

––––– "Foundations of Intuitionistic Logic," in *Logic, Methodology and Philosophy of Science*, ed. by E. Nagel, P. Suppes, and A. Tarski. Stanford, Calif.: Stanford Univ. Press, 1962.

Lakatos, I. "The Foundations of Mathematics," *Arist. Soc. Supp.*, vol. 36, 1962.

Langford, C. H. and C. I. Lewis. *Symbolic Logic*, 2nd ed. New York: Dover, 1959.

Lewis, C. I. *A Survey of Mathematical Logic*, Berkeley, Calif.: Univ. of California Press, 1918.

Lewis, C. I. and C. H. Langford. *Symbolic Logic*, 2nd ed. New York: Dover, 1959.

Lewy, C. "Why are the Calculuses of Logic and Mathematics Applicable to Reality?" *Arist. Soc. Supp.*, vol. 20, 1946.

Lorenzen, P. *Einführung in die operative Logik und Mathematik*, Berlin: Göttingen & Heidelberg, 1955.

––––– "Wie ist Philosophie der Mathematik möglich?" *Philosophia Naturalis* **4** (1957).

––––– *Metamathematik*, Mannheim: Bibliographisches Institut, 1962.

Lucas, J. R. "Minds, Machines and Gödel," *Philosophy* **36** (1961).

Lukasiewicz, J. "Die Logik und das Grundlagenproblem," *Les entretiens de Zurich sur les fondements et la méthode des sciences mathématiques*, 1938.

McNaughton, R. "Conceptual Schemes in Set Theory," *Phil. Review* **66** (1957).

Marshall, W. "Frege's Theory of Functions and Objects," *Phil. Review* **62** (1953).

Martin, R. M. *Truth and Denotation*, Chicago: Univ. of Chicago Press, 1958.

Mehlberg, H. "The Present Situation in the Philosophy of Mathematics," in *Logic and Language: Studies dedicated to Professor Rudolf Carnap on the occasion of his seventieth birthday*. Dordrecht: Reidel, 1962.

Menger, K. "Der Intuitionismus," *Blätter für deutsche Philosophie* **4** (1930).

Mill, J. S. *A System of Logic*, London: Longmans, 1843.

Moore, G. E. "Wittgenstein's Lectures in 1930–33," in *Philosophical Papers*, London: G. Allen, 1959.

Mostowski, A., A. Tarski, and R. M. Robinson. *Undecidable Theories*, Amsterdam: North–Holland, 1953.

Myhill, J. "Two Ways of Ontology in Modern Logic," *Review of Metaphysics* **5** (1951–52).

––––– "Some Philosophical Implications of Mathematical Logic," *Review of Metaphysics* **6** (1952–53).

Nagel, E. "Logic Without Ontology," in *Naturalism and the Human Spirit*, ed. by Y. H. Krikorian. New York: Columbia University Press, 1944. Reprinted in this anthology, pp. 302–21.

––––– *Logic Without Metaphysics*, New York: Free Press, 1956.

Nagel, E. and M. R. Cohen. *An Introduction to Logic and Scientific Method*, New York: Harcourt, 1934.

Nagel, E. and J. R. Newman. *Gödel's Proof*, New York: New York Univ. Press, 1958.

Neumann, J. v. "Die formalistische Grundlegung der Mathematik," *Erkenntnis* **2** (1931). Translated in this anthology, pp. 50–4.

Newman, J. R. and E. Nagel. *Gödel's Proof*, New York: New York Univ. Press, 1958.

Oppenheim, P. and C. G. Hempel. *Der Typusbegriff im Lichte der Neuen Logik*, Leiden: Sijthoff, 1936.

Pap, A. *Semantics and Necessary Truth*, New Haven: Yale Univ. Press, 1958.
——— "Types and Meaninglessness," *Mind* **69**, 1960.

Peirce, C. S. *Collected Papers*, vols. I–VIII, ed. by C. Hartshorne, P. Weiss, and A. W. Burks. Cambridge, Mass: Harvard Univ. Press, 1931–58.

Poincaré, H. *The Foundations of Science*, trans. by G. B. Halstead. New York: Science Press, 1913, including *Science and Hypothesis* and *Science and Method*.
——— *Science and Hypothesis*, trans. by "W. J. G." New York: Dover, 1952.
——— *Science and Method*, trans. by F. Maitland. New York: Dover, n.d.
——— *Dernières Pensees*, Paris: Flammarion, 1913.

Popper, K. "Why are the Calculuses of Logic and Mathematics Applicable to Reality?" *Arist. Soc. Supp.*, vol. 20, 1946.
——— "Logic Without Assumptions," *Proc. Arist. Soc.* **47** (1946–47).
——— "New Foundations for Logic," *Mind* 56–57 (1947–48).
——— "What can Logic do for Philosophy?" *Arist. Soc. Supp.*, vol. 22 (1948).

Putnam, H. "Mathematics and the Existence of Abstract Entities," *Phil. Studies* **7** (1956).
——— "The Analytic and the Synthetic," *Minnesota Studies in the Phil. of Sci.* III, Minneapolis: Univ. of Minnesota Press, 1962.
——— "The Thesis that Mathematics is Logic," to appear in a volume in honor of Bertrand Russell on his 93rd birthday. London: G. Allen, 1964.

Quine, W. V. "Truth by Convention," in *Philosophical Essays for A. N. Whitehead*, ed. by O. H. Lee. New York: McKay, 1936. Reprinted in this anthology, pp. 322–45.
——— "Designation and Existence," *Jour. of Phil.* 36 (1939).
——— "Notes on Existence and Necessity," *Jour. of Phil.* 40 (1943).
——— "Whitehead and the Rise of Modern Logic," in *The Philosophy of Alfred North Whitehead*, ed. by P. A. Schilpp. New York: Tudor, 1951.
——— "Semantics and Abstract Objects," *Proc. of the Amer. Acad. of Arts and Sciences* **80** (1951).
——— "Ontology and Ideology," *Phil. Studies* **2** (1951).
——— "On What There Is" (reply to Ayer and Geach), *Arist. Soc. Supp.*, vol. 25, 1951. Reprinted in this anthology, pp. 183–96.
——— "On Carnap's Views on Ontology," *Phil. Studies* **2** (1951).
——— "On an Application of Tarski's Theory of Truth," *Proc. of the Nat'l. Acad. of Sci.* **38** (1951).
——— *From a Logical Point of View*, Cambridge, Mass.: Harvard Univ. Press, 1953.
——— "On Mental Entities," *Proc. of the Amer. Acad. of Arts and Sciences* **80** (1953).
——— "On Frege's Way Out," *Mind* **64** (1955).
——— "Speaking of Objects," *Proc. and Addresses of the Amer. Phil. Assoc.* **31** (1958).
——— *Word and Object*, Cambridge, Mass., and New York: The Technology Press of M.I.T., and Wiley, 1960.
——— "Carnap and Logical Truth," in *Logic and Language: Studies dedicated to Professor Rudolf Carnap on the occasion of his seventieth birthday*, Dordrecht: Reidel, 1962.

Quine, W. V. and N. Goodman. "Steps toward a Constructive Nominalism," *Jour. of Symbolic Logic* **12** (1947).

Ramsey, F. P. *The Foundations of Mathematics*, New York: Harcourt, 1931, including "The Foundations of Mathematics," "Mathematical Logic," "Universals," etc.

Reichenbach, H. "Bertrand Russell's Logic," in *The Philosophy of Bertrand Russell*, ed. by P. A. Schilpp. New York: Tudor, 1944.

Richard, J. "Les Principes des Mathématiques et le Problème des Ensembles," *Revue Générale des Sciences* **16** (1905).

Robinson, R. M., A. Tarski, and A. Mostowski. *Undecidable Theories*, Amsterdam: North–Holland, 1953.

Rosser, J. B. "Constructibility as a Criterion for Existence," *Jour. of Symbolic Logic* **1** (1936).
—— "An Informal Exposition of the Proofs of Gödel's Theorem and Church's Theorem," *Jour. of Symbolic Logic* **4** (1939).

Russell, B. "Some Difficulties in the Theory of Transfinite Numbers and Order Types," *Proc. London Math. Soc.* (2) **4** (1906).
—— "The Theory of Implication," *Amer. Jour. of Math.* **28** (1906).
—— "Les Paradoxes de la Logique," *Revue de Métaphysique et de la Morale* **14** (1906).
—— *Introduction to Mathematical Philosophy*, London: G. Allen, 1919. Excerpts reprinted in this anthology, pp. 113–33.
—— *The Principles of Mathematics*, 2nd ed., London: G. Allen, 1937.
—— *An Inquiry into Meaning and Truth*, London: G. Allen, 1940.
—— *Logic and Knowledge*, ed. by R. C. Marsh. London: G. Allen, 1956, including "On Denoting," "Mathematical Logic as based on the Theory of Types," "The Philosophy of Logical Atomism," etc.

Russell, B. and A. N. Whitehead. *Principia Mathematica*, New York: Cambridge Univ. Press, vol. 1 (1910), vol. 2 (1912), vol. 3 (1913); 2nd ed., vol. 1 (1925), vol. 2 (1927), vol. 3 (1927).

Ryle, G. "Why are the Calculuses of Logic and Mathematics Applicable to Reality?" *Arist. Soc. Supp.*, vol. 20 (1946).

Rynin, D. "The Dogma of Logical Pragmatism," *Mind* **65** (1956).

Scheffler, I. and N. Chomsky. "What is said to be," *Proc. Arist. Soc.* **59** (1958–59).

Searle, J. R. "Russell's Objections to Frege's Theory of Sense and Reference," *Analysis* **18** (1957–58).

Sellars, W. and H. Feigl. *Readings in Philosophical Analysis*, New York: Appleton, 1949.

Shwayder, D. S. *Modes of Referring and the Problem of Universals*, University of California Publications in Philosophy, vol. 35, Berkeley and Los Angeles: Univ. of Calif. Press, 1961.

Skolem, T. "Über die Nicht–charakterisierbarkeit der Zahlenreihe mittels endlich oder abzählbar unendlich vieler Aussagen ausschliesslich mit Zahlenvariabeln," *Fundamenta Mathematica* **23** (1934).

Smart, J. J. C. "Whitehead and Russell's Theory of Types," *Analysis* **10** (1949–50).

Strawson, P. F. "On Referring," *Mind* **59** (1950).
—— *Introduction to Logical Theory*, London: Methuen, 1952.
—— "Singular Terms, Ontology and Identity," *Mind* **65** (1956).
—— *Individuals*, London: Methuen, 1959.

Strawson, P. F. and H. P. Grice. "In Defense of a Dogma," *Phil. Review* **65** (1956).

Tarski, A. "On Undecidable Statements in Enlarged Systems of Logic and the Concept of Truth," *Jour. of Symbolic Logic* **4** (1939).
—— *Introduction to Logic and to the Methodology of the Deductive Sciences*, New York: Oxford Univ. Press, 1941.
—— "The Semantic conception of Truth and the Foundations of Semantics," in *Readings in Philosophical Analysis*, ed. by H. Feigl and W. Sellars. New York: Appleton, 1949.
—— *Logic, Semantics, Metamathematics*, trans. by J. H. Woodger. Oxford: Clarendon Press, 1956, including "The Concept of Truth in Formalized Languages," "On the Concept of Logical Consequence," etc.

Tarski, A., A. Mostowski, and R. M. Robinson. *Undecidable Theories*, Amsterdam: North–Holland, 1953.

Thomson, J. F. "What Achilles should have said to the Tortoise," *Ratio* **3** (1960–61).
—— "On some Paradoxes," in *Analytical Philosophy*, ed. by R. J. Butler. Oxford: Blackwell, 1963.

Turing, A. M. "Solvable and Unsolvable Problems," *Science News* (Penguin Books) **31** (1954).

Waismann, F. "Die Natur des Reduzibilitätsaxioms," *Monatshefte für Mathematik und Physik* **35** (1928).
—— "Ist die Logik eine deduktive Theorie?" *Erkenntnis* **7** (1937–38).
—— "Are there Alternative Logics?" *Proc. Arist. Soc.* **46** (1945–46).
—— "Analytic-Synthetic," *Analysis* **10–13** (1949–53).
—— *Introduction to Mathematical Thinking*, trans. by J. Benac. New York: Ungar, 1951.

Wang, H. "What is an Individual?" *Phil. Review* **62** (1953).
—— "On Formalization," *Mind* **64** (1955).
—— "Eighty Years of Foundational Studies," *Dialectica* **12** (1958).
—— "Process and Existence in Mathematics," in *Essays on the Foundations of Mathematics, dedicated to A. A. Fränkel on his seventieth anniversary*, ed. by Y. Bar-Hillel. Jerusalem: Magnes Press, 1961.
—— *A Survey of Mathematical Logic*, Amsterdam: North-Holland, 1963.

Warnock, G. J. "Metaphysics in Logic," in *Essays in Conceptual Analysis*, ed. by A. Flew. London: Macmillan, 1956.

Weyl, H. *Das Kontinuum*, Leipzig: Gruyter, 1918.
—— "Über die neue Grundlagenkrise der Mathematik," *Mathematische Zeitschrift* **10** (1919).
—— "The Mathematical Way of Thinking," *Science* **92** (1940).
—— "David Hilbert and his Mathematical Work," *Bull. Amer. Math. Soc.* **50** (1944).
—— "Mathematics and Logic: A Brief Survey serving as a Preface to a Review of *The Philosophy of Bertrand Russell*," *Amer. Math. Monthly* **53** (1946).
—— *Philosophy of Mathematics and Natural Science*, Princeton, N.J.: Princeton Univ. Press, 1949.

White, M. G. "The Analytic and the Synthetic: An Untenable Dualism," in *Semantics and the Philosophy of Language*, ed. by L. Linsky. Urbana, Ill.: Univ. of Illinois Press, 1952.

Whitehead, A. N. and B. Russell. *Principia Mathematica*, New York: Cambridge Univ. Press, vol. 1 (1910), vol. 2 (1912), vol. 3 (1913); 2nd ed., vol. 1 (1925), vol. 2 (1927), vol. 3 (1927).

Wilder, R. L. *Introduction to the Foundations of Mathematics*, New York: Wiley, 1952.

Wittgenstein, L. "Some Remarks on Logical Form," *Arist. Soc. Supp.*, vol. 9 (1929).
—— *Philosophical Investigations*, trans. by G. E. M. Anscombe. Oxford: Blackwell, 1953.
—— *Remarks on the Foundations of Mathematics*, ed. by G. H. von Wright, R. Rhees, and G. E. M. Anscombe, trans. by G. E. M. Anscombe. Oxford: Blackwell, 1956. Excerpts reprinted in this anthology, pp. 421–80.
—— *The Blue and Brown Books*, Oxford: Blackwell, 1958.
—— *Notebooks: 1914–1916*, ed. by G. H. von Wright and G. E. M. Anscombe, trans. by G. E. M. Anscombe. Oxford: Blackwell, 1961.
—— *Tractatus Logico–Philosophicus*, trans. by D. Pears and B. McGuinness, with an introduction by B. Russell. London: Routledge, 1961.

Wood, O. P. "On being Forced to a Conclusion," *Arist. Soc. Supp.*, vol. 35 (1961).

Zermelo, E. "Beweis, dass jede Menge wohlgeordnet werden kann," *Mathematische Annalen* **59** (1904).